PSYCHOLOGY INFORMATION GUIDE SERIES

Series Editors: Sydney Schultz, M.L.S., Consultant, Library and Publications Services, and Duane Schultz, Adjunct Professor of Psychology, American University, Washington, D.C.

Also in this series:

ABNORMAL BEHAVIOR—*Edited by Henry Leland and Marilyn Deutsch**

ADULT DEVELOPMENT AND AGING—*Edited by Elizabeth Ann Robertson-Tchabo**

ALTERED STATES OF CONSCIOUSNESS—*Edited by Milton V. Kline**

ANIMAL BEHAVIOR—*Edited by Ethel Tobach**

B.F. SKINNER AND BEHAVIORISM—*Edited by Carol Filipczak**

CHILD AND ADOLESCENT DEVELOPMENT—*Edited by Dorothy E. Eichorn**

COMMUNICATION—*Edited by A. George Gitter and Robert Grunin**

CRIMINAL JUSTICE AND BEHAVIOR—*Edited by Harold J. Vetter**

EDUCATIONAL AND SCHOOL PSYCHOLOGY—*Edited by John F. Feldhusen**

FREUD AND PSYCHOANALYSIS—*Edited by Reuben Fine**

GROUP BEHAVIOR—*Edited by Gloria Behar Gottsegen*

HUMANISTIC PSYCHOLOGY—*Edited by Gloria Behar Gottsegen and Abby J. Gottsegen**

HUMAN MOTIVATION—*Edited by Charles N. Cofer**

PERSONALITY—*Edited by Robert B. Meagher, Jr.**

PHYSIOLOGICAL PSYCHOLOGY—*Edited by David L. Margules**

PSYCHOLOGY AND INDUSTRY—*Edited by Sydney Schultz and Duane Schultz**

PSYCHOLOGY IN HEALTH AND REHABILITATION—*Edited by Durand F. Jacobs and Jack G. Wiggins, Jr.**

PSYCHOLOGY OF WOMEN—*Edited by Helen R. Kearney**

PSYCHOPHARMACOLOGY—*Edited by David L. Margules**

*in preparation

The above series is part of the
GALE INFORMATION GUIDE LIBRARY

The Library consists of a number of separate series of guides covering major areas in the social sciences, humanities, and current affairs.

General Editor: Paul Wasserman, Professor and former Dean, School of Library and Information Services, University of Maryland

Managing Editor: Denise Allard Adzigian, Gale Research Company

History of Psychology

A GUIDE TO INFORMATION SOURCES

Volume 1 in the Psychology Information Guide Series

Wayne Viney

Professor of Psychology
Colorado State University
Fort Collins

Michael Wertheimer

Professor of Psychology
University of Colorado
Boulder

Marilyn Lou Wertheimer

Reference Librarian and Bibliographer
University of Colorado
Boulder

Gale Research Company
Book Tower, Detroit, Michigan 48226

Library of Congress Cataloging in Publication Data

Viney, Wayne.
    History of psychology.

    (Psychology information guide series ; v. 1) (Gale
information guide library)
    Includes indexes.
    1. Psychology—History—Bibliography. I. Wertheimer,
Michael, joint author. II. Wertheimer, Marilyn Lou,
joint author. III. Title. IV. Series.
Z7204.H57V56 [BF81]   016.5'09   79-9044
ISBN 0-8103-1442-8

VITAE

Wayne Viney received his Ph.D. degree in general experimental psychology from the University of Oklahoma, and has published extensively in the psychology of learning. At Colorado State University in Fort Collins, he served as head of the department of psychology from 1967 to 1973, and as associate dean of the College of Natural Sciences and director of the biological core curriculum from 1973 to 1976. In 1976 he took a sabbatical leave and studied the history of psychology at the University of Colorado. Currently professor of psychology at Colorado State University, he teaches courses in general psychology, theories of motivation, the psychology of religion, and the history of psychology.

Michael Wertheimer received his B.A. degree from Swarthmore College, his M.A. from Johns Hopkins, and his Ph.D. from Harvard; he has specialized in experimental psychology, general psychology, and the history of psychology. Among his books are A BRIEF HISTORY OF PSYCHOLOGY and FUNDAMENTAL ISSUES IN PSYCHOLOGY; he has also published many articles on the history of psychology. He taught at Wesleyan University before coming to the University of Colorado in 1955, where he has been professor of psychology since 1961. In 1977-78 Wertheimer was president of Division 26, the Division of the History of Psychology, of the American Psychological Association.

Marilyn Lou Wertheimer holds a B.A. degree from Stanford University and M.A. degrees from Columbia University and the University of California at Los Angeles, the latter in library science. She also holds a certificate of the Russian Institute from Columbia University, and has done graduate work at the University of California, Berkeley. She was employed by the library at the University of California at San Diego before coming to the University of Colorado, where she has been a reference librarian and bibliographer since 1968.

CONTENTS

Contents

Contents

Contents

PREFACE

This bibliography on the history of psychology was constructed with the hope that it will serve as a guide for students, teachers, reference librarians, and other interested persons. The usefulness of a bibliography depends, among other things, upon its organization and its content. A review of some of the deliberations pertaining to these areas may be of interest to the user.

A bibliography on the history of psychology could be appropriately organized in a variety of ways. One possibility, discussed at length by the present bibliographers in the early stages of this project, is an organization based on temporal periods. Such a scheme has considerable merit but was rejected, partly because a given period, such as 1910-19, is not historically very meaningful. Further, an organization based on temporal periods would call for too many arbitrary decisions regarding the particular period to which a given individual or idea should be assigned. Does William James, for example, belong to the nineteenth or the twentieth century? Obviously, he belongs to both centuries, but that fact in itself demonstrates the difficulty of a temporal organization.

We chose instead an organization which focuses on general reference materials, specific reference materials on psychology, general histories of psychology, major systems or schools of thought, histories of specific content areas, and histories of related fields such as philosophy, psychiatry, and biology. This scheme utilizes familiar categories, but it does not avoid the necessity of making some arbitrary decisions. Indeed, any organization will require some arbitrary decisions. Each major section of the bibliography is preceded by a brief explanatory statement which is intended to provide perspective for use of that section.

This bibliography contains almost 3,000 entries, over 1,200 of which are annotated. Although a bibliography on the history of psychology should contain articles in other languages, especially German, in accordance with guidelines established for the Gale Information Guide Library, only English-language sources have been included; even with this limitation a complete bibliography would contain many thousand more entries than are in this book. Because of space considerations there was no choice but to be selective. We must, accordingly, offer apologies to authors of many worthy works which have not been included. The only categories for which we sought a near complete complement of entries were reference works specifically designed for the history of psychology and general histories of psychology.

Our search and selection strategies involved examining all issues of journals which have had a tradition of publishing articles on the history of psychology, such as JOURNAL OF THE HISTORY OF THE BEHAVIORAL SCIENCES, PSYCHOLOGICAL REVIEW, JOURNAL OF GENERAL PSYCHOLOGY, and AMERICAN PSYCHOLOGIST. In addition, we searched PSYCHOLOGICAL ABSTRACTS from 1927 to 1977 and PSYCHOLOGICAL INDEX from 1894 to 1935. In PSYCHOLOGICAL ABSTRACTS we examined such topics as history of psychology, history of psychiatry, behaviorism, functionalism, Gestalt psychology, psychoanalysis, and structuralism. It should be noted that this kind of search of the PSYCHOLOGICAL ABSTRACTS undoubtedly fails to uncover some valuable historical articles. To try partially to compensate for this problem we examined all entries in each issue of the ABSTRACTS listed under "general." Cards were filled out for all articles which appeared to be appropriate to the history of psychology. At the end, we deleted more than 1,000 entries on historical books or articles as inappropriate for inclusion, for reasons detailed below.

The search for general histories of psychology was conducted by examining our personal libraries, the card catalogs of the University of Colorado libraries, the Colorado State University Library, and the Library of Congress, and the HARVARD LIST OF BOOKS IN PSYCHOLOGY. We sent requests for assistance to over fifty psychologists who are recognized authorities in the history of psychology, asking them to forward their ideas regarding unusual or little-known historical works not likely to be encountered in usual search procedures. We also wrote to over fifty major publishers asking for lists of their publications in the history of psychology. We are grateful to the many individuals and publishers who took the trouble to respond to our rather difficult request.

Our search resulted in far more references than could be included. Accordingly, selection procedures had to be established. As noted, we attempted to compile an exhaustive set of entries on reference materials specifically designed for the history of psychology and on general histories of psychology. The entries in other categories were selected in terms of our judgments of their historical importance and their presumed availability to the typical user. If two similar articles were of equal historical importance but one appeared in a more accessible journal, that article would be the more likely candidate for inclusion in this work.

It was our intention to annotate all entries, but economical use of space and time dictated the trading of some annotations for additional entries. All but a few dozen annotations are based on firsthand examination of the work in question (the few exceptions are from PSYCHOLOGICAL ABSTRACTS or publishers' flyers). Decisions as to what to annotate and what not to annotate were based on such considerations as the adequacy of a title for revealing the content of an item and the length of a work. In general, we attempted to annotate longer books, major classical items, and articles with major historical significance.

A comment is in order regarding our treatment of biographical materials. An annotated bibliography of biographies of major psychologists would itself be a mammoth volume. Accordingly, we have concentrated on sources of biographical materials, and have included only a few major book-length biographies and books of collected shorter biographies. Our section on biography includes hints for finding biographical materials on individuals who may be of interest.

Nor was an attempt made to include complete bibliographies of the published works of famous psychologists. Instead, we focus on how and where to locate such bibliographies.

We wish to express our special gratitude and appreciation to Michael M. Sokal for his careful reading of an early draft of this manuscript and for his hundreds of detailed suggestions. Helpful comments and recommendations were also received from the following, to whom we are greatly indebted: Rudolf Arnheim, David Avery, David Bakan, Paul Bell, Thomas Bennett, Patrick Capretta, Henry Cross, Solomon Diamond, Rand B. Evans, Amedeo Giorgi, Mary Henle, Ernest R. Hilgard, Larry Jacobson, Julian Jaynes, Stuart Johnson, Cedric Larson, Gardner Lindzey, Ivan D. London, Ross Loomis, T.P. McConahay, Melvin Marx, Joseph D. Matarazzo, Richard Morehouse, C. Roger Myers, Klaus Riegel, Robert Romanyshyn, William Sahakian, Duane Schultz, Sydney Schultz, Peggy Sweitzer, George Thornton, Steven Vandenberg, Thom Verhave, Robert I. Watson, William H. Webb, Wilse B. Webb, Richard Weigel, Theta Wolf, and Leonard Zusne. Wynona Viney donated many hours to checking on countless details. Agnes Conley was rapid--and accurate--in typing both an early and the final draft of the manuscript. Needless to say, with so much capable assistance, the errors that remain in this book must be seen as our own responsibility, and as the result of an insufficiency in our collective compulsiveness.

Wayne Viney
Michael Wertheimer
Marilyn Wertheimer

Section A
GENERAL REFERENCES

This section includes general sources, many of them not specific to psychology, but all of which contain material relevant to psychology or its history. There are seven subsections: biographical sources, bibliographical sources, dictionaries and encyclopedias, directories, abstracts and indexes, guides and sourcebooks, and book review indexes and sources.

1. BIOGRAPHICAL SOURCES

Rather than listing hundreds of biographies and autobiographies, this section identifies major sources of biographical information. Particularly useful are the Benjamin and Zusne works; if the reader knows the date of death of the biographee sought, then PSYCHOLOGICAL ABSTRACTS (during the year or two following date of death) and NEW YORK TIMES OBITUARY INDEX are also likely to be useful sources of information.

AMERICAN JOURNAL OF PSYCHOLOGY.

> See section B3, p. 45 for annotation; early volumes of this journal carried many necrologies of prominent psychologists.

AMERICAN MEN AND WOMEN OF SCIENCE. New York: R.R. Bowker, 1973-- .

> First eleven editions published irregularly from 1906 to 1968 under the title AMERICAN MEN OF SCIENCE. Issued in two sections beginning with ninth edition in 1956: Physical and Biological Sciences, and Social and Behavioral Sciences. Among over 34,000 biographies in the twelfth edition are many of psychologists. Gives brief biographical information on living scientists including education, positions held, and publications. Contains a necrology, a geographic index, and an index by discipline.

American Psychological Association. DIRECTORY OF THE AMERICAN PSYCHOLOGICAL ASSOCIATION. Washington, D.C.: 1969-- . Triennial. (ix, 1,449 p.,1978).

From 1916 to 1947 titled YEARBOOK; from 1948 to 1969 titled DIRECTORY and published annually. Self-reported biographical information in 1978 edition on almost 47,000 fellows, members, and associates of the American Psychological Association. Contains information on the structure and bylaws of the association, ethical standards of psychologists, standards for providers of psychological services, psychology laws in the United States and Canada, membership in the various divisions of the association, lists of practicing psychologists who are diplomates, a geographical index, and guides to the use of the directory.

Benjamin, Ludy T., Jr. "Prominent Psychologists: A Selected Bibliography of Biographical Sources." JOURNAL SUPPLEMENT ABSTRACT SERVICE, CATALOG OF SELECTED DOCUMENTS IN PSYCHOLOGY, 4, no. 1 (1974). MS No. 535. 32 p.

Over seven hundred references to biographical or autobiographical materials on more than three hundred prominent psychologists living and deceased, arranged in alphabetical order.

Benjamin, Ludy T., Jr., and Heider, Kathryn L. "History of Psychology in Biography: A Bibliography." JOURNAL SUPPLEMENT ABSTRACT SERVICE, CATALOG OF SELECTED DOCUMENTS IN PSYCHOLOGY, 6, no. 61 (1976). MS No. 1276. 21 p.

Lists alphabetically about ninety prominent figures in the history of psychology with references to over two hundred relevant biographies and autobiographies.

BIOGRAPHY INDEX: A CUMULATIVE INDEX TO BIOGRAPHICAL MATERIAL IN BOOKS AND MAGAZINES. New York: H.W. Wilson, 1947-- . Quarterly, with annual and three-year cumulations.

Indexes biographical material, primarily on Americans, appearing in books and about 1,700 periodicals. Includes obituaries, collections of letters, diaries, memoirs, and bibliographies, arranged alphabetically by name of biographee. An index to professions and occupations lists psychiatrists, psychoanalysts, and psychologists.

CURRENT BIOGRAPHY. New York: H.W. Wilson, 1940-- . Annual.

Lengthy biographies (average about three pages), occasionally updated, of "living leaders in all fields of human accomplishment the world over." References at the end of each article. Classified list by profession (including psychologists). Three decennial indexes have been compiled in CURRENT BIOGRAPHY CUMULATED INDEX 1940-1970.

DICTIONARY OF AMERICAN BIOGRAPHY. 11 vols. Edited by Allen Johnson et al. New York: Charles Scribner's Sons, 1946?-58. Reprint of original 20 vol. ed. published 1928-37 with supplementary vols. 21-22 which were added in 1944 and 1958. Index to vols. 1-10 published 1958; supplement 3, 1973; supplement 4, 1974.

Compiled under the auspices of the American Council of Learned Societies. Includes biographies of persons "who have made some significant contribution to American life in its manifold aspects." Signed articles, of less than a page to several pages, on many persons prominent in the history of psychology. Bibliography at the end of each article.

DICTIONARY OF SCIENTIFIC BIOGRAPHY. Edited by Charles C. Gillispie. 14 vols. New York: Charles Scribner's Sons, 1970-76.

Biographies of prominent scientists who are no longer living, worldwide from classical antiquity to modern times. Articles vary in length from less than a page to thirty pages. Includes bibliographies of original works and secondary literature.

A HISTORY OF PSYCHOLOGY IN AUTOBIOGRAPHY. 6 vols. Vol. 1. Edited by Carl Murchison. 1930. Reprint. New York: Russell and Russell, 1961. Vol. 2. Edited by Carl Murchison. 1932. Reprint. New York: Russell and Russell, 1961. Vol. 3. Edited by Carl Murchison. 1936. Reprint. New York: Russell and Russell, 1961. Vol. 4. Edited by Edwin G. Boring, Herbert S. Langfeld, Heinz Werner, and Robert M. Yerkes. 1952. Reprint. New York: Russell and Russell, 1968. Vol. 5. Edited by Edwin G. Boring and Gardner Lindzey. New York: Irvington, 1967. Vol. 6. Edited by Gardner Lindzey. Englewood Cliffs, N.J.: Prentice-Hall, 1974. Index in Vol. 4.

Autobiographies of eighty-six distinguished psychologists from America and numerous European countries who were invited by a committee to prepare materials for these volumes. Additional volumes are in preparation.

Krawiec, T.S., ed. THE PSYCHOLOGISTS. 2 vols. New York: Oxford University Press, 1972, 1974.

Autobiographies of twenty-one contemporary psychologists who have distinguished themselves in various areas of psychology. Bibliographies follow each entry. Biographical index identifies individuals named as influential in the lives of the autobiographers. Additional volumes in preparation.

_____. THE PSYCHOLOGISTS: AUTOBIOGRAPHIES OF DISTINGUISHED LIVING PSYCHOLOGISTS. Volume 3. Brandon, Vt.: Clinical Psychology Publishing Co., 1978.

Contains autobiographies of George Albee, Edwin Ghiselli, Molly Harrower, Starke Hathaway, R. Duncan Luce, Lois B. Murphy, J.B. and Louisa E. Rhine, Lorrin Riggs, Joseph Royce, Patrick Suppes, Leona Tyler, and Philip Vernon.

McGRAW-HILL ENCYCLOPEDIA OF WORLD BIOGRAPHY. 12 vols. New York: McGraw-Hill, 1973.

Contains five thousand biographies of men and women, including psychologists, "whose achievements are important to our understanding of social and cultural history" from classical to contemporary times. Level suitable for high school students and college undergraduates. Articles average eight hundred words and are accompanied by a portrait or illustration. Volume 12 includes a comprehensive index which lists persons according to their association with places, battles, inventions, pictures, ideas, philosophies, styles, and movements, as well as by occupation and discipline.

McGRAW-HILL MODERN MEN OF SCIENCE. 2 vols. New York: McGraw-Hill, 1966-68.

Volume 1 contains biographies of 426 "leading contemporary scientists," including some psychologists, and "describe[s] not only what each man did but why and how as well." Volume 2 updates biographies in Volume 1 and presents 420 additional ones. Combined table of contents in Volume 2. Analytical index in both volumes "to persons, subjects, books, institutions and so forth mentioned in the text." Classified index includes experimental psychology.

Murchison, Carl, ed. THE PSYCHOLOGICAL REGISTER. Vols. 1 and 3. Worcester, Mass.: Clark University Press, 1929, 1932. Vol. 2 never published.

Contains biographical data on psychologists from thirty-two countries. Criteria for inclusion varied by country. For the United States, all Ph.D.-level members of the American Psychological Association were included.

Murchison, Carl, and Harden, Luberta, eds. THE PSYCHOLOGICAL REGISTER. Vol. 3. Worcester, Mass.: Clark University Press, 1932.

Endeavors to provide complete bibliographies of all people who identified themselves as psychologists and who were living in 1932.

National Academy of Sciences. BIOGRAPHICAL MEMOIRS. New York: Columbia University Press, 1877-- . Irregular.

A series of volumes containing biographies averaging twenty to thirty pages in length "of deceased members of The National

Academy of Sciences and bibliographies of their published scientific contributions." Articles written by persons knowledgeable about the discipline and the biographee. Includes some psychologists.

NATIONAL CYCLOPEDIA OF AMERICAN BIOGRAPHY. 53 vols. New York: James T. White, 1892-1971.

Broader coverage than DICTIONARY OF AMERICAN BIOGRAPHY. Aims to "perpetuate . . . American civilization through its chief personalities." Includes numerous psychologists. Because entries are in rational and not alphabetical order, it is necessary to consult the index. Loose-leaf indexes superseded by the REVISED INDEX, PERMANENT AND CURRENT SERIES. Compiled by H.A. Harvey and Raymond D. McGill. New York: James T. White, 1971. 537 p.

NATIONAL CYCLOPEDIA OF AMERICAN BIOGRAPHY. Current vols., A-L. New York: James T. White, 1930-72. In progress.

Includes biographies of living persons. Although volumes are lettered A-L, each includes the full alphabet of names and has its own index. The REVISED INDEX indexes the permanent series through volume 52 and the current series through volume K.

NEW YORK TIMES OBITUARY INDEX: 1858-1968. New York: New York Times Co., 1970. 1,136 p.

Lists obituaries and occasional articles about funerals and memorial services that appeared in the NEW YORK TIMES. Entries provide year, date, section (if any), page, and column number. Includes many psychologists.

Nordby, Vernon J., and Hall, Calvin S. A GUIDE TO PSYCHOLOGISTS AND THEIR CONCEPTS. San Francisco: W.H. Freeman, 1974. 187 p.

Brief biographies followed by descriptions of the major concepts of forty-two psychologists influential in contemporary psychology. References. Index.

WHO'S WHO. London: C. and A. Black, 1849.

Gives biographical information about education, career, publications, and so forth, of prominent British and a few other nationalities in many fields, including psychology.

WHO'S WHO IN AMERICA. Chicago: Marquis, 1899-1900-- . Biennial.

Criteria for inclusion based on "position or responsibility held" or "level of significant achievement." Concise biographies cover an individual's outstanding activities. Thirty-ninth edition of over

70,000 entries has a necrology of those who died since the previous edition. Names of those appearing in regional WHO'S WHO are listed at the back.

WHO WAS WHO, 1897-1915, 1916-28, 1929-40, 1941-50, 1951-60, 1961-70. A COMPANION TO WHO'S WHO CONTAINING THE BIOGRAPHIES OF THOSE WHO DIED DURING THE PERIOD. 6 vols. London: C. and A. Black, 1929-72.

Contains biographies of prominent British individuals from previous WHO'S WHO (see above, this section) which were deleted because of death, with occasional additional information. Future volumes are planned for the close of each decade.

WHO WAS WHO IN AMERICA: A COMPANION BIOGRAPHICAL REFERENCE WORK TO WHO'S WHO IN AMERICA. 5 vols. Chicago: Marquis, 1942-73.

These volumes, covering 1897-1973, together with WHO WAS WHO IN AMERICA: HISTORICAL VOLUME, 1607-1896, form the series WHO'S WHO IN AMERICAN HISTORY. Series contains over 90,000 brief biographies of "American notables," including numerous psychologists. Biographies are those removed from WHO'S WHO IN AMERICA because of death. Volume 5 has a cumulated index to the full series.

WHO WAS WHO IN AMERICA: HISTORICAL VOLUME, 1607-1896. A COMPONENT VOLUME OF WHO'S WHO IN AMERICAN HISTORY. Chicago: Marquis, 1963. 670 p.

See WHO WAS WHO IN AMERICA: A COMPANION BIOGRAPHICAL REFERENCE WORK TO WHO'S WHO IN AMERICA.

WORLD WHO'S WHO IN SCIENCE: A BIOGRAPHICAL DICTIONARY OF NOTABLE SCIENTISTS FROM ANTIQUITY TO THE PRESENT. Edited by Allen G. Debus. Chicago: Marquis, 1968. xvi, 1,855 p.

Provides approximately 30,000 "sketches" of prominent scientists, including many psychologists. About half of the biographies are of people living at the time the book was published.

Zusne, Leonard. "Five Hundred Seventy-Eight Names in the History of Psychology: Computer Tabulations of Biographic Data." JOURNAL SUPPLEMENT ABSTRACT SERVICE, CATALOG OF SELECTED DOCUMENTS IN PSYCHOLOGY 5 (Spring 1975). MS No. 915. 265 p.

Includes the following biographic information on 578 persons important in the history of psychology who lived from antiquity to 1973: alphabetic list of names; year, month, and day of birth and of death; age at death; country of birth and of death; nationality;

highest earned academic degree; primary and secondary fields of specialization; contribution to psychology (up to four areas per individual); eminence rating; and sex. Tabular data for each of the data fields above are arranged in twenty tables for comparative purposes.

_____. NAMES IN THE HISTORY OF PSYCHOLOGY: A BIOGRAPHICAL SOURCEBOOK. New York: Halsted Press, 1975. xvii, 489 p.

Brief biographies in standard format of 526 individuals, selected largely on the basis of experts' ratings of eminence in the history of psychology. Additional biographical sources are provided for each entry. Index.

2. BIBLIOGRAPHICAL SOURCES

Although many of these sources are standard reference tools, a number of them are especially useful for psychology (e.g., PSYCHOLOGICAL ABSTRACTS), and particularly for the history of psychology (Benjamin and Heider, Brožek, Rand, and Watson's two books). See section A6, p. 27, for additional sources focusing primarily on psychology.

ABS GUIDE TO RECENT PUBLICATIONS IN THE SOCIAL AND BEHAVIORAL SCIENCES. New York: Merton, 1965. xxi, 781 p.

Annotated bibliography of books, articles, government reports and pamphlets, and unbound items arranged alphabetically by author. Title and subject indexes. Annual supplements entitled RECENT PUBLICATIONS IN THE SOCIAL AND BEHAVIORAL SCIENCES (1966-).

Annan, Gertrude L., and Felter, Jacqueline W., eds. HANDBOOK OF MEDICAL LIBRARY PRACTICE. 3d ed. Chicago: Medical Library Association, 1970. xi, 411 p.

Contains much relevant reference material for medicine and allied sciences, but only a small number of references for psychology.

Benjamin, Ludy T., Jr., and Heider, Kathryn L. "History of Psychology in Biography: A Bibliography." JOURNAL SUPPLEMENT ABSTRACT SERVICE, CATALOG OF SELECTED DOCUMENTS IN PSYCHOLOGY, 1976, 6, no. 61. MS No. 1276. 21 p.

See section A1, p. 2, for annotation.

BIBLIOGRAPHICAL INDEX: A CUMULATIVE BIBLIOGRAPHY OF BIBLIOGRAPHIES. New York: H.W. Wilson, 1938-- . 3/year.

Published in April and August with a cumulative volume in December. Subject listing of bibliographies which contain at least fifty entries, published separately or found in books, periodicals, and pamphlets. Over two thousand periodicals examined regularly.

BIBLIOGRAPHY OF THE HISTORY OF MEDICINE. Bethesda, Md.: U.S. Department of Health, Education, and Welfare, Public Health Service. No. 1, 1965--. Annual, five-year cumulations.

Part I, Biographies; part II, Subject Index; part III, Authors. Each part includes bibliographic citations. "All chronologic periods and geographic areas are covered. Journal articles, monographs, and analytic entries for symposia, congresses, and similar composite publications, as well as historical chapters in general monographs are included." Cumulated volumes for 1964-69 and for 1970-74 each devote approximately fifteen pages to psychology.

Bolton, Henry Carrington. CATALOGUE OF SCIENTIFIC AND TECHNICAL PERIODICALS, 1665-1895. 2d ed. Washington, D.C.: Smithsonian Institution, 1897. vii, 1,247 p.

BOOKS IN PRINT: AN AUTHOR-TITLE-SERIES INDEX TO THE PUBLISHERS' TRADE LIST ANNUAL. New York: R.R. Bowker, 1948--. Annual.

This is an alphabetically arranged author and title index giving bibliographic information about books published by U.S. publishers. The 29th edition in 1976 lists approximately 450,000 titles from over 4,600 publishers. Contains a list of publishers with addresses. A BOOKS IN PRINT SUPPLEMENT gives price changes and lists newly published and announced books since the latest BOOKS IN PRINT was published. See also SUBJECT GUIDE TO BOOKS IN PRINT, below, p. 17.

British Museum. Department of Printed Books. GENERAL CATALOGUE OF PRINTED BOOKS. 263 vols. Photolithographic ed. to 1955. London: Trustees, 1959-66.

This enormous collection of some five-and-a-half to six million entries contains works related to the history of psychology published world-wide. Supplements have been issued.

_____. SUBJECT INDEX OF THE MODERN WORKS ADDED TO THE LIBRARY, 1881-1900. Edited by G.K. Forescue. 3 vols. London: Trustees, 1902-3.

Continued by 5-year supplements.

Brožek, Josef. "Contemporary West European Historiography of Psychology." HISTORY OF SCIENCE 13 (Part 1, no. 19) (1975): 29-60.

Provides information on historically relevant materials such as dictionaries, encyclopedias, bibliographies, anthologies, indexes, monographs, and historical treatises recently produced in Europe

(including French-speaking areas, German-speaking areas, "So-
vietica," Great Britain, Holland, Italy, and Scandinavia). Bibliography with over 175 entries.

Buros, Oscar Krisen, ed. MENTAL MEASUREMENTS YEARBOOK. Highland
Park, N.J.: Gryphon Press, 1938-- . Irregular. 7th ed., 1972 in 2 vols.
Title and publisher vary.

Supersedes EDUCATIONAL, PSYCHOLOGICAL, AND PERSON-
ALITY TESTS, 1933/34-36 by Buros. Each yearbook supplements
earlier ones. Seventh yearbook lists tests by subject, including
psychology and related subjects, and provides reviews and references. "Books and Reviews" section has a classified index. Separate indexes include Periodical Directory and Index, Publishers Directory and Index, Index of Book Titles, Index of Test Titles,
Index of Names, and Classified Index of Tests.

_____. TESTS IN PRINT: A COMPREHENSIVE BIBLIOGRAPHY OF TESTS
FOR USE IN EDUCATION, PSYCHOLOGY, AND INDUSTRY. Highland Park,
N.J.: Gryphon Press, 1961. 479 p.

_____. TESTS IN PRINT II: AN INDEX TO TESTS, TEST REVIEWS, AND
THE LITERATURE ON SPECIFIC TESTS. Highland Park, N.J.: Gryphon Press,
1974. 1,107 p.

Bibliography of tests in print arranged by subject, "published as
separates for use with English-speaking subjects." Indexes information in MENTAL MEASUREMENTS YEARBOOKS, PERSONALITY
TESTS AND REVIEWS, and READING TESTS AND REVIEWS, and
provides supplementary references. Out-of-print tests included in
Index of Titles and Index of Names. Contains standards of the
American Psychological Association, the American Educational Research Association, and the National Council on Measurement in
Education; a Publishers Directory and Index; and a Scanning Index.

CHILD DEVELOPMENT ABSTRACTS AND BIBLIOGRAPHY. Chicago: University
of Chicago Press, Society for Research in Child Development, 1927-- . 3/year.

Two numbers published in each issue. About 150 periodicals regularly searched. Subject matter may vary but often includes material on such subjects as developmental and comparative psychology,
experimental psychology, including learning phenomena, personality,
sociology and social psychology, education, educational psychology,
counseling, psychiatry, clinical psychology, and other clinical
studies. "Book Notices" section in each issue provides short evaluative book reviews and a list of "Books Received." Author and
subject indexes.

CUMULATIVE BOOK INDEX. New York: H.W. Wilson, 1898-- . 11/year.

An author-subject-title listing in a single alphabet of books in the English language published anywhere in the world. Published monthly (except August) with cumulations at various intervals until 1969, when it began cumulating annually. It was issued as a supplement to the four editions of THE UNITED STATES CATALOG: BOOKS IN PRINT in 1899, 1902, 1912, 1928.

CURRENT CONTENTS. Philadelphia: Institute for Scientific Information, 1961-- . Weekly.

Beginning with volume 6, no. 2, January 2, 1974, issued weekly as CURRENT CONTENTS: SOCIAL AND BEHAVIORAL SCIENCES. Lists titles of "papers and all other substantive material from more than 1,100 journals" covering the social and behavioral sciences. Separate sections for education and for the behavioral, social, and management sciences, prior to this date. Weekly subject index.

Daniel, Robert S., and Louttit, C[hauncey].M. PROFESSIONAL PROBLEMS IN PSYCHOLOGY. New York: Prentice-Hall, 1953. xv, 416 p.

Detailed discussion of psychology as a career. Describes the literature in psychology, how to report psychological research, and problems of the professional psychologist. Contains extensive and useful appendixes: annotated list of reference books in psychology; bibliography of psychology journals; sources for books, tests, apparatus, equipment, and supplies; and glossary of abbreviations useful to psychologists. Name and subject indexes.

Dennis, Wayne. "Bibliographies of Eminent Psychologists." AMERICAN PSYCHOLOGIST 9 (January 1954): 35-36.

Lists the number of publications of seventeen eminent psychologists and comments on their productivity.

Erickson, Ralph Waldo. "Contemporary Histories of Psychology." In PRESENT-DAY PSYCHOLOGY, edited by A[braham].A. Roback, pp. 487-506. New York: Philosophical Library, 1955.

Reviews some important histories of psychology by American, British, German, and French authors.

Estey, Helen Grace. A BIBLIOGRAPHY ON PSYCHOLOGY. Gardner, Mass.: Author, 1926. 69 p.

Lists approximately two thousand books on such topics as applied, comparative, educational, general, pathological, physiological, religious, and social psychology.

Freides, Thelma. LITERATURE AND BIBLIOGRAPHY OF THE SOCIAL SCIENCES. Los Angeles: Melville Publishing Co., 1973. xviii, 284 p.

Describes "the literature and bibliography of the social sciences, and the strategy of literature searching, against a background of some basic ideas about communication in science." Deals with several disciplines, including psychology.

Grinstein, Alexander. THE INDEX OF PSYCHOANALYTIC WRITINGS. See section C12a, p. 198.

GUIDE TO REFERENCE BOOKS. Compiled by Eugene P. Sheehy. 9th ed. Chicago: American Library Association, 1976. xviii, 1,015 p.

First six editions are by Isadore Gilbert Mudge, the seventh and eighth by Constance Mabel Winchell. This is a bibliography of reference works, including general reference works, the humanities, social sciences, history and area studies, .pure and applied sciences. Gives a brief description of each work, including numerous ones on psychology.

HANDBOOK OF MEDICAL LIBRARY PRACTICE. See Annan, Gertrude L., and Felter, Jacqueline W., eds., p. 7.

HARVARD LIST OF BOOKS IN PSYCHOLOGY. 4th ed. Compiled and annotated by the Psychologists in Harvard University. Cambridge, Mass.: Harvard University Press, 1971. viii, 108 p.

Highly selective list of hundreds of books in psychology chosen for inclusion by the faculty members at Harvard University. Books grouped by topic; many on the history of psychology.

Hoselitz, B.F., ed. A READER'S GUIDE TO THE SOCIAL SCIENCES. New York: Free Press, 1970. xiv, 425 p.

Chapters devoted to seven disciplines in the social sciences; the one on psychology is by Walter R. Reitman. Each chapter includes a brief essay mentioning some of the classic works as well as a sampling of the literary output of the discipline.

THE INDEX-CATALOGUE OF THE LIBRARY OF THE SURGEON GENERAL'S OFFICE. 61 vols. Washington, D.C.: U.S. Department of Health, Education, and Welfare, Public Health Service, 1880-1961.

A mammoth publication in five multivolume series which attempts to list all publications, including some in psychology, relevant to the field of medicine. Superseded by INDEX MEDICUS, the CATALOG OF THE NATIONAL LIBRARY OF MEDICINE, and other bibliographical publications.

INDEX MEDICUS. Washington, D.C.: National Library of Medicine, 1960-- . Monthly.

An author and subject index to the world's periodical biomedical literature, prepared by the National Library of Medicine. Yearly cumulated volume consisting of eight books. Includes a bibliography of medical reviews, medical subject headings, and a list of journals indexed (over two thousand in 1976).

INDEX TO THE ENGLISH CATALOGUE OF BOOKS, 1837-1889. 4 vols. London: S. Low, 1858-93.

This is the subject index for the first four volumes of the ENGLISH CATALOGUE OF BOOKS.

INTERNATIONAL BIBLIOGRAPHY OF SOCIAL AND CULTURAL ANTHROPOLOGY. Paris: United Nations Educational, Scientific and Cultural Organization, 1955-59; Chicago: Aldine, 1960-- . Annual.

Subject matter is mainly anthropology, but includes entries in psychology. Indexes many foreign as well as English-language periodicals. Classified arrangement with general subject index.

INTERNATIONAL BIBLIOGRAPHY OF SOCIOLOGY. New York: United Nations Educational, Scientific and Cultural Organization, 1953-59; Chicago: Aldine, 1960-- . Annual.

Subject matter is mainly sociology, but includes some entries in psychology. Indexes many foreign as well as English-language periodicals. Classified arrangement with general subject index.

INTERNATIONAL INDEX. See SOCIAL SCIENCES INDEX.

ISIS CRITICAL BIBLIOGRAPHY OF THE HISTORY OF SCIENCE AND ITS CULTURAL INFLUENCES. Title varies. Currently issued annually as the May issue of the journal ISIS. Washington, D.C.: History of Science Society, Vol. 1, 1913-14-- . Publisher varies.

A large major classified bibliography of books and periodical articles. New classification scheme beginning with volume 46 (1955) lists works on psychology under sections on the sciences of man (see next entry).

ISIS CUMULATIVE BIBLIOGRAPHY OF THE HISTORY OF SCIENCE. Edited by Magda/Whitrow. 2 vols. London: Mansell, 1971.

A massive reference source indexing the critical biographies printed in ISIS between 1913 and 1965. References classified by civilization and period, and by subject field (including psychology).

Langfeld, Herbert S. "The Realm of Behavior: Books on Psychology." In THE FIRST ONE HUNDRED AND FIFTY YEARS: A HISTORY OF JOHN WILEY

AND SONS, INCORPORATED 1807-1957, edited by the publishers, pp. 194-
201. New York: John Wiley and Sons, 1957.

> Discusses the publisher's impressive record of issuing books on psy-
> chology, beginning with Johann Casper Lavater's THE SCIENCE
> OF PHYSIOGNOMY (1918).

LIBRARY OF CONGRESS CATALOG. BOOKS: SUBJECTS. Publisher varies.
1950-- . Quarterly.

> Annual and five-year cumulations. This is a vast subject bibliog-
> raphy of works received and catalogued by the Library of Congress
> which are represented by Library of Congress printed cards. Lists
> a very large number of books, including many in psychology.

Lins, Leon Joseph, and Rees, R.A., eds. SCHOLARS' GUIDE TO JOURNALS
OF EDUCATION AND EDUCATIONAL PSYCHOLOGY. Madison, Wis.: Dem-
bar Educational Research Services, 1965. 150 p.

> Lists major journals in education and educational psychology with
> subscription data and manuscripts information for each. Includes
> some psychology journals. Index.

Louttit, Chauncey [M.]. BIBLIOGRAPHY OF BIBLIOGRAPHIES ON PSYCHOL-
OGY, 1900-1927. Washington, D.C.: National Research Council Bulletin
No. 65, 1928. 108 p.

> Lists bibliographies on psychology and allied subjects. A useful
> source of early twentieth-century material. Subject index.

_____. HANDBOOK OF PSYCHOLOGICAL LITERATURE. Bloomington, Ind.:
Principia Press, 1932. 200 p.

> An annotated guide to the literature of psychology, including
> chapters on journal literature, institution publications, general
> reference works, literature guides, and other materials and sources.
> Appendixes include a list of journals in psychology and related
> subjects, and a list of special psychological collections in U.S.
> and British libraries, arranged by subject.

_____. "The Use of Bibliographies in Psychology." PSYCHOLOGICAL RE-
VIEW 36 (July 1929): 341-47.

> Summarizes the author's work on a BIBLIOGRAPHY OF BIBLIOG-
> RAPHIES ON PSYCHOLOGY, 1900-1927 (see above, this section)
> and classifies six types of bibliographies. Offers suggestions for
> how to use a bibliography.

Meissner, William W. ANNOTATED BIBLIOGRAPHY IN RELIGION AND
PSYCHOLOGY. New York: Academy of Religion and Mental Health, 1961.
xi, 235 p.

Almost three thousand items, most of them annotated (largely drawn from PSYCHOLOGICAL ABSTRACTS), relevant to "psychological aspects of religion or religious aspects of psychology." Most items published in the twentieth century and arranged under forty-seven categories. Author index.

MENTAL MEASUREMENTS YEARBOOK. See above, this section, under Buros, Oscar Krisen, ed.

Mott, Frank Luther. A HISTORY OF AMERICAN MAGAZINES. 5 vols. Cambridge, Mass.: Harvard University Press, 1938-68.

NATIONAL UNION CATALOG. Washington, D.C.: Library of Congress, 1961-- . 9 monthly issues, 3 quarterly cumulations, annual cumulations for 4 years, quinquennial in the 5th. Publisher varies.

"The NATIONAL UNION CATALOG is designed as a current and cumulative continuation of A CATALOG OF BOOKS REPRESENTED BY LIBRARY OF CONGRESS PRINTED CARDS and its supplements." It is an author and main entry catalog. A four-year supplement, THE NATIONAL UNION CATALOG, 1952-1955 IMPRINTS, was published in 1961. The first quinquennial cumulation covered the years 1953-57. Symbols are used to indicate National Union Catalog participating libraries which hold the title.

NATIONAL UNION CATALOG OF MANUSCRIPT COLLECTIONS, 1959/61-- . Irregular, mostly annual. Hamden, Conn.: Shoe String Press, 1962-- . Publisher varies.

Lists manuscript holdings in public or quasi-public repositories in the United States. Each entry includes physical description of the manuscript, location, scope and content, and so forth. "The index provides in one alphabet references to the names, places, subjects, and named historical periods reported in the catalog entries." Some entries pertain to psychology. With the 1976 catalog, descriptions of approximately 37,600 collections located in 990 different repositories had been published.

THE NATIONAL UNION CATALOG PRE-1956 IMPRINTS. London: Mansell, 1968-- . Volumes through "S" available; "T-Z" in press.

A catalog of items in the Library of Congress printed or (in the case of manuscripts) written before 1956 for which the Library of Congress has printed cards, plus items reported to the National Union Catalog by the several hundred participating libraries. It is an author and main entry catalog, and, when completed, will consist of approximately 610 volumes with some ten million entries. Symbols are used to indicate libraries owning a title.

NEW SERIALS TITLES; A UNION LIST OF SERIALS COMMENCING PUBLICA-
TION AFTER DECEMBER 31, 1949. Washington, D.C.: Library of Congress,
January 1953-- . 8 monthly issues, 4 quarterly issues, annual cumulation.

> See UNION LIST OF SERIALS. Several cumulations covering four
> or more years have appeared. Supplements the UNION LIST OF SERI-
> ALS; it lists "new" serials alphabetically by title and provides
> date of beginning volume and holdings of "participating libraries."
> A section entitled "Changes in serials" includes such information
> as title changes, cessations, suspensions, and so forth.

NEW SERIALS TITLES--CLASSED SUBJECT ARRANGEMENT. Washington, D.C.
Library of Congress, Card Div., 1955-- . Monthly.

> No cumulation; entries are arranged in subject sequence according
> to the Dewey Decimal Classification system.

POOLE'S INDEX TO PERIODICAL LITERATURE, 1802-1881. Rev. ed. Boston:
Houghton, 1891. 2 vols. 5 supplements, January 1882-January 1, 1907.

> A general subject index (including writers treated as subjects) to
> over two hundred mainly American and some British periodicals.
> Numerous entries relate to psychology.

PSYCHOLOGICAL ABSTRACTS. Washington, D.C.: American Psychological
Association, 1927-- . Monthly.

> See section A5, p. 25, for annotation.

PSYCHOLOGICAL INDEX, 1894-1935, AN ANNUAL BIBLIOGRAPHY OF THE
LITERATURE OF PSYCHOLOGY AND COGNATE SUBJECTS. 42 vols. Princeton, N.J.: Psychological Review Co., 1895-1936.

> See section A5, p. 26, for annotation.

QUARTERLY CHECK-LIST OF PSYCHOLOGY. Darien, Conn.: American Bibliographic Service, 1961-- .

> Provides bibliographic data on "new and recent nonperiodical mate-
> rials" in psychology "in the Western languages as published through-
> out the world." Translations, reprints, revised editions, and paper-
> backs included. Annual index of authors, editors, and translators.

Rand, Benjamin, comp. BIBLIOGRAPHY OF PHILOSOPHY, PSYCHOLOGY, AND
COGNATE SUBJECTS. 2d ed. New York: Macmillan, 1928.

> Published in two parts in 1905 as volume 3 of DICTIONARY OF
> PHILOSOPHY AND PSYCHOLOGY edited by James Baldwin (see
> Baldwin, section A3, p. 19).

General References

READER'S GUIDE TO PERIODICAL LITERATURE. New York: H.W. Wilson, 1905-- . Semi-monthly, annual cumulations.

This is an "author-subject index to periodicals of general interest [not primary scholarly journals] published in the United States." Many headings pertain to psychology.

The Royal Society of London. CATALOGUE OF SCIENTIFIC PAPERS, 1800-1900. 19 vols. London: C.J. Clay and Sons, 1867-1902; Cambridge: At the University Press, 1914-25.

Contains author-title listings, including dates and pages of articles appearing in transactions and proceedings of scientific societies and in scientific journals, including those of some psychologists. Volumes 1 to 6 (1800-1863); Volumes 7 and 8 (1864-73); Volumes 9 to 11 (1874-83); Volume 12 (supplementary volume covering 1800-1883); Volumes 13 to 19 (1884-1900).

_____. CATALOGUE OF SCIENTIFIC PAPERS, 1800-1900. SUBJECT INDEX. 3 vols. Cambridge: At the University Press, 1908-14.

This index to the preceding entry is divided by subject as follows: volume 1: Pure Mathematics; volume 2: Mechanics; volume 3: Physics, part 1, generalities, heat, light, sound; part 2, electricity and magnetism. Each volume contains a list of serial publications and a schedule of classification.

SCIENCE CITATION INDEX. Philadelphia: Institute for Scientific Information, 1961-- . Quarterly, annual cumulation.

See section A5, p. 26, for annotation.

SOCIAL SCIENCES AND HUMANITIES INDEX. See SOCIAL SCIENCES INDEX.

SOCIAL SCIENCES CITATION INDEX. Philadelphia: Institute for Scientific Information, 1973-- . 3/year, annual cumulation.

See section A5, p. 27, for annotation.

SOCIAL SCIENCES INDEX. New York: H.W. Wilson, April 1974-- . Quarterly.

Formerly part of INTERNATIONAL INDEX (Vols. 1-18, 1907-March 1965) and SOCIAL SCIENCES AND HUMANITIES INDEX (Vols. 19-27, April 1965-March 1974). A major bibliographic publication that provides indexes by author and subject to the contents of many English-language periodicals in anthropology, social studies, economics, political science, psychology, public administration, sociology, and related subjects. Index to book reviews.

SOCIOLOGICAL ABSTRACTS. New York: Sociological Abstracts, 1952-- .
6/year.

> See section A5, p. 27, for annotation.

STANDARD PERIODICAL DIRECTORY. 5th ed. New York: Oxbridge Publishing Co., 1977. 1,715 p.

> More than 62,000 U.S. and Canadian periodicals, including ones
> on psychology and psychiatry, are listed alphabetically by subject.
> Usually provides name of journal, address, name of editor, sub-
> scription rate, circulation, as well as other information. Alpha-
> betical title index at the back. Published irregularly since 1964.

SUBJECT GUIDE TO BOOKS IN PRINT. New York: R.R. Bowker, 1957-- .
Annual.

> Lists books in print by subject according to headings used by the
> Library of Congress. The 1977-78 edition includes over 400,000
> books under more than 62,000 headings. Most fiction (except
> biographical and historical) is omitted.

ULRICH'S INTERNATIONAL PERIODICALS DIRECTORY. 17th ed. New York:
R.R. Bowker, 1977. 2,096 p.

> Contains a classified list of and a title index for approximately
> 60,000 periodicals published throughout the world. Most entries
> provide address of publisher, name of editor, subscription rate,
> circulation, and indexing information. Supplements are issued
> between editions.

UNION LIST OF SERIALS IN LIBRARIES OF THE UNITED STATES AND CAN-
ADA. 3d ed. 5 vols. Edited by Edna Brown Titus. New York: H.W.
Wilson, 1965.

> Lists serials alphabetically by title and includes place, volumes,
> and dates of publication as well as holdings of "cooperating li-
> braries."

U.S. Department of Health, Education, and Welfare. Specialized bibliographies.

> Sample bibliographies listed in Bell, James Edward. A GUIDE
> TO LIBRARY RESEARCH IN PSYCHOLOGY, section A6, p. 27.

U.S. Library of Congress. A CATALOG OF BOOKS REPRESENTED BY LIBRARY
OF CONGRESS PRINTED CARDS ISSUED TO JULY 31, 1942. 167 vols. Ann
Arbor, Mich.: Edwards Brothers, 1942-46.

> Nearly two million cards from a depository card catalog have been
> arranged alphabetically by author and photographically reproduced

in this catalog. Many of the cards were catalogued by libraries other than the Library of Congress, and not all the books represented are in that library. A 42-volume supplement representing cards issued August 1, 1942-December 31, 1947 was published in 1948, and in 1953 a 24-volume supplement was issued, entitled LIBRARY OF CONGRESS AUTHOR CATALOG; A CUMULATIVE LIST OF WORKS REPRESENTED BY LIBRARY OF CONGRESS PRINTED CARDS, 1948-1952. For additional supplements see NATIONAL UNION CATALOG.

Watson, Robert I., Sr. THE HISTORY OF PSYCHOLOGY AND THE BEHAV-IORAL SCIENCES: A BIBLIOGRAPHIC GUIDE. New York: Springer Publishing Co., 1978. ix, 241 p.

A work on the resources available for the study of the history of psychology. Contains annotated lists of bibliographies, biographies, and archival collections as well as sections on historical accounts of social and behavioral science; verbal and quantitative historical methodology; the history of history; and the philosophy, psychology, and sociology of science.

_____, ed. EMINENT CONTRIBUTORS TO PSYCHOLOGY. 2 vols. New York: Springer Publishing Co., 1974, 1976.

Volume 1 is a bibliography of primary sources, including bibliographies of major publications by over five hundred individuals living between 1600 and 1969 who contributed to psychology, selected for eminence by a panel of experts. Volume 2 is a bibliography of secondary sources, containing over 50,000 references to the works of individuals listed in volume 1.

White, Carl M., and associates. SOURCES OF INFORMATION IN THE SO-CIAL SCIENCES: A GUIDE TO THE LITERATURE. 2d ed. Chicago: American Library Association, 1973. xviii, 702 p.

A chapter on social science literature is followed by separate chapters on each of the social science disciplines. Each includes an introductory essay about the discipline, descriptive and evaluative comments on basic works, guides to the literature, and a list of reference sources. Contains chapters on history, geography, economics, business administration, sociology, anthropology, psychology, education, and political science. The psychology chapter (pp. 375-424) was prepared by Robert I. Watson and Carl M. White. Index.

Whitrow, Magda, ed. ISIS CUMULATIVE BIBLIOGRAPHY OF THE HISTORY OF SCIENCE. 2 vols. London: Mansell, 1971.

See above in this section, p. 12, under ISIS CUMULATIVE BIB-LIOGRAPHY OF THE HISTORY OF SCIENCE.

3. DICTIONARIES AND ENCYCLOPEDIAS

This section lists primarily dictionaries and encyclopedias specifically devoted to psychology. Comparison of earlier and later encyclopedia and dictionary entries provides useful historical information.

Baldwin, James Mark, ed. DICTIONARY OF PHILOSOPHY AND PSYCHOLOGY. 3 vols. in 4. New York: Macmillan, 1901-5.

> Defines basic words and terms and includes biographies as well as articles on philosophy and psychology. International editorial board and contributors representing such disciplines as philosophy, philology, anthropology, biology, economics, law, education, neurology, and psychology. Volume 3, BIBLIOGRAPHY OF PHILOSOPHY, PSYCHOLOGY, AND COGNATE SUBJECTS, compiled by Benjamin Rand (see Rand, section A2, p. 15).

Chaplin, J.P. DICTIONARY OF PSYCHOLOGY. New York: Dell Publishing Co., 1968. xxx, 537 p.

> Brief articles on standard psychological terms and on "famous men of the prescientific period who contributed to psychology, founders of schools, and prominent contemporary theorists." Five appendixes: abbreviations commonly used in psychology; Hull's major symbolic constructs; standard Rorschach scoring symbols; Greek letter symbols often used in psychology; and prefixes, suffixes, and combining forms common in psychological terminology.

Drever, James. A DICTIONARY OF PSYCHOLOGY. Rev. ed., by Harvey Wallerstein. Baltimore: Penguin Books, 1964. 320 p.

> A standard source of concise definitions of terms relevant to psychology.

ENCYCLOPAEDIA BRITANNICA. See THE NEW ENCYCLOPAEDIA BRITANNICA.

ENCYCLOPEDIA OF THE SOCIAL SCIENCES. New York: Macmillan, 1930-35.

> See Seligman, E., and Johnson, A., eds., this section, p. 22.

English, Horace B. A STUDENT'S DICTIONARY OF PSYCHOLOGICAL TERMS. 4th ed. New York: Harper and Brothers, 1934. vii, 131 p.

> An early and relatively brief dictionary intended for students and the lay public.

English, Horace B., and English, Eva Champney. A COMPREHENSIVE DIC-

TIONARY OF PSYCHOLOGICAL AND PSYCHOANALYTIC TERMS: A GUIDE TO USAGE. New York: Longmans, Green, 1958. xiv, 594 p.

> A leading but dated dictionary with over 11,000 entries. Includes sources of selected foreign terms and entries associated with specific schools of thought, cross references, groupings of related terms, pronunciation keys for selected words, and notes and comments on usage.

Eysenck, H.-J.;Arnold, W.; and Neili, R., eds. ENCYCLOPEDIA OF PSYCHOLOGY. 3 vols. New York: Herder and Herder, 1972.

> Includes definitions of standard terms, brief articles on selected concepts accompanied by bibliographies, and brief biographical accounts of important figures in psychology, in a single alphabetical arrangement. Published in English, German, French, Spanish, Portuguese, and Italian editions. Contributors from twenty-two countries.

Goldenson, Robert M. THE ENCYCLOPEDIA OF HUMAN BEHAVIOR: PSYCHOLOGY, PSYCHIATRY, AND MENTAL HEALTH. 2 vols. Garden City, N.Y.: Doubleday, 1970.

> Over a thousand alphabetized articles, most starting with a concise definition. Some photographs and drawings. Index in volume 1 classifies articles under such headings as fields of psychology and psychiatry, history of psychology, history of psychiatry, theories, systems, schools, areas of psychology, mental disorders and mental health, miscellaneous terms, and illustrative cases. Volume 2 includes an extensive reference list and a general index with over 5,000 entries.

Gould, Julius, and Kolb, W.L., eds. A DICTIONARY OF THE SOCIAL SCIENCES. New York: Free Press, 1964. xiv, 761 p.

> Compiled by 270 social scientists from the United Kingdom and the United States. Defines terms used in the social sciences, including social psychology, not normally found in a standard encyclopedia. Entries are divided into sections: section A gives the core meaning or meanings; the following sections provide historical background and/or more detailed discussion.

Harriman, Philip L[awrence]., ed. DICTIONARY OF PSYCHOLOGY. 3d ed. London: Peter Owen, 1972. iii, 364 p.

_____. ENCYCLOPEDIA OF PSYCHOLOGY. New York: Philosophical Library, 1946. vii, 897 p.

> A comprehensive source book with authoritative information provided by over eighty expert contributors. Emphasizes major trends and

the historical development of the field as of the middle 1940s.
References.

_____. HANDBOOK OF PSYCHOLOGICAL TERMS. Totowa, N.J.: Little-
field, Adams, 1969. 222 p.

_____. THE NEW DICTIONARY OF PSYCHOLOGY. New York: Philosophi-
cal Library, 1947. 364 p.

Heidenreich, Charles A. A DICTIONARY OF PERSONALITY: BEHAVIOR AND
ADJUSTMENT TERMS. Dubuque, Iowa: Wm. C. Brown, 1968. vii, 213 p.

Alphabetically-arranged reference source with over 1,400 definitions intended for students, faculty, professional personnel, and
lay persons. Covers many terms commonly encountered in social
science disciplines. Index. Cross references. Brief bibliography.

Hopke, William, ed. DICTIONARY OF PERSONNEL AND GUIDANCE TERMS:
INCLUDING PROFESSIONAL AGENCIES AND ASSOCIATIONS. Chicago:
J.G. Ferguson, 1968. xix, 464 p.

Terms with definitions followed by reference sources which present
the terms in context. Bibliography provides page number(s) where
the terms appear. Addresses and brief statements about services
and objectives of professional agencies and associations. Classified list of terms in such categories as group work, guidance,
employment counseling, and student personnel services.

INTERNATIONAL ENCYCLOPEDIA OF THE SOCIAL SCIENCES. 16 vols. and
index vol. New York: Macmillan, 1968.

See Sills, David L., ed., this section, p. 22.

Klein, Barry T., ed. REFERENCE ENCYCLOPEDIA OF AMERICAN PSYCHOL-
OGY AND PSYCHIATRY. Rye, N.Y.: Todd Publications, 1975. 459 p.

Contains ten sections pertaining to psychology, psychiatry, and
mental health: associations, societies, and organizations; research
centers; periodicals; special libraries; foundations and associations
which provide grants, scholarships, and loans; audiovisual aids;
psychiatric hospitals; mental health centers; psychology graduate
schools; and psychiatric training programs. Subject index.

THE NEW ENCYCLOPAEDIA BRITANNICA. 15th ed. 30 vols. Chicago:
Encyclopaedia Britannica, 1974.

The fifteenth edition of this widely consulted encyclopedia deviates
from earlier editions, in which articles were arranged in a single
sequence. This edition is in three parts: Propedia, Macropedia,

and Micropedia. The first is an outline of human knowledge and refers the reader to articles in the Macropedia. The Macropedia is designed for the reader who wants to read more extensively on the subject. Its articles are longer and broader than most in the Micropedia, which provides brief information on specific subjects.

Seligman, E., and Johnson, A., eds. ENCYCLOPEDIA OF THE SOCIAL SCIENCES. 15 vols. New York: Macmillan, 1930-35.

See also Sills, David L., ed. INTERNATIONAL ENCYCLOPEDIA OF THE SOCIAL SCIENCES, next entry. Comprehensive articles on various topics in the social sciences. Bibliographies.

Sills, David L., ed. INTERNATIONAL ENCYCLOPEDIA OF THE SOCIAL SCIENCES. 16 vols. and index vol. New York: Macmillan, 1968.

Biographies and articles on topics in the broad range of the social sciences, written by prominent social scientists, including psychologists. Each article contains a bibliography. Supplements but does not replace the ENCYCLOPEDIA OF THE SOCIAL SCIENCES (see Seligman and Johnson, eds., just above).

Tuke, D.H., ed. A DICTIONARY OF PSYCHOLOGICAL MEDICINE. 2 vols. London: Churchill, 1892.

Provides "the definition, etymology and synonyms of the terms used in medical psychology with the symptoms, treatment, and pathology of insanity." Includes short definitions as well as longer articles with occasional bibliographies. Bibliography of English psychological medicine in volume 2.

Warren, Howard C[rosby]., ed. DICTIONARY OF PSYCHOLOGY. Boston: Houghton Mifflin, 1934. x, 372 p.

A substantial, early dictionary, prepared with the help of a distinguished advisory board and a large number of well-known collaborators. Includes extensive appendixes as well as glossaries of French and German terms.

White, Owen R., ed. A GLOSSARY OF BEHAVIORAL TERMINOLOGY. Champaign, Ill.: Research Press, 1971. xxv, 220 p.

Definitions of over 1,000 key words and phrases commonly used in behavioral science and technology. Appendix.

Wilkening, Howard. THE PSYCHOLOGY ALMANAC: A HANDBOOK FOR STUDENTS. Monterey, Calif.: Brooks/Cole, 1973.

Wolman, Benjamin B., comp., ed. DICTIONARY OF BEHAVIORAL SCIENCE. New York: Van Nostrand Reinhold, 1973. ix, 478 p.

Ninety prominent scholars (mainly psychologists and psychiatrists) collaborated on this broad-ranging dictionary. Includes brief entries intended to cover all areas of psychology as well as psychiatry, biochemistry, psychopharmacology, and clinical practice. Two appendixes: American Psychiatric Association's classification of mental disorders and American Psychological Association's statement of ethical standards of psychologists.

_____, ed. INTERNATIONAL ENCYCLOPEDIA OF PSYCHIATRY, PSYCHOLOGY, PSYCHOANALYSIS, AND NEUROLOGY. 12 vols. New York: Van Nostrand Reinhold and Aesculapius Publishers, 1977.

Title annotates. Also includes entries in related fields such as biochemistry, ergonomics, genetics, and psychosomatic medicine.

Zadrozny, John Thomas. DICTIONARY OF SOCIAL SCIENCE. Washington, D.C.: Public Affairs Press, 1959. 367 p.

Gives short definitions of terms used in the major social sciences, including psychology.

4. DIRECTORIES

This section contains lists of members of major associations in psychology, a list of non-U.S. psychologists, and the major reference tool for associations in general (ENCYCLOPEDIA OF ASSOCIATIONS).

American Psychological Association. AMERICAN PSYCHOLOGICAL ASSOCIATION 1977 MEMBERSHIP REGISTER. Washington, D.C.: 1977. vi, 444 p.

Published in years in which no new edition of the DIRECTORY OF THE AMERICAN PSYCHOLOGICAL ASSOCIATION (see Section A1, p. 1, under American Psychological Association) is produced, contains mailing addresses, membership status, divisional affiliations, and diplomate status of members of the association.

_____. DIRECTORY OF THE AMERICAN PSYCHOLOGICAL ASSOCIATION. Washington, D.C.: 1978. 1,509 p.

See Section A1, p. 1, for annotation.

CANADIAN PSYCHOLOGICAL ASSOCIATION: MEMBERSHIP DIRECTORY. Ottawa: The Association, 1965. 110 p.

Presents ethical standards of psychologists, bylaws, and lists of officers and representatives, as well as a brief biographical directory of the members of the Canadian Psychological Association.

Duijker, H.C.J., and Jacobson, E.H., eds. INTERNATIONAL DIRECTORY OF PSYCHOLOGISTS, EXCLUSIVE OF THE U.S.A. 2d ed. Assen, The Netherlands: Royal VanGorcum; New York: Humanities Press, 1966. xxiv, 575 p.

> Brief biographical entries on approximately 8,000 psychologists in countries other than the United States. Individuals listed by country of residence. Index of names.

ENCYCLOPEDIA OF ASSOCIATIONS. 13th ed. Edited by Nancy Yakes and Denise Akey. 3 vols. Detroit: Gale Research Co., 1979.

> Volume 1, national organizations of the U.S.; volume 2, geographic and executive index; volume 3, new associations and projects. Volume 1 lists primarily "non-profit American membership organizations of national scope," many of which pertain to psychology, and includes for each organization such information as address, chief official and title, founding date, number of members, description, publications, and meetings. Eighteen sections cover different types of organizations. Alphabetical and key word index.

5. ABSTRACTS AND INDEXES

By far the most important source of abstracts in psychology is PSYCHOLOGICAL ABSTRACTS, which lists and indexes items under headings such as "History of Psychology," but there are other useful reference guides as well.

Ansbacher, H.L., ed. PSYCHOLOGICAL INDEX. ABSTRACT REFERENCES OF VOLS. 1-35, 1894-1928. 2 vols. American Psychological Association, Ohio State University, 1940-41.

> These volumes indicate where items listed in the PSYCHOLOGICAL INDEX were abstracted. Abstracts were found for about half the items, in a wide variety of journals; this work directs the reader to those abstracts. Entries are coded in such a way that this list can be used only in conjunction with the volumes of the PSYCHOLOGICAL INDEX itself.

AUTHOR INDEX TO PSYCHOLOGICAL INDEX 1894 TO 1935 AND PSYCHOLOGICAL ABSTRACTS 1927 TO 1958. Compiled by the Psychology Library, Columbia University. 5 vols. Boston: G.K. Hall, 1960.

> See annotation for PSYCHOLOGICAL ABSTRACTS in this section, p. 25.

BIOLOGICAL ABSTRACTS. Philadelphia: BioSciences Information Service of Biological Abstracts, 1926-- . Semimonthly.

> Contains abstracts covering articles from approximately 7,600 journals published worldwide. Includes author, biosystematic, generic,

cross, and subject indexes. Over six hundred subject categories, including many relating to psychology and psychiatry.

Columbia University Psychology Library. AUTHOR INDEX TO PSYCHOLOGI-CAL INDEX 1894 TO 1935 AND PSYCHOLOGICAL ABSTRACTS 1927 TO 1958.

See Psychology Library of Columbia University, AUTHOR INDEX TO PSYCHOLOGICAL INDEX 1894 TO 1935 AND PSYCHOLOGICAL ABSTRACTS 1927 TO 1958, this section, p. 24.

COMPREHENSIVE DISSERTATION INDEX 1861-1972. 37 vols. Ann Arbor, Mich.: University Microfilms, 1973.

Lists over 400,000 dissertations accepted for academic doctoral degrees (not professional or honorary degrees) granted by U.S. and some foreign educational institutions. Arranged by discipline (including psychology) with key word, subject, and author indexes. Annual supplementary volumes.

DISSERTATION ABSTRACTS INTERNATIONAL. Ann Arbor, Mich.: University Microfilms, 1938-- . Monthly.

From 1938 to 1951 was titled MICROFILM ABSTRACTS; 1952-June 1969, DISSERTATION ABSTRACTS. Beginning in July 1966, issued in two sections: A. The Humanities and Social Sciences, and B. The Sciences and Engineering. Most psychology entries are in section B. By 1976 included abstracts of doctoral dissertations from over 375 institutions, mainly in the United States, with a few in Canada and Europe. Cooperating institutions listed with date each began submitting dissertations. Key word, title, and author indexes.

EDUCATION INDEX. New York: H.W. Wilson, 1929-30-- . Monthly, with annual and triennial cumulations.

Cumulative author and subject index to educational material in over two hundred English-language serial publications. Includes some monographs and materials published by the U.S. government. "Subject fields indexed include the arts, applied science and technology, audio-visual education, business education, comparative and international education, exceptional children and special education, health and physical education, languages and linguistics, mathematics, psychology and mental health, religious education, [and] social studies."

MICROFILM ABSTRACTS. See DISSERTATION ABSTRACTS INTERNATIONAL.

PSYCHOLOGICAL ABSTRACTS. Washington, D.C.: American Psychological Association, 1927-- . Monthly.

The major bibliographic source for all literature in psychology published since the 1920s. Purports to cover "the world's literature
in psychology and related disciplines," averaging 30,000 entries
per year by the 1970s. Each monthly issue contains full bibliographic information on articles and books, brief nonevaluative
abstracts of the contents of most entries, and brief subject and
author indexes. Classified arrangement. Extensive subject and
author indexes for each volume (two volumes per year since 1971).
Volume subject indexes carry a form entry for bibliographies. Indexes available as follows: AUTHOR INDEX TO PSYCHOLOGICAL
INDEX 1894 TO 1935 and PSYCHOLOGICAL ABSTRACTS 1927 TO
1958 compiled by the Psychology Library, Columbia University,
published in 5 volumes by G.K. Hall, 1960; first supplement covering PSYCHOLOGICAL ABSTRACTS 1959-63 compiled by the Psychology Library, Columbia University; second supplement (2 volumes) covering 1964-68 compiled by G.K. Hall; subsequent volumes covering 1969-71 and 1972-74 published by American Psychological Association; cumulative subject indexes published at irregular intervals. Recent volumes accessible by computer.

PSYCHOLOGICAL INDEX, 1894-1935, AN ANNUAL BIBLIOGRAPHY OF THE
LITERATURE OF PSYCHOLOGY AND COGNATE SUBJECTS. 42 vols. Princeton, N.J.: Psychological Review Co., 1895-1936.

Classified bibliography of books and periodical articles published
worldwide. Topics covered vary with the growth of the field and
changes in editorial policy. Author index. Number of titles
listed ranges from 1,312 in volume 1 to 5,927 in volume 42, at
which time PSYCHOLOGICAL ABSTRACTS assumed the bibliographical services of this index. See also in this section Ansbacher,
H.L., ed. PSYCHOLOGICAL INDEX. ABSTRACT REFERENCES
OF VOLS. 1-35, 1894-1928.

Psychology Library of Columbia University. AUTHOR INDEX TO PSYCHOLOGI-
CAL INDEX 1894 TO 1935 AND PSYCHOLOGICAL ABSTRACTS 1927 TO 1958.
5 vols. Boston, Mass.: G.K. Hall, 1960.

A vast compilation of the author entries of 42 volumes of the
PSYCHOLOGICAL INDEX and 33 volumes of the PSYCHOLOGICAL
ABSTRACTS that makes it unnecessary to consult 75 different vol-
umes to find out what a particular author has published.

SCIENCE CITATION INDEX. Philadelphia: Institute for Scientific Information,
1961-- . Quarterly, annual cumulation.

Processes more than 2,700 journals and books. Issued in three
parts: Citation Index lists the works of authors who have been
cited within the time period indexed and tells who has done the
citing; Source Index is an author index containing bibliographic
details of the sources that cited those authors listed in the Citation

Index, and also lists source journals, many of which are in psychology; Permuterm Subject Index pairs words from article titles so that users may find other articles that use the same combination of key words.

SOCIAL SCIENCES CITATION INDEX. Philadelphia: Institute for Scientific Information, 1973-- . 3/year, annual cumulation.

Processes about 70,000 articles in approximately 2,000 periodicals. Issued in three parts; see SCIENCE CITATION INDEX above for description.

SOCIOLOGICAL ABSTRACTS. New York: Sociological Abstracts, 1952-- . 6/year.

A major index for sociology, with some overlap with psychology. Includes a section on social psychology. Classified arrangement with a cumulative author and subject index for each annual volume.

Tompkins, Margaret, and Shirley, Norma, eds. SERIALS IN PSYCHOLOGY AND ALLIED FIELDS. 2d ed., rev. Troy, N.Y.: Whitston, 1976. xi, 472 p.

Extensive annotated list of journals. Presents name of editor, editorial and business address, price, date of first issue, information about indexing (whether it has an index and what other sources index it), statement of objectives, fields of interest, and miscellaneous information.

6. GUIDES AND SOURCEBOOKS

This section includes general guides and sourcebooks in psychology. For the history of psychology in particular, Watson's works listed in section A2 are especially helpful. For additional guides and sourcebooks, see the other entries in section A2, p. 9, "Bibliographical Sources."

Bell, James Edward. A GUIDE TO LIBRARY RESEARCH IN PSYCHOLOGY. Dubuque, Iowa: Wm. C. Brown, 1971. xii, 211 p.

Comprehensive guide for undergraduates to information sources. Contains lists of journals, textbooks, books of readings, book review sources, dictionaries, handbooks, encyclopedias, bibliographies of bibliographies, and abstracts and indexes. Many entries annotated. Appendixes contain information on style manuals and guides, Graduate Record Examinations, graduate education, and the Library of Congress classification.

General References

Elliott, Charles K. A GUIDE TO THE DOCUMENTATION OF PSYCHOLOGY.
Hamden, Conn.: Linnett Books, 1971. 134 p.

> A brief guide to the psychological literature intended as a refer-
> ence source to "some of the more common materials." Contains
> chapters on psychology and related subjects, libraries and classifi-
> cation, documentary aids, and searching strategies. Ten appen-
> dixes. Index.

Hamer, Philip M. A GUIDE TO ARCHIVES AND MANUSCRIPTS IN THE
UNITED STATES. New Haven, Conn.: Yale University Press, 1961. xxiii,
775 p.

> Provides a geographical guide to over a thousand collections con-
> taining hundreds of millions of primary items, throughout the United
> States. One hundred thirty-two-page index makes it possible to
> find out where papers of particular individuals, organizations, and
> groups are deposited. Second edition in preparation, to be pub-
> lished by the National Historical Publications and Records Commis-
> sion of the National Archives.

Harvard University Library. PHILOSOPHY AND PSYCHOLOGY. 2 vols.
Widener Library Shelflist 42, 43. Cambridge, Mass.: Harvard University Press,
1973.

> A catalogue of the philosophy and psychology holdings of this
> major library. Volume 1 contains the classification schedule, a
> classified listing by call number, and a chronological listing of
> works, including monographs and serials. Volume 2 contains an
> author and title listing.

Hawes, Marion E. WHAT TO READ IN PSYCHOLOGY. Chicago: American
Library Association, 1942. 36 p.

> A brief reading guide for the early 1940s public-library user with
> little knowledge of psychology. Annotations are highly evaluative;
> many indicate level of difficulty.

Higginson, G.D. GUIDE FOR PSYCHOLOGY. New York: Macmillan, 1937.
98 p.

Latham, A.J. "Guides to Pyschological Literature." AMERICAN PSYCHOLO-
GIST 9 (January 1954): 21-28.

> Discusses general and specific indexes, bibliographies, abstract
> journals, book review sources, and miscellaneous publications perti-
> nent in the early 1950s.

Sarbin, Theodore R., and Coe, William C. THE STUDENT PSYCHOLOGIST'S
HANDBOOK; A GUIDE TO SOURCES. Cambridge, Mass.: Schenkman, 1969.
104 p.

Tompkins, Margaret, and Shirley, Norma, eds. SERIALS IN PSYCHOLOGY AND ALLIED FIELDS. 2d ed., rev. Troy, N.Y.: Whitston, 1976. xi, 472 p.

See section A5, p. 27, for annotation.

7. BOOK REVIEW INDEXES AND SOURCES

There are no book review indexes specific to the history of psychology. Some general book review indexes list reviews of books in the history of psychology. The Bry work and the MENTAL HEALTH BOOK REVIEW INDEX, pertinent to psychology in general, include psychiatry and psychoanalysis as well. CONTEMPORARY PSYCHOLOGY is the American Psychological Association's primary outlet for book reviews, and other journals (for example, JOURNAL OF THE HISTORY OF THE BEHAVIORAL SCIENCES, ISIS, AMERICAN JOURNAL OF PSYCHOLOGY) occasionally carry reviews of books on the history of psychology.

BOOK REVIEW DIGEST. New York: H.W. Wilson, 1905-- . Monthly, annual cumulations.

An index to reviews in selected periodicals of fiction and nonfiction published or distributed in the United States. Author, subject, and title indexes.

BOOK REVIEW INDEX. Detroit: Gale Research Co., 1965-- . Bimonthly, quarterly and annual cumulations.

A "current guide to current reviews of current books." The 1976 annual cumulation lists over 75,000 reviews of almost 40,000 books, including many in psychology, appearing in 270 periodicals. Primarily an author-title index until 1976, when a separate title index was added.

Bry, Ilse, et al. MENTAL HEALTH BOOK REVIEW INDEX: PSYCHOLOGY, PSYCHIATRY, PSYCHOANALYSIS. Psychology Newsletter, New York University, vol. 8, no. 6, supplement no. 4 (1957). 21 p.

CONTEMPORARY PSYCHOLOGY: A JOURNAL OF REVIEWS. Washington, D.C.: American Psychological Association, 1956-- . Monthly.

Reviews books and films and carries editorials on topics of interest to users and consumers of psychological literature. Reviews typically provide good exposition along with critical and appreciative comment. Author and reviewer index in December issue. Contains a list of books received each month.

MENTAL HEALTH BOOK REVIEW INDEX: AN ANNUAL BIBLIOGRAPHY OF BOOKS AND BOOK REVIEWS IN THE BEHAVIORAL SCIENCES. New York:

New York University, Council on Research Bibliography, 1956-72.

Lists books reviewed in at least three periodicals and provides references to the book reviews, many of which are in psychology journals. Number of journals indexed varies from about 50 in the first issue to over 200 in the last. Arranged alphabetically by author.

TECHNICAL BOOK REVIEW INDEX. 12 vols. Pittsburgh: Carnegie Library, 1917-29. Quarterly. Resumed publication in 1935, Vol. 1-- . Compiled and edited in the Technology Dept., Carnegie Library of Pittsburgh, Special Libraries Association. Monthly (except July and August), since 1935.

Lists books in science and technology alphabetically by author. Quotes excerpts from reviews in current scientific, technical, and trade journals. Classified subject arrangements beginning with volume 39, no. 1, January 1973. Expanded coverage includes "all scientific, technical and medical (except clinical) subjects, including life sciences and mathematics. Management and behavioral sciences will be included in cases where they interface with science or technology."

Section B

REFERENCES IN THE HISTORY OF PSYCHOLOGY

This section includes general works specifically on the history of psychology, as well as ones on more limited topics in the area. Works on the major schools and systems of psychology are listed in section C, p. 127, and ones on the history of particular subfields of psychology are contained in section D, p. 249. In this section, the subcategories are general works on the history of psychology, brief general discussions of the history of psychology, major periodical sources on the history of psychology, books of readings in the history of psychology, articles on psychology in different geographical locations and times, specialized histories, and historiography (the study of historical methodology).

1. GENERAL WORKS ON THE HISTORY OF PSYCHOLOGY

The standard text on the history of experimental psychology is still Boring's work (1950 edition). Broader, more general, recent histories of psychology include Flugel and West, Klein, Lundin, Misiak and Sexton, Murphy and Kovach, Peters, Robinson, Schultz, Thomson, and Watson. Concentrating on the schools of psychology are Heidbreder, Krantz, and Woodworth and Sheehan. Broad, briefer introductions to the history of psychology are offered by Bruno, Capretta, Chaplin and Krawiec, Lowry, Marx and Hillix, Murphy, O'Neil, and Wertheimer.

Baldwin, James Mark. HISTORY OF PSYCHOLOGY; A SKETCH AND AN INTERPRETATION. 2 vols. New York: G.P. Putnam's Sons, 1913.

> An early, brief, popular account in two small 200-page illustrated volumes. Divides the history of psychology into the periods before and after John Locke. Contains a short list of secondary sources. Index.

Beloff, John. PSYCHOLOGICAL SCIENCES: A REVIEW OF MODERN PSYCHOLOGY. London: Crosby Lockwood Staples, 1973. xi, 361 p.

> Examines the historical background, major problems, and controversies in such areas as comparative psychology, differential psychol-

ogy, behavioristics, cognitive psychology, social psychology, depth psychology, and para-psychology. Notes and annotations follow each chapter. Bibliography. Index.

Boring, Edwin G. A HISTORY OF EXPERIMENTAL PSYCHOLOGY. 2d ed. New York: Appleton-Century-Crofts, 1950. xxi, 777 p.

The standard, classic source on the history of experimental psychology. Detailed notes and bibliographic information follow each chapter. Index.

Brennan, R.E. HISTORY OF PSYCHOLOGY FROM THE STANDPOINT OF A THOMIST. New York: Macmillan, 1945. xvi, 277 p.

A systematic text with a Catholic orientation presenting a brief history of psychology from Greek thought to twentieth-century trends. Descriptive as well as critical discussions of the major systems of psychology. Includes material on the interface between psychology and philosophy. Bibliography. Index.

Brett, George Sidney. A HISTORY OF PSYCHOLOGY. 3 vols. London: George Allen & Co., 1912-21.

A classic history of psychology covering ancient and patristic contributions in volume 1, the medieval and early modern period in volume 2, and modern psychology (including the first few years of the twentieth century) in volume 3. This work is obviously dated but may be of considerable help to those interested in pre-twentieth-century psychology. Emphasis on contributions from medical, political, religious, and philosophical thought. Abridged and updated version edited by R.S. Peters (see below, this section, p. 38). Index follows volume 1; author index follows volumes 2 and 3.

_____. PSYCHOLOGY: ANCIENT AND MODERN. Our Debt to Greece and Rome Series. Edited by G.D. Hadzsits and D.M. Robinson. New York: Cooper Square Publishers, 1963. ix, 164 p.

Examines the contributions of classical thought to such areas as the physiological basis of psychology, cognition, conduct, education, society and politics, and abnormal states. Bibliography.

Bruno, Frank J. THE STORY OF PSYCHOLOGY. New York: Holt, Rinehart and Winston, 1972. xiv, 209 p.

A brief, elementary, historical text tracing psychological thought from ancient times to twentieth-century developments. Includes anecdotes and examples as well as test questions and answers following each chapter. References. Index.

Capretta, Patrick J. A HISTORY OF PSYCHOLOGY IN OUTLINE: FROM

ITS ORIGINS TO THE PRESENT. New York: Dell, 1967. xiv, 226 p.

A short overview of psychological thought from primitive times to recent developments. Appendix A contains an annotated bibliography of selected works in the history of psychology and a list of great psychologists and their contributions. Appendix B discusses recurrent concepts in the history of psychology. Appendix C provides a glossary of key terms. Notes and bibliographic sources. Index.

Chaplin, James P., and Krawiec, T.S. SYSTEMS AND THEORIES OF PSYCHOLOGY. 3d ed. New York: Holt, Rinehart and Winston, 1974. x, 739 p.

Historical introduction to the major systems and theories of psychology. Substantive content areas of contemporary psychology are viewed from the perspective of the schools of psychology. References. Index.

Dessoir, Max. OUTLINES OF THE HISTORY OF PSYCHOLOGY. Translated by Donald Fisher. New York: Macmillan, 1912. xxix, 278 p.

Brief examination of psychological inquiry from the Greek period to the early twentieth century. Four main chapters organized chronologically: ancient times, Middle Ages, seventeenth and eighteenth centuries, and recent times. A final section traces developments in France, England, and Germany. Bibliography. Index.

Esper, Erwin A. A HISTORY OF PSYCHOLOGY. Philadelphia: W.B. Saunders, 1964. xi, 368 p.

An analysis of the historical development of psychology emphasizing the importance of early thinkers. Traces influences from philosophy, biology and physiology, and social theory. References. Index.

Flugel, J[ohn].C[arl]. A HUNDRED YEARS OF PSYCHOLOGY: 1833-1933. New York: Macmillan, 1933. 384 p.

Landmarks in the history of psychology examined in the time periods: 1833-60, 1860-1900, and 1900-1933. Discusses the major systems of thought, applications, and influences from philosophy, physiology, and biology. Bibliography. Index.

_____. A HUNDRED YEARS OF PSYCHOLOGY: 1833-1933. With an additional part: 1933-63 by Donald J. West. 3d ed. New York: Basic Books, 1964. 394 p. Reprint. New York: International Universities Press, 1970.

The supplement (covering 1933-63) is a revision of the supplement in the second edition, which covered 1933-47. Contains a bibliography for the first edition and the supplement, and a chronological table of major ideas and discoveries since 1807. Index.

Ford, Adelbert. THE STORY OF SCIENTIFIC PSYCHOLOGY. New York: Sears Publishing Co., 1932. xii, 307 p.

A simplified history of psychology written primarily for a popular audience. Focuses on late nineteenth-century and early twentieth-century developments. Index.

Griffith, Coleman R. PRINCIPLES OF SYSTEMATIC PSYCHOLOGY. Urbana: University of Illinois Press, 1943. xv, 718 p.

An appraisal of various major schools of psychological thought emphasizing the search for a system which does justice to the richness of the subject matter of psychology. Bibliography. Index.

Heidbreder, Edna. SEVEN PSYCHOLOGIES. New York: Appleton-Century-Crofts, 1933. viii, 450 p.

A classic work that offers a brief, general history of psychology followed by a descriptive and evaluative treatment of the major schools of thought of the first third of the twentieth century. Still remarkably useful. References. Index.

Hulin, Wilbur S. A SHORT HISTORY OF PSYCHOLOGY. New York: Holt, 1934. vi, 189 p.

A nontechnical overview discussing psychology from earliest thought to major systems which flourished early in the twentieth century. Bibliographic materials. Index.

Kantor, Jacob R. THE SCIENTIFIC EVOLUTION OF PSYCHOLOGY. 2 vols. Chicago: Principia Press, 1963, 1969.

A survey of the history of psychology as an "interbehavioral science," with emphasis on early Greek thought to the scholastic transformation of Aristotle's psychology (volume 1), and on the evolution of psychology as a science and as a general cultural institution (volume 2). Volume 1 also discusses problems and perspectives in studying the history of science and psychology. Volume 2 contains appendixes. References. Index.

Keller, Fred S. THE DEFINITION OF PSYCHOLOGY. 2d ed. New York: Appleton-Century-Crofts, 1973. ix, 149 p.

The first edition covered the various academic systems of psychology. The second edition adds material on such topics as contemporary behaviorism, psychoanalysis, hormic psychology, and the history of the conditioned reflex. Index.

_____. THE HISTORY OF PSYCHOLOGY: A PERSONALIZED SYSTEM OF INSTRUCTION COURSE. 2 vols. Roanoke, Va.: The Scholars Press, 1973.

> Treats selected individuals and excerpts from primary literature in the history of psychology in the format of a self-paced, individualized instructional package (known as "PSI" or the "Keller plan").

Klein, David B. A HISTORY OF SCIENTIFIC PSYCHOLOGY: ITS ORIGINS AND PHILOSOPHICAL BACKGROUNDS. New York: Basic Books, 1970. xii, 907 p.

> A survey of the intellectual and philosophical influences that contributed to the development of scientific psychology. Covers history from Grecian thought to Wundt. References. Index.

Klemm, Otto. A HISTORY OF PSYCHOLOGY. Translated by Emil Carl Wilm and Rudolf Pintner. New York: Charles Scribner's Sons, 1914. xiv, 380 p.

> An early text covering the history and major theories of such topics as sensation, perception, feeling, psychophysics, consciousness, and association. References in footnotes. Index.

Krantz, David L., ed. SCHOOLS OF PSYCHOLOGY: A SYMPOSIUM. New York: Appleton-Century-Crofts, 1969. ix, 134 p.

> Structuralism, functionalism, behaviorism, Gestalt psychology, and psychoanalysis are explored in papers presented as part of a symposium at the 1967 American Psychological Association convention. Includes a paper on the Baldwin-Titchener controversy and a final integrative discussion. References. Index.

Lowry, Richard. THE EVOLUTION OF PSYCHOLOGICAL THEORY: 1650 TO THE PRESENT. Chicago: Aldine-Atherton, 1971. xviii, 237 p.

> Traces psychological thought from Descartes to major twentieth-century systems with emphasis on psychoanalysis, behaviorism, and Gestalt theory. Notes and suggestions for further reading. Index.

Lundin, Robert W. THEORIES AND SYSTEMS OF PSYCHOLOGY. Lexington, Mass.: D.C. Heath, 1972. 324 p.

> A text on the history of psychology from ancient times to the present. Emphasizes antecedents of psychology and provides detailed coverage of selected twentieth-century theories including structuralism, functionalism, associationism, Gestalt psychology, behaviorism, psychoanalysis, and existential psychology. Bibliography. Index.

MacLeod, Robert B. THE PERSISTENT PROBLEMS OF PSYCHOLOGY. Pittsburgh: Duquesne University Press, 1975. x, 207 p.

An unfinished history of psychology with emphasis on major philosophical and psychological issues. Places psychology within the
heritage of the history of ideas. Appendix. Index.

Marx, Melvin H., and Hillix, William A. SYSTEMS AND THEORIES IN
PSYCHOLOGY. 2d ed. New York: McGraw-Hill, 1973. xv, 626 p.

General discussions of the nature of science followed by a survey
of the historical systems of psychology and contemporary theories.
Includes appendixes on European, Soviet, and Oriental psychology.
References. Index.

Miller, George A., and Buckhout, Robert. PSYCHOLOGY: THE SCIENCE
OF MENTAL LIFE. 2d ed. New York: Harper and Row, 1973. 561 p.

See section D1, p. 253, for annotation.

Misiak, Henryk, and Sexton, Virginia Staudt. HISTORY OF PSYCHOLOGY:
AN OVERVIEW. New York: Grune and Stratton, 1966. x, 499 p.

Traces the history of psychology from ancient thought to recent
developments. Emphasizes the evolution of psychology and schools
of thought in various countries. Includes a bibliography of major
works published after 1900 and summaries of the international congresses of psychology and applied psychology. References follow
each chapter. Index.

Moore, Jared Sparks, and Gurnee, Herbert. THE FOUNDATIONS OF PSY-
CHOLOGY. 2d ed. Princeton, N.J.: Princeton University Press, 1933.
xix, 239 p.

An early book on philosophical psychology from the perspective of
philosophy. Contains historical material on several major systems
of psychology. Bibliography.

Mueller-Freienfels, Richard. THE EVOLUTION OF MODERN PSYCHOLOGY.
Translated by W. Beran Wolfe. New Haven, Conn.: Yale University Press,
1935. xiii, 513 p.

A history of psychological thought with emphasis on the major systems of the late nineteenth and early twentieth centuries. Bibliography. Index.

Murchison, Carl, ed. PSYCHOLOGIES OF 1930. Worcester, Mass.: Clark
University Press, 1930. Reprint. New York: Arno Press, 1973. xix, 495 p.

Twenty-five papers by eminent psychologists on various schools of
psychological thought: hormic, act, functional, structural, configurational, Russian, behavioristic, dynamic, factor, and analytic.

_____. PSYCHOLOGIES OF 1925. Worcester, Mass.: Clark University Press, 1926. 412 p.

> Articles by the well-known psychologists Watson, Hunter, Woodworth, Koffka, Koehler, Prince, McDougall, Dunlap, and Bentley. Presents thoughts and work characteristic of behaviorism, dynamic psychology, Gestalt psychology, purposive psychology, reaction psychology, and structuralism.

Murphy, Gardner. PSYCHOLOGICAL THOUGHT FROM PYTHAGORAS TO FREUD: AN INFORMAL INTRODUCTION. New York: Harcourt, Brace & World, 1968. ix, 211 p.

> Discusses in lecture format ideas and personalities pivotal in the development of psychology. Bibliographic materials in footnotes. Index.

Murphy, Gardner, and Kovach, Joseph K. HISTORICAL INTRODUCTION TO MODERN PSYCHOLOGY. 3d ed. New York: Harcourt Brace Jovanovich, 1972. xiv, 526 p.

> A comprehensive introductory text tracing the development of psychology from its origins in Greek philosophy to the present. References after each chapter. Recommendations for further reading. Index.

Murphy, Gardner, and Murphy, Lois B., eds. WESTERN PSYCHOLOGY: FROM THE GREEKS TO WILLIAM JAMES. New York: Basic Books, 1969. x, 296 p.

> Editorial comments introduce selections from the writings of prominent figures in the history of Western psychological thought. Bibliographic information in footnotes. Companion volume to the editors' ASIAN PSYCHOLOGY (see section B5ii, p. 62). Index.

Neel, Ann. THEORIES OF PSYCHOLOGY: A HANDBOOK. 2d ed. New York: John Wiley and Sons, 1977. 650 p.

> Provides "a summary acquaintance, a feel, if you will, for the various theories and ideas it presents." Covers over twenty major theories and systems including structuralism, functionalism, several behavioristic approaches, several psychoanalytic systems, field theories, individual psychologies, and physiological theories. Examines methods employed, basic unit of study, views of specific content areas, and major constructs. References. Index.

O'Neil, W.M. THE BEGINNINGS OF MODERN PSYCHOLOGY. Baltimore: Penguin Books, 1968. 157 p.

> A brief survey of the history of psychology beginning with Descartes

and concluding with developments in the first quarter of the twentieth century. Bibliography. Index.

Peters, R.S., ed. BRETT'S HISTORY OF PSYCHOLOGY. 2d ed. Cambridge:
M.I.T. Press, 1962. 778 p.

The abridged version of Brett's classic three-volume work (see above,
this section, p. 32). Provides a comprehensive history of psychology from primitive times to the early twentieth century with emphasis on influences from other sciences, religion, and philosophy.
The editor's final chapter on twentieth-century theories extends the
scope of the original work. Includes editorial introductions to
each chapter, a list of sections omitted from the original three-
volume work, and bibliographic materials. Index.

Pillsbury, W.B. THE HISTORY OF PSYCHOLOGY. New York: W.W.
Norton, 1929. x, 326 p.

Development of psychological thought from early Greek times to
the major schools which characterized psychology during the first
third of the twentieth century. Bibliography. Index.

Reeves, Joan Wynn. BODY AND MIND IN WESTERN THOUGHT: AN IN-
TRODUCTION TO SOME ORIGINS OF MODERN PSYCHOLOGY. Baltimore:
Penguin Books, 1958. 403 p.

Roback, Abraham Aaron. HISTORY OF PSYCHOLOGY AND PSYCHIATRY.
New York: Philosophical Library, 1961. xiii, 422 p.

An analysis of the historical development of psychological sciences
emphasizing individuals and their contributions from Aristotle to
early twentieth-century thinkers. Presents major trends of thought
in the United States and several European countries. Brief bibliographies. Index.

Roback A[braham].A[aron]., and Kiernan, Thomas. PICTORIAL HISTORY OF
PSYCHOLOGY AND PSYCHIATRY. New York: Philosophical Library, 1969.
294 p.

Brief descriptions of psychologists and their concepts and contributions accompanied by illustrations and photographs. Covers a time
span from Aristotle to the twentieth century, although living psychologists are generally not included. Footnotes.

Robinson, Daniel N. AN INTELLECTUAL HISTORY OF PSYCHOLOGY. New
York: Macmillan, 1976. xiii, 434 p.

Analysis of the history of ideas that contributed to the development of scientific psychology, with emphasis on Hellenic through nine-teenth-century thought. Bibliography. Index.

Sahakian, William S. HISTORY AND SYSTEMS OF PSYCHOLOGY. New York: Schenkman, 1975. xvii, 494 p.

A history of psychology organized primarily around universities and other centers of thought. Contains extensive quotations from original sources. Includes sections on Soviet psychology, Oriental psychology, and Latin American psychology. References. Index.

Sargent, S. Stansfeld, in collaboration with Kenneth Stafford. THE BASIC TEACHINGS OF THE GREAT PSYCHOLOGISTS. Rev. ed. New York: Doubleday, 1965. 382 p.

Chronologically treats developments in such areas as learning, perception, thought, motivation, and emotion, and contrasts positions of the major systems. Brief biographical notes on over two hundred famous psychologists follow the text. Index.

Schultz, Duane. A HISTORY OF MODERN PSYCHOLOGY. 2d ed. New York: Academic Press, 1975. xvii, 395 p.

A widely-used undergraduate text emphasizing the history of psychology from Descartes to recent developments. Covers such classical systems of psychology as structuralism, functionalism, behaviorism, Gestalt psychology, and psychoanalysis. Bibliography. Index.

Spearman, Charles Edward. PSYCHOLOGY DOWN THE AGES. 2 vols. New York: Macmillan, 1937.

A large-scale critical and systematic work, cast to some extent in the form of a history of psychology, that attempts "to outline how far scientific psychology has really made progress," and to present "what wisdom it has through all the ages attained, accumulated, and preserved." Extensive notes. Subject and name indexes.

Thomson, Robert. THE PELICAN HISTORY OF PSYCHOLOGY. Baltimore: Penguin Books, 1968. 464 p.

Examines the history of psychology from developments in seventeenth-century empiricist philosophy to mid-twentieth-century thought. Emphasis on psychology from Wundt to World War II, with only a brief treatment of post-World War II developments. Bibliography. Index.

Villa, Guido. CONTEMPORARY PSYCHOLOGY. Rev. ed. Translated by Harold Manacorda. New York: Macmillan, 1903. xv, 396 p.

A historical introduction to psychology from Descartes to the latter part of the nineteenth century. Emphasis on the scope of psychology, methods, and philosophical problems. Bibliographical materials in footnotes. Index.

Watson, Robert I. THE GREAT PSYCHOLOGISTS. 4th ed. Philadelphia: J.B. Lippincott, 1978. xiv, 645 p.

A history of psychology from early Greek thought to the present, organized primarily around the contributions of individuals. Biographical information and references after each chapter. Index.

Wertheimer, Michael. A BRIEF HISTORY OF PSYCHOLOGY. Rev. ed. New York: Holt, Rinehart and Winston, 1979. viii, 168 p.

A condensed, integrated overview of the history of psychology emphasizing contributions from science and philosophy. Discusses the great twentieth-century schools of psychology. Index.

Woodworth, Robert S., and Sheehan, Mary R. CONTEMPORARY SCHOOLS OF PSYCHOLOGY. 3d ed. New York: Ronald Press, 1964. viii, 457 p.

The revised and enlarged edition of Woodworth's classic work. Traces the early development and evolution of the major systems of psychology. Includes a chapter on Soviet psychology as a school of thought. Bibliography of Robert S. Woodworth's works. References. Index.

2. BRIEF GENERAL DISCUSSIONS

This section includes shorter general articles on the history of psychology such as entries in major encyclopedias, discussions of general developments over a period of several decades, and capsule summaries of major events in the history of psychology.

Adams, Grace. "The Rise and Fall of Psychology." ATLANTIC MONTHLY, (January 1934), 82-92.

A brief analysis of psychology from after the First World War to the early 1930s.

Atkinson, Richard C. "Reflections on Psychology's Past and Concern About Its Future." AMERICAN PSYCHOLOGIST 32 (March 1977): 205-10.

Focuses on psychology's progress during the past twenty-five years and outlines possible reasons for the decline in financial support for science in general and psychology in particular.

Baldwin, J. Mark. "Psychology Past and Present." PSYCHOLOGICAL RE-
VIEW (July 1894): 363-91.

> Discusses the then recent history of psychology with emphasis on
> contributions from various countries, the major divisions of experi-
> mental psychology, and the exhibits in experimental psychology at
> the Columbian Exposition in Chicago.

_____. "Sketch of the History of Psychology." PSYCHOLOGICAL REVIEW
12 (March-May 1905): 144-65.

> An examination of the history of psychology as "the history of the
> stages or modes of the evolution of reflective consciousness of self."
> Includes sections on Greek psychology, the dualistic tradition,
> postulates of "modern" scientific psychology, history of nineteenth-
> century psychology, nineteenth-century naturalism, nineteenth-
> century positivism, and speculation on probable lines of develop-
> ment in early twentieth-century psychology.

Bartlett, F.C. "Changing Scene." BRITISH JOURNAL OF PSYCHOLOGY
(May 1956): 81-87.

> Presidential address delivered to the British Psychological Society
> in 1951. Focuses on selected developments in psychology since
> the first informal meeting of the society in 1901.

Ben-David, Joseph, and Collins, Randall. "Social Factors in the Origins of
a New Science: The Case of Psychology." AMERICAN SOCIOLOGICAL RE-
VIEW 31 (August 1966): 451-65.

> See also Ross, this section, p. 44.

Brett, G.S. "History of Psychology." ENCYCLOPAEDIA BRITANNICA, 14th
ed. 18 (1929): 706-20.

Britt, Steuart Henderson. "European Background (1600-1900) for American
Psychology." JOURNAL OF GENERAL PSYCHOLOGY 27 (October 1942):
311-29.

> Provides "a 'bird's eye view' of the names, dates, and publications
> of the important British, French, and German thinkers who exerted
> a significant influence on the development of modern psychology."

Cantril, Hadley. "Psychology." SCIENTIFIC AMERICAN, September 1950,
79-84.

> A brief overview of trends in psychology from 1900 to 1950. This
> issue of the journal is entirely devoted to progress in the sciences
> during the first half of the twentieth century.

Dolby, R.G.A. "The Transmission of Two New Scientific Disciplines from Europe to North America in the Late Nineteenth Century." ANNALS OF SCIENCE 34 (May 1977): 287-310.

> Describes how experimental psychology and physical chemistry were transmitted to the United States from Germany; the former underwent more of a change in this process than the latter.

Drever, James. "The Present Position in Psychology." PHILOSOPHY, THE JOURNAL OF THE BRITISH INSTITUTE OF PHILOSOPHY 7 (July 1932): 311-19.

> An overview in lecture format of the history of psychology from 1879 to about 1930 and a description of the chief schools of psychological thought.

Dunton, Larkin; Munsterberg, Hugo; Harris, W.T.; and Hall, G. Stanley. THE OLD PSYCHOLOGY AND THE NEW: ADDRESSES BEFORE THE MASSACHUSETTS SCHOOLMASTERS' CLUB, APRIL, 27, 1895. 38 p.

Goodenough, Florence L. "Trends in Modern Psychology." THE PSYCHOLOGICAL BULLETIN 31 (February 1934): 81-97.

> Trends are indicated by graphs showing number of publications from 1894 to 1931 in several content areas.

Griffith, Coleman R. "Contributions to the History of Psychology--1916-1921." PSYCHOLOGICAL BULLETIN 19 (August 1922): 411-28.

> Focuses on the founding of new journals and laboratories, addresses of presidents of the American Psychological Association, deaths of leading psychologists during this six-year period, and significant publications pertaining to the history of psychology (e.g., Baldwin's HISTORY OF PSYCHOLOGY and volumes 2 and 3 of Brett's HISTORY OF PSYCHOLOGY). Includes one hundred twenty references.

Humphrey, George. ON PSYCHOLOGY TODAY. Oxford, Engl.: Clarendon Press, 1949. 24 p.

> A lecture delivered at Oxford University in 1949 briefly characterizing developments of the recent past and noting contributions of such individuals as McDougall, Watson, Freud, and Bartlett.

Huxley, Julian, et al. "Centenary of Psychology: 1856-1956." AMERICAN PSYCHOLOGIST 11 (October 1956): 558-62.

> Summarizes four addresses delivered at Washington University, St. Louis, Missouri: psychology in evolutionary perspective by Huxley, the role of consciousness in the emergence of a scientific psychol-

ogy by Edwin G. Boring, organic disorder and mental disorder by Winifred Overholser, and the cultural matrix of the unconscious by Saul Rosenzweig.

Jastrow, J. "Psychology." ENCYCLOPEDIA OF THE SOCIAL SCIENCES 12 (1934): 588-96.

Louttit, C[hauncey].M. "Publication Trends in Psychology: 1894-1954." AMERICAN PSYCHOLOGIST 12 (January 1957): 14-21.

A posthumous article based upon examination of every fifth volume of PSYCHOLOGICAL INDEX and PSYCHOLOGICAL ABSTRACTS over the years indicated in the title. Analyzes total number of publications, number of publications in each of twelve content areas, and number of publications in various languages. Publications in applied areas and in English were increasing dramatically, while publications in basic areas and in German and French were decreasing during this period.

McKinney, Fred. "Fifty Years of Psychology." AMERICAN PSYCHOLOGIST 31 (December 1976): 834-42.

Examines the growth and development of psychology from the 1920s to the 1970s. Presents growth curves for APA membership, published titles, and departments offering graduate work. Contrasts interest areas over time.

Maller, J.B. "Forty Years of Psychology. A Statistical Analysis of American and European Publications, 1894-1933." PSYCHOLOGICAL BULLETIN 31 (October 1934): 533-59.

Reports and analyzes trends of publications listed in the PSYCHOLOGICAL INDEX in terms of number of publications per country and number of publications per content area (e.g. general psychology, social psychology, abnormal psychology).

Marks, Robert W., ed. GREAT IDEAS IN PSYCHOLOGY. New York: Bantam Books, 1966. 534 p.

Miles, W.R. "Psychology." In DEVELOPMENT OF THE SCIENCES: SECOND SERIES, edited by L.L. Woodruff, pp. 247-90. New Haven, Conn.: Yale University Press, 1941.

A brief overview of the historical development of psychology from the time of the Greeks to the twentieth century.

Murphy, Gardner. "Pyschology and the Post-War World." PSYCHOLOGICAL REVIEW 49 (July 1942): 298-318.

See section B7e, p. 120, for annotation.

Overstreet, H.A. "A Quarter-Century of Psychology: A Science That Has Only Just Been Born." CENTURY MAGAZINE 113 (March 1927): 526-35.

Pillsbury, W[alter].B[owers]. "The New Developments in Psychology in the Past Quarter Century." PHILOSOPHICAL REVIEW 26 (January 1917): 56-59.

> Complements the Washburn article listed below, this section. Recounts advances in such areas as educational psychology, child psychology, abnormal psychology, and animal psychology.

Robinson, Daniel N. THE MIND UNFOLDED: ESSAYS ON PSYCHOLOGY'S HISTORIC TEXTS. Washington, D.C.: University Publications of America, 1978. xi, 539 p.

> A collection of all the prefaces written by the author for the twenty-eight volumes of SIGNIFICANT CONTRIBUTIONS TO THE HISTORY OF PSYCHOLOGY, 1750-1920, that he edited (see section B4, p. 51). Appendix lists the contents of all the volumes, which are composed of five series: Orientations (11 books), Psychometrics and educational psychology (4 volumes), Medical psychology (5 volumes), Comparative psychology (4 books), and Physiological psychology (4 volumes).

Ross, Dorothy. "On the Origins of Psychology." AMERICAN SOCIOLOGICAL REVIEW 32 (1967): 466-69.

> Discusses social factors in the origins of psychology (see Ben-David and Collins, this section).

Sahakian, W.S., ed. "Psychology, History of." ENCYCLOPAEDIA BRITANNICA 15 (1974): 151-58.

Saugstad, Per. AN INQUIRY INTO THE FOUNDATIONS OF PSYCHOLOGY. New York: Bedminster Press, 1965. 104 p.

> A highly critical examination of the philosophical underpinnings of scientific psychology. Includes an 8-page chapter on the "history of psychology in outline."

Walk, R.D. "Developments in Psychology Since 1900." In AN INTELLECTUAL AND CULTURAL HISTORY OF THE WESTERN WORLD, edited by H.E. Barnes, pp. 1167-75. 3d ed. New York: Dover, 1965.

Washburn, Margaret Floy. "Some Thoughts on the Last Quarter Century in Psychology." PHILOSOPHICAL REVIEW 26 (January 1917): 46-55.

> Recounts such advances in psychology as the founding of journals, the development of new tests and statistical methods, and the emergence of new subdisciplinary areas such as social psychology and animal learning. Discusses the status of introspection as a method.

Webb, Wilse B. "The Antecedents of Contemporary Psychology." In his THE PROFESSION OF PSYCHOLOGY, pp. 20-33. New York: Holt, Rinehart and Winston, 1962.

_____. "Progress in Psychology: 1903-1907." AMERICAN PSYCHOLOGIST 29 (December 1974): 897-902.

> Each year, from 1904 through 1908, Franklin Buchner, then editor of PSYCHOLOGICAL BULLETIN, published a section entitled "Psychological Progress," reviewing significant developments in the previous year. Based on Buchner's work, Webb provides data (e.g., number of doctorates and types of publications) pertaining to the young discipline of psychology; brief descriptions of the work of such figures as Binet, Titchener, James, Wundt, and Spencer; and characterizations of work in such areas as comparative psychology, clinical psychology, and social psychology.

Woodworth, R[obert].S[essions]. "Psychology." In A QUARTER CENTURY OF LEARNING 1904-1929, edited by Dixon Ryan Fox, pp. 129-46. New York: Columbia University Press, 1931.

> Examines the present status of psychology, points of view, and progress of the discipline during the early twentieth century.

3. MAJOR PERIODICALS

Many journals occasionally publish articles on the history of psychology. Listed here are those journals that contain a relatively large number of such articles. The early volumes of the PSYCHOLOGICAL REVIEW had more historical articles than later volumes. A large number of the articles in the JOURNAL OF THE HISTORY OF THE BEHAVIORAL SCIENCES have been on the history of psychology.

AMERICAN JOURNAL OF PSYCHOLOGY. Urbana: University of Illinois Press, 1887-- . Quarterly.

> A venerable journal founded by G. Stanley Hall. Includes a broad range of articles in general psychology. Early volumes contain many historical items including necrologies, and later volumes still carry a few such articles. Book reviews.

AMERICAN PSYCHOLOGIST. Washington, D.C.: American Psychological Association, 1946-- . Monthly.

> Contains a broad range of materials of interest to the psychological community: archival documents; announcements on various topics such as deaths, awards, convention calendars, and training program information; comments; occasional specifically historical articles; and articles of general interest to psychologists. Annual index.

ANNUAL REVIEW OF PSYCHOLOGY. Palo Alto, Calif.: Annual Reviews, 1950-- .

> Each volume contains reviews and summaries of characteristic research and theoretical work in several major content areas. Topics may vary from year to year. Author and subject index.

ARCHIVES OF PSYCHOLOGY. Available in microfiche from Johnson Associates Inc., PO Box 1017, 321 Greenwich Avenue, Greenwich, Connecticut 06830.

> A microform set reproducing the forty-one volumes, containing three hundred monographs, published in this journal that was founded by R.S. Woodworth, from 1906 to 1945. Represents a sound primary source on the evolution of psychology during the forty years of the periodical's existence.

CATALOG OF SELECTED DOCUMENTS IN PSYCHOLOGY. Washington, D.C.: Journal Supplement Abstract Service of the American Psychological Association. 1971-- . Quarterly.

> Provides access to some literature reviews and bibliographies, as well as to occasional articles with a historical focus.

HISTORY OF EDUCATION QUARTERLY. New York: New York University, 1961-- .

> The official publication of the History of Education Society. Publishes articles on a wide range of topics such as influence of individuals, historiography, scientific knowledge of a given era, characterization of college students of particular times, curriculum development and evolution, and educational issues. Announcements, comments, and book reviews.

HISTORY OF SCIENCE. New York: Neale Watson Academic Publications, 1962-- . Quarterly.

> An international journal reviewing recent literature providing reassessments of selected topics in the history of science and articles dealing with prospective research topics. Book reviews, annotated bibliographies of books to be reviewed, and brief notes on contributors. Accounts of developments in training opportunities in the history of science. Volumes 1-10 were published annually.

ISIS. London: History of Science Society, 1913-- . 5/year.

> An international journal "devoted to the history of science and its cultural influences." Contains articles on a broad range of historical topics, as well as documents and translations, bibliographies, notes and correspondence, book reviews, notes on contributors, and administrative documents. Annual index.

JOURNAL OF GENERAL PSYCHOLOGY. Provincetown, Mass.: Journal Press, 1928-- . Quarterly.

A journal founded by Edward Bradford Titchener and Carl Murchison. Publishes original research and theoretical papers on a very broad range of topics in experimental, physiological, and comparative psychology. Occasionally publishes articles on the history of psychology.

JOURNAL OF THE HISTORY OF BIOLOGY. Cambridge, Mass.: Belknap Press of Harvard University Press, 1968-- . Semiannual.

Publishes papers characterizing biological thought during all periods of history; emphasizes developments during the past 100 years. Notes, book reviews, and annual index.

JOURNAL OF THE HISTORY OF IDEAS. Philadelphia: Journal of the History of Ideas, 1940-- . Quarterly.

Publishes a wide spectrum of papers on such topics as the influence of early thought on contemporary events; the impact of philosophical ideas on science, religion, and social thought; the influence of scientific thought on other intellectual domains; and the impact of widely accepted doctrines such as relativism or evolution on other ideas. Contains original articles, notes, and book reviews.

JOURNAL OF THE HISTORY OF THE BEHAVIORAL SCIENCES. Brandon, Vt.: Clinical Psychology Publishing Co., 1965-- . Quarterly.

A major outlet for historical studies in the behavioral sciences. Publishes a broad range of historical articles along with book reviews, news and notes, announcements, editorial comments, and brief biographical sketches of authors.

JOURNAL SUPPLEMENT ABSTRACT SERVICE.

See CATALOG OF SELECTED DOCUMENTS IN PSYCHOLOGY, this section, p. 46.

PSYCHOLOGICAL REVIEW. Washington, D.C.: American Psychological Association, 1894-- . Bimonthly.

Currently specializes in articles which advance theory in any of the subspecialties of scientific psychology. Earlier issues, broader in scope, contained many classic articles in the discipline now of interest to the historian of psychology: obituaries, appreciations, brief biographies of recently deceased psychologists, and papers on specific topics in the history of psychology.

SOCIAL RESEARCH: AN INTERNATIONAL QUARTERLY OF THE SOCIAL SCIENCES. New York: New School for Social Research, 1934-- .

A general periodical containing papers on a variety of topics in social sciences, broadly conceived. Occasional articles on the history of psychology.

4. BOOKS OF READINGS

Most anthologies in the history of psychology reprint excerpts from significant primary sources. Among such works are Dennis, Sahakian, and Shipley. The Diamond, and the Herrnstein and Boring books provide extensive and useful annotations. Some of the books of readings listed here contain different types of material (e.g., Boring's essays on the history of psychology, Evans's transcripts of interviews with eminent psychologists, and Postman's chapters on the history of specific research areas).

Averill, James R., ed. PATTERNS OF PSYCHOLOGICAL THOUGHT: READINGS IN HISTORICAL AND CONTEMPORARY TEXTS. Washington, D.C.: Hemisphere Publishing Corp., distributed by Halsted Press, New York, 1976. xii, 603 p.

An anthology of selections from the works of ten historical figures (Plato, Aristotle, Plotinus, Augustine, Aquinas, Descartes, Hume, Kant, Darwin, and Marx) on such topics as psychological explanation, consciousness, emotion, perception, and evolution. Also includes selections on the same topics from the writings of such recent theorists as Kohlberg, Chomsky, Gordon Allport, Lorenz, Skinner, and Luria. The unique arrangement permits comparison and appreciation of the insights and contributions of the early figures. Editorial comments introduce major subdivisions. Index.

Beck, Samuel J., and Molish, Herman B., eds. REFLEXES TO INTELLIGENCE: A READER IN CLINICAL PSYCHOLOGY. Glencoe, Ill.: Free Press, 1959. xiv, 669 p.

See section D13a, p. 353, for annotation.

Boring, Edwin G. HISTORY, PSYCHOLOGY AND SCIENCE: SELECTED PAPERS BY EDWIN G. BORING, HARVARD UNIVERSITY. Edited by Robert I. Watson and Donald T. Campbell. New York: John Wiley and Sons, 1963. xii, 372 p.

Contains thirty of Boring's seminal papers on the history, sociology, and psychology of science in five major sections: the Zeitgeist and the psychology of science, the history of psychology, the scientific method, the mind-body problem, and the psychology of communicating science. Editorial perspectives introduce each section. References. Index.

_____. PSYCHOLOGIST AT LARGE: AN AUTOBIOGRAPHY AND SELECTED ESSAYS. New York: Basic Books, 1961. 371 p.

Autobiography of the dean of historians of psychology, highlighting his work with Titchener, his personal psychoanalysis, and his career at Harvard. Includes letters and papers on a broad range of topics such as the moon illusion, Edward Bradford Titchener, Lewis Madison Terman, a history of introspection, and learning versus training of graduate students. Bibliography of Boring's principal publications, 1912–60. Index.

Bringmann, Wolfgang C., and Balance, William D.G., advisory eds. ORIGINS OF PSYCHOLOGY: A COLLECTION OF EARLY WRITINGS. New York: Alan R. Liss, 1975-- . Annual.

Two volumes published each year include facsimile reproductions of classic contributions covering a wide spectrum of topics in early psychology. Volumes available through 1977: works by Morton Prince, I. Kant, Charles A. Strong, F.A. von Hartsen (volume 1); David Ferrier, Karl Schaffner, P. Jousset, Baron de Richemont, H. Helmholtz (volume 2); Adolf Kussmaul, v. Krafft-Ebing, E. Kraepelin, G.Th. Fechner, J.-M. Charcot, and A. Pitres (volume 3); and H.M. Bernheim, Wilhelm Wundt, George Henry Lewes, G.Th. Fechner (volume 4).

Brožek, Josef, and Evans, Rand B., eds. R.I. WATSON'S SELECTED PAPERS ON THE HISTORY OF PSYCHOLOGY. Hanover, N.H.: University Press of New England, 1976. 420 p.

Reprints some of the papers of a major historian of psychology together with an introduction, an autobiography, and a bibliography of Watson's writings. Index.

Dennis, Wayne, ed. READINGS IN THE HISTORY OF PSYCHOLOGY. New York: Appleton-Century-Crofts, 1948. xi, 587 p.

Contains sixty-one classic articles and excerpts from monographs and books on a broad range of topics, representing a time span from Aristotle to Clark Hull, selected by the editor and a panel of fourteen other psychologists. Name index.

Diamond, Solomon, ed. THE ROOTS OF PSYCHOLOGY: A SOURCEBOOK IN THE HISTORY OF IDEAS. New York: Basic Books, 1974. xvii, 781 p.

Over 300 brief selections in twenty-eight topic areas in the history of psychology. Includes works not widely anthologized. Offers useful commentary to provide continuity and context preceding each selection. Bibliographical materials. Appendixes on vocabulary and on titles of works excerpted. Index.

Evans, Richard I. THE MAKING OF PSYCHOLOGY: DISCUSSIONS WITH CREATIVE CONTRIBUTORS. New York: Alfred A. Knopf, 1976. xvii, 381 p.

Transcripts of interviews with twenty-eight eminent individuals who have made outstanding contributions in areas such as ethology, development, learning, motivation, emotion, physiological psychology, personality, and social psychology. Includes a biographical sketch of each interviewee and a brief statement summarizing the main points of the interview. Index.

Henle, Mary; Jaynes, Julian; and Sullivan, John J., eds. HISTORICAL CONCEPTIONS OF PSYCHOLOGY. New York: Springer Publishing Co., 1973. xii, 323 p.

Twenty-one articles on such topics as approaches to history, psychological movements, and theories and theorists. Includes an annotated bibliography of sources in the history of psychology and a bibliography of the published writings of Edna Heidbreder. Index.

Herrnstein, Richard J., and Boring, Edwin G., eds. A SOURCE BOOK IN THE HISTORY OF PSYCHOLOGY. Cambridge, Mass.: Harvard University Press, 1966. xvii, 636 p.

Extensively annotated readings organized into chapters on such traditional topics in the history of experimental psychology as sensation, psychophysics, perception of size and distance, cerebral localization, the reflex, association, evolution, and learning. Indexes.

Hilgard, Ernest R., ed. AMERICAN PSYCHOLOGY IN HISTORICAL PERSPECTIVE: ADDRESSES OF THE PRESIDENTS OF THE AMERICAN PSYCHOLOGICAL ASSOCIATION, 1892-1977. Washington, D.C.: American Psychological Association, 1978. viii, 558 p.

Hillix, William A., and Marx, Melvin H., eds. SYSTEMS AND THEORIES IN PSYCHOLOGY: A READER. St. Paul, Minn.: West Publishing, 1974. viii, 437 p.

Organized to complement the Marx and Hillix text, SYSTEMS AND THEORIES IN PSYCHOLOGY (see section B1, p. 36). Includes fifty classic papers on such topics as association, structuralism, functionalism, behaviorism, neobehaviorism, Gestalt psychology, psychoanalysis, and personality theory. Editorial comments introduce each section. Provides a brief biographical statement on the author of each paper. Index.

Matson, F.W., ed. BEING, BECOMING AND BEHAVIOR. New York: George Braziller, 1967. xii, 288 p.

Thirty-one readings in the history of psychology organized in five parts: psychology as philosophy; psychology as experimental science, with readings from such pioneers as Fechner, Wundt, and Pavlov; humanistic psychology, with readings from such individuals as James, Allport, and Maslow; psychotherapy, with readings from nine major theorists; and philosophy as psychology, with readings from Nietzsche, Jaspers, Cassirer, and Tillich. Helpful editorial introductions to each major section. Index.

Murphy, Gardner, and Murphy, Lois B., eds. WESTERN PSYCHOLOGY: FROM THE GREEKS TO WILLIAM JAMES. New York: Basic Books, 1969. x, 296 p.

See section B1, p. 37, for annotation.

ORIGINS OF PSYCHOLOGY: A COLLECTION OF EARLY WRITINGS. New York: Alan R. Liss, 1975-- .

See Bringmann, Wolfgang C., and Balance, William D.G., advisory eds. ORIGINS OF PSYCHOLOGY: A COLLECTION OF EARLY WRITINGS, this section, p. 49.

Postman, Leo, ed. PSYCHOLOGY IN THE MAKING: HISTORIES OF SE-LECTED RESEARCH PROBLEMS. New York: Alfred A. Knopf, 1962. viii, 785, xxxiv p.

Original essays presenting historical perspective on topics in several areas of experimental psychology: biological foundations; perception, learning, and memory; and individual differences and personality. References follow each chapter. Index.

Rand, Benjamin, ed. THE CLASSICAL PSYCHOLOGISTS: SELECTIONS ILLUS-TRATING PSYCHOLOGY FROM ANAXAGORAS TO WUNDT. Boston: Houghton Mifflin, 1912. xxi, 734 p.

A large collection of milestone psychological and philosophical excerpts representing Greek, patristic, medieval, and modern thought from Hobbes to Wundt. Sparse bibliographical materials in footnotes. Index.

Robinson, Daniel N., ed. SIGNIFICANT CONTRIBUTIONS TO THE HISTORY OF PSYCHOLOGY, 1750-1920. 28 vols. Washington, D.C.: University Publications of America, 1977.

A massive publication venture that provides access to the seminal works that led to modern psychology. Selected by a leading historian of science, the texts and treatises are prefaced by him with helpful comments that place each work into its scientific, intellectual, and social context. Five series: Series A, Orientations, consists of eleven volumes, reprinting works by such figures as Condillac, Bain, Herbart, Fichte, Ward, Dewey, Cattell, Thorndike, and Wertheimer. Series B, Psychometrics and Educational Psychology, four volumes, has works by Herbart, Pestalozzi, Froebel, Sully, Binet, Galton, and Stern. The five volumes of Series C, Medical Psychology, reprint contributions by Ribot,

Janet, Pinel, Maudsley, and Binet. Series D, Comparative Psychology, four volumes, contains works by such psychologists as Wundt, Morgan, Jennings, Angell, and Galton. The four volumes of Series E, Physiological Psychology, consist of writings by such contributors as Whytt, Hall, Flourens, Ferrier, Magendie, Binet, and Huxley.

Sahakian, William S., ed. HISTORY OF PSYCHOLOGY: A SOURCE BOOK IN SYSTEMATIC PSYCHOLOGY. Itasca, Ill.: F.E. Peacock, 1968. xiv, 559 p.

A reader composed of classical papers and excerpts in a variety of areas including personality theory, experimental psychology, psychotherapy, child psychology, and others. Contains a calendar of important events in the history of psychology. Index.

Sexton, Virginia Staudt, and Misiak, Henryk, eds. HISTORICAL PERSPECTIVES IN PSYCHOLOGY: READINGS. Monterey, Calif.: Brooks/Cole, 1971. ix, 452 p.

Articles of recent origin examine such topics in the history of psychology as the relation of psychology to other sciences, theoretical issues in psychology, American psychology, psychology in other countries, and psychology's future. Editorial comments introduce subdivisions and provide brief biographical sketches of each author. References follow each selection. Index.

_____. PSYCHOLOGY AROUND THE WORLD. Monterey, Calif.: Brooks/ Cole, 1976. viii, 470 p.

Describes the development and current status of psychology in forty countries. Each chapter written by an authority on psychology in the country in question. Extensive name index. Subject index.

Shipley, Thorne, ed. CLASSICS IN PSYCHOLOGY. New York: Philosophical Library, 1961. xx, 1,342 p.

A massive volume of thirty-six influential papers in the history of psychology on such areas as sensation and perception, psychopathology, neurology, psychoanalysis, behavior theory, individual differences, child psychology, Gestalt psychology, and social psychology. Brief biographies and lists of important publications of or about the author follow each paper. Index.

Watson, Robert I., Sr. BASIC WRITINGS IN THE HISTORY OF PSYCHOLOGY. New York: Oxford University Press, 1979. 366 p.

An annotated selection of fifty of the most eminent contributions to psychology from Descartes through Skinner. Chronological orientation serves to illustrate the influence of earlier works on those that came later.   Statements of context precede each excerpt, and each is followed by an editorial examination of its significance in relation to the historical development of psychology.

Wolman, Benjamin B., ed.   HISTORICAL ROOTS OF CONTEMPORARY PSY-CHOLOGY.   New York: Harper and Row, 1968.   viii, 376 p.

Sixteen papers intended to elucidate developments in three histori-cal content areas: association and learning; thought processes (with focus on James, Janet, and Freud); and personalistic and cultural psychology.

Zimbardo, Philip, and Maslach, Christina, eds.   PSYCHOLOGY FOR OUR TIMES: READINGS.   2d ed.   Glenview, Ill.:   Scott, Foresman, 1977.   424 p.

5.   DEVELOPMENT OF PSYCHOLOGY IN DIFFERENT GEOGRAPHICAL LOCATIONS AND TIMES

Many articles try to characterize psychology in a particular place or time. This section includes works on early psychology (ancient, medieval, and Renais-sance), followed by subcategories specific to different parts of the world. Broader works often refer to psychology in different locations and times as well; see the listings in section B1, p. 31.   Special attention is called to the book of readings entitled PSYCHOLOGY AROUND THE WORLD, edited by Virginia S. Sexton and Henryk Misiak, listed in section B4, p. 52.   The geographical sub-categories in the present section include Africa, Asia and India, Australia and New Zealand, Austria and Germany, Canada, Eastern Europe, England, France, Italy, Mexico and Central and South America, the Soviet Union, the United States (including a supplementary section containing discussions of the history of selected psychology departments in U.S. institutions), and other western Euro-pean countries.

a.   Ancient, Medieval, and Renaissance

Materials in this section are supplemented by some of the entries in section E1b, p. 382, which lists articles on the psychological teachings of major philosophers.

Cohen, Morris R., and Drabkin, I.E.   A SOURCE BOOK IN GREEK SCIENCE. New York: McGraw-Hill, 1948.   xxi, 579 p.

A comprehensive work covering Greek achievements in mathematics, astronomy, geography, physics, chemistry, geology, biology, medi-cine, and psychology.   Within psychology covers such topics as animal traits, animal senses, human senses, association, and emo-tions.   Lists important books on Greek science.   Notes.   Index.

Crombie, A.C.   "Early Concepts of the Senses and the Mind."   SCIENTIFIC

AMERICAN 210 (May 1964): 108-16.

> Presents an overview of seventeenth-century ideas of such thinkers as Kepler, Descartes, and Duverney. These and others "separated answerable physical questions from unanswerable metaphysical questions."

_____. MEDIEVAL AND EARLY MODERN SCIENCE. 2d ed., rev. 2 vols. New York: Doubleday-Anchor Books, 1959. Originally published in 1953 by Harvard University Press as AUGUSTINE TO GALILEO: THE HISTORY OF SCIENCE A.D. 400-1650.

> Provides a thorough grounding in the history of science, including some psychological thought, up to the Newtonian revolution. Index for each volume (Science in the Middle Ages: 5th-13th Centuries; and Science in the Later Middle Ages and Early Modern Times: 13th-17th Centuries).

Cruttwell, Patrick. "Physiology and Psychology in Shakespeare's Age." JOURNAL OF THE HISTORY OF IDEAS 12 (January 1951): 75-89.

Diamond, Solomon. "Marin Cureau De La Chambre (1594-1669)." JOURNAL OF THE HISTORY OF THE BEHAVIORAL SCIENCES 4 (January 1968): 40-54.

> An overview of selected topics in La Chambre's work on emotions, animal reason and instinct, and memory and muscular movement. Describes La Chambre's work as a physician.

Dowden, Edward. "Elizabethan Psychology." ATLANTIC MONTHLY 100 (September 1907): 388-99.

> Outlines some of the psychological concepts of such thinkers as Spenser, Shakespeare, John Davies, and Thomas Wright.

Eng, Erling W. "The Significance of the Self-portrait and the Mirror in Renaissance Developments in Psychology." PROCEEDINGS OF THE XTH INTERNATIONAL CONGRESS OF THE HISTORY OF SCIENCE 2 (1964): 1045-47.

Fernberger, Samuel W. "Fundamental Categories as Determiners of Psychological Systems: An Excursion into Ancient Chinese Psychologies." PSYCHOLOGICAL REVIEW 42 (November 1935): 544-54.

> Compares Greek and early Chinese thought, and describes the relation of Chinese psychologies to cosmological elements prominent in ancient Chinese thought.

Forest, Louise C. Turner. "A Caveat for Critics Against Invoking Elizabethan Psychology." PUBLICATIONS OF THE MODERN LANGUAGE ASSOCIATION OF AMERICA 61 (September 1946): 651-72.

Claims there was no single Elizabethan psychology, but rather a variety of Elizabethan psychologies.

Gardiner, Judith Kegan. "Elizabethan Psychology and Burton's Anatomy of Melancholy." JOURNAL OF THE HISTORY OF IDEAS 38 (July–September 1977): 373–88.

A general overview of Elizabethan psychology followed by an analysis of Burton's position on such key issues as the mind–body problem, motivation, the nature of personality, and the characteristics of melancholy.

Gerard, Eugene O. "Medieval Psychology: Dogmatic Aristotelianism or Observational Empiricism." JOURNAL OF THE HISTORY OF THE BEHAVIORAL SCIENCES 2 (October 1966): 315–29.

Notes that recent historical research indicates greater contributions of medieval science to observational empiricism than heretofore thought. Describes some medieval contributions to observational empiricism and reviews the thought of Aquinas on such topics as methodology in the study of behavior, cognition, emotion, and social processes.

Harvey, Ruth E. THE INWARD WITS: PSYCHOLOGICAL THEORY IN THE MIDDLE AGES AND THE RENAISSANCE. London: Warburg Institute, University of London, 1975. 79 p.

Presents a brief overview of contributions of leading thinkers of the Middle Ages on topics such as dreams, magic, senses, memory, and intellect. Notes. Index.

Hershenson, David B. "Vocational Development Theory Before 1400." JOURNAL OF THE HISTORY OF THE BEHAVIORAL SCIENCES 10 (April 1974): 170–79.

Describes the theory of vocational development found in Geoffrey Chaucer's THE CANTERBURY TALES, written between 1387 and 1394.

Jaynes, Julian. "The Problem of Animate Motion in the Seventeenth Century." JOURNAL OF THE HISTORY OF IDEAS 31 (April–June 1970): 219–34.

Jaynes, Julian, and Woodward, William. "In the Shadow of the Enlightenment: 1. Reimarus Against the Epicureans." JOURNAL OF THE HISTORY OF THE BEHAVIORAL SCIENCES 10 (January 1974): 3–15.

Provides information on the life of Reimarus as well as on his thought on topics such as motivation, animal instincts, and the origin of life.

_____. "In the Shadow of the Enlightenment: II. Reimarus and his Theory of Drives." JOURNAL OF THE HISTORY OF THE BEHAVIORAL SCIENCES 10 (April 1974): 144-59.

Describes Reimarus's work on animal behavior with special emphasis on drives. Offers a critique of his work and an assessment of his influence.

Juhasz, Joseph B. "Greek Theories of Imagination." JOURNAL OF THE HISTORY OF THE BEHAVIORAL SCIENCES 7 (January 1971): 39-58.

Discusses the thought on imagination of the Milesians, the Pythagoreans, the Eleatics, the Atomists, and the Sophists, and of such individuals as Hippocrates, Socrates, Plato, and Aristotle.

Lang, Frederick R. "Psychological Terminology in the Tusculans." JOURNAL OF THE HISTORY OF THE BEHAVIORAL SCIENCES 8 (October 1972): 419-36.

Presents Latin psychological terms found in books three and four of the TUSCULAN DISPUTATIONS and Greek originals or equivalents provided by Cicero.

Laver, A.B. "D'Assigny and the Art of Memory." JOURNAL OF THE HISTORY OF THE BEHAVIORAL SCIENCES 9 (July 1973): 240-50.

A brief biographical sketch of D'Assigny (1643-1717) and a discussion of his book, THE ART OF MEMORY, which contains prescriptions for developing and improving memory.

_____. "Precursors of Psychology in Ancient Egypt." JOURNAL OF THE HISTORY OF THE BEHAVIORAL SCIENCES 8 (April 1972): 181-95.

Reviews ancient Egyptian thought on a broad variety of topics such as the function of the heart, the relation between cardiac and psychological activities, the function of the brain, and the significance of names.

Mesulam, Marek M., and Perry, Jon. "The Diagnosis of Love-Sickness: Experimental Psychophysiology Without the Polygraph." PSYCHOPHYSIOLOGY 9 (September 1972): 546-51.

Describes work by the ancient physicians Galen and Avicenna.

Moore, Kate Gordon. "Aurelius Augustine on Imagination." JOURNAL OF PSYCHOLOGY 23 (1947): 161-68.

_____. "Johannes Scotus Erigena on Imagination." JOURNAL OF PSYCHOLOGY 23 (1947): 169-78.

_____. "Some Arab Doctrines on Imagination: A Chapter in the History of Psychology." JOURNAL OF PSYCHOLOGY 41 (1956): 127-33.

Ramul, Konstantin. "Some Early Measurements and Ratings in Psychology." AMERICAN PSYCHOLOGIST 18 (October 1963): 653-59.

    Describes measurements and ratings of such dimensions as visual acuity in the early eighteenth century, memory in Greek times, span of attention in the fifth century A.D., and personality in the early eighteenth century.

Reinmuth, O.W. "Greek Contributions to the Terminology of Psychology." PSYCHOLOGICAL REVIEW 41 (September 1934): 403-23.

Simon, Bennett. "Models of Mind and Mental Illness in Ancient Greece: II. The Platonic Model. Section 1." JOURNAL OF THE HISTORY OF THE BEHAVIORAL SCIENCES 8 (October 1972): 389-404.

    Provides background materials on early Greek philosophy and an exposition of Plato's views of mind and madness. Argues that "the Platonic 'model' of mind and madness is described in language pointing to an important unconscious assumption."

_____. "Models of Mind and Mental Illness in Ancient Greece: II. The Platonic Model. Section 2." JOURNAL OF THE HISTORY OF THE BEHAVIORAL SCIENCES 9 (January 1973): 3-17.

    Examines Plato's views on the treatment of mental illness and the similarities between Plato and Freud.

Simon, Bennett, and Weiner, Herbert. "Models of Mind and Mental Illness in Ancient Greece: 1. The Homeric Model of Mind." JOURNAL OF THE HISTORY OF THE BEHAVIORAL SCIENCES 2 (October 1966): 303-14.

    The first of three papers (see preceding two entries) dealing with explanations of mental illness and recommended treatment procedures in Greece from 700 to 300 B.C. The Homeric (poetic) model, presented in this article, is followed by the Platonic (philosophical) and Hippocratic (medical) models.

Smith, Noel W. "The Ancient Background to Greek Psychology and Some Implications for Today." PSYCHOLOGICAL RECORD 24 (Summer 1974): 309-24.

    Reviews aspects of belief systems, especially about mind-body relations, held by Egyptians, Mesopotamians, and peoples of smaller early tribes, and traces their influence on Greek thought. Argues that naturalistic modes of thought prevailed in ancient civilizations and in Greece. Dualistic notions, which still impede the progress of scientific psychology, emerged "in the escapist philosophies of the turbulent and socially inimical Hellenistic period."

_____ . "Belief Systems and Psychological Concepts of Ancient Egypt to the End of the Old Kingdom (2700 B.C.)." PROCEEDINGS OF THE ANNUAL CONVENTION OF THE AMERICAN PSYCHOLOGICAL ASSOCIATION 6, pt. 2 (1971): 721-22.

Strong, Charles A. "A Sketch of the History of Psychology Among the Greeks." AMERICAN JOURNAL OF PSYCHOLOGY 4 (December 1891): 177-97.

> Discusses selected psychological thought of pre-Socratic philosophers, Socrates, Plato, and Aristotle.

Thornton, Harry. "Socrates and the History of Psychology." JOURNAL OF THE HISTORY OF THE BEHAVIORAL SCIENCES 5 (October 1969): 326-39.

> Presents a critical analysis of selected topics in a chapter on "Socratic Anthropology" in volume 1 of J.R. Kantor's THE SCIENTIFIC EVOLUTION OF PSYCHOLOGY (see section B, p. 34), and sets forth alternative interpretations of Socratic thought.

Watson, Foster. "The Father of Modern Psychology." PSYCHOLOGICAL REVIEW 22 (September 1915): 333-53.

> Discusses the possible claims of Aristotle as father of psychology and of Descartes as father of modern psychology. Concludes that in terms of methods employed (empirical-inductive and introspective) and problems investigated (association, memory, thought, feeling), Juan Luis Vives (1492-1540) is the true originator of modern psychology.

b. Different Geographical Locations

Sexton, Virginia Staudt, and Misiak, Henryk, eds. PSYCHOLOGY AROUND THE WORLD. Monterey, Calif.: Brooks/Cole, 1976. viii, 470 p.

> See section B4, p. 52, for annotation.

Webb, Wilse B. "Psychologists in Other Countries." In his THE PROFESSION OF PSYCHOLOGY, pp. 267-81. New York: Holt, Rinehart and Winston, 1962.

> Briefly discusses psychology in the Soviet Union, other countries in the Soviet orbit, Great Britain, Italy, West Germany, Eire, Northern Ireland, Egypt, Greece, Sweden, Finland, and Japan.

i. AFRICA

Abdi, Yusuf Omer. "The Problems and Prospects of Psychology in Africa." INTERNATIONAL JOURNAL OF PSYCHOLOGY 10 (1975): 227-34.

Speculates about why psychology did not develop substantially in
Africa and evaluates the present status of African psychology.

Hoorweg, J.C., and Marais, H.C. PSYCHOLOGY IN AFRICA: A BIBLIOG-
RAPHY. Leyden, The Netherlands: Afrika-Studiecentrum, 1969. 139 p.

Marais, H.C., and Hoorweg, J.C. "Psychology in Africa: A Bibliographical
Survey." INTERNATIONAL JOURNAL OF PSYCHOLOGY 6 (1971): 329-35.

   Provides an analysis of numbers of African publications in psychology from 1880 to 1969 and provides breakdowns by language, content area, and geographic part of Africa.

Oliensis, David G. "Psychology in Uganda." PSYCHOLOGIA 9 (December
1966): 210.

   Reports on the work of a few expatriate psychologists working in
   Uganda.

Prothro, E. Terry, and Melikian, Levon H. "Psychology in the Arab Near
East." PSYCHOLOGICAL BULLETIN 52 (July 1955): 303-10.

   Briefly describes psychology and psychologists in Egypt, Lebanon,
   Syria, Iraq, and the Persian Gulf area.

Wickert, Frederic R., ed. READINGS IN AFRICAN PSYCHOLOGY FROM
FRENCH LANGUAGE SOURCES. East Lansing: Michigan African Studies
Center, State University, 1967. x, 381 p.

   Fifty-two papers exploring topics in testing and African culture,
   personnel work, attitudes and attitude change, education and psychology, and child psychology. Bibliographical materials. Index.

ii. ASIA AND INDIA

Akhilananda, Swami. HINDU PSYCHOLOGY; ITS MEANING FOR THE WEST.
Introduction by Gordon W. Allport. New York: Harper, 1946. xviii, 241 p.

   A nontechnical introduction to Hindu psychology discussing such
   topics as cognition, emotion, meditation, superconscious experience, religion, psychotherapy, and philosophy of life. Bibliography.
   Index.

Ayman, Iraj. "Industrial and Organizational Psychology in Iran." AMERICAN
PSYCHOLOGIST 32 (November 1977): 905-9.

Bagchi, Amalendu. "The Indian Approach to Psychology." EDUCATION AND
PSYCHOLOGY, DELHI 3 (1956): 1-16.

Banerji, Manmatha Nath. "Hindu Psychology: Physiological Basis and Experimental Methods." AMERICAN JOURNAL OF PSYCHOLOGY 50 (November 1937): 328–46.

Chang, Y.H., ed. SELECTED PAPERS FROM THE CHINESE JOURNAL OF PSYCHOLOGY. Vol. 1. Shanghai: Chung Hwa Book Co., 1932. 398 p.

Chin, Robert, and Chin, Ai-li S. PSYCHOLOGICAL RESEARCH IN COMMUNIST CHINA: 1949-1966: Cambridge: M.I.T. Press, 1969. xii, 274 p.

> An overview of the historical origins and evolution of the field of psychology in China from 1949 to 1966. Describes such major areas of research as medical psychology, labor psychology, educational psychology, and research on moral character and individuality. Glossary of Chinese terms and compilation of psychological terms published by the Chinese Academy of Sciences. Bibliography. Index.

Chou, Siegen K. "The Present Status of Psychology in China." AMERICAN JOURNAL OF PSYCHOLOGY 38 (October 1927): 664–66.

_____. "Psychological Laboratories in China." AMERICAN JOURNAL OF PSYCHOLOGY 44 (April 1932): 372–74.

_____. "Trends in Chinese Psychological Interest Since 1922." AMERICAN JOURNAL OF PSYCHOLOGY 38 (July 1927): 487–88.

De Vos, George A.; Murakami, Eiji; and Murase, Takao. "Recent Research, Psychodiagnosis, and Therapy in Japan." In PROGRESS IN CLINICAL PSYCHOLOGY, edited by Lawrence Edwin Abt and Bernard F. Riess, vol. 6, pp. 226–234. New York: Grune and Stratton, 1964.

Ganguli, H[arish].C. "Developments in Industrial Psychology in India." INTERNATIONAL REVIEW OF APPLIED PSYCHOLOGY 20 (October 1971): 121–42.

_____. "Psychological Research in India: 1920-1967." INTERNATIONAL JOURNAL OF PSYCHOLOGY 6 (1971): 165–77.

Gardiner, Harry W. "Psychology in Thailand." PSYCHOLOGIA 11 (June 1968): 122–24.

Gilbert, Albin R. "An Essay on the History of Asian Psychology." PSYCHOLOGIA 17 (September 1974): 121–25.

> Briefly contrasts Eastern and Western approaches to introspection and personality. Comments on Eastern goals to heighten or illumine personality.

Guthrie, George M., and Jaime, Bulatao, "Psychology in the Philippines." PSYCHOLOGIA 11 (December 1968): 201-6.

Hake, Harold W. "Japanese Experimental Psychology Viewed from America." PSYCHOLOGIA 1 (June 1958): 184-86.

Hirota, Kimiyoshi. "Development of Social Psychology in Japan." PSYCHOLOGIA 2 (December 1959): 216-28.

Hsiao, Sigmund. "Psychology in China." AMERICAN PSYCHOLOGIST 32 (May 1977): 374-76.

> Brief overview of major areas of psychological research in the People's Republic of China.

Jayasuriya, D. Laksiri. "Recent Psychological Research in Ceylon." PSYCHOLOGIA 8 (September 1965): 169-74.

Jayasuriya, J.E. "Psychology in Ceylon." PSYCHOLOGIA 1 (December 1957): 127-28.

Kaketa, Katsumi. "Psychoanalysis in Japan." PSYCHOLOGIA 1 (December 1958): 247-52.

Kido, Mantaro. "Origin of Japanese Psychology and Its Development." PSYCHOLOGIA 4 (March 1961): 1-10.

> An overview of the history of Japanese psychology from early times to the modern era.

Kilby, Richard W. "Impressions of Psychology in India." PSYCHOLOGIA 11 (December 1968): 207-10.

Kirihara, Shigemi H. "Industrial Psychology in Japan." PSYCHOLOGIA 2 (December 1959): 206-15.

Kuo, You-Yuh. "Psychology in Communist China." PSYCHOLOGICAL RECORD 21 (Winter 1971): 95-105.

> Emphasizes areas of research, the philosophical basis of Chinese Communist psychology, and the questions raised by the Chinese regarding the capitalistic basis of some of American psychology.

Lloyd, Van Voorhees. "Psychology in Colleges and Universities in Japan and the Republic of Korea." JOURNAL OF PSYCHOLOGY 61 (November 1965): 183-91.

References in History of Psychology

McGinnies, Elliott. "Psychology in Japan: 1960." AMERICAN PSYCHOLO-
GIST 15 (August 1960): 556–62.

Melikian, Levon. "Clinical Psychology in the Arab Middle East." In PROG-
RESS IN CLINICAL PSYCHOLOGY, edited by Lawrence Edwin Abt and
Bernard F. Riess, vol. 6, pp. 242–49. New York: Grune and Stratton, 1964.

Mitra, S.C. "Progress of Psychology in India." INDIAN JOURNAL OF PSY-
CHOLOGY 30 (1955): 1–21.

Mitra, S.C., and Mukhopadhyay, P.K. "Development of Psychological Studies
in India. From 1916-1950." PSYCHOLOGIA 1 (June 1958): 191-202.

A brief historical overview accompanied by over 400 references.

Motoyoshi, Ryoji, and Iwahara, Shinkuro. "Japanese Studies on Animal Behavior in the Last Decade." PSYCHOLOGIA 3 (September 1960): 135–48.

Murphy, Gardner, and Murphy, Lois B., eds. ASIAN PSYCHOLOGY. New
York: Basic Books, 1968. xv, 238 p.

Selections from traditional literature which characterize psychological thought in India, China, and Japan. Editorial comments precede the sections on each of the three countries. Bibliographic
information in footnotes. Companion volume to the editors' WEST-
ERN PSYCHOLOGY (see section B2, p. 37). Index.

Nandy, Ashis. "The Non-paradigmatic Crisis of Indian Psychology: Reflections
on a Recipient Culture of Science." INDIAN JOURNAL OF PSYCHOLOGY
49 (March 1974): 1–20.

A discussion of the problems of psychology in the Indian culture.

Okamoto, S. "Dr. Matataro Matsumoto: His Career and Achievements."
JOURNAL OF THE HISTORY OF THE BEHAVIORAL SCIENCES 12 (1976): 31-38.

Biographical information on Dr. Matsumoto, "the most eminent fig-
ure in the history of psychology in Japan." Describes his achievements as an author, teacher, founder of journals, and organizer of
the Japanese Psychological Association.

Pan, Shuh. "China's Recent Research Work on Psychology (Mainland)." PSY-
CHOLOGIA 2 (December 1959): 193-201.

Pandey, R.E. "Psychology in India." AMERICAN PSYCHOLOGIST 24 (October 1969): 936-39.

Provides an overview of psychology in India with materials on historical developments, growth of psychology departments in universities (1920-64), student enrollments in graduate programs, and theoretical trends.

Pareek, Udai. "Psychology in India." PSYCHOLOGIA 1 (June 1957): 55-59.

Prabhu, G.G. "Clinical Psychology in India: In Retrospect and Prospect." INDIAN JOURNAL OF CLINICAL PSYCHOLOGY 1 (1974): 3-7.

Saradatta, L., and Miyake, K. "Psychology in Thailand." PSYCHOLOGIA 2 (June 1959): 120-23.

Sastry, N.S.N. "Growth of Psychology in India." INDIAN JOURNAL OF PSYCHOLOGY 7 (1932): 1-40.

_____. "Trends of Psychological Research in India." INDIAN JOURNAL OF PSYCHOLOGY 30 (1955): 25-33.

Sato, K., and Graham, C.H. "Psychology in Japan." PSYCHOLOGICAL BULLETIN 51 (September 1954): 443-64.

Surveys the history of psychology in Japan and provides an overview of work in major content areas such as social psychology, personality, clinical psychology, general psychology, experimental psychology, and developmental psychology. 222 references.

Sen, I. "The Standpoint of Indian Psychology." INDIAN JOURNAL OF PSYCHOLOGY 26 (1951): 89-95.

Su, Hsiang-Yu. "Psychological Activities in Taiwan." PSYCHOLOGIA 2 (December 1959): 202-5.

Sukemane, Seisah; Haruk, Kataka; and Kashiwagi, Keiko. "Studies on Social Learning in Japan." AMERICAN PSYCHOLOGIST (November 1977): 924-33.

Tanaka, Yoshihisa. "Status of Japanese Experimental Psychology." ANNUAL REVIEW OF PSYCHOLOGY 17 (1966): 233-72.

An overview of the history of psychological studies in Japan. Discusses training procedures and examines work in vision and perception. One hundred ninety references.

Thwin, Hla, comp. "Department of Psychology, University of Rangoon, Burma." PSYCHOLOGIA 5 (June 1962): 107-11.

Historical development of the psychology department at the University of Rangoon.

Tomoda, Fujio. "Client-centered Therapy in Japan." PSYCHOLOGIA 1 (December 1958): 237-41.

Tsushima, Tadashi. "Notes on Trends and Problems of Psychotherapy in Japan." PSYCHOLOGIA 1 (December 1958): 231-36.

Whittaker, James O. "Psychology in China: A Brief Survey." AMERICAN PSYCHOLOGIST 25 (August 1970): 757-59.

> Reviews recent developments in psychology in Communist China including areas of emphasis, locus of research, and levels of interest.

Yoda, Arata, and Hidano, Tadashi. "Development of Educational Psychology in Japan." PSYCHOLOGIA 2 (September 1959): 137-49.

Zaidi, S.M. Hafeez. "Pakistan Psychology." AMERICAN PSYCHOLOGIST 14 (August 1959): 532-36.

_____. "Psychology in Pakistan." PSYCHOLOGIA 1 (June 1958): 187-90.

iii. AUSTRALIA AND NEW ZEALAND

Brown, L.B., and Fuchs, Alfred H. "Early Experimental Psychology in New Zealand: The Hunter-Titchener Letters." JOURNAL OF THE HISTORY OF THE BEHAVIORAL SCIENCES 7 (January 1971): 10-22.

> Notes the early British influence on psychology in New Zealand and, through the Hunter-Titchener letters, traces themes in the development of experimental psychology.

Hunter, Thomas. "The Development of Psychology in New Zealand." QUARTERLY BULLETIN OF THE BRITISH PSYCHOLOGICAL SOCIETY 3 (1952): 101-11.

Latham, John. "Psychology Sixty Years Ago in Melbourne." BULLETIN OF THE BRITISH PSYCHOLOGICAL SOCIETY 31 (1957): 33-34.

> A brief account of the beginnings of psychology as a discipline at the University of Melbourne.

McElwain, D.W. "A Review of Psychology in Australia." OCCUPATIONAL PSYCHOLOGY, LONDON 24 (1950): 141-52.

Martin, A.H. THE PRESENT STATUS OF PSYCHOLOGY. Sydney, Australia: Sydney University Reproductions, (1926). 12 p. Also in AUSTRALASIAN JOURNAL OF PSYCHOLOGY AND PHILOSOPHY 3 (1926): 40-51.

An address delivered in 1925 to the Australian Association for Philosophy and Psychology. Reviews the growth of psychology in Australian and New Zealand universities.

Thornton, Henry. "Synthesis: Some Reflections on the History of Psychology." AUSTRALIAN JOURNAL OF PSYCHOLOGY 11 (1959): 99-105.

Winterbourn, R.A. "A Review of Psychology in New Zealand." AUSTRALIAN JOURNAL OF PSYCHOLOGY 5 (1953): 17-27.

iv. AUSTRIA AND GERMANY

Adams, James F. "Current Developments in Germanic Academic Psychology." JOURNAL OF THE HISTORY OF THE BEHAVIORAL SCIENCES 2 (April 1966): 168-70.

_____. "A Developmental and Historical Analysis of Psychology Within the Universities of Austria and Germany Over a Ten-Year Period: 1955-1965." TRANSACTIONS OF THE NEW YORK ACADEMY OF SCIENCES 28 (April 1966): 754-60.

_____."The Status of Psychology in the Universities of Austria and Germany, 1955-1956." JOURNAL OF GENERAL PSYCHOLOGY 56 (April 1957): 147-57.

_____. "The Status of Psychology in the Universities of Austria and Germany, 1960-61." JOURNAL OF GENERAL PSYCHOLOGY 67 (October 1962): 337-47.

Angermeier, W.F. "Psychology in East Germany." AMERICAN PSYCHOLOGIST 19 (November 1964): 846.

Bondy, Curt, in cooperation with Klaus Riegel. SOCIAL PSYCHOLOGY IN WESTERN GERMANY. Washington, D.C.: Library of Congress, Reference Department, 1956. viii, 84 p.

A brief narrative about social psychology in Germany before 1945. Annotated bibliography of articles from 1945-55, information about teaching and research institutions, and lists of books, articles, dissertations, and periodicals.

Chestnut, Robert W. "Psychotechnik: Industrial Psychology in the Weimar Republic 1918-1924." PROCEEDINGS OF THE ANNUAL CONVENTION OF THE AMERICAN PSYCHOLOGICAL ASSOCIATION 7, pt. 2 (1972): 781-82.

Cocks, Geoffrey. "Psychotherapy in the Third Reich: A Research Note." JOURNAL OF THE HISTORY OF THE BEHAVIORAL SCIENCES 14 (January 1978): 33-36.

Cox, Frank. "A Visit to Leipzig and Prague Psychological Institutes." AMERICAN PSYCHOLOGIST 21 (November 1966): 1,076.

A brief comment on library holdings and current work in two institutions in locations of historical importance to psychology.

Crannell, Clark W. "Wolfgang Koehler." JOURNAL OF THE HISTORY OF THE BEHAVIORAL SCIENCES 6 (July 1970): 267-68.

Recounts Koehler's courage during the political repression in Germany in 1933.

Dobson, Velma, and Bruce, Darryl. "The German University and the Development of Experimental Psychology." JOURNAL OF THE HISTORY OF THE BEHAVIORAL SCIENCES 8 (April 1972): 204-7.

Credit for the founding of experimental psychology is often given to individuals, but this article emphasizes the freedom of teaching and learning in German higher education as a condition conducive to the development of the new discipline.

Hall, G. Stanley. FOUNDERS OF MODERN PSYCHOLOGY. New York: Appleton, 1912. vii, 471 p.

Based on six lectures delivered at Columbia University in 1912. Describes the life and work of six eminent German scholars with whom the author studied: Eduard Zeller, Rudolph Hermann Lotze, Gustav Theodor Fechner, Eduard von Hartmann, Hermann von Helmholtz, and Wilhelm Wundt. Bibliographies of each man's published works follow the chapters. Index.

Henle, Mary. "One Man Against the Nazis--Wolfgang Koehler." AMERICAN PSYCHOLOGIST 33 (October, 1978): 939-44.

Hunsdahl, Jørgen B. "Concerning Einfuehlung (Empathy): A Concept Analysis of Its Origin and Early Development." JOURNAL OF THE HISTORY OF THE BEHAVIORAL SCIENCES 3 (April 1967): 180-91.

Focuses largely on the period 1900-1925 when German authors such as Theodore Lipps, Antonin Prandtl, Theodore A. Meyer, Max Deri, and Richard Mueller-Freienfels debated the meaning of Einfuehlung in a series of monographs.

Klix, Friedhart. "Some Recent Trends and Prospects of Psychological Research in the German Democratic Republic." PSYCHOLOGIA 10 (June 1967): 89-92.

Langer, Walter C., and Gifford, Sanford. "An American Analyst in Vienna During the Anschluss." JOURNAL OF THE HISTORY OF THE BEHAVIORAL SCIENCES 14 (January 1978): 37-54.

> Discusses the experiences and recollections of Walter C. Langer in Vienna prior to and during Nazi occupation. Comments, among other things, on Langer's contributions in assisting Jews to escape from Vienna and on the problem of lay analysis.

Langfeld, Herbert S. "Stumpf's 'Introduction to Psychology.'" AMERICAN JOURNAL OF PSYCHOLOGY 50 (November 1937): 33-56.

> A brief description of a psychology course taught by Stumpf at the University of Berlin, winter semester, 1906-7.

Leary, David E. "The Philosophical Development of the Conception of Psychology in Germany, 1780-1850." JOURNAL OF THE HISTORY OF THE BEHAVIORAL SCIENCES 14 (April 1978): 113-21.

> Traces both the positive and the negative impact of Kant's thought on such early contributors to psychology as Friedrich Edward Beneke, Jakob Friedrich Fries, and Johann Friedrich Herbart.

Mandler, Jean Matter, and Mandler, George. "The Diaspora of Experimental Psychology: The Gestaltists and Others." In THE INTELLECTUAL MIGRATION: EUROPE AND AMERICA 1930-1960, edited by Donald Fleming and Bernard Bailyn, pp. 371-419. Cambridge, Mass.: Belknap Press of Harvard University Press, 1969.

> Discusses the immigration to the United States of German experimental psychologists including Koffka, Wertheimer, Koehler, Lewin, Heider, Goldstein, Buehler, Brunswik, Stern, Werner, and Scheerer.

Marshall, Marilyn E. "G.T. Fechner: Premises Toward a General Theory of Organisms (1823)." JOURNAL OF THE HISTORY OF THE BEHAVIORAL SCIENCES (October 1974): 438-47.

> Presents selected themes in Fechner's conceptual development followed by an outline of the contents of his paper, "Premises Toward a General Theory of Organisms." The paper is discussed in terms of the post-Kantian idealistic tradition.

Metzger, Wolfgang. "The Historical Background for National Trends in Psychology: German Psychology." JOURNAL OF THE HISTORY OF THE BEHAVIORAL SCIENCES 1 (January 1965): 109-15.

> Part of a symposium at the 17th International Congress of Psychology. Outlines major traits of German psychology: inclination to phenomenology, and distrust of purely empiristic views, elementarism and extreme objectivism. Highlights major contributions such as the first laboratory of psychology, the initiation of act psychol-

ogy, and the founding of psychophysics, of psychoanalysis, of the Wuerzburg school, and of the holistic approach in psychology.

Ribot, Théodule Armand. GERMAN PSYCHOLOGY OF TODAY: THE EMPIRI-CAL SCHOOL. Translated from the 2d French edition by James Mark Baldwin. New York: Charles Scribner's Sons, 1886. xxi, 307 p.

Captures some of the spirit of the German psychology of the late nineteenth century by examining representative topics in the psychologies of such individuals as Herbart, Lotze, Mueller, Weber, Stumpf, Fechner, and Wundt. The first chapter compares German and English psychologies, and the final chapter attempts to characterize the condition of German psychology. Some bibliographical materials in footnotes.

Russell, Wallace A. "A Note on Lotze's Teaching of Psychology, 1842-1881." JOURNAL OF THE HISTORY OF THE BEHAVIORAL SCIENCES 2 (January 1966): 74-75.

Relates some of the course titles, frequency of class meetings, and numbers of students enrolled in courses taught by Lotze during the period 1842-81.

Stern, W. "Psychological Science in Germany." SCANDINAVIAN SCIENTIFIC REVIEW 2 (1923): 225-29.

Stratton, George M. "Wundt and Leipzig in the Association's Early Days." PSYCHOLOGICAL REVIEW 50 (January 1943): 68-70.

Stumpf, C. "Hermann von Helmholtz and the New Psychology." PSYCHOLOGICAL REVIEW 2 (January 1895): 1-12.

A brief account of the accomplishments of Helmholtz, especially as they bear upon psychology.

Turner, R. Steven. "Hermann von Helmholtz and the Empiricist Vision." JOURNAL OF THE HISTORY OF THE BEHAVIORAL SCIENCES 13 (January 1977): 48-58.

Discusses the effect of Helmholtz's philosophical convictions upon his research and the influence on Helmholtz of J.G. Fichte and, to a lesser extent, of Kant.

von Bracken, Helmut. "Recent Trends in German Psychology." JOURNAL OF GENERAL PSYCHOLOGY 47 (October 1952): 165-79.

Briefly describes the effects of World War II on German psychology and postwar developments in Gestalt psychology, experimental studies on the will, the theory of Schichten, expressive movements, projective tests, and social adjustment.

Watson, Goodwin. "Psychology in Germany and Austria." PSYCHOLOGICAL BULLETIN 31 (December 1934): 755-76.

_____. "Psychology Under Hitler." SCHOOL AND SOCIETY 38 (December 2, 1933): 732-36.

Wehner, Ernst G. "The Development of German Psychology Since 1945." INTERNATIONAL REVIEW OF APPLIED PSYCHOLOGY 23 (1974): 47-53.

Wellek, Albert. "The Impact of the German Immigration on the Development of American Psychology." JOURNAL OF THE HISTORY OF THE BEHAVIORAL SCIENCES 4 (July 1968): 207-29.

See entry under United States, section B5bxii, p. 92.

Wenzl, A. "Contemporary German Psychology." MONIST 38 (January 1928): 120-57.

Provides an overview of various trends in German psychology including major content areas such as comparative, differential, general and experimental psychology, and theoretical approaches such as Gestalt, phenomenological, and psychoanalytic psychology.

Wesley, Frank. "Masters and Pupils Among the German Psychologists." JOURNAL OF THE HISTORY OF THE BEHAVIORAL SCIENCES 1 (January 1965): 252-58.

Follows the design of an earlier study by E.G. Boring on masters and pupils among American psychologists. Fifty-three prominent German psychologists were asked to name the person or persons who influenced them most up to the time of their doctorate. Results presented in tabular form.

Woodward, William R. "Fechner's Panpsychism: A Scientific Solution to the Mind-Body Problem." JOURNAL OF THE HISTORY OF THE BEHAVIORAL SCIENCES 8 (October 1972): 367-86.

Explores Fechner's use of analogy as a solution to the problem of the relation of the spiritual to the material world.

Wyatt, Frederick, and Teuber, Hans Lukas. "German Psychology Under the Nazi System: 1933-1940." PSYCHOLOGICAL REVIEW 51 (July 1944): 229-47.

v. CANADA

Two major collections concerned with the history of psychology in Canada are located in the Public Archives of Canada in Ottawa. They are the Archives of the Canadian Psychological Association, Head Office (consisting of papers, documents, and reports accumulated since 1939) and the "Oral History of Psychology in Canada" (a series of tapes and transcripts recording the reminiscences of veteran psychologists).

Appley, M.H., and Rickwood, Jean. PSYCHOLOGY IN CANADA. Ottawa: Science Secretariat, Privy Council Office, 1967. xii, 131 p.

> A status report on the field of psychology in Canada in 1966 commissioned by the Canadian Psychological Association at the request of the publisher. Detailed charts and tables.

Arvidson, Robert M., and Nelson, Thomas M. "Sixty Years of Psychology at the University of Alberta." CANADIAN PSYCHOLOGIST 9 (1968): 500-504.

Bernhardt, Karl S. "Canadian Psychology--Past, Present and Future." CANADIAN JOURNAL OF PSYCHOLOGY 1 (June 1947): 49-60.

Bringmann, Wolfgang G.; Fehr, Robert C.; and Mueller, Ronald H. "Psychology at Windsor." CANADIAN PSYCHOLOGIST 10 (1969): 371-82.

Laver, A. Bryan. "The Historiography of Psychology in Canada." JOURNAL OF THE HISTORY OF THE BEHAVIORAL SCIENCES 13 (July 1977): 243-51.

> Provides an overview of developments since 1950 for such topics as undergraduate history of psychology courses, graduate history programs, recent Canadian research in the history of psychology, and publishing outlets in the history of psychology.

Myers, C.R. "Edward Alexander Bott." CANADIAN PSYCHOLOGIST 15 (July 1974): 292-302.

_____. "Notes on the History of Psychology in Canada." CANADIAN PSYCHOLOGIST 6 (January 1965): 4-19.

> Outlines the historical development of psychology in Canada from the 1840s, when psychology was first treated as a separate subject in university courses, through the founding of the first Canadian experimental psychology laboratory by James Mark Baldwin in the early 1890s, to the founding of the Canadian Psychological Association. Concludes with a brief description of the Canadian Psychological Association.

_____. "R.B. MacLeod (1907-1972) Talks About Psychology in Canada."

CANADIAN PSYCHOLOGIST 15 (April 1974): 105-11.

> Brief, edited excerpts of conversations with MacLeod focusing primarily on his experiences as a student at McGill University and later as chairman of that psychology department.

Scarborough, Barron B., and Platt, Charles E. "Ten Years of Psychological Research in the United States and Canada." JOURNAL OF GENERAL PSYCHOLOGY 68 (January 1963): 21-36.

> See entry under United States, section B5bxii, p. 91.

Wright, M.J. "Canadian Psychology Comes of Age." CANADIAN PSYCHOLOGIST 10 (1969): 229-53.

vi. EASTERN EUROPE

Brožek, Josef. "Contemporary East European Historiography of Psychology." HISTORY OF SCIENCE 15 (December 1977): 233-51.

> Describes recent and current historiography of psychology in Czechoslovakia, Poland, Yugoslavia, and Romania. Includes a brief bibliography for each country.

_____. "Quantitative Explorations in the History of Psychology in Yugoslavia: Translations." PSYCHOLOGICAL REPORTS 31 (October 1972): 397-98.

Brožek, Josef, and Hoskovec, J. "Contemporary Psychology in Czechoslovakia: The General Setting." PSYCHOLOGIA 9 (March 1966): 53-60.

> Reports on such topics as book reviews, periodicals, educational institutions, research centers, institutes, and clinics to provide an overview of psychological activities in Czechoslovakia.

Budkiewicz, Janina. "Psychological Concepts of Jan Wladyslaw Dawid in Relation to European Psychology of His Day." POLISH PSYCHOLOGICAL BULLETIN 1 (1971): 51-59.

Choynowski, M. "Psychology in Poland: Past and Present." POLISH REVIEW 3 (Autumn 1958): 88-103.

Rapoport, Anatol. "Modern Developments in Behavioral Science in Poland." BEHAVIORAL SCIENCE 7 (1962): 379-89.

Rosca, Al. "Current State of Psychology in Romania." REVUE ROUMAINE DES SCIENCES SOCIALES--SERIE DE PSYCHOLOGIE 17 (1973): 3-10.

Rouček, J.S., ed. SLAVONIC ENCYCLOPEDIA. 4 vols. New York: Philosophical Library, 1949.

> Volume 3 (pp. 1062-1067) contains brief descriptions of psychology in Czechoslovakia, Poland, and Russia.

Zajonc, Robert B., excerpter and trans. "Psychology in Poland: From M. Choynowski's 'On the Awakening of Polish Psychology.'" AMERICAN PSYCHOLOGIST 12 (December 1957): 730-33.

> Excerpts from an article appearing in a Polish journal which describe the demise of psychology in Poland in terms of its removal from the curricula of most universities; elimination of psychological laboratories, clinics, and journals; and the downgrading of the roles of psychologists. Argues that psychology should be restored because, among other reasons, it is not simply an ideological science, and notes that Pavlovism does not constitute a sufficiently broad theoretical base for psychology.

Zusne, Leonard. "Development of Psychology in Latvia." JOURNAL SUPPLEMENT ABSTRACT SERVICE, CATALOG OF SELECTED DOCUMENTS IN PSYCHOLOGY, 61 (August 1976). Manuscript no. 1277. 17 p.

vii. ENGLAND

Bartlett, Frederic Charles. "Cambridge, England: 1887-1937." AMERICAN JOURNAL OF PSYCHOLOGY 50 (November 1937): 97-110.

_____. SOME RECENT DEVELOPMENTS OF PSYCHOLOGY IN GREAT BRITAIN. Istanbul, Turkey: Baha Matbaasi, 1957. viii, 92 p.

> Six lectures covering historical developments in psychology from 1914-30 with special emphasis on military psychology and on the importance of psychology.

Burt, Cyril. "Francis Galton and His Contributions to Psychology." BRITISH JOURNAL OF STATISTICAL PSYCHOLOGY 15 (May 1962): 1-49.

> An overview of Galton's life and his pioneering psychological studies.

Drever, James. "The Historical Background for National Trends in Psychology: On the Non-existence of English Associationism." JOURNAL OF THE HISTORY OF THE BEHAVIORAL SCIENCES 1 (April 1965): 123-30.

> Outlines the major associationist trends of thought and the contributions of such individuals as Locke, Berkeley, Hume, Molyneux, Hartley, Reid, and Bartlett.

Flugel, J.C.   "A Hundred Years or So of Psychology at University College, London."   BULLETIN OF THE BRITISH PSYCHOLOGICAL SOCIETY 23 (1954): 21-31.

Foss, Brian M., ed.   PSYCHOLOGY IN GREAT BRITAIN.   London: British Psychological Society, 1970. 48 p.

   A pamphlet prepared for the 19th International Congress of Psychology. Contains a historical essay and describes developments and
   recent trends in British psychology.

Hearnshaw, L.S.   "Sherrington, Burt and the Beginnings of Psychology in Liver-
pool."   BULLETIN OF THE BRITISH PSYCHOLOGICAL SOCIETY 27 (1974): 9-
14.

_____. A SHORT HISTORY OF BRITISH PSYCHOLOGY 1840-1940. New
York: Barnes & Noble, 1964. xi, 331 p.

   Traces psychological thought in Great Britain from Alexander Bain
   to World War II. Includes influences from other countries and
   from related disciplines such as physiology, statistics, sociology,
   and medicine. Bibliographical materials. Index.

Hetherington, Ralph.   "Twenty Years of Psychology at the Chrichton Royal,
Dumfries: A Personal Account."   BULLETIN OF THE BRITISH PSYCHOLOGICAL
SOCIETY 22 (1969): 303-6.

Kantor, J.R.   "Newton's Influence on the Development of Psychology."   PSY-
CHOLOGICAL RECORD 20 (Winter 1970): 83-92.

   Focuses on Isaac Newton's "lamentable" influence on the field of
   sensation and perception. Newton, under the influence of dualism,
   advanced a theory which "has dominated psychological thinking for
   centuries in complete variance from fact and naturalistic theory."

Knight, Rex.   "Present-day Trends in British Psychology."   ADVANCEMENT OF
SCIENCE 5 (October 1948): 254-61.

Mace, C.A.   "The Permanent Contribution to Psychology of George Frederick
Stout."   BRITISH JOURNAL OF EDUCATIONAL PSYCHOLOGY 24 (June 1954):
64-67.

Mace, C.A., and Vernon, D.E., eds.   CURRENT TRENDS IN BRITISH PSY-
CHOLOGY.   London: Methuen and Co. Ltd., 1953. viii, 262 p.

   As part of the contribution of the British Association for the Advancement of Science to a Festival of Britain, the psychology
   section of the Association presented papers written by outstanding

scholars on current trends in such areas as industrial psychology, vocational guidance, educational psychology, clinical psychology, social psychology, learning, and personality. Index.

Mace, Marjorie, ed. C.A. MACE: SELECTED PAPERS. London: Methuen and Co. Ltd., 1973. xiii, 429 p. Index.

Mischel, Theodore. "'Emotion' and 'Motivation' in the Development of English Psychology: D. Hartley, James Mill, A. Bain." JOURNAL OF THE HISTORY OF THE BEHAVIORAL SCIENCES 2 (April 1966): 123-44.

Briefly sketches the philosophical context of eighteenth- and nineteenth-century England and describes the concepts of motivation and emotion in the works of Hartley, Mill, and Bain.

Poser, Ernest G. "Impressions of Psychology in England." CANADIAN JOURNAL OF PSYCHOLOGY 2 (June 1948): 85-87.

Ribot, Th[éodule Armand]. ENGLISH PSYCHOLOGY. Translator unknown. New York: Appleton, 1874 (French edition 1870). viii, 328 p.

A distinguished French psychologist examines the basic psychological thought of Hartley, Spencer, Bain, Lewes, Bailey, James Mill, and John Stuart Mill. Concludes with a characterization of the psychology of the time.

Sokal, Michael M. "Psychology at Victorian Cambridge--The Unofficial Laboratory of 1887-1888." PROCEEDINGS OF THE AMERICAN PHILOSOPHICAL SOCIETY 116 (April 1972): 145-47.

Describes the work of James McKeen Cattell in establishing an unofficial and temporary psychological laboratory at Cambridge University in England.

Summerfield, A. "Clinical Psychology in Britain." AMERICAN PSYCHOLOGIST 13 (April 1948): 171-76.

Zangwill, O.L. "The Cambridge Psychological Laboratory." BULLETIN OF THE BRITISH PSYCHOLOGICAL SOCIETY 48 (1962): 22-24.

viii. FRANCE

Delay, Jean. "Jacksonism and the Works of Ribot." AMA ARCHIVES OF NEUROLOGY AND PSYCHIATRY 78 (1957): 505-15.

Goldsmith, Margaret. FRANZ ANTON MESMER: A HISTORY OF MESMERISM. Garden City, N.Y.: Doubleday, 1934. 308 p.

A popular, sympathetic biography of Mesmer, with an account of the spread of Mesmerism and related ideas in Europe and elsewhere during the nineteenth century.

Goshen, Charles E. "The Psychology of Jean Louis Alibert, 1768-1837." JOURNAL OF THE HISTORY OF THE BEHAVIORAL SCIENCES 2 (October, 1966): 357-70.

An overview of the psychological thought of Jean Louis Alibert, a French dermatologist, followed by selected translations from his two-volume PHYSIOLOGIE DES PASSIONS on such topics as attention, perception, the inner life, fear, and laziness.

Kopell, Bert S. "Pierre Janet's Description of Hypnotic Sleep Provoked from a Distance." JOURNAL OF THE HISTORY OF THE BEHAVIORAL SCIENCES 4 (April 1968): 119-23.

A brief introduction and background to Janet's early interest and work in hypnosis.

Littman, Richard L. "Henri Piéron and French Psychology: A Comment on Professor Fraisse's Note." JOURNAL OF THE HISTORY OF THE BEHAVIORAL SCIENCES 7 (July 1971): 261-68.

An account of some of Piéron's accomplishments followed by speculation as to why John B. Watson rather than Piéron is generally considered the founder of behaviorism.

Mayo, Elton. SOME NOTES ON THE PSYCHOLOGY OF PIERRE JANET. Cambridge, Mass.: Harvard University Press, 1948. vii, 132 p.

These notes, primarily on society and on industry, are organized under the following headings: psychopathology and social study, hysteria and hypnosis, the complexity of the attentive act, obsessive thinking, obsession and the equilibrium hypothesis, and the psychology of adaptation. Index.

Pollack, Robert H., and Brenner, Margaret W., eds. THE EXPERIMENTAL PSYCHOLOGY OF ALFRED BINET. New York: Springer Publishing Co., 1969. xiv, 235 p.

In the United States Binet is known for his pioneering work in intelligence testing, but is not given due credit for his early work in experimental psychology. This book includes fourteen of Binet's papers on such topics as threshold determination, illusions of movement, visual memory in children, perception of duration, fear in children, and imageless thought. Bibliography of Binet's writings.

Reuchlin, M. "The Historical Background for National Trends in Psychology: France." JOURNAL OF THE HISTORY OF THE BEHAVIORAL SCIENCES 1 (January 1965): 115-23.

Part of a symposium at the 17th International Congress of Psychology. Outlines contributions of such French scholars as Ribot, Piéron, Binet, Charcot, Janet, and Piaget.

Silverman, H.L., and Krenzel, K. "Alfred Binet: Prolific Pioneer in Psychology." PSYCHIATRIC QUARTERLY SUPPLEMENT 38 (1964): 323-35.

Varon, E[dith].J[udith]. THE DEVELOPMENT OF ALFRED BINET'S PSYCHOLOGY. PSYCHOLOGICAL MONOGRAPHS, Vol. 46, no. 207. Princeton, N.J. and Albany, N.Y.: Psychological Review Co., 1935. 129 p.

Wesley, Frank, and Hurtig, Michel. "Masters and Pupils Among French Psychologists." JOURNAL OF THE HISTORY OF THE BEHAVIORAL SCIENCES 5 (October 1969): 320-35.

Follows the model of earlier studies conducted in the United States and Germany, and traces the influence of the preceding intellectual generation on psychologists currently prominent in France.

Winters, Barbara. "Franz Anton Mesmer: An Inquiry Into the Antecedents of Hypnotism." JOURNAL OF GENERAL PSYCHOLOGY 43 (July 1950): 63-75.

Traces selected intellectual antecedents of Mesmerism and highlights some of the fortunes and vicissitudes of the movement in eighteenth-century France.

Wolf, Theta H. ALFRED BINET. Chicago: University of Chicago Press, 1973. xiii, 376 p.

Based partly on interviews with Theodore Simon and Henri Piéron, this biography presents the development of Binet's thought, his work, and his personal qualities and circumstances. References to letters and unpublished manuscripts. Chronological list of Binet's publications and of publications about Binet before 1911. Bibliography. Index.

_____. "An Individual Who Made A Difference." AMERICAN PSYCHOLOGIST 16 (May 1961): 245-48.

Based on conversations between the author and Theodore Simon in 1959 and 1960. Describes selected topics in the lives and works of Binet and Simon.

ix. ITALY

Brožek, Josef, and Dazzi, Nino. "Contemporary Historiography of Psychology: Italy." JOURNAL OF THE HISTORY OF THE BEHAVIORAL SCIENCES 13 (January 1977): 33-40.

Describes Italian approaches to the history of psychology and attempts to "supplement and bring up to date the information on
events and publications relevant to the 'coming of age' of the
historiography of psychology in Italy."

De Sanctis, S. "Psychological Science in Italy." SCANDINAVIAN SCIENCE
REVIEW 2 (1963): 114-18.

Lazzeroni, Virgilio, and Marzi, Alberto. "Psychology in Italy from 1945 to
1957." ACTA PSYCHOLOGICA 14 (1958): 54-80.

Misiak, Henryk, and Staudt, Virginia M. "Psychology in Italy." PSYCHO
LOGICAL BULLETIN 50 (September, 1953): 347-61.

Plottke, Paul. "Psychology in Italy." INDIVIDUAL PSYCHOLOGY BULLETIN
5 (1946): 89-91.

Standing, E.M. MARIA MONTESSORI: HER LIFE AND WORK. New York:
New American Library, 1962. 382 p.

x. MEXICO, CENTRAL AMERICA, AND SOUTH AMERICA

Abt, Lawrence Edwin. "Clinical Psychology in Latin America." In PROGRESS
IN CLINICAL PSYCHOLOGY, edited by Lawrence Edwin Abt and Bernard F.
Riess, vol. 6, pp. 235-41. New York: Grune and Stratton, 1964.

Ardila, Ruben. "Historical Development of the Colombian Federation of Psychology." INTERNATIONAL JOURNAL OF PSYCHOLOGY 5 (1970): 143-44.

Describes the development and aims of Colombia's professional association for psychologists.

_____. "José Ingenieros, Psychologist." JOURNAL OF THE HISTORY OF
THE BEHAVIORAL SCIENCES 6 (January 1970): 41-47.

A brief overview of the accomplishments of Argentina's José
Ingenieros. Discusses his publications, his work as a professor and
editor, and the outlines of his psychological system.

_____. "Landmarks in the History of Latin American Psychology." JOURNAL
OF THE HISTORY OF THE BEHAVIORAL SCIENCES 6 (April 1970): 140-45.

A brief outline of over one hundred landmark events and dates in
Latin American psychology from 1567 to 1969.

_____. "Psychology in Latin America." AMERICAN PSYCHOLOGIST 23
(August 1968): 567-74.

Beebe-Center, J.G., and McFarland, Ross A. "Psychology in South America." PSYCHOLOGICAL BULLETIN 38 (October 1941): 627-67.

Diaz-Guerrero, Rogelio. "A Mexican Psychology." AMERICAN PSYCHOLOGIST 32 (November 1977): 934-44.

Dreikurs, Rudolf. "The Development of Individual Psychology in Brazil." INDIVIDUAL PSYCHOLOGY BULLETIN 5 (1946): 91-93.

Hall, Margaret E. "The Present Status of Psychology in South America." PSYCHOLOGICAL BULLETIN 43 (September 1946): 441-76.

> Reviews the status of psychology in ten South American countries and provides names of selected organizations and individuals active in the field.

Hereford, C.F. "Current Status of Psychology in Latin America." LATIN AMERICAN RESEARCH REVIEW 1 (Spring 1966): 97-108.

Kinnaird, Lucia Burk, and Nichols, Madaline W. "A Bibliography of Articles in Psychology: NOSOTROS, Volumes I-LXXVI." PSYCHOLOGICAL BULLETIN 32 (March 1935): 237-42.

Ribes-Iñesta, Emilio. "Psychology in Mexico." AMERICAN PSYCHOLOGIST 23 (August 1968): 565-66.

Sutter, Christian, and Morales, Manuel. "Present Status of Industrial Psychology in Colombia." INTERNATIONAL JOURNAL OF PSYCHOLOGY 6, no. 4 (1971): 323-27.

Vernon, W.H.D. "Psychology in Cuba." PSYCHOLOGICAL BULLETIN 41 (February 1944): 73-89.

xi. SOVIET UNION

Ananiev, B. "Achievements of Soviet Psychologists." JOURNAL OF GENERAL PSYCHOLOGY 38 (1948): 257-62.

> A brief summary of accomplishments of such Soviet scholars as Luria, Teplov, Rubinstein, and Vygotsky in such areas as speech mechanisms, hearing, and thought processes.

Bauer, Raymond A. THE NEW MAN IN SOVIET PSYCHOLOGY. Cambridge, Mass.: Harvard University Press, 1952. xxiii, 229 p.

> Presents the new view of human beings, the "New Man," which has emerged in Soviet society. Rich in materials on the history of

psychology in post-revolutionary Russian society. Provides many insights into the relationship between psychology and the Soviet system. Notes and bibliographical materials. Index.

_____, ed. SOME VIEWS ON SOVIET PSYCHOLOGY. Washington, D.C.: American Psychological Association, 1962. ix, 285 p.

The views of a group of well-known American psychologists who visited the Soviet Union in the summer of 1960. Discusses such areas as personality development, thinking, mental health facilities, clinical work with children, physiological psychology, educational psychology, and industrial psychology. The opening chapter provides a historical overview, and the concluding chapter focuses on Soviet life and Soviet psychology. References. Index.

Beach, Edward L., Jr. "The Historical Significance of Pavlov's Experiments on Conditional Reflexes." CONDITIONAL REFLEX: A PAVLOVIAN JOURNAL OF RESEARCH AND THERAPY 1 (1966): 281-87.

Bieliauskas, Vytautas J. "Mental Health Care in the USSR." AMERICAN PSYCHOLOGIST 32 (May 1977): 376-79.

Comments, based on a visit to the USSR in 1976, on mental hospitals, treatment procedures, research, and mental health professionals in the USSR.

Borovski, V.M. "Psychology in the U.S.S.R." JOURNAL OF GENERAL PSYCHOLOGY 2 (April-July 1929): 177-86.

See annotation in section C10, p. 178.

Brožek, Josef. "Soviet Historiography of Psychology: Sources of Biographic and Bibliographic Information." JOURNAL OF THE HISTORY OF THE BEHAVIORAL SCIENCES 9 (April 1973): 152-61.

A valuable reference source for those interested in Soviet psychology. Includes information on bibliographies, archival reference works, sources of biographic data, and articles in VOPROSY PSIKHOLOGII, a major medium which publishes historical papers. An addendum includes titles of recent historical articles published in VOPROSY PSIKHOLOGII.

_____. "Soviet Historiography of Psychology. II. Contributions of Non-Russian Authors." JOURNAL OF THE HISTORY OF THE BEHAVIORAL SCIENCES 9 (July 1973): 213-16.

Describes the history of psychology in the Ukraine and lists important conferences and essays.

_____. "Soviet Historiography of Psychology. III. Between Philosophy and History." JOURNAL OF THE HISTORY OF THE BEHAVIORAL SCIENCES 10 (April 1974): 195-201.

> Outlines the contents of works on philosophical and historical topics written by such individuals as S.L. Rubenshtein (Rubinstejn), E.A. Budilova, A.V. Brushlinskii, and A.I. Karamyan.

_____. "Soviet Psychology's Coming of Age." AMERICAN PSYCHOLOGIST 25 (November 1970): 1057-58.

_____. "Spectrum of Soviet Psychology: 1968 Model." AMERICAN PSYCHOLOGIST 24 (October 1969): 944-46.

_____. "To Test or Not to Test: Trends in the Soviet Views." JOURNAL OF THE HISTORY OF THE BEHAVIORAL SCIENCES 8 (April 1972): 243-48.

> Psychological tests are banned in the Soviet Union because they represent a capitalist attempt to justify class character and, in the case of projective techniques, because their interpretation is based on the Freudian theory of the unconscious. Nevertheless, tests are used in the space program and in the detection of brain disease, although quantification is not emphasized. The author cites a recent Soviet paper which seems more open to the question of testing.

Brožek, Josef, and Herz, Anna Pirscenok, comps. "Recent Russian Books in Psychology." CONTEMPORARY PSYCHOLOGY 19 (May 1974): 421-25.

Brožek, Josef, and Hoskovec, Jiri. "Soviet Psychology in English: Translations of Books." SOVIET PSYCHOLOGY AND PSYCHIATRY 4 (Spring-Summer 1966): 100-104.

Brožek, Josef; Hoskovec, Jiri; and Slobin, Dan I[saac]. "Reviews in English of Recent Soviet Psychology: A Bibliography." SOVIET PSYCHOLOGY AND PSYCHIATRY 4 (Spring-Summer 1966): 95-99.

Brožek, Josef, and Mecacci, Luciano. "New Soviet Research Institute of Psychology: A Milestone in the Development of Psychology in the U.S.S.R." AMERICAN PSYCHOLOGIST 29 (June 1974): 475-78.

Brožek, Josef, and Slobin, Dan I[saac]., eds. PSYCHOLOGY IN THE U.S.S.R.: AN HISTORICAL PERSPECTIVE. White Plains, N.Y.: International Arts and Sciences Press, 1972. x, 301 p.

> A collection of papers, representing basic and applied psychology and Georgian psychology, written by Russian psychologists in commemoration of the fiftieth anniversary of the Soviet revolution in

Russia. Papers cover such topics as vision, child development, labor, military psychology, sport psychology, and psychology in Georgia. Editors provide an orientation as well as a section on sources of information (e.g., bibliographies, readings, handbooks, and Russian books on the history of psychology). Materials on the current spectrum of Soviet psychology including contributions to its history and to the study of brain and behavior.

Cole, Michael, and Maltzman, Irving, eds. A HANDBOOK OF CONTEMPO-RARY SOVIET PSYCHOLOGY. New York: Basic Books, 1969. xviii, 887 p.

Thirty chapters in sections on developmental psychology, abnormal and social psychology, general experimental psychology, and higher nervous activity. Provides a representative cross-section of recent research in the Soviet Union. Brief historical overview, and editorial comments with each chapter. References follow each chapter. Index.

Corson, Samuel A., ed., and Corson, Elizabeth O'Leary, assoc. ed. PSYCHI-ATRY AND PSYCHOLOGY IN THE U.S.S.R. New York: Plenum Publishing Corp., 1976. 296 p.

Includes an overview of diverse topics such as philosophical and historical roots of Pavlov's psychology, history of Soviet psychology, psychotherapy in the U.S.S.R., drinking patterns in Soviet and American societies, hospitalization of political dissidents, and Soviet approaches to intelligence testing.

Gibbons, J., ed. I.P. PAVLOV: SELECTED WORKS. Translated by S. Belsky. Moscow: Foreign Languages Publishing House, n.d. 662 p.

See annotation in section C10, p. 179.

Hac, Pham Minh. "View of Soviet Psychologists on Behaviorism." PSYCHOLO-GIA 19 (September 1976): 163-72.

See annotation in section C10, p. 179.

Holowinsky, Ivan Z. "Contemporary Psychology in the Ukranian Soviet Socialist Republic." AMERICAN PSYCHOLOGIST 33 (February 1978): 185-89.

Kimble, Gregory A. "Sechenov and the Anticipation of Conditioning Theory." In his FOUNDATIONS OF CONDITIONING AND LEARNING, pp. 3-21. New York: Appleton-Century-Crofts, 1967.

London, Ivan D. "A Historical Survey of Psychology in the Soviet Union." PSYCHOLOGICAL BULLETIN 46 (July 1949): 241-77.

See annotation in section C10, p. 179.

References in History of Psychology

_____. "Contemporary Psychology in the Soviet Union." SCIENCE 114, (August 1951): 227-33.

_____. "Psychology in the U.S.S.R." AMERICAN JOURNAL OF PSYCHOL-OGY 64 (July 1951): 422-28.

A brief overview of selected research topics in the Soviet Union.

McLeish, John. "Psychology in the Soviet Union: Three Recent Contributions." QUARTERLY BULLETIN OF THE BRITISH PSYCHOLOGICAL SOCIETY 2 (1951): 47-52.

_____. SOVIET PSYCHOLOGY: HISTORY, THEORY, CONTENT. London: Methuen and Co. Ltd., 1975. xxi, 308 p.

See annotation in section C10, p. 179.

Miller, Jessie L., and Miller, James G. "Behavioral Scientists Visit the Soviet Union." BEHAVIORAL SCIENCE 7 (1962): 344-78.

An overview of the Soviet Union and Soviet people. Includes sections on psychology and psychiatry, based on discussions among numerous eminent behavioral scientists who visited the Soviet Union.

Mintz, Alexander. "Further Developments in Psychology in the U.S.S.R." ANNUAL REVIEW OF PSYCHOLOGY 10 (1959): 455-87.

An extension of an article appearing in the previous volume of the ANNUAL REVIEW OF PSYCHOLOGY (see below, next entry).

_____. "Recent Developments in Psychology in the U.S.S.R." ANNUAL RE-VIEW OF PSYCHOLOGY 9 (1958): 453-504.

Reviews the general Soviet view of psychology based on materials from recent textbooks, published proceedings of meetings, and published papers. 220 references.

"Noted Figures in the History of Soviet Psychology: Pictures and Brief Biographies." SOVIET PSYCHOLOGY AND PSYCHIATRY 4 (Spring-Summer 1966): 105-12.

Brief biographies and pictures of such Soviet psychologists as Boris M. Teplov, Vladimir M. Bekhterev, Konstantin N. Kornilov, Ivan P. Pavlov, Ivan M. Sechenov, and Lev S. Vygotskiy.

O'Connor, N[eil]. PRESENT-DAY RUSSIAN PSYCHOLOGY. New York: Pergamon Press, 1966. xv, 201 p.

Surveys the following topics in Russian psychological literature: attention, consciousness, and voluntary control; psychotherapy; statistical and cybernetic models; abnormal psychology; psycholinguistics; mental development of the child; and contemporary Soviet psychology. References follow each chapter. Index.

_____, ed. RECENT SOVIET PSYCHOLOGY. Translated by Ruth Kisch, R. Crawford, and H. Asher. New York: Liveright, 1961. 334 p.

A collection of papers representative of Russian work in such areas as physiology, speech, and education by such authors as Teplov, Luria, Anokhin, and Merlin. Introduction by the editor provides perspective on Russian psychology. Index.

O'Neil, William F., and Demos, George D. "Sanity of the Soviets: The Communist Approach to Mental Illness." ETC 33 (March 1976): 7-26.

Piaget, Jean. "Some Impressions of a Visit to Soviet Psychologists." ACTA PSYCHOLOGICA 12 (1956): 216-19.

Rahmani, Levy. SOVIET PSYCHOLOGY: PHILOSOPHICAL, THEORETICAL, AND EXPERIMENTAL ISSUES. New York: International Universities Press, 1973. viii, 440 p.

See annotation in section C10, p. 181.

Razran, Gregory H.S. "Psychology in the U.S.S.R." JOURNAL OF PHILOSOPHY 32 (January 1935): 19-24.

Discusses theoretical and methodological trends in psychology in the Soviet Union.

_____. "Soviet Psychology and Psychophysiology." SCIENCE 128 (November 1958): 1187-94.

_____. "Soviet Psychology and Psychophysiology." BEHAVIORAL SCIENCE 4 (1959): 35-48.

See annotation in section C10, p. 181.

_____. "Soviet Psychology Since 1950." SCIENCE 126 (November 1957): 1100-1107.

Simon, Brian, ed. PSYCHOLOGY IN THE SOVIET UNION. Stanford, Calif.: Stanford University Press, 1957. viii, 305 p.

Twenty papers by Soviet psychologists A.R. Luria, A.A. Smirnov, E.N. Sokolov, S.L. Rubinstejn (Rubenstein), and others describing work and thought on memory, educational psychology, methods in psychology, language formation, and perception. Introduction by the editor provides an overview. Appendixes describe psychopatho-logical research in the Soviet Union and the Fourteenth Interna-tional Congress of Psychology. Index.

Slobin, Dan Isaac, ed. HANDBOOK OF SOVIET PSYCHOLOGY. SPECIAL ISSUE OF SOVIET PSYCHOLOGY AND PSYCHIATRY 4, nos. 3-4 (1966): 1-146.

Ziferstein, Isidore. "Group Psychotherapy in the Soviet Union." AMERICAN JOURNAL OF PSYCHIATRY 129 (November 1972): 595-600.

xii. UNITED STATES

Items in this section are supplemented by section E1, which contains numerous entries on American philosophical thought as it helped shape the development of American psychology.

Adams, James F., and Hoberman, Arnold A. "Joseph Buchanan, 1785-1829: Pioneer American Psychologist." JOURNAL OF THE HISTORY OF THE BEHAV-IORAL SCIENCES 5 (October 1969): 340-48.

Argues that Buchanan has not received the attention he deserves as an early psychologist in the United States and provides an over-view of his life and contributions.

Adler, Helmut E. "The Vicissitudes of Fechnerian Psychophysics in America." ANNALS OF THE NEW YORK ACADEMY OF SCIENCES 291 (18 April 1977): 21-32.

Bakan, David. "Political Factors in the Development of American Psychology." ANNALS OF THE NEW YORK ACADEMY OF SCIENCES 291 (18 April 1977): 222-32.

Beit-Hallahmi, Benjamin. "Psychology of Religion 1880-1930: The Rise and Fall of a Psychological Movement." JOURNAL OF THE HISTORY OF THE BE-HAVIORAL SCIENCES 10 (January 1974): 84-90.

Outlines the contributions of such pioneers in the psychology of re-ligion as G. Stanley Hall, J.H. Leuba, E.D. Starbuck, and William James, and speculates about the reasons for the rise and fall of interest in the psychology of religion during the period 1880-1930.

Berlyne, D.E. "American and European Psychology." AMERICAN PSYCHOLO-GIST 23 (June 1968): 447-52.

Focuses on the growth and dominance of American psychology.

Blumenthal, Arthur L. "Wilhelm Wundt and Early American Psychology: A Clash of Two Cultures." ANNALS OF THE NEW YORK ACADEMY OF SCIENCES 291 (18 April 1977): 13-20.

Boring, Edwin G. "The Influence of Evolutionary Theory Upon American Psychological Thought." In EVOLUTIONARY THOUGHT IN AMERICA, edited by Stow Persons, pp. 268-98. New Haven, Conn.: Yale University Press, 1950. x, 462 p.

In its early development, psychology in the United States followed traditions in German psychology and British biology but imposed its own brand of pragmatism on them. This article discusses contributions of such American pioneers as William James, John Dewey, G. Stanley Hall, James Mark Baldwin, and John B. Watson, and comments on the influence of Darwin on their thought.

Bringman, Wolfgang G. "The European Roots of American Psychology: Questions of Import." ANNALS OF THE NEW YORK ACADEMY OF SCIENCES 291 (18 April 1977): 56-65.

Britt, Steuart Henderson. "European Background (1600-1900) for American Psychology." JOURNAL OF GENERAL PSYCHOLOGY 27 (October 1942): 311-29.

See annotation in section B2, p. 41.

Bruner, Jerome S., and Allport, Gordon W. "Fifty Years of Change in American Psychology." PSYCHOLOGICAL BULLETIN 37 (December 1940): 757-76.

Buchner, Edward Franklin. "A Quarter Century of Psychology in America: 1878-1903." AMERICAN JOURNAL OF PSYCHOLOGY 14 (July-October 1903): 666-80.

Burnham, John Chynoweth. "The New Psychology: From Narcissism to Social Control." In CHANGE AND CONTINUITY IN TWENTIETH-CENTURY AMERICA: THE 1920's, edited by John Braeman, Robert H. Bremner, and David Brody, pp. 351-98. Columbus: Ohio State University Press, 1968.

Describes such movements in the 1920s as the rise of behaviorism, advances in testing, the emphasis in popular psychology on the self, the influence of psychoanalysis, and the growing focus in all of psychology on the possibilities of social control.

Camfield, Thomas M. "The Professionalization of American Psychology, 1870-1917." JOURNAL OF THE HISTORY OF THE BEHAVIORAL SCIENCES 9 (January 1973): 66-75.

See annotation in section D16, p. 374.

Cardno, J.A. "Imagination: Some Early American Approaches Evaluated." PSYCHOLOGICAL RECORD 17 (January 1967): 65-76.

> Theories of imagination of early American psychologists Upham, Wayland, Haven, and Mahan are compared with theories advanced by Reid, James, and Bain.

Carlson, Eric T. "Benjamin Rush and Mental Health." ANNALS OF THE NEW YORK ACADEMY OF SCIENCES 291 (18 April 1977): 94-103.

Cattell, J[ames]. McKeen. "Psychology in America." SCIENCE 70 (October 1929): 335-47.

> A brief overview of the history of American psychology delivered as a presidential address to the Ninth International Congress of Psychology, Yale University, September 2, 1929.

_____. "Psychology in America." SCIENTIFIC MONTHLY 30 (February 1930): 115-26.

> A shorter version of the paper described in the preceding entry. Includes excellent pictures of some of America's pioneer psychologists.

Cravens, Hamilton, and Burnham, John C[hynoweth]. "Psychology and Evolutionary Naturalism in American Thought, 1890-1940." AMERICAN QUARTERLY 23 (December 1971): 635-57.

> Explores the impact of Darwinian and Lamarckian thought on American psychologists William James, James Mark Baldwin, G. Stanley Hall, Edward L. Thorndike, John B. Watson, and others.

Dain, Norman. "Nineteenth Century Institutional Mental Care." ANNALS OF THE NEW YORK ACADEMY OF SCIENCES 291 (18 April 1977): 74-82.

Davies, Arthur Ernest. "The Influence of Biology on the Development of Modern Psychology in America." PSYCHOLOGICAL REVIEW 30 (May 1923): 164-75.

Davis, R.C. "American Psychology, 1800-1885." PSYCHOLOGICAL REVIEW 43 (November 1936): 471-93.

Diamond, Solomon. "Francis Galton and American Psychology." ANNALS OF THE NEW YORK ACADEMY OF SCIENCES 291 (18 April 1977): 47-55.

Fay, Jay Wharton. AMERICAN PSYCHOLOGY BEFORE WILLIAM JAMES. New Brunswick, N.J.: Rutgers University Press, 1939. Reprint. New York: Octagon Books, 1966. x, 240 p.

A survey of psychological thought in America from 1640 to 1890. Discusses the work of Samuel Johnson, Jonathan Edwards, Benjamin Rush, and Thomas C. Upham, among others. Contends that scientific psychology existed in America prior to 1890. Chronological table of American works and foreign sources. Bibliography of primary sources in American psychology before 1890. Notes. Index.

Fernberger, Samuel W. "The Publications of American Psychologists." PSYCHOLOGICAL REVIEW 37 (November 1930): 526-44.

_____. "The Scientific Interests and Scientific Publications of the Members of APA." PSYCHOLOGICAL BULLETIN 35 (May 1938): 261-81.

Finison, Lorenz J. "Unemployment, Politics, and the History of Organized Psychology." AMERICAN PSYCHOLOGIST 31 (November 1976): 747-55.

An analysis of the fate of psychology and psychologists during the Great Depression of the 1930s. Shows how the pressures of the times led to the founding of new organizations of psychologists and to changes in the American Psychological Association. Draws parallels with problems of the mid-1970s.

Franz, S.I. "The Scientific Productivity of American Professional Psychologists." PSYCHOLOGICAL REVIEW 24 (May 1917): 197-219.

Fulcher, J. Rodney. "Puritans and the Passions: The Faculty Psychology in American Puritanism." JOURNAL OF THE HISTORY OF THE BEHAVIORAL SCIENCES 9 (April 1973): 123-39.

Explores Puritan thought on the passions, the will, and the intellect.

Garvey, C.R. "List of American Psychology Laboratories." PSYCHOLOGICAL BULLETIN 26 (October 1929): 652-60.

Gengerelli, J.A. "Graduate School Reminiscences: Hull and Koffka." AMERICAN PSYCHOLOGIST 31 (October 1976): 685-88.

The author describes his experiences as a graduate student at the University of Wisconsin during the years 1925-27, and discusses the personality characteristics of Clark Hull and Kurt Koffka.

"The Growth of Psychological Journals in America." PSYCHOLOGICAL REVIEW 50 (January 1943): 80.

Characterizes the growth of American psychology journals by quinquennia from 1890, when only one journal (AMERICAN JOURNAL

OF PSYCHOLOGY) was published, to 1940 when twenty-six journals were published.

Hall, G. Stanley. LETTERS OF G. STANLEY HALL TO JONAS GILMAN
CLARK. Edited by Norwin Rush. Worcester, Mass.: Clark University Library,
1948. 38 p.

Hardesty, Francis P. "William Stern and American Psychology: A Preliminary
Analysis of Contributions and Contexts." ANNALS OF THE NEW YORK ACAD-
EMY OF SCIENCES 291 (18 April 1977): 33–46.

Harms, Ernest. "America's First Major Psychologist: Laurens Perseus Hickok."
JOURNAL OF THE HISTORY OF THE BEHAVIORAL SCIENCES 8 (January 1972):
120–23.

> Summarizes themes from two major books by Hickok, RATIONAL
> PSYCHOLOGY (1849) and EMPIRICAL PSYCHOLOGY (1854) (see
> below), and advances the position that Hickok "deserves the claim
> of having been the first to develop a real science of psychology
> in America."

Henle, Mary. "The Influence of Gestalt Psychology in America." ANNALS
OF THE NEW YORK ACADEMY OF SCIENCES 291 (18 April 1977): 3–12.

Hickok, Laurens P[erseus]. EMPIRICAL PSYCHOLOGY; OR, THE HUMAN
MIND AS GIVEN IN CONSCIOUSNESS. FOR THE USE OF COLLEGES AND
ACADEMIES. 2d ed. New York: Ivison, Blakeman, Taylor and Co., 1871.
xii, 400 p.

> A typical pre-Jamesian U.S. psychology text.

_____. RATIONAL PSYCHOLOGY; OR, THE SUBJECTIVE IDEA AND THE
OBJECTIVE LAW OF ALL INTELLIGENCE. A facsimile reproduction with an
introduction by Ernest Harms. Delmar, N.Y.: Scholars' Facsimiles & Reprints,
1973. xix, 717 p.

> A classic work, one of the earliest on psychology. Complements
> the author's later EMPIRICAL PSYCHOLOGY (see above), and
> covers introspective method or self observation as well as intuition,
> knowledge, and reason.

Hulin, Wilbur S. "Psychology." In AMERICAN YEAR BOOK: A RECORD OF
EVENTS AND PROGRESS. YEAR 1928, edited by Hart, Albert Bushnell,
pp. 751–56.

> A review of psychology for the year 1928. Includes lists of signif-
> icant books, major meetings, films, necrologies, and leading
> articles.

Jahoda, Marie. "Some Notes on the Influence of Psychoanalytic Ideas on American Psychology." HUMAN RELATIONS 16 (May 1963): 111-29.

Jastrow, Joseph. "American Psychology in the '80's and '90's. PSYCHOLOGICAL REVIEW 50 (January 1943): 65-67.

Jastrow, Joseph, et al. "Psychology in American Colleges and Universities." AMERICAN JOURNAL OF PSYCHOLOGY 3 (April 1890): 275-86.

   Offers brief descriptions of psychology (mostly experimental) as of the late 1880s at Wisconsin (by Jastrow), Nebraska (Wolfe), Teachers College (Hervey), Columbia (Butler), Harvard (James), Yale (Ladd), the Office of the Surgeon General (anonymous), Pennsylvania (Cattell), Indiana (Bryan), Clark (Sanford), and Toronto (Baldwin).

Kockelmans, Joseph J. "Phenomenological Psychology in the United States: A Critical Analysis of the Actual Situation." JOURNAL OF PHENOMENOLOGICAL PSYCHOLOGY 1 (1971): 139-72.

Koehler, Wolfgang. "A Perspective on American Psychology." PSYCHOLOGICAL REVIEW 50 (January 1943): 77-79.

_____. "The Scientists and Their New Environment." In THE CULTURAL MIGRATION: THE EUROPEAN SCHOLAR IN AMERICA, edited by W. Rex Crawford, pp. 112-37. Philadelphia: University of Pennsylvania Press, 1953.

   A brief discussion of the impact of European immigrant psychologists on U.S. psychology, primarily in the first half of the twentieth century. Concentrates on McDougall and Gestalt psychology.

Ladd, George Trumbull. "On Certain Hinderances to the Progress of Psychology in America." PSYCHOLOGICAL REVIEW 6 (March 1899): 121-33.

   Originally read as a paper before the American Psychological Association in 1898. The author here discusses such hinderances to the progress of psychology as: aloofness on the part of psychologists from the mental life of the average human being, multiplication of books which popularize psychology, and the "commercial spirit" causing, for example, premature publication.

Langfeld, H.S. "The Development of American Psychology." SCIENTIA 86 (August-September 1951): 264-69.

McKeachie, Wilbert J. "Psychology in America's Bicentennial Year." AMERICAN PSYCHOLOGIST 31 (December 1976): 819-33.

   A discussion of selected topics in the development of psychology in the United States and of recent trends in cognitive psychology. Argues that "psychologists now are coming to share a view of human nature that, as compared with earlier stimulus-response views, is more compatible with that of Jefferson and the founders of our republic."

Pillsbury, W[alter].B[owers].   "The Present Status of Psychology in the United States." SCANDINAVIAN SCIENTIFIC REVIEW 3 (1924-25): 199-208.

Rieber, R[obert].W. "Thomas C. Upham and the Making of an Indigenous American Psychology." ANNALS OF THE NEW YORK ACADEMY OF SCIENCES 291 (18 April 1977): 186-202.

Rieber, R[obert].W., and Salzinger, Kurt, eds. THE ROOTS OF AMERICAN PSYCHOLOGY: HISTORICAL INFLUENCES AND IMPLICATIONS FOR THE FUTURE. Annals of the New York Academy of Sciences, vol. 291. New York: New York Academy of Sciences, 1977. 394 p.

Proceedings of a conference attended by contemporary writers on the history of psychology. Separate parts on European influences on U.S. psychology, early U.S. approaches to mental health, nineteenth- and twentieth-century trends in the psychology of self, socioeconomic and political factors in the development of U.S. psychology, historical aspects of the psychology of language and cognition, and psychological systems--past, present, and future.

Roback, Abraham A. HISTORY OF AMERICAN PSYCHOLOGY. Rev. ed. New York: Collier Books, 1964. 575 p.

A survey of American psychology covering both preexperimental and experimental eras. Discusses major systems of thought and important historical figures. Bibliographical materials. Index.

_____. "Psychology as an American Science." MONIST 36 (October 1926): 667-77.

Argues that, unlike some other disciplines, psychology has advanced in America "without needing the support of Europe." Sketches selected trends in American psychology.

Ruckmich, C[hristian]. A. "The History and Status of Psychology in the United States." AMERICAN JOURNAL OF PSYCHOLOGY 32 (October 1912): 517-31.

Ruckmick, C[hristian].A. "Development of Laboratory Equipment in Psychology in the United States." AMERICAN JOURNAL OF PSYCHOLOGY 37 (October 1926): 582-92.

Scarborough, Barron B., and Platt, Charles E. "Ten Years of Psychological Research in the United States and Canada." JOURNAL OF GENERAL PSYCHOLOGY 68 (January 1963): 21-36.

Presents the number of articles per year (1948-57) abstracted in PSYCHOLOGICAL ABSTRACTS carrying the names of forty-two major agencies and institutions in the United States and Canada. Shows the number and percent of articles published in each of twelve content areas for each institution or agency.

Shakow, David, and Rapaport, David. THE INFLUENCE OF FREUD ON AMERICAN PSYCHOLOGY. Psychological Issues, vol. 4, no. 1. Monograph 13. New York: International Universities Press, 1964. v, 243 p.

Upham, Thomas Cogswell. ELEMENTS OF INTELLECTUAL PHILOSOPHY. Portland, Maine: W. Hyde, 1827. 504 p.

A standard textbook in the tradition of British empiricism written by an early American philosopher-psychologist before psychology emerged as a scientific discipline.

_____. MENTAL PHILOSOPHY; EMBRACING THE THREE DEPARTMENTS OF THE INTELLECT, SENSIBILITIES, AND WILL. 2 vols. New York: Harper and Brothers, 1869.

A revision of Upham's earlier textbooks in the form of a 561-page volume on the intellect, with an appendix on language, and a 705-page volume on the sensibilities and the will.

_____. A PHILOSOPHICAL AND PRACTICAL TREATISE ON THE WILL. New York: Harper and Brothers, 1841. 411 p.

A text for college courses on mental philosophy. Provides the flavor of preexperimental American philosophical psychology. Includes extensive arguments for the freedom of the will.

Van Hoorn, Willem, and Verhave, Thom. "Socioeconomic Factors and the Roots of American Psychology 1865-1914. An Exploratory Essay." ANNALS OF THE NEW YORK ACADEMY OF SCIENCES 291 (18 April 1977): 203-21.

Verhave, Thom, and Van Hoorn, Willem. "The Temporalization of Ego and Society During the Nineteenth Century: A View from the Top." ANNALS OF THE NEW YORK ACADEMY OF SCIENCES 291 (18 April 1977): 140-48.

Wallin, J.E.W[allace]. "Reminiscences from Pioneering Days in Psychology, With a Few Personality Portraits." JOURNAL OF GENERAL PSYCHOLOGY 67 (July 1962): 121-40.

Recounts educational experiences at the turn of the century in laboratories at Yale, Clark, Michigan, and Princeton universities. Personality sketches of G. Stanley Hall, Edward W. Scripture, George T. Ladd, and others.

Warden, C.J., and Warner, L.H. "The Development of Animal Psychology in the United States During the Past Three Decades." PSYCHOLOGICAL REVIEW 34 (May 1927): 196-205.

Watson, Robert I. "The Historical Background for National Trends in Psychology: United States." JOURNAL OF THE HISTORY OF THE BEHAVIORAL SCIENCES 1 (January 1965): 130-38.

Traces broad developments from about 1880 and comments on selected contributions of James, Hall, Cattell, Titchener, Thurstone, Lashley, Boring, J.B. Watson, and others. Summarizes major trends during ninety years of psychology in the United States.

Wellek, Albert. "The Impact of the German Immigration on the Development of American Psychology." JOURNAL OF THE HISTORY OF THE BEHAVIORAL SCIENCES 4 (July 1968): 207-29.

Outlines the effects of the Nazi regime on psychologists, and discusses major figures involved in the German-American emigration and their impact on American psychology.

Woodward, William R. "Lotze, the Self, and American Psychology." ANNALS OF THE NEW YORK ACADEMY OF SCIENCES 291 (18 April 1977): 168-77.

Woodworth, Robert S. "The Adolescence of American Psychology." PSYCHOLOGICAL REVIEW 50 (January 1943): 10-32.

Yerkes, Robert M. "Report of the Psychology Committee of the National Research Council." PSYCHOLOGICAL REVIEW 26 (March 1919): 83-149.

Reports by numerous psychology committees (on topics such as examination of recruits, recreation, shellshock and reeducation, propaganda, and problems of vision and audition) active during World War I. Provides a brief historical overview of the services of psychologists in solving military problems.

aa. Histories of U.S. Psychology Departments

There are quite a few small-circulation or exotic items in this category; many departments have published their own histories in limited editions. A number of these have been deposited at the Archives for the History of American Psychology at the University of Akron, Akron, Ohio 44325.

Benjamin, Ludy T., Jr. "Psychology at the University of Nebraska, 1889-1930." NEBRASKA HISTORY 56 (Fall 1975): 375-87.

Traces the early history of psychology at the University of Nebraska. Appendix lists names and brief biographies of some of
the outstanding students who took their bachelor's degrees at Nebraska.

Benjamin, Ludy T., Jr., and Bertelson, Amy D. "The Early Nebraska Psychology Laboratory, 1889-1930: Nursery for Presidents of the American Psychological Association." JOURNAL OF THE HISTORY OF THE BEHAVIORAL SCI-
ENCES 11 (April 1975): 142-48.

Nebraska leads all other schools as the undergraduate training
ground for presidents of the American Psychological Association.
This paper describes conditions in Nebraska's early laboratories
and speculates about its impact on Walter B. Pillsbury, Madison
Bentley, Harry Levi Hollingworth, Edwin R. Guthrie, J.P. Guilford,
and Joseph McVicker Hunt--all of whom became APA presidents.

Bronk, Detlev W., et al. "Twenty-five Years Later: Retrospective Comments
by Members of the Original Harvard Commission." AMERICAN PSYCHOLO-
GIST 25 (May 1970): 411-20.

In 1947, Harvard University set up a commission to advise on the
future of psychology in the university. This article contains retrospective comments by five of the commission members.

Cattell, James McKeen. "Psychology at the University of Pennsylvania."
AMERICAN JOURNAL OF PSYCHOLOGY 3 (April 1890): 281-83.

"Chronology, Vineland Laboratory." TRAINING SCHOOL BULLETIN 28 (1931):
137-38.

Dollard, John A. "Yale's Institute of Human Relations: What Was It?" VEN-
TURES (Magazine of the Yale Graduate School) Winter 1964, pp. 32-40.

Jastrow, Joseph, et al. "Psychology in American Colleges and Universities."
AMERICAN JOURNAL OF PSYCHOLOGY 3 (April 1890): 275-86.

See annotation in section B5bxii, p. 89.

Kingsbury, Forest A. "A History of the Department of Psychology at the University of Chicago." PSYCHOLOGICAL BULLETIN 43 (May 1946): 259-71.

Meyer, Ronald W. "Psychology, Psychologists, and the University of California:
The First Twenty Years, 1880-1900." PROCEEDINGS OF THE ANNUAL CON-
VENTION OF THE AMERICAN PSYCHOLOGICAL ASSOCIATION 7, pt. 2,
pp. 777-78. Washington, D.C.: American Psychological Association, 1972.

Murchison, Carl. "Recollections of a Magic Decade at Clark: 1925-1935." JOURNAL OF GENERAL PSYCHOLOGY 61 (July 1959): 3-12.

Nyman, Lawrence. RECOLLECTIONS: AN ORAL HISTORY OF THE PSYCHOLOGY DEPARTMENT OF THE CITY COLLEGE OF THE CITY UNIVERSITY OF NEW YORK: INTERVIEWS WITH JOSEPH E. BARMACK. New York: Nyman, 1976. viii, 187 p.

Patrick, George T.W. "Founding the Psychological Laboratory at the State University of Iowa: An Historical Sketch." IOWA JOURNAL OF HISTORY AND POLITICS 30 (July 1932): 404-16.

Peixotto, Helen E. "A History of Psychology at Catholic University." CATHOLIC EDUCATIONAL REVIEW 66 (April 1969): 844-49.

> Traces the development of psychology at Catholic University in Washington, D.C., since 1891, when Edward A. Pace founded the laboratory and began teaching there.

Raphelson, Alfred C. PSYCHOLOGY AT THE UNIVERSITY OF MICHIGAN, 1852-1950. 2 vols. Ann Arbor: University of Michigan, Flint College, 1968.

Riegel, K.F. "A Structural Developmental Analysis of the Department of Psychology at the University of Michigan." HUMAN DEVELOPMENT 13, no. 4 (1970): 269-79.

Sanford, Nevitt. "Graduate Education Then and Now." AMERICAN PSYCHOLOGIST 31 (November 1976): 756-64.

> Contrasts graduate education in the 1930s, especially at Harvard University and the University of California at Berkeley, with present-day graduate education. Examines faculty-student relations, general academic climate, Ph.D. requirements, sexism, and racism.

Seashore, Carl E. PIONEERING IN PSYCHOLOGY. University of Iowa Studies, No. 398; Series on Aims and Progress of Research, No. 70. University of Iowa Press, 1942. vi, 232 p.

> This work is primarily a description of psychology at the University of Iowa from 1897 to 1937, written by the distinguished psychologist who was head of the psychology department and dean of the graduate college for three decades.

Sheldon, H.D. "Clark University, 1897-1900." JOURNAL OF SOCIAL PSYCHOLOGY 24 (November 1946): 227-47.

Woodworth, R.S. THE COLUMBIA UNIVERSITY PSYCHOLOGICAL LABORATORY: A FIFTY-YEAR RETROSPECT. New York: Author, Columbia University, 1942. 23 p.

A history of the Columbia University laboratory. Discusses Ph.D. alumni from 1891 to 1941, department organization, and degree requirements.

Zeigler, May. "Growth and Development of Psychology at the University of Georgia." JOURNAL OF GENETIC PSYCHOLOGY 75 (September 1949): 51-59.

xiii. OTHER EUROPEAN COUNTRIES

Bjerstedt, A. TWELVE YEARS OF EDUCATIONAL AND PSYCHOLOGICAL RE-SEARCH IN SWEDEN; A BIBLIOGRAPHY OF PUBLICATIONS IN ENGLISH 1955-1966. Lund, Sweden: Gleerup, 1968.

Brožek, Josef. "Contemporary West European Historiography of Psychology." HISTORY OF SCIENCE 13 (March 1975): 29-60.

Surveys developments in historiography of psychology in French-speaking, German-speaking, and English-speaking areas as well as for Holland, Italy, and Scandinavia.

From, F. "Psychology in Denmark; Psychology as a Science." NORDISK PSYKOLOGI 3 (1951): 75-78.

Heymans, G. "Psychological Science in Holland." SCANDINAVIAN SCIENTIFIC REVIEW 2 (1923): 124-25.

Ley, A. "The Present Status of Psychology in Belgium." SCANDINAVIAN SCIENTIFIC REVIEW 3 (1924-25): 188-95.

Muller, Ph. "Contemporary Psychology in Switzerland." ACTA PSYCHOLOGICA 18, no. 1 (1961): 29-66.

Nuttin, Joseph. PSYCHOLOGY IN BELGIUM. Louvain, Belgium: Publications Universitaires, 1961. 80 p.

6. SPECIALIZED HISTORIES

Several specialized areas in the history of psychology, other than standard histories of the great schools or systems of psychology (section C, p. 127) or of major research fields (section D, p. 249), have been the subject of research. These include the following topics, into which the present section is divided: the origin of the word "psychology"; the history of the American Psychological Association; histories of other specialized groups (such as black psychologists and Catholic psychologists) and associations (such as the Society of Experimental

Psychologists and the Southern Society for Philosophy and Psychology); and histories of particular journals in psychology.

a. Origin of Psychological Terms

Boring, Edwin G. "A Note on the Origin of the Word 'Psychology.'" JOURNAL OF THE HISTORY OF THE BEHAVIORAL SCIENCES 2 (April 1966): 167.

    Reports evidence that the word "psychology" was used in a lost manuscript of Marko Marulic (1450-1524).

Lapointe, Francois H. "Origin and Evolution of the Term 'Psychology.'" AMERICAN PSYCHOLOGIST 25 (July 1970): 640-46.

    Traces the word "psychology" from its appearance in the sixteenth century to its first use in a systematic textbook in 1855. A table identifies the evolution of the term from 1530 to 1855.

_____. "The Origin and Evolution of the Term 'Psychology.'" PSYCHOLOGIA 16 (March 1973): 1-16.

    Argues that there is no evidence that Melanchthon was the first to use the term "psychology." Discusses the early use of the term by Marko Marulič and Johannes Thomas Freigius as well as the evolution of the term from around 1520 to 1855. Complements preceding entry.

_____. "Who Originated the Term 'Psychology'?" JOURNAL OF THE HISTORY OF THE BEHAVIORAL SCIENCES 8 (July 1972): 328-35.

    Traces the early use of the term "psychology" and argues that there is no evidence "that Melanchthon ever used the term 'psychology' 'als Vorlesungstitel' ('as the title for a lecture')." Discusses the use of the term by other individuals such as Marko Marulic, Freigius, Taillepied, Goeckel, and Casmann.

Senn, Peter R. "What is 'Behavioral Science'?--Notes Toward a History." JOURNAL OF THE HISTORY OF THE BEHAVIORAL SCIENCES 2 (April 1966): 107-22.

    Follows the development of the phrase "behavioral science" in textbook titles, journal titles, and government sources. Suggests guidelines for the use of the term.

b. Histories of the American Psychological Association

Boring, E[dwin].G. "Statistics of the American Psychological Association in 1920." PSYCHOLOGICAL BULLETIN 17 (July 1920): 271-78.

Cattell, James McKeen. "The Founding of the Association and of the Hopkins and Clark Laboratories." PSYCHOLOGICAL REVIEW 50 (January 1943): 61-64.

Dennis, Wayne, and Boring, Edwin G. "The Founding of the APA." AMERICAN PSYCHOLOGIST 7 (March 1952): 95-97.

    A brief account of selected topics relevant to the meeting on July 8, 1892 of the founders of the American Psychological Association. Discusses those who attended and were appointed to offices.

Farrand, L. "The American Psychological Association." SCIENCE 5 (February 1897): 206-15.

Fernberger, S[amuel].W. "The American Psychological Association: A Historical Summary, 1892-1930." PSYCHOLOGICAL BULLETIN 29 (January 1932): 1-89.

_____. The American Psychological Association: 1892-1942." PSYCHOLOGICAL REVIEW 50 (January 1943): 33-60.

_____. "Statistical Analysis of the Members and Associates of the American Psychological Association, Inc., in 1928. A Cross Section of American Professional Psychology." PSYCHOLOGICAL REVIEW 35 (November 1928): 447-65.

Habbe, S. "A Comparison of the American Psychological Association Membership of 1929 and 1939; An Analysis of Changes During the Past Decade With a Few Suggestions for the Next Decade." PSYCHOLOGICAL RECORD 4 (March 1941): 215-32.

Littman, Richard A. "Format of Publication and Election to the Presidency of the American Psychological Association." JOURNAL OF THE HISTORY OF THE BEHAVIORAL SCIENCES 8 (April 1972): 216-21.

    Describes presidents of the American Psychological Association in terms of such variables as the number who had published books before election, the mean age at the time of election, and the mean age at which the highest degree was earned. Characteristics of the first forty presidents are compared with those of the next forty presidents.

Moore, Clyde B. "Notes on the Presidents of the American Psychological Association." AMERICAN JOURNAL OF PSYCHOLOGY 29 (July 1918): 347-49.

Sokal, Michael M. "APA's First Publication: Proceedings of the American Psychological Association, 1892-1893." AMERICAN PSYCHOLOGIST 28 (April 1973): 277-92.

A reproduction of the proceedings of the 1892 and 1893 meetings preceded by a brief explanatory note and information about publication of some of the subsequent proceedings.

Wallin, J.E. Wallace. "Facts of Interest Regarding the Oldest APA Ph.D.s Born in the Seventies and Still Alive." JOURNAL OF THE HISTORY OF THE BEHAVIORAL SCIENCES 4 (July 1968): 245-48.

Biographical data (e.g., birth date, year PhD granted, PhD school, and number of publications) on seventeen APA members born in the 1870s and still living in the mid-1960s.

c. Histories of Other Specialized Associations and Groups

Benjamin, Ludy T., Jr. "The Psychological Round Table: Revolution of 1936." AMERICAN PSYCHOLOGIST 32 (July 1977): 542-49.

An account of the organization, early years, and early membership of the exclusive "Society of Experimenting Psychologists," formed partly in rebellion against the APA and the older Society of Experimental Psychologists.

Boring, Edwin G. "The Society of Experimental Psychologists: 1904-1938." AMERICAN JOURNAL OF PSYCHOLOGY 51 (April 1938): 410-23.

_____. "Titchener's Experimentalists." JOURNAL OF THE HISTORY OF THE BEHAVIORAL SCIENCES 3 (October 1967): 315-25.

Canaday, Herman G. "Psychology in Negro Institutions." JOURNAL OF NEGRO EDUCATION 7 (April 1938): 165-71.

Surveys the status of psychology in Negro institutions, courses offered, laboratory equipment and research, and teaching personnel.

Evans, Rand B., and Scott, Frederick J. Down. "The 1913 International Congress of Psychology: The American Congress that Wasn't." AMERICAN PSYCHOLOGIST 33 (August 1978): 711-23.

Traces a power struggle among eminent American psychologists that resulted in the cancellation of what would have been the first International Congress of Psychology to be held in the United States.

Finison, Lorenz J. "Psychologists and Spain: A Historical Note." AMERICAN PSYCHOLOGIST 32 (December 1977): 1080-84.

Describes the activities of a group headed by T.C. Schneirla and organized as the Psychologists' Committee of the Medical Bureau to aid Spanish Democracy.

Guthrie, Robert V. EVEN THE RAT WAS WHITE: A HISTORICAL VIEW OF
PSYCHOLOGY. New York: Harper and Row, 1976. xii, 224 p.

> Provides racial and historical perspectives on the background of
> mental testing and the warnings of black psychologists against the
> dangers of mass testing. Presents contributions and biographies of
> distinguished black psychologists in the United States, and surveys
> the growth of psychology and education in black colleges and uni-
> versities. Includes statistical information on the roles, opportuni-
> ties, contributions, and education of blacks in psychology. Bibli-
> ography. Index.

Hollander, Edwin P. "The Society of Experimental Social Psychology: An Historical Note." JOURNAL OF PERSONALITY AND SOCIAL PSYCHOLOGY 9
(July 1968): 280-82.

Lindsley, Donald B., and Harrell, Thomas W. "History of the Western Psychological Association." AMERICAN PSYCHOLOGIST 19 (April 1964): 290-91.

Martinez, Joe L., Jr., ed. CHICANO PSYCHOLOGY. New York: Academic Press, 1977. xiv, 367 p.

> Contains twenty-one papers on such topics as bilingualism, psycho-
> logical testing, psychotherapy, and social psychology. Includes
> some history of Chicano psychology. Index.

Miner, J.B. "The Past Ten Years of Psychology in the Southern Society for
Philosophy and Psychology." PSYCHOLOGICAL REVIEW 48 (November 1941):
552-64.

> Examines some of the trends in the psychology of the 1930s evi-
> denced in convention programs of the Southern Society for Philoso-
> phy and Psychology.

Misiak, Henryk, and Staudt, Virginia M. CATHOLICS IN PSYCHOLOGY:
A HISTORICAL SURVEY. New York: McGraw-Hill, 1954. xv, 309 p.

> Focuses on the contributions of Catholic scholars to psychology and
> describes the work of Joseph Froebes, Albert E. Michotte,
> Thomas V. Moore, and Edward A. Pace, among others. Contains
> materials on schools, organizations, and periodicals; Catholic
> pioneers in Europe and America; bibliographies on the history of
> psychology in English, and a list of major Catholic textbooks.
> Notes and references follow each chapter. Index.

Poffenberger, A.T. "A History of the National Research Council, 1919-1933.
VIII. Division of Anthropology and Psychology." SCIENCE 78 (August 1933):
158-61.

Salzinger, Kurt, ed. PSYCHOLOGY IN PROGRESS: AN INTERIM REPORT. New York: New York Academy of Sciences, 1976. 151 p.

> Papers on selected historical and current research topics. Historical themes include: an overview of the history of the psychology section of the New York Academy of Sciences, reappraisals of Wundt, and William Stern's work at Hamburg.

Symonds, J.P. "I. Historical Sketch of Applied Organizations." JOURNAL OF APPLIED PSYCHOLOGY 21 (1937): 322-25.

> Part I of a larger article on a proposed American Association of Applied and Professional Psychology. Explores the formation of earlier organizations of applied psychologists.

Whitney, E. Arthur. "The American Association of Mental Deficiency: Brief History and Purposes." JOURNAL OF CLINICAL PSYCHOLOGY 2 (October 1946): 394-96.

d. Histories of Psychology Journals

Allport, G.W. "An Editorial." JOURNAL OF ABNORMAL AND SOCIAL PSYCHOLOGY 33 (January 1938): 3-13.

> Reviews the history of the JOURNAL OF ABNORMAL AND SOCIAL PSYCHOLOGY and outlines editorial policy.

Bolton, Henry Carrington. CATALOGUE OF SCIENTIFIC AND TECHNICAL PERIODICALS, 1665-1896. 2d ed. Washington, D.C.: Smithsonian Institution, 1897. vii, 1,247 p.

Chaison, Gary N. "Changes in Authorship, Affiliation and Research Support Patterns of JOURNAL OF APPLIED PSYCHOLOGY Articles, 1917-1969." JOURNAL OF APPLIED PSYCHOLOGY 55 (October 1971): 484-86.

> Documents trends toward multiple authorship, increased diversity of funding sources, and changes in institutional affiliations of authors.

Cofer, Charles N. "Origins of the Journal of Verbal Learning and Verbal Behavior." JOURNAL OF VERBAL LEARNING AND VERBAL BEHAVIOR 17 (February 1978): 113-26.

Dallenbach, Karl M. "The American Journal of Psychology: 1887-1937." AMERICAN JOURNAL OF PSYCHOLOGY 50 (November 1937): 489-506.

> In commemoration of the Golden Jubilee of this oldest psychology journal. A brief history by the journal's editor discussing G. Stanley Hall, the journal's founder, and the journal's scope, publishers, printers, editors, indexes, and special issues.

_____. "An Interdisciplinary Journal of the History of the Behavioral Sciences." AMERICAN JOURNAL OF PSYCHOLOGY 77 (December 1964): 674.

> Announcement of the publication of the JOURNAL OF THE HISTORY OF THE BEHAVIORAL SCIENCES, Robert I. Watson, editor.

Darley, John G. "1917: A Journal Is Born." JOURNAL OF APPLIED PSYCHOLOGY 52, pt. 1 (February 1968): 1-9.

Eng, Erling. "Karl Philipp Moritz's MAGAZIN ZUR ERFAHRUNGSSEELENKUNDE [Magazine for Empirical Psychology] 1783-1793." JOURNAL OF THE HISTORY OF THE BEHAVIORAL SCIENCES 9 (October 1973): 300-305.

> General information on the editor, contributors, and major focus of what may have been the first journal of psychology and psychiatry.

Evans, Rand B. "The JOURNAL OF AMERICAN PSYCHOLOGY: A Pioneering Psychological Journal." JOURNAL OF THE HISTORY OF THE BEHAVIORAL SCIENCES 7 (July 1971): 283-84.

> Describes some of the general purposes and contents of the JOURNAL OF AMERICAN PSYCHOLOGY, an early publication discontinued after its seventh number.

Hall, G.S[tanley]. "The American Journal of Psychology." AMERICAN JOURNAL OF PSYCHOLOGY 32 (January 1921): 1-3.

Langfeld, H[erbert].S. "Jubilee of the PSYCHOLOGICAL REVIEW: Fifty Volumes of the PSYCHOLOGICAL REVIEW." PSYCHOLOGICAL REVIEW 50 (January 1943): 143-55.

Symonds, J.P[ercival]. "Ten Years of Journalism in Psychology, 1937-1946; First Decade of the JOURNAL OF CONSULTING PSYCHOLOGY." JOURNAL OF CONSULTING PSYCHOLOGY 10 (November-December 1946): 335-74.

e. Histories of Psychology Instruments

Burnham, John C. "Thorndike's Puzzle Boxes." JOURNAL OF THE HISTORY OF THE BEHAVIORAL SCIENCES 8 (April 1972): 159-67.

> Discusses the theory and impact of Thorndike's work with puzzle boxes and reproduces eight photographs of the boxes.

Carmichael, L. "The History of Mirror Drawing as a Laboratory Method." PEDAGOGICAL SEMINARY 34 (1927): 90-91.

References in History of Psychology

Popplestone, John A., and McPherson, Marion White. "Prolegomenon to the Study of Apparatus in Early Psychology Laboratories Circa 1875-1915." AMERICAN PSYCHOLOGIST 26 (July 1971): 656-57.

> Notes the importance of technology and equipment in shaping the history of a science and suggests sources of information on early equipment in psychology laboratories: stock lists of manufacturers, laboratory and university inventories, photographs, laboratory manuals, journal articles, and reminiscences of psychologists. The Archives of the History of American Psychology at the University of Akron (Ohio), with which the authors are affiliated, contains many "manufacts" and is thus a valuable source of information.

Ruckmick, C[hristian].A. "Development of Laboratory Equipment in Psychology in the United States." AMERICAN JOURNAL OF PSYCHOLOGY 37 (October 1926): 582-92.

Sanford, Edmund C. "Some Practical Suggestions on the Equipment of a Psychology Laboratory." AMERICAN JOURNAL OF PSYCHOLOGY 5 (July 1893): 429-38.

> Discusses rooms, furniture, and types of apparatus needed for a psychological laboratory. Offers suggestions on how to use a laboratory.

Sokal, Michael M.; Davis, Audrey B.; and Merzbach, Uta C. "Laboratory Instruments in the History of Psychology." JOURNAL OF THE HISTORY OF THE BEHAVIORAL SCIENCES 12 (January 1976): 59-64.

> A brief discussion of the importance of early laboratory equipment in historical research and teaching. Reviews Cattell's work with the Hipp chronoscope.

. "A National Inventory of Historic Psychological Apparatus." JOURNAL OF THE HISTORY OF THE BEHAVIORAL SCIENCES 11 (July 1975): 284-86.

> Describes efforts to locate and preserve historic psychological apparatus by the Archives of the History of American Psychology at the University of Akron, the American Psychological Association, and the Department of Psychology at Cornell University. Notes the sponsorship by the National Museum of History and Technology of the Smithsonian Institution of a National Inventory of Historic Psychological Apparatus.

f. Histories of Women in Psychology

Astin, Helen S. "Employment and Career Status of Women Psychologists." AMERICAN PSYCHOLOGIST 27 (May 1972): 371-81.

Bachtold, Louise M., and Werner, Emmy E. "Personality Profiles of Gifted Women Psychologists." AMERICAN PSYCHOLOGIST 25 (March 1970): 234-43.

    Compares personality characteristics of academic women in psychology with those of academic men, college women, and women in the general population.

Benjamin, Ludy T., Jr. "The Pioneering Work of Leta Hollingworth in the Psychology of Women." NEBRASKA HISTORY 56 (Winter 1975): 493-505.

    An excellent overview of Leta Hollingworth's research, primarily on the variability of men and women.

Bernstein, Maxine D., and Russo, Nancy Felipe. "The History of Psychology Revisited, or, Up With Our Foremothers." AMERICAN PSYCHOLOGIST 29 (February 1974): 130-34.

    Notes that awareness of historical and contemporary contributions of women in psychology is generally deficient. Describes briefly the contributions of selected women and offers suggestions for improving insight into the contributions of women.

Boring, Edwin G. "The Woman Problem." AMERICAN PSYCHOLOGIST 6 (December 1951): 679-82.

    Discusses unequal recognition and unequal employment opportunities for women in psychology and considers possible reasons for this situation.

Boring, Edwin G., and Bryan, Alice L. "Women in American Psychology: Factors Affecting Their Professional Careers." PI LAMBDA THETA JOURNAL 25 (1946): 92-95.

Bryan, Alice L., and Boring, Edwin G. "Women in American Psychology: Factors Affecting Their Professional Careers." AMERICAN PSYCHOLOGIST 2 (January 1947): 3-20.

    Based on 440 questionnaire responses. Compares women PhDs in psychology with a matched group of men on such topics as family background, salary status, how they became interested in psychology, satisfaction with professional training, and job satisfaction.

_____. "Women in American Psychology: Prolegomenon." PSYCHOLOGICAL BULLETIN 41 (July 1944): 447-54.

_____. "Women in American Psychology: Statistics From the OPP Questionnaire." AMERICAN PSYCHOLOGIST 1 (March 1946): 71-79.

    Based on data collected by the Office of Psychological Personnel. Provides information for women in American psychology such as where they took their PhD, employment status, and salary.

_____. Women in Psychology: Factors Affecting Their Careers." TRANSAC-
TIONS OF THE NEW YORK ACADEMY OF SCIENCES, SERIES 11 9 (November
1946): 19-23.

Davis, Audrey B. BIBLIOGRAPHY ON WOMEN, WITH SPECIAL EMPHASIS
ON THEIR ROLES IN SCIENCE AND SOCIETY. New York: Science History
Publications, 1974. 50 p.

Kimmel, E. "Contributions to the History of Psychology, XXIV: Role of Women
Psychologists in the History of Psychology in the South." PSYCHOLOGICAL
REPORTS 38 (April 1976): 611-18.

Lonsdale, Kathleen. "Women in Science: Reminiscences and Reflections."
IMPACT OF SCIENCE ON SOCIETY 20 (January-March 1970): 45-59.

Lowie, Robert H., and Hollingworth, Leta Stetter. "Science and Feminism."
SCIENTIFIC MONTHLY 3 (September 1916): 277-84.

Challenges the hypothesis that males are more variable than females.
Argues that women are well suited to do scientific work and other
work from which they have been excluded.

Mitchell, Mildred B. "Status of Women in the American Psychological Association." AMERICAN PSYCHOLOGIST 6 (June 1951): 193-201.

Shows membership status and administrative appointments in the
American Psychological Association by sex for 1923-49, and officers
of APA by sex for 1892-1949.

NOTABLE AMERICAN WOMEN 1607-1950. A BIOGRAPHICAL DICTIONARY.
3 vols. Cambridge, Mass.: Belknap Press of Harvard University Press, 1971.

Pratola, Stephanie. "Up With Our Foremother." AMERICAN PSYCHOLOGIST
29 (October 1974): 780.

A brief note outlining some of the contributions of Mary Whiton
Calkins.

Rosenberg, Charles, and Smith-Rosenberg, Carroll. "The Bitter Fruit: Heredity,
Disease and Social Thought in Nineteenth Century America." PERSPECTIVES
IN AMERICAN HISTORY 8 (1974): 189-235.

Rossiter, Margaret W. "Women Scientists in America Before 1920." AMERICAN
SCIENTIST 62 (May-June 1974): 312-23.

Shows percentage of women working in various disciplines, including
psychology, and numbers of women in academic institutions. Outlines achievements of selected women.

Shields, Stephanie A. "Ms. Pilgrim's Progress: The Contributions of Leta Stetter Hollingworth to the Psychology of Women." AMERICAN PSYCHOLOGIST 30 (August 1975): 852-57.

> Discusses Hollingworth's early work on the variability hypothesis (that men are more variable than women), and presents biographical information.

Strunk, Orlo, Jr. "The Self-Psychology of Mary Whiton Calkins." JOURNAL OF THE HISTORY OF THE BEHAVIORAL SCIENCES 8 (April 1972): 196-203.

> Presents an overview of Calkins' self theory and provides biographical information, including comments on her work at Harvard with William James. Notes the sexism of the day that denied her a PhD in spite of strong support from prominent figures.

Zuckerman, Harriet, and Cole, Jonathan R. "Women in American Science." MINERVA 13 (Spring 1975): 82-102.

7. HISTORIOGRAPHY

Writers on the history of psychology, like other writers of history, devote attention to their craft itself. For example, how should one go about writing the history of a particular subject, movement, event, or group of people? Such issues are the focus of historiography, and the items listed in this section concern such questions. The section contains the following subcategories: the history of psychology as a special field, the teaching of the history of psychology, studies of eminence in the history of psychology, methods and resources for research in the history of psychology, methodological and philosophical issues in the historiography of psychology, and psychohistory (the use of developmental and psychoanalytic concepts in writing interpretive history).

a. History of Psychology as a Specialty

Brožek, Josef. "Current and Anticipated Research in the History of Psychology." JOURNAL OF THE BEHAVIORAL SCIENCES 4 (April 1968): 180-85.

> Reports the research interests and activities of fifty-eight members of the Division of the History of Psychology (Division 26) of the American Psychological Association.

_____. "History of Psychology: Diversity of Approaches and Uses." TRANSACTIONS OF THE NEW YORK ACADEMY OF SCIENCES, SERIES 11 31 (February 1969): 115-27.

Cardno, J.A. "Natural Limits and Change of Content in the History of Psychology." PSYCHOLOGICAL RECORD 12 (July 1962): 289-98.

Krantz, David L. "Toward a Role for Historical Analysis: The Case of Psychology and Physiology." JOURNAL OF THE HISTORY OF THE BEHAVIORAL SCIENCES 1 (January 1965): 278-83.

Uses historical controversies over physiological and psychological explanations to buttress the argument that knowledge of the past clarifies present perspectives and heightens awareness.

Swartz, Paul. "Perspectives in Psychology: V. Psychology in the Historical Sense." PSYCHOLOGICAL RECORD 8 (January 1958): 17-20.

Argues that psychology has not achieved a historical sense, and that content and methods in the young discipline were too narrowly conceived. Ends with a plea that dissertations in the history of psychology be acceptable.

Watson, Robert I. "The History of Psychology: A Neglected Area." AMERICAN PSYCHOLOGIST 15 (April 1960): 251-55.

Documents the neglect of history, showing that only 38 of 2,800 articles published in three leading psychology journals over a twenty-year period (1938-57) dealt explicitly with the history of the field. Notes that few psychologists in the 1958 APA Directory list history as an interest area, and suggests that psychologists give greater attention to the history of their discipline.

_____. The History of Psychology as a Specialty: A Personal View of Its First 15 Years." JOURNAL OF THE HISTORY OF THE BEHAVIORAL SCIENCES 11 (January 1975): 5-14.

Traces developments in the history of psychology as a discipline with emphasis on the establishment of the JOURNAL OF THE HISTORY OF THE BEHAVIORAL SCIENCES, the founding of the Archives of the History of American Psychology at the University of Akron, the establishment of doctoral training programs in the history of psychology, and the founding of the Division of the History of Psychology in the American Psychological Association.

_____. "A Note on the History of Psychology as a Specialization." JOURNAL OF THE HISTORY OF THE BEHAVIORAL SCIENCES 3 (April 1967): 192-93.

Notes increasing acceptance of the history of psychology as a discipline, as evidenced by the establishment of the JOURNAL OF THE HISTORY OF THE BEHAVIORAL SCIENCES, increasing postdoctoral training in the history of psychology, and growing tolerance of psychological dissertations based on historical research.

b. Teaching the History of Psychology

Brožek, Josef. "Breadth and Depth in Teaching History." AMERICAN PSY-

CHOLOGIST 21 (November 1966): 1075-76.

> A brief comment on the philosophy of teaching history of psychology, and the texts used, at Lehigh University.

Brožek, Josef, and Schneider, Leslie S. "Second Summer Institute on the History of Psychology." JOURNAL OF THE HISTORY OF THE BEHAVIORAL SCIENCES 9 (April 1973): 91-101.

> Describes major goals of the 1971 conference, activities of the director and participants, and the topics presented by panels and guest speakers.

Brožek, Josef; Watson, Robert I.; and Ross, Barbara. "A Summer Institute on the History of Psychology: Part I." JOURNAL OF THE HISTORY OF THE BEHAVIORAL SCIENCES 5 (October 1969): 307-19.

> Report of a conference at the University of New Hampshire in 1968. Discusses group activities of the participants, pedagogical aspects of the history of psychology, and characteristics of the ideal history textbook. (See also the Weyant item in this subsection, p. 109.)

_____. "A Summer Institute on the History of Psychology: Part II." JOURNAL OF THE HISTORY OF THE BEHAVIORAL SCIENCES 6 (January 1970): 25-35.

> Summarizes the presentations of staff members of the summer institute and provides notes on guest lecturers. (See also the Weyant item in this subsection, p. 109.)

Carlson, Eric T., and Simpson, Meribeth M. "A Program on the History of Psychiatry and the Behavioral Sciences at Cornell University Medical College." JOURNAL OF THE HISTORY OF THE BEHAVIORAL SCIENCES 3 (October 1967): 370-72.

> A brief overview of the development, activities, and library holdings of the history of psychiatry section at Cornell University.

Dunlap, Knight. "The Historical Method in Psychology." JOURNAL OF GENERAL PSYCHOLOGY 24 (January 1941): 49-62.

> Argues that historical methods are neglected in psychology and points to the need for more thematic histories, such as Fearing's HISTORY OF REFLEX ACTION. Comments on source books, biographies, general histories, and surveys of periods, and pleads for more adequate training for historians of psychology.

Erickson, Ralph Waldo. "Contemporary Histories of Psychology." In PRESENT-DAY PSYCHOLOGY, edited by A[braham].A[aron]. Roback, pp. 487-506. New York: Philosophical Library, 1955.

Reviews history textbooks by Murphy, Boring, Roback, Brett, Spearman, Flugel, and Mueller-Freienfels. Includes comments about historical writing in the United States, England, Germany, and France.

Helson, Harry. "What Can We Learn From the History of Psychology?" JOURNAL OF THE HISTORY OF THE BEHAVIORAL SCIENCES 8 (January 1972): 115-19.

Enumerates some of the values of the study of history and discusses characteristics of ideas which have proved to be influential.

Henle, Mary, and Sullivan, John. "Seven Psychologies Revisited." JOURNAL OF THE HISTORY OF THE BEHAVIORAL SCIENCES 10 (January 1974): 40-46.

A review of and a tribute to the classic text by Edna Heidbreder (see section B1, p. 34) which, after forty years, leaves the "impression that one is reading a contemporary book."

Nance, R. Dale. "Current Practices in Teaching History of Psychology." AMERICAN PSYCHOLOGIST 17 (May 1962): 250-52.

Reports the results of a survey of major psychology departments on topics pertinent to the history of psychology: whether a course in history is taught, whether it is required, number of credits for the course, and textbook used.

_____. "Student Reactions to the History of Psychology." AMERICAN PSYCHOLOGIST 16 (April 1961): 189-91.

Reports the results of a student survey in a course in the history of psychology at the University of Wisconsin at Milwaukee. Shows student preference for various topic areas and student opinion on the great contributors to psychology.

Perloff, Robert, and Perloff, Linda S. "The Fair--An Opportunity for Depicting Psychology and for Conducting Behavioral Research." AMERICAN PSYCHOLOGIST 32 (March 1977): 220-29.

Provides examples of how psychology has been depicted at fairs and expositions over the past ninety years and encourages the development of psychological exhibits at fairs of all kinds.

Reidel, Robert G. "The Current Status of the History and Systems of Psychology Courses in American Colleges and Universities." JOURNAL OF THE HISTORY OF THE BEHAVIORAL SCIENCES 10 (October 1974): 410-12.

Questionnaire data returned by 393 of 600 registrars of American colleges and universities. Provides information on number and percentage of schools offering and requiring courses in the history of psychology, and number of students enrolled in such courses during the years 1966-71.

Shaklee, Alfred B. "Autobiography in Teaching History of Psychology." AMERICAN PSYCHOLOGIST 12 (May 1957): 282-83.

> Describes role-playing techniques used to make a course in the history of psychology more meaningful. Students familiarized themselves with famous psychologists and presented materials as if they were the person they had studied. Student reactions were positive, both to the role-playing technique and to W.C. Dampier's A HISTORY OF SCIENCE (see section E5, p. 416), used as a supplemental textbook.

Watson, Robert I. "The Role and Use of History in the Psychology Curriculum." JOURNAL OF THE HISTORY OF THE BEHAVIORAL SCIENCES 2 (January 1966): 64-69.

Weigel, Richard G., and Gottfurcht, James W. "Faculty Genealogies: A Stimulus for Student Involvement in History and Systems." AMERICAN PSYCHOLOGIST 27 (October 1972): 981-83.

> Describes projects in which students trace the intellectual genealogies of faculty members.

Weyant, Robert G. "Some Reflections on the NSF Summer Institute in the History of Psychology." CANADIAN PSYCHOLOGIST 9, no. 4 (1968): 505-10.

> A discussion of the summer institute reported in the papers by Brožek, Schneider, Watson, and Ross (see above, this section, p. 107).

c. Studies of Eminence

Annin, Edith L.; Boring, Edwin G.; and Watson, Robert I. "Important Psychologists, 1600-1967." JOURNAL OF THE HISTORY OF THE BEHAVIORAL SCIENCES 4 (October 1968): 303-15.

> Lists 538 nonliving psychologists selected by an international panel of experts from 1,040 names rated for eminence in the history of psychology. This list has been used extensively in later works such as Watson (see section A2, p. 18) and Zusne (see section A1, p. 6).

Becker, Russell J. "Outstanding Contributors to Psychology." AMERICAN PSYCHOLOGIST 14 (June 1959): 297-98.

> In two spearate surveys, a random sample of members and fellows of the American Psychological Association ranked American psychologists, and psychologists without regard to national location, for their contributions to the field. The top-rated individuals in each survey are listed.

References in History of Psychology

Bentley, Madison. "The 'Best' Psychologists." AMERICAN JOURNAL OF PSYCHOLOGY 54 (July 1941): 439.

A brief note criticizing rating procedures used by Science Service for determining the "best" or "most outstanding" psychologists.

Boring, Mollie D., and Boring, Edwin G. "Masters and Pupils Among the American Psychologists." AMERICAN JOURNAL OF PSYCHOLOGY 61 (October 1948): 527-34.

A well-known article showing the intellectual genealogy of famous American psychologists.

Coan, Richard W., and Zagona, Salvatore V. "Contemporary Ratings of Psychological Theorists." PSYCHOLOGICAL RECORD 12 (July 1962): 315-22.

Reports the results of a survey of forty-two judges knowledgeable in the history of psychology who rated psychologists with respect to the importance of their contributions. Ratings presented for eight decades, from 1880 to 1959.

Duncan, Carl P. "Recognition of Names of Eminent Psychologists." JOURNAL OF THE HISTORY OF THE BEHAVIORAL SCIENCES 12 (October 1976): 325-29.

Recognition of the names of 228 eminent but deceased psychologists was surprisingly low in a sample of currently-active psychologists, and even lower among graduate students, undergraduate psychology majors, and students enrolled in introductory psychology courses. Discusses results in terms of both the number of psychologists who have never had a course in the history of psychology, and the effects of specialization in PhD programs.

Grove, Carl, and Radford, John. "Dear Colleague . . .: A Replication." BULLETIN OF THE BRITISH PSYCHOLOGICAL SOCIETY 26 (April 1973): 129-30.

Presents a list of people who contributed greatly to twentieth-century psychology, based on a survey of British psychologists.

Kassinove, Howard. "A Second Note on the Question, How Well Known Are APA Award Winners?" JOURNAL OF THE HISTORY OF THE BEHAVIORAL SCIENCES 8 (April 1972): 249-51.

Psychology faculty members indicated the extent of their knowledge of APA award winners for 1956-68. There was wide variability in knowledge and a .79 correlation between faculty rankings and graduate student rankings from an earlier study (see Yuker below, this section, p. 111).

Merrifield, Marilyn, and Watson, Robert I. "Eminent Psychologists: Corrections and Additions." JOURNAL OF THE HISTORY OF THE BEHAVIORAL SCIENCES 6 (July 1970): 261–62.

A few corrections and additions to the list of important psychologists, 1600–1967, published in 1968 by Annin, Boring, and Watson (see above, this section, p. 109).

Visher, Stephen S. "Recently Starred Psychologists." AMERICAN JOURNAL OF PSYCHOLOGY 57 (October 1944): 573–74.

A note on geographic distribution, location of doctorate, and birthplaces for psychologists starred in the six editions of AMERICAN MEN OF SCIENCE.

Walker, Ronald E. "An Indirect Communication of Psychology's History to Undergraduates." JOURNAL OF THE HISTORY OF THE BEHAVIORAL SCIENCES 5 (April 1969): 182–84.

Reports a study of the extent to which undergraduates and academicians interested in the history of psychology agree on who is eminent in psychology. Agreement improved as a function of number of courses completed by the undergraduate subjects.

Watson, Robert I., and Merrifield, Marilyn. "Characteristics of Individuals Eminent in Psychology in Temporal Perspective: Part I." JOURNAL OF THE HISTORY OF THE BEHAVIORAL SCIENCES 9 (October 1973): 339–59.

Five hundred thirty-eight individuals rated for eminence in psychology by a panel of knowledgeable judges (see Annin, Boring, and Watson, above, this section, p. 109) presented here in terms of their major field (philosophy, psychology, physiology), nationality, and the temporal period during which they made their contribution.

Wispé, Lauren G. "Some Social and Psychological Correlates of Eminence in Psychology." JOURNAL OF THE HISTORY OF THE BEHAVIORAL SCIENCES 1 (January 1965): 88–98.

Reports the results of a study of ninety-five eminent and ninety-five matched control psychologists to determine social and psychological correlates of eminence. Eminents came from smaller families and had better-educated parents who were above-average financially.

_____. "Traits of Eminent American Psychologists." SCIENCE 141 (September 1963): 1256–61.

Yuker, Harold E. "A Note on the Question: How Well Known Are APA Award Winners?" JOURNAL OF THE HISTORY OF THE BEHAVIORAL SCIENCES 6 (July 1970): 265–66.

Zusne, Leonard. "Contributions to the History of Psychology: XXI. History of Rating of Eminence in Psychology Revisited." PSYCHOLOGICAL REPORTS 36 (April 1975): 492-94.

> Offers a critique of the earlier eminence study by Annin, Boring, and Watson (see above, this section, p. 109) and reports on an alternate study which purports to correct scaling biases.

_____. "Five Hundred Seventy-eight Names in the History of Psychology: Computer Tabulations of Biographic Data." JOURNAL SUPPLEMENT ABSTRACT SERVICE, CATALOG OF SELECTED DOCUMENTS IN PSYCHOLOGY 5 (Spring 1975). MS No. 915. 265 p.

> See annotation in section A1, p. 6.

d. Methods and Resources for Research

i. GENERAL

Briskman, L.B. "Is a Kuhnian Analysis Applicable to Psychology?" SCIENCE STUDIES 2 (1972): 87-97.

Brooks, G.P. "Some Thoughts on Historical Study in Psychology, or At Last An Historian Who Reads More Than He Writes." PAPERS IN PSYCHOLOGY 5 (April 1971): 16-18.

Cardno, J.A. "The Experimental Upsurge: 1797-1874." AMERICAN JOURNAL OF PSYCHOLOGY 75 (September 1962): 499-501.

> Based on entries in Rand's bibliography of physiology, psychology, and cognate subjects. Shows specific publications for each of eight-time periods (1797-1874) for such subdisciplinary areas as sight, comparative psychology, abnormal and clinical psychology, and experimental and physiological psychology.

_____. "Inclusion, Exclusion, Emphasis: Selection in the History of Psychology." PSYCHOLOGICAL RECORD 11 (October 1961): 321-31.

> Comments on a major historiographical problem: the ratio of material selected to available material as one writes about a given time. Discusses principles of selection.

_____. "Victorian Psychology: A Biographical Approach." JOURNAL OF THE HISTORY OF THE BEHAVIORAL SCIENCES 1 (April 1965): 165-77.

> Designates some of the contributions to psychology in the Victorian era (1837-1901), discusses methods for assessing contributions, and points out historical errors pertaining to under- and over-evaluation of contributions.

Dashiell, John F. "The Unreliability of Secondary Sources: With Examples From Jung." PSYCHOLOGICAL RECORD 12 (July 1962): 331-34.

Goodman, Elizabeth S. "Citation Analysis as a Tool in Historical Study: A Case Study Based on F.C. Donders and Mental Reaction Times." JOURNAL OF THE HISTORY OF THE BEHAVIORAL SCIENCES 7 (April 1971): 187-91.

Employs a quantitative method to assess use and recognition by modern investigators of Donders's pioneering work on reaction time.

Littman, Richard A. "The Need for Accuracy in Historiography." JOURNAL OF THE HISTORY OF THE BEHAVIORAL SCIENCES 12 (April 1976): 178-80.

Points out numerous errors in a previous paper by John R. Wettersten, "The Historiography of Scientific Psychology: A Critical Study" (see section B7e, p. 122) and stresses the importance of accuracy in historiography.

Mountjoy, Paul T. "Methodological Note: The United States Patent Office As A Source of Historical Documents." JOURNAL OF THE HISTORY OF THE BEHAVIORAL SCIENCES 10 (January 1974): 119-20.

Provides information on how the Patent Office can be a source of important historical documents for historians of the behavioral sciences.

Palermo, David S. "Is A Scientific Revolution Taking Place in Psychology?" SCIENCE STUDIES 1 (1971): 135-55.

Reingold, Nathan, and Watson, Robert I. "The Organization and Preservation of Personal Papers." AMERICAN PSYCHOLOGIST 21 (October 1966): 971-72.

Notes efforts by professional societies such as the American Psychological Association to select and preserve unpublished papers. Offers suggestions concerning the preservation of documents of individual psychologists.

Roeckelein, Jon E. "Contributions to the History of Psychology: XVI. Eponymy in Psychology: Early Versus Recent Textbooks." PSYCHOLOGICAL REPORTS 34 (April 1974): 427-32.

Compares early texts published between 1920 and 1939 with texts published between 1968 and 1971 for amount of naming of theorists. Recent textbooks had higher naming ratios (frequency of naming divided by number of pages) than earlier books.

Sedlow, Walter A., Jr., and Sedlow, Sally Keates. "Formalized Historiography, the Structure of Scientific and Literary Texts: Part I. Some Issues Posed by Computational Methodology." JOURNAL OF THE HISTORY OF THE BEHAVIORAL SCIENCES 14 (July 1978): 247-63.

Argues that computer techniques (including content analysis and syntactic analysis) are becoming for the formalized analysis of historical writing what microscopy and telescopes are for the "subvisual" and for astronomic phenomena.

Shapiro, S.I., and Miller, Anne C. "A Pictorial Concordance to Important Psychologists, 1600-1967." JOURNAL OF THE HISTORY OF THE BEHAVIORAL SCIENCES 13 (October 1977): 326-27.

Describes a project in which portraits of 440 of the 538 eminent psychologists identified by Annin, Boring, and Watson have been located. (Original 61-page bibliography available from ASIS/NAPS, c/o Microfiche Publications, P.O. Box 3513, Grand Central Station, New York, N.Y. 10017.)

Toynbee, Arnold. "The Value of C.G. Jung's Work for Historians." JOURNAL OF ANALYTIC PSYCHOLOGY 1 (1956): 193-94.

Weimer, Walter B. "The History of Psychology and Its Retrieval From Historiography, I. The Problematic Nature of History." SCIENCE STUDIES 4 (1974): 235-58.

_____. "The History of Psychology and Its Retrieval From Historiography, II. Some Lessons From the Methodology of Scientific Research." SCIENCE STUDIES 4 (1974): 367-96.

Weimer, Walter B., and Palermo, David S. "Paradigms and Normal Science in Psychology." SCIENCE STUDIES 3 (1973): 211-44.

Wettersten, John R. "Response to Littman: The Need for Recognition of Theory in Historiography." JOURNAL OF THE HISTORY OF THE BEHAVIORAL SCIENCES 12 (April 1976): 181-82.

Response to a criticism by Richard Littman (see above this section, p. 113) of his earlier paper, "The Historiography of Scientific Psychology: A Critical Study " (see section B7e, p. 122). Argues for a "broadminded" historiography that is factually accurate and distinguishes between conjecture and fact.

Wurtz, Kenneth R. "A Survey of Important Psychological Books." AMERICAN PSYCHOLOGIST 16 (April 1961): 192-94.

Yerkes, R.M. "Plan for a History of Psychological Services in the War." PSYCHOLOGICAL BULLETIN 42 (February 1945): 87-90.

ii. ORAL HISTORY

Berman, Leo H. "Oral History As Source Material for the History of Behavioral

Sciences." JOURNAL OF THE HISTORY OF THE BEHAVIORAL SCIENCES 3 (January 1967): 58-59.

Cites the advantages of tape-recorded conversations with eminent persons as a historical source.

Evans, Richard I. "Contributions to the History of Psychology: X. Filmed Dialogues With Notable Contributors to Psychology." PSYCHOLOGICAL RE-PORTS 25 (August 1969): 159-64.

Discusses the uses and archival value of a series of 30- to 50-minute films of dialogues with the notable psychologists Jung, Fromm, Skinner, Hilgard, Allport, and others.

McPherson, Marion White. "Some Values and Limitations of Oral Histories." JOURNAL OF THE HISTORY OF THE BEHAVIORAL SCIENCES 11 (January 1975): 34-36.

Comments on the origin and extent of use of interviews (oral histories) of prominent persons recorded on audio devices. Outlines values and limitations of the practice.

McPherson, Marion White, and Popplestone, John A. PROBLEMS AND PRO-CEDURES IN ORAL HISTORIES AT THE ARCHIVES OF THE HISTORY OF AMERI-CAN PSYCHOLOGY. Akron, Ohio: Archives of the History of American Psychology, University of Akron, August 1967.

Myers, C.R. "The Collection, Preservation and Use of Oral History Materials." CANADIAN PSYCHOLOGICAL REVIEW 16 (April 1975): 130-33.

Wozniak, R.H. "Need for Verification of References in Recorded Interviews." JOURNAL OF THE HISTORY OF THE BEHAVIORAL SCIENCES 14 (July 1978): 264.

Provides examples of inaccurate references in recorded interviews.

iii. ARCHIVES AND MANUSCRIPTS

Balance, William D.G. "Frustrations and Joys of Archival Research." JOUR-NAL OF THE HISTORY OF THE BEHAVIORAL SCIENCES 11 (January 1975): 37-40.

Attempts "to refute Roback's account of Muensterberg's call to the University of Zurich" as a way of illustrating the problems of archival research.

Bringmann, Wolfgang G. "Design Questions in Archival Research." JOURNAL OF THE HISTORY OF THE BEHAVIORAL SCIENCES 11 (January 1975): 23-26.

Defines archives and distinguishes between archives and library collections. Explores archival research procedures and demonstrates their value, using biographical materials on Wilhelm Wundt as an example.

Brożek, Josef. "Contemporary West European Historiography of Psychology." HISTORY OF SCIENCE 13, pt. 1 (March 1975): 29-60.

Surveys historiographic literature (including historical treatises, biographies, and bibliographies) for French-speaking areas, German-speaking areas, Great Britain, Holland, Italy, and Scandinavia. Lengthy bibliography.

_____. "Irons in the Fire: Introduction to a Symposium on Archival Research." JOURNAL OF THE HISTORY OF THE BEHAVIORAL SCIENCES 11 (January 1975): 15-19.

Describes the author's archival research in such areas as correspondence among scientists, biographical research, and the search for unpublished scientific manuscripts.

Brożek, Josef, and McPherson, Marion W[hite]. "Pavloviana in the USA: Archives of the History of American Psychology, University of Akron." CONDITIONED REFLEX 8 (1973): 236-44.

Cadwallader, Thomas C. "Unique Values of Archival Research." JOURNAL OF THE HISTORY OF THE BEHAVIORAL SCIENCES 11 (January 1975): 27-33.

Defines archives and discusses values of archival research: the potential for uncovering unsuspected facets of history, the genesis of ideas and of unsuspected personal influences, and the discovery of the role of politics in shaping lives and careers.

Hamer, Philip M. A GUIDE TO ARCHIVES AND MANUSCRIPTS IN THE UNITED STATES. New Haven, Conn.: Yale University Press, 1961. xxiii, 775 p.

See annotation in section A6, p. 28.

Harrower, Molly. "A Note on the Koffka Papers." JOURNAL OF THE HISTORY OF THE BEHAVIORAL SCIENCES 7 (April 1971): 141-53.

See annotation in section C11A, p. 183.

Popplestone, John A. "Retrieval of Primary Sources." JOURNAL OF THE HISTORY OF THE BEHAVIORAL SCIENCES 11 (January 1975): 20-22.

Discusses the frequently negative attitudes of scientists toward history, along with the problems encountered by archivists in obtaining primary or original sources.

Popplestone, John A., and Kult, Milton. "The Archives of the History of American Psychology January 1965–August 1966." JOURNAL OF THE HISTORY OF THE BEHAVIORAL SCIENCES 3 (January 1967): 60–63.

> Describes the founding of the Archives, lists the names of the initial board of supervisors, and describes some of the initial activities.

Popplestone, John A., and McPherson, Marion White. "Ten Years at the Archives of the History of American Psychology." AMERICAN PSYCHOLOGIST 31 (July 1976): 533–34.

> A comment on the history, holdings, and activities of the Archives of the History of American Psychology.

Sokal, Michael M. "Discussion: F.M. Urban and the Value of Archival Material." JOURNAL OF THE HISTORY OF THE BEHAVIORAL SCIENCES 14 (April 1978): 170–72.

> Draws from archival records, and amplifies an earlier article "The Real F.M. Urban" by Jutta E. Ertle, Robert C. Bushong, and William A. Hillix published in the JOURNAL OF THE HISTORY OF THE BEHAVIORAL SCIENCES 13 (October 1977): 379–83.
>
> Documents the value of primary archival materials.

_____, comp. GUIDE TO MANUSCRIPTS IN THE UNITED STATES IN THE HISTORY OF PSYCHOLOGY AND RELATED AREAS. Wellesley, Mass.: Wellesley College Colloquium in the History of Psychology, 1977. 70 p.

> A collection of entries from the National Union Catalog of Manuscript Collections, 1959–75, including a listing and description of 224 collections in the United States important to researchers in the history of psychology and in areas such as neurology, mental deficiency and hygiene, and philosophical psychology. Subject and repository indexes.

e. Methodological and Philosophical Issues

Boring, Edwin G. "On the Subjectivity of Important Historical Dates." JOURNAL OF THE HISTORY OF THE BEHAVIORAL SCIENCES 1 (January 1965): 5–9.

> Comments on the subjectivity of dating in history and discusses dates and priorities of specific events such as the founding of the first psychological laboratory and of the Society of Experimental Psychologists.

Brooks, G.P. "Some Thoughts on Historical Study in Psychology, or, at Last an Historian Who Reads More Than He Writes." PAPERS IN PSYCHOLOGY 5 (April 1971): 16–18.

Brunswik, Egon. "The Conceptual Framework of Psychology." In INTERNA-TIONAL ENCYCLOPEDIA OF UNIFIED SCIENCE, edited by Otto Neurath, vol. 1, no. 10. Chicago: University of Chicago Press, 1952.

> Presents selected historical approaches to such problems as conscious-ness as a unit of study, subject-object separation, and descriptive vs. reductive theories. Appropriate for advanced students.

Buss, Allan R. "In Defense of a Critical-Presentist Historiography: The Fact-Theory Relationship and Marx's Epistemology." JOURNAL OF THE HISTORY OF THE BEHAVIORAL SCIENCES 13 (July 1977): 252-260.

> Argues that a critical presentism, consistent with Marx's epistemol-ogy and contemporary philosophy of science, is more defensible than older historiographies, which were unduly influenced by early twentieth-century positivist philosophy of science.

Cardno, J.A. "'The Birds are Rather Big for Ducks': Criterion and Materials in History." JOURNAL OF THE HISTORY OF THE BEHAVIORAL SCIENCES 5 (January 1969): 68-72.

> Contrasts the views of three historians--G.S. Brett, J.W. Fay, and A.A. Roback--on the contributions of Thomas Cogswell Upham. Explores the question whether Upham anticipated the James-Lange theory of emotion, and concludes that he did not. Contains sug-gestions for improving the accuracy of historical research.

_____. "Judgment in the History of Psychology: Literature, Science, or Understanding." AUSTRALIAN JOURNAL OF PSYCHOLOGY 13 (1961): 175-83.

_____. "The Network of Reference: Comparison in the History of Psychology." JOURNAL OF GENERAL PSYCHOLOGY 68 (January 1963): 141-56.

Fischer, Constance T. "Historical Relations of Psychology as an Object-Science and a Subject-Science: Toward Psychology as a Human Science." JOURNAL OF THE HISTORY OF THE BEHAVIORAL SCIENCES 13 (October 1977): 369-78.

> Argues that historical sources have overemphasized psychology's de-velopment as an object science and neglected the human-as-subject aspect of the science which has been present throughout the history of the discipline.

Griffith, Coleman R. "Some Neglected Aspects of a History of Psychology." PSYCHOLOGICAL MONOGRAPHS 30 (1921): 17-29.

> Argues that the history of psychology should be written from the perspective of the history of science, not of the "history of the functions of the soul or of the problem of knowledge or of the na-ture of the ego."

References in History of Psychology

Gruba-McCallister, Frank P. "Efficient Causality in Boring's Work and Thought: A Case of One-Sided Determinism." JOURNAL OF THE HISTORY OF THE BEHAVIORAL SCIENCES 14 (July 1978): 207-12.

> Boring's emphasis on efficient-cause determinism influenced his discussions of history, science, and the content areas of psychology, and because of Boring's eminence, his biases have influenced later psychology.

Harvey, O.J. "The History of Psychology as Sociology of Thought." JOURNAL OF THE HISTORY OF THE BEHAVIORAL SCIENCES 1 (January 1965): 196-202.

> Argues that there are possible parallels between the development of a discipline such as psychology and the general cognitive and intellectual development of an individual. Groups, like individuals, may move from simpler to more complex cognitive structures, from "undifferentiation through differentiation to integration," and from concrete thinking to more abstract thinking.

Hitt, William D. "Two Models of Man." AMERICAN PSYCHOLOGIST 24 (July 1969): 651-58.

> Presents a set of dimensions similar to Watson's "prescriptions" (see Watson, below, this section, p. 122) and Wertheimer's "issues" (see Wertheimer, below, this section, p. 122) for categorizing major positions on psychological questions. Contrasts behaviorism and phenomenology on the dimensions.

Jascalevich, Alexander A. "The Idea of Continuity in the History of Psychology." JOURNAL OF PHILOSOPHY 21 (November 1924): 645-63.

> Discusses the problems of intellectual isolation of systems and the difficulties they create for the writing of the history of psychology.

Kantor, J.R. "History of Psychology: What Benefits? A Review of Three Books." PSYCHOLOGICAL RECORD 14 (1964): 433-43.

> Reviews books dealing with historical materials (Postman's [ed.] PSYCHOLOGY IN THE MAKING; Beach, Hebb, Morgan, and Nissen's THE NEUROPSYCHOLOGY OF LASHLEY; and Esper's A HISTORY OF PSYCHOLOGY) and briefly discusses historiographical issues on the uses of history, and on the assumption often made by historians that "the brain and its operations are the central features of psychological events."

_____. "Perspectives in Psychology: XV. History of Science as Scientific Method." PSYCHOLOGICAL RECORD 10 (July 1960): 187-89.

> Argues that "the employment of history as a genuine method of science instead of a scientific support for institutional ways of

thinking would provide all theoretical scientists with more naturalistic and more rational ideas concerning scientific data and con-
structions about them."

Kirsch, Irving. "Demonology and the Rise of Science: An Example of the
Misperception of Historical Data." JOURNAL OF THE HISTORY OF THE BE-
HAVIORAL SCIENCES 14 (April 1978): 149–57.

Argues that demonology was relatively weak during the Middle
Ages but gained strength in the Renaissance and reached its apogee
during the seventeenth century. It therefore corresponded in time
with much of the early scientific revolution.

McGuire, William J. "Historical Comparisons: Testing Psychological Hypotheses
with Cross-Era Data." INTERNATIONAL JOURNAL OF PSYCHOLOGY 11,
no. 3 (1976): 161–83.

MacKenzie, Brian B., and MacKenzie, S. Lynne. "The Case for a Revised
Systematic Approach to the History of Psychology." JOURNAL OF THE HIS-
TORY OF THE BEHAVIORAL SCIENCES 10 (July 1974): 324–47.

Presents an overview of behaviorism and argues that the historiography of psychology has been conditioned by the presence of behaviorism, and that the treatment of the history of psychology
should not contain a behavioristic bias.

Marx, Otto M. "History of Psychology: A Review of the Last Decade."
JOURNAL OF THE HISTORY OF THE BEHAVIORAL SCIENCES 13 (January
1977): 41–47.

Argues that historians of psychology should avoid isolation from
mainstream psychology and should make their prejudices explicit.
Refers, for support, to numerous recent historiographical articles in
the JOURNAL OF THE HISTORY OF THE BEHAVIORAL SCIENCES.

Murphy, Gardner. "Psychology and the Post-War World." PSYCHOLOGICAL
REVIEW 49 (July 1942): 298–318.

Provides examples from Germany, France, Great Britain, and the
United States of how social pressures have conditioned the historical development of psychology. Discusses trends in future challenges to, and opportunities for, psychology.

Pastore, Nicholas. "On Plagiarism: Buffon, Condillac, Porterfield, Schopenhauer." JOURNAL OF THE HISTORY OF THE BEHAVIORAL SCIENCES 9
(October 1973): 378–92.

Discusses types of plagiarism and offers several historical examples
of paraphrasing and plagiarism.

Riegel, Klaus F. "History as a Nomothetic Science: Some Generalizations From Theories and Research in Developmental Psychology." JOURNAL OF SOCIAL ISSUES 25 (Fall 1969): 99-127.

_____. PSYCHOLOGY OF DEVELOPMENT AND HISTORY. New York: Plenum Publishing Corp., 1976. ix, 263 p.

A collection of essays on topics such as nomothetic interpretations of history, structure and transformation in modern intellectual history, structural analysis of the history of experimental psychology, and the recall of events from the individual and collective past. Index.

Ross, Dorothy. "The 'Zeitgeist' and American Psychology." JOURNAL OF THE HISTORY OF THE BEHAVIORAL SCIENCES 5 (July 1969): 256-62.

Explores the origins of the term "Zeitgeist" and outlines its ambiguities as an explanatory concept with illustrations from developments in American psychology.

Sarup, Gian. "Historical Antecedents of Psychology: The Recurrent Issue of Old Wine in New Bottles." AMERICAN PSYCHOLOGIST 33 (May 1978): 478-85.

Discusses some of the problems associated with the search for the historical roots of major concepts. Emphasizes the importance of the distinction between anticipations--ideas which are similar to but discontinuous with a subsequent concept, and foundations--ideas which are similar to and clearly continuous with subsequent concepts.

Stocking, George W., Jr. "On the Limits of 'Presentism' and 'Historicism' in the Historiography of the Behavioral Sciences (An Editorial)." JOURNAL OF THE HISTORY OF THE BEHAVIORAL SCIENCES 1 (January 1965): 211-17.

Discusses implications of historicism (understanding history for its own sake) and presentism (understanding history for the sake of the present).

Thorne, Frederick C. "Historical Research: An Observation." JOURNAL OF THE HISTORY OF THE BEHAVIORAL SCIENCES 14 (January 1978): 55-56.

Comments that a reading of T.S. Krawiec's THE PSYCHOLOGISTS (see section A1, p.3) demonstrates the value of "living history" and orientations of eminent psychologists, and provides a clue as to what psychology should study: "the whole person living in a real world."

Wallin, J.E. Wallace. "Historical Inaccuracies." JOURNAL OF CLINICAL PSYCHOLOGY 11 (April 1955): 197-200.

Challenges various earlier articles on such topics as the date of the founding of the American Association of Clinical Psychologists, the introduction of the Binet-Simon scale in the United States, and the date of first advocacy for internship and practicum training.

Watson, Robert I. "Prescriptions as Operative in the History of Psychology." JOURNAL OF THE HISTORY OF THE BEHAVIORAL SCIENCES 7 (October 1971): 311-22.

Examines approaches to historical inquiry with an eye to "providing a framework in which to carry on research and to write in the field." Specifies a series of bipolar "prescriptions" which can be used to characterize the positions of prominent figures in the history of psychology.

_____. "A Prescriptive Analysis of Descartes' Psychological Views." JOURNAL OF THE HISTORY OF THE BEHAVIORAL SCIENCES 7 (July 1971): 223-48.

Characterizes the orientations and assumptions of Descartes on such topics as methodology, the mind-body problem, the structure of the mind, and the will, using the author's bipolar descriptive dimensions for basic issues in psychology ("prescriptions"; see preceding and following entries).

_____. "Psychology: A Prescriptive Science." AMERICAN PSYCHOLOGIST 22 (June 1967): 435-43.

Argues that psychology is still in a "preparadigmatic stage," and outlines a set of bipolar "prescriptions" (such as peripheralism vs. centralism, determinism vs. indeterminism, and rationalism vs. irrationalism) for characterizing various theories, developments, and positions in psychology's history.

Wertheimer, Michael. FUNDAMENTAL ISSUES IN PSYCHOLOGY. New York: Holt, Rinehart and Winston, 1972. ix, 278 p.

A historical, philosophical, and conceptual introduction to psychology oriented around such classic issues as freedom vs. determinism, mind vs. body, and nature vs. nurture. These issues can be considered as an alternative set of dimensions to Watson's "prescriptions" (see preceding entries). Index.

Wettersten, John R. "The Historiography of Scientific Psychology: A Critical Study." JOURNAL OF THE HISTORY OF THE BEHAVIORAL SCIENCES 11 (April 1975): 157-71.

Argues that historians have not solved the problem of how to present the evolution of psychology as "a steady development culminating in current theory." Instead of focusing on mistakes, problems, and errors, historians of psychology engage in the presentation of facts and techniques regardless of their significance, discussion of careers, and uncritical praise of theory.

Weyant, Robert G. "Helvétius and Jefferson: Studies of Human Nature and Government in the Eighteenth Century." JOURNAL OF THE HISTORY OF THE BEHAVIORAL SCIENCES 9 (January 1973): 29-41.

> "Relationships between psychological theory and governmental policy in the eighteenth and early nineteenth centuries." Examines contrasting views of human nature and discusses implications for the study of the history of psychology.

Wolf, Friedrich O. "Marxian Approaches to the History of Psychology." JOURNAL OF THE HISTORY OF THE BEHAVIORAL SCIENCES 14 (April 1978): 122-23.

> A brief note, presented as the concluding remarks at a workshop held in conjunction with the 1975 meeting of CHEIRON, stresses the importance of the relationship between societal development and progress in social science.

f. Psychohistory

de Mause, Lloyd. "The Independence of Psychohistory: A Symposium." HISTORY OF CHILDHOOD QUARTERLY: THE JOURNAL OF PSYCHOHISTORY 3 (Fall 1975): 163-200.

> An exposition by de Mause on the background, status, and goals of psychohistory followed by evaluative comments by historians and social scientists Barbara Tuchman, Richard Lyman, Jr., Patrick Dunn, Fred Greenstein, Everett Hagen, and others with a final response by de Mause.

_____, ed. THE NEW PSYCHOHISTORY. New York: Psychohistory Press, 1975. 313 p.

> A foreword by the editor outlines the development of psychohistory, followed by ten papers originally published in HISTORY OF CHILDHOOD QUARTERLY: THE JOURNAL OF PSYCHOHISTORY on topics in the history of childhood, psychobiography, and group psychodynamics of the Victorian family, infanticide, Kissinger's impact on foreign policy, psychohistory, and psychotherapy.

de Mause, Lloyd; Sinofsky, Faye; Fitzpatrick, John J.; and Potts, Louis W. A BIBLIOGRAPHY OF PSYCHOHISTORY. New York: Garland STPM Press, 1975. 81 p.

Dunn, Patrick P. "Who Stole the Hyphen From Psycho-History?" BOOK FORUM 1 (1974): 248-53.

> A brief discussion on the meanings and values of the term "psychohistory." Short list of suggested readings.

Eissler, K.R. "Freud and the Psychoanalysis of History." JOURNAL OF THE AMERICAN PSYCHOANALYTIC ASSOCIATION 11, no. 4 (1963): 675-703.

Feinstein, Howard. "An Application of the Concept of Identification for the Historian." JOURNAL OF THE HISTORY OF THE BEHAVIORAL SCIENCES 6 (April 1970): 147-50.

    Of interest to those engaged in psychohistorical research. Shows
    how a psychological process, in this case identification, was used
    in establishing an appropriate historical date.

JOURNAL OF PSYCHOHISTORY. New York: Association for Psychohistory Inc., 1974-- . Quarterly.

    Affiliated with the Institute for Psychohistory, Psychohistory Press,
    and JOURNAL OF PSYCHOLOGICAL ANTHROPOLOGY. Pub-
    lishes articles on psychohistory including work on childhood and
    the family, historical development of belief systems and social
    movements, and applications of psychoanalysis to individuals and
    groups. Book reviews.

Kren, George M., and Rappoport, Leon H., eds. VARIETIES OF PSYCHO-HISTORY. New York: Springer Publishing Co., 1976. 370 p.

    Explores the nature of psychohistory, psychobiography, the history
    of conceptions of childhood, and group processes and historical
    trends.

Lifton, Robert Jay. "On Psychohistory." In PSYCHOANALYSIS AND CON-TEMPORARY SCIENCE: AN ANNUAL OF INTEGRATIVE AND INTERDISCIPLIN-ARY STUDIES, edited by Robert R. Holt and Emanuel Peterfreund, vol. 1., pp. 355-72. New York: Macmillan, 1972.

Malkin, Edward E. "Reich and Rousseau: An Essay in Psycho-history." AMERI-CAN JOURNAL OF PSYCHOANALYSIS 34 (1974): 63-72.

Manuel, Frank E. "The Use and Abuse of Psychology in History." DAEDALUS 100 (Winter 1971): 187-213.

    A searching discussion of the problems in writing psychohistory.

Mazlish, Bruce, ed. PSYCHOANALYSIS AND HISTORY. Rev. ed. New York: Universal Library, 1971. vi, 217 p.

Mollinger, Robert N. "Introduction: On Psychohistory." PSYCHOANALYTIC REVIEW 62 (Summer, 1975): 315-19.

PSYCHOHISTORY REVIEW. Springfield, Ill.: Sangamon State University, 1972-- . Quarterly.

Weinstein, Fred, and Platt, Gerald M. THE WISH TO BE FREE: SOCIETY, PSYCHE, AND VALUE CHANGE. Berkeley and Los Angeles: University of California Press, 1969. viii, 319 p.

Examines social change from perspectives in history, psychoanalysis, and sociology. Notes. Index.

Section C

SYSTEMS AND SCHOOLS OF PSYCHOLOGY

Much of the history of psychology, particularly during the first half of the twentieth century, concerns the great schools or systems. A school or system is a way of looking at the discipline with a characteristic delineation of the appropriate subject matter of psychology, methods of investigation, research topics, and implicit or explicit philosophic assumptions. While historians of psychology are not fully agreed on how many schools there were, most concur that the following were among the major systems: structuralism, functionalism, behaviorism, Gestalt psychology, and psychoanalysis. This section includes these five major systems along with several others which made important contributions to the development of psychology. Excellent overviews of the schools are provided by relevant chapters in many of the works listed under section B1, p. 31, longer works broadly covering the history of psychology, especially the books by Heidbreder, and by Woodworth and Sheehan. Other categories in this section list articles that discuss fundamental issues, compare the various schools of psychology, or discuss systems or schools of psychology that do not readily fall into the other categories.

1. PRE-WUNDTIAN PSYCHOLOGIES

There were psychologies prior to that of Wilhelm Wundt, and many of these are found in section B5a, p. 53, and E1b, p. 382. Two specific systems that might qualify as schools, faculty psychology and phrenology, are listed in this section.

a. Faculty Psychologies

Some of the earliest psychologies emphasized "faculties" consisting of independent regions or powers, each of which was responsible for a given function of the mind. Examples of faculty psychology are found in the works of the Scottish philosopher Thomas Reid (see section E1b, p. 393) and in the ideas of the early American psychiatrist Benjamin Rush (see section E2, p. 406, and this section). This section presents a few journal-length articles on faculty psychology. Other relevant references, particularly on localization of function, are found in section D4, p. 274. References to additional major works are found in articles by Albrecht and Pratt (see below, this section, p. 128).

Systems and Schools of Psychology

Albrecht, Frank M. "A Reappraisal of Faculty Psychology." JOURNAL OF THE HISTORY OF THE BEHAVIORAL SCIENCES 6 (January 1970): 36-40.

> Reviews some of the intellectual background of faculty psychology and argues that "faculty psychology was the first fully empirical psychology."

Blight, James G. "Solomon Stoddard's 'Safety of Appearing' and the Dissolution of the Puritan Faculty Psychology." JOURNAL OF THE HISTORY OF THE BEHAVIORAL SCIENCES 10 (April 1974): 238-50.

> An overview of Puritan thought on rational and affective faculties, especially as they pertain to religious conversion, followed by a summary of Stoddard's background, his ministry, and the thoughts advanced in his religious tract, SAFETY OF APPEARING (1729), which contributed to the demise of Puritan faculty psychology.

Fulcher, J. Rodney. "Puritans and the Passions: The Faculty Psychology in American Puritanism." JOURNAL OF THE HISTORY OF THE BEHAVIORAL SCIENCES 9 (April 1973): 123-39.

> Explores tensions between Puritan views of emotions and appetite (motivation) and other Puritan doctrines such as moral responsibility and the primacy of reason.

Noel, Patricia S., and Carlson, Eric T. "The Faculty Psychology of Benjamin Rush." JOURNAL OF THE HISTORY OF THE BEHAVIORAL SCIENCES 9 (October 1973): 369-77.

> Notes some of the individuals and circumstances that influenced Rush. Outlines his faculty psychology, with emphasis on the psychology of sleep and dreaming.

Pratt, Carroll C. "Faculty Psychology." PSYCHOLOGICAL REVIEW 36 (March 1929): 142-71.

> Presents some of the history of faculty psychology, outlines typical criticisms leveled against faculty psychology, and argues that faculties as measurable mental capacities are important to psychology.

b. Phrenology

The extreme expression of faculty psychology was found in phrenology, founded by Franz Joseph Gall, who taught that there were specifiable loci in the brain for specific powers of the mind. A more extensive bibliography on phrenology is available in "Contributions to the History of Psychology: XIII. Bibliographia Phrenologica," by Anthony Walsh (see below, this section, p. 129).

Bakan, David. "The Influence of Phrenology on American Psychology." JOUR-

NAL OF THE HISTORY OF THE BEHAVIORAL SCIENCES 2 (July 1966): 200-220.

> Argues that while phrenology was discredited, it nevertheless had a profound effect on the intellectual trends that molded twentieth-century psychology such as positivism, concern with individual differences, and liberalism.

_____. "Is Phrenology Foolish?" PSYCHOLOGY TODAY 1 (May 1968): 44-51.

> A brief historical overview followed by an examination of the scientific and cultural dimensions of phrenology, which stimulated valuable scientific hypotheses and interests.

Bentley, M. "The Psychological Antecedents of Phrenology." PSYCHOLOGICAL MONOGRAPHS 21 (1916): 102-15.

Cooter, R.J. "Phrenology: The Provocation of Progress." HISTORY OF SCIENCE 14 (December 1976): 211-34.

Davies, John D. PHRENOLOGY, FAD AND SCIENCE: A 19TH CENTURY AMERICAN CRUSADE. New Haven, Conn.: Yale University Press, 1955. xv, 203 p.

Hollander, B. "The Centenary of Franz Joseph Gall." MEDICAL PRESS 126, no. 5 (1928): 7-10.

Joynt, Robert J. "Phrenology in New York State." NEW YORK STATE JOURNAL OF MEDICINE 73 (October 1973): 2382-84.

Noel, Patricia S., and Carlson, Eric T. "Origins of the Word 'Phrenology.'" AMERICAN JOURNAL OF PSYCHIATRY 127 (November 1970): 694-97.

Spurzheim, Johann Caspar. OBSERVATIONS ON THE DERANGED MANIFESTATIONS OF THE MIND OR INSANITY, 1833. Reprint. Gainesville, Fla.: Scholars' Facsimiles & Reprints, 1970. xiv, viii, 260 p.

> The classic phrenological interpretation of mental illness. Covers such topics as disorders of voluntary motion; diseases of the senses; diseases of the brain; internal functions of the mind; and the causes, prognosis, and treatment of insanity. Includes plates showing shapes of heads associated with various forms of mental deficiency and a plan for a mental hospital. Bibliography.

Walsh, Anthony A. "Contributions to the History of Psychology: XIII. Bibliographia Phrenologica." PSYCHOLOGICAL REPORTS 28 (April 1971): 641-42.

Calls attention to bibliographic sources for those interested in research in the history of phrenology.

_____. "Is Phrenology Foolish? A Rejoinder." JOURNAL OF THE HISTORY OF THE BEHAVIORAL SCIENCES 6 (October 1970): 358-61.

Emphasizes the significance of phrenology and offers both appreciative and critical comment on an earlier article entitled "Is Phrenology Foolish?" (See Bakan, above, this section, p. 129).

_____. "Phrenology and the Boston Medical Community in the 1830's." BULLETIN OF THE HISTORY OF MEDICINE 50 (Summer 1976): 261-73.

Wester, William C. "The Phreno-Magnetic Society of Cincinnati, 1842." AMERICAN JOURNAL OF CLINICAL HYPNOSIS 18 (April 1976): 277-81.

2. WILHELM WUNDT—SELECTED MAJOR WORKS AND SECONDARY SOURCES

Wundt is generally considered the founder of the first laboratory for experimental psychology in the world; his laboratory at Leipzig was flourishing by the late 1870s. Recent work (e.g., Blumenthal's article in this section) suggests that Wundt was far more than the figurehead for the new experimental psychology; he was deeply interested in cultural psychology (Voelkerpsychologie) and can also be seen as an ancestor of recent developments in social psychology, cognitive psychology, and psycholinguistics.

Anderson, Richard J. "The Untranslated Content of Wundt's GRUNDZUEGE DER PHYSIOLOGISCHEN PSYCHOLOGIE." JOURNAL OF THE HISTORY OF THE BEHAVIORAL SCIENCES 21 (October 1975): 381-86.

Notes that Titchener translated those parts of Wundt's GRUNDZUEGE which he felt best characterized Wundt's primary interests and which, not incidentally, supported Titchener's structuralism, leading to an incomplete and perhaps misleading view of Wundt's psychology.

Baldwin, Bird T., introducer. "In Memory of Wilhelm Wundt By His American Students." PSYCHOLOGICAL REVIEW 28 (May 1921): 153-58.

Seventeen of Wundt's American students, including such distinguished individuals as G. Stanley Hall, J. McKeen Cattell, E.B. Titchener, James R. Angell, and Charles H. Judd, pay tribute to their former teacher in this collection of brief statements.

Benerji, M. "Expansion of Wundt's Definition, Method and Scope of Experimental Psychology." INDIAN JOURNAL OF PSYCHOLOGY 7 (1932): 30-52.

Bhattacharyya, H.D. "Wundt and Modern Tendencies in Psychology." INDIAN JOURNAL OF PSYCHOLOGY 7 (1932): 71-75.

_____. "Wundt's Doctrine of Creative Synthesis." INDIAN JOURNAL OF PSYCHOLOGY 7 (1932): 82-99.

Blumenthal, Arthur L. "A Reappraisal of Wilhelm Wundt." AMERICAN PSY-CHOLOGIST 30 (November 1975): 1081-88.

> Discusses Wundt's method, theoretical system, and the relationship of his psychology to contemporary psychology, arguing that Wundt's theoretical system has been misunderstood. For example, Wundt did not use the label "structuralist"; his psychology was voluntaristic, with an emphasis on selective volitional, attentional processes. Because of the cognitive emphasis in modern psychology, Wundt can be better understood today than he could a few years ago.

Bringmann, Wolfgang G. "Wundt in Heidelberg: 1845-1874." CANADIAN PSYCHOLOGICAL REVIEW 16 (April 1975): 124-29.

Bringmann, Wolfgang G.; Balance, William D.G.; and Evans, Rand B. "Wilhelm Wundt 1832-1920: A Brief Biographical Sketch." JOURNAL OF THE HISTORY OF THE BEHAVIORAL SCIENCES 11 (July 1975): 287-97.

> Reviews the life of "the senior psychologist in the history of psychology," exploring early years, education, and scientific and professional activities. Describes Wundt's relationships with students and friends. Fifty-seven references.

Feldman, S. "Wundt's Psychology." AMERICAN JOURNAL OF PSYCHOLOGY 44 (November 1932): 615-29.

> Wundt's theoretical stance on such topics as sensation, perception, consciousness, emotion, and esthetic feelings is summarized. Materials are based on Wundt's GRUNDZUEGE DER PHYSIOLOGISCHEN PSYCHOLOGIE (1874).

Fernberger, Samuel W. "Wundt's Doctorate Students." PSYCHOLOGICAL BULLETIN 30 (January 1933): 80-83.

> Presents a statistical breakdown of Wundt's doctorate students on such topics as achievement of prominence, where the students located, and the number who pursued psychology as a career.

Haeberlin, Herman K. "The Theoretical Foundations of Wundt's Folk-Psychology." PSYCHOLOGICAL REVIEW 23 (July 1916): 279-302.

> A critical treatment of Wundt's "folk-psychology" (or cultural psychology) preceded by an overview of selected themes in his philosophical system.

Systems and Schools of Psychology

Raphelson, Alfred C. "Lincoln Steffens at the Leipzig Psychological Institute, 1890-1891." JOURNAL OF THE HISTORY OF THE BEHAVIORAL SCIENCES 3 (January 1967): 38-42.

> Lincoln Steffens, later an influential American journalist, spent two semesters working in Wundt's laboratory. This article relates Steffens's largely negative opinions both of Wundt and of the atmosphere in the laboratory.

Samanta, M.N. "Wundt on Apperception." INDIAN JOURNAL OF PSYCHOLOGY 7 (1932): 67-70.

Stratton, George M. "The New Psychology Laboratory at Leipzig." SCIENCE 4 (December 1896): 867-68.

Tinker, M.A. "Wundt's Doctorate Students and their Theses (1875-1920)." AMERICAN JOURNAL OF PSYCHOLOGY 44 (October 1932): 630-37.

> Lists the 186 theses written under Wundt's direction.

Titchener, Edward Bradford. "Brentano and Wundt: Empirical and Experimental Psychology." AMERICAN JOURNAL OF PSYCHOLOGY 32 (January 1921): 108-20.

_____. "Wilhelm Wundt." AMERICAN JOURNAL OF PSYCHOLOGY 32, no. 2 (April 1921): 161-178.

Wundt, Wilhelm. ELEMENTS OF FOLK PSYCHOLOGY. Translated by Edward Leroy Schaub. New York: Macmillan, 1916. xxiii, 532 p.

> This shorter version of Wundt's massive VOELKERPSYCHOLOGIE attempts to provide "a psychological history of development" of the human species from its primitive beginnings to the emergence of modern humanity. Index.

_____. AN INTRODUCTION TO PSYCHOLOGY. 2d ed. Translated by Rudolph Pintner. London: George Allen & Co., 1912. Reprint. New York: Arno Press, 1973. xi, 198 p.

> A nontechnical introduction by the founder of experimental psychology. Presents major thoughts and discoveries of psychology in five chapters covering consciousness and attention, elements of consciousness, association, apperception, and laws of psychical life. Omits philosophical and methodological discussion and minimizes references to experiments.

_____. LECTURES ON HUMAN AND ANIMAL PSYCHOLOGY. 2d ed. Translated by J.E. Creighton and E[dward].B[radford]. Titchener. New York: Macmillan, 1907. xi, 459 p.

Thirty lectures provide a comprehensive introduction to the "new" psychology of the late nineteenth century. Topics include sensation, measurement of sensations, reflex movements, attention, feelings, association, dreams, animal psychology, instincts, and philosophical problems. The translators claim this is the first of Wundt's writings made available to the English-speaking public. Index.

_____. OUTLINES OF PSYCHOLOGY. Translated by Charles Hubbard Judd. New York: Gustav E. Stechert, 1897. Reprint. Scholarly Press, [1969?]. xviii, 342 p.

A systematic introduction to psychology covering the definition of the discipline, general theories, methods, "psychical elements" including "pure sensations" and "simple feelings," "psychical compounds," and psychical development including development in animals and children. A Glossary includes selected German-English equivalents. Index.

_____. PRINCIPLES OF PHYSIOLOGICAL PSYCHOLOGY. Vol. 1. Translated by E[dward].B[radford]. Titchener. London: Swan Sonnenschein; from 5th German ed. (1902). New York: Macmillan, 1910. Reprint. New York: Krause Reprint Co., 1969. xvi, 347 p.

A pivotal book in the history of psychology, attempting "to mark out a new domain of science." Consists of an introductory survey of physiological psychology followed by a consideration of the structural and functional characteristics of the nervous system. Index.

3. WUNDT'S CONTEMPORARIES

Numerous individuals were conducting psychological investigations contemporaneously with Wilhelm Wundt, but two individuals are particularly noteworthy because they represent systems of thought which were competitive with Wundt's system: Franz Brentano, founder of act psychology; and Oswald Kuelpe, known primarily for the work on higher thought processes conducted at Wuerzburg. This section includes articles and major works characterizing their positions.

a. Franz Brentano

Barclay, James R. "Franz Brentano and Sigmund Freud." JOURNAL OF EXISTENTIALISM 5 (1964): 1-36.

_____. "Themes of Brentano's Psychological Thought and Philosophical Overtones." NEW SCHOLASTICISM 33 (July 1959): 300-318.

Brentano, Franz. PSYCHOLOGY FROM AN EMPIRICAL STANDPOINT. Edited by Oskar Kraus and Linda L. McAlister. Translated by Antos C. Rancurello, D.B. Terrell, and Linda L. McAlister. London: Routledge and Kegan Paul; New York: Humanities Press, 1973. xx, 415 p.

Fancher, Raymond E. "Brentano's PSYCHOLOGY FROM AN EMPIRICAL STAND-POINT and Freud's Early Metapsychology." JOURNAL OF THE HISTORY OF THE BEHAVIORAL SCIENCES 13 (July 1977): 207-27.

See annotation in section C15, p. 240.

Rancurello, Antos C. A STUDY OF FRANZ BRENTANO: HIS PSYCHOLOGI-CAL STANDPOINT AND HIS SIGNIFICANCE IN THE HISTORY OF PSYCHOL-OGY. New York: Academic Press, 1968. xiv, 178 p.

A biography of Brentano followed by an examination of his position on psychological issues and his historical significance. Partially annotated bibliography of Brentano's works and writings about his work. Index.

Sussman, Edward J. "Franz Brentano--Much Alive, Though Dead." AMERI-CAN PSYCHOLOGIST 17 (July 1962): 504-6.

Points to the influence of Brentano's thinking on specific trends and individuals, such as phenomenology, Gestalt psychology, and British act psychology. Notes that Brentano's ideas remain influ-ential in modern psychology.

Titchener, E[dward].B[radford]. "Brentano and Wundt: Empirical and Experi-mental Psychology." AMERICAN JOURNAL OF PSYCHOLOGY 32 (January 1921): 108-20.

_____. "Empirical and Experimental Psychology." JOURNAL OF GENERAL PSYCHOLOGY 1 (January 1928): 176-77.

_____. "Functional Psychology and the Psychology of Act, II." AMERICAN JOURNAL OF PSYCHOLOGY 33 (January 1922): 43-83.

b. Oswald Kuelpe

Dallenbach, K.M. "Oswald Kuelpe: 1862-1915." AMERICAN JOURNAL OF PSYCHOLOGY 64 (January 1951): 3.

Erikson, R.W. "Some Historical Connections Between Existentialism, Daseins-analysis, Phenomenology, and the Wuerzburg School." JOURNAL OF GENERAL PSYCHOLOGY 76 (January 1967): 3-24.

Kuelpe, Oswald. INTRODUCTION TO PHILOSOPHY: A HANDBOOK FOR

STUDENTS OF PSYCHOLOGY, LOGIC, ETHICS, AESTHETICS AND GENERAL
PHILOSOPHY. 4th ed. Translated by W[alter].B. Pillsbury and E[dward].
B[radford]. Titchener. New York: Macmillan, 1915. x, 256 p.

_____. OUTLINES OF PSYCHOLOGY: BASED UPON THE RESULTS OF
EXPERIMENTAL INVESTIGATION. 3d ed. Translated by E[dward.B[radford].
Titchener. New York: Macmillan, 1909. Reissued. New York: Arno Press,
1973. xi, 462 p. Index.

_____. "The Problem of Attention." MONIST 13 (October 1902): 36-68.

Lindenfeld, David. "Oswald Kuelpe and the Wuerzburg School." JOURNAL
OF THE HISTORY OF THE BEHAVIORAL SCIENCES 14 (April 1978): 132-41.

   A brief overview of Kuelpe's importance and eminence in his time
   followed by an analysis of his psychology as it related to the
   shift in his philosophical views from Machian phenomenalism to
   realism.

Ogden, R.M. "Oswald Kuelpe and the Wuerzburg School." AMERICAN
JOURNAL OF PSYCHOLOGY 64 (January 1951): 4-19.

   Bibliographical materials on Kuelpe followed by descriptions of
   some of the thought and work which characterized the Wuerzburg
   school.

4. STRUCTURALISM

Structuralism was the first major modern school of psychology. It was initially,
and perhaps erroneously, identified with Wilhelm Wundt at the University of
Leipzig in Germany; the major founder and proponent of structuralism was
Edward Bradford Titchener at Cornell University in the United States. This
section includes selected basic works and secondary sources as well as sources
on consciousness and introspection (concepts which were central to structuralist
thought).

Adams, Grace. "Titchener at Cornell." AMERICAN MERCURY 2 (1951): 440-
46.

   A brief and nontechnical account of Titchener's contributions to
   psychology and his work at Cornell.

Angell, Frank. "Titchener at Leipzig." JOURNAL OF GENERAL PSYCHOL-
OGY 1 (April 1928): 195-98.

   Recounts experiences with Titchener during their time together in
   Wundt's laboratory and discusses some of Titchener's work and personality traits.

Boring, Edwin G. "A History of Introspection." PSYCHOLOGICAL BULLETIN 50 (May 1953): 169-89.

> Discusses such topics as the classical introspection of structuralism, phenomenological description in Gestalt psychology, and the verbal report in behaviorism. Concludes that consciousness is still employed in psychology, although often under other names. Ninety-nine references.

_____. THE PHYSICAL DIMENSIONS OF CONSCIOUSNESS. New York: Century, 1933. xii, 251 p.

> Explores a perennial problem in the philosophy of science: reduction. Examines specifically the relationship between physiological and psychological levels of explanation. Index.

_____. "Titchener and the Existential." AMERICAN JOURNAL OF PSYCHOLOGY 50 (November 1937): 470-83.

_____. "Titchener, Meaning and Behaviorism." In SCHOOLS OF PSYCHOLOGY: A SYMPOSIUM, edited by D.L. Krantz, pp. 21-34. New York: Appleton-Century-Crofts, 1969.

> Describes Titchener's shift toward behaviorist thought with respect to the problem of meaning.

_____. "Titchener on Meaning." PSYCHOLOGICAL REVIEW 45 (January 1938): 92-95.

Brown, L.B., and Fuchs, A.H. "The Letters Between Sir Thomas Hunter and E.B. Titchener." VICTORIA UNIVERSITY OF WELLINGTON PUBLICATIONS IN PSYCHOLOGY 23 (1969): 4-60.

Burt, Cyril. "The Concept of Consciousness." BRITISH JOURNAL OF PSYCHOLOGY 53 (August 1962): 229-42.

De Silva, H.R. "The Common Sense of Introspection." PSYCHOLOGICAL REVIEW 37 (January 1930): 71-87.

Dunlap, Knight. "The Case Against Introspection." PSYCHOLOGICAL REVIEW 19 (September 1912): 404-13.

> Reviews several definitions of introspection, notes inconsistencies between how the term is defined and how it is used in experiments, and concludes that it would be best to discard the term altogether.

Eccles, Sir John Carew, ed. BRAIN AND CONSCIOUS EXPERIENCE: STUDY WEEK, SEPTEMBER 28 TO OCTOBER 4, 1964, OF THE PONTIFICIA ACADEMIA

SCIENTIARUM. New York: Springer-Verlag, 1966. xxi, 591 p.

A collection of twenty-one papers by such leading authorities as J.C. Eccles, W. Penfield, R.W. Sperry, R.A. Granit, and H.L. Teuber. Explores a considerable range of topics such as brain injury, brain stimulation, brain bisection, and neurophysiological and neurochemical influences as they relate to consciousness. Index.

Erickson, Ralph W. "An Examination of Prof. Edwin G. Boring's System of Psychology." JOURNAL OF GENERAL PSYCHOLOGY 24 (January 1941): 63-79.

Describes Boring's transition from structuralism to a more eclectic system which reflects the influence of behaviorism.

Evans, Rand B. "E.B. Titchener and His Lost System." JOURNAL OF THE HISTORY OF THE BEHAVIORAL SCIENCES 8 (April 1972): 168-80.

Traces the evolution of Titchener's thought from 1910 to 1927, discusses the decline in Titchener's productivity during his last ten years, and speculates about what a final Titchenerian system might have been like.

_____. "The Origins of Titchener's Doctrine of Meaning." JOURNAL OF THE HISTORY OF THE BEHAVIORAL SCIENCES 21 (October 1975): 334-41.

Outlines Titchener's theory of meaning and argues that the theory was developed gradually through the 1890s, not developed simply as a means of rejecting the Wuerzburg school and its notion of imageless thought.

Frost, Elliot Park. "Cannot Psychology Dispense With Consciousness?" PSYCHOLOGICAL REVIEW 21 (May 1914): 204-11.

Discusses some of the problems associated with the study of consciousness and argues that psychic terminology is confusing.

Heidbreder, Edna. "Mary Whiton Calkins: A Discussion." JOURNAL OF THE HISTORY OF THE BEHAVIORAL SCIENCES 8 (January 1972): 56-58.

Explores dimensions of Calkins's self psychology, its paradigmatic qualities, and its relation to philosophy. A paper originally read in abbreviated form to the Cheiron Society in 1970.

Henle, Mary. "Did Titchener Commit the Stimulus Error? The Problem of Meaning in Structural Psychology." JOURNAL OF THE HISTORY OF THE BEHAVIORAL SCIENCES 7 (July 1971): 279-82.

Argues that Titchener himself could not "keep from falling into the territory of logical analysis." Suggests that inconsistencies in his system may have accounted for his later decline in productivity.

_____ . "E.B. Titchener and the Case of the Missing Element." JOURNAL OF THE HISTORY OF THE BEHAVIORAL SCIENCES 10 (April 1974): 227-37.

> Traces the evolution of Titchener's thought regarding the affective element and speculates on the time of and reasons for the disappearance of that element from his system.

Hindeland, Michael J. "Edward Bradford Titchener: A Pioneer in Perception." JOURNAL OF THE HISTORY OF THE BEHAVIORAL SCIENCES 7 (January 1971): 23-28.

> Outlines Titchener's general approach to perception and emphasizes some of his work with specific senses.

Holt, Edwin B. THE CONCEPT OF CONSCIOUSNESS. 1914. Reprint. New York: Arno Press, 1973. xvi, 343 p.

> A classic work which identifies formal and empirical properties of consciousness and attempts to provide a definition of it. Discusses such topics as memory, imagination, thought, and volition in the light of the author's definition. Brief bibliography. Index.

James, William. See articles on consciousness in section C5.

Jaynes, Julian. THE ORIGIN OF CONSCIOUSNESS IN THE BREAKDOWN OF THE BICAMERAL MIND. Boston: Houghton Mifflin, 1977. v, 467 p.

King, C.D. THE PSYCHOLOGY OF CONSCIOUSNESS. New York: Harcourt Brace, 1932. xv, 256 p.

Langfeld, H.S. "Titchener's System of Psychology." MONIST 21 (October 1911): 624-30.

Natsoulas, Thomas. "Concerning Introspective Knowledge." PSYCHOLOGICAL BULLETIN 73 (February 1970): 89-111.

> Discusses such topics as afterimages, pain, and sense impressions, as well as some major theories of introspective awareness.

Ornstein, Robert E., ed. THE NATURE OF HUMAN CONSCIOUSNESS: A BOOK OF READINGS. New York: Viking Press, 1974. xiii, 514 p.

> Forty-one readings on a broad spectrum of topics on the nature of consciousness including physiological studies, biofeedback studies, drug-induced altered states of consciousness, Eastern meditation studies, and theoretical papers. Editor notes that the predominant

paradigm in psychology during the past sixty years has ruled out such studies, but they now form part of a new trend in psychology. Index.

Radford, John. "Reflections on Introspection." AMERICAN PSYCHOLOGIST 29 (April 1974): 245-50.

Reviews selected historical views regarding introspection and suggests that both Titchener and John B. Watson were in the observation-alist tradition. Introspection is useful because it yields data about experience.

ten Hoor, Marten. "A Critical Analysis of the Concept of Introspection." JOURNAL OF PHILOSOPHY 29 (June 1932): 322-31.

Titchener, Edward Bradford. A BEGINNER'S PSYCHOLOGY. New York: Macmillan, 1915. xvi, 362 p.

A systematic structuralist introduction to psychology presenting major areas of inquiry and laying "less stress . . . upon knowledge and more on point of view." This is not a revision of the author's primer of psychology, although its purposes are similar. References. Index.

_____. EXPERIMENTAL PSYCHOLOGY: A MANUAL OF LABORATORY PRACTICE. VOL. I. QUALITATIVE EXPERIMENTS. PART I. STUDENT'S MANUAL; PART II. INSTRUCTOR'S MANUAL. New York: Macmillan, 1901. xx, 214 p.; xxxiii, 456 p.

These manuals outline procedures for conducting laboratory exercises in such areas as visual, cutaneous, gustatory, olfactory, and organic sensation as well as attention, space perception, and association. In the student's manual, a general orientation to each area pre-cedes suggested exercises. The instructor's manual includes instruc-tions for repeating laboratory exercises and illustrations of apparatus. References.

_____. EXPERIMENTAL PSYCHOLOGY: A MANUAL OF LABORATORY PRACTICE. VOL. II. QUANTITATIVE EXPERIMENTS. PART I. STUDENT'S MANUAL; PART II. INSTRUCTOR'S MANUAL. New York: Macmillan, 1905. xli, 208 p.; clxxi, 453 p.

These and the preceding volumes were widely used as laboratory manuals in experimental psychology courses in the early decades of the twentieth century. The parallel with chemistry laboratory man-uals (one volume on qualitative experiments and one on quantitative experiments) was explicitly intended by Titchener.

_____. "Experimental Psychology: A Retrospect." AMERICAN JOURNAL OF PSYCHOLOGY 36 (July 1925): 313-23.

. LECTURES ON THE ELEMENTARY PSYCHOLOGY OF FEELING AND ATTENTION. New York: Macmillan, 1908. ix, 404 p.

Based on lectures delivered at Columbia University in 1908, this work discusses such topics as attributes of sensation, the tridimensional theory of feeling, the laws of attention, and affection. Extensive notes. Index.

. LECTURES ON THE EXPERIMENTAL PSYCHOLOGY OF THE THOUGHT-PROCESSES. New York: Macmillan, 1909. ix, 318 p.

Five lectures given at the University of Illinois on the recent experimental work on thought processes. Extensive notes and bibliographical materials. Index.

. AN OUTLINE OF PSYCHOLOGY. 2d ed. New York: Macmillan, 1897. xiv, 352 p.

An early introductory structuralist text based on lectures to second- and third-year college students. Focuses on introspective methods and on experiments on elementary and complex mental processes.

. "The Past Decade in Experimental Psychology." AMERICAN JOURNAL OF PSYCHOLOGY 21 (July 1910): 404-21.

. "The Postulates of a Structural Psychology." PHILOSOPHICAL REVIEW 7 (September 1898): 449-65.

. A PRIMER OF PSYCHOLOGY. Rev. ed. New York: Macmillan, 1912. xvi, 316 p.

A nontechnical and systematic structuralist textbook on general psychology emphasizing methods and established generalizations within such major content areas as attention, feeling, emotion, action, memory, and thought. Questions, exercises, and references. Index.

. SYSTEMATIC PSYCHOLOGY: PROLEGOMENA. Foreword by Rand B. Evans and Robert B. MacLeod. 1929. Reprint. Ithaca, N.Y.: Cornell University Press, 1972. xxiii, 280 p.

The major work on systematic psychology which was to have followed this introduction was never begun. The prolegomena, itself incomplete, consists of an introduction comparing the conceptions of psychology represented by Wundt and Brentano, and three chapters. Chapter 1 characterizes the nature of science and scientists. Chapters 2 and 3 deal with the definition of psychology and provide both a point of view and extensive historical perspective on the topic. Bibliographical materials in footnotes. Index.

_____. A TEXT-BOOK OF PSYCHOLOGY. Enl. ed. New York: Macmillan, 1913. xx, 565 p.

Intended to replace Titchener's earlier AN OUTLINE OF PSYCHOL-OGY. Covers major content areas of general psychology from a structuralist point of view. The first chapter discusses the subject matter, method, and problems of psychology; a final chapter comments on the status of psychology. Emphasizes "experimental methods and experimental results in the forefront of discussion." References for further reading. Index.

Washburn, Margaret Floy. "Introspection as an Objective Method." PSYCHO-LOGICAL REVIEW 29 (March 1922): 89-112.

A discussion of similarities between structuralism and behaviorism followed by a defense of introspection. A presidential address delivered to the American Psychological Association in 1921.

Wood, Ledger. "Inspection and Introspection." PHILOSOPHY OF SCIENCE (April 1940): 220-28.

5. WILLIAM JAMES

William James is considered by many as the first major modern American psychologist. His writings brought the "new" psychology of Germany to the attention of the English-speaking world and contained many seminal ideas that were taken over by functionalism and later systems.

Aldrich, E.P., ed. AS WILLIAM JAMES SAID: EXTRACTS FROM THE PUB-LISHED WRITINGS OF WILLIAM JAMES. New York: Vanguard Press, 1942. ix, 242 p.

A brief biographical sketch of William James precedes selections from a broad spectrum of his writings. One of many similar works.

Allport, Gordon W. "William James and the Behavioral Sciences." JOURNAL OF THE HISTORY OF THE BEHAVIORAL SCIENCES 2 (April 1966): 145-47.

Comments on the catholicity of James's interests and his search for unity among disciplines. Reprint of a brief address delivered as part of the ceremonies at the hanging of a portrait of James in William James Hall at Harvard University in 1965.

Ames, Van Meter. "William James and Zen." PSYCHOLOGICA 2 (June 1959): 114-19.

Notes similarities in Zen writings and James's thought.

Baum, M. "The Attitude of William James Toward Science." MONIST 42 (October 1932): 585-604.

> Traces background factors which shaped James's view of the prestige of science (because of the excellence of its method) and of the limitations of science (because the method is not universally applicable).

_____. "The Development of James's Pragmatism Prior to 1879." JOURNAL OF PHILOSOPHY 30 (January 1933): 43-51.

Bentley, Arthur F. "The Jamesian Datum." JOURNAL OF PSYCHOLOGY 16 (1943): 35-79.

> An attack on previous misstatements and misinterpretations of James followed by a characterization of Jamesian thought, with emphasis on James's empiricism and love of fact.

Boring, Edwin G. "Human Nature vs. Sensation: William James and the Psychology of the Present." AMERICAN JOURNAL OF PSYCHOLOGY 55 (July 1942): 310-27.

> Comments on James's dislike of the old sensory psychology and suggests James would like the then-current psychologies of Hocking, Murray, and Koehler.

Brett, G[eorge]. S[idney]. "The Psychology of William James in Relation to Philosophy." In IN COMMEMORATION OF WILLIAM JAMES 1842-1942, edited by Brand Blanshard and Herbert W. Schneider, pp. 81-94. New York: Columbia University Press, 1942.

Burkhart, Frederick H., gen. ed. THE WORKS OF WILLIAM JAMES. Cambridge, Mass.: Harvard University Press, 1975-- . In progress.

> Sponsored by the American Council of Learned Societies. This series will, when completed, provide a definitive edition of James's work, each preceded by an authoritative introduction.

"Century of the Birth of William James." PSYCHOLOGICAL REVIEW 50 (January 1943): 81-139.

> Articles by J.R. Angell, E.L. Thorndike, G.W. Allport, J. Dewey, R.B. Perry, E.B. Delabarre, E.D. Starbuck, and R.P. Angier on selected themes in the life and thought of James. Preceded by a portrait of James and concluded with reproductions of letters from James to Stumpf and Muensterberg.

Compton, Charles H., ed. WILLIAM JAMES, PHILOSOPHER AND MAN: QUOTATIONS AND REFERENCES IN 652 BOOKS. New York: Scarecrow Press, 1957. xxiv, 229 p.

Statements about William James and quotations from James's work
by 146 men and women, many of considerable distinction, followed
by references to James's work in 652 books. Index to titles of
works by James.

Doud, Robert M. "The Will and the Right to Believe: A Study in the Philosophy of William James." PENNSYLVANIA PSYCHIATRIC QUARTERLY 7, no. 4
(1968): 14-41.

Evans, Elizabeth Glendower. "William James and his Wife." ATLANTIC
MONTHLY, July 1929, pp. 374-87.

Reminiscences by the author intermingled with correspondence from
James to the author in a warm appreciation of James and his wife
Alice.

Fishman, Stephen M. "James and Lewes on Unconscious Judgment." JOUR-
NAL OF THE HISTORY OF THE BEHAVIORAL SCIENCES 4 (October 1968):
335-48.

An evaluation of James's criticisms of the theory of unconscious
judgment advanced by G.H. Lewes.

Foster, G. "The Psychotherapy of William James." PSYCHOANALYTIC RE-
VIEW 32 (1945): 300-318.

Gurwitsch, A. "William James' Theory of the 'Transitive Parts' of the Stream
of Consciousness." PHILOSOPHY AND PHENOMENOLOGICAL RESEARCH 3
(June 1943): 449-77.

Hardwick, Elizabeth, ed. THE SELECTED LETTERS OF WILLIAM JAMES. New
York: Farrar, Straus, 1960. xxix, 271 p.

Includes some duplication of letters found in previous works (see
Henry James and Ralph Barton Perry below, this section) and some
not included in these works.

Holt, E.B. "William James as Psychologist." In IN COMMEMORATION OF
WILLIAM JAMES 1842-1942, edited by Brand Blanshard and Herbert W. Schneider,
pp. 34-47. New York: Columbia University Press, 1942.

IN COMMEMORATION OF WILLIAM JAMES 1842-1942. Edited by Brand
Blanshard and Herbert W. Schneider. New York: Columbia University Press,
1942. 147 p.

Jacks, L.P. "William James and his Letters." ATLANTIC MONTHLY, August
1921, pp. 197-203.

Provides an overview of selected themes in James's philosophy.
Notes that James's letters reveal his philosophy.

James, Henry, ed. "Familiar Letters of William James I." ATLANTIC
MONTHLY, July 1920, pp. 1–15; August 1920, pp. 163–75; September 1920,
pp. 305–17.

Selected letters from three periods in James's life: the student days
and the years immediately following, his "sabbatical" time right after
publication of the PRINCIPLES OF PSYCHOLOGY, and the last
decade of James's life.

_____. THE LETTERS OF WILLIAM JAMES. 2 vols. in 1. Boston: Little,
Brown, 1926.

Includes a large variety of letters to family, friends, and colleagues
on psychological, philosophical, and personal matters.

James, William. "Great Men, Great Thoughts, and the Environment." ATLAN-
TIC MONTHLY, October 1880, pp. 441–49.

A brief treatise on causation in human affairs that also provides a
philosophy of history. James argues against the extreme determinism
of Herbert Spencer and his followers and for a balanced view which
emphasizes the causal roles of the person, the Zeitgeist, and the
physical environment in human affairs.

_____. THE MEANING OF TRUTH: A SEQUEL TO PRAGMATISM. New
York: Longmans, Green, 1909. xxii, 298 p.

A collection of James's papers from 1884 to 1909 dealing with the
question of truth. Two papers previously unpublished.

_____. A PLURALISTIC UNIVERSE. New York: Longmans, Green, 1925
(1909). vi, 405 p.

Eight lectures in which James gave an overview of then-current
trends in philosophy. Of special interest to psychologists are lectures on Fechner's and Bergson's philosophies.

_____. PRAGMATISM: A NEW NAME FOR SOME OLD WAYS OF THINKING.
New York: Longmans, Green, 1907. xiii, 309 p.

Eight unabridged lectures delivered at the Lowell Institute in Boston
(December 1906) and Columbia University (January 1907), dealing
with such problems as the meaning of pragmatism, pragmatism's conception of truth, pragmatism and humanism, and pragmatism and religion.

_____. THE PRINCIPLES OF PSYCHOLOGY. 2 vols. New York: Holt,

1890. Reprint. New York: Dover, 1957.

The first major modern American psychology textbook. Discusses
such topics in general psychology as the scope of psychology, the
functions of the brain, habit, the nature of thought, attention,
association, memory, sensation, imagination, perception, reason,
the emotions, the will, and hypnotism. Reflects James's pragmatic
orientation. Extensive notes. Index.

_____. PSYCHOLOGY: BRIEFER COURSE. New York: Holt, 1892. xiii,
478 p.

An abridgment of James's classic two-volume PRINCIPLES OF PSY-
CHOLOGY (see preceding entry), omitting historical and philosophical material and many bibliographic sources. Index.

_____. TALKS TO TEACHERS ON PSYCHOLOGY: AND TO STUDENTS ON
SOME OF LIFE'S IDEALS. 1899. Reprint. New York: Dover Publications,
1962. vi, 146 p.

See annotation in section D14, p. 365.

_____. THE VARIETIES OF RELIGIOUS EXPERIENCE: A STUDY IN HUMAN
NATURE. 1929. Reprint, with new introduction by Reinhold Niebuhr. New
York: Collier Books, 1973. 416 p.

Twenty lectures delivered at Edinburgh in 1901-2, considered by
many to be the classic work in psychology of religion. Examines
varieties of experiences which can be viewed as religious. Warns
against the dangers of reductionism and outlines a systematic approach (pragmatism) to religious experience. Index.

_____. THE WILL TO BELIEVE AND OTHER ESSAYS IN POPULAR PHILOSO-
PHY. 1896. Reprint. Gloucester, Mass.: Peter Smith, 1973.

Explores such topics as psychical research, morality, determinism,
and the importance of individuals. The first four chapters constitute an exploration and defense of religious faith.

Kantor, J.R. "Jamesian Psychology and the Stream of Psychological Thought."
In IN COMMEMORATION OF WILLIAM JAMES 1842-1942, edited by Brand
Blanshard and Herbert W. Schneider, pp. 143-56. New York: Columbia
University Press, 1942.

Kraushaar, Otto F. "Lotze's Influence on the Psychology of William James."
PSYCHOLOGICAL REVIEW 43 (January 1936): 235-57.

LeClair, Robert C., ed. THE LETTERS OF WILLIAM JAMES AND THEODORE

FLOURNOY. Madison: University of Wisconsin Press, 1966. xix, 252 p.

An exchange of seventy letters from James and fifty-four from Flournoy, first professor of psychology at the University of Geneva, written between 1890 and 1910.

Levinson, Ronald B. "Gertrude Stein, William James, and Grammar." AMERI-CAN JOURNAL OF PSYCHOLOGY 54 (January 1941): 124-28.

Marshall, M.E. "William James, Gustav Fechner, and the Question of Dogs and Cats in the Library." JOURNAL OF THE HISTORY OF THE BEHAVIORAL SCIENCES 10 (July 1974): 304-12.

"Shows something of James's general conceptual development through the focus of his changing receptivity to Fechnerian philosophy. . . ."

Murphy, Gardner, and Ballou, Robert O., eds. and comps. WILLIAM JAMES ON PSYCHICAL RESEARCH. New York: Viking Press, 1960. viii, 339 p.

A collection of articles, with helpful editorial introductions, il-lustrating the range of James's interest in psychical phenomena and his impatience with a narrow definition of scientifically legitimate topics. Identifies original sources. Index.

Pastore, Nicholas. "William James: A Contradiction." JOURNAL OF THE HISTORY OF THE BEHAVIORAL SCIENCES 13 (April 1977): 126-30.

Describes a contradiction between text material and a footnote in James's PRINCIPLES OF PSYCHOLOGY. The text material supports a Helmholtzian view of interest and discrimination, and the foot-note repudiates Helmholtz's views. The contradiction is discussed in terms of James's general ambivalence toward Helmholtz. Offers suggestions for further research.

Perry, Ralph Barton. ANNOTATED BIBLIOGRAPHY OF THE WRITINGS OF WILLIAM JAMES. Darby, Pa.: Darby Books, 1920. Reprint. Folcroft, Pa.: Folcroft Press, 1969. 69 p.

Annotated bibliography of James's short essays, reviews, notes, open letters, journal articles, and major works.

_____. THE THOUGHT AND CHARACTER OF WILLIAM JAMES: AS RE-VEALED IN UNPUBLISHED CORRESPONDENCE AND NOTES, TOGETHER WITH HIS PUBLISHED WRITINGS. Vol. 1, INHERITANCE AND VOCATION; Vol. 2, PHILOSOPHY AND PSYCHOLOGY. Boston: Little, Brown, 1935.

A mammoth biographical contribution on William James as a human being, a philosopher, and a psychologist.

_____. THE THOUGHT AND CHARACTER OF WILLIAM JAMES. BRIEFER

VERSION. New York: George Braziller, 1954. x, 402 p.

An abridgment of Perry's 1935 two-volume work on James's thought and development (see preceding entry). Organized around family background, friends, and major interest area. Rich in direct quotations and letters. Index.

Putnam, James Jackson. "William James." ATLANTIC MONTHLY, December 1910, pp. 835-48.

A typical appreciative obituary of James.

Roback, A[braham].A. WILLIAM JAMES: HIS MARGINALIA, PERSONALITY AND CONTRIBUTION. Cambridge, Mass.: Sci-Art, 1942. 336 p.

Ross, Barbara. "William James and the New England Medical Scene." In PSYCHOANALYSIS, PSYCHOTHERAPY AND THE NEW ENGLAND MEDICAL SCENE: 1894-1944, edited by G. Gifford, pp. 10-23. New York: Neale Watson, 1978.

Skrupskelis, Ignas K. WILLIAM JAMES: A REFERENCE GUIDE. Boston, Mass.: G.K. Hall, 1977. xviii, 250 p.

An annotated bibliography of writings by and about James.

Spoerl, Howard Davis. "Abnormal and Social Psychology in the Life and Work of William James." JOURNAL OF ABNORMAL AND SOCIAL PSYCHOLOGY 37 (January 1942): 3-19.

WILLIAM JAMES: THE MAN AND THE THINKER. Editor varies. Madison: University of Wisconsin Press, 1942. 147 p.

Ten public addresses honoring the centenary of the birth of James given at the University of Wisconsin and reprinted here. Addresses covered such topics as James's philosophy, his views on religion, and his views on psychoanalysis.

6. FUNCTIONALISM

This loosely-knit school flourished primarily at the University of Chicago. Several major figures were identified with it, and much has been written about its origins, influence, and approach to various psychological phenomena. This section includes materials of functional orientation on origins, influence, and particular approaches to specific psychological topics. Selected materials on John Dewey, James Roland Angell, and Harvey Carr are also included. For brief, chapter-length discussions of functionalism, we recommend some of the books listed in section B1, p. 31 (e.g., Heidbreder, Schultz, Woodworth and Sheehan).

Abel, Theodora Mead. "Washburn's Motor Theory: A Contribution to Functional Psychology." AMERICAN JOURNAL OF PSYCHOLOGY 39 (December 1927): 91-105.

>   Notes that Washburn's theory emphasizes function and performance as opposed to structural descriptions of sensations, ideas, emotions, and images.

Allport, Gordon W. "Dewey's Individual and Social Psychology." In LIBRARY OF LIVING PHILOSOPHERS, edited by P.A. Schilpp, vol. 1, pp. 265-90. Evanston, III.: Northwestern University, 1939.

Angell, James Rowland. "Behavior as a Category of Psychology." PSYCHOLOGICAL REVIEW 20 (July 1913): 255-70.

>   Comments on the problems associated with the term "consciousness" and argues that consciousness and introspection should be retained, respectively, as appropriate subject matter and tool for psychology.

_____. CHAPTERS FROM MODERN PSYCHOLOGY. New York: Longmans, Green, 1912. vii, 308 p.

>   Eight nontechnical lectures by an early functionalist designed to characterize the psychology of the day. Includes topics such as general, experimental, physiological, animal, social and racial, applied, and genetic psychology. References.

_____. "Imageless Thought." PSYCHOLOGICAL REVIEW 18 (September 1911): 295-323.

>   Explores representative work in imageless thought, addresses the question of the existence of imageless thought, and raises several questions which challenge the doctrine.

_____. "The Influence of Darwin on Psychology." PSYCHOLOGICAL REVIEW 16 (May 1909): 152-69.

>   Examines the effects of Darwin's thought on the study of instinct and intelligence, of the evolution of mind, and of the expression of emotions. Other articles in the same issue of PSYCHOLOGICAL REVIEW deal with Darwin's influence in such areas as historical and political thought, sociology, and ethics.

_____. AN INTRODUCTION TO PSYCHOLOGY. New York: Holt, 1918. vi, 281 p.

>   A brief introductory text which emphasizes a biological interpretation of mental life. Reflects the influence of behaviorism and thus departs somewhat from Angell's earlier and larger work, PSYCHOLOGY, 4th ed. (see below, this section, p. 149).

_____. "The Province of Functional Psychology." PSYCHOLOGICAL REVIEW 14 (March 1907): 61-91.

A classic statement of the position of the functionalist school of psychology devoting particular attention to the definition of the subject matter of psychology.

_____. PSYCHOLOGY. AN INTRODUCTION TO THE STRUCTURE AND FUNCTION OF HUMAN CONSCIOUSNESS. 4th ed. New York: 1908. ix, 468 p.

A major early introductory text. Provides a comprehensive coverage of the content areas of psychology and distinguishes between the methods of structuralism and functionalism. Suggested readings. Index.

Baldwin, J. Mark. "The Limits of Pragmatism." PSYCHOLOGICAL REVIEW 11 (January 1904): 30-60.

A summary of the major ideas of pragmatism followed by a discussion of certain epistemological problems which the pragmatic theory of truth must answer, such as the meaning of undiscovered realities and the possibilities of realities whose meanings are "not exhausted in the statement of their pragmatic origin."

Boydston, Jo Ann, ed. GUIDE TO THE WORKS OF JOHN DEWEY. Rev. ed. Carbondale: Southern Illinois University Press, 1972. xv, 395 p.

Twelve sections by various authors, summarizing Dewey's contributions. Section 1, by Herbert W. Schneider, is on Dewey's psychology. A checklist of relevant works by Dewey follows each section. Index.

_____. JOHN DEWEY: THE MIDDLE WORKS, 1899-1924. Multiple vols. Carbondale: Southern Illinois University Press, 1976-- .

Cadwallader, Thomas C. "Charles S. Peirce (1839-1914): The First American Experimental Psychologist." JOURNAL OF THE HISTORY OF THE BEHAVIORAL SCIENCES 10 (July 1974): 291-98.

Biographical materials on Peirce followed by an overview of his work in experimental psychology on such topics as the perception of color, difference limens, and the experimental method.

Carr, Harvey A. AN INTRODUCTION TO SPACE PERCEPTION. New York: Longmans, Green, 1935. xi, 413 p.

Summarizes selected experimental work in auditory and visual space perception from a functionalist perspective. Examines major issues and theories. References. Index.

_____. "The Nature of Mental Process." PSYCHOLOGICAL REVIEW 24 (May 1917): 181-87.

Argues that psychology should study consciousness and neural events.

_____. PSYCHOLOGY: A STUDY OF MENTAL ACTIVITY. New York: Longmans, Green, 1925. v, 432 p.

An early functionalist introductory text. Index.

Coughlan, Neil. YOUNG JOHN DEWEY: AN ESSAY IN AMERICAN INTELLECTUAL HISTORY. Chicago: University of Chicago Press, 1975. xii, 187 p.

Brief biographical materials followed by chapters on such topics as Dewey's psychology, ethics, politics, and pragmatism. Bibliographical materials in notes. Index.

Crissman, Paul. "The Psychology of John Dewey." PSYCHOLOGICAL REVIEW 49 (September 1942): 441-62.

A description and critique of such key concepts in Dewey's psychology as habit, character, impulse, emotion, motive, desire, thought, mind, consciousness, and meaning.

Dewey, John. "Body and Mind." MENTAL HYGIENE 12 (January 1928): 1-17.

_____. THE EARLY WORKS OF JOHN DEWEY, 1882-1898. 5 vols. Edited by Fredson Bowers, Jo Ann Boydston, et al. Carbondale: Southern Illinois University Press, 1967-72.

_____. EXPERIENCE AND EDUCATION. 1938. Reprint. New York: Collier Books, 1963. 91 p.

_____. EXPERIENCE AND NATURE. 2d ed. La Salle, Ill.: Open Court Publishing Co., 1958. xvii, 360 p.

_____. "How is Mind to be Known?" JOURNAL OF PHILOSOPHY 39 (January 1942): 29-35.

_____. HOW WE THINK: A RESTATEMENT OF THE RELATION OF REFLECTIVE THINKING TO THE EDUCATIVE PROCESS. Rev. ed. Boston: D.C. Heath, 1933. x, 301 p.

A revision of Dewey's earlier functionalist classic on the nature of thinking and on methods of special usefulness to teachers for training thought. Index.

_____. HUMAN NATURE AND CONDUCT; AN INTRODUCTION TO SOCIAL PSYCHOLOGY. New York: Modern Library, 1930. ix, 336 p.

A classic work exploring the roles of habit, impulse, and intelligence in conduct. Argues that habit should be a central concept in social psychology. Index.

_____. "The Need for Social Psychology." PSYCHOLOGICAL REVIEW 24 (July 1917): 266-77.

Reviews selected developments in social psychology and argues that this field is important to general psychology and to a more complete understanding of human beings. Based on an address celebrating the twenty-fifth anniversary of the American Psychological Association.

_____. PROBLEMS OF MEN. New York: Philosophical Library, 1946. Reprint. New York: Greenwood Press, 1968. 424 p.

A collection of essays on such topics as democracy and education, religion, science, value, and the philosophical thought of James Marsh, William James, and Alfred North Whitehead. Index.

_____. PSYCHOLOGY. 3d ed., rev. New York: Harper, 1898. xii, 427 p.

An early introductory text discussing the methods and major content areas of psychology from a functionalist point of view.

_____. "The Reflex Arc Concept in Psychology." PSYCHOLOGICAL REVIEW 3 (July 1896): 357-70.

A classic article challenging the psychological adequacy of the reflex arc concept, arguing that it merely replaces the old mind-body dualism with a new dualism of stimulus and response, resulting in a disjointed, overly simplistic psychology. Notes that unifying and coordinating processes lend value and coherence to acts.

Dykhuizen, George. THE LIFE AND MIND OF JOHN DEWEY. Edited by Jo Ann Boydston. Carbondale: Southern Illinois University Press, 1973. xxv, 429 p.

Feldman, W.T. THE PHILOSOPHY OF JOHN DEWEY. Baltimore: Johns Hopkins Press, 1934. 127 p.

Feuer, Lewis S. "John Dewey's Reading at College." JOURNAL OF THE HISTORY OF IDEAS 19 (June 1958): 415-21.

Fite, Warner. "The Place of Pleasure and Pain in the Functional Psychology." PSYCHOLOGICAL REVIEW 10 (November 1903): 633-44.

An outline of the functionalist system followed by an account of

the manner in which it treats pleasure and pain. Discusses implications for experimental investigations and ethics.

Handy, Rollo, and Harwood, E.C. USEFUL PROCEDURES OF INQUIRY.
Great Barrington, Mass.: Behavioral Research Council, 1973. vii, 232 p.

A broad treatment of epistemological problems examining scientific
inquiry, logic, and authoritarianism. Includes a section by Joseph
Radner on John Dewey's philosophy, and reprints the paper "Know-
ing and the Known" by Dewey and Arthur F. Bentley. Also includes several reprints of shorter papers by the authors. Index.

Harrison, Ross. "Functionalism and Its Historical Significance." GENETIC
PSYCHOLOGY MONOGRAPHS 68 (November 1963): 387–423.

Hartshorne, Charles; Weiss, Paul; and Burks, Arthur W., eds. COLLECTED
PAPERS OF CHARLES SANDERS PEIRCE. 8 vols. Vols. 1–6 edited by Charles
Hartshorne and Paul Weiss; vols. 7 and 8 edited by Arthur W. Burks. Cambridge, Mass.: Belknap Press of Harvard University Press (vols. 1–6) and Harvard University Press (vols. 7–8), 1931–58.

The major works of one of the founders of pragmatism, also an
early U.S. experimental psychologist. Of interest to psychologists
is volume 7 on scientific method and various psychological topics
under the heading "Philosophy of Mind," volume 5 on pragmatism,
and volume 8 containing reviews and comments on the works of
various psychologists. Volume 8 contains a bibliography of Peirce's
works. Editorial notes. Indexes.

Hocking, William Ernest. "Dewey's Concepts of Experience and Nature." THE
PHILOSOPHICAL REVIEW 49 (March 1940): 228–44.

James, William. "The Chicago School." PSYCHOLOGICAL BULLETIN 1 (January 1904): 1–5.

Kaminsky, Jack. "Dewey's Concept of an Experience." PHILOSOPHY AND
PHENOMENOLOGICAL RESEARCH 17 (March 1957): 316–30.

Kantor, J[acob].R. "A Functional Interpretation of Human Instincts." PSYCHO-
LOGICAL REVIEW 27 (January 1920): 50–72.

Discusses the nature of instincts and considers such topics as the
range of instinctive conduct, the intelligence of instinctive behavior,
the specificity of instincts, and the relation of instincts to emotion.

Lynch, J.A. "A Criticism of Dewey's Theory of Stimulus." PHILOSOPHICAL
REVIEW 49 (May 1940): 356–60.

McKinney, Fred. "Functionalism at Chicago--Memories of a Graduate Student:
1929-1931." JOURNAL OF THE HISTORY OF THE BEHAVIORAL SCIENCES
14 (April 1978): 142-48.

> Characterizes the philosophical climate, the faculty, courses, and
> students at Chicago. Notes that the functionalist tradition is
> manifested in much of contemporary American psychology.

Madden, Edward H. "Chauncey Wright's Functionalism." JOURNAL OF THE
HISTORY OF THE BEHAVIORAL SCIENCES 10 (July 1974): 281-90.

> A brief review of Wright's essay, "The Evolution of Self-Conscious-
> ness," followed by a discussion of his influence on other American
> functionalists, the implications of his work, and his contributions to
> symbolic interactionism.

Morris, Charles W. "Peirce, Mead, and Pragmatism." PHILOSOPHICAL RE-
VIEW 47 (March 1938): 109-27.

Raphelson, Alfred C. "The Pre-Chicago Association of the Early Functionalists."
JOURNAL OF THE HISTORY OF THE BEHAVIORAL SCIENCES 9 (April 1973):
115-22.

> Notes that the origins of functionalism can be traced partly to
> early acquaintances among functionalists, particularly at Johns
> Hopkins University and the University of Michigan.

Riley, I. Woodbridge. AMERICAN THOUGHT FROM PURITANISM TO PRAG-
MATISM AND BEYOND. 2d ed. Gloucester, Mass.: P. Smith, 1959 (1915).
x, 438 p.

Shields, Stephanie A. "Functionalism, Darwinism, and the Psychology of
Women: A Study of Social Myth." AMERICAN PSYCHOLOGIST 30 (July 1975):
739-54.

> Discusses selected topics in the psychology of women from the latter
> half of the nineteenth century through the first third of the twenti-
> eth century. Presents ideas from Gall, Spurzheim, Bain, Galton,
> and G. Stanley Hall, and documents the influence of functionalism
> and Darwinism.

Sohn, David. "Two Concepts of Adaptation: Darwin's and Psychology's."
JOURNAL OF THE HISTORY OF THE BEHAVIORAL SCIENCES 12 (October
1976): 367-75.

> Presents evidence that Darwin's theory of species adaptation is
> irreconcilable with psychological notions of individual adaptation.
> Argues that Darwin's notions of individual adaptation had minimal
> influence on psychology.

Thomas, Milton H., ed. JOHN DEWEY: A CENTENNIAL BIBLIOGRAPHY. Chicago: University of Chicago Press, 1962. xiii, 370 p.

Townsend, H.G. "Some Sources and Early Meanings of American Pragmatism As Reflected in Volume V of the Collected Papers of Charles Sanders Peirce." JOURNAL OF PHILOSOPHY 32 (March 1935): 181–87.

Washburn, Margaret Floy. MOVEMENT AND MENTAL IMAGERY: OUTLINES OF A MOTOR THEORY OF THE COMPLEXER MENTAL PROCESSES. Boston: Houghton Mifflin, 1916. xv, 252 p.

> Work by a major early functionalist advancing a motor theory of mental processes. Attempts to bridge the gap between the study of mental processes and the study of movement, which is "the ultimate fact of physical science." References. Index.

Whitely, Paul L. "A New Name for an Old Idea? A Student of Harvey Carr Reflects." JOURNAL OF THE HISTORY OF THE BEHAVIORAL SCIENCES 12 (July 1976): 260–74.

> Outlines Carr's systematic approach to psychology and describes his work as a teacher. Extracts from letters of students and comments by the author provide insight into Carr's personal characteristics.

7. THE COLUMBIA SCHOOL (Thorndike, Woodworth, Cattell)

This section includes representative works of James McKeen Cattell, Edward L. Thorndike, and Robert Sessions Woodworth, and articles about psychology at Columbia University. The Columbia school does not represent a well-defined system of thought. Indeed, Woodworth, often associated with what came to be called "dynamic psychology," had a disdain for systems and did not wish to establish a school. The Columbia school might nevertheless be viewed as being broadly within the American functionalist tradition. An excellent chapter-length characterization of psychology at Columbia is contained in chapter 8 of Edna Heidbreder's SEVEN PSYCHOLOGIES (see section B1, p. 34).

Bitterman, M.E. "Thorndike and the Problem of Animal Intelligence." AMERICAN PSYCHOLOGIST 24 (April 1969): 444–53.

> Reviews Thorndike's academic background and provides a succinct overview of his work on the problem-solving ability of various species.

Cattell, James McKeen. JAMES McKEEN CATTELL: MAN OF SCIENCE. Vol. 1, PSYCHOLOGICAL RESEARCH; Vol. 2, ADDRESSES AND FORMAL PAPERS. Edited by A.T. Poffenberger. Lancaster, Pa.: Science Press, 1947.

Joncich, Geraldine [M.]. "Complex Forces and Neglected Acknowledgments in the Making of a Young Psychologist: Edward L. Thorndike and His Teachers." JOURNAL OF THE HISTORY OF THE BEHAVIORAL SCIENCES 2 (January 1966): 43-50.

> Notes that Thorndike failed to acknowledge the sources of influence that led him into psychology. Reviews major influences including Andrew C. Armstrong (an undergraduate teacher at Wesleyan University), James Sully's OUTLINES OF PSYCHOLOGY (see section D14, p. 367), and William James.

_____. "E.L. Thorndike: The Psychologist as Professional Man of Science." AMERICAN PSYCHOLOGIST 23 (June 1968): 434-46.

> Examines Thorndike's professional contributions and also characterizes the early twentieth-century scientific community, emphasizing attempts at professionalization, zeal, disputes, and personal characteristics of people such as Thorndike, Titchener, James, and Cattell.

_____. THE SANE POSITIVIST: A BIOGRAPHY OF EDWARD L. THORNDIKE. Middletown, Conn.: Wesleyan University Press, 1968. 634 p.

> A major biography of Edward L. Thorndike emphasizing his times and his principal contributions. Includes an essay on sources.

Loughnan, H.B. "What is the Value of Woodworth's Psychology?" AUSTRALASIAN JOURNAL OF PSYCHOLOGY AND PHILOSOPHY 13 (1935): 161-87.

Poffenberger, A.T., ed. JAMES McKEEN CATTELL: MAN OF SCIENCE. 1860-1944. 2 vols. Lancaster, Pa.: Science Press, 1947. Reprint. New York: Arno Press, 1973.

Sokal, Michael M. "The Unpublished Autobiography of James McKeen Cattell." AMERICAN PSYCHOLOGIST 26 (July 1971): 626-35.

> A discussion of conflicts and issues pertinent to Cattell's refusal to contribute to Murchison's HISTORY OF PSYCHOLOGY IN AUTOBIOGRAPHY (cf. section A1, p. 3) followed by a printing of an unfinished autobiography by Cattell found among the Cattell papers at the manuscript division of the Library of Congress.

Thorndike, Edward L. ANIMAL INTELLIGENCE: EXPERIMENTAL STUDIES. New York: Macmillan, 1911. viii, 297 p.

> Consists mostly of papers published in scientific journals. The collection represents the first "application of the experimental method in animal psychology," and covers such topics as experiments with cats, dogs, and chicks; the instinctive reactions of chicks; and the mental life of monkeys. The first chapter compares the study

of consciousness with the study of behavior, and a final chapter deals with the evolution of human intelligence.

_____. THE ELEMENTS OF PSYCHOLOGY. 2d ed. New York: A.G. Seiler, 1911. xix, 351 p.

An introduction to general principles of psychology including such topics as the subject matter of psychology, feelings, the physiological basis of mental life, association, and dynamic psychology. Contains a chapter on the relation of psychology to other disciplines. References and suggestions for further study.

_____. HUMAN NATURE AND THE SOCIAL ORDER. Edited and abridged by Geraldine [M.] Joncich. Cambridge: M.I.T. Press, 1969. xxv, 373 p. Index.

Discusses general facts and principles of human behavior and applications of psychology to such topics as human welfare, economics, labor and wages, the psychology of capitalism and alternative systems, and law and human nature. A classic in applied social psychology.

_____. AN INTRODUCTION TO THE THEORY OF MENTAL AND SOCIAL MEASUREMENTS. New York: Science Press, 1904. xii, 212 p.

_____. "The Law of Effect." AMERICAN JOURNAL OF PSYCHOLOGY 39 (December 1927): 212-22.

Results of experiments designed to investigate "whether the aftereffects of a connection do in fact strengthen or weaken it."

_____. MAN AND HIS WORKS. Cambridge, Mass.: Harvard University Press, 1943. Reprint. Port Washington, N.Y.: Kennikat Press, 1969. v, 212 p.

Preserves the author's ten 1942 William James Lectures at Harvard; devoted to mental genetics, learning, human relations, and the psychology of language, government, punishment, and welfare. Index.

_____. PSYCHOLOGY AND THE SCIENCE OF EDUCATION: SELECTED WRITINGS OF EDWARD L. THORNDIKE. Edited by Geraldine M. Joncich. New York: Teachers College, Columbia University, 1962. vi, 158 p.

Includes Thorndike's brief autobiography, his paper on Darwin's contribution to psychology, and papers on education as a science, intelligence, and measurement.

_____. SELECTED WRITINGS FROM A CONNECTIONIST'S PSYCHOLOGY.

New York: Appleton-Century-Crofts, 1949. vii, 370 p.

Includes some of Thorndike's most important writings, primarily on topics of educational interest: law of effect, influences of punishment, heredity and environment, mental fatigue, personality, language, science and values, and Darwin's contributions to psychology. Introduced with a brief autobiography. Minimal bibliographical materials. Index.

Thorne, Frederick C. "Reflections on the Golden Age of Columbia's Psychology." JOURNAL OF THE HISTORY OF THE BEHAVIORAL SCIENCES 12 (April 1976): 159-65.

Describes the leadership, faculty, organization, philosophical orientation, and research foci of the psychology department at Columbia University from 1920 to 1940.

Woodworth, Robert Sessions. THE COLUMBIA UNIVERSITY PSYCHOLOGICAL LABORATORY: A FIFTY-YEAR RETROSPECT. New York: Author, 1942. 23 p.

See section B5bxiiaa, p. 94, for annotation.

_____. DYNAMIC PSYCHOLOGY. New York: Columbia University Press, 1918. 210 p.

Eight lectures by an early functionalist providing a systematic treatment of topics such as problems and methods of psychology, native equipment of man, originality, drive and mechanism in abnormal behavior, and drive and mechanism in social behavior.

_____. "Dynamic Psychology." In PSYCHOLOGIES OF 1930, edited by C[arl]. Murchison, pp. 327-36. Worcester, Mass.: Clark University Press, 1930.

_____. DYNAMICS OF BEHAVIOR. New York: Holt, Rinehart and Winston, 1958. x, 403 p.

Preserves and updates the point of view in Woodworth's earlier book, DYNAMIC PSYCHOLOGY (see above, this section), and supplements his EXPERIMENTAL PSYCHOLOGY (see section D2, p. 261). Emphasizes "dynamic interactions of motivation, learning, perception, and problem solving." Extensive references. Index.

_____. EXPERIMENTAL PSYCHOLOGY. New York: Holt, 1938. xi, 889 p. Index.

_____. "Professor Cattell's Psychophysical Contributions." ARCHIVES OF PSYCHOLOGY No. 30, 1914, pp. 60-74.

_____. PSYCHOLOGICAL ISSUES: SELECTED PAPERS OF ROBERT S.

WOODWORTH. New York: Columbia University Press, 1939. x, 421 p.

See section C14, p. 236 for annotation.

Woodworth, Robert Sessions, and Marquis, Donald G. PSYCHOLOGY. 5th ed. New York: Holt, 1947. x, 677 p.

A standard introductory textbook since its first edition in 1921 under the authorship of Woodworth. Covers such topics as individual differences, the nervous system, development, motives, feeling and emotion, the senses, learning, memory, and thinking. References. Index.

8. WILLIAM McDOUGALL

William McDougall, perhaps the most neglected pioneer psychologist, advanced a systematic approach to the discipline and at the same time made important contributions to areas such as social psychology, psychopathology, and physiological psychology (see section D, pp. 281, 336, and 349). This section includes representative major works, works which characterize McDougall's system, and works which assess McDougall's contributions to psychology.

Boden, Margaret A. "McDougall Revisited." JOURNAL OF PERSONALITY 33 (March 1965): 1-19.

Elucidates key concepts in McDougall's psychology such as cognition, instincts, sentiments, and personality. Notes that he anticipated "many important contemporary views on cognition, social psychology, and personality."

_____. PURPOSIVE EXPLANATION IN PSYCHOLOGY. Cambridge, Mass.: Harvard University Press, 1972. 408 p.

Discusses McDougall's general approach to purpose and the relation of purpose to such topics as instincts, sentiments, self, consciousness, and freedom. Includes brief accounts of behaviorist interpretations of purpose as advanced by J.B. Watson, Tolman, Hull, Spence, Skinner, and others. Extensive bibliography and notes. Index.

Burt, Cyril. "The Permanent Contributions of McDougall to Psychology." BRITISH JOURNAL OF EDUCATIONAL PSYCHOLOGY 25 (February 1955): 10-22.

Krantz, David L., and Allen, David. "The Rise and Fall of McDougall's Instinct Doctrine." JOURNAL OF THE HISTORY OF THE BEHAVIORAL SCIENCES 3 (October 1967): 326-38.

Reviews arguments raised against instinct theory in the 1920s, factors responsible for the decline of the doctrine, and contemporary implications of McDougall's theory.

Krantz, David L.; Hall, Richard; and Allen, David. "William McDougall and the Problem of Purpose." JOURNAL OF THE HISTORY OF THE BEHAVIORAL SCIENCES 5 (January 1969): 25-38.

> Contrasts approaches to the concept of purpose of psychologists William McDougall and Howard C. Warren, radical behaviorists such as John B. Watson and Z.Y. Kuo, and reconciliationists such as E.C. Tolman and R.B. Perry.

Langfeld, Herbert S. "Professor McDougall's Contributions to the Science of Psychology." BRITISH JOURNAL OF PSYCHOLOGY 31 (October 1940): 107-14.

McDougall, William. BODY AND MIND: A HISTORY AND A DEFENSE OF ANIMISM. 3d ed. London: Methuen, 1915. xix, 384 p.

> Explores the history of animistic concepts from ancient times to the early twentieth century. Examines late nineteenth- and early twentieth-century developments such as the influence of Darwinian thought. Emphasizes the inadequacy of materialistic concepts and defends the idea of the causal efficacy of psychic processes. Notes and bibliographical materials. Index.

_____. "A Contribution Towards An Improvement in Psychological Method." MIND 7 (January, April, July 1898): 15-33, 159-78, 364-87.

_____. THE ENERGIES OF MEN: A STUDY OF THE FUNDAMENTALS OF DYNAMIC PSYCHOLOGY. New York: Charles Scribner's Sons, 1932. xii, 395 p.

> An updated and abridged version of McDougall's earlier OUTLINE OF PSYCHOLOGY (see below, this page) and OUTLINE OF ABNORMAL PSYCHOLOGY (see section D12b, p. 349).

_____. "The Hormic Psychology." In PSYCHOLOGIES OF 1930, edited by C[arl]. Murchison, pp. 3-36. Worcester, Mass.: Clark University Press, 1930.

_____. MODERN MATERIALISM AND EMERGENT EVOLUTION. New York: D. Van Nostrand, 1929. x, 249 p.

> Argues for teleological causation and explores problems of efficient causation associated with atomic materialism. Intended as a supplement to his earlier BODY AND MIND (see above, this page). Extensive notes. Bibliographical materials. Index.

_____. OUTLINE OF PSYCHOLOGY. New York: Charles Scribner's Sons, 1924. xvi, 456 p.

> A comprehensive early introductory text covering traditional topics,

and devoting considerable space to topics in comparative psychology. Emphasizes purposive rather than mechanistic psychology. Index.

_____. "Prolegomena to Psychology." PSYCHOLOGICAL REVIEW 29 (January 1922): 1-43.

Criticizes narrow definitions of psychology as merely the study of consciousness or behavior. Argues that psychology can be viewed as the study of the mind, but data both from the facts of introspection and from behavior must be admissible.

_____. PSYCHOLOGY: THE STUDY OF BEHAVIOR. 2d ed. London: Oxford University Press, 1959. xxix, 177 p.

_____. "Purposive or Mechanical Psychology?" PSYCHOLOGICAL REVIEW 30 (July 1923): 273-88.

9. BEHAVIORISM

The behaviorist system of psychology has been considered by many historians as the most peculiarly American of the schools, but its concerns can be traced to other countries as well. Primarily identified in its early years with John B. Watson, it later became widely known under the championship of B.F. Skinner. Writings on this school appear to fall naturally into the subcategories used in this section: major statements of behavioristic systems, the origin and development of behaviorism, criticisms of behaviorism (it has been a controversial school since its inception), and behavioristic interpretations of specialized subject matter areas in psychology. Particularly helpful chapter-length overviews of behaviorism may be found in books listed in section B1 (e.g., Heidbreder, chapter 7; Watson, chapter 18) and in Skinner's book ABOUT BEHAVIORISM listed in section C9a, p. 162.

a. Major Statements of Behavioristic Systems

Bawden, H. Heath. "The Presuppositions of a Behaviorist Psychology." PSYCHOLOGICAL REVIEW 25 (May 1918): 171-90.

Discusses selected assumptions of behavioral psychology, focusing on the meaning of behavior, the problem of introspection, and various conceptions of mental processes.

Bry, Adelaide. A PRIMER OF BEHAVIORAL PSYCHOLOGY. New York: Mentor Books, 1975. 128 p.

Presents a history of behaviorism including discussion of Pavlov, Sechenov, Watson, Thorndike, Hull, Guthrie, Tolman, Skinner, and others. Bibliography. Glossary. Notes.

Calkins, Mary Whiton. "The Truly Psychological Behaviorism." PSYCHOLOGI-
CAL REVIEW 28 (January 1921): 1-18.

Outlines two types of behaviorism: radical or extreme behaviorism
as advanced by John B. Watson, and a modified behaviorism as
promoted by H.C. Warren. Discusses the possibility of a behavioristic self psychology.

Dunlap, K. ELEMENTS OF SCIENTIFIC PSYCHOLOGY. St. Louis, Mo.:
C.V. Mosby, 1922. 368 p.

Honig, Werner K., ed. OPERANT BEHAVIOR: AREAS OF RESEARCH AND
APPLICATION. New York: Appleton-Century-Crofts, 1966. xi, 865 p.

Surveys research on and applications of operant conditioning in
eighteen areas including superstition, sensory reinforcement, animal sensory processes, punishment, drugs, altered psychological
states, space technology, human verbal behavior, and programmed
environments. Editorial comments precede and references follow
each chapter. Index.

Hull, Clark Leonard. A BEHAVIOR SYSTEM: AN INTRODUCTION TO BE-
HAVIOR THEORY CONCERNING THE INDIVIDUAL ORGANISM. 1952. Reprint. New York: John Wiley and Sons, 1964. ix, 372 p.

A presentation of Hull's well-known behavior system covering such
topics as trial-and-error learning, discrimination learning, behavioral chains, complex maze learning, and problem solving. Glossary of symbols. Index.

_____. ESSENTIALS OF BEHAVIOR. New Haven, Conn.: Yale University
Press, 1951. viii, 144 p.

Hull presents his views on "the basic primary laws (postulates) of
mammalian behavior." Index.

_____. PRINCIPLES OF BEHAVIOR: AN INTRODUCTION TO BEHAVIOR
THEORY. New York: Appleton-Century-Crofts, 1943. x, 422 p.

A systematic, quantitative, hypothetico-deductive approach to psychology as a natural science. Index.

Hunter, Walter S. HUMAN BEHAVIOR. Rev. ed. Chicago: University of
Chicago Press, 1928. x, 355 p.

An introductory text written from a behavioristic point of view.
References. Index.

_____. "The Psychological Study of Behavior." PSYCHOLOGICAL REVIEW
39 (January 1932): 1-24.

Kantor, J.R. "Behaviorism in the History of Psychology." PSYCHOLOGICAL RECORD 18 (April 1968): 151-66.

_____. "In Defense of Stimulus-Response Psychology." PSYCHOLOGICAL REVIEW 40 (May 1933): 324-36.

Kendler, Howard H., and Spence, Janet T., eds. ESSAYS IN NEOBEHAVIOR-ISM: A MEMORIAL VOLUME TO KENNETH W. SPENCE. New York: Appleton-Century-Crofts, 1971. xii, 345 p.

> A volume honoring the memory of Kenneth W. Spence. Includes a brief necrology, a paper by the editors on the tenets of neobehaviorism, and papers by Spence's students on such topics as conditioning, discrimination learning, motivation, and memory. Index.

Mowrer, O. Hobart. "The Present State of Behaviorism: I." EDUCATION 97 (Fall 1976): 4-23.

Pepper, Stephen C. "The Conceptual Framework of Tolman's Purposive Behaviorism." PSYCHOLOGICAL REVIEW 41 (March 1934): 108-33.

Skinner, B[urrhus].F[rederic]. ABOUT BEHAVIORISM. New York: Alfred A. Knopf, 1974. viii, 256 p.

> Behavioristic explanations of such psychological topics as perceiving, thinking, the self, knowing, and motivation and emotion. Contrasts behavioristic and mentalistic explanations and defends behaviorism. Bibliographical information. Index.

_____. THE BEHAVIOR OF ORGANISMS: AN EXPERIMENTAL ANALYSIS. New York: Appleton-Century, 1938. ix, 457 p.

> A well-known work by one of the world's foremost psychologists describing experiments in such areas as conditioning, extinction, discrimination, and drive. Presents the first detailed version of Skinner's influential system and discusses its implications. References. Index.

_____. CUMULATIVE RECORD; A SELECTION OF PAPERS. 3d ed. New York: Appleton-Century-Crofts, 1972. xi, 604 p.

_____. PARTICULARS OF MY LIFE. New York: Alfred A. Knopf, 1976. 319 p.

> An intimate autobiographical account of Skinner's family background, boyhood, adolescence, and college experiences.

_____. SCIENCE AND HUMAN BEHAVIOR. New York: Macmillan, 1953. x, 461 p.

A systematic approach to psychology dealing with the possibility of a science of human behavior; the analysis of behavior with emphasis on such topics as operant behavior, punishment, and emotion; the individual, with discussion of private events and the self; group behavior; and the control of behavior including discussion of such control agencies as law, religion, and education. Index.

Spence, Kenneth W. "The Postulates and Methods of Behaviorism." PSYCHO-LOGICAL REVIEW 55 (March 1948): 67-78.

Modifications of Watson's original behavioristic system go by such labels as purposive behaviorism, operational behaviorism, and molecular behaviorism. Spence characterizes common behavioristic approaches to such topics as conceptions of psychological events, the nature of scientific concepts, and levels of analysis (molar vs. molecular), and concludes by contrasting behaviorism and Gestalt psychology with respect to field theory. Originally given as an address as part of a symposium on "The Postulates and Methods of Gestalt Psychology, Behaviorism and Psychoanalysis."

Stephenson, William. "Postulates of Behaviorism." PHILOSOPHY OF SCIENCE 20 (April 1953): 110-20.

Tolman, Edward Chase. COLLECTED PAPERS IN PSYCHOLOGY. Berkeley and Los Angeles: University of California Press, 1961. xiv, 269 p.

Nineteen selected papers covering the period 1922-48 characterize the growth and development of Tolman's neobehavioristic system. Bibliography of Tolman's published work.

_____. "A New Formula for Behaviorism." PSYCHOLOGICAL REVIEW 29 (January 1922): 44-53.

Argues for a nonphysiological behaviorism that will provide a more adequate treatment of such problems as motivation, purpose, and emotion.

_____. PURPOSIVE BEHAVIOR IN ANIMALS AND MEN. New York: Century, 1932. xiv, 463 p.

Tolman's major systematic statement outlining a neobehavioristic psychology which incorporates features of Gestalt psychology and McDougall's hormic psychology. Outlines his position on a variety of issues and presents research findings pertinent to the theory. References. Glossary. Index.

Watson, John B. "Animal Education: An Experimental Study on the Psychical Development of the White Rat, Correlated With the Growth of Its Nervous System." Ph.D. dissertation, University of Chicago, 1903. 122 p.

_____. "An Attempted Formulation of the Scope of Behavior Psychology."
PSYCHOLOGICAL REVIEW 24 (September 1917): 329-52.

A behavioristic approach to the field of psychology followed by a
delineation of divisions of psychology and a discussion of the relation of psychology to other disciplines such as physics, neurology,
medicine, and physiology.

_____. BEHAVIORISM. Rev. ed. New York: W.W. Norton, 1930. xi,
308 p.

A text contrasting behaviorism with older psychologies. Outlines
the methods of behaviorism and treats substantive areas such as
instincts, emotions, habits, talking and thinking, and personality.
Watson offers a brief analysis of why behaviorism is the subject of
so much criticism. Index.

_____. "Behaviorism: A Psychology Based on Reflex-Action." JOURNAL
OF PHILOSOPHICAL STUDIES 1 (October 1926): 454-66.

_____. "Behaviorism: A Psychology Based on Reflexes." ARCHIVES OF
NEUROLOGY AND PSYCHIATRY 15 (1926): 185-204.

_____. "The Place of the Conditioned-Reflex in Psychology." PSYCHOLOGI-
CAL REVIEW 23 (March 1916): 89-116.

Distinguishes between conditioned secretion and motor reflexes, discusses general characteristics of the reflex, and outlines methods
of using the reflex to obtain differential reactions. (Presidential
address to the American Psychological Association in 1915.)

_____. "Psychology as the Behaviorist Views It." PSYCHOLOGICAL REVIEW
20 (March 1913): 158-77.

A classic article providing a succinct statement of the position of
behaviorism on the definition of psychology, the proper methods of
study, the failures of earlier psychologies such as structuralism and
functionalism, and appropriate areas of inquiry for psychology.
Sometimes referred to as "the behaviorist manifesto."

_____. PSYCHOLOGY FROM THE STANDPOINT OF A BEHAVIORIST. 3d
ed. Philadelphia: J.B. Lippincott, 1929. 458 p.

An elementary text by the founder of behaviorism presenting a systematic behavioristic approach to psychology. Emphasis is on
"the human animal." Index.

_____. THE WAYS OF BEHAVIORISM. New York: Harper, 1928. 144 p.

_____. "What is Behaviorism?" HARPER'S MAGAZINE, May 1926, pp. 723-
29.

A brief popular defense of behaviorism; claims that it may help solve many human problems.

Weigel, John A. B.F. SKINNER. Boston, Mass.: Twayne, 1977. 125 p.

Provides an overview of Skinner's contributions, biographical materials, reviews, tributes, critiques, and interviews.

Weiss, Albert P. "Behavior and the Central Nervous System." PSYCHOLOGICAL REVIEW 29 (September 1922): 329-43.

A definition of behaviorism accompanied by a proposal that the study of a typical behavioral problem include: the stimulus situation, sensory-cerebro-motor conditions, and overt reaction. Criticizes an earlier conception of psychology proposed by H.C. Warren (see section C14, p. 235).

_____. "Behaviorism and Behavior, I." PSYCHOLOGICAL REVIEW 31 (January 1924): 32-50.

_____. Behaviorism and Behavior, II." PSYCHOLOGICAL REVIEW 31 (March 1924): 118-149.

Williams, Katherine A. "Five Behaviorisms." AMERICAN JOURNAL OF PSYCHOLOGY 43 (July 1931): 337-60.

Reviews the major concepts of Watson, Weiss, Lashley, Hunter, and Tolman and notes the striking differences among them.

Woodworth, R[obert].S[essions]. "Four Varieties of Behaviorism." PSYCHOLOGICAL REVIEW 31 (July 1924): 257-64.

b. Origin and Development

Bakan, David. "Behaviorism and American Urbanization." JOURNAL OF THE HISTORY OF THE BEHAVIORAL SCIENCES 2 (January 1966): 5-28.

Traces the development of behaviorism in the United States and advances the thesis that urbanization shaped American ideology and had an impact on the development of behaviorism.

Bergmann, Gustav. "The Contribution of John B. Watson." PSYCHOLOGICAL REVIEW 63 (July 1956): 265-76.

Focuses on the work of John B. Watson in historical perspective and outlines some of Watson's basic positions on psychological matters. Suggests that Watson's importance in the history of psychology is second only to Freud's, "though at a rather great distance." Based on addresses given to psychology clubs at Northwestern University and the University of Chicago.

Birnbaum, Lucille T. "Behaviorism in the 1920's." AMERICAN QUARTERLY 7 (Spring 1955): 15-30.

Burnham, John C. "The New Psychology: From Narcissism to Social Control." In CHANGE AND CONTINUITY IN TWENTIETH-CENTURY AMERICA: THE 1920S, edited by John Braeman, Robert H. Bremner, and David Brody, pp. 351-98. Columbus: Ohio University Press, 1968.

_____. "On the Origins of Behaviorism." JOURNAL OF THE HISTORY OF THE BEHAVIORAL SCIENCES 4 (April 1968): 143-51.

Argues that the origins of behaviorism were complex, and many individuals other than John B. Watson contributed to its origin and development. "Rather than founder, Watson is better viewed as the charismatic leader of behaviorism."

Calverton, V.F. "The Rise of Objective Psychology." PSYCHOLOGICAL REVIEW 31 (September 1944): 418-26.

Dzendolet, Ernest. "Behaviorism and Sensation in the Paper by Beer, Bethe, and Von Uexkuell (1899)." JOURNAL OF THE HISTORY OF THE BEHAVIORAL SCIENCES 3 (July 1967): 256-61.

Presents a translation of an 1899 paper, "Proposals Toward an Objective Nomenclature in the Psychology of the Nervous System," which contributed to the development of comparative psychology and anticipated behavioristic psychology.

Fraisse, Paul. "French Origins of the Psychology of Behavior: The Contribution of Henri Piéron." JOURNAL OF THE HISTORY OF THE BEHAVIORAL SCIENCES 6 (April 1970): 111-19.

Points out how provincial the interpretation of the origins of behaviorism typically is in the United States. Mentions Russian contributions and the origins, development, and major ideas of the behaviorism of Henri Piéron who, as early as "1907, claimed that psychology could only be the science of behavior."

Gottlieb, Gilbert. "Zing-Yang Kuo: Radical Scientific Philosopher and Innovative Experimentalist (1809-1970)." JOURNAL OF COMPARATIVE AND PHYSIOLOGICAL PSYCHOLOGY 80, no. 1 (1972): 1-10.

Gussin, Arnold E.S. "Jacques Loeb: The Man and His Tropism Theory of Animal Conduct." JOURNAL OF THE HISTORY OF MEDICINE AND ALLIED SCIENCES 18 (October 1963): 321-36.

Discusses Loeb's theory of tropisms and some of the philosophical positions with which the theory differed.

Guttman, Norman. "On Skinner and Hull: A Reminiscence and Projection."
AMERICAN PSYCHOLOGIST 32 (May 1977): 321-28.

Harrell, Willard, and Harrison, Ross. "The Rise and Fall of Behaviorism."
JOURNAL OF GENERAL PSYCHOLOGY 18 (April 1938): 367-421.

> Traces the development of behaviorism, outlines its contributions, and
> prematurely talks of its demise. Excellent 426-item bibliography.

Kantor, J.R. "Behaviorism: Whose Image?" PSYCHOLOGICAL RECORD 13
(October 1963): 499-512.

> Discusses the metamorphosis of behaviorism from its early formal
> development and advances a systematic position that behaviorism
> and science are synonymous.

_____. "Behaviorism in the History of Psychology." PSYCHOLOGICAL
RECORD 18 (April 1968): 151-66.

> Presents a systematic account of the evolution of behaviorism in psy-
> chology. Behaviorism is defined as equivalent to the term "science,"
> and all sciences have their behaviorisms (for example, astronomy stud-
> ies interactions of stars, planets, and galaxies; biology studies organic
> processes such as photosynthesis and metabolism). Argues that behav-
> iorism has evolved through six stages from what is called archaic be-
> haviorism through Watsonian behaviorism to authentic or field behav-
> iorism.

Loeb, Jacques. "Concerning the Theory of Tropisms." JOURNAL OF EXPERI-
MENTAL ZOOLOGY 4 (February 1907): 151-56.

_____. THE MECHANISTIC CONCEPTION OF LIFE. Edited by Donald Fleming.
Cambridge, Mass.: Belknap Press of Harvard University Press, 1964. xlii, 216 p.

> Ten essays, written as lectures or journal articles, outline Loeb's deter-
> ministic and mechanistic approach. Of interest to psychologists are
> chapters on "The Significance of Tropisms for Psychology," and "Ex-
> perimental Study of the Influence of Environment on Animals." Edito-
> rial introduction and notes provide helpful perspective. Index.

_____. THE ORGANISM AS A WHOLE. FROM A PHYSICOCHEMICAL
VIEWPOINT. New York: Putnam, 1916. x, 379 p.

> A classic treatment of living organisms from the point of view of
> a leading mechanistic biologist. Index.

Muckler, Frederick A. "On the Reason of Animals: Historical Antecedents to
the Logic of Modern Behaviorism." PSYCHOLOGICAL REPORTS 12 (June 1963):
863-82.

Explores the historical background to the question of reason in animals in the works of Aristotle, Montaigne, Descartes, Bayle, and Hume.

O'Neil, W.M. "Realism and Behaviorism." JOURNAL OF THE HISTORY OF THE BEHAVIORAL SCIENCES 4 (April 1968): 152-60.

Distinguishes among realism, phenomenalism, and idealism and demonstrates the influence of the new realism upon the thought of some of the early behaviorists.

Palmer, Dorothy E. "Jacques Loeb: A Contribution to the History of Psychology." JOURNAL OF GENERAL PSYCHOLOGY 2 (January 1929): 97-114.

An appreciation of Loeb's biological and mechanistic approach to topics such as instincts, associative memory, consciousness, heredity, and human nature.

Rosenfield, Leonora Cohen. FROM BEAST-MACHINE TO MAN-MACHINE: ANIMAL SOUL IN FRENCH LETTERS FROM DESCARTES TO LA METTRIE. Enl. ed. New York: Octagon Books, 1968. xxviii, 385 p.

See section D3, p. 264, for annotation.

Skinner, B.F. "The Concept of the Reflex in the Description of Behavior." JOURNAL OF GENERAL PSYCHOLOGY 5 (October 1931): 427-58.

Contrasts the historical definition of reflex with an alternative definition. Contains considerable historical material on the concept of the reflex.

_____. "The Experimental Analysis of Operant Behavior." ANNALS OF THE NEW YORK ACADEMY OF SCIENCES 291 (18 April 1977): 374-85.

Brief overview of the development of the thought of one of America's best-known scientists.

Suppes, Patrick. "From Behaviorism to Neobehaviorism." THEORY AND DECISION 6 (August 1975): 269-85.

Swartz, Paul. "A Rose for Behaviorism." PSYCHOLOGICAL REPORTS 27 (October 1970): 364.

Notes that Marcel Proust in his LE COTE DE GUERMANTES anticipated behavioristic thought on the reinforcing effects of anxiety reduction.

Walsh, Anthony A. "George Combe: A Portrait of a Heretofore Generally Unknown Behaviorist." JOURNAL OF THE HISTORY OF THE BEHAVIORAL SCIENCES 7 (July 1971): 269-78.

Provides a brief review of the life and works of Combe with emphasis on his commitment to phrenology and his anticipation of behaviorism.

Wesley, Frank. "Was Raehlmann the First Behaviorist?" JOURNAL OF THE HISTORY OF THE BEHAVIORAL SCIENCES 4 (April 1968): 161-62.

> Reports on the work of E. Raehlmann, a German ophthalmologist, who conducted infant conditioning experiments in color vision as early as 1890, and who embraced axioms that anticipated behaviorism.

c. Criticisms of Behaviorism

Alston, William P. "Can Psychology Do Without Private Data?" BEHAVIOR-ISM 1 (1972): 71-102.

Berman, Louis. THE RELIGION CALLED BEHAVIORISM. New York: Boni and Liveright, 1927. viii, 153 p.

> A simplistic, popular low-level critique.

Bode, B.H. "Psychology as a Science of Behavior." PSYCHOLOGICAL RE-VIEW 21 (January 1914): 46-61.

> Comments on some of the methodological and philosophical problems encountered by behavioral and structural psychologies.

Braud, William. "Mannheim's Critique of Behaviorism." PSYCHOLOGICAL RECORD 17 (April 1967): 251-56.

> Argues that a critique of behaviorism found in Karl Mannheim's MAN AND SOCIETY IN AN AGE OF RECONSTRUCTION; STUDIES IN MODERN SOCIAL STRUCTURE (London: K. Paul, Trench, Trubner and Co., 1940), shows a "misunderstanding of the abstract nature of scientific explanation." Suggests that Mannheim fails to discriminate between critical terms such as "ideology" and "rationale" and that this failure leads to simplification and inconsistency.

Burt, Cyril. "The Concept of Consciousness." BRITISH JOURNAL OF PSY-CHOLOGY 53 (August 1962): 229-42.

> A critique of an exclusively behavioristic psychology arguing that consciousness as a subject, and introspection as a method of observation, should be included as part of psychological science.

_____. "Consciousness and Behaviourism: A Reply." BRITISH JOURNAL OF PSYCHOLOGY 55 (February 1964): 93-96.

> A response to Keehn's article (see below, this section, p. 170) and a reiteration of Burt's earlier position (in "The Concept of Consciousness," see above, this page) regarding the inability of behaviorism to account for human experience.

Carini, Louis. "The Aristotelian Basis of Hull's Behavior Theory." JOURNAL OF THE HISTORY OF THE BEHAVIORAL SCIENCES 4 (January 1968): 109-18.

Aruges that Hull's behavior system is Aristotelian and that it must be "discarded if psychology is to become a science in the sense that physics can be said to be scientific." Contrasts Hull's theory with Newtonian physics.

Erickson, Ralph W. "An Examination of Edward C. Tolman's System of Psychology." JOURNAL OF GENERAL PSYCHOLOGY 39 (July 1948): 73-90.

Identifies the major constructs of Tolman's behaviorism and contrasts selected constructs with classical behaviorism. Concludes that Tolman's system is beset with confusion and contradictions and, in general, is less desirable than Watsonian behaviorism.

Eysenck, H.J. "The Concept of Mind: A Behaviouristic Approach." JOURNAL OF PSYCHOLOGICAL RESEARCHES 5 (1961): 37-47.

Fine, Reuben. "The Logic of Psychology." PSYCHOANALYSIS AND THE PSYCHOANALYTIC REVIEW 45 (Winter 1958-59): 15-41.

An exposition and discussion of what the author views as errors in the experimentalist-behaviorist tradition followed by an outline of a more inclusive and positive approach to psychology.

Gregory, J.C. "Three Witnesses Against Behaviorism." PHILOSOPHICAL REVIEW 31 (November 1922): 581-92.

Gundlach, R. "Some Difficulties with Weiss's Behavioristic Postulates." AMERICAN JOURNAL OF PSYCHOLOGY 38 (July 1927): 469-75.

Ions, Edmund. AGAINST BEHAVIOURALISM: A CRITIQUE OF BEHAVIOURAL SCIENCE. Totowa, N.J.: Rowman and Littlefield, 1977. xiii, 165 p.

A broad critique not only of the thought of specific behaviorists such as B.F. Skinner, but also of the application of behavioristic thought to such areas as jurisprudence, political science, anthropology, and psychology. Index.

Johnson, Rochelle J. "Discussion: A Commentary on 'Radical Behaviorism.'" PHILOSOPHY OF SCIENCE 30 (July 1963): 274-85.

Criticizes an earlier critique of Skinner by M. Scriven (see below, this section, p. 172) for its failure to recognize the positive features in Skinner's methodology and for its apparent confusion between ordinary meanings of words and the scientific-explanatory values of terms.

Keehn, J.D. "Consciousness and Behaviourism." BRITISH JOURNAL OF PSYCHOLOGY 55 (February 1964): 89-91.

Argues that Skinnerian behaviorism can account for conscious experience and that "private events" can be brought under control.

King, William P., ed. BEHAVIORISM: A BATTLE LINE. Nashville, Tenn.: Cokesbury Press, 1930. 376 p.

Seventeen symposium papers attack presumed weaknesses of behaviorism under three topic areas: general principles, behaviorism and value, and behaviorism and metaphysics. Minimal reference material.

Knopfelmacher, F. "Types of Behaviour Theory." AUSTRALIAN JOURNAL OF PSYCHOLOGY 17 (December 1965): 167-78.

Examines introspective, behavioristic, and sociological approaches to behavior theory with emphasis on a critique of behaviorism.

Locke, Edwin A. "Critical Analysis of the Concept of Causality in Behavioristic Psychology." PSYCHOLOGICAL REPORTS 31 (August 1972): 175-97.

MacKenzie, Brian D. "Behaviorism and Positivism." JOURNAL OF THE HISTORY OF THE BEHAVIORAL SCIENCES 8 (April 1972): 222-31.

Documents disillusionment with behaviorism in citations of published critiques, attrition in the ranks of behaviorists, development of the "third force," and changes in kinds of published articles. Concludes that behaviorism did not provide a paradigmatic base for psychology and that it "is not a scientific system and has hitherto prevented one from developing."

Mischel, Theodore. "Psychology and Explanations of Human Behaviour." PHILOSOPHY AND PHENOMENOLOGICAL RESEARCH 23 (June 1963): 578-94.

Argues that behavioral explanations are inadequate.

Mishler, Elliot G. "Skinnerism: Materialism Minus the Dialectic." JOURNAL FOR THE THEORY OF SOCIAL BEHAVIOR 6 (April 1976): 21-47.

Mursell, James L. "The Stimulus Response Relation." PSYCHOLOGICAL REVIEW 29 (March 1922): 146-62.

Notes that the basic assumption of behaviorism is that all the subject matter of psychology can be reduced to stimulus-response relations. Argues for a broader conception of behaviorism which includes experience, as well as for a tolerant view which admits the legitimacy of both structuralism and behaviorism.

Prytula, Robert E.; Oster, Gerald D.; and Davis, Stephen F. "The 'Rat-Rabbit' Problem: What Did John B. Watson Really Do?" TEACHING OF PSYCHOLOGY 4 (February 1977): 44-46.

Richelle, Marc. "Formal Analysis and Functional Analysis of Verbal Behavior: Notes on the Debate Between Chomsky and Skinner." BEHAVIORISM 4 (Fall 1976): 209-21.

Rife, David C., and Snyder, Laurence H. "Studies in Human Inheritance. VI. A Genetic Refutation of the Principles of 'Behavioristic' Psychology." HUMAN BIOLOGY, A RECORD OF RESEARCH 3 (December 1931): 547-59.

Roback A[braham].A. BEHAVIORISM AND PSYCHOLOGY. Cambridge, Mass.: University Bookstore, 1923. 284 p.

   Discussions of the antecedents and varieties of behaviorism followed by a critique of behaviorism. Relates behaviorism to ethics, jurisprudence, medicine, religion, intelligence, and group processes. Predicts inaccurately a dim future for behaviorism. Reference list of 238 items. Index.

_____. BEHAVIORISM AT TWENTY-FIVE. Cambridge, Mass.: Sci-Art Publishers, 1937. 256 p.

   A strongly-worded polemic designed to expose the weaknesses of behaviorism. Bibliography. Index.

Santayana, George. "Living Without Thinking." FORUM 68 (September 1922): 731-35.

Scriven, Michael. "A Study of Radical Behaviorism." In MINNESOTA STUDIES IN THE PHILOSOPHY OF SCIENCE. Vol. 1, THE FOUNDATIONS OF SCIENCE AND THE CONCEPTS OF PSYCHOLOGY AND PSYCHOANALYSIS, edited by Herbert Feigl and Michael Scriven, pp. 88-130. Minneapolis: University of Minnesota Press, 1956.

   A critique of major assumptions and implications of Skinner's theory.

Smedslund, Jan. "The Epistemological Foundations of Behaviorism. A Critique." ACTA PSYCHOLOGICA 11 (1955): 412-31.

Thurstone, L.L. "The Stimulus-Response Fallacy in Psychology." PSYCHOLOGICAL REVIEW 30 (September 1923): 354-69.

   Comments on the simplistic character of S-R psychology and argues for a more complex psychology that considers the psychological act in terms of such processes as deliberate ideation, energy sources, internal and external stimuli, and needs.

Titchener, E[dward].B[radford]. "On Psychology as the Behaviorist Views It." PROCEEDINGS OF THE AMERICAN PHILOSOPHICAL SOCIETY 53 (January-May 1914): 1-17.

Varvel, Walter A. "A Gestalt Critique of Purposive Behaviorism." PSYCHO-
LOGICAL REVIEW 41 (July 1934): 381-99.

Watson, John B., and Durant, Will. "Is Man a Machine? A Socratic Dialogue." FORUM 82 (November 1929): 264-70.

> A famous philosopher and the founder of behaviorism argue about
> the mechanistic approach to human beings.

Watson, John B., and McDougall, William. THE BATTLE OF BEHAVIORISM:
AN EXPOSITION AND EXPOSURE. New York: W.W. Norton, 1929. v,
96 p.

> Contains materials presented as a debate before the Washington,
> D.C., Psychological Club in 1924. In the first part John B. Watson
> outlines the essential features of behaviorism. In the second part
> in a postscript William McDougall offers a strongly-worded critique
> of behaviorism with emphasis upon areas such as daydreams, think-
> ing, and purposive striving which, in McDougall's opinion, are
> troublesome for behaviorism.

Wickham, Harvey. THE MISBEHAVIORISTS: PSEUDOSCIENCE AND THE MOD-
ERN TEMPER. New York: Lincoln Mac Veagh, Dial Press, 1928. 294 p.

> A polemical work directed not only against classical behaviorism
> but also against McDougall's psychology, psychoanalysis, and
> other systems. Other critiques that are academically more sound
> are available.

Wiest, William M. "Some Recent Criticisms of Behaviorism and Learning
Theory: With Special Reference to Breger and McGaugh and to Chomsky."
PSYCHOLOGICAL BULLETIN 67 (March 1967): 214-25.

> A defense of behaviorism pointing to weaknesses in earlier criti-
> cisms of the system.

d. Behavioristic Interpretations of Selected Subject Matter Areas in Psychology

Broadbent, D.E. BEHAVIOUR. New York: Basic Books, 1961. 215 p.

> An overview of progress in the understanding of behavior with
> emphasis on such topics as conflict, anxiety, problem solving,
> brain and behavior, and motivation. Index.

Champagne, Paul, and Tausky, Curt. "Alternative Perspectives in Education:
The Radical School or Reinforcement Theory?" BEHAVIORISM 4 (Fall 1976):
231-43.

Chandra, Satish. "Repression, Dreaming and Primary Process Thinking: Skinnerian Formulations of Some Freudian Facts." BEHAVIORISM 4 (Spring 1976): 53-75.

Cullen, C.N. "'Behaviorism and Education': A Reply." ASSOCIATION OF EDUCATIONAL PSYCHOLOGISTS JOURNAL 3 (Summer 1975): 35-38.

Dashiell, J.F. "A Physiological-Behavioristic Description of Thinking." PSYCHOLOGICAL REVIEW 32 (January 1925): 54-73.

De Laguna, Grace A. "Emotion and Perception From the Behaviorist Standpoint." PSYCHOLOGICAL REVIEW 26 (November 1919): 409-27.

> Points out that behaviorism has studied the behavior of lower animals and stirred controversy over the problem of consciousness, but has failed to deal effectively with classical topics such as sensation, perception, emotion, volition, and thought. Notes that there are signs of progress in dealing with these topics and contributes a brief behavioristic account of perception and emotion.

Goss, Albert E. "Early Behaviorism and Verbal Mediating Responses." AMERICAN PSYCHOLOGIST 16 (July 1961): 285-98.

> Describes positions of such early behaviorists as Watson, Tolman, Hull, Meyer, Hunter, Dashiell, and Kantor on such topics as verbal mediation, language and symbolism, consciousness, purpose, and thinking.

Graham, C.H. "Sensation and Perception in an Objective Psychology." PSYCHOLOGICAL REVIEW 65 (March 1958): 65-76.

Gray, George W. "Thinking Machines." HARPER'S MAGAZINE, March 1936, pp. 416-25.

> A popular article describing some learning robots, largely based on Clark Hull's theory.

Gray, J. S[tanley]. "A Behavioristic Interpretation of Concept Formation." PSYCHOLOGICAL REVIEW 38 (January 1931): 65-72.

> Reviews Thorndike's account of concept formation and contrasts it with Gray's behavioristic view.

_____. "A Behavioristic Interpretation of Intelligence." PSYCHOLOGICAL REVIEW 39 (May 1932): 271-78.

Gray, Philip Howard. "Prerequisite to an Analysis of Behaviorism: The Conscious Automaton Theory from Spalding to William James." JOURNAL OF THE HISTORY OF THE BEHAVIORAL SCIENCES 4 (October 1968): 365-76.

Discusses materialistic approaches to the mind-body problem and the related problem of free will and determinism. Comments on the contributions of Spinoza, La Mettrie, Tyndall, Spalding, Thomas Huxley, James, and others.

Greenspoon, Joel, and Brownstein, Aaron J. "Psychotherapy from the Standpoint of a Behaviorist." PSYCHOLOGICAL RECORD 17 (July 1967): 401-16.

Defines the terms "behavior" and "abnormal behavior" and the nature of psychotherapeutic problems and types of controlling stimuli, with emphasis on verbal stimuli. Unlike some earlier behaviorist writings, this position recognizes contributions from other disciplines such as genetics, neurology, and biochemistry.

Herrnstein, R.J. "Nature as Nurture: Behaviorism and the Instinct Doctrine." BEHAVIORISM 1 (1972): 23-52.

Hunter, Walter S. "The Problem of Consciousness." PSYCHOLOGICAL REVIEW 31 (January 1924): 1-31.

_____. "A Reformulation of the Law of Association." PSYCHOLOGICAL REVIEW 24 (May 1917): 188-96.

A "semibehaviorist" account of association. Attempts to "render explicit certain facts and points of view that the writer finds implicit in current psychological thinking." Brief statements on views of association advanced by Aristotle, Hartley, Titchener, Angell, Calkins, and others.

Hunter, W[alter].S., and Hudgins, C.V. "Voluntary Activity from the Standpoint of Behaviorism." ACTA PSYCHOLOGICA, HAGUE 1 (1935): 111-18.

Jones, Mary Cover. "Albert, Peter, and John B. Watson." AMERICAN PSYCHOLOGIST 29 (August 1974): 581-83.

Brief reminiscences on research on desensitization of a fear response and on Watson's personal qualities.

Krantz, David L.; Hall, Richard; and Allen, David. "William McDougall and the Problem of Purpose." JOURNAL OF THE HISTORY OF THE BEHAVIORAL SCIENCES 5 (January 1969): 25-38.

See annotation in section C8, p. 159.

Kuo, Zing-Yang. "The Net Result of the Anti-Hereditary Movement in Psychology." PSYCHOLOGICAL REVIEW 36 (May 1929): 181-99.

Discusses the salient arguments by those who defend and those who attack the concept of instinct. Concludes with a restatement of the author's systematic anti-heredity position.

_____. "A Psychology Without Heredity." PSYCHOLOGICAL REVIEW 31 (November 1924): 427–48.

Lachman, Sheldon J. PSYCHOSOMATIC DISORDERS: A BEHAVIORISTIC INTERPRETATION. New York: John Wiley and Sons, 1972. xi, 208 p.

Lashley, K.S. "The Behavioristic Interpretation of Consciousness I." PSYCHOLOGICAL REVIEW 30 (July 1923): 237–72.

   A brief resume of behavioristic approaches to consciousness followed by a detailed attempt to show that the problems of consciousness are no more insurmountable for the behaviorist than for the mentalist. Notes "as complete an account of the attributes of consciousness can be given in behavioristic terms as can be given in subjective terms as the result of introspective study."

_____. "The Behavioristic Interpretation of Consciousness II." PSYCHOLOGICAL REVIEW 30 (September 1923): 329–53.

   Continues the argument of the preceding entry.

Miles, T.R. ELIMINATING THE UNCONSCIOUS: A BEHAVIORIST VIEW OF PSYCHOANALYSIS. Long Island City, N.Y.: Pergamon Press, 1966. xviii, 171 p.

   See section 12C, p. 211, for annotation.

Norris, Orland O. "A Behaviorist Account of Consciousness." JOURNAL OF PHILOSOPHY 26 (January 1929): 29–43, 57–67.

   Part I treats the awareness aspects of consciousness; part II treats its qualitative aspect.

_____. "A Behaviorist Account of Intelligence." JOURNAL OF PHILOSOPHY 25 (December 1928): 701–14.

O'Brien, G.E. "Behaviorism and Explanation." AUSTRALIAN JOURNAL OF PSYCHOLOGY 18 (December 1966): 197–209.

   Argues in support of a behavioristic methodology in psychology.

Perry, Ralph Barton. "A Behavioristic View of Purpose." JOURNAL OF PHILOSOPHY 18 (February 1921): 85–105.

Seeman, William. "On a Behavioristic Approach to the Concept of Wish-Fulfillment." JOURNAL OF ABNORMAL AND SOCIAL PSYCHOLOGY 47 (January 1952): 17–24.

Throne, John M. "Learning Disabilities: A Radical Behaviorist Point of View." SCHOOL PSYCHOLOGY DIGEST 5 (Winter 1976): 41–45.

Tolman, Edward Chace. "Behaviorism and Purpose." JOURNAL OF PHILOSO-
PHY 22 (January 1925): 36-41.

_____. "A Behaviorist Account of the Emotions." PSYCHOLOGICAL REVIEW
30 (May 1923): 217-27.

_____. "A Behavioristic Theory of Ideas." PSYCHOLOGICAL REVIEW 33
(September 1926): 352-69.

_____. "A Behaviorist's Definition of Consciousness." PSYCHOLOGICAL RE-
VIEW 34 (November 1927): 433-39.

_____. "Concerning the Sensation Quality: A Behavioristic Account." PSY-
CHOLOGICAL REVIEW 29 (March 1922): 140-45.

Tolman argues that "raw feels" or "qualia" themselves do not get
into psychological science; what does get in is behavioral manifestations or potentialities of "qualia."

Turner, M[erle].B. PSYCHOLOGY AND THE PHILOSOPHY OF SCIENCE.
New York: Appleton-Century-Crofts, 1968. xi, 240 p.

Examines the philosophical aspects of and problems with behavioristic psychology. Extensive scholarly notes and a lengthy list of
references. Index.

Watson, John B. "The Behaviorist Looks at Instincts." HARPER'S MAGAZINE,
July 1927, pp. 228-35.

_____. "How We Think: A Behaviorist's View." HARPER'S MAGAZINE,
June 1926, pp. 40-45.

A brief, popular account of Watson's well-known motor theory of
thinking.

_____. "Memory as the Behaviorist Sees It." HARPER'S MAGAZINE, July
1926, pp. 244-50.

_____. "The Myth of the Unconscious: A Behavioristic Explanation." HARP-
ER'S MAGAZINE, September 1927, pp. 507-8.

_____. "Recent Experiments with Homing Birds." HARPER'S MAGAZINE,
August 1915, pp. 457-64.

Watson, John B., and Durant, Will. "Can We Make Our Children Behave?
John B. Watson vs. Will Durant." THE FORUM 82 (December 1929): 346-50.

_____. "Is Man a Machine?: A Socratic Dialogue. John B. Watson vs. Will Durant." THE FORUM 82 (November 1929): 264-70.

Welch, Livingston. "A Behaviorist Explanation of Concept Formation." JOURNAL OF GENETIC PSYCHOLOGY 71 (December 1947): 201-22.

_____. "The Inclusion of Both Physiological and Acquired Needs in a Behavioristic System." JOURNAL OF GENERAL PSYCHOLOGY 35 (July 1946): 87-97.

   Argues that acquired needs fit within a behavioristic framework as easily as physiological needs, and that all motivation can be explained in terms of physiological and acquired needs.

Woolbert, C[harles].H. "A Behavioristic Account of Intellect and Emotions." PSYCHOLOGICAL REVIEW 31 (July 1924): 265-72.

_____. "A Behavioristic Account of Sleep." PSYCHOLOGICAL REVIEW 27 (November 1920): 420-28.

10. RUSSIAN MATERIALISTIC PSYCHOLOGIES

ACADEMY OF SCIENCES OF THE USSR: SCIENTIFIC SESSION ON THE PHYSIOLOGICAL TEACHINGS OF ACADEMICIAN I.P. PAVLOV, JUNE 28-JULY 4, 1950; INAUGURAL ADDRESS, REPORTS, RESOLUTION. Moscow: Foreign Languages Publishing House, 1951. 173 p.

Bechterev, Vladimir Michailovitch. GENERAL PRINCIPLES OF HUMAN REFLEXOLOGY: AN INTRODUCTION TO THE OBJECTIVE STUDY OF PERSONALITY. Translated by Emma and William Murphy. New York: International Publishers, 1932. 467 p.

Borovski, V.M. "Psychology in the U.S.S.R." JOURNAL OF GENERAL PSYCHOLOGY 2 (April-July 1929): 177-86.

   Discusses problems and progress in the development of a psychology consistent with the dialectical materialist philosophy.

Brožek, Josef, and Slobin, Dan I., eds. PSYCHOLOGY IN THE U.S.S.R.: AN HISTORICAL PERSPECTIVE. White Plains, N.Y.: International Arts and Sciences Press, 1972. x, 301 p.

   See annotation in section B5bxi, p. 80.

Frolov, Y.P. PAVLOV AND HIS SCHOOL. New York: Oxford University

Press, 1931. Reprint. Chicago, Ill.: Johnson Reprint Corp., 1970. xix, 291 p.

Gibbons, J., ed. I.P. PAVLOV: SELECTED WORKS. Translated by S. Belsky. Moscow: Foreign Languages Publishing House, n.d. 662 p.

> A somewhat haphazard collection of a brief autobiography, letters, public addresses, lectures, and statements from Pavlov's "Wednesday gatherings" on such topics as digestion, sleep and hypnosis, theory of types, physiology and psychology, experimental pathology of the higher nervous system, and criticisms of Gestalt psychology.

Hac, Pham Minh. "View of Soviet Psychologists on Behaviorism." PSYCHOLOGIA 19 (September 1976): 163-72.

> Reviews criticisms of behaviorism by such Russian psychologists as Kornilov, Vygotski, and Rubinstein.

Kimble, Gregory A. "Sechenov and the Anticipation of Conditioning Theory." In FOUNDATIONS OF CONDITIONING AND LEARNING, edited by G.A. Kimble, pp. 3-21. New York: Appleton-Century-Crofts, 1967.

Liddell, H.S. "Pavlov's Contribution to Psychology." PSYCHOLOGICAL BULLETIN 33 (October 1936): 583-90.

> Notes Pavlov's contribution to learning theory, his influence on behaviorism, and his role in sensitizing psychologists to the importance of physiology.

London, Ivan D. "A Historical Survey of Psychology in the Soviet Union." PSYCHOLOGICAL BULLETIN 46 (July 1949): 241-77.

> Traces the historical development of psychology in the Soviet Union from pre-Marxist thought to the gradual development of a dialectical psychology based on Marxist assumptions. Sets forth basic principles of that psychology. References.

Lowry, Richard. "The Reflex Model in Psychology: Origins and Evolution." JOURNAL OF THE HISTORY OF THE BEHAVIORAL SCIENCES 6 (January 1970): 64-69.

> See annotation in section D6, p. 292.

McLeish, John. SOVIET PSYCHOLOGY: HISTORY, THEORY, CONTENT. London: Methuen and Co., Ltd., 1975. xii, 308 p.

> "This is the first book in any language, including Russian, to provide a detailed analysis of the relationship between Russian philosophy and psychology, as it developed from 1750, and contemporary Soviet psychology." Topics investigated include Tsarist ideology, origins of Soviet psychology, methodological foundations of Soviet

psychology, Soviet psychology in the Stalin era, Soviet work on
selected content areas such as emotion, speech, and individual differences. A final chapter briefly compares Soviet, British, American, and European psychologies. Bibliography. Index.

O'Connor, N[eil]., ed. RECENT SOVIET PSYCHOLOGY. Translated by Ruth
Kisch, R. Crawford, and H. Asher. New York: Liveright, 1961. 334 p. Index.

See annotation in section B5bxi, p. 82.

Pavlov, Ivan P. CONDITIONED REFLEXES: AN INVESTIGATION OF THE
PHYSIOLOGICAL ACTIVITY OF THE CEREBRAL CORTEX. Translated by G.V.
Anrep. London: Oxford University Press, 1927. Reprint. New York: Dover
Publications, 1960. xv, 430 p. Index.

_____. EXPERIMENTAL PSYCHOLOGY AND OTHER ESSAYS. New York:
Philosophical Library, 1957. 653 p.

Includes Pavlov's autobiography, a comment by Kh.S. Koshtoyants
on the significance of Pavlov's work, and papers representing
Pavlov's work on blood circulation, digestion, higher nervous activity, theory of types, sleep and hypnosis, physiology and psychology,
pathology of the nervous system, physiology and psychiatry, and
statements from his Wednesday gatherings.

_____. LECTURES ON CONDITIONED REFLEXES. 2 vols. Translated and
edited by W. Horsley Gantt. New York: International Publishers, 1928, 1941.
414 p.; 199 p.

Volume 1, a brief biographical sketch of Pavlov written by the
editor. Followed by Pavlov's lectures on such topics as experimental neuroses, sleep, results of removal of parts of the cerebral
hemispheres, hypnotism, and the physiology of the cerebral hemispheres. Volume 2, Pavlov's writings after his seventy-fifth birthday. Focuses on applications of his work to psychiatry. Indexes
follow each volume.

_____. "The Reply of a Physiologist to Psychologists." PSYCHOLOGICAL RE-
VIEW 39 (March 1932): 91-127.

Criticizes theories and procedures advanced by psychologists Guthrie,
Lashley, and Koehler.

Payne, T.R. S.L. RUBENSTEJN AND THE PHILOSOPHICAL FOUNDATIONS OF
SOVIET PSYCHOLOGY. Dordrecht, Holland: D. Reidel, 1968. x, 184 p.

Discusses historical origins and philosophical bases of Soviet psychological theory. The works of S.L. Rubenstejn (1889-1960), one
of the most important psychological writers in the Soviet Union,

constitute the primary source. Includes a selected bibliography and
a list of books and articles by Rubenstejn. Index.

Phillips, Shelley. "The Contributions of L.S. Vygotsky to Cognitive Psychology." ALBERTA JOURNAL OF EDUCATIONAL RESEARCH 23 (March 1977):
31-42.

Rahmani, Levy. SOVIET PSYCHOLOGY: PHILOSOPHICAL, THEORETICAL,
AND EXPERIMENTAL ISSUES. New York: International Universities Press,
1973. viii, 440 p.

    Describes selected topics in Soviet psychology such as the nature
    of the psyche, sensory processes, thought and language, memory,
    emotions, will and voluntary activity, and personality. Includes
    an overview of the history of twentieth-century Soviet psychology.

Razran, G[regory].H.S. "K.N. Kornilov, Theoretical and Experimental Psychologist." SCIENCE 128 (July 1958): 74-75.

_____. "Psychology in the U.S.S.R." JOURNAL OF PHILOSOPHY 32 (Janu-
ary 1935): 19-24.

_____. "Russian Physiologists' Psychology and American Experimental Psychol-
ogy: A Historical and a Systematic Collation and a Look Into the Future."
PSYCHOLOGICAL BULLETIN 63 (January 1965): 42-64.

    An overview of contributions of such Russian scholars as Bekhterev,
    Sechenov, and Pavlov with special emphasis on Pavlov's influence
    on American psychological thought.

_____. "Soviet Psychology and Psychophysiology." BEHAVIORAL SCIENCE
4 (January 1959): 35-48.

    An account of a visit by Razran with Pavlov in 1934 followed by
    an overview of Russian psychology and its primary areas of research
    and doctrine. Compares Russian and American psychology.

Schniermann, A.L. "Present-Day Tendencies in Russian Psychology." JOUR-
NAL OF GENERAL PSYCHOLOGY 1 (July-October 1928): 397-404.

    Outlines the materialistic approaches of Pavlov, Bekhterev,
    and Kornilov.

Sechenov, Ivan Mikhailovich. I.M. SECHENOV: BIOGRAPHICAL SKETCH
AND ESSAYS. New York: Arno Press, 1973. xxxvi, 489 p.

Subkov, A.A., ed. MEMORIAL VOLUME OF SELECTED WORKS OF I.
SECHENOV. Moscow, Leningrad: State Publishing House for Biological and
Medical Literature, 1935. xxxvi, 489 p.

Selected works of Sechenov on such topics as thinking, reflex activity, and method accompanied by a brief biographical sketch.

Wells, Harry K. PAVLOV AND FREUD. New York: International Publications, 1956. 223 p.

Part 1, entitled "Ivan P. Pavlov: Toward a Scientific Psychology and Psychiatry," introduces Pavlovian concepts and applies them to clinical problems. Emphasizes the significance of Pavlov's contribution. Part 2 entitled "Sigmund Freud: A Pavlovian Critique."

11. GESTALT PSYCHOLOGY

The Gestalt approach in psychology (not to be confused with gestalt psychotherapy as developed by Frederick Perls and others) flourished independently of structuralism, functionalism, and behaviorism, and contrasted itself with them. Devoted to the experimental method just as much as the other three schools, it nevertheless developed a different theoretical approach. This section is subdivided into origins, basic works, and general overviews; a small set of anthologies; evaluations, critiques, and replies; and Gestalt interpretations of selected topics in psychology.

a. Origins, Basic Works, and General Overviews

Anderson, Robert M. "Wholistic and Particulate Approaches in Neuropsychology." In COGNITION AND THE SYMBOLIC PROCESSES, edited by Walter B. Weimer, Jr., and David S. Palmero, pp. 388-96. Hillsdale, N.J.: Lawrence Erlbaum, 1974.

Asch, Solomon E. "Max Wertheimer's Contribution to Modern Psychology." SOCIAL RESEARCH 13 (March 1946): 81-102.

Blackburn, J.M. "A Review of Gestalt Psychology." JOURNAL OF MENTAL SCIENCE 86 (1940): 1-28.

Boring, Edwin G. "The Gestalt Psychology and the Gestalt Movement." AMERICAN JOURNAL OF PSYCHOLOGY 42 (April 1930): 308-15.

Carini, Louis. "A Reassessment of Max Wertheimer's Contribution to Psychological Theory." ACTA PSYCHOLOGICA, AMSTERDAM 32 (August 1970): 377-85.

Commins, W.D. "Some Early Holistic Psychologists." JOURNAL OF PHILOSOPHY 29 (April 1932): 208-17.

Reviews holistic concepts found in the thought of such theorists as Herbart, Wundt, Kuelpe, James, and Dewey.

Freeman, Frank S. "The Beginnings of Gestalt Psychology in the United States." JOURNAL OF THE HISTORY OF THE BEHAVIORAL SCIENCES 13 (October 1977): 352-53.

> Points out that Robert Morris Ogden was instrumental in bringing Gestalt psychology to America through his writing and translating, and by inviting Gestalt psychologists to fill academic positions at Cornell University.

Gibson, James J. "The Legacies of Koffka's Principles." JOURNAL OF THE HISTORY OF THE BEHAVIORAL SCIENCES 7 (January 1971): 3-9.

> A commemorative article on selected topics in Koffka's PRINCIPLES OF GESTALT PSYCHOLOGY (see below, this section, p. 186).

Goldstein, Kurt. THE ORGANISM, A HOLISTIC APPROACH TO BIOLOGY DERIVED FROM PATHOLOGICAL DATA IN MAN. 2d ed. Boston: Beacon Press, 1963. xx, 553 p.

> A classic work in the Gestalt tradition which emphasizes a holistic approach to the understanding of life processes.

Harlow, R.F. "Philosophy's Contribution to Gestalt Psychology." JOURNAL OF PSYCHOLOGY 5 (1938): 185-200.

Harrower, Molly. "A Note on the Koffka Papers." JOURNAL OF THE HISTORY OF THE BEHAVIORAL SCIENCES 7 (April 1971): 141-53.

> Outlines materials which were in the research laboratory at Smith College at the time of Koffka's death, including unpublished lectures, letters, notes on experiments, and a play written by Koffka concerning his own death. The author served as executrix of Koffka's estate.

Hartmann, George Wilfried. GESTALT PSYCHOLOGY: A SURVEY OF FACTS AND PRINCIPLES. New York: Ronald Press, 1935. xiii, 325 p.

Heider, Fritz. "Gestalt Theory: Early History and Reminiscences." JOURNAL OF THE HISTORY OF THE BEHAVIORAL SCIENCES 6 (April 1970): 131-39.

> Focuses on the contributions of such pioneers as Ehrenfels, Meinong, Benussi, Wertheimer, Koehler, and Koffka with particular attention to the "relation of Ehrenfels to the Graz school and the relation of Graz to Berlin."

_____. "On Lewin's Methods and Theory." JOURNAL OF SOCIAL ISSUES, Suppl. no. 13 (1959). 13 p.

Helson, Harry. "The Fundamental Propositions of Gestalt Psychology." PSYCHOLOGICAL REVIEW 40 (January 1933): 13-32.

_____. "The Psychology of Gestalt." AMERICAN JOURNAL OF PSYCHOL-
OGY 36 and 37 (July 1925 and January 1926): 342-70, 494-526, 189-223.

These articles (published by the author at Urbana, Illinois, in a
single volume in 1926) provided the first relatively thorough introduction of Gestalt thought to the English-speaking world.

_____. THE PSYCHOLOGY OF GESTALT. Urbana, Ill.: Author, 1926.   131 p.

Published originally as three separate articles; see preceding entry.

_____. "Why Did Their Precursors Fail and the Gestalt Psychologists Succeed?
Reflections on Theories and Theorists." AMERICAN PSYCHOLOGIST 24 (November 1969):   1006-11.

Attributes the successes of Gestalt theory to its radical departure from
established psychologies, its experimental approach with strong emphasis on facts, its focus on physiological thinking, its concentration on
descriptive theory as opposed to constructive theory, and its simplicity.

Hsiao, H.H.   "A Suggestive Review of Gestalt Psychology." PSYCHOLOGICAL
REVIEW 35 (July 1928):   280-97.

Reviews central concepts in Gestalt psychology; discusses Gestalt
treatment of such topics as learning, thought, intelligence, and
habit; and examines criticisms of Gestalt psychology.

Kantor, J[acob].R.   "The Significance of the Gestalt Conception in Psychology."
JOURNAL OF PHILOSOPHY 22 (April 1925):   234-41.

An appreciative article outlining the general characteristics and
significance of Gestalt psychology.

Katz, David.   GESTALT PSYCHOLOGY: ITS NATURE AND SIGNIFICANCE.
Translated from the 2d German edition by Robert Tyson.   New York: Ronald
Press, 1950.   x, 175 p.

Examines the Gestalt system in such content areas as thinking, memory,
space perception, and social psychology.   Discusses Gestalt methods
and contrasts Gestalt and atomistic psychology.   Bibliography.   Index.

Knox, G.W.   "Where is the Confusion?"   JOURNAL OF PSYCHOLOGY 7
(1939):   17-27.

Koehler, W[olfgang].   DYNAMICS IN PSYCHOLOGY.   1940.   Reprint.   New
York: Liveright, 1973.   158 p.

Discusses Gestalt theory and the resulting research on perception
and memory.   (An elaboration of three lectures delivered at the
University of Virginia in 1938).

_____. GESTALT PSYCHOLOGY. New York: Liveright, 1929. x, 403 p.

A comprehensive exposition of Gestalt psychology and one of the first available to the English-speaking world. Contrasts Gestalt thought with behaviorism and introspection, the major trends of the time. Bibliographies. Index.

_____. GESTALT PSYCHOLOGY. London: Bell, 1930. 312 p.

_____. GESTALT PSYCHOLOGY: AN INTRODUCTION TO NEW CONCEPTS IN MODERN PSYCHOLOGY. Rev. ed. New York: Liveright, 1947. 369 p.

_____. "Gestalt Psychology Today." AMERICAN PSYCHOLOGIST 14 (December 1959): 727-34.

Explores selected topics in the history of Gestalt psychology and various trends in American psychology with emphasis on behavioristic and Gestalt approaches to problems.

_____. THE MENTALITY OF APES. Translated from 2d. rev. ed. by Ella Winter. London: Routledge and Kegan Paul Ltd., 1956. vii, 336 p.

See section C11d, p. 195, for annotation.

_____. "The New Psychology and Physics." YALE REVIEW 19 (March 1930): 560-76.

_____. THE PLACE OF VALUE IN A WORLD OF FACTS. New York: Liveright, 1938. ix, 418 p.

Explores the problem of fact and value from the perspectives of science and philosophy. Emphasizes the inadequacies of positivism and argues for a phenomenological approach, which has a greater potential for providing a coherent framework for fact-value questions. Index.

_____. THE TASK OF GESTALT PSYCHOLOGY. Princeton, N.J.: Princeton University Press, 1969. vii, 164 p.

A posthumous book discussing early developments in Gestalt psychology, relationships between Gestalt psychology and natural science, recent developments in Gestalt psychology, and the psychology of thinking. An introduction by Carroll C. Pratt provides a brief biography. Based on four lectures delivered at Princeton University in 1966.

Koehler, W[olfgang]., and Wallach, H. "Figural Aftereffects: An Investigation of Visual Processes." PROCEEDINGS OF THE AMERICAN PHILOSOPHICAL SOCIETY 88, no. 4 (1944): 269-357.

Koffka, Kurt. THE GROWTH OF THE MIND: AN INTRODUCTION TO CHILD PSYCHOLOGY. 2d rev. ed. Translated by Robert Morris Ogden. New York: Harcourt, Brace, 1928. xix, 427 p.

> An early comprehensive text providing a survey of psychological principles useful for developmental psychologists and educators. It helped introduce Gestalt theory and research to the English-speaking world. Notes. Index.

_____. "Perception: An Introduction to the Gestalt-Theorie." PSYCHOLOGI-CAL BULLETIN 19 (October 1922): 531-85.

> The first major publication on Gestalt theory in English.

_____. PRINCIPLES OF GESTALT PSYCHOLOGY. New York: Harcourt, Brace, 1935. xi, 720 p.

> A classic systematic text, the fullest statement of the Gestalt school of psychology, discussing such topics as the task of psychology, perception, reflexes, memory, learning, society, and personality. Bibliography. Index.

Lewin, Kurt. "The Conflict Between Aristotelian and Galileian Modes of Thought in Contemporary Psychology." JOURNAL OF GENERAL PSYCHOLOGY 5 (April 1931): 141-77.

> Treats a problem in the philosophy of science relevant to the schools of psychology, namely, the contrast between Aristotelian and Galileian modes of thought and how these modes dictate procedures and problems. Argues that the Galileian will soon replace the Aristotelian mode of thought in contemporary psychology.

_____. PRINCIPLES OF TOPOLOGICAL PSYCHOLOGY. Translated by Fritz Heider and Grace M. Heider. New York: McGraw-Hill, 1936. Reprint. New York: Johnson Reprint Corp., 1969. xv, 231 p.

> The major classic statement of the influential Lewinian systematic approach to psychology, the field theory of personality, motivation, and social psychology that grew out of Gestalt theory. Bibliography. Index.

Line, W. "Gestalt Psychology in Relation to Other Psychological Systems." PSYCHOLOGICAL REVIEW 38 (September 1931): 375-91.

> Outlines intellectual antecedents of and major trends in Gestalt thought. Argues that a full evaluation of the system "must await the development of a positive program."

Miller, Arthur I. "Albert Einstein and Max Wertheimer: A Gestalt Psychologist's View of the Genesis of Special Relativity Theory." HISTORY OF SCIENCE 13 (1975): 75-103.

Moore, T.V. "Gestalt Psychology and Scholastic Philosophy. I." NEW SCHOLASTICISM 7 (1933): 298-325.

Morgan, Conwy Lloyd. EMERGENT EVOLUTION: THE GIFFORD LECTURES. New York: Holt, 1926. xii, 313 p.

Sets forth Morgan's known systematic position that collections of simple elements may have emergent qualities which could not have been predicted from the simple elements themselves. (Lectures delivered at the University of St. Andrews in 1922). Index.

Murphy, Gardner. "Kurt Lewin and Field Theory." BULLETIN OF THE MENNINGER CLINIC 30 (November 1966): 358-67.

Pastore, Nicholas. "Reevaluation of Boring on Kantian Influence, Nineteenth Century Nativism, Gestalt Psychology, and Helmholtz." JOURNAL OF THE HISTORY OF THE BEHAVIORAL SCIENCES 10 (October 1974): 375-90.

Rejects Boring's interpretation of the influence of Kant's nativism on Mueller, Hering, Stumpf, Helmholtz, Wertheimer, Koffka, and Koehler, and notes that Koffka and Koehler "disclaimed any Kantianism in the Gestalt theory of perception."

Peterman, B. THE GESTALT THEORY AND THE PROBLEM OF CONFIGURATION. Translated by M. Fortes. New York: Harcourt, Brace, 1932. xi, 344 p.

Purdy, D.M. "The Biological Psychology of Kurt Goldstein." CHARACTER AND PERSONALITY 5 (June 1937): 321-30.

Reiser, Oliver L. "Aristotelian, Galilean and Non-Aristotelian Modes of Thinking." PSYCHOLOGICAL REVIEW 46 (March 1939): 151-62.

Welcomes the rapprochement of psychology and logic brought about by Gestalt psychology, but argues that Gestalt theory still retains elements of Aristotelianism. Outlines directions for modes of thinking which are non-Aristotelian.

_____. "The Logic of Gestalt Psychology." PSYCHOLOGICAL REVIEW 38 (July 1931): 359-68.

Examines selected logical problems associated with Gestalt psychology and argues that among the various systems of psychological thought, "Gestalt theory holds out the greatest promise of being developed into a system which can explain itself in terms of its own configurational principles."

Sato, Koji. "Fifty Years of Gestalt Psychology and Behaviorism." PSYCHOLOGIA 6 (March-June 1963): 1-65.

Seven papers present general and specific overviews of Gestalt psychology and behaviorism. Authors are Wolfgang Koehler, Koji Sato, Wolfgang Metzger, Shin Nozawa, Toshio Iritani, Chu Hsiliang, and Shinkuro Iwahara and Osamu Fujita.

Squires, P.C. "A New Psychology After the Manner of Einstein." SCIENTIFIC MONTHLY 30 (February 1930): 156-63.

_____. "Some Observations by Dostoievsky and Their Bearing on the Gestalt Psychology." AUSTRALASIAN JOURNAL OF PSYCHOLOGY AND PHILOSOPHY 14 (1936): 295-300.

Taylor, H. "The Method of Gestalt Psychology." AMERICAN JOURNAL OF PSYCHOLOGY 44 (1932): 356-61.

Von Ehrenfels, Christian. "On Gestalt-Qualities." Translated by Mildred Focht. PSYCHOLOGICAL REVIEW 44 (November 1937): 521-24.

Outlines the theory of Gestalt-qualities and traces some of its origins.

Wertheimer, Max. "Gestalt Theory." SOCIAL RESEARCH 11 (February 1944): 78-99.

_____. PRODUCTIVE THINKING. Enl. ed. Ed. by Michael Wertheimer. New York: Harper and Row, 1959. x, 302 p.

See annotation in section C11d, p. 197.

Wertheimer, Michael. "Relativity and Gestalt: A Note on Albert Einstein and Max Wertheimer." JOURNAL OF THE HISTORY OF THE BEHAVIORAL SCIENCES 1 (January 1965): 86-87.

Discusses the friendship between Albert Einstein and Max Wertheimer and notes their common Weltanschauungen, including similar interests, theoretical orientations, and moral and political views.

Wheeler, R.H. "Gestalt Psychology in the Light of History." PSYCHOLOGICAL BULLETIN 32 (October 1935): 548.

_____. THE LAWS OF HUMAN NATURE: A GENERAL VIEW OF GESTALT PSYCHOLOGY. New York: Appleton, 1932. xv, 235 p.

A brief popular account of general psychology from a Gestalt perspective. Includes Wheeler's rather idiosyncratic version of what Gestalt psychology is all about. Index.

White, Ralph K. "Two Basic Postulates of Field Theory, and Their Experimental Justification." PSYCHOLOGICAL BULLETIN 38 (July 1941): 523.

Williams, R.D. "Studies in Contemporary Psychological Theory: II. What is Gestalt Psychology?" JOURNAL OF PSYCHOLOGY 6 (1938): 99-114.

b. Anthologies

Ellis, Willis D. A SOURCE BOOK OF GESTALT PSYCHOLOGY. New York: Humanities Press, 1967. xiv, 403 p.

> Condensed translations of thirty-four classic papers written between 1915 and 1929 by Gestalt psychologists on Gestalt theory in general, and on perception, animal research, thought, motivation, and pathological phenomena. Concludes with replies by Koehler and Koffka to criticisms of Gestalt theory. Index.

Henle, Mary, ed. DOCUMENTS OF GESTALT PSYCHOLOGY. Berkeley and Los Angeles: University of California Press, 1961. xi, 352 p.

> An anthology of Gestalt contributions, mainly from the 1950s, on topics in philosophy, cognitive processes, general theory, social psychology and motivation, and psychology of expression and art. References.

_____. THE SELECTED PAPERS OF WOLFGANG KOEHLER. New York: Liveright, 1971. x, 465 p.

> Selected papers covering the span of Koehler's productive life representing a range of interests such as Gestalt theory, cognitive processes, animal psychology, psychology and physiology of the brain, and natural science. Includes papers published in English for the first time. Bibliography of Koehler's writings. Index.

c. Evaluations, Critiques, and Replies

Calkins, Mary Whiton. "Critical Comments on the 'Gestalt-Theorie.'" PSYCHOLOGICAL REVIEW 33 (March 1926): 135-58.

De Laguna, G.A. "Dualism and Gestalt Psychology." PSYCHOLOGICAL REVIEW 37 (May 1930): 187-213.

Eng, Erling. "Looking Back on Kurt Lewin: From Field Theory to Action Research." JOURNAL OF THE HISTORY OF THE BEHAVIORAL SCIENCES 14 (July 1978): 228-32.

> Traces common themes in Lewin's work from 1917 to post-World War II and discusses the impact on his thought and work of the move from Germany to America.

Frank, Jerome D. "Kurt Lewin in Retrospect--A Psychiatrist's View." JOURNAL OF THE HISTORY OF THE BEHAVIORAL SCIENCES 14 (July 1978): 223-27.

> Surveys some of Lewin's achievements in theory and research, and his "largely unacknowledged" indirect contributions in application of psychological knowledge to such areas as psychotherapy, mental deficiency, and group dynamics.

Freeman, G.L. "Concerning the 'Field' in 'Field' Psychology." PSYCHOLOGICAL REVIEW 47 (September 1940): 416-24.

Garrett, Henry E. "Lewin's 'Topological' Psychology: An evaluation." PSYCHOLOGICAL REVIEW 46 (November 1939): 517-24.

> Argues that Lewin has not demonstrated that pictorial analogies and mathematical-spatial concepts contribute to understanding psychological events. Questions Lewin's characterization of certain psychological concepts as Aristotelian.

Gregg, F.M. "Materializing the Ghost of Koehler's Gestalt Psychology." PSYCHOLOGICAL REVIEW 39 (May 1932): 257-70.

Hamlyn, D.W. "Psychological Explanation and the Gestalt Hypothesis." MIND 60 (October 1951): 506-20.

Helson, Harry. "Some Remarks on Gestalt Psychology By Kurt Koffka." JOURNAL OF THE HISTORY OF THE BEHAVIORAL SCIENCES 3 (January 1967): 43-46.

> Contains a letter from Koffka to Helson which answers certain objections to Gestalt theory raised by Helson in an early series of articles on Gestalt psychology.

Henle, Mary. "The Influence of Gestalt Psychology in America." ANNALS OF THE NEW YORK ACADEMY OF SCIENCES 291 (April 1977): 3-12.

Herr, V.V. "Gestalt Psychology: Empirical or Rational?" NEW SCHOLASTICISM 17 (1943): 358-79.

Higginson, G.D. "Apparent Visual Movement and the Gestalt. I. Nine Observations Which Stand Against Wertheimer's Cortical Theory. II. The Effect Upon Visual Movement of Colored Stimulus Objects." JOURNAL OF EXPERIMENTAL PSYCHOLOGY 9 (June 1926): 228-52.

Knox, G.W. "Some Contemporary Evaluations of Current Gestalt Psychology." JOURNAL OF PSYCHOLOGY 6 (1938): 261-63.

Koffka, K[urt]. "Purpose and Gestalt: A Reply to Professor McDougall." CHARACTER AND PERSONALITY 6 (1938): 218-38.

> A reply to four earlier criticisms offered by William McDougall (see below, this page).

La Fave, Lawrence. "The Holism-Atomism Controversy: Gestalt Psychology Confronts the Revised Law of Inverse Variation." PSYCHOLOGICAL REPORTS 24 (June 1969): 699-704.

> Notes the ambiguity of the Gestalt holistic view that "the whole is equal to something besides the sum of its parts." Argues that emergent properties are psychologically but not logically new.

Lashley, K.S.; Chow, K.L.; and Semmes, Josephine. "An Examination of the Electrical Field Theory of Cerebral Integration." PSYCHOLOGICAL REVIEW 58 (March 1951): 123-56.

Leeper, R.W. LEWIN'S TOPOLOGICAL AND VECTOR PSYCHOLOGY: A DIGEST AND CRITIQUE. Eugene: University of Oregon, 1943. ix, 218 p.

Lindworsky, J. THEORETICAL PSYCHOLOGY. Translated by H.R. DeSilva. St. Louis, Mo.: Herder, 1932. viii, 145 p.

> A critique of Gestalt points of view. Advances a system based on "laws of content" and "laws of process."

Luchins, Abraham S. "An Evaluation of Some Current Criticisms of Gestalt Psychological Work on Perception." PSYCHOLOGICAL REVIEW 58 (March 1951): 69-95.

> Notes some misinterpretations of Gestalt theory by advocates of the "new look" movement in perception. Criticizes selected theoretical and empirical trends within the "new look" theory.

Lund, Frederick H. "The Phantom of the Gestalt." JOURNAL OF GENERAL PSYCHOLOGY 2 (April-July 1929): 307-21.

> An outline of major contentions of Gestalt theory followed by the criticism that Gestalt theory is ambiguous and has a nonempirical origin. Also discusses other weaknesses.

Lundholm, Helge. "Phenomenon and Observer in the Natural Philosophy of Wolfgang Koehler." CHARACTER AND PERSONALITY 11 (1942): 128-44.

McDougall, William. "Dynamics of the Gestalt Psychology." CHARACTER AND PERSONALITY 4 (1935): 232-44, 319-34; 5 (1936): 61-82, 131-48.

Maher, Brendan. "Information Redundancy and Gestalt Psychology: An His-

torical Note and Translation." JOURNAL OF THE HISTORY OF THE BEHAV-
IORAL SCIENCES 9 (January 1973): 76-85.

> A translation of "On Redundancy and Overdetermination" by Edgar
> Rubin, a Danish psychologist who worked in the Gestalt tradition,
> and of notes by Rubin's assistant Edgar Tranekjaer Rasmussen.
> Shows that they worked on information and redundancy in human
> speech many years before Shannon's 1948 work.

Margineanu, Nicolas. "Professor Lewin's Conception of Laws." JOURNAL OF
GENERAL PSYCHOLOGY 12 (1935): 397-415.

> A critique of Kurt Lewin's conception of scientific law, particularly
> of certain notions set forth in his paper on "The Conflict Between
> Aristotelian and Galileian Modes of Thought in Contemporary Psy-
> chology."

Metzger, Wolfgang. "Certain Implications of the Concept of Gestalt." AMERI-
CAN JOURNAL OF PSYCHOLOGY 40 (January 1928): 162-66.

Murphy, Gardner. "The Geometry of Mind: An Interpretation of Gestalt Psychology." HARPER'S MAGAZINE, October 1931, pp. 584-93.

> A sympathetic, popular account of Gestalt theory.

Oeser, O.A. "Critical Notice. Gestalt and the Gestalt Theory." BRITISH
JOURNAL OF PSYCHOLOGY 21 (July 1930): 73-94.

O'Neil, W.M., and Landauer, A.A. "The Phi-Phenomenon: Turning Point
or Rallying Point." JOURNAL OF THE HISTORY OF THE BEHAVIORAL SCI-
ENCES 2 (October 1966): 335-40.

> Reviews the meaning and implications of the term "phi phenomenon"
> and comments on misinterpretations of Wertheimer's classic paper on
> this kind of apparent motion.

Pillsbury, W[alter].B[owers]. "Gestalt vs. Concept as a Principle of Explanation in Psychology." JOURNAL OF ABNORMAL AND SOCIAL PSYCHOLOGY
21 (April 1926): 14-18.

_____. "The Units of Experience--Meaning or Gestalt." PSYCHOLOGICAL
REVIEW 40 (November 1933): 481-97.

Rashevsky, N. "Physico-Mathematical Aspects of the Gestalt Problem."
PHILOSOPHICAL SCIENCE 1 (1934): 409-19.

Rescher, Nicholas, and Oppenheim, Paul. "Logical Analysis of Gestalt Concepts." BRITISH JOURNAL OF THE PHILOSOPHY OF SCIENCE 6 (1955):
89-106.

Rock, Irvin. "The Present Status of Gestalt Psychology." In FESTSCHRIFT FOR GARDNER MURPHY, edited by John G. Peatman and Eugene L. Hartley, pp. 117-44. New York: Harper and Row, 1960.

> A brief overview and critique of selected concepts from Gestalt theory such as part-whole relationships, perceptual learning, problem solving, brain theory, and the law of Praegnanz. References. Index.

Spearman, Charles E. "The Confusion That is Gestalt-Psychology." AMERICAN JOURNAL OF PSYCHOLOGY 50 (November 1937): 369-83.

Squires, Paul Chatham. "A Criticism of the Configurationist's Interpretation of 'Structuralism.'" AMERICAN JOURNAL OF PSYCHOLOGY 42 (January 1930): 134-40.

Wei-tu. "A Criticism of Gestalt Psychology and Its Learning Theory." ACTA PSYCHOLOGICA SINICA 3, no. 5 (1959): 347-53.

Wheeler, Raymond Holder; Perkins, F. Theodore; and Bartley, S. Howard. "Errors in Recent Critiques of Gestalt Psychology. I. Sources of Confusion." PSYCHOLOGICAL REVIEW 38 (March 1931): 109-36.

_____. "Errors in the Critiques of Gestalt Psychology. II. Confused Interpretation of the Historical Approach." PSYCHOLOGICAL REVIEW 40 (May 1933): 221-45.

_____. "Errors in the Critiques of Gestalt Psychology. III. Inconsistencies in Thorndike's System." PSYCHOLOGICAL REVIEW 40 (July 1933): 303-23.

_____. "Errors in the Critiques of Gestalt Psychology. IV. Inconsistencies in Woodworth, Spearman and McDougall." PSYCHOLOGICAL REVIEW 40 (September 1933): 412-33.

White, Ralph K. "Has Field Theory Been 'Tried and Found Wanting?'" JOURNAL OF THE HISTORY OF THE BEHAVIORAL SCIENCES 14 (July 1978): 242-46.

> Comments on other papers in the same journal issue by Eng, Frank, and Henle (see this section, pp. 189 and 190), and concludes that, while terms such as "valence" and "vector" have been largely dropped from contemporary psychology, the essential ideas in Lewin's theory are "very much alive."

Winthrop, Henry. "Major Errors of Configurationism, With Special Reference to Gestalt Psychology." JOURNAL OF GENERAL PSYCHOLOGY 36 (1947): 139-49.

Focuses on "obscurantism" in configurationist literature with special emphasis on the concepts of "emergence" and "non-predictability."

Wyatt, Horace G. "The Gestalt Enigma." PSYCHOLOGICAL REVIEW 35 (July 1928): 298-310.

A critique of Gestalt psychology emphasizing Gestalt tendencies to substitute description for explanation.

d. Gestalt Interpretations of Selected Topics in Psychology

Arnheim, Rudolf. ART AND VISUAL PERCEPTION. Rev. ed. Berkeley and Los Angeles: University of California Press (1954), 1974. x, 508 p.

_____. "Gestalt and Art." JOURNAL OF AESTHETICS 2, no. 8 (1943): 71-75.

Chou, Siegen K. "Gestalt in Reading Chinese Characters." PSYCHOLOGICAL REVIEW 37 (January 1930): 54-70.

Ellis, Willis Davis. GESTALT PSYCHOLOGY AND MEANING. Berkeley, Calif.: Sather Gate Book Shop, 1930. xi, 172 p.

An early attempt to provide a relatively systematic overview of the Gestalt school. Concentrates on the Gestalt approach to the problem of meaning. Bibliography. Index.

Gates, Arthur I. "The Gestalt Theory in Educational Psychology." JOURNAL OF EDUCATIONAL PSYCHOLOGY 17 (December 1926): 631-37.

Goldstein, Kurt. "Organismic Approach to the Problem of Motivation." TRANSACTIONS OF THE NEW YORK ACADEMY OF SCIENCES 9 (1947): 218-30.

Hammond, Marjorie. "'Gestalttheorie': Its Significance for Teaching." BRITISH JOURNAL OF EDUCATIONAL PSYCHOLOGY 2 (June 1932): 153-72.

Heims, Steve. "Kurt Lewin and Social Change." JOURNAL OF THE HISTORY OF THE BEHAVIORAL SCIENCES 14 (July 1978): 238-41.

A brief discussion of some of Lewin's thoughts on social change and their political implications.

Henle, Mary. "Gestalt Psychology and Gestalt Therapy." JOURNAL OF THE HISTORY OF THE BEHAVIORAL SCIENCES 14 (January 1978): 23-32.

Points out major differences between classical Gestalt psychology

and the gestalt therapy described in the writings of Fritz Perls.
After demonstrating fundamental differences in philosophical assumptions, attitudes, and uses of concepts, concludes that Gestalt psychology and gestalt therapy have nothing in common.

_____. "Kurt Lewin as Metatheorist." JOURNAL OF THE HISTORY OF THE
BEHAVIORAL SCIENCES 14 (July 1978): 233-37.

A discussion of Lewin's work in motivation and personality. Argues
that Lewin was less interested in formulating a formal theory of
personality than in establishing the formal requirements for such a
theory.

_____. "On Field Forces." JOURNAL OF PSYCHOLOGY 43 (1957): 239-
49.

Discusses the importance of field forces in motivation theory.

Josey, Charles C. "The Self in the Light of Gestalt Psychology." JOURNAL
OF ABNORMAL AND SOCIAL PSYCHOLOGY 30 (April-June 1935): 47-56.

Koehler, Wolfgang. THE MENTALITY OF APES. Translated from 2d rev. ed.
by Ella Winter. London: Routledge and Kegan Paul Ltd., 1956. vii, 336 p.

Describes Koehler's classic research on intelligence, insight, and
problem-solving abilities in chimpanzees carried out on the Isle of
Tenerife from 1913 to 1917. Introduces a variety of thinking problems which chimpanzees solve in a manner consistent with the Gestalt view of the nature of thought.

_____. "On the Nature of Associations." PROCEEDINGS OF THE AMERI-
CAN PHILOSOPHICAL SOCIETY 84 (June 1941): 489-502.

_____. THE PLACE OF VALUE IN A WORLD OF FACTS. New York: Live-
right, 1938. ix, 418 p.

See section C11a, p. 185, for annotation.

_____. "Value and Fact." JOURNAL OF PHILOSOPHY 41 (April 1944):
197-212.

Lewin, Miriam A. "Kurt Lewin's View of Social Psychology: The Crisis of
1977 and the Crisis of 1927." PERSONALITY AND SOCIAL PSYCHOLOGY
BULLETIN 3 (Spring 1977): 159-72.

Luchins, Abraham S., and Luchins, Edith H. REVISITING WERTHEIMER'S
SEMINARS. Vol. 1, VALUE, SOCIAL INFLUENCE, AND POWER; Vol. 2,
PROBLEMS IN SOCIAL PSYCHOLOGY. Lewisburg, Pa.: Bucknell University
Press, 1978.

Madden, Edward H. "The Philosophy of Science in Gestalt Theory." PHILOS-
OPHY OF SCIENCE 19 (1952): 228-38.

Maier, Norman R.F. "A Gestalt Theory of Humour." BRITISH JOURNAL OF
PSYCHOLOGY 23 (July 1932): 69-74.

Miller, Arthur I. "Albert Einstein and Max Wertheimer: A Gestalt Psychologist's View of the Genesis of Special Relativity Theory." HISTORY OF SCI-
ENCE 13 (June 1975): 75-103.

O'Connell, Daniel C. "A Gestalt Law of Mental Work." JOURNAL OF
GENERAL PSYCHOLOGY 58 (January 1958): 105-9.

Ogden, R.M. "The Gestalt Psychology of Learning." JOURNAL OF GENETIC
PSYCHOLOGY 38 (1930): 280-87.

_____. "The Gestalt Theory of Learning." SCHOOL AND SOCIETY 41
(April 1935): 527-33.

_____. "Sociology and Gestalt Psychology." AMERICAN JOURNAL OF
PSYCHOLOGY 46 (October 1934): 651-55.

Schiller, Paul. "A Configurational Theory of Puzzles and Jokes." JOURNAL
OF GENERAL PSYCHOLOGY 18 (April 1938): 217-34.

Scott, Ray R. "Some Suggestions on Learning From the Point of View of Gestalt Psychology." JOURNAL OF EDUCATIONAL PSYCHOLOGY 21 (May
1930): 361-66.

Usher, Abbott Payson. A HISTORY OF MECHANICAL INVENTIONS. Rev.
ed. Cambridge, Mass.: Harvard University Press, 1954. xi, 450 p.

   Surveys the development of mechanical inventions from pre-Christian
   antiquity such as water wheels, mechanical clocks, the printing
   press, textile machinery, and machine tools. Takes a Gestalt approach to a discussion of historical, philosophical, and psychological problems associated with invention and the emergence of novel-
   ty. Bibliography. Index.

Vernon, P.E. "Auditory Perception. I. The Gestalt Approach." BRITISH
JOURNAL OF PSYCHOLOGY 25 (October 1934): 123-39.

_____. "Auditory Perception. II. The Evolutionary Approach." BRITISH
JOURNAL OF PSYCHOLOGY 25 (January 1935): 265-83.

Wertheimer, Max. PRODUCTIVE THINKING. Enl. ed. Edited by Michael Wertheimer. New York: Harper and Row, 1959. x, 302 p.

> Expands Max Wertheimer's classic work, PRODUCTIVE THINKING (1945), with previously unpublished materials found among his papers and notes. Examines thinking processes from a Gestalt view which has both theoretical and applied implications. Bibliography of Max Wertheimer's works. Index.

Woodworth, R[obert].S[essions]. "Gestalt Psychology and the Concept of Reaction Stages." AMERICAN JOURNAL OF PSYCHOLOGY 39 (December 1927): 62-69.

12. PSYCHOANALYSIS

Because another volume in this series (Reuben Fine, FREUD AND PSYCHOANALYSIS, Detroit: Gale Research Co., forthcoming) is entirely devoted to psychoanalysis, this section is relatively brief and focuses primarily on the history of the school rather than on its major concepts. Because psychoanalysis is not really central to general psychology, many articles have been written on the relation of psychoanalysis to psychology proper. This section is subdivided as follows: general reference sources for psychoanalysis; the origin and development of psychoanalysis; Sigmund Freud's major works, secondary sources on Freud, and critiques and evaluations of Freud; the influence of Freud and psychoanalysis on psychology; and post-Freudian psychoanalysis.

a. General Reference Sources

AMERICAN IMAGO: A PSYCHOANALYTIC JOURNAL FOR CULTURE, SCIENCE AND THE ARTS. Detroit, Mich.: Wayne State University Press, for the Association of Applied Psychoanalysis Inc., 1939-- . Quarterly.

> Includes articles on applications of psychoanalytic theory to a broad range of social, humanistic, cultural, artistic, and scientific topics. Index in final issue of each volume.

ANNUAL OF PSYCHOANALYSIS. Edited by the Chicago Institute for Psychoanalysis. New York: International Universities Press, 1973-- .

> Contains comprehensive and topical papers by well-known authors, including materials on psychoanalytic history.

ANNUAL SURVEY OF PSYCHOANALYSIS. New York: International Universities Press, 1950-- .

> A comprehensive survey of psychoanalytic theory and practice. Includes materials on criticisms, methodology, child analysis, psychoanalytic training and practice, and reviews of psychoanalytic books. First chapter surveys publications on the history of psychoanalysis.

CONTEMPORARY PSYCHOANALYSIS. New York: Academic Press, 1964-- . Quarterly.

> Journal of the William Alanson White Psychoanalytic Society. Publishes articles on the theory and practice of psychoanalysis as well as on contemporary issues. Includes book reviews, letters, comments from readers, and news items. An index to the annual volume follows the fourth issue each year.

Fodor, Nandor, and Gaynor, F., eds. FREUD: DICTIONARY OF PSYCHO-ANALYSIS. New York: Philosophical Library, 1950. xii, 208 p.

> A dictionary of terms and phrases introduced or used by Freud. Gives his original definitions and shows how he modified the use of some then-current terms. Identifies original sources.

Grinstein, Alexander. THE INDEX OF PSYCHOANALYTIC WRITINGS. 14 vols. New York: International Universities Press, 1956-73.

> A revision and updating of Rickman's INDEX PSYCHOANALYTICUS (see below, this section, p. 199). Lists tens of thousands of books and articles on psychoanalysis or by psychoanalysts in probably the most extensive reference source available for that literature. Successive sets of volumes added more recent works as well as supplementary material to earlier volumes.

_____, comp. SIGMUND FREUD'S WRITINGS: A COMPREHENSIVE BIBLIOG-RAPHY. New York: International Universities Press, 1976. 300 p.

> A thorough work providing a catalog of all of Freud's writings: abstracts, articles, books, introductions, letters, postscripts, prefaces, publications honoring his friends and colleagues, obituaries, reviews, and translations.

JOURNAL OF THE AMERICAN PSYCHOANALYTIC ASSOCIATION. New York: International Universities Press, January 1953-- . Quarterly.

> Publishes original articles on clinical issues and problems and broader applications of psychoanalysis, as well as proceedings, book reviews, and book notices. Index.

Kahn, Samuel. PSYCHOLOGICAL AND NEUROLOGICAL DEFINITIONS AND THE UNCONSCIOUS. Boston: Meador, 1940. 219 p.

> A brief description and chronology of the development of Freudian psychoanalysis followed by a glossary of almost 600 items and a bibliography of 800 items relevant to neurology, psychiatry, and psychoanalysis. Index.

Laplanche, J[ean]., and Pontalis, J.B. THE LANGUAGE OF PSYCHOANALYSIS. Translated by Donald Nicholson-Smith. New York: W.W. Norton, 1973. xv, 510 p.

Presents the major concepts of psychoanalysis in alphabetical sequence. Gives the history of many terms and provides German, Spanish, French, Italian, and Portuguese equivalents for each entry. Index.

Lorand, Sandor, et al., eds. THE YEARBOOK OF PSYCHOANALYSIS. New York: International Universities Press, 1945-- .

Moore, Burness, and Fine, B., eds. A GLOSSARY OF PSYCHOANALYTIC TERMS AND CONCEPTS. 2d ed. New York: American Psychoanalytic Association, 1968. 102 p.

PSYCHOANALYTIC QUARTERLY. New York: Psychoanalytic Quarterly, 1932-- .

Includes original manuscripts on a wide range of psychoanalytic research, problems, and issues, as well as book reviews, abstracts, and notes. Index.

PSYCHOANALYTIC REVIEW. New York: National Psychological Association for Psychoanalysis, 1913-- . Quarterly.

Later volumes combine PSYCHOANALYSIS (founded in 1952) and THE PSYCHOANALYTIC REVIEW (founded in 1913). Devoted to the psychoanalytic study of behavior and culture. Publishes book review.

PSYCHOANALYTIC STUDY OF THE CHILD. New York: International Universities Press, 1945-- . Annual.

A major psychoanalytic repository of clinical reports, research, and thought on the development and psychology of children. Abstracts and index for volumes 1-25 published by Yale University Press in 1975.

Rickman, John. INDEX PSYCHOANALYTICUS, 1893-1926. London: Hogarth Press and the Institute of Psychoanalysis, 1928. 276 p.

Rothgeb, Carrie Lee, ed. ABSTRACTS OF THE STANDARD EDITION OF THE COMPLETE PSYCHOLOGICAL WORKS OF SIGMUND FREUD, WITH AN INTRODUCTION ON READING FREUD. New York: Jason Aronson, 1973. 315 p.

A helpful introduction on reading Freud by Robert R. Holt. Provides, among other things, hints for understanding Freud, an overview of Freud's basic assumptions, and an analysis of Freud's writing style. Abstracts are generally clear and long enough to provide a good sense of the original work. Index.

Rycroft, Charles. A CRITICAL DICTIONARY OF PSYCHOANALYSIS. New York: Basic Books, 1968. xxvi, 189 p.

Gives formal dictionary definitions of terms as well as information about their origins and "connections with other terms and concepts

used in analytical theory, and of the controversies relating to them
that exist among analysts themselves." Although emphasis is on
Freudian concepts (Rycroft was trained in the Freudian school),
those of other schools are included. Bibliography.

b. Origin and Development

Amacher, Peter. "The Concepts of the Pleasure Principle and Infantile Erogenous
Zones Shaped by Freud's Neurological Education." PSYCHOANALYTIC QUAR-
TERLY 43 (April 1974): 218-23.

_____. FREUD'S NEUROLOGICAL EDUCATION AND ITS INFLUENCE ON
PSYCHOANALYTIC THEORY. Monograph 16. New York: International Universities Press, 1965. 93 p.

Andersson, Ola. STUDIES IN THE PREHISTORY OF PSYCHOANALYSIS. THE
ETIOLOGY OF PSYCHONEUROSES AND SOME RELATED THEMES IN SIGMUND
FREUD'S SCIENTIFIC WRITINGS AND LETTERS 1886-1896. Stockholm: Svenska
Bokfoerlaget, 1962. viii, 238 p.

Traces sources of influence and development of Freud's early
thought on the etiology of the psychoneuroses. References.

Anthony, E. James. "The History of Group Psychotherapy." In THE ORIGINS
OF GROUP PSYCHOANALYSIS, edited by Harold I. Kaplan and Benjamin J.
Sadock, pp. 1-26. New York: Jason Aronson, 1972.

Bailey, P. "Janet and Freud." AMA ARCHIVES OF NEUROLOGY AND
PSYCHIATRY 76 (1956): 76-89.

Bakan, David. SIGMUND FREUD AND THE JEWISH MYSTICAL TRADITION.
Princeton, N.J.: D. Van Nostrand, 1958. xix, 326 p.

Argues that the intellectual history of psychoanalysis cannot be
understood apart from Freud's Jewish identity and his participation
"in the struggles and issues of Jewish mysticism. . . ."

Beharriell, Frederick J. "Freud's Debts to Literature." PSYCHOANALYSIS 4
nos. 4-5 (1957): 18-27.

Bergman, Paul. "The Germinal Cell of Freud's Psychoanalytic Psychology and
Therapy." PSYCHIATRY 12 (August 1949): 265-78.

Bergmann, Martin S., and Hartman, Frank R., eds. THE EVOLUTION OF
PSYCHOANALYTIC TECHNIQUE. New York: Basic Books, 1976. xiv, 497 p.

Berkower, Lary. "The Enduring Effect of the Jewish Tradition Upon Freud." AMERICAN JOURNAL OF PSYCHIATRY 125 (February 1969): 1067-73.

Bjerre, Paul. THE HISTORY AND PRACTICE OF PSYCHOANALYSIS. [?]. Reprint. Translated by Elizabeth N. Barrow. Boston: Richard G. Badger, 1916. 294 p.

    Discussion of historical influences on psychoanalysis from Kant and the Nancy School followed by a brief outline of Freudian thought and a comparison of Freud's and Adler's theories. Index.

Brill, A.A. "The Freudian Epoch." In THE MARCH OF MEDICINE: THE NEW YORK ACADEMY OF MEDICINE LECTURES TO THE LAITY, 1942, editor varies, pp. 68-99. New York: Columbia University Press, 1943.

Brome, Vincent. FREUD AND HIS EARLY CIRCLE. New York: William Morrow, 1968. xii, 275 p.

    An examination of the interpersonal relations and conflicts of such psychoanalytic pioneers as Sigmund Freud, Sandor Ferenczi, Karl Abraham, Alfred Adler, and Carl Gustav Jung. Index.

Burchard, Edward M.L. "The Evolution of Psychoanalytic Tasks and Goals: A Historical Study of Freud's Writings and Technique." PSYCHIATRY 21 (November 1958): 341-57.

Burnham, John Chynoweth. "The Beginnings of Psychoanalysis in the United States." AMERICAN IMAGO 13 (Spring 1956): 65-68.

_____. "The Medical Origins and Cultural Use of Freud's Instinctual Drive Theory." PSYCHOANALYTIC QUARTERLY 43 (April 1974): 193-217.

    Argues that Freud's instinctual drive theory developed from medical literature and his own practice, independently of the biological theory of his day.

_____. PSYCHOANALYSIS AND AMERICAN MEDICINE, 1894-1918: MEDICINE, SCIENCE, AND CULTURE. Psychological Issues vol. 5, no. 4. Monograph 20. New York: International Universities Press, 1967. v, 249 p.

Calogeras, Roy C., and Schupper, Fabian X. "Origins and Early Formations of the Oedipus Complex." JOURNAL OF THE AMERICAN PSYCHOANALYTIC ASSOCIATION 20 (October 1972): 751-75.

Capps, Donald. "Hartmann's Relationship to Freud: A Reappraisal." JOURNAL OF THE HISTORY OF THE BEHAVIORAL SCIENCES 6 (April 1970): 162-75.

Argues that "Hartmann played a crucial role in reminding Freud of the potentialities of Jewish mysticism," and that Jewish mysticism played a greater role in the origin and development of Freud's ideas than German philosophical and scientific traditions.

Conn, Jacob H. "The Rise and Decline of Psychoanalysis." PSYCHIATRIC OPINION 10 (October 1973): 34-38.

Cranefield, Paul. "Freud and the School of Helmholtz." GESNERUS 23 (1966): 35-39.

Drager, Kaethe. "Psychoanalysis in Hitler Germany: 1933-1949." AMERICAN IMAGO (Fall 1972): 199-214.

Ekstein, Rudolf. "Psychoanalytic Precursors in Greek Antiquity." BULLETIN OF THE MENNINGER CLINIC 39 (1975): 246-67.

Ellenberger, Henri F. THE DISCOVERY OF THE UNCONSCIOUS: THE HISTORY AND EVOLUTION OF DYNAMIC PSYCHIATRY. New York: Basic Books, 1970. xvi, 932 p.

_____. "Fechner and Freud." BULLETIN OF THE MENNINGER CLINIC 20 (1956): 201-14.

Fancher, Raymond E. "The Neurological Origin of Freud's Dream Theory." JOURNAL OF THE HISTORY OF THE BEHAVIORAL SCIENCES 7 (January 1971): 59-74.

Presents evidence that Freud's "neurological assumptions pervaded, and perhaps even determined," his well-known theory of dreams.

_____. PSYCHOANALYTIC PSYCHOLOGY: THE DEVELOPMENT OF FREUD'S THOUGHT. New York: W.W. Norton, 1973. xi, 241 p.

Freud, Sigmund. ON THE HISTORY OF THE PSYCHO-ANALYTIC MOVEMENT. Translated by Joan Riviere. Revised and edited by James Strachey. New York: W.W. Norton, 1966. 79 p.

A brief sketch of the historical development of psychoanalysis and its fundamental concepts followed by a strongly-worded statement on the inconsistencies and weaknesses in the revisionist thought of Adler and Jung; Freud argued that it would be inappropriate to apply the term "psychoanalysis" to Adlerian and Jungian thought. Index.

Friedman, Lawrence. "Reasons for the Freudian Revolution." PSYCHOANALYTIC QUARTERLY 46 (October 1977): 623-49.

_____. "A View of the Background of Freudian Theory." PSYCHOANALYTIC QUARTERLY 46 (July 1977): 425-65.

Reviews nineteenth-century developments in biology, the human sciences and psychology, and argues that developments in "hypnotism gave Freud the opportunity to isolate objective entities within the mind and to found a psychology on that basis."

Gedo, John E., and Pollock, George H., eds. FREUD: THE FUSION OF SCIENCE AND HUMANISM. THE INTELLECTUAL HISTORY OF PSYCHOANALYSIS. Psychological Issues vol. 9, nos. 2-3. Monographs 34-35. New York: International Universities Press, 1976. 447 p.

A collection of papers dealing with Freud's cultural and personal background, the intellectual influence of such individuals as Breuer and Charcot, the creation of psychoanalysis, Freud's mature working methods, and his relations with the psychoanalytic community.

Grotjahn, Martin. "Psychoanalysis Twenty Five Years After the Death of Sigmund Freud." PSYCHOLOGICAL REPORTS 16 (June 1965): 965-68.

Notes the growth of psychoanalysis in neighboring fields, its value as a tool for exploring the unconscious, and the growth of societies and training centers. Although the treatment technique has not lived up to expectations, according to Grotjahn, psychodynamic training is of value to psychotherapists.

_____. "The Rundbriefe between Sigmund Freud and the Committee during the Years 1920-1924." ANNALS OF PSYCHOANALYSIS 2 (1974): 24-39.

Discusses an exchange of letters between Freud and trusted colleagues during the years 1920-24.

Gupta, R.K. "Freud and Schopenhauer." JOURNAL OF THE HISTORY OF IDEAS 36 (October-December 1975): 721-28.

Points out similarities in the thought of Freud and Schopenhauer on such topics as sex, repression, human nature, and attitude toward life.

Hale, Nathan G., Jr. FREUD AND THE AMERICANS: THE BEGINNINGS OF PSYCHOANALYSIS IN THE UNITED STATES, 1876-1917. New York: Oxford University Press, 1971. xvi, 574 p.

Explores Freud's early influence and reception in the United States beginning with the Clark Conference in 1909 and the intellectual climate at that time, followed by an examination of Freud's immediate influence (1909-1918). The author hopes to detail Freud's later influence in a subsequent volume. Index.

Harms, Ernest. "Simon-Andred Tissot (1728-1797): The Freudian Before Freud." AMERICAN JOURNAL OF PSYCHIATRY 112 (March 1956): 744.

Hoenig, J. "Sigmund Freud's Views on the Sexual Disorders in Historical Perspective." BRITISH JOURNAL OF PSYCHIATRY 129 (September 1976): 193-200.

Jones, Ernest. "The Early History of Psychoanalysis." JOURNAL OF MENTAL SCIENCE 100 (1954): 198-200.

_____. THE LIFE AND WORK OF SIGMUND FREUD. 3 vols. New York: Basic Books, 1953, 1955, 1957. Indexes.

For annotation see section C12c, p. 210.

Kaplan, Harold I., and Sadock, Benjamin J., eds. THE ORIGINS OF GROUP PSYCHOANALYSIS. New York: Dutton, 1972. x, 100 p.

For annotation see section D13b, p. 359.

Kern, Stephen. "The Prehistory of Freud's Theory of Castration Anxiety." PSYCHOANALYTIC REVIEW 62 (Summer 1975): 309-14.

Lampl-de Groot, Jeanne. "Personal Experience with Psychoanalytic Technique and Theory during the Last Half Century." PSYCHOANALYTIC STUDY OF THE CHILD 31 (1976): 283-96.

Describes the author's psychoanalysis with Freud and presents observations on the development of psychoanalysis from 1922 to 1976.

Lorand, Sandor. "Historical Aspects and Changing Trends in Psychoanalytic Therapy." PSYCHOANALYTIC REVIEW 59 (Winter 1972-73): 497-525.

Lowenberg, Peter. "'Sigmund Freud as a Jew': A Study in Ambivalence and Courage." JOURNAL OF THE HISTORY OF THE BEHAVIORAL SCIENCES 7 (October 1971): 363-69.

Explores the effects of Freud's Jewish background on his interpersonal relations, his theory, and his world view.

Lowry, Richard. "Psychoanalysis and the Philosophy of Physicalism." JOURNAL OF THE HISTORY OF THE BEHAVIORAL SCIENCES 3 (April 1967): 156-67.

Documents the influence of the philosophy of physicalism on Freud's psychological theorizing.

Martindale, Colin. "A Note on an Eighteenth Century Anticipation of Freud's Theory of Dreams." JOURNAL OF THE HISTORY OF THE BEHAVIORAL

SCIENCES 6 (October 1970); 362-64.

> Several essays on dreams written in 1714 attributed to John Byrom, a poet, clearly anticipate Freud's notions of the wish fulfilling nature of dreams and the self understanding which can come from dream analysis.

Mayo, Elton. SOME NOTES ON THE PSYCHOLOGY OF PIERRE JANET. Cambridge, Mass.: Harvard University Press, 1948. vii, 132 p.

> Covers Janet's views on such topics as hysteria and hypnosis, obsessions, and the psychology of adaptation. Many consider Janet's psychology a forerunner of Freud's. Index.

Miller, Julian A., et al. "Some Aspects of Charcot's Influence on Freud." JOURNAL OF THE AMERICAN PSYCHOANALYTIC ASSOCIATION 17 (April 1969): 608-23.

Munroe, Ruth L. SCHOOLS OF PSYCHOANALYTIC THOUGHT: AN EXPOSITION, CRITIQUE, AND ATTEMPT AT INTEGRATION. New York: Dryden Press, 1955. xvi, 670 p.

> See annotation in section C12eiii, p. 220.

Oberndorf, C.P. A HISTORY OF PSYCHOANALYSIS IN AMERICA. New York: Grune and Stratton, 1953. Reprint. New York: Harper Torchbooks, 1964. 280 p.

> Traces the origin and development of the psychoanalytic movement in America. Appendixes include key events, a list of former officers and meetings of the American Psychoanalytic Society (APS), approved affiliate societies of the APS, and a list of the congresses of the International Psychoanalytic Association to 1953. Bibliographical notes. Index.

Parkin, Alan. "Feuchtersleben: A Forgotten Forerunner to Freud." CANADIAN PSYCHIATRIC ASSOCIATION JOURNAL 20 (October 1975): 477-81.

Ramzy, Ishak. "From Aristotle to Freud: A Few Notes on the Roots of Psychoanalysis." BULLETIN OF THE MENNINGER CLINIC 20 (1956): 112-23.

Ritvo, Lucille B. "Carl Claus as Freud's Professor of the New Darwinian Biology." INTERNATIONAL JOURNAL OF PSYCHO-ANALYSIS 53 (1972): 277-83.

_____. "The Impact of Darwin on Freud." PSYCHOANALYTIC QUARTERLY 43 (April 1974): 177-92.

> Notes Freud's generally positive attitude toward Darwin, Darwinian

influences in Freud's education, and parallels in Freud's and
Darwin's thought.

Robert, Marthe. FROM OEDIPUS TO MOSES: FREUD'S JEWISH IDENTITY.
Translated by Ralph Manheim. Garden City, N.Y.: Anchor, 1976. 229 p.

Rosen, George. "Freud and Medicine in Vienna: Some Scientific and Medical
Sources of His Thought." PSYCHOLOGICAL MEDICINE 2 (1972): 332–44.

Sandler, Joseph; Dare, Christopher; and Holder, Alex. "Frames of Reference
in Psychoanalytic Psychology." BRITISH JOURNAL OF MEDICAL PSYCHOLOGY
45 (June 1972): 127-31, 133-42, 143-47.

> The first of these three articles provides a general introduction and
> orientation, the second presents historical materials and phases in
> the development of psychoanalysis, and the third is a note on as-
> sumptions in psychoanalytic theory.

Sauri, Jorge J. "From Looking to Listening." JOURNAL OF THE HISTORY
OF THE BEHAVIORAL SCIENCES 9 (October 1973): 306-12.

> Traces selected therapeutic procedures from Charcot to Freud with
> a focus on the change from acting out to talking as a means of
> achieving catharsis. Describes this change of emphasis for the
> therapist as listening rather than looking.

Schneck, Jerome M. "A Reevaluation of Freud's Abandonment of Hypnosis."
JOURNAL OF THE HISTORY OF THE BEHAVIORAL SCIENCES 1 (April 1965):
191-95.

> Argues that Freud's ambition and desire for fame, recognition, and
> originality contributed to his abandonment of hypnosis, a technique
> which already had a long tradition of use and research.

Serota, Herman M. "The Ego and the Unconscious: 1784-1884." PSYCHO-
ANALYTIC QUARTERLY 43 (April 1974): 224–42.

> Traces developments in thought on the ego and the unconscious as
> well as evidence for the unconscious found in hypnotic phenomena
> from the 1784 Royal Commission on Mesmer's animal magnetism to
> Bernheim's book DE LA SUGGESTION published in 1884.

Sherman, Murray H., ed. PSYCHOANALYSIS IN AMERICA: HISTORICAL
PERSPECTIVES. Springfield, Ill.: Charles Thomas, 1966. xii, 518 p.

Simon, Bennett. "Plato and Freud: The Mind in Conflict and the Mind in
Dialogue." PSYCHOANALYTIC QUARTERLY 42 (January 1973): 91-122.

Stepansky, Paul E. A HISTORY OF AGGRESSION IN FREUD. Psychological Issues vol. 10, no. 3. Monograph 39. New York: International Universities Press, 1977. ix, 201 p.

> Traces the development of Freud's theory of aggression and specu-
> lates about the personal, political, and social forces which influ-
> enced the theory. References. Index.

Sterba, Richard F. "The Humanistic Wellspring of Psychoanalysis." PSYCHO-ANALYTIC QUARTERLY 43 (April 1974): 167-76.

> Attempts to demonstrate the effect of a humanistic world view on
> the development of Freud's thought.

Stewart, Larry. "Freud Before Oedipus: Race and Heredity in the Origins of Psychoanalysis." JOURNAL OF THE HISTORY OF BIOLOGY 9 (1976): 215-28.

> Traces the development of Freud's rejection of the possible role of
> heredity in the etiology of the neuroses.

Thompson, Clara. PSYCHOANALYSIS: EVOLUTION AND DEVELOPMENT. New York: Hermitage House, 1950. xii, 252 p.

> A sympathetic treatment of Freudian and neo-Freudian psychoanaly-
> sis. Reviews the history of these schools in four main periods:
> 1885 to 1900, 1900 to 1910, 1910 to 1925, and 1925 to about
> 1945. Bibliography. Index.

Tourney, Garfield. "Freud and the Greeks: A Study of the Influence of Classical Greek Mythology and Philosophy Upon the Development of Freudian Thought." JOURNAL OF THE HISTORY OF THE BEHAVIORAL SCIENCES 1 (January 1965): 67-85.

> Discusses Freud's "use of Greek concepts and their application as
> designations of his scientific hypotheses, the resemblance between
> Freud's theories and certain Greek concepts, and his identification
> with Oedipus."

Tridon, Andre. PSYCHOANALYSIS: ITS HISTORY, THEORY AND PRACTICE. New York: Huebsch, 1923. 272 p.

Trosman, Harry, and Simmons, Roger D. "The Freud Library." JOURNAL OF THE AMERICAN PSYCHOANALYTIC ASSOCIATION 21 (1973): 646-87.

_____. "Freud's Cultural Background." ANNALS OF PSYCHOANALYSIS 1 (1973): 318-35.

Vranich, S.B. "Sigmund Freud and 'The Case History of Berganza.'" PSYCHO-ANALYTIC REVIEW 63 (Spring 1976): 73-82.

Weisz, George. "Scientists and Sectarians: The Case of Psychoanalysis." JOURNAL OF THE HISTORY OF THE BEHAVIORAL SCIENCES 21 (October 1975): 350-64.

> Uses themes in the history of the psychoanalytic movement to illustrate sectarian tendencies observed in scientists.

Whyte, Lancelot Law. THE UNCONSCIOUS BEFORE FREUD. New York: Basic Books, 1960. xiii, 219 p.

> Traces the lengthy background of ideas about the unconscious advanced by a host of thinkers before Freud. Index.

Wittels, Fritz. "Freud's Scientific Cradle." AMERICAN JOURNAL OF PSYCHIATRY 100 (January 1944): 521-28.

> Provides an overview of the influences encountered by Freud during his work as a student in the Viennese medical school.

Wyss, Dieter. DEPTH PSYCHOLOGY: A CRITICAL HISTORY, DEVELOPMENT, PROBLEMS, CRISES. Translated by Gerald Onn. New York: W.W. Norton, 1966. 568 p.

> Covers selected themes in the history of psychoanalytic psychology with emphasis on developments since the early 1930s. Includes the contributions of a very large number of theorists, thus sacrificing depth of coverage. Critical treatment focuses on the scientific status of psychoanalytic theory and on problems associated with specific concepts such as the pleasure principle, the theory of repression, and the theory of drives. Concludes with a brief examination of relationships among schools of depth psychology. References in footnotes. Index.

c. Freud's Major Works, Selected Secondary Sources, and Critiques

Rather than listing all of Freud's many works separately in this section, we refer to the standard edition of Freud's writings, edited by Strachey (see below, this section, p. 210).

Abraham, Hilda C., and Freud, Ernest L., eds. A PSYCHO-ANALYTIC DIALOGUE: THE LETTERS OF SIGMUND FREUD AND KARL ABRAHAM 1907-1926. Translated by Bernard Marsh and Hilda C. Abraham. New York: Basic Books, 1965. xvii, 406 p.

> Includes 367 letters exchanged between Freud and his pupil, Karl Abraham.

Alexander, Franz. "A Jury Trial of Psychoanalysis." JOURNAL OF ABNORMAL AND SOCIAL PSYCHOLOGY 35 (July 1940): 305-23.

A well-known psychoanalyst responds to a symposium on psychoanalysis as seen by analyzed psychologists (see next entry).

Allport, Gordon W., ed. "Symposium: Psychoanalysis as Seen by Analyzed Psychologists." JOURNAL OF ABNORMAL AND SOCIAL PSYCHOLOGY 35 (January–April 1940): 3–55, 139–225.

Several well-known psychologists including Edwin G. Boring, Carney Landis, J.F. Brown, Raymond B. Willoughby, Percival M. Symonds, Henry A. Murray, Else Frenkel-Brunswik, and David Shakow offer evaluations of psychoanalysis based on their personal experiences in psychoanalysis. Includes a comment on Boring's paper by his analyst Hanns Sachs. Symposium followed by a comment by Franz Alexander (see above).

Bakan, David. "The Authenticity of the Freud Memorial Collection." JOURNAL OF THE HISTORY OF THE BEHAVIORAL SCIENCES 21 (October 1975): 365–67.

Presents facts regarding the acquisition and authenticity of the Freud Memorial Collection in the New York Psychiatric Institute's library. Bakan doubts that all of the books were actually part of Freud's library.

Brill, A.A. FUNDAMENTAL CONCEPTIONS OF PSYCHOANALYSIS. New York: Harcourt, Brace, 1921. vii, 344 p.

A nontechnical discussion of such topics in psychoanalysis as catharsis, forgetting, wit, dreaming, forms of insanity, the only child, and selected vocations. Index.

Eliasberg, Wladimir G. "Early Criticisms of Freud's Psychoanalysis. The Conscious vs. the Unconscious." PSYCHOANALYTIC REVIEW 41 (October 1954): 347–63.

Freeman, Lucy, and Small, Marvin. THE STORY OF PSYCHOANALYSIS. New York: Pocket Books, 1960. xiv, 178 p.

Freud, Ernest L., ed. THE LETTERS OF SIGMUND FREUD AND ARNOLD ZWEIG. Translated by Elaine Robson-Scott and William Robson-Scott. New York: Harcourt, Brace and World, 1970. ix, 190 p.

Selected letters between Freud and the novelist Zweig, some of which describe the latter's neurosis. Index.

Freud, Sigmund. COLLECTED PAPERS. 5 vols. Edited by Ernest Jones. Authorized translation under the supervision of Joan Riviere. New York: International Psychoanalytic Press, 1924–50; New York: Basic Books, 1959.

Contains early papers and materials on the history of the psycho-

analytic movement (volume 1); clinical papers and papers on technique (volume 2); case histories (volume 3); papers on metapsychology and on applied psychoanalysis (volume 4); and miscellaneous
papers, 1888-1938 (volume 5). Index for volumes 4 and 5 only.

_____. THE STANDARD EDITION OF THE COMPLETE PSYCHOLOGICAL
WORKS OF SIGMUND FREUD. 24 vols. Edited by James Strachey in collaboration with Anna Freud. Translated by James Strachey and Alan Tyson. Editorial Assistant, Angela Richards. London: Hogarth Press and The Institute of
Psycho-Analysis, 1953-74.

Includes Freud's published psychoanalytic and prepsychoanalytic
writings but does not include his early publications in the physical
sciences, his correspondence, lectures, unpublished papers, or reports. Extensive notes and commentary provided by the editor.
Translations mainly based on last German editions.

Grotjahn, Martin. "Collector's Items From the Correspondence Between Sigmund
Freud and Otto Rank, and From the First 'Rundbriefe' of the 'Ring Holders.'"
JOURNAL OF THE OTTO RANK ASSOCIATION 6 (June 1971): 7-31.

Hall, Calvin S. A PRIMER OF FREUDIAN PSYCHOLOGY. Cleveland: World
Publishing Co., 1954. 137 p.

Hendrick, Ives. FACTS AND THEORIES OF PSYCHOANALYSIS. 3d ed. New
York: Alfred A. Knopf, 1958. xii, 385, xvii p.

A concise overview of psychoanalysis devoted to "facts," theories,
therapy, and the psychoanalytic movement. Suggestions for further
reading. Glossary of psychoanalytic terms.

Izenberg, Gerald N. THE EXISTENTIALIST CRITIQUE OF FREUD: THE CRISIS
OF AUTONOMY. Princeton, N.J.: Princeton University Press, 1976. xii,
354 p.

An overview of critiques of classic psychoanalytic theory offered by
such existentialist thinkers as Binswanger, Sartre, Boss, and
Heidegger. Index.

Johnson, Hiram K. "Psychoanalysis: A Critique." PSYCHIATRIC QUARTERLY
22 (1948): 321-338.

Jones, Ernest. THE LIFE AND WORK OF SIGMUND FREUD. 3 vols. New
York: Basic Books, 1953, 1955, 1957.

A definitive biography of Freud discussing the formative years and
great discoveries (volume 1), the years of maturity (volume 2), and
the last phase of Freud's work and life (volume 3). Includes numerous illustrations and case histories. Discusses Freud's major ideas

and his contributions in fields such as religion, art, biology, and literature. Notes and bibliographical materials. Brief appendixes present extracts from correspondence, surgical notes, and an extract of a case history. Indexes.

_____. SIGMUND FREUD; FOUR CENTENARY ADDRESSES. New York: Basic Books, 1956. 150 p.

Klein, D[avid].B[allin]. THE UNCONSCIOUS: INVENTION OR DISCOVERY? A HISTORICOCRITICAL INQUIRY. Santa Monica, Calif.: Goodyear, 1977.

Levitt, Morton, ed. READINGS IN PSYCHOANALYTIC PSYCHOLOGY. New York: Appleton-Century-Crofts, 1959. xiv, 413 p.

Twenty-four contributing authors explore topics in developmental processes, defense mechanisms, diagnosis, and theory. Includes a biographical sketch of Freud. A section on applied psychoanalysis includes papers on Freud and literature, psychoanalysis and education, and psychoanalysis and medicine. Index.

Ludwig, Emil. DOCTOR FREUD: AN ANALYSIS AND A WARNING. New York: Hellman, Williams, 1947. 317 p.

A popular critique of Freud and his theories by a professional writer who was not favorably impressed by Freud.

Miles, T.R. ELIMINATING THE UNCONSCIOUS: A BEHAVIORIST VIEW OF PSYCHOANALYSIS. New York: Pergamon Press, 1966. xviii, 171 p.

Argues that the scientific status of psychoanalysis would improve if it could avoid dualistic terminology. Suggests a more behavioristic terminology. References. Index.

Moore, Jared S. "Some Defects in Psychoanalysis." PSYCHOLOGICAL REVIEW 30 (November 1923): 461-75.

Criticizes three psychoanalytic concepts: the complex, the libido, and the censor.

Mullahy, Patrick. OEDIPUS: MYTH AND COMPLEX. New York: Grove Press, 1955. xii, 370 p.

Provides an overview of central concepts in Freud's theory and the theories of Adler, Jung, Rank, Horney, Fromm, and Sullivan. Includes brief critical and appreciative comments on all of the theories. Notes. Bibliography.

Roazen, Paul. BROTHER ANIMAL: THE STORY OF FREUD AND TAUSK. New York: Alfred A. Knopf, 1969. xx, 221, v p.

A partial biography of Tausk exploring possible reasons for his suicide and his relationship to Freud. Index.

Ruitenbeek, Hendrik M., ed. FREUD AS WE KNEW HIM. Detroit: Wayne State University Press, 1973. 524 p.

A collection of reminiscences, documents, impressions, and accounts of encounters written by students, colleagues, friends, family members, and others, "to put the man Freud in perspective." Index.

Salter, Andrew. THE CASE AGAINST PSYCHOANALYSIS. Rev. ed. New York: Citadel Press, 1963. ix, 179 p.

A severe, brief, popular critique of Freudian psychoanalysis by a writer steeped in the behaviorist tradition.

Silverman, Lloyd H. "Psychoanalytic Theory: 'The Reports of my Death Are Greatly Exaggerated.'" AMERICAN PSYCHOLOGIST 31 (September 1976): 621-37.

Describes two, independent, long-term research projects on the relationship between unconscious wishes and psychopathology. Claims that the findings of both projects support the predictions of psychoanalytic theory.

Skinner, B.F. "Critiques of Psychoanalytic Concepts and Theories." SCIENTIFIC MONTHLY 79 (November 1954): 300-305.

Stafford-Clark, David. WHAT FREUD REALLY SAID. New York: Schocken Books, 1967. 260 p.

Szasz, Thomas. KARL KRAUS AND THE SOUL-DOCTORS: A PIONEER CRITIC AND HIS CRITICISM OF PSYCHIATRY AND PSYCHOANALYSIS. Baton Rouge: Louisiana State University Press, 1976. xviii, 180 p.

Timpanaro, Sebastiano. THE FREUDIAN SLIP: PSYCHOANALYSIS AND TEXTUAL CRITICISM. Translated by Kate Soper. Atlantic Highlands, N.J.: Humanities Press, 1976. 236 p.

Critique of psychoanalytic interpretation of slips and of psychoanalysis as a whole.

Waelder, Robert. BASIC THEORY OF PSYCHOANALYSIS. New York: Schocken Books, 1964. xiii, 273 p.

Includes materials on the historical development of psychoanalysis, a survey of basic concepts, and a discussion of the problems of scientific validation. Offers a brief discussion of common misunderstandings of psychoanalytic concepts. Bibliography. Index.

_____, ed. THE LIVING THOUGHTS OF FREUD. New York: Longmans, Green, 1941. 168 p.

Wells, Harry K. THE FAILURE OF PSYCHOANALYSIS: FROM FREUD TO FROMM. New York: International Publishers Co., 1963. 252 p. Index.

d. Influence of Freud on Psychology

Bruner, Jerome S. "Freud and the Image of Man." AMERICAN PSYCHOLO-GIST 11 (September 1956): 463-66.

Explores the influence of Freud (and to a lesser extent of Darwin) on modern views of human nature.

Burnham, J.C. "Sigmund Freud and G. Stanley Hall: Exchange of Letters." PSYCHOANALYTIC QUARTERLY 29 (1960): 307-16.

DeVoto, Bernard. "Freud's Influence on Literature." SATURDAY REVIEW OF LITERATURE 20 (7 October 1939): 10-11.

A brief popular and appreciative comment on Freud's extensive impact on literature.

Fisher, Seymour, and Greenberg, Roger P. THE SCIENTIFIC CREDIBILITY OF FREUD'S THEORIES AND THERAPY. New York: Basic Books, 1977. x, 502 p.

An attempt at a dispassionate evaluation of psychoanalytic theory and therapy in light of the massive evidence that has been accumulated over the last decades. Cites about 2,000 references. Indexes.

Heidbreder, Edna. "Freud and Psychology." PSYCHOLOGICAL REVIEW 47 (May 1940): 185-95.

Hilgard, Ernest R. "Freud and Experimental Psychology." BEHAVIORAL SCIENCE 2 (January 1957): 74-79.

Explores relationships between psychoanalytic thought and behaviorism and the gradual assimilation of Freudian psychology into American psychology.

Jastrow, Joseph. "Contributions of Freudism to Psychology: IV. The Neurological Concept of Behavior." PSYCHOLOGICAL REVIEW 31 (May 1924): 203-18.

Klein, David Ballin. "Psychology and Freud: An Historico-Critical Appraisal." PSYCHOLOGICAL REVIEW 40 (September 1933): 440-56.

Lashley, K.S. "Contributions of Freudism to Psychology: III. Physiological Analysis of the Libido." PSYCHOLOGICAL REVIEW 31 (May 1924): 192-202.

Lee, S.G.M., and Herbert, Martin, eds. FREUD AND PSYCHOLOGY: SELECTED READINGS. Baltimore: Penguin Books, 1970. 308 p.

Leuba, James H. "Contributions of Freudism to Psychology: II. Freudian Psychology and Scientific Inspiration." PSYCHOLOGICAL REVIEW 31 (May 1924): 184-91.

Macalpine, Ida. "Tribute to Freud." JOURNAL OF THE HISTORY OF MEDICINE AND ALLIED SCIENCES 11 (July 1956): 347-60.

Comments, on the hundredth anniversary of Freud's birth, on his contributions to the understandings of the mind.

Mann, Thomas. "Freud and the Future." SATURDAY REVIEW OF LITERATURE 14, no. 13 (July 25, 1936): 3-4, 14-15.

An appreciation of Freud based on an address prepared for Freud's eightieth birthday.

Murphy, Gardner. "The Current Impact of Freud Upon Psychology." AMERICAN PSYCHOLOGIST 11 (December 1956): 663-72.

Traces selected influences on Freud's thought and rates Freud's influence on sixteen areas in psychology such as physiological psychology, perception, memory, thinking, and personality.

Park, Dorothy G. "Freudian Influence on Academic Psychology." PSYCHOLOGICAL REVIEW 38 (January 1931): 73-85.

Analyzes the influence of Freud on academic psychology, based on a content analysis of fifty general psychology textbooks published between 1910 and 1930. Notes percent of pages devoted to Freudianism and authors' positive or negative attitude toward Freud and his concepts. Clearly demonstrates the growth of Freud's influence.

Shakow, David, and Rapaport, David. THE INFLUENCE OF FREUD ON AMERICAN PSYCHOLOGY. Psychological Issues, vol. 4, no. 1. Monograph 13. New York: International Universities Press, 1964. v, 243 p.

Thurstone, L.L. "Contributions of Freudism to Psychology: I. Influence of Freudism on Theoretical Psychology." PSYCHOLOGICAL REVIEW 31 (May 1924): 175-83.

e. Post-Freudian Psychoanalysis

i. ALFRED ADLER

Adler, Alfred. "Individual Psychology." In PSYCHOLOGIES OF 1930, edited by C[arl]. Murchison, pp. 395-405. Worcester, Mass.: Clark University Press, 1930.

_____. THE PRACTICE AND THEORY OF INDIVIDUAL PSYCHOLOGY. 2d ed., rev. New York: Humanities Press, 1951. viii, 352 p.

_____. UNDERSTANDING HUMAN NATURE. New York: Greenberg Publishers, 1927. xiii, 286 p.

Adler, Kurt A. "The Relevance of Adler's Psychology to Present Day Theory." AMERICAN JOURNAL OF PSYCHIATRY 127 (December 1970): 773-76.

Allen, Thomas W. "The Individual Psychology of Alfred Adler: An Item of History and a Promise of a Revolution." COUNSELING PSYCHOLOGIST 3 (1971): 3-24.

Ansbacher, Heinz L. "Adler's Interpretation of Early Recollections: Historical Account." JOURNAL OF INDIVIDUAL PSYCHOLOGY 29 (November 1973): 135-45.

_____. "Alfred Adler: A Historical Perspective." AMERICAN JOURNAL OF PSYCHIATRY 127 (December 1970): 777-82.

_____. "Alfred Adler and G. Stanley Hall: Correspondence and General Relationship." JOURNAL OF THE HISTORY OF THE BEHAVIORAL SCIENCES 7 (October 1971): 337-52.

> The Hall-Adler letters are published here for the first time, accompanied by an assessment of Hall's relationship with Adler and with Freud.

_____. "Life Style: A Historical and Systematic Review." JOURNAL OF INDIVIDUAL PSYCHOLOGY 23 (November 1967): 191-212.

_____. "Was Adler a Disciple of Freud? A Reply." JOURNAL OF INDIVIDUAL PSYCHOLOGY 18 (November 1962): 126-35.

Ansbacher, H[einz].L., and Ansbacher, Rowena, eds. THE INDIVIDUAL PSYCHOLOGY OF ALFRED ADLER. New York: Basic Books, 1956. xxiii, 503 p.

Bornemann, Aenne, and Ansbacher, H.L. "Indvidual Psychology in Germany." INDIVIDUAL PSYCHOLOGY BULLETIN 7 (1949): 30-32.

Dolliver, Robert H. "Alfred Adler and the Dialectic." JOURNAL OF THE HISTORY OF THE BEHAVIORAL SCIENCES 10 (January 1974): 16-20.

> Discusses "Adler's use of the dialectic as an apperceptive mode, his descriptions of psychological processes which reflect dialectical movement, and Adler's eventual shift from the dialectic."

Federn, Ernest. "Was Adler a Disciple of Freud? A Freudian View." JOURNAL OF INDIVIDUAL PSYCHOLOGY 19 (May 1963): 80-82.

Ledermann, E.K. "A Review of the Principles of Adlerian Psychology." INTERNATIONAL JOURNAL OF SOCIAL PSYCHIATRY 2 (1956): 172-84.

Maslow, A.H. "Was Adler a Disciple of Freud? A Note." JOURNAL OF INDIVIDUAL PSYCHOLOGY 18 (November 1962): 125.

Mosak, Harold H., ed. ALFRED ADLER: HIS INFLUENCE ON PSYCHOLOGY TODAY. Park Ridge, N.J.: Noyes, 1973. 306 p.

Papanek, Helene. "Adler's Psychology and Group Psychotherapy." AMERICAN JOURNAL OF PSYCHIATRY 127 (December 1970): 783-86.

Rayner, Doris. "Adler and His Psychology." MENTAL HEALTH, LONDON 16 (1957): 58-62.

Wilder, Joseph. "Alfred Adler in Historical Perspective." AMERICAN JOURNAL OF PSYCHOTHERAPY 24 (July 1970): 450-60.

ii. CARL GUSTAV JUNG

Adler, Gerhard. "Aspects of Jung's Personality and Work." PSYCHOLOGICAL PERSPECTIVES 6 (Spring 1975): 11-21.

_____, ed., in collaboration with Aniela Jaffe. C.G. JUNG LETTERS. 2 vols. Translated by R.F.C. Hull. Princeton, N.J.: Princeton University Press, 1973.

> Selected letters written by the distinguished analytical psychologist during a time span of over fifty years. Editorial notes with many of the letters. Lists the collected works of Jung. Indexes.

Bancroft, Mary. "Jung and His Circle." PSYCHOLOGICAL PERSPECTIVES 6 (Fall 1975): 114-27.

Clark, Robert A. "Jung and Freud: A Chapter in Psychoanalytic History." AMERICAN JOURNAL OF PSYCHOTHERAPY 9 (October 1955): 605-11.

Cohen, Edmund D. C.G. JUNG AND THE SCIENTIFIC ATTITUDE. Totowa, N.J.: Littlefield, Adams, 1976. xii, 167 p.

Dry, Avis M. THE PSYCHOLOGY OF JUNG: A CRITICAL INTERPRETATION. New York: Wiley, 1961. 329 p.

A dispassionate scholarly examination of Jung and his work, particularly from the perspective of the history of ideas.

Evans, R.I. CONVERSATIONS WITH CARL GUSTAV JUNG. Princeton, N.J.: D. Van Nostrand, 1964. viii, 173 p.

Fordham, Frieda. AN INTRODUCTION TO JUNG'S PSYCHOLOGY. 2d ed. Baltimore: Penguin Books, 1959. 127 p.

Gray, H., and Wheelwright, J.B. "Jung's Psychological Types, Including the Four Functions." JOURNAL OF GENERAL PSYCHOLOGY 33 (October 1945): 265-84.

Seeks to clarify Jung's notions of introversion and extraversion and the four functions of sensation, intuition, thinking, and feeling.

_____. "Jung's Psychological Types: Their Frequency of Occurrence." JOURNAL OF GENERAL PSYCHOLOGY 34 (January 1946): 3-17.

Explores evidence for introversion and extraversion in previous literature and from their experience with a questionnaire intended to measure the pair of perception functions (sensation vs. intuition), and the pair of judgment functions (thinking vs. feeling).

Hall, Calvin S[pringer]., and Nordby, Vernon J. A PRIMER OF JUNGIAN PSYCHOLOGY. New York: Taplinger Publishing Co., 1973. 142 p.

An exposition, based on Jung's published writings, of his theory of the normal personality. Discusses the structure, dynamics, and development of personality as well as the theory of psychological types and of symbols and dreams. Includes a brief biography of Jung and an estimate of his place in psychology. Lists Jung's published works. Suggestions for further reading. Index.

Harms, E. "Carl Gustav Jung--Defender of Freud and the Jews." PSYCHIATRIC QUARTERLY 20 (1946): 199-230.

Explores the relationship between Freud and Jung and argues against the contentions of those who accused Jung of anti-Semitism.

Jacobi, Jolande. THE PSYCHOLOGY OF C.G. JUNG. 6th ed., rev. New Haven, Conn.: Yale University Press, 1962. 192 p.

_____, ed. C.G. JUNG: PSYCHOLOGICAL REFLECTIONS; A NEW AN-THOLOGY OF HIS WRITINGS, 1905-1961. Princeton, N.J.: Princeton University Press, 1970. xvi, 391 p.

An anthology of brief (typically a paragraph) reflections on a range of topics under the general headings of nature and activity of the psyche, man and his relation to others, the world of values, and ultimate things. Includes a list of sources and a bibliography of Jung's works.

Jung, Carl Gustav. THE BASIC WRITINGS OF C.G. JUNG. Edited by Violet Staub de Laszlo. New York: Modern Library, 1959. xxiii, 552 p.

_____. COLLECTED WORKS. 18 vols. Edited by Herbert Read, Michael Fordham, and Gerhard Adler. Most vols. translated by R.F.C. Hull. New York: Pantheon Books; Princeton, N.J.: Princeton University Press, 1957-- .

Presents Jung's works in a sequence corresponding, in the main, to the development of his interests. All materials based on the most recent versions of Jung's work, but references are given to earlier versions. (Undertaking by the Bollingen Foundation Inc.) Indexes.

Kawai, Hayao. "Professor Carl G. Jung and Japanese Psychology." PSYCHO-LOGIA 5 (March 1962): 8-10.

Kelman, Harold. "Eastern Influences on Psychoanalytic Thinking." PSYCHO-LOGIA 2 (June 1959): 71-78.

Kirsch, James. "Affinities Between Zen and Analytical Psychology." PSYCHO-LOGIA 3 (June 1960): 85-91.

McGuire, William, ed. THE FREUD/JUNG LETTERS: THE CORRESPONDENCE BETWEEN SIGMUND FREUD AND C.G. JUNG. Bollingen Series no. 94. Translated by Ralph Manheim and R.F.C. Hull. Princeton, N.J.: Princeton University Press, 1974. xiii, 650 p.

_____. "The Freud/Jung Letters: 'You Have Not Been Injured By My Neuro-sis.'" PSYCHOLOGY TODAY 7 (February 1974): 37-42, 86-94.

Neumann, Erich. THE ORIGINS AND HISTORY OF CONSCIOUSNESS. Translated by R.F.C. Hull. New York: Harper and Row, 1962. xxiv, 493 p.

Explores the evolution of consciousness, based on Jungian theory, in terms of such constructs as the creation myth, the hero myth, and the transformation myth. Discusses psychological stages in the development of personality. Bibliography. Index.

Progoff, Ira. JUNG'S PSYCHOLOGY AND ITS SOCIAL MEANING. New York: Grove Press, 1953. xviii, 299 p. Index.

Selesnick, S.T. "C.G. Jung's Contributions to Psychoanalysis." AMERICAN JOURNAL OF PSYCHIATRY 120 (October 1963): 350-56.

Stepansky, Paul E. "The Empiricist as Rebel: Jung, Freud and the Burdens of Discipleship." JOURNAL OF THE HISTORY OF THE BEHAVIORAL SCIENCES 12 (July 1976): 216-39.

> Traces some of the details of the controversy between Freud and Jung and argues that Jung's modifications of Freudian theory were legitimate within the context of his liberal interpretation of discipleship. Concludes that "Jung never 'broke' with Freud" and that "he continued even after the rupture to be a loyal disciple of Freud on the modest grounds in which he conceived of discipleship."

Stern, Paul J. C.G. JUNG: THE HAUNTED PROPHET. New York: Braziller, 1976. 267 p. Bibliography.

Valett, R.W. "Jung's Effect on Psychology." BULLETIN OF THE BRITISH PSYCHOLOGICAL ASSOCIATION 46 (1962): 58-66.

Vincie, Joseph F., and Rathbauer-Vincie, Margreta. C.G. JUNG AND AN-ALYTIC PSYCHOLOGY: A COMPREHENSIVE BIBLIOGRAPHY. New York: Garland, 1977. xiv, 297 p.

iii. OTHER PSYCHOANALYTIC SCHOOLS

Abraham, Karl. SELECTED PAPERS OF KARL ABRAHAM. Translated by Doug Bryan and Alix Strachey. New York: Basic Books, 1968. 527 p.

> A collection of "Abraham's more important psychoanalytic work, except his TRAUM UND MYTHUS which has already appeared in English, and his study on Amenhotep, for which room could not, unfortunately, be found." Includes a memoir by Ernest Jones and bibliography of Abraham's scientific writings. Index.

_____. SELECTED PAPERS OF KARL ABRAHAM. Vol. 2. CLINICAL PAPERS AND ESSAYS ON PSYCHO-ANALYSIS. Edited by Hilda Abraham. Translated by Hilda Abraham, D.R. Ellison et al. New York: Basic Books, 1955. 336 p.

Alexander, Franz; Eisenstein, Samuel; and Grotjahn, Martin, eds. PSYCHO-ANALYTIC PIONEERS. New York: Basic Books, 1966. xvii, 616 p.

Brief biographies and evaluations of the contributions of forty-one psychoanalytic pioneers followed by chapters tracing the development of psychoanalysis in England and the United States. References. Index.

Alexander, Franz, and Ross, Helen, eds. TWENTY YEARS OF PSYCHOANALY-SIS: A SYMPOSIUM IN CELEBRATION OF THE TWENTIETH ANNIVERSARY OF THE CHICAGO INSTITUTE FOR PSYCHOANALYSIS. New York: W.W. Norton, 1953. 309 p.

Bergmann, Martin S. "Theodor Reik's Contributions to Psychoanalysis." PSYCHOANALYTIC REVIEW 57 (Winter 1970-71): 549-53.

Brown, J.A.C. FREUD AND THE POST-FREUDIANS. Baltimore, Md.: Penguin Books, 1961. xiii, 225 p.

Coles, Robert. ERIK H. ERIKSON: THE GROWTH OF HIS WORK. Boston: Little, Brown, 1970. xxi, 440 p.

Discusses Erikson's philosophical roots, thought, and writings. Bibliography of Erikson's writings. Bibliographical notes. Index.

Ekstein, Rudolf. "The Birth and the First Fifty Years of Otto Rank's THE TRAUMA OF BIRTH." JOURNAL OF THE OTTO RANK ASSOCIATION 8 (Winter 1973-74): 92-104.

Freud, Anna. THE EGO AND THE MECHANISMS OF DEFENSE. 2d ed. Translated by Cecil Baines. London: Hogarth Press and Institute of Psychoanalysis, 1954. x, 196 p.

Hartmann, H[einz]. ESSAYS ON EGO PSYCHOLOGY: SELECTED PROBLEMS IN PSYCHOANALYTIC THEORY. New York: International Universities Press, 1964. xv, 492 p.

Horney, Karen. THE COLLECTED WORKS OF KAREN HORNEY. 2 vols. New York: W.W. Norton, 1963. Index.

Miller, H.C. PSYCHO-ANALYSIS AND ITS DERIVATIVES. New York: Holt, 1933. 256 p.

Munroe, Ruth L. SCHOOLS OF PSYCHOANALYTIC THOUGHT: AN EXPOSITION, CRITIQUE, AND ATTEMPT AT INTEGRATION. New York: Dryden Press, 1955. xvi, 670 p.

Discusses and criticizes the major ideas of classical Freudian psychoanalysis and the schools of thought advanced by Adler, Horney, Fromm, Sullivan, Jung, and Rank. Bibliography. Index.

Progoff, Ira. "Otto Rank and the Step Beyond Psychology." JOURNAL OF THE OTTO RANK ASSOCIATION 9 (Summer 1974): 46-60.

Roazen, Paul. ERIK H. ERIKSON: THE POWER AND LIMITS OF A VISION. New York: Free Press, 1976. x, 246 p.

Examines Erikson's contributions in selected areas, his relationship with Freud, and his revitalization of Freud. Notes. Index.

_____. FREUD AND HIS FOLLOWERS. New York: Alfred A. Knopf, 1975. xxxiv, 602 p.

Reich, Wilhelm. EARLY WRITINGS: I. Translated by P. Schmitz. New York: Farrar, Straus and Giroux, 1975. xvii, 332 p.

Covers the years 1920 to 1925. Includes Reich's work on such topics as the incest taboo, motivation, and "The Impulsive Character."

Schwartz, Albert. "The Trauma of Birth and Rank's Departure From Freud." REVIEW OF EXISTENTIAL PSYCHOLOGY AND PSYCHIATRY 12 (1973): 75-92.

Silverman, Hirsch Lazaar. "The Psychology and Psychiatry of Harry Stack Sullivan." PSYCHIATRIC QUARTERLY SUPPLEMENT 29 (1955): 7-22.

13. EXISTENTIAL, PHENOMENOLOGICAL, AND HUMANISTIC PSYCHOLOGIES

In recent years existential, phenomenological, and humanistic psychologies have emerged as alternatives to behavioristic and psychoanalytic psychologies. Following are representative statements and historical surveys of these movements.

Arnold, Magda B. "The Phenomenological Approach in Psychology." PHILOSOPHICAL PSYCHOLOGIST 10 (Spring 1976): 12-14.

Berg, Jan Hendrick van den. THE CHANGING NATURE OF MAN: INTRODUCTION TO A HISTORICAL PSYCHOLOGY (METABLETICA). Translated from the Dutch by H.F. Cross. New York: W.W. Norton, 1961. 252 p.

Characterizes changes in human experience and behavior occurring over time. Not a history of psychology but a systematic study in historical psychology.

_____. A DIFFERENT EXISTENCE: PRINCIPLES OF PHENOMENOLOGICAL PSYCHOPATHOLOGY. Pittsburgh: Duquesne University Press, 1972. 141 p.

_____. THE PHENOMENOLOGICAL APPROACH TO PSYCHIATRY; AN IN-TRODUCTION TO RECENT PHENOMENOLOGICAL PSYCHOPATHOLOGY. Springfield, Ill.: Charles C Thomas, 1955. 105 p.

Binswanger, L. "On the Relationship Between Husserl's Phenomenology and Psychological Insight." PHILOSOPHY AND PHENOMENOLOGICAL RESEARCH 2 (December 1941): 199-210.

Blauner, Jacob. "Existential Analysis: L. Binswanger's Daseinsanalyse." PSYCHOANALYTIC REVIEW 44 (January 1957): 51-64.

Bucklew, John. "Perspectives in Psychology. VIII. The Three Worlds of Daseinsanalyse." PSYCHOLOGICAL RECORD 8 (October 1958): 101-4.

Explores selected trends of thought in phenomenological-existential theory and Daseinsanalysis. A central theme of these psychologies is that we must learn to relate to the Umwelt; the natural; and Mitwelt, the world of other humans; and the Eigenwelt, the self world. Notes some philosophical problems in Daseinsanalysis.

_____. "The Subjective Tradition in Phenomenological Psychology." PHILOS-OPHY OF SCIENCE 22 (October 1955): 289-99.

Bugental, J.F.T. "The Third Force in Psychology." JOURNAL OF HUMAN-ISTIC PSYCHOLOGY 4 (Spring 1964): 19-26.

Buss, Allan R. "Development of Dialectics and Development of Humanistic Psychology." HUMAN DEVELOPMENT 19, no. 4 (1976): 248-60.

_____. "Karl Mannheim's Legacy to Humanistic Psychology." JOURNAL OF HUMANISTIC PSYCHOLOGY 16 (Fall 1976): 79-81.

Child, Irvin L. HUMANISTIC PSYCHOLOGY AND THE RESEARCH TRADITION: THEIR SEVERAL VIRTUES. New York: John Wiley and Sons, 1973. vi, 213 p.

Traces the weakness and strengths of traditional research psychology and humanistic psychology as well as areas where the two are com-plementary. Index.

Dolezal, Hubert. "In Honor of Robert Brodie MacLeod: Psychological Phenom-enology Face to Face With the Persistent Problems of Psychology." JOURNAL OF THE HISTORY OF THE BEHAVIORAL SCIENCES 11 (July 1975): 223-34.

Reviews basic methods, goals, and assumptions of the psychological phenomenology of MacLeod, noting three recurrent themes: the self, communicating meanings linguistically, and value properties. Includes personal observations about MacLeod. (An invited address to Division 26 [History of Psychology] of the American Psychological Association).

Erikson, R.W. "Some Historical Connections Between Existentialism, Daseinsanalysis, Phenomenology, and the Wuerzburg School." JOURNAL OF GENERAL PSYCHOLOGY 76 (January 1967): 3-24.

Farber, M. "Edmund Husserl and the Background of His Philosophy." PHILOSOPHY AND PHENOMENOLOGICAL RESEARCH 1 (1940): 1-20.

_____. THE FOUNDATION OF PHENOMENOLOGY: EDMUND HUSSERL AND THE QUEST FOR A RIGOROUS SCIENCE OF PHILOSOPHY. Cambridge, Mass.: Harvard University Press, 1943. xi, 585 p.

Describes the background of Husserl's philosophy, his early interests in logic and mathematics, and selected themes of special interest to psychologists such as expression and meaning, analysis of wholes and parts, intentionality, and sensibility and understanding. Bibliographical materials in footnotes. Index.

Fischer, Constance I. "The Meaning of Phenomenological Psychology." PHILOSOPHICAL PSYCHOLOGIST 10 (Spring 1976): 14-19.

Fluckiger, Fritz A., and Sullivan, John J. "Husserl's Conception of a Pure Psychology." JOURNAL OF THE HISTORY OF THE BEHAVIORAL SCIENCES 1 (July 1965): 262-77.

Discusses Husserl's idea of psychology and such related topics as reductionism, rationalism, and empiricism. Based primarily on Husserl's unfinished work, THE CRISIS OF EUROPEAN SCIENCES AND TRANSCENDENTAL PHENOMENOLOGY (see below, this section, p. 224).

Frankl, Viktor E. "On Logotherapy and Existential Analysis." AMERICAN JOURNAL OF PSYCHOANALYSIS 18 (1958): 28-37.

Gavin, Eileen A. "What is Phenomenological Psychology?" PHILOSOPHICAL PSYCHOLOGIST 10 (Spring 1976): 1-4

Gilbert, Albin R. "Franz Brentano in the Perspective of Existential Psychology." JOURNAL OF THE HISTORY OF THE BEHAVIORAL SCIENCES 4 (July 1968): 249-53.

Supports the idea that "Brentano's thinking is congenial with an optimistic existentialism."

Giorgi, Amedeo. "Phenomenology and the Foundations of Psychology." NE-BRASKA SYMPOSIUM ON MOTIVATION 23 (1975): 281-348.

Golomb, Jacob. "Psychology from the Phenomenological Standpoint of Husserl." PHILOSOPHY AND PHENOMENOLOGICAL RESEARCH 36 (June 1976): 451-71.

Gurwitsch, Aron. STUDIES IN PHENOMENOLOGY AND PSYCHOLOGY. Evanston, Ill.: Northwestern University Press, 1966. xxv, 452 p.

> A collection of previously published papers on phenomenology and on topics such as the affinities and relationships between phenomenology and Gestalt theory, the psychology of William James, and the work of Gelb and Goldstein on brain disorders. Reference is also made to some of Piaget's theories. A final chapter discusses Husserl's last work on THE CRISIS OF THE EUROPEAN SCIENCES AND TRANSCENDENTAL PHENOMENOLOGY, then untranslated, but now available in English (see below, this section). Index.

Henle, Mary, and Baltimore, Gertrude. "Portraits in Straw." PSYCHOLOGICAL REVIEW 74 (July 1967): 325-29.

> Contends that Brody and Oppenheim (see section C15, p. 238), in an earlier critique of phenomenology, misunderstood phenomenological views of conceptualized and nonconceptualized experiences, and that behaviorism cannot logically be disinterested in private experience. Discusses the problem of the reconciliation of phenomenology and behaviorism.

Husserl, Edmund. THE CRISIS OF EUROPEAN SCIENCES AND TRANSCENDENTAL PHENOMENOLOGY: AN INTRODUCTION TO PHENOMENOLOGICAL PHILOSOPHY. Translated by David Carr. Evanston, Ill.: Northwestern University Press, 1970. x, iii, 405 p.

> Unlike Husserl's earlier introductions to phenomenology, this unfinished book is a historical introduction with discussions of Greek philosophy, the scientific revolution, and the work of Descartes and Kant. Of interest to psychologists are the materials on Wundt and Brentano. Appendixes. Index.

_____. IDEAS: GENERAL INTRODUCTION TO PURE PHENOMENOLOGY. Translated by W.R.B. Gibson. New York: Macmillan, 1931. 466 p.

Kahn, Eugen. "An Appraisal of Existential Analysis." PSYCHIATRIC QUARTERLY 31 (1957): 203-27.

Kelman, H. "A Phenomenological Approach to Dream Interpretation: I. Phenomenology--An Historical Perspective." AMERICAN JOURNAL OF PSYCHOANALYSIS 25, no. 2 (1965): 188-202.

Kockelmans, Joseph J. EDMUND HUSSERL'S PHENOMENOLOGICAL PSY-
CHOLOGY: A HISTORICO-CRITICAL STUDY. Translated by Bernd Jager.
Pittsburgh: Duquesne University Press, 1967. 359 p.

> An overview of the history of psychology from its genesis in Greek
> philosophy to the twentieth century followed by such topics as an
> appraisal of the development of Husserl's thought, characteristics
> of phenomenological psychology, relations of empirical psychology
> and phenomenological psychology, the meaning of Husserl's last
> work ("Krisis"), and specific issues in phenomenological psychology.
> Bibliography.

_____. "Phenomenological Psychology in the United States: A Critical Analy-
sis of the Actual Situation." JOURNAL OF PHENOMENOLOGICAL PSYCHOL-
OGY 1 (Spring 1971): 139-72.

Kohyama, Iwao. "Existential Philosophy and Psychology in the East and the
West." PSYCHOLOGIA 9 (March 1966): 2-6.

> An overview of selected Buddhistic thought and related teachings
> of Schelling, Heidegger, and Jaspers.

Kuenzli, Alfred E., ed. THE PHENOMENOLOGICAL PROBLEM. New York:
Harper and Row, 1959. x, 321 p.

> An anthology of papers by such psychologists as Donald Snygg,
> Carl Rogers, Robert MacLeod, and M. Brewster Smith. Focuses
> on attempts to describe human experience from the perspective of
> the person experiencing it. Selected bibliography. Index.

Landsman, Ted. "Four Phenomenologies." JOURNAL OF INDIVIDUAL PSY-
CHOLOGY 14 (May 1958): 29-37.

La Pointe, Francois H. "Merleau-Ponty's Phenomenological Critique of Psychology." JOURNAL OF PHENOMENOLOGICAL PSYCHOLOGY 2 (Spring 1972):
237-55.

Linschoten, Hans. ON THE WAY TOWARD A PHENOMENOLOGICAL PSY-
CHOLOGY: THE PSYCHOLOGY OF WILLIAM JAMES. Pittsburgh: Duquesne
University Press, 1968. 319 p.

McGill, V.J. "The Bearing of Phenomenology on Psychology." PHILOSOPHY
AND PHENOMENOLOGICAL RESEARCH 7 (March 1947): 357-68.

MacLeod, Robert B[rodie]. "The Phenomenological Approach to Social Psychology." PSYCHOLOGICAL REVIEW 54 (July 1947): 193-210.

Maddi, Salvatore R., and Costa, Paul T. HUMANISM IN PERSONOLOGY:

ALLPORT, MASLOW, AND MURRAY. Chicago: Aldine/Atherton, 1972. xviii, 200 p.

May, Rollo. "Gregory Bateson and Humanistic Psychology." JOURNAL OF HUMANISTIC PSYCHOLOGY 16 (Fall 1976): 33-51.

_____, ed. EXISTENTIAL PSYCHOLOGY. New York: Random House, 1961. 126 p.

> Papers presented by May, Maslow, Feifel, Rogers, and Allport at a symposium at the 1959 convention of the American Psychological Association. Discusses the interests of psychologists in existentialism and the contributions of existentialism to psychology. Partially annotated bibliography by Joseph Lyons.

May, Rollo; Angel, Ernest; and Ellenberger, Henri F., eds. EXISTENCE: A NEW DIMENSION IN PSYCHIATRY AND PSYCHOLOGY. New York: Basic Books, 1958. x, 445 p.

> Includes an introduction by May on the origins and significance of the existential movement in psychology, and a clinical introduction by Ellenberger on psychiatric phenomenology and existential analysis. Contains translations of important phenomenological papers by such figures as Ludwig Binswanger, Eugene Minkowski, Erwin W. Strauss, V.E. von Gebsattel, and Ronald Kuhn, followed by brief biographical notes on the contributors. Index.

Misiak, Henryk, and Sexton, Virginia Staudt. PHENOMENOLOGICAL, EXISTENTIAL, AND HUMANISTIC PSYCHOLOGIES: A HISTORICAL SURVEY. New York: Grune and Stratton, 1973. x, 162 p.

> Examines historical and philosophical foundations of phenomenological and existential psychology as a background for understanding contemporary humanistic psychology. Bibliography. Index.

Morrison, James C. "Husserl and Brentano on Intentionality." PHILOSOPHY AND PHENOMENOLOGICAL RESEARCH 31 (September 1970): 27-46.

Moustgaard, I.K. "Phenomenological Descriptions after the Manner of Edgar Rubin." JOURNAL OF PHENOMENOLOGICAL PSYCHOLOGY 6 (Fall 1975): 31-61.

> Reviews Rubin's influence on Gestalt, descriptive, and phenomenological psychology.

Muuss, Rolf. "Existentialism and Psychology." EDUCATIONAL THEORY 6 (July 1956): 135-53.

Nath, Prem. "Existential Trends in American Psychology." PSYCHOLOGIA 6 (September 1963): 125-30.

Outlines major existential premises and reviews the thought of such Americans as Maslow and Allport.

Nord, Walter. "A Marxist Critique of Humanistic Psychology." JOURNAL OF HUMANISTIC PSYCHOLOGY 17 (Winter 1977): 75-83.

Osborn, Andrew D. "Some Recent German Critics of Phenomenology." JOURNAL OF PHILOSOPHY 31 (July 1934): 377-82.

Patterson, C.H. "Phenomenological Psychology." PERSONNEL AND GUIDANCE JOURNAL 43 (June 1965): 997-1005.

Romanyshyn, Robert D. "Phenomenological Psychology." PHILOSOPHICAL PSYCHOLOGIST 10 (Spring 1976): 4-11.

Rychlak, Joseph F. "Psychological Science as a Humanist Views it." NEBRASKA SYMPOSIUM ON MOTIVATION 23 (1975): 205-29.

Traces the history of the controversy between behavioristic and humanistic theories and proposes a humanistic learning theory.

_____. THE PSYCHOLOGY OF RIGOROUS HUMANISM. New York: John Wiley and Sons, 1977. xi, 547 p.

Sartre, Jean Paul. BEING AND NOTHINGNESS: AN ESSAY IN PHENOMENOLOGICAL ONTOLOGY. Special abridged edition. Translated and with an introduction by Hazel E. Barnes. New York: Citadel Press, 1971. lxvii, 553 p.

A well-known philosophic work and a classic in phenomenological psychology. Details Sartre's position on consciousness, freedom, the existence of others, and our relations with others.

_____. EXISTENTIAL PSYCHOANALYSIS. Translated and with an introduction by Hazel E. Barnes. New York: Philosophical Library, 1953. viii, 275 p.

A translation of a portion of Sartre's major work, BEING AND NOTHINGNESS (see above), with a lengthy translator's introduction. Index.

Severin, Frank T., ed. HUMANISTIC VIEWPOINTS IN PSYCHOLOGY: A BOOK OF READINGS. New York: McGraw-Hill, 1965. xvii, 430 p.

Sonnemann, Ulrich. EXISTENCE AND THERAPY: AN INTRODUCTION TO PHENOMENOLOGICAL PSYCHOLOGY AND EXISTENTIAL ANALYSIS. New York: Grune and Stratton, 1954. xi, 372 p.

A rather difficult treatise examining the thought of Binswanger, Heidegger, Jaspers, Sartre, and other phenomenologists and existentialists. Part 1: "The Crisis of Knowledge and the Rise of Phenomenology," Part 2: "The Spectre of Nothingness and the Janus Face of Reflection," and Part 3: "The Peril to Man, and Psychotherapy: The Freedom to Be." Notes. Bibliography. Index.

Spiegelberg, Herbert. PHENOMENOLOGY IN PSYCHOLOGY AND PSYCHIATRY. Evanston, Ill.: Northwestern University Press, 1972. xiv, 411 p.

Provides a historical overview of the influence of phenomenological thought in the major schools of psychology and psychiatry. Bibliography.

Strasser, Stephan. "Phenomenological Trends in European Psychology." PHILOSOPHY AND PHENOMENOLOGICAL RESEARCH 18 (September 1957): 18-34.

_____. PHENOMENOLOGY AND THE HUMAN SCIENCES: A CONTRIBUTION TO A NEW SCIENTIFIC IDEAL. Pittsburgh: Duquesne University Press, 1963. Distributed by Humanities Press, Atlantic Highlands, 1974. xiii, 339 p.

An elaboration and defense of phenomenology examining mythical, scientific, and philosophical attitudes toward knowledge.

Strauss, Erwin Walter. PHENOMENOLOGICAL PSYCHOLOGY. Translated in part by Erling Eng. New York: Basic Books, 1966. xiii, 353 p.

Three parts: phenomenological studies, anthropological studies, and clinical studies. Presents a collection of selected papers on such topics as spatiality, remembering, awakeness, the upright posture, Descartes's significance for modern psychology, shame, the pathology of compulsion, and the pseudo-reversibility of catatonic stupor. A helpful sourcebook for those seeking phenomenological approaches to specific problems. References. Index.

Sutich, Anthony J. "Transpersonal Psychology: An Emerging Force." JOURNAL OF HUMANISTIC PSYCHOLOGY 8 (Spring 1968): 77-78.

Sutich, Anthony J., and Vich, Miles A., eds. READINGS IN HUMANISTIC PSYCHOLOGY. New York: Free Press, 1969. xv, 440 p.

Van Spaendonck, J.A. "An Analysis of the Metabletical Method." JOURNAL OF PHENOMENOLOGICAL PSYCHOLOGY 6 (Fall 1975): 89-108.

Examines J.H. van den Berg's theory of history and psychology.

Welch, E. Parl. EDMUND HUSSERL'S PHENOMENOLOGY. Los Angeles, Calif.: University of Southern California Press, 1939. 100 p.

Presents an overview of Husserl's fundamental concepts and a comparison of realism and phenomenology. Bibliography.

_____. THE PHILOSOPHY OF EDMUND HUSSERL: THE ORIGIN AND DEVELOPMENT OF HIS PHENOMENOLOGY. New York: Columbia University Press, 1941. xxiv, 337 p.

Wertheimer, Michael. "Humanistic Psychology and the Humane but Tough-Minded Psychologist." AMERICAN PSYCHOLOGIST 33 (1978): 739-45.

Argues that the phrase "humanistic psychology" is typically used in a very vague manner, and that there is little agreement about its definition.

Winthrop, Henry. "Some Considerations Concerning the Status of Phenomenology." JOURNAL OF GENERAL PSYCHOLOGY 68 (January 1963): 127-40.

Characterizes typical criticisms of phenomenology and outlines some of its strengths and weaknesses.

Young, Paul Thomas. "The Phenomenological Point of View." PSYCHOLOGICAL REVIEW 31 (July 1924): 288-96.

Zaner, Richard M. "Criticism of 'Tensions in Psychology Between the Methods of Behaviorism and Phenomenology.'" PSYCHOLOGICAL REVIEW 74 (July 1967): 318-24.

A critique of an earlier paper charging that Brody and Oppenheim (see section C15, p. 238) are incorrect when they claim that phenomenological method does without any concepts at all. Points to logical difficulties in the assertion that the behaviorist can appeal to publicly verifiable data. Contrary to Brody and Oppenheim, the author claims that rapprochement between phenomenology and behaviorism is still open.

14. ISSUES IN SYSTEMATIC PSYCHOLOGY

Issues in the philosophy of science and the philosophy of psychology are explored in the following references. These include the role of theory in science, vitalistic and mechanistic explanation, pure vs. applied science, and wholistic vs. elementaristic psychologies. Listed here are also a few works on systems other than those to which previous subsections have been devoted.

Anthony, James. "The System Makers: Piaget and Freud." BRITISH JOURNAL OF MEDICAL PSYCHOLOGY 30 (1957): 255-69.

Bakan, David. "Volition as a Problem in Psychology." ONTARIO PSYCHOLOGIST 7 (December 1975): 5-8.

Outlines historical treatment of volition in psychology and argues
that volitional processes should be reexamined by psychologists.
Lists sources on the free will–determinism issue.

Bergmann, Gustav, and Spence, Kenneth W. "Operationism and Theory in
Psychology." PSYCHOLOGICAL REVIEW 48 (January 1941): 1-14.

A general discussion of some of the problems associated with applications of operationism and theory in psychology followed by a
discussion of Hull's theory in the light of such problems.

Bertocci, Peter A. "The Partners that Cannot be Divorced: Psychology and
Philosophy." PSYCHOLOGIA 14 (December 1971): 148-52.

A comment on hidden philosophical biases in psychology.

Borger, Robert, and Cioffi, Frank, eds. EXPLANATION IN THE BEHAVIORAL
SCIENCES. Cambridge: Cambridge University Press, 1970. xii, 520 p.

A distinguished group of contributors from such disciplines as sociology, philosophy, psychology, and linguistics explore fundamental
issues pertaining to explanation in the behavioral sciences. Discusses issues such as purposive vs. mechanistic explanation and
reasons vs. causes. References. Index.

Braginsky, D.D., and Braginsky, B.M. MAINSTREAM PSYCHOLOGY: A
CRITIQUE. New York: Holt, Rinehart, and Winston, 1974. xv, 206 p.

Argues that the methods and theories of scientific psychology are
conditioned by the values, assumptions, and ideology of mainstream
society. References. Index.

Bretscher, Theodore Adolph. "A Paradox in Psychological Theorizing." PSY-
CHOLOGICAL REVIEW 38 (January 1931): 14-26.

Argues that mechanistic views are compatible with scientific methodology but assume a mental being which is foreign to experience;
organismic or configurational views create a mental being which is
consistent with experience but less compatible with the requirements
of scientific methodology.

Brunswik, Egon. "The Conceptual Framework of Psychology." In INTERNA-
TIONAL ENCYCLOPEDIA OF UNIFIED SCIENCE, edited by Otto Neurath,
vol. 1, no. 10. Chicago: University of Chicago Press, 1952.

See section B7e, p. 118, for annotation.

Coan, Richard W. "Dimensions of Psychological Theory." AMERICAN PSY-
CHOLOGIST 23 (November 1968): 715-22.

Traces trends in such dimensions of psychological theory as methodological emphasis, basic assumptions, and mode of conceptualization from the 1880s to the 1950s.

Cohen, David. PSYCHOLOGISTS ON PSYCHOLOGY. New York: Taplinger, 1977. 360 p.

Based on interviews with thirteen well-known contemporary psychologists (including David McClelland, Donald Broadbent, Noam Chomsky, H.J. Eysenck, Leon Festinger, Neal Miller, B.F. Skinner, and Niko Tinbergen). Explores some of the major systematic and theoretical issues which divide modern psychology. Cohen provides helpful background material and considerable biographical materials. Concludes with a summary of the various positions relating to such matters as methodology, humanistic psychology, and the paradigm of psychology. Bibliography.

Dennis, Wayne, et al. CURRENT TRENDS IN PSYCHOLOGICAL THEORY: A BICENTENNIAL PROGRAM. Pittsburgh: University of Pittsburgh Press, 1961. ix, 229 p.

Driesch, Hans. "Critical Remarks on Some Modern Types of Psychology." PEDAGOGICAL SEMINARY 34 (March 1927): 3-13.

Brief but strong critical commentary on Watsonian behaviorism and on Gestalt psychology.

Eacker, Jay N. PROBLEMS OF PHILOSOPHY AND PSYCHOLOGY. Chicago: Nelson-Hall, 1975. 216 p.

Examines such perennial philosophical problems as causality, purpose, freedom, knowledge, and mind-brain relations. Glossary. References. Index.

English, Horace B. "The Ghostly Tradition and the Descriptive Categories of Psychology." PSYCHOLOGICAL REVIEW 40 (November 1933): 498-513.

_____. "Illusion as a Problem in Systematic Psychology." PSYCHOLOGICAL REVIEW 58 (January 1951): 52-53.

Erickson, Ralph W. "An Examination of the System of Professor K.S. Lashley." JOURNAL OF GENERAL PSYCHOLOGY 42 (1950): 243-60.

Fodor, Jerry A. PSYCHOLOGICAL EXPLANATION: AN INTRODUCTION TO THE PHILOSOPHY OF PSYCHOLOGY. New York: Random House, 1968. xxi, 165 p.

Examines philosophical problems which confront psychological theories. Contains chapters on whether psychology is possible, behaviorism and mentalism, materialism, and the logic of simulation. Notes. References. Index.

Gilbert, Albin R. "Whatever Happened to the Will in American Psychology." JOURNAL OF THE HISTORY OF THE BEHAVIORAL SCIENCES 6 (January 1970): 52-58.

> Reviews interpretations of the will by Locke, Leibniz, and psychologists representing phenomenological, behavioristic, and existential approaches.

Guthrie, Edwin R. "The Status of Systematic Psychology." AMERICAN PSYCHOLOGIST 5 (April 1950): 97-101.

> Contrasts the goals of science and applied disciplines such as medicine, and argues that the emphasis in psychology should be on basic science.

Hammond, Kenneth R., ed. THE PSYCHOLOGY OF EGON BRUNSWIK. New York: Holt, Rinehart and Winston, 1966. x, 549 p.

> A memorial volume based on the collaborative efforts of numerous psychologists. Includes essays and studies which clarify Brunswik's views on such topics as memory, perception, psychological tests, and the nature of the environment. Contains thoughtful criticisms of Brunswik's work as well as four of his papers, including one on historical and thematic relations of psychology to other sciences. Lists Brunswik's papers, monographs, and books. References. Index.

Hecht, Selig. "The Uncertainty Principle and Human Behavior." HARPER'S MAGAZINE, January 1935, pp. 237-49.

> A sophisticated examination of the issue of free will and determinism in physics, biology, and psychology.

Kantor, J.R. INTERBEHAVIORAL PSYCHOLOGY: A SAMPLE OF SCIENTIFIC SYSTEM CONSTRUCTION. Bloomington, Ind.: Principia Press, 1958. xvi, 238 p.

_____. "Psychology as a Science of Critical Evaluation." PSYCHOLOGICAL REVIEW 26 (January 1919): 1-15.

> Argues that the scientist should attempt to describe facts wherever they are found and that the preconceived notions of some of the schools of thought (for example, that consciousness must be broken down into its elements, or that psychology is the study of behavior alone) may obscure important facts and impede the progress of the science.

Kirsch, Irving. "Psychology's First Paradigm." JOURNAL OF THE HISTORY OF THE BEHAVIORAL SCIENCES 13 (October 1977): 317-25.

Argues that psychology was organized around a unifying mentalist paradigm by the end of the nineteenth century. Early behaviorists overthrew the mental model, but it reappeared with the work of Tolman and Hebb.

Klein, David Ballin. "Eclecticism versus System-Making in Psychology." PSYCHOLOGICAL REVIEW 37 (November 1930): 488-96.

Koch, Sigmund. "Theoretical Psychology, 1950: An Overview." PSYCHOLOGICAL REVIEW 58 (July 1951): 295-301.

Lana, Robert E. THE FOUNDATIONS OF PSYCHOLOGICAL THEORY. Hillsdale, N.J.: Lawrence Erlbaum, 1976. Distributed by John Wiley and Sons, New York. xii, 177 p.

A specialized history focusing on the historical development of epistemological positions and their interplay with psychological theory and method. Presents selected historical materials from the Greeks to the present. References. Index.

London, Ivan D. "The Need for Reorientation in Psychology in the Light of Modern Physics." JOURNAL OF GENERAL PSYCHOLOGY 40 (April 1949): 219-28.

McGeoch, John A. "The Formal Criteria of a Systematic Psychology." PSYCHOLOGICAL REVIEW 40 (January 1933): 1-12.

Madden, Edward H. PHILOSOPHICAL PROBLEMS OF PSYCHOLOGY. New York: Odyssey Press, 1962. vii, 149 p.

Examines selected philosophical problems associated with Gestalt theory, learning theory, and psychoanalysis in chapters on wholes vs. parts, isomorphism, lawfulness, psychoanalytic propositions, and psychoanalysis and responsibility. Bibliographic materials. Index.

Marx, Melvin H., ed. PSYCHOLOGICAL THEORY. New York: Macmillan 1951. xi, 585 p.

Twenty-three papers dealing with problems of theory construction in psychology followed by twenty-four papers describing representative theories within such specialty areas as perception, learning, psychodynamics, personality, and social interaction. Index.

_____. THEORIES IN CONTEMPORARY PSYCHOLOGY. New York: Macmillan, 1963. xi, 628 p.

Theory and the role of theory in specialty areas are discussed in thirty-five papers on the role of models, mathematical and statistical models, theoretical constructs, levels of explanation, development and social psychology, personality and psychodynamics, learning and sensation and perception. Editorial comments introduce each major area. With the editor's 1951 PSYCHOLOGICAL THEORY (see preceding entry), provides an overview of the evolution of theory in psychology from 1951 to 1963. References. Index.

Marx, Melvin H., and Goodson, Felix H., eds. THEORIES IN CONTEMPORARY PSYCHOLOGY. 2d ed. New York: Macmillan, 1976. x, 642 p.

Selected articles on the philosophical and methodological problems of contemporary psychology. Emphasizes the paradigm shift which occurred since the 1963 edition (see preceding entry).

Marx, Melvin H., and Hillix, William A. SYSTEMS AND THEORIES IN PSYCHOLOGY. 2d ed. New York: McGraw-Hill, 1973. xv, 626 p.

A widely-used systematic text divided into three parts: psychology as science, systems of psychology, and contemporary theories. Appendixes describe psychology in various countries. Index.

Matson, Floyd W. THE IDEA OF MAN. New York: Delacorte Press, 1976. xxii, 249 p.

Discusses historic views about human nature.

Oppenheim, Frank M. "Royce's Community: A Dimension Missing in Freud and James?" JOURNAL OF THE HISTORY OF THE BEHAVIORAL SCIENCES 13 (April 1977): 173-90.

A brief outline of Royce's contributions to psychology: courses in psychology at Harvard and Radcliffe, publication of over forty journal articles on psychological topics, public lectures on psychology, interest in Harvard's psychological laboratory and in psychopathology. Discusses some of Royce's substantive views, especially of the development of social consciousness, and compares them with those of Baldwin, Freud, and James.

Sarason, Seymour B. "Psychology: To the Finland Station in the Heavenly City of the Eighteenth Century Philosophers." AMERICAN PSYCHOLOGIST 30 (November 1975): 1072-88.

A provocative article pointing to themes of method, authority, truth, tradition, and dogmatism in Carl Becker's book THE HEAVENLY CITY OF THE EIGHTEENTH CENTURY PHILOSOPHERS (New Haven, Conn.: Yale University Press, 1959) and Edmund Wilson's book TO THE FINLAND STATION (New York: Farrar,

Straus and Giroux, 1972), which are relevant to the intellectual history of psychology and to contemporary psychology.

Schultz, Duane P., ed. THE SCIENCE OF PSYCHOLOGY: CRITICAL REFLECTIONS. New York: Appleton-Century-Crofts, 1970. ix, 402 p.

An anthology raising questions concerning the potential narrowness and futility of strictly scientific psychology. Calls for a continuation of scientific psychology but with new emphasis on a critical appraisal of the previous philosophical and methodological constraints which have resulted in artificial and trivial concerns. Index.

Seward, Georgene S., and Seward, John P., eds. CURRENT PSYCHOLOGICAL ISSUES: ESSAYS IN HONOR OF ROBERT S. WOODWORTH. New York: Holt, 1958. viii, 360 p.

Contains papers by psychologists whose work was influenced by Woodworth and includes a brief biography. References. Indexes.

Stevens, S.S. "Psychology and the Science of Science." PSYCHOLOGICAL BULLETIN 36 (April 1939): 221-63.

An overview of logical positivism with emphasis on operationism and its use in psychology.

Troland, Leonard T. THE PRINCIPLES OF PSYCHOPHYSIOLOGY: A SURVEY OF MODERN SCIENTIFIC PSYCHOLOGY. 3 vols. New York: Van Nostrand, 1929. Reprint. New York: Greenwood Press, 1969.

A systematic examination of the problems and methods of psychology and important facts and theories. Volume 1 devoted to problems of psychology and perception, volume 2 to sensation, and volume 3 to cerebration and action. Troland seeks to outline a system which will serve as an integration of behaviorism and introspection. Bibliography. Index.

Vanderplas, James M., ed. CONTROVERSIAL ISSUES IN PSYCHOLOGY. New York: Houghton Mifflin, 1966. x, 438 p.

Examines selected issues in academic psychology and presents classic position papers. Issues are the role of theory, the definition of psychology, continuity versus noncontinuity in learning, theories of emotion, and the scientific status of psychoanalytic theory. References and bibliographic materials.

Warren, Howard C. "Psychology and the Central Nervous System." PSYCHOLOGICAL REVIEW 28 (July 1921): 249-69.

Argues for a balanced conception of psychology concerned with environmental stimulation, activity of the central nervous system, and

Systems and Schools of Psychology

responses. Notes that behavior and conscious experiences are the result of nervous system activity.

Wertheimer, Michael. FUNDAMENTAL ISSUES IN PSYCHOLOGY. New York: Holt, Rinehart and Winston, 1972. ix, 278 p.

See section B7E, p. 122, for annotation.

Wheeler, R[aymond].H[older]. "Persistent Problems in Systematic Psychology. V. Attention and Association." PSYCHOLOGICAL REVIEW 35 (January 1928): 1-18.

_____. "Persistent Problems in Systematic Psychology. IV. Structural versus Functional Analysis." JOURNAL OF GENERAL PSYCHOLOGY 1 (January 1928): 91-107.

_____. "Persistent Problems in Systematic Psychology. I. A Philosophical Heritage." PSYCHOLOGICAL REVIEW 32 (May 1925): 179-91.

_____. "Persistent Problems in Systematic Psychology. III. Stimulus-Error and Complete Introspection." PSYCHOLOGICAL REVIEW 32 (November 1925): 443-56.

_____. "Persistent Problems in Systematic Psychology. II. The Psychological Datum." PSYCHOLOGICAL REVIEW 32 (July 1925): 251-65.

Wolman, Benjamin B., ed., and Nagel, Ernest, consult. ed. SCIENTIFIC PSYCHOLOGY: PRINCIPLES AND APPROACHES. New York: Basic Books, 1965. xv, 620 p.

Thirty original articles on philosophical problems associated with the science of psychology. Suggested readings. Index.

Woodworth, R[obert].S[essions]. PSYCHOLOGICAL ISSUES: SELECTED PAPERS OF ROBERT S. WOODWORTH. New York: Columbia University Press, 1939. x, 421 p.

An anthology of major papers by Woodworth, including his autobiography, presented to the author as a surprise by admiring colleagues at Columbia University on the occasion of his seventieth birthday. Sections devoted to systematic problems, abnormal psychology, differential psychology, motor phenomena, and educational psychology. Bibliography of Woodworth's articles and books. Index.

15. COMPARISONS AMONG SYSTEMS

This section contains references to books and articles which explore similarities and differences among the various systems of psychology. The topics investigated include philosophical assumptions, definition of psychology, and methods of inquiry. Some entries in the preceding section (C14) have similar themes.

Alonzo, Thomas M.; LaCagnina, Giulia R.; and Olsen, Bob G. "Behaviorism vs. Humanism: Two Contrasting Approaches to Learning Theory." SOUTHERN JOURNAL OF EDUCATIONAL RESEARCH 11 (Summer 1977): 135-51.

Angell, James Rowland. "The Relations of Structural and Functional Psychology to Philosophy." PHILOSOPHICAL REVIEW 12 (May 1903): 243-71.

Bash, K.W. "Consciousness and the Unconscious in Depth and Gestalt Psychology." ACTA PSYCHOLOGICA 6 (1949): 213-88.

Bentley, Madison. "The Major Categories of Psychology." PSYCHOLOGICAL REVIEW 33 (March 1926): 71-105.

> Explores some of the fundamental categories of inquiry in structuralism, behaviorism, and Gestalt psychology. (Presidential address to the American Psychological Association in 1925).

Bixler, Julius Seelye. "Reappraisals: The Existentialists and William James." AMERICAN SCHOLAR 28 (Winter 1958-59): 80-90.

> Compares selected existentialist thought with the philosophy of William James. Notes that "everything they have said he has said better."

Bode, B.H. "What is Psychology?" PSYCHOLOGICAL REVIEW 29 (July 1922): 250-58.

> Discusses problems associated with behaviorism and older psychologies which emphasized experience. Argues that psychology must include experience as part of its subject matter if it is to be distinguished from physiology or physics.

Boring, Edwin G. "The Psychologist's Circle." PSYCHOLOGICAL REVIEW 38 (March 1931): 177-82.

> An exploration of problems associated with definitions of psychology proposed by the structuralist, Gestalt, and behaviorist schools. Argues for a broad conception of psychology which includes both experience and physiological facts.

Boss, Medard. PSYCHOANALYSIS AND DASEINSANALYSIS. Translated by Ludwig B. Lefebre. New York: Basic Books, 1963. viii, 295 p.

> An exposition of the daseinsanalytic view followed by daseinsanalytic reevaluations of psychoanalytic therapy and selected psychoana-

lytic handling of such topics as transference, dreams, and counter-transference. Index.

Brody, Nathan, and Oppenheim, Paul. "Tensions in Psychology between the Methods of Behaviorism and Phenomenology." PSYCHOLOGICAL REVIEW 73 (July 1966): 295-305.

Brandt, Lewis W. "Phenomenology, Psychoanalysis, and Behaviorism: [E = S] vs. [E ≠ S]?" JOURNAL OF PHENOMENOLOGICAL PSYCHOLOGY 1 (1970): 7-18.

Burns, Hobert W. "Pragmatism and the Science of Behavior." PHILOSOPHY OF SCIENCE 27 (January 1960): 58-74.

Burt, Cyril. "Consciousness and Behaviorism: A Reply." BRITISH JOURNAL OF PSYCHOLOGY 55 (February 1964): 93-96.

Buss, Allan R. "The Structure of Psychological Revolutions." JOURNAL OF THE HISTORY OF THE BEHAVIORAL SCIENCES 14 (January 1978): 57-64.

> Briefly characterizes the paradigms of structuralism, behaviorism, psychoanalysis, cognitive psychology, and humanistic psychology in terms of their positions on subject-object relationships. Argues for a psychological revolution to end psychological revolutions, namely "a dialectical paradigm [which] emphasizes the reciprocal, interactive relationship between the person and reality such that each may serve as both subject and object."

Butler, Clark. "Hegel and Freud: A Comparison." PHILOSOPHY AND PHENOMENOLOGICAL RESEARCH 36 (June 1976): 506-22.

Calkins, Mary Whiton. "A Reconciliation Between Structural and Functional Psychology: President's Address." PSYCHOLOGICAL REVIEW 13 (March 1906): 61-81.

> Points to the interest of the physicist in the ultimate parts of matter and of the biologist in adaptation of organisms, and to the legitimacy of both interests. Argues that both structural and functional analysis are essential to an adequate psychology of self. (Presidential address at the 1905 meeting of the American Psychological Association).

Cameron, Edward Herbert, ed. VIEWPOINTS IN EDUCATIONAL PSYCHOLOGY: A BOOK OF SELECTED READINGS. New York: Century, 1930. xxv, 511 p. Index.

> See section D14, p. 365, for annotation.

Carmichael, L. "Scientific Psychology and the Schools of Psychology." AMERI-CAN JOURNAL OF PSYCHIATRY 11 (1932): 955-68.

Notes that despite the various systems of psychology, experimental psychologists still seek an understanding of human nature.

Catania, A. Charles. "The Psychologies of Structure, Function, and Development." AMERICAN PSYCHOLOGIST 28 (May 1973): 434-43.

Suggests that differences among various systems of psychology should not be viewed as revolutionary paradigm clashes "because it is not clear that the controversies have grown out of incompatible treat-ments of common problems." Argues that systems of psychology have been concerned with essentially different subject matter.

Chou, Siegen K. "Cinematography of Psychologies." PSYCHOLOGICAL RE-VIEW 38 (May 1913): 254-75.

Argues that the various schools of psychology are somewhat analo-gous to several camera operators taking pictures of the same scene but from different vantage points. Suggests the possibility of ec-lecticism, similar to a panoramic view.

Cobliner, W. Godfrey. "Psychoanalysis and the Geneva School of Genetic Psychology: Parallels and Counterparts." INTERNATIONAL JOURNAL OF PSYCHIATRY 3 (1967): 82-129.

Correnti, Samuel. "A Comparison of Behaviorism and Psychoanalysis with Existentialism." JOURNAL OF EXISTENTIALISM 5 (1965): 379-88.

Corriveau, Michael. "Phenomenology, Psychology, and Radical Behaviorism: Skinner and Merleau-Ponty on Behavior." JOURNAL OF PHENOMENOLOGI-CAL PSYCHOLOGY 3 (Fall 1972): 7-34.

Couzin, Robert. "Leibnitz, Freud and Kabbala." JOURNAL OF THE HISTORY OF THE BEHAVIORAL SCIENCES 6 (October 1970): 335-48.

Presents evidence for a possible equation of the so-called Lockean-Leibnitzian and behavioristic-psychoanalytic dichotomies.

Dallenbach, Karl M. "Phrenology versus Psychoanalysis." AMERICAN JOUR-NAL OF PSYCHOLOGY 68 (December 1955): 511-25.

Suggests similarities in the development and philosophy of phrenol-ogy and psychoanalysis.

Dunlap, Knight. OLD AND NEW VIEWPOINTS IN PSYCHOLOGY. St. Louis, Mo.: C.V. Mosby, 1925. 166 p.

239

Five lectures on schools of psychology, mental measurements, spiritualism, humor, and character reading. Index.

Ellis, Albert. "Theoretical Schools of Psychology." In CONTRIBUTIONS TO-WARD MEDICAL PSYCHOLOGY: THEORY AND PSYCHODIAGNOSTIC METH-ODS, edited by Arthur Weider, pp. 31-50. New York: Ronald Press, 1953.

Chapter includes brief and dated overviews of such systems as behaviorism, Gestalt psychology, psychoanalysis, and the psychologies of Adler, Jung, Rank, Horney, Fromm, Sullivan, and Rogers. Index.

English, Horace B. "Is a Synthesis of Psychological Schools to be Found in a Personalistic Act-Psychology?" PSYCHOLOGICAL REVIEW 33 (July 1926): 298-307.

Erickson, Ralph W. "Some Historical Connections Between Existentialism, Daseinsanalysis, Phenomenology, and the Wuerzburg School." JOURNAL OF GENERAL PSYCHOLOGY 76 (January 1967): 3-24.

Outlines selected contributions of leading figures such as Sartre, Kierkegaard, Nietzsche, Jaspers, Husserl, Brentano, Kuelpe, and Heidegger, and emphasizes major influences and disagreements.

Fancher, Raymond E. "Brentano's PSYCHOLOGY FROM AN EMPIRICAL STANDPOINT and Freud's Early Metapsychology." JOURNAL OF THE HIS-TORY OF THE BEHAVIORAL SCIENCES 13 (July 1977): 207-27.

An overview of the debate regarding the extent of Brentano's influence on Freud's thought followed by a discussion of similarities in Brentano's book PSYCHOLOGY FROM AN EMPIRICAL STAND-POINT (see section C3a, p. 133) and Freud's psychology as set forth in his PROJECT FOR A SCIENTIFIC PSYCHOLOGY, in James Strachey, ed., STANDARD EDITION OF THE COMPLETE WORKS OF SIGMUND FREUD, vol. 1, pp. 283-410 (see p. 210).

Fernberger, Samuel W. "Behavior versus Introspective Psychology." PSYCHO-LOGICAL REVIEW 29 (November 1922): 409-13.

Feuer, Lewis S. "The Standpoints of Dewey and Freud: A Contrast and Analy-sis." JOURNAL OF INDIVIDUAL PSYCHOLOGY 16 (November 1960): 119-36.

Frey-Rohn, Liliane. FROM FREUD TO JUNG: A COMPARATIVE STUDY OF THE PSYCHOLOGY OF THE UNCONSCIOUS. Translated by Fred E. Engreen and Evelyn K. Engreen. New York: Putnam, 1974. xiv, 345 p. Index.

Fuchs, Alfred H., and Kawash, George F. "Prescriptive Dimensions for Five Schools of Psychology." JOURNAL OF THE HISTORY OF THE BEHAVIORAL SCIENCES 10 (July 1974): 352-66.

Behaviorism, functionalism, Gestalt psychology, psychoanalysis, and structuralism were ranked by sixty-eight knowledgeable judges (members of Division 26, APA) on each of thirty-six philosophical or value orientation dimensions such as nativism, centralism, and determinism. Ratings were reasonably reliable and the method provides a workable consensual approach to characterizing the stance of the systems on the various dimensions.

Furfey, P.H. "Psychoanalysis, Behaviorism, and the Gestalt." THOUGHT 4 (1929): 237-53.

Geissler, L.R. "The Objectives of Objective Psychology." PSYCHOLOGICAL REVIEW 36 (September 1929): 353-74.

Notes some of the problems of a purely introspective and a purely behavioristic psychology and argues for a psychology based on both consciousness and behavior.

Giorgi, Amedeo. "Convergences and Divergences Between Phenomenological Psychology and Behaviorism: A Beginning Dialog." BEHAVIORISM 3 (1975): 200-212.

Guilford, J.P. "A Psychology with Act, Content, and Form." JOURNAL OF GENERAL PSYCHOLOGY 90 (January 1974): 87-100.

Reviews traditional psychologies (functionalism, behaviorism, psychoanalysis, structuralism) and shows that they typically emphasized either act, content, or form to the exclusion of the other two. Proposes an operational-informational viewpoint which involves all three.

Harrower, M.R. "Gestalt versus Associationism." PSYCHE 9 (July 1928): 55-71.

Heims, Steve. "Encounter of Behavioral Sciences with New Machine-Organism Analogies in the 1940's." JOURNAL OF THE HISTORY OF THE BEHAVIORAL SCIENCES 21 (October 1975): 368-73.

Describes an encounter between Wolfgang Koehler and a group of early cyberneticists.

Hinkelman, Emmet Arthur, and Aderman, Morris. "Apparent Theoretical Parallels Between G. Stanley Hall and Carl Jung." JOURNAL OF THE HISTORY OF THE BEHAVIORAL SCIENCES 4 (July 1968): 254-57.

Presents evidence from statements, letters, and personal contacts between Jung and Hall that Hall's psychology had a considerable impact on Jung's system of thought.

Hull, Clark L. "Modern Behaviorism and Psychoanalysis." TRANSACTIONS OF THE NEW YORK ACADEMY OF SCIENCES 1 (1939): 78-82.

Jastrow, Joseph. "Concepts and 'Isms' in Psychology." AMERICAN JOURNAL OF PSYCHOLOGY 39 (December 1927): 1-6.

> Argues that "barren interest in 'isms'" should be replaced by interest in concepts. Scientists should be identified more in terms of their interests than in terms of their system or school of thought.

_____. "The Current Chaos in Psychology: And the Way Out Via Psyche's Design for Living." SCIENTIFIC MONTHLY 41 (August 1935): 97-110.

Kawash, George, and Fuchs, Alfred H. "A Factor Analysis of Ratings of Five Schools of Psychology on Prescriptive Dimensions." JOURNAL OF THE HISTORY OF THE BEHAVIORAL SCIENCES 10 (October 1974): 426-37.

> Discusses five systems of psychology in terms of seven factors (naturalism, dynamicism, inductivism, peripheralism, dualism, idiographicism, and molarism) derived from a factor analysis of data from an earlier study in which sixty-eight knowledgeable judges ranked each of the five systems on thirty-six philosophical or value dimensions (see Fuchs and Kawash, above, this section, p. 240).

Krantz, David L. "The Baldwin-Titchener Controversy: A Case Study in the Functioning and Malfunctioning of Schools." In SCHOOLS OF PSYCHOLOGY: A SYMPOSIUM, edited by D.L. Krantz, pp. 1-20. New York: Appleton-Century-Crofts, 1969.

> Traces the development of a controversy over the meaning of reaction time. Comments on how the controversy is exacerbated, perhaps in inappropriate ways, by the "single mindedness" of the early schools of psychology.

_____. "Schools and Systems: The Mutual Isolation of Operant and Non-operant Psychology as a Case Study." JOURNAL OF THE HISTORY OF THE BEHAVIORAL SCIENCES 8 (January 1972): 86-102.

> Distinguishes between the terms "systems" and "schools" and discusses the evidence for the causes and implications of the mutual isolation of operant and non-operant psychology.

Krasner, Leonard. "The Future and the Past in the Behaviorism-Humanism Dialogue." AMERICAN PSYCHOLOGIST 33 (September 1978): 799-804.

> Traces the roots of the behaviorism-humanism dialogue in post World War II developments, and argues that the future will bring greater agreement between adherents of the two systems.

Kubie, Lawrence S. "Pavlov, Freud and Soviet Psychiatry." BEHAVIORAL SCIENCE 4 (1959): 29-34.

Focuses on areas of agreement between Pavlov and Freud.

Langfeld, Herbert Sidney. "Consciousness and Motor Response." PSYCHOLOG-
ICAL REVIEW 34 (January 1927): 1-9.

Larson, Cedric A., and Sullivan, John J. "Watson's Relation to Titchener."
JOURNAL OF THE HISTORY OF THE BEHAVIORAL SCIENCES 1 (October
1965): 338-54.

> Traces through letters, published writings, and personal comments
> the affable personal relationship maintained between the proponents
> of two psychologies which were poles apart. Explores reasons for
> the friendly relationship between Watson and Titchener.

Laswell, H.D. "Approaches to Human Personality: William James and Sigmund
Freud." PSYCHOANALYSIS AND THE PSYCHOANALYTIC REVIEW 47, no. 3
(Fall 1960): 52-68.

Leeper, R.[W.]. "The Relation Between Gestalt Psychology and the Behavioristic Psychology of Learning." TRANSACTIONS OF THE KANSAS ACADEMY
OF SCIENCE 34 (1931): 268-73.

Levine, Albert J. CURRENT PSYCHOLOGIES: A CRITICAL SYNTHESIS.
Cambridge, Mass.: Sci-Art Publishers, 1940. 270 p.

> Describes and appraises the contributions of selected schools of
> psychology. Appendix on the philosophical and educational im-
> plications of the schools. Bibliography. Index.

Levitt, Morton. FREUD AND DEWEY ON THE NATURE OF MAN. New York:
Philosophical Library, 1960. 180 p.

> Includes brief biographical materials on Freud and Dewey and
> considers major intellectual influences in their lives. Discusses
> selected themes in their systems as well as similarities and differ-
> ences, especially with reference to method of investigation and
> positions on such areas as thought processes, instinct, conflict
> theory of mental disorder, defense mechanisms, and symbolism.
> References. Index.

Line, W. "Three Recent Attacks on Associationism." JOURNAL OF GENERAL
PSYCHOLOGY 5 (October 1931): 495-512.

> Summarizes the work of Lashley, Koehler, and Spearman that
> challenged atomistic associationism.

McDougall, W[illiam]. "The Present Chaos in Psychology and the Way Out."
JOURNAL OF PHILOSOPHICAL STUDIES 5 (July 1930): 353-63.

_____. "Purposive or Mechanical Psychology?" PSYCHOLOGICAL REVIEW 30 (July 1923): 273-88.

McGill, V.J. "Behaviorism and Phenomenology." PHILOSOPHY AND PHE-NOMENOLOGICAL RESEARCH 26 (June 1966): 578-88.

MacLeod R[obert].B[rodie]. "Newtonian and Darwinian Conceptions of Man, and Some Alternatives." JOURNAL OF THE HISTORY OF THE BEHAVIORAL SCIENCES 6 (July 1970): 207-18.

Melrose, J.A. "The Crux of the Psychological Problem." PSYCHOLOGICAL REVIEW 29 (March 1922): 113-31.

    Discusses methods, theories, and problems of behaviorism and older psychologies (such as structuralism) in terms of the problem of consciousness.

Myers, Charles S. "Aspects of Modern Psychology." SCIENCE 94 (July 1941): 75-81; (August 1941): 102-05.

    Provides an overview of major systems of psychology and their role in the late 1930s.

Ogden, R.M. "Gestalt Psychology and Behaviorism." AMERICAN JOURNAL OF PSYCHOLOGY 45 (January 1933): 151-55.

Osheroff, Steven S. "Wittgenstein: Psychological Disputes and Common Moves." PHILOSOPHY AND PHENOMENOLOGICAL RESEARCH 36 (March 1976): 339-63.

    Compares theories and systems of psychology in terms of "language games."

Pillsbury, W.B. "Suggestions for a Compromise of Existing Controversies in Psychology." PSYCHOLOGICAL REVIEW 29 (July 1922): 259-66.

_____. "Titchener and James." PSYCHOLOGICAL REVIEW 50 (January 1943): 71-73.

    Speculates about Titchener's general evaluation of James and his reaction to James's theory of emotion.

Rahn, Carl. THE RELATION OF SENSATION TO OTHER CATEGORIES IN CONTEMPORARY PSYCHOLOGY: A STUDY IN THE PSYCHOLOGY OF THINK-ING. Psychological Monographs, vol. 16, no. 1. Princeton, N.J. and Lancaster, Pa.: Psychological Review Co., 1913. vi, 131 p.

Rasmussen, E. Tranekjaer. "Bridging Physiology and Phenomenology in Dynamic Psychology." SCANDINAVIAN JOURNAL OF PSYCHOLOGY 2, no. 4 (1961): 161-66.

Reeves, Margaret Pegram. "The Psychologies of McDougall and Adler; A Comparison." INDIVIDUAL PSYCHOLOGY BULLETIN 7 (1949): 147-61.

Reiser, O.L. "Behaviorism and Gestalt-Psychology." PSYCHE 8 (1928): 60-62.

Rosenzweig, Saul. "Schools of Psychology: A Complementary Pattern." PHILOSOPHY OF SCIENCE 4 (January 1937): 96-106.

Ryback, David. "Existentialism and Behaviorism: Some Differences Settled." CANADIAN PSYCHOLOGIST 13 (January 1972): 53-60.

Savage, C. Wade. "Introspectionist and Behaviorist Interpretations of Ratio Scales of Perceptual Magnitudes." PSYCHOLOGICAL MONOGRAPHS: GENERAL AND APPLIED 80, no. 19 (1966): 1-32.

Schubert, Joseph. "S-R Theory and Dynamic Theory." JOURNAL OF PHENOMENOLOGICAL PSYCHOLOGY 1 (Spring 1971): 173-84.

Simon, Robert I. "Great Paths Cross: Freud and James at Clark University, 1909." AMERICAN JOURNAL OF PSYCHIATRY 124 (December 1967): 831-34.

Smith, Stevenson. "The Schools of Psychology." PSYCHOLOGICAL REVIEW 38 (November 1931): 461-73.

> Explores subject matter and methodological differences in the schools of psychology and concludes that "the real difference is one of emphasis, and emphasis is a matter of rhetoric, not of science."

Stern, Alfred. "Existential Psychoanalysis and Individual Psychology." JOURNAL OF INDIVIDUAL PSYCHOLOGY 14 (May 1958): 38-50.

Stevenson, Leslie. SEVEN THEORIES OF HUMAN NATURE. New York: Oxford University Press, 1974. 136 p.

> A brief overview of the teachings of Plato, Christianity, Marx, Freud, Sartre, Skinner, and Lorenz.

Tiebout, H.M., Jr. "Freud and Existentialism." JOURNAL OF NERVOUS AND MENTAL DISEASE 126 (April 1958): 341-52.

Titchener, Edward Bradford. "Functional Psychology and the Psychology of Act: I." AMERICAN JOURNAL OF PSYCHOLOGY 32 (October 1921): 519-42.

_____. "Functional Psychology and the Psychology of Act: II." AMERICAN JOURNAL OF PSYCHOLOGY 33 (January 1922): 43-83.

Troland, L.T. "Optics as Seen by a Psychologist." JOURNAL OF THE OPTICAL SOCIETY OF AMERICA 18 (March 1929): 223-36.

Contrasts behavioristic and introspectionist approaches to vision. Advocates a correlative "psycho-physiological optics."

Wandersman, Abraham; Poppen, Paul; and Ricks, David, eds. HUMANISM AND BEHAVIORISM: DIALOGUE AND GROWTH. New York: Pergamon Press, 1976. 439 p.

A broad survey of relations between humanism and behaviorism. Includes debates, attempts at synthesis, and prospects for the two schools.

Wann, T.W., ed. BEHAVIORISM AND PHENOMENOLOGY: CONTRASTING BASES FOR MODERN PSYCHOLOGY. Chicago: University of Chicago Press, 1964. xi, 190 p.

Six papers by distinguished authors show how behaviorism and phenomenology complement and contrast with each other. References.

Washburn, Margaret F. "Gestalt Psychology and Motor Psychology." AMERICAN JOURNAL OF PSYCHOLOGY 37 (October 1926): 516-20.

Weiss, A.P. "Relation between Functional and Behavioral Psychology." PSYCHOLOGICAL REVIEW 24 (September 1917): 353-68.

Compares functionalism and behaviorism noting some inadequacies of all functionalism and some strengths of behaviorism.

_____. "Relation between Structural and Behavioral Psychology." PSYCHOLOGICAL REVIEW 24 (July 1917): 301-17.

Contrasts assumptions and methods of structuralism and behaviorism. Shows how a behavioristic approach can be applied to problems normally investigated by the structuralist.

Weitz, Lawrence J. "Jung's and Freud's Contributions to Dream Interpretation: A Comparison." AMERICAN JOURNAL OF PSYCHOTHERAPY 30 (April 1976): 289-93.

Welch, Livingston. "An Integration of Some Fundamental Principles of Modern Behaviorism and Gestalt Psychology." JOURNAL OF GENERAL PSYCHOLOGY 39 (October 1948): 175-90.

Enumerates fundamental principles and hypotheses which should be agreeable to both behaviorists and Gestaltists. Maintains that integration is possible in many instances and that controversy is helpful when disagreements are substantive but counterproductive when "antagonists fail to realize that they are arguing about that which both believe."

_____. "The Theoretical Basis of Psychotherapy: Psychoanalysis, Behaviorism, and Gestalt Psychology." AMERICAN JOURNAL OF ORTHOPSYCHIATRY 15 (April 1945): 256-66.

Wheeler, Raymond Holder. "Introspection and Behavior." PSYCHOLOGICAL REVIEW 30 (March 1923): 103-15.

_____. "Persistent Problems in Systematic Psychology, I-V." See section C14, p. 236.

White, C.M. "Behaviorism, Psychoanalysis, and the Psychology of P-Function." AMERICAN JOURNAL OF PSYCHOLOGY 44 (1932): 263-74.

Winetrout, Kenneth. "Adlerian Psychology and Pragmatism." JOURNAL OF INDIVIDUAL PSYCHOLOGY 24 (May 1968): 5-24.

Section D

HISTORIES AND MAJOR WORKS
IN SELECTED CONTENT AREAS OF PSYCHOLOGY

Histories have been written about content areas within psychology such as motivation, learning, or psychopathology. The focus of the materials in this section is on histories of specific content areas, major older textbooks, laboratory manuals, and handbooks which summarize the state of the art at a given time. It is beyond the scope of the present work to provide a bibliography for each subdisciplinary area of psychology. Accordingly, we have tried to emphasize historical works and major articles and monographs associated with these areas.

1. GENERAL PSYCHOLOGY

Since the establishment of psychology as a separate discipline, great numbers of general psychology textbooks have been published. Before that time, psychological topics were often discussed in books on mental philosophy. This section includes a few representative texts from Upham's two-volume MENTAL PHILOSOPHY through James's two-volume PRINCIPLES OF PSYCHOLOGY to Boring, Langfeld, and Weld's FOUNDATIONS OF PSYCHOLOGY and beyond. Wolman's HANDBOOK OF GENERAL PSYCHOLOGY, published in 1973, is also included, but we have largely limited the entries to items published before 1950.

Bain, Alexander. MENTAL SCIENCE. New York: American Book Co., 1868. 10, xxii, 428, 101 p.

> An early introductory text designed for high school and college students and covering topics in content areas such as the nervous system, instincts, sensation, the intellect, perception, emotions, and the will. Lengthy appendix on issues in philosophical psychology.

Baldwin, James M. ELEMENTS OF PSYCHOLOGY. New York: Holt, 1893. xvi, 372 p.

> A condensed introductory text based on Baldwin's earlier two-volume HANDBOOK OF PSYCHOLOGY.

Berelson, Bernard, and Steiner, Gary A. HUMAN BEHAVIOR: AN INVEN-
TORY OF SCIENTIFIC FINDINGS. New York: Harcourt, Brace and World,
1964. xxiii, 712 p.

> An attempt, by a sociologist and a psychologist, to inventory veri-
> fied knowledge as of the early 1960s in such behavioral science
> areas as development, perception, learning and thinking, motiva-
> tion, the family, small and large groups, ethnic relations, opinions,
> society, and culture. Bibliographical materials. Index.

Boring, Edwin G.; Langfeld, Herbert S.; Weld, Harry P.; and contributors.
FOUNDATIONS OF PSYCHOLOGY. New York: John Wiley and Sons, 1948.
xv, 632 p.

> One of the leading post-World War II comprehensive introductory
> textbooks. Provides excellent coverage of traditional topics in ex-
> perimental psychology and of such applied topics as personal adjust-
> ment, vocational selection, social relations of the individual, and
> human efficiency. References. Index.

_____. INTRODUCTION TO PSYCHOLOGY. New York: John Wiley and
Sons, 1939. xxii, 627 p.

> A classic, leading introductory textbook covering traditional areas
> in experimental psychology as well as selected applied topics in
> personality and social psychology. References. Index.

Calkins, Mary Whiton. AN INTRODUCTION TO PSYCHOLOGY. New York:
Macmillan, 1901. xv, 511 p.

> One of the earlier introductory textbooks that treats psychology as
> the study of consciousness. Includes a chapter on the history of
> psychological systems and an appendix on selected topics. Bibliog-
> raphy. Index.

Coffield, Kenneth E., and Engle, T.L. "High School Psychology: A History
and Some Observations." AMERICAN PSYCHOLOGIST 15 (June 1960): 350-52.

> Results of a questionnaire sent to school officials in forty-six states.
> Shows that psychology was taught in high schools long before 1900.
> Presents trends from 1895 to 1960 regarding the teaching of psychol-
> ogy in high schools.

Dashiell, J.F. FUNDAMENTALS OF OBJECTIVE PSYCHOLOGY. New York:
Houghton Mifflin, 1928. xviii, 588 p.

> An influential early text often used in medical schools.

Davis, Robert A., and Gould, Silas E. "Changing Tendencies in General Psychology." PSYCHOLOGICAL REVIEW 36 (July 1929): 320-31.

An analysis of 110 introductory textbooks in psychology written between 1890 and 1928. Reports trends in topical coverage and makes recommendations on standardization of terminology and on topical coverage.

Ebbinghaus, Hermann. PSYCHOLOGY: AN ELEMENTARY TEXTBOOK. Translated and edited by Max Meyer. Boston: D.C. Heath, 1908. viii, 215 p.

Includes a historical chapter presenting the commonly accepted areas of psychological inquiry at the turn of the century. Concludes with a chapter on the "highest accomplishments of consciousness"--religion, art, and morality. Index.

Engle, T.L., and Snellgrove, Louis. PSYCHOLOGY: ITS PRINCIPLES AND APPLICATIONS. 6th ed. New York: Harcourt Brace Jovanovich, 1974. ix, 535 p.

The most widely used high school psychology text in the United States for several decades, which sold more than one million copies in its first six editions; seventh edition planned for 1978.

Guilford, J.P. GENERAL PSYCHOLOGY. New York: D. Van Nostrand, 1939. xii, 630 p.

_____, ed. FIELDS OF PSYCHOLOGY. New York: D. Van Nostrand, 1940. x, 695 p.

Written by authorities eminent in their fields at the time as a text for a second semester course in psychology. Discusses such fields as animal, child, social, abnormal, educational, clinical, industrial, vocational, and physiological psychology. References. Index.

_____. FIELDS OF PSYCHOLOGY. 3d ed. New York: D. Van Nostrand, 1966. x, 350 p.

A brief examination of the classic schools of psychology followed by descriptions of special areas such as experimental psychology, developmental psychology, social psychology, and abnormal behavior. Surveys such professional fields as clinical, educational, employment, managerial, and engineering psychology. References. Index.

Helson, Harry, ed. THEORETICAL FOUNDATIONS OF PSYCHOLOGY. New York: D. Van Nostrand, 1951. xix, 787 p.

Fifteen chapters by authorities on major theories in motivation, emotion, learning, perception, thinking, measurement, intelligence, personality, social psychology, abnormal psychology, and physiological psychology. Rich in historical materials. References. Index.

Helson, Harry, and Bevan, William, eds. CONTEMPORARY APPROACHES TO PSYCHOLOGY. New York: D. Van Nostrand, 1967. xii, 596 p.

> Emphasizes methods, issues, and theories in fourteen major areas of psychology. Some include historical perspective. Primarily for advanced students. References. Index. Succeeds Helson's earlier THEORETICAL FOUNDATIONS OF PSYCHOLOGY (see above, this section, p. 251).

Hunter, Walter S. HUMAN BEHAVIOR. New rev. ed. Chicago: University of Chicago Press, 1928. x, 355 p.

> An early text covering such topics as abnormal behavior, the nervous system, instincts, habit, thinking, and receptor processes from a behavioristic point of view (what Hunter calls "anthroponomy").

James, William. PRINCIPLES OF PSYCHOLOGY. See in section C5a, p. 144.

Judd, Charles Hubbard. PSYCHOLOGY: GENERAL INTRODUCTION. New York: Charles Scribner's Sons, 1907. xii, 389 p.

> An early introductory psychology text. Leans heavily on the writings of Wilhelm Wundt and William James, and intends to help "diffuse . . . the functional explanations of mental life." Index.

Koch, Sigmund, ed. PSYCHOLOGY: A STUDY OF A SCIENCE. 6 vols. New York: McGraw-Hill, 1959-63.

> A massive endeavor written by leading psychologists that surveys scientific psychology as of the late 1950s. Two major sections: "Conceptual and Systematic" (volumes 1-3) and "Empirical Substructure and Relations with Other Sciences" (volumes 4-6). Extensive bibliographies. Index.

Ladd, George Trumbull. PSYCHOLOGY: DESCRIPTIVE AND EXPLANATORY. A TREATISE OF THE PHENOMENA, LAWS, AND DEVELOPMENT OF HUMAN MENTAL LIFE. New York: Charles Scribner's Sons, 1894. xiii, 676 p.

> A basic text designed "to give a clear, accurate, and comprehensive picture of the mental life of the individual." Reasonably comprehensive coverage of the categories of inquiry common to the time. Bibliographical materials. Index.

MacDougall, William. OUTLINE OF PSYCHOLOGY. New York: Charles Scribner's Sons, 1923. xvi, 456 p.

> A systematic introduction to psychology with strong emphasis on purposive striving and against mechanistic and "mosaic" psychologies. Covers traditional content areas (perception, instincts, atten-

tion, emotions) and discusses the behavior of lower animals (including insects), belief systems in humans, and the organization of character. Index.

Meyer, Max F. PSYCHOLOGY OF THE OTHER-ONE: AN INTRODUCTORY TEXTBOOK OF PSYCHOLOGY. 2d ed., rev. Columbia, Mo.: Missouri Book Co., 1922. 439 p.

An early introductory text written from an objectivist standpoint. Index.

Miller, George A., and Buckhout, Robert. PSYCHOLOGY: THE SCIENCE OF MENTAL LIFE. 2d ed. New York: Harper and Row, 1973. 561 p.

An introduction to the science of psychology and its historical development. Intersperses biographical chapters on some of the early founders of psychology with chapters on traditional subject matter in the field. Bibliography and suggestions for further reading. Glossary. Index.

Moore, Jared Sparks. THE FOUNDATIONS OF PSYCHOLOGY. Princeton, N.J.: Princeton University Press, 1921. xix, 239 p.

A text in general psychology containing much historical material as well as discussions of systems of psychology. References. Index.

Muensterberg, H. PSYCHOLOGY: GENERAL AND APPLIED. New York: Appleton, 1914. xiv, 487 p.

An introductory textbook by an early American pioneer. One of the first to include extensive discussions of the applications of psychology to education, law, industry, commerce, health, hygiene, art, and science. Also among the first to place substantial emphasis on social psychology and purposivism. Bibliography. Index.

Ogden, R.M. AN INTRODUCTION TO GENERAL PSYCHOLOGY. New York: Longmans, Green, 1914. xviii, 270 p.

Pillsbury, W.B. THE FUNDAMENTALS OF PSYCHOLOGY. Rev. ed. New York: Macmillan, 1922. xvi, 590 p.

An eclectic introductory text covering such major content areas as sensation, perception, memory, reasoning, instinct, feeling, emotion, and the self.

Pillsbury, W.B., and Pennington, L.A. A HANDBOOK OF GENERAL PSYCHOLOGY: A SUMMARY OF ESSENTIALS AND A DICTIONARY OF TERMS. New York: Dryden Press, 1942. xiv, 400 p.

A brief historical section followed by chapters on major content areas such as sensation, intelligence, learning, motivation, attention, memory, and reasoning. Over seventy pages devoted to dictionary of terms. Brief biographical statements for over one hundred major contributors to psychology. References. Index.

Roback, A[braham].A[aron]. PRESENT-DAY PSYCHOLOGY. New York: Philosophical Library, 1955. xiv, 995 p.

Includes forty chapters covering developments in many academic branches of psychology such as child psychology, educational psychology, animal and comparative psychology and psychometrics; trends in dynamic and clinical psychology; methodological developments; and trends in such related areas as the psychology of religion, of literature, and of art, and parapsychology. Index.

Robinson, E.S., and Richardson-Robinson, F. READING IN GENERAL PSYCHOLOGY. 2d ed. Chicago: University of Chicago Press, 1929. xix, 812 p.

Ruch, Floyd L. PSYCHOLOGY AND LIFE. See Zimbardo, Philip G., and Ruch, Floyd L., below.

Stout, G[eorge].F[rederick]. A MANUAL OF PSYCHOLOGY. 3d ed. London: W.B. Clive, University Tutorial Press, 1924. xvii, 769 p.

An exposition of such topics in psychology as consciousness, attention, sensation, perception, thinking, instinct, and emotion.

Upham, Thomas C. MENTAL PHILOSOPHY. 2 vols. New York: Harper, 1869, 1875.

An early eclectic work (an enlarged version of Upham's 1840 book) exploring such topics as sensation, attention, dreaming, association, memory, reasoning, and insanity in volume 1, and emotions, instinct, motivation, and volition in volume 2. Appendix on language is in volume 1.

Weld, H.P. PSYCHOLOGY AS A SCIENCE: ITS PROBLEMS AND POINTS OF VIEW. New York: Holt, 1928. xi, 297 p.

An early introductory text limited to topics within the scientific domain. Includes discussions of the meaning of science, science and technology, general psychology, abnormal psychology, animal psychology, developmental psychology, social psychology, and applied psychology. Index.

Wheeler, Raymond Holder, ed. READINGS IN PSYCHOLOGY. New York: Thomas Y. Crowell, 1930. x, 597 p.

Presents twenty-five readings on experimental investigations in such content areas as social behavior, intelligence, emotion, learning, perception, and the nervous system. Editorial comments introduce each selection. Technical terms defined in glossaries following each selection. References. Index.

Wolman, Benjamin B., ed. HANDBOOK OF GENERAL PSYCHOLOGY. Englewood Cliffs, N.J.: Prentice-Hall, 1973. xv, 1006 p.

A survey of major trends and developments within such content areas of general psychology as biological bases of behavior, perception, learning; language, thought, and development; motivation and emotion; and personality. Briefer treatment of such areas as social, developmental, and industrial psychology. An introductory section discusses history, theory, and methodology common to all the content areas. References. Index.

Woodworth, Robert Sessions, and Marquis, Donald G. PSYCHOLOGY. 5th ed. New York: Holt, 1947. x, 677 p. Index.

See section C7, p. 158, for annotation.

Yerkes, Robert M. INTRODUCTION TO PSYCHOLOGY. New York: Holt, 1911. xii, 427 p.

An outline of psychology emphasizing the aims and methods of the discipline and the description, development, and facts of consciousness. Index.

Zimbardo, Philip G., and Ruch, Floyd L. PSYCHOLOGY AND LIFE. 9th ed. Glenview, Ill.: Scott, Foresman, 1975. 788 p.

A comprehensive and eclectic introductory text, first published by Ruch in 1937 and widely adopted by American colleges and universities. References. Glossary. Index.

2. EXPERIMENTAL PSYCHOLOGY

In addition to listing selected early texts, laboratory manuals, and handbooks, this section includes articles on early psychological laboratories and on early courses in experimental psychology.

Boring, Edwin G. "The Beginning and Growth of Measurement in Psychology." In QUANTIFICATION: A HISTORY OF THE MEANING OF MEASUREMENT IN THE NATURAL AND SOCIAL SCIENCES, edited by Harry Woolf, pp. 108-27. Indianapolis: Bobbs-Merrill, 1961.

_____. "An Operational Restatement of G.E. Mueller's Psychophysical Axioms."

PSYCHOLOGICAL REVIEW 48 (November 1941): 457-64.

> Restates in operational language three of Mueller's axioms referring to psychoneural isomorphism and discusses implications. Because the axioms refer to presumed correspondences between mental processes and brain processes, Boring notes that the term "psychophysiological" is more appropriate than "psychophysical."

Brožek, Josef. "Contributions to the History of Psychology: XII. Wayward History: F.C. Donders (1818-1889) and the Timing of Mental Operations." PSYCHOLOGICAL REPORTS 26 (April 1970): 563-69.

> Details a "comedy of errors" relating to typesetting and to the historical accounts of Donders's work on the timing of mental operations.

Cardno, J.A. "Experimental and Physiological Psychology: Historical Relations." AMERICAN JOURNAL OF PSYCHOLOGY 76 (September 1963): 509-11.

> Shows trends in publications in physiological psychology and experimental psychology from 1797 to 1896. Data derived from Rand's bibliography of philosophy, psychology, and cognate subjects in J.M. Baldwin (ed.), DICTIONARY OF PHILOSOPHY AND PSYCHOLOGY (see section A3, p. 19).

Cason, Hulsey. "The Courses in Experimental Psychology." JOURNAL OF GENERAL PSYCHOLOGY 13 (1935): 176-85.

> Characterizes courses in experimental psychology during the early 1930s in terms of reading materials, laboratory projects, subjects stressed, and course requirements. Based on responses of thirty-seven psychologists to an inquiry from Cason.

Cattell, James McKeen. "Early Psychological Laboratories." In FEELINGS AND EMOTIONS: THE WITTENBERG SYMPOSIUM, pp. 427-33. Worcester, Mass.: Clark University Press, 1928. Also published in SCIENCE 67 (June 1928): 543-48.

_____. "The Founding of the Association and of the Hopkins and Clark Laboratories." PSYCHOLOGICAL REVIEW 50 (January 1943): 61-64.

Crafts, Leland W., et al. RECENT EXPERIMENTS IN PSYCHOLOGY. New York: McGraw-Hill, 1938. xiv, 417 p.

> Nontechnical descriptions of twenty-eight experiments representing a cross-section of such topics in experimental psychology as instinct, emotion, learning, intelligence, memory, thinking, and handwriting. Cites original sources and other reference materials. Index.

Ertle, Jutta E.; Bushong, Roger C.; and Hillix, William A. "The Real F.M. Urban." JOURNAL OF THE HISTORY OF THE BEHAVIORAL SCIENCES 13 (October 1977): 379-83.

A brief sketch of the life and career of Urban.

Fernberger, S.W. "Some European Psychological Laboratories--1951." AMERICAN JOURNAL OF PSYCHOLOGY 65 (October 1952): 619-26.

Describes physical facilities, personnel, and work in selected laboratories in Italy, France, Belgium, and Britain.

Forrest, Derek. "The First Experiments on Word Association." BULLETIN OF THE BRITISH PSYCHOLOGICAL SOCIETY 30 (February 1977): 40-42.

Foster, William S. EXPERIMENTS IN PSYCHOLOGY. New York: Holt, 1923. x, 309 p.

Discusses experimental methods and presents twenty-four experiments on classical topics as laboratory exercises for a first course in experimental psychology. References. Appendix on instructions for obtaining materials for the experiments.

Garrett, Henry E. GREAT EXPERIMENTS IN PSYCHOLOGY. 3d ed. New York: Appleton-Century-Crofts, 1951. xvii, 358 p.

Describes sixteen classic experiments in psychology and presents bibliographic information on each. Index.

Garvey, C.R. "List of American Psychology Laboratories." PSYCHOLOGICAL BULLETIN 26 (November 1929): 652-60.

Lists 117 psychology laboratories along with such information as the date the laboratory was established, initial appropriation, and the name of the person originally in charge of the laboratory.

Gulliksen, Harold. "Louis Leon Thurstone, Experimental and Mathematical Psychologist." AMERICAN PSYCHOLOGIST 23 (November 1968): 786-802.

Reviews Thurstone's work on such topics as test theory, psychophysics, psychological scaling, and factor analysis.

Harper, Robert S. "The First Psychological Laboratory." ISIS 41, pt. 2,(July 1950): 158-61.

_____. "The Laboratory of William James." HARVARD ALUMNI BULLETIN 52 (1949): 169-73.

Jaager, John Jacob de. ORIGINS OF PSYCHOMETRY: JOHAN JACOB DE

JAAGER, STUDENT OF F.C. DONDERS ON REACTION TIME AND MENTAL PROCESSES. Edited and translated by Josef Brožek and O. Marten S. Sibinga. 1865. Reprint. Nieuwkook, The Netherlands: B. de Graaf, 1970. 76 p.

A facsimile reproduction (in Dutch) of de Jaager's celebrated doctoral thesis accompanied by an English translation and an editorial introduction reviewing the history of the measurement of the speed of mental processes. Provides biographical information and sources on de Jaager and Donders. References. Index.

Judd, Charles Hubbard. LABORATORY EQUIPMENT FOR PSYCHOLOGICAL EXPERIMENTS. New York: Charles Scribner's Sons, 1907. xi, 257 p.

The final volume in Judd's series of textbooks. Keyed to the second volume in the series, the laboratory manual. Describes apparatus and procedures in sufficient detail to construct and operate the equipment; alternatively, the author indicates that "Correspondence is invited from any who wish to make purchases, and a detailed price list will be mailed on application." Index.

_____. LABORATORY MANUAL OF PSYCHOLOGY. New York: Charles Scribner's Sons, 1907. xii, 127 p.

Discusses how to do experiments in psychology and how to write them up. Includes twenty-five suggested sets of exercises. Index.

Kirsch, Irving. "The Impetus to Scientific Psychology: A Recurrent Pattern." JOURNAL OF THE HISTORY OF THE BEHAVIORAL SCIENCES 12 (April 1976): 120-29.

Discusses the impact of "the personal equation" on the development of experimental psychology, and notes that modern problems in theoretical physics have also influenced developments in psychology. Notes implications of parallels between the history of physical science and the history of psychology.

Ladd, George Trumbull, and Woodworth, Robert Sessions. ELEMENTS OF PHYSIOLOGICAL PSYCHOLOGY: A TREATISE ON THE ACTIVITIES AND NATURE OF THE MIND, FROM THE PHYSICAL AND EXPERIMENTAL POINTS OF VIEW. Rev. ed. New York: Charles Scribner's Sons, 1911. xix, 704 p.

See section D4b, p. 281, for annotation.

Langfeld, H.S. "Princeton Psychological Laboratory." JOURNAL OF EXPERIMENTAL PSYCHOLOGY 9 (June 1926): 259-70.

Mintz, Alexander. "An Eighteenth Century Attempt at an Experimental Psychology." JOURNAL OF GENERAL PSYCHOLOGY 50 (January 1954): 63-77.

Provides an overview of a book by J.C. Krueger, ATTEMPT AT AN

EXPERIMENTAL PSYCHOLOGY, published in 1756. Speculates
as to why the book had little influence.

Murchison, Carl, ed. THE FOUNDATIONS OF EXPERIMENTAL PSYCHOLOGY.
Worcester, Mass.: Clark University Press, 1929. Reprint. New York: Johnson Reprint Corp., 1969. x, 907 p.

A comprehensive exposition of the major areas of inquiry in experimental psychology as of the end of the first quarter of the twentieth century. References.

_____. A HANDBOOK OF GENERAL EXPERIMENTAL PSYCHOLOGY. Wor-
cester, Mass.: Clark University Press, 1934. xii, 1125 p.

A revision and extension of the general experimental section of
Murchison's 1929 THE FOUNDATIONS OF EXPERIMENTAL PSY-
CHOLOGY (see above). Provides a comprehensive overview of
the experimental psychology of the early 1930s. Major topic
areas include heredity, motivation, emotion, learning, vision,
audition, chemoreception, and skin senses. References. Index.

Newman, Edwin B. "Newton, Physics and the Psychology of the Nineteenth
Century." AMERICAN JOURNAL OF PSYCHOLOGY 82 (September 1969):
400-406.

Osgood, Charles E. METHOD AND THEORY IN EXPERIMENTAL PSYCHOLOGY.
New York: Oxford University Press, 1953. vi, 800 p.

A major classic reference source in experimental psychology. Reviews experimental literature selected for its relevance to basic
issues and theories. Four sections cover sensory processes, perceptual processes, learning, and symbolic processes.

Popplestone, John A., and McPherson, Marion White. "Prolegomenon to the
Study of Apparatus in Early Psychology Laboratories Circa 1875-1915." AMERI-
CAN PSYCHOLOGIST 26 (July 1971): 656-57.

See section B6e, p. 102, for annotation.

Postman, Leo. "Hermann Ebbinghaus." AMERICAN PSYCHOLOGIST 23 (March
1968): 149-57.

Focuses on Ebbinghaus's contributions to the development of experimental psychology. Based on a commemorative address at the
American Psychological Association convention in 1967.

Ramul, Konstantin. "The Problem of Measurement in the Psychology of the
Eighteenth Century." AMERICAN PSYCHOLOGIST 15 (1960): 256-65.

The author explores "hitherto largely unknown opinions of a number of eighteenth century philosophical and nonphilosophical writers regarding the possibilities and methods of psychological measurements." Writers included are Christian von Wolff, Andrew Michael Ramsay, Gottfried Ploucquet, Charles Bonnet, Johann Heinrich Lambert, and Gottlieb Friedrich Hagen.

Ruckmick, C.A. "Development of Laboratory Equipment in Psychology in the United States." AMERICAN JOURNAL OF PSYCHOLOGY 37 (October 1926): 582–92.

Sanford, Edmund C. A COURSE IN EXPERIMENTAL PSYCHOLOGY. PART I. SENSATION AND PERCEPTION. Boston: D.C. Heath, 1897. iv, 183 p.

Includes laboratory demonstrations in the dermal senses, kinaesthetic senses, taste, smell, audition, and vision.

Scripture, E.W. "Methods of Laboratory Mind-Study." THE FORUM 17 (August 1894): 721–28.

A brief summary of techniques of experimental psychology emphasizing practical applications, especially in education.

Seashore, Carl E. ELEMENTARY EXPERIMENTS IN PSYCHOLOGY. New York: Holt, 1908. xi, 218 p.

Designed for the first course in psychology. Outlines individual experiments on such topics as after-images, Weber's law, association, memory, affective tone, and reaction time. Students can conduct these experiments without laboratory equipment.

Siegel, Michael H., and Zeigler, H. Philip, eds. PSYCHOLOGICAL RESEARCH: THE INSIDE STORY. New York: Harper and Row, 1976. xi, 412 p.

Stevens, S.S., ed. HANDBOOK OF EXPERIMENTAL PSYCHOLOGY. New York: John Wiley and Sons, 1951. xi, 1,436 p.

Exhaustive technical exposition and analysis of the state of experimental psychology in midcentury in six major content areas: physiological mechanisms, growth and development, motivation, learning and adjustment, sensory processes, and human performance. References. Index.

Stratton, George Malcolm. EXPERIMENTAL PSYCHOLOGY AND ITS BEARING UPON CULTURE. New York: Macmillan, 1903. vii, 331 p.

Reviews the history of psychology and describes the character of psychological experiments. Provides a nontechnical overview of selected research on such topics as mental measurements, the un-

conscious, illusions, space perception, memory, imitation, and
suggestion. Discusses mind-body relations and spiritual implications of experimental work. Minimal references in footnotes.
Index.

Titchener, Edward Bradford. EXPERIMENTAL PSYCHOLOGY: A MANUAL
OF LABORATORY PRACTICE.

See in section C4, p. 139.

_____. "Experimental Psychology: A Retrospect." AMERICAN JOURNAL
OF PSYCHOLOGY 36 (July 1925): 313-23.

Outlines some negative effects of the Herbartian empirical and
philosophical traditions upon the development of experimental psychology. Address delivered to the twenty-second annual meeting
of experimental psychologists in 1925.

_____. "A Psychological Laboratory." MIND 7 (July 1898): 311-31.

Comments on progress in laboratories since the founding of Wundt's
laboratory, contrasts American and German laboratories, and provides a plan (including a sketch of a floor plan) for a psychological laboratory.

Watson, Robert I. "The Content of Experimental Manuals in Psychology."
JOURNAL OF GENERAL PSYCHOLOGY 24 (January 1941): 183-94.

Discusses the results of a content analysis of ten laboratory manuals
in terms of the kinds of problems included, the kinds of instruments
used, and the percent of each manual devoted to subdisciplinary
areas.

Witmer, Lightner. ANALYTIC PSYCHOLOGY: A PRACTICAL MANUAL FOR
COLLEGES AND NORMAL SCHOOLS, PRESENTING THE FACTS AND PRIN-
CIPLES OF MENTAL ANALYSIS. Boston: Ginn, 1902. xxvi, 251 p.

A series of laboratory exercises and experiments on mental processes
designed primarily for beginning students. Index.

Woodworth, Robert S[essions]. THE COLUMBIA UNIVERSITY PSYCHOLOGICAL
LABORATORY: A FIFTY-YEAR RETROSPECT. New York: Author, Columbia
University, 1942.

See section B5bxiiaa, p. 94, for annotation.

Woodworth, Robert S[essions]., and Schlosberg, Harold. EXPERIMENTAL PSY-
CHOLOGY. Rev. ed. New York: Holt, 1954 (1st ed. 1938). xi, 948 p.

An outgrowth of the text by Ladd and Woodworth (see above, this section, p. 258). Served for years as the authoritative source on the methods and findings of experimental psychology. Index.

Yerkes, R.M. "The Yale Laboratories of Primate Biology." SCIENCE MONTHLY, NEW YORK 56 (1943): 287-90.

Zupan, M.L. "The Conceptual Development of Quantification in Experimental Psychology." JOURNAL OF THE HISTORY OF THE BEHAVIORAL SCIENCES 12 (April 1976): 145-58.

> An overview of psychology in eighteenth- and nineteenth-century Germany followed by an examination of the development of quantification, with emphasis on the contributions of Herbart, Fechner, and Wundt.

3. COMPARATIVE PSYCHOLOGY

Contributions to comparative psychology can be found in the works of such philosophers as Aristotle and Descartes. Modern scientific approaches to the area begin with Darwin and C. Lloyd Morgan. Included here are references to histories of comparative psychology, selected textbooks and treatises, books of readings, articles dealing with the problems of comparative psychology, and histories of work with specific species.

a. Histories of Comparative Psychology

Adler, Helmut E.; Adler, Leonore L.; and Tobach, Ethel. "Past, Present, and Future of Comparative Psychology." ANNALS OF THE NEW YORK ACADEMY OF SCIENCES 223 (1973): 184-92.

Altmann, Margaret. "How Early Was 'Imprinting' Observed?" AMERICAN PSYCHOLOGIST 19 (August 1964): 684.

> A description of what in modern times is called imprinting can be found as early as 1515 in Sir Thomas More's UTOPIA.

Aronson, Lester R., ed. DEVELOPMENT AND EVOLUTION OF BEHAVIOR: ESSAYS IN MEMORY OF T.C. SCHNEIRLA. San Francisco: W.H. Freeman, 1970. xviii, 656 p.

Beach, Frank A. "The Snark was a Boojum." AMERICAN PSYCHOLOGIST 5 (April 1950): 115-24.

> Focuses on historical trends in comparative psychology, discussing early work on a variety of species with a subsequent and lamentable narrowing of focus to the learning of the laboratory rat. Examines advantages and disadvantages of concentration on one species as well as advantages of a truly comparative approach.

Chiszar, David. "Historical Continuity in the Development of Comparative Psychology: Comment on Lockard's 'Reflections.'" AMERICAN PSYCHOLOGIST 27 (July 1972): 665-70.

> Challenges some of Lockard's conclusions (see below, this page), and identifies the following eras of textbook writing in comparative psychology: the Darwinian (1880-1930), the "classical" (1930s), and the "edited" (1940-70).

Eaton, R.L. "An Historical Look at Ethology: A Shot in the Arm for Comparative Psychology." JOURNAL OF THE HISTORY OF THE BEHAVIORAL SCIENCES 6 (April 1970): 176-87.

> Examines the historical roots of comparative psychology and ethology, evaluates their methods, and points to the new role of biological theory in American psychology.

Gray, Philip H. "Comparative Psychology and Ethology: A Saga of Twins Reared Apart." ANNALS OF THE NEW YORK ACADEMY OF SCIENCES 223 (1973): 49-53.

Howard, D.T. "The Influence of Evolutionary Doctrine on Psychology." PSYCHOLOGICAL REVIEW 34 (July 1927): 305-12.

Jaynes, Julian. "The Historical Origins of 'Ethology' and 'Comparative Psychology.'" ANIMAL BEHAVIOUR 17 (November 1969): 601-6.

Klopfer, Peter H. AN INTRODUCTION TO ANIMAL BEHAVIOUR: ETHOLOGY'S FIRST CENTURY. 2d ed. Englewood Cliffs, N.J.: Prentice-Hall, 1974. xiv, 332 p.

> A textbook of ethology organized chronologically with sections on foundations of ethology, 1850-1900; the structure of ethology, 1900-1950; and contributions of related disciplines, 1900-1950. A final section covers more recent developments in ethology. Extensive reference list. Indexes.

Lockard, Robert B. "Reflections on the Fall of Comparative Psychology: Is There a Message for Us All?" AMERICAN PSYCHOLOGIST 26 (February 1971): 168-79.

> Discusses the beginnings of comparative psychology in the work of Darwin, the demise of the area during the 1930s, 1940s, and 1950s as theorists became overly narrow and dogmatic, and the subsequent ascendancy of behavioral biology. Reviews basic premises of the comparative psychology of the 1950s and contemporary behavioral biology along with their implications for comparative psychology, developmental psychology, human psychology, and animal learning.

Mountjoy, Paul T., and Sears, Gary W. "Historical Note: An Observation of Territoriality in Birds which Predates Scientific Reports." PSYCHOLOGICAL RECORD 20 (Winter 1970): 93-95.

> Annie Martin, writing on life on an ostrich farm, reported territoriality in ostriches in 1891, twenty years prior to scientific reports of such territoriality.

Munn, N.L. "Animal Psychology." ENCYCLOPEDIA AMERICANA 1 (1947): 699-703.

> A brief history of comparative psychology.

Richards, Robert J. "Lloyd Morgan's Theory of Instinct: From Darwinism to Neo-Darwinism." JOURNAL OF THE HISTORY OF THE BEHAVIORAL SCIENCES 13 (January 1977): 12-32.

> An overview of the instinct theories of Darwin and Romanes followed by examination of the philosophical assumptions embraced by Morgan and Morgan's specific contributions to instinct theory. Discusses briefly subsequent developments in the work of McDougall and the modern work of Lorenz.

Rosenfield, Leonora Cohen. FROM BEAST-MACHINE TO MAN-MACHINE: ANIMAL SOUL IN FRENCH LETTERS FROM DESCARTES TO LA METTRIE. Enl. ed. New York: Octagon Books, 1968. xxviii, 385 p.

> Examines French theological, philosophical, and scientific literature dealing with questions on the animal soul and animal automatism. Index.

Tinbergen, N. THE STUDY OF INSTINCT. Oxford, Engl.: Clarendon Press, 1951. Reprint. Oxford: Oxford University Press, 1974. xx, 228 p.

> A nontechnical introduction to early ethological research conducted in Europe. Includes chapters on such topics as external stimuli, internal stimuli, development, adaptiveness of behavior, and evolution. Bibliography. Index.

Warden, Carl John. "The Historical Development of Comparative Psychology." PSYCHOLOGICAL REVIEW 34 (January and March 1927): 57-85, 135-68.

Warden, Carl J[ohn].; Jenkins, Thomas N.; and Warner, Lucien H. COMPARATIVE PSYCHOLOGY. 3 vols. New York: Ronald Press, 1935, 1936, 1940.

> See section D3b, p. 271, for annotation.

Yerkes, Robert M. "Early Days of Comparative Psychology." PSYCHOLOGICAL REVIEW 50 (January 1943): 74-76.

b. Major Textbooks, Treatises, Articles, and Books of Readings

Allee, Warder Clyde. THE SOCIAL LIFE OF ANIMALS. Rev. ed. Boston: Beacon Press, 1958. 233 p.

> A significant work on the evolution of social behavior. Argues that cooperation and competition can coexist in the same society. Index.

Baerends, Gerard; Beer, Colin; and Manning, Aubrey, eds. FUNCTION AND EVOLUTION IN BEHAVIOUR: ESSAYS IN HONOUR OF PROFESSOR NIKO TINBERGEN, F.R.S. Oxford, Engl.: Clarendon Press, 1975. xxxi, 393 p.

> Seventeen papers by leading authorities on topics in the function of behavior (part I) and in comparison and evolution (part II). Topics include behavior genetics, social hunting, aggression, learning, and predatory behavior. This collection published in honor of Tinbergen's retirement from the chair of animal behavior at the University of Oxford. Selected bibliography of Tinbergen's works.

Brewer, T.M. "Can a Bird Reason?" ATLANTIC MONTHLY, July 1871, pp. 41-44.

> Argues that birds, in adapting their nesting patterns to human invasion of their territories, exhibit the capacity to reason or learn.

Burroughs, John. "The Animal Mind." ATLANTIC MONTHLY, November 1910, pp. 622-31.

_____. "Do Animals Think?" HARPER'S MAGAZINE, February 1905, pp. 354-58.

> Argues against the idea that animals think in any sense as humans do.

Carr, Harvey. "The Interpretation of the Animal Mind." PSYCHOLOGICAL REVIEW 34 (March 1927): 87-106.

> A discussion of the anthropomorphism of early animal psychology.

Darwin, Charles. THE EXPRESSION OF THE EMOTIONS IN MAN AND ANIMALS. New York: Greenwood Press, 1955 (1872). xi, 372 p.

> See section D7, p. 298, for annotation.

Davis, H.B. "The Raccoon: A Study in Animal Intelligence." AMERICAN JOURNAL OF PSYCHOLOGY 18 (October 1907): 447-89.

Denny, M. Ray, and Ratner, Stanley C., eds. COMPARATIVE PSYCHOLOGY:

RESEARCH IN ANIMAL BEHAVIOR. Rev. ed. Homewood, Ill.: Dorsey Press, 1970. xiv, 869 p.

Papers written by authorities in comparative psychology illustrate research methods and the variety of topical areas within comparative psychology. Major subsections devoted to such topics as behavioral genetics, innate behaviors, early experience, animal group behavior, conditioning, and effects of aversive stimulation. Extensive reference materials. Index.

Eibl-Eibesfeldt, Irenaeus. ETHOLOGY: THE BIOLOGY OF BEHAVIOR. 2d ed. Translated by Erich Klinghammer. New York: Holt, Rinehart and Winston, 1975. xiv, 625 p.

A text providing fairly comprehensive coverage of the subject matter of ethology. Presents most topics from a Lorenzian viewpoint but includes other views as well. Brief introductory chapter on the history of ethology. Extensive reference list. Index.

Evans, Richard I. KONRAD LORENZ: THE MAN AND HIS IDEAS. New York: Harcourt Brace Jovanovich, 1975. xviii, 302 p.

Transcriptions of discussions between Evans and Lorenz on such topics as ethology and imprinting, motivation, aggression, and contemporary issues. Contains reprints of four early papers by Lorenz and a bibliography of his major published works. References. Index.

Fischer, Ronald A. THE GENETICAL THEORY OF NATURAL SELECTION. London: Oxford University Press, 1930. Reprint. New York: Dover, 1958. xiv, 291 p. Index.

Griffin, Donald R. THE QUESTION OF ANIMAL AWARENESS: EVOLUTIONARY CONTINUITY OF MENTAL EXPERIENCE. New York: Rockefeller University Press, 1976. viii, 135 p.

Explores both contemporary and historical positions on questions of animal thought and awareness. Bibliography. Index.

Haggerty, M.E. "Animal Intelligence." ATLANTIC MONTHLY, May 1907, pp. 599-607.

An early popular account of scientific work in comparative psychology and in animal conditioning and learning; argues for the value of such endeavors.

Herrick, Charles Judson. NEUROLOGICAL FOUNDATIONS OF ANIMAL BEHAVIOR. New York: Holt, 1924. Reprint. New York: Hafner, 1962. xii, 334 p.

A reprint of Herrick's classic work (also reprinted in 1952) exploring the relationship between the nervous systems of animals and their behaviors. Bibliography. Glossary. Index.

Hinde, R.A. ANIMAL BEHAVIOUR: A SYNTHESIS OF ETHOLOGY AND COMPARATIVE PSYCHOLOGY. 2d ed. New York: McGraw-Hill, 1970. xvi, 876 p.

A massive attempt to bring together the work of psychologists, zoologists, physiologists, anatomists, geneticists, ecologists, and others as it bears on the understanding of animal behavior. More than 2,500 references. Indexes.

Hobhouse, L.T. MIND IN EVOLUTION. 3d ed. New York: Macmillan, 1926. xix, 483 p.

An early influential textbook of comparative psychology. Index.

Klopfer, Peter H., and Hailman, Jack P., eds. CONTROL AND DEVELOPMENT OF BEHAVIOR: AN HISTORICAL SAMPLE FROM THE PENS OF ETHOLOGISTS. Reading, Mass.: Addison-Wesley, 1972. xiii, 281 p.

A collection of historical papers complementing Klopfer's earlier book, AN INTRODUCTION TO ANIMAL BEHAVIOR: ETHOLOGY'S FIRST CENTURY (see entry in preceding section, p. 263). Includes selected papers and excerpts on "innate releasing mechanisms," displacement activities and drives, critical periods, and the role of experience in parental feeding. Brief biographical sketches of authors. References.

Koehler, Wolfgang. THE MENTALITY OF APES.

See section C4d, p. 195, for annotation.

Loeb, Jacques. COMPARATIVE PHYSIOLOGY OF THE BRAIN, AND COMPARATIVE PSYCHOLOGY. Translated by Anne Leonard Loeb. New York: G.P. Putnam's Sons, 1900. x, 309 p.

A classic introduction to comparative physiology and psychology. Outlines experiments on animals from many phyla and concludes with a discussion of memory and localization of psychic functions. Loeb argues, in the tradition of Ernst Mach, that physiological processes can substitute for metaphysical interpretations of brain functions. Index.

_____. FORCED MOVEMENTS, TROPISMS, AND ANIMAL CONDUCT. Philadelphia: J.B. Lippincott, 1918. 209 p.

Outlines Loeb's mechanistic theory of animal conduct and presents experiments which support his theory, performed on a variety of animals. Extensive references. Index.

Long, William J. "The Question of Animal Reason." HARPER'S MAGAZINE, September 1905, pp. 588-94.

A popular, anecdotal defense of the proposition that animals can indeed reason.

Lorenz, Konrad. EVOLUTION AND MODIFICATION OF BEHAVIOR. Chicago: University of Chicago Press, 1965. 121 p.

Explores theoretical attitudes toward the concept of the "innate" and criticizes behavioristic arguments and attitudes of early and modern ethologists. Discusses values and limitations of deprivation experiments. References. Index.

_____. KING SOLOMON'S RING: NEW LIGHT ON ANIMAL WAYS. New York: Thomas Y. Crowell, 1952. xix, 202 p.

A popular account of the ethological approach to the study of animal behavior covering such topics as instinct, aggression, sexual behaviors, and social structures. Index.

_____. ON AGGRESSION. Translated by Marjorie Kerr Wilson. New York: Harcourt, Brace and World, 1966. xiv, 306 p.

A major controversial ethological treatise concerning "the fighting instinct in beast and man which is directed against members of the same species."

Lorenz, Konrad, and Leyhausen, Paul. MOTIVATION OF HUMAN AND ANIMAL BEHAVIOR: AN ETHOLOGICAL VIEW. New York: Van Nostrand Reinhold, 1973. xix, 423 p.

A collection of eleven papers published between 1939 and 1967. The first paper, by Lorenz, is on the comparative study of behavior. Papers by Leyhausen explore topics in sexual motivation, fear, territoriality, and social organization. Outlines a theory of motivation. Notes. References. Index.

Maier, N.R.F., and Schneirla, T.C. PRINCIPLES OF ANIMAL PSYCHOLOGY. New York: McGraw-Hill, 1935. Reprint. New York: Dover, 1964. xvi, 683 p.

An expanded and corrected version of the classic systematic text published in 1935. Examines comparative behavior of animals, principles of animal adjustment, and modification of behavior in mammals. This edition includes a supplement exploring such topics as instinct, frustration, and conditioning. Bibliography. Index.

Maier, Richard A., and Maier, Barbara M. COMPARATIVE ANIMAL BEHAVIOR. Monterey, Calif.: Brooks/Cole, 1970. viii, 459 p.

A text on comparative psychology examining the physiological foundations of behavior; such functional behavior patterns as feeding, defense, reproduction, social organization, and navigation; and such dynamic features of behavior as emotion, learning, and the effects of early experience. Includes chapters on behavior genetics and on evolution and behavior. Bibliography. Glossary. Index.

Marler, Peter Robert, and Hamilton, William J. III. MECHANISMS OF ANIMAL BEHAVIOR. New York: John Wiley and Sons, 1966. x, 771 p.

Morgan, Conwy Lloyd. THE ANIMAL MIND. New York: Longmans, Green, 1930. xii, 275 p.

Explores such topics in animal psychology as instincts, memory, learning, and levels of mentality. Index.

_____. HABIT AND INSTINCT. New York: Edward Arnold, 1896. 351 p. Index.

_____. INSTINCT AND EXPERIENCE. New York: Macmillan, 1912. xvii, 299 p. Index.

See section C3b, p. 305, for annotation.

_____ AN INTRODUCTION TO COMPARATIVE PSYCHOLOGY. London: Walter Scott, 1894. vii, 382 p.

A classic, highly systematic work in comparative psychology. Explores relationships between human and animal psychology and the evolution of consciousness, and is significant for its philosophical and methodological perspective. Morgan sets forth his parsimonious canon that actions should not be interpreted in terms of higher psychical faculties if they can be interpreted in terms of lower ones. Minimal bibliographical materials in footnotes. Index.

Moss, R.A., ed. COMPARATIVE PSYCHOLOGY. Englewood Cliffs, N.J.: Prentice-Hall, 1951. (1934, 1942). xvii, 525 p.

Munn, Norman L. AN INTRODUCTION TO ANIMAL PSYCHOLOGY: THE BEHAVIOR OF THE RAT. New York: Houghton Mifflin, 1933. xxii, 439 p.

A standard introduction to the methods, issues, and areas of investigation in animal psychology. Munn's later HANDBOOK OF PSYCHOLOGICAL RESEARCH ON THE RAT (see section D3c, p. 273), which is both an extensive survey and a text, replaced this work. Index.

Porter, James P. "A Preliminary Study of the Psychology of the English Sparrow." AMERICAN JOURNAL OF PSYCHOLOGY 15 (July 1904): 313-46.

Romanes, George John. ANIMAL INTELLIGENCE. 7th ed. London: Kegan Paul, Trench, Trubner and Co., 1898. xiv, 520 p.

A classic work in comparative psychology. Presents empirical observations on animal intelligence in relation to evolutionary theory. Describes the behaviors and habits of animals in a wide range of phyla and sometimes numerous species within a phylum.

_____. MENTAL EVOLUTION IN ANIMALS. New York: Appleton, 1884. 411 p.

An extension of the author's earlier work, ANIMAL INTELLIGENCE (see preceding entry), via anecdote and large inferential leaps. Attempts to trace the emergence in the phylogenetic scale of such mental phenomena as consciousness, sensation, perception, and reason, and thus to establish the mental evolution of animals. An appendix includes a posthumously published essay on instinct by Charles Darwin. Index.

_____. MENTAL EVOLUTION IN MAN: ORIGIN OF HUMAN FACULTY. New York: Appleton, 1889. viii, 452 p.

Romanes's earlier work on animal intelligence and mental evolution (see preceding two entries) is extended in this work, which attempts to trace the origin and development of human thought processes. Chapters are devoted to such topics as language and its origin, speech, self-consciousness, gestures, and ideas. Bibliographical materials in footnotes. Index.

Schneirla, T[heodore].C[hristian]. ARMY ANTS: A STUDY IN SOCIAL ORGANIZATION. Edited by Howard R. Topoff. San Francisco: W.H. Freeman, 1971. xx, 349 p.

A posthumous work by a pioneer comparative psychologist. Presents the results of his classic studies of the social behavior of ants carried out over four decades. Index.

Stone, Calvin P., ed. COMPARATIVE PSYCHOLOGY. 3d ed. Englewood Cliffs, N.J.: Prentice-Hall, 1951. xvii, 525 p. Index.

Thorndike, Edward L. ANIMAL INTELLIGENCE: EXPERIMENTAL STUDIES. New York: Macmillan, 1911. viii, 297 p.

See section C7, p. 155, for annotation.

_____. "The Instinctive Reaction of Young Chicks." PSYCHOLOGICAL REVIEW 6 (May 1899): 282-91.

Thorpe, W.H. LEARNING AND INSTINCT IN ANIMALS. Rev. and enl. ed. Cambridge, Mass.: Harvard University Press, 1966. x, 558 p.

Surveys instinctual responses and learning abilities in such animal groups as protozoa, worms, arthropods, fish, amphibians, birds, and mammals. Examines numerous learning paradigms. References. Index.

Thorpe, W.H., and Zangwill, O.L., eds. CURRENT PROBLEMS IN ANIMAL BEHAVIOUR. Cambridge: Cambridge University Press, 1961. xiv, 424 p. References. Index.

Tinbergen, Niko. THE ANIMAL IN ITS WORLD: EXPLORATIONS OF AN ETHOLOGIST 1932-1972. 2 vols. Cambridge, Mass.: Harvard University Press, 1972.

Volume 1 reprints ten articles reporting field studies. Volume 2 reprints eight general papers and papers reporting laboratory experiments. The Foreword, by Sir Peter Medawar, notes that these papers "will give the historian of ideas an insight into the early days of one of the most influential movements in modern science." References.

_____. SOCIAL BEHAVIOUR IN ANIMALS: WITH SPECIAL REFERENCE TO VERTEBRATES. New York: John Wiley and Sons, 1953. xi, 150 p.

A well-known book illustrating the ethological approach to the study of animal behavior. Explores such social behaviors as mating, family and group life, fighting, interspecies relationships, and the growth of social organizations. Bibliography. Index.

_____. THE STUDY OF INSTINCT. Oxford, Engl.: Clarendon Press, 1951. xii, 228 p.

Designed to acquaint Anglo-Americans with research done on the European continent and to present a coherent overview of ethological problems and research. Based on a series of lectures. Bibliography. Index.

Warden, Carl J.; Jenkins, Thomas N.; and Warner, Lucien H. COMPARATIVE PSYCHOLOGY. 3 vols. New York: Ronald Press, 1935, 1936, 1940.

This massive work discusses the historical development, methods, and principles of comparative psychology in volume 1; receptive capacities and reactive characteristics of plants and animals representing the various phyla up to Arthropoda in volume 2; and receptive and reactive characteristics of vertebrates (Pisces, Amphibia, Reptilia, Aves, Mammalia) in volume 3.

_____. INTRODUCTION TO COMPARATIVE PSYCHOLOGY. New York: Ronald Press, 1934. x, 581 p.

An abridged version of the three-volume work by the same authors (see preceding entry). Index.

Washburn, Margaret Floy. THE ANIMAL MIND: A TEXT-BOOK OF COMPARATIVE PSYCHOLOGY. 4th ed. New York: Macmillan, 1936. x, 333 p.

A classic work emphasizing experimental findings, especially as they relate to sensory and reactive capacities of animals, memory, and attention. Bibliography. Index.

Waters, Rolland, H.; Rethlingshafer, D.A.; and Caldwell, Willard E., eds. PRINCIPLES OF COMPARATIVE PSYCHOLOGY. New York: McGraw-Hill, 1960. ix, 453 p. Index.

Watson, John B. BEHAVIOR: AN INTRODUCTION TO COMPARATIVE PSYCHOLOGY. New York: Holt, Rinehart and Winston, 1967. xxxvi, 439 p.

Sets forth the behavioristic position on the subject matter, methods, and problems of psychology followed by chapters devoted to characteristics of learning, sensory processes, and instinct in a variety of species. Based on a series of lectures delivered at Columbia University in 1913. This edition includes an introduction by R.J. Herrnstein tracing selected themes in the development of behaviorism and in the life of John B. Watson.

_____. "How Animals Find their Way Home." HARPER'S MAGAZINE, October 1909, pp. 685-89.

A brief popular account of homing behavior in birds.

_____. "Imitation in Monkeys." PSYCHOLOGICAL BULLETIN 5 (June 1908): 169-78.

_____. "The New Science of Animal Behavior." HARPER'S MAGAZINE, February 1910, pp. 346-53.

A popular early plea for an objective science of animal behavior; describes mazes and other apparatus for such work.

Yerkes, Robert M., and Learned, Blanche W. CHIMPANZEE INTELLIGENCE AND ITS VOCAL EXPRESSIONS. Baltimore: Williams and Wilkins, 1925. 157 p.

An influential work in comparative psychology. Examines physical and mental traits of chimpanzees, evidence of insight in chimpanzees, and chimpanzee vocalizations associated with a variety of specific environmental stimuli. Minimal references.

c. Problems in Comparative Psychology and Histories of Work
   with Specific Species

Gray, Philip Howard. "Historical Notes on the Aerial Predator Reaction and
the Tinbergen Hypothesis." JOURNAL OF THE HISTORY OF THE BEHAVIORAL
SCIENCES 2 (October 1966): 330-34.

> Reviews some of the early work on the aerial predator reaction
> and discusses four variables not accounted for in previous experiments.

Gregson, E.D., and Gregson, R.A.M. "A Note on a Seventeenth-Century
Distinction Between Feral Man and Man-Like Apes." JOURNAL OF THE HIS-
TORY OF THE BEHAVIORAL SCIENCES 6 (April 1970): 159-61.

> Notes that A. Kircher in 1667 drew a distinction between feral
> humans and anthropoid apes which is fairly consistent with modern
> views. Concludes that Linneaus's classification of 1758 in his
> SYSTEMA NATURAE "must now be seen as a retrograde step."

Miles, Walter R. "On the History of Research with Rats and Mazes: A Collection of Notes." JOURNAL OF GENERAL PSYCHOLOGY 3 (April 1930):
324-37.

> Reprints of letters from individuals acquainted with early maze re-
> search with rats. Attempts to trace this research back to its
> founder, and concludes that E.C. Sanford was the first to use the
> maze as an apparatus for studying the behavior of the rat.

Mountjoy, Paul T., et al. "Falconry: Neglected Aspect of the History of
Psychology." JOURNAL OF THE HISTORY OF THE BEHAVIORAL SCIENCES
5 (January 1969): 59-67.

> Provides a brief overview of the history of falconry, explores simi-
> larities between medieval falconry and modern operant techniques,
> and suggests closer historical scrutiny of the possible influences of
> early animal training techniques on modern psychology.

Munn, Norman L. HANDBOOK OF PSYCHOLOGICAL RESEARCH ON THE
RAT: AN INTRODUCTION TO ANIMAL PSYCHOLOGY. Boston: Houghton
Mifflin, 1950. xxvi, 598 p.

> A well-illustrated, classic survey. Includes materials on the care
> and handling of rats and on types of problems which can be ex-
> plored with rats in such content areas as unlearned behavior, ac-
> tivity, motivation, sensory processes, learning, and abnormal and
> social behavior. Extensive bibliography. Index.

Ruch, T.C., and Fulton, J.F. "Growth of Primate Literature Since 1800."
SCIENCE 95 (January 1942): 47-48.

Waters, R.H. "Morgan's Canon and Anthropomorphism." PSYCHOLOGICAL REVIEW 46 (November 1939): 534-40.

> Outlines the historical effect of Morgan's canon on psychological research and argues that current violations of the canon are neces-sary if interpretations of some forms of animal behavior are to be intelligible.

White, Geoffrey K.; Juhasz, Joseph B.; and Wilson, Peter J. "Is Man No More Than This?: Evaluative Bias in Interspecies Comparison." JOURNAL OF THE HISTORY OF THE BEHAVIORAL SCIENCES 9 (July 1973): 203-12.

> Reviews historical conceptions of human and animal behavior that have led to biases in comparative psychology. Argues that dif-ferences between human and animal behavior are in kind, not in degree. "Man is neither more nor less than any other animal."

4. PHYSIOLOGICAL PSYCHOLOGY

Most of the works included here describe historical developments in specific topical areas of physiological psychology. An excellent example is Fearing's book on reflex action. After the first subsection devoted to historical articles, a second (D4b) lists a few major textbooks in physiological psychology. For general orientation, see relevant chapters in Stevens's HANDBOOK or in Osgood's or Woodworth's texts (all in section D2).

a. Histories of Physiological Psychology

Anderson, Robert M. "Wholistic and Particulate Approaches in Neuropsychol-ogy." In COGNITION AND THE SYMBOLIC PROCESSES, edited by Walter B. Weimer and David S. Palermo, pp. 389-96. Hillsdale, N.J.: Lawrence Erlbaum, 1974. xii, 450 p.

Beck, Adolf. "The Determination of Localizations in the Brain and Spinal Cord With the Aid of Electrical Phenomena." ACTA NEUROBIOLOGIAE EX-PERIMENTALIS.Suppl. 3 (1973). 59 p.

> An English edition of one of the classic discoveries of electrical currents in the brain.

Brazier, Mary A.B. "Cerebral Localization: The Search for Functional Repre-sentation in the Cortex." ACTA NEUROBIOLOGIAE EXPERIMENTALIS 35, nos. 5-6 (1975): 529-35.

_____. "The Growth of Concepts Relating to Brain Mechanisms." JOURNAL OF THE HISTORY OF THE BEHAVIORAL SCIENCES 1 (July 1965): 218-34.

Traces empirical approaches to the understanding of brain mechanisms with emphasis on the work of such pioneers as Locke, Condillac, DeTracy, and Cabanis.

_____. "The Historical Development of Neurophysiology." In HANDBOOK OF PHYSIOLOGY, edited by John Field. Section 1, NEURO-PHYSIOLOGY, edited by H.W. Magoun, pp. 1-58. Baltimore: Williams and Wilkins, 1959-60.

_____. A HISTORY OF THE ELECTRICAL ACTIVITY OF THE BRAIN: THE FIRST HALF CENTURY. London: Pitman Medical Publishers; New York: Macmillan, 1961. vii, 119 p.

An illustrated monograph detailing the history of the study of the electrical nature of neural activity, including the discovery of the electroencephalogram. References. Index.

Brooks, Chandler McC., and Cranefield, Paul F., eds. THE HISTORICAL DEVELOPMENT OF PHYSIOLOGICAL THOUGHT; A SYMPOSIUM HELD AT THE STATE UNIVERSITY OF NEW YORK DOWNSTATE MEDICAL CENTER. New York: Hafner, xiii, 401 p.

An anthology of papers by leading scholars on selected topics including some of special interest to psychologists, for example development of ideas on the relation of mind and brain, the biology of consciousness, and backgrounds of neurophysiology. Index.

Brožek, Josef, and Joffe, Matthew. "Documenting the History of Psychology: De Maupertuis on the Planning of Research, 1752." JOURNAL OF THE HISTORY OF THE BEHAVIORAL SCIENCES 12 (April 1976): 141-44.

Translates selections from a letter on the progress of the sciences written in 1752 by Pierre-Louis Moreau de Maupertuis. Includes a foreword and section XVII on proposed psychological experiments on such topics as sleep, direct stimulation of the brain of accident victims and those condemned to death, and language development.

Caldwell, Willard E. "Some Historical Notes and a Brief Summary of the Experimental Method and Findings of Ferdinando Cazzamalli." JOURNAL OF GENERAL PSYCHOLOGY 60 (January 1959): 121-29.

Describes selected topics in the experimental psychology of Cazzamalli at the University of Rome including his attempts in 1925 to measure the electrical activity of the brain.

Cardno, J.A. "Bain and Physiological Psychology." AUSTRALIAN JOURNAL OF PSYCHOLOGY 7 (1956): 108-20.

Carmichael, Leonard. "Robert Whytt: A Contribution to the History of Physiological Psychology." PSYCHOLOGICAL REVIEW 34 (July 1927): 287-304.

Clarke, Edwin, and Dewhurst, Kenneth. AN ILLUSTRATED HISTORY OF BRAIN FUNCTION. Berkeley and Los Angeles: University of California Press, 1972.

Clarke, Edwin, and O'Malley, C.D. THE HUMAN BRAIN AND SPINAL CORD: A HISTORICAL STUDY ILLUSTRATED BY WRITINGS FROM ANTIQUITY TO THE TWENTIETH CENTURY. Berkeley and Los Angeles: University of California Press, 1968.

Clements, Raymond D. "Physiological-Psychological Thought in Juan Luis Vives." JOURNAL OF THE HISTORY OF THE BEHAVIORAL SCIENCES 3 (July 1967): 219-35.

> Reviews Vives's thought on such topics as the emotions, education, memory, and association.

Creed, R.S., et al. REFLEX ACTIVITY OF THE SPINAL CORD. Oxford, Engl.: Clarendon Press, 1932. 183 p.

> Presents technical and physiological features of reflex action. Specifically avoids questions of the biological and philosophical significance of the reflex. References. Index.

DeSilva, Harry R., and Ellis, Willis D. "Changing Conceptions in Physiological Psychology." JOURNAL OF GENERAL PSYCHOLOGY 11 (July 1934): 145-59.

> Outlines the shift from reflex arc and single-unit analysis to the view that the nervous system is dynamically organized. Special emphasis on the contributions of Paul Weiss.

Fearing, Franklin. "Jan Swammerdam: A Study in the History of Comparative and Physiological Psychology of the 17th Century." AMERICAN JOURNAL OF PSYCHOLOGY 41 (July 1929): 442-55.

_____. REFLEX ACTION: A STUDY IN THE HISTORY OF PHYSIOLOGICAL PSYCHOLOGY. Cambridge: M.I.T. Press, 1970 (1930). xv, 350 p.

> Presents a detailed historical analysis of the development of the reflex arc concept in philosophic traditions and as an outgrowth of the neuroanatomical and neurophysiological discoveries of the seventeenth, eighteenth, and nineteenth centuries. Concludes with a chapter on modern (early twentieth century) concepts. Bibliography. Index.

_____. "René Descartes: A Study in the History of the Theories of Reflex Action." PSYCHOLOGICAL REVIEW 36 (September 1929): 375-88.

Outlines Descartes's theory of movement, including such topics as automatic action, animal spirits, and reflex action.

Giannitrapani, Duilio. "Developing Concepts of Lateralization of Cerebral Functions." CORTEX 3 (1967): 353-70.

Goldstein, Melvin L. "Physiological Theories of Emotions: A Critical Historical Review from the Standpoint of Behavior Theory." PSYCHOLOGICAL BULLETIN 69 (January 1968): 23-40.

Hall, G.S. "A Sketch of the History of Reflex Action." AMERICAN JOURNAL OF PSYCHOLOGY 3 (January 1890): 71-86.

Hoff, Hebbel E., and Kellaway, Peter. "The Early History of the Reflex." JOURNAL OF THE HISTORY OF MEDICINE AND ALLIED SCIENCES 7 (Summer 1952): 211-49.

Discusses contributions of such theorists as Galen, Hippocrates, Descartes, Whytt, and Unzer to the development of the concept of the reflex.

King, Lester S. "Stahl and Hoffman: A Study of Eighteenth Century Animism." JOURNAL OF THE HISTORY OF MEDICINE AND ALLIED SCIENCES 19 (April 1964): 118-30.

Presents similarities and contrasts between the approaches to animism advanced by George Ernest Stahl and Fridericus Hoffman.

Lachman, Sheldon J. HISTORY AND METHODS OF PHYSIOLOGICAL PSYCHOLOGY: A BRIEF OVERVIEW. Detroit: Hamilton Press, 1963. 64 p.

Brief survey of the development of physiological psychology with emphasis on nineteenth- and twentieth-century thought. Includes a short and elementary discussion of biological, clinical, and experimental methods. Transcription of informal lectures to graduate students. Minimal references. Index.

Lipton, Morris A.; DiMascio, Alberto; and Killam, Keith F., eds. PSYCHOPHARMACOLOGY: A GENERATION OF PROGRESS. New York: Raven Press, 1978. 1,750 p.

Livingston, Robert B. "How Man Looks at His Own Brain: An Adventure Shared by Psychology and Neurophysiology." In PSYCHOLOGY: A STUDY OF A SCIENCE, edited by Sigmund Koch, vol. 4, pp. 51-99. New York: McGraw-Hill, 1962.

McMalton, Carol E. "Harvey On the Soul: A Unique Episode in the History

of Psycho-physiological Thought." JOURNAL OF THE HISTORY OF THE BE-
HAVIORAL SCIENCES 11 (July 1975): 276-83.

> Argues that Harvey's theory of the circulation of the blood was
> consistent with earlier notions of psychosomatic medicine in which
> a biological soul served as a basis for the unification of the men-
> tal and the physiological. Unfortunately for the development of
> psychophysiology and psychosomatic medicine, Cartesian mind-body
> dualism gained ascendancy following Harvey's death.

Meyer, Alfred. HISTORICAL ASPECTS OF CEREBRAL ANATOMY. London:
Oxford University Press, 1971. ix, 230 p.

> A book "complementary to the work of Clarke and O'Malley" (see
> entry earlier in this section, p. 276) concentrating on historical de-
> velopments since Galen in knowledge about morphology (especially
> of the basal ganglia), the diencephalon, the "olfactory brain," and
> the cerebral convolutions and fissures. A chapter on problems
> concerning the discovery of the neurons of special interest to psy-
> chologists. References. Index.

O'Neil, W.M. "Mueller's Theory of the Specific Energies of the Sensory
Nerves." PSYCHOLOGIA 14 (December 1971): 131-35.

> Presents an overview of principles which guided Mueller's thought
> and a comment on Mueller's influence on the development of ex-
> perimental psychology.

Pastore, Nicholas, and Klibbe, Helene. "The Orientation of the Cerebral
Image in Descartes' Theory of Visual Perception." JOURNAL OF THE HISTORY
OF THE BEHAVIORAL SCIENCES 5 (October 1969): 385-89.

> Argues that diagrams appearing in the posthumously published
> L'HOMME (1664) are "the basis for erroneous interpretations of
> Descartes' psychophysiology" because the diagrams were not con-
> structed by Descartes, but by other individuals.

Penfield, Wilder. THE CEREBRAL CORTEX OF MAN: A CLINICAL STUDY OF
LOCALIZATION OF FUNCTION. New York: Hafner, 1968. xv, 248 p.

> A brief historical note on neurophysiology followed by an examina-
> tion of the role of the cortex in sensorimotor functions, speech,
> vision, hearing, and memory. Bibliography. Index.

Porter, Langley. "The Beginnings of Modern Thinking About Neurology."
JOURNAL OF NERVOUS AND MENTAL DISEASE 99 (May 1944): 808-24.

Pubols, Benjamin H., Jr. "Jan Swammerdam and the History of Reflex Action."
AMERICAN JOURNAL OF PSYCHOLOGY 72 (March 1959): 131-35.

Outlines "Swammerdam's experimental and conceptual contributions in the history of reflex action."

Rather, L.J. MIND AND BODY IN EIGHTEENTH CENTURY MEDICINE. Berkeley and Los Angeles: University of California Press, 1965. xii, 275 p.

Translations of two Latin treatises, published in The Netherlands in 1747 and 1763 by Jerome Gaub, provide the flavor of medical thought on the classic mind-body problem in mid-eighteenth century Europe. Extensive introductory comments and notes, bibliography. Index.

Ribot, Th. HEREDITY: A PSYCHOLOGICAL STUDY OF ITS PHENOMENA, LAWS, CAUSES, AND CONSEQUENCES. Translator not named. New York: Appleton, 1915. x, 393 p.

A largely anecdotal early work attempting to demonstrate the hereditary basis of such characteristics as sensory abilities, imagination, intelligence, the will, and national character. Part two considers laws of heredity; parts three and four explore more philosophical issues such as how psychological states could have hereditary bases, eugenics, and heredity and liberty. Minimal references.

Riese, Walther. "The Principle of Integration: Its History and Its Nature." JOURNAL OF NERVOUS AND MENTAL DISEASE 96 (September 1942): 296-312.

Riese, Walther, and Hoff, Ebbe C. "A History of the Doctrine of Cerebral Localization: Sources, Anticipations, and Basic Reasoning." JOURNAL OF THE HISTORY OF MEDICINE AND ALLIED SCIENCES 5 (Winter 1950): 50-71.

_____. "A History of the Doctrine of Cerebral Localization, Second Part: Methods and Main Results." JOURNAL OF THE HISTORY OF MEDICINE AND ALLIED SCIENCES 6 (Autumn 1951): 439-70.

Sheer, Daniel E. "Brain and Behavior: The Background of Interdisciplinary Research." In ELECTRICAL STIMULATION OF THE BRAIN: AN INTERDISCIPLINARY SURVEY OF NEUROBEHAVIORAL INTEGRATIVE SYSTEMS, edited by Daniel E. Sheer, pp. 3-21. Austin: University of Texas Press, 1961.

Traces contributions in neuropsychology, neurophysiology, neurology, and electrophysiology made by sixteen pioneers working primarily in the eighteenth and nineteenth centuries. Includes descriptions of the work of Luigi Galvani, Pierre Flourens, Charles S. Sherrington, Pierre Paul Broca, and Karl S. Lashley. Offers brief comments on the work of other pioneers such as Hippocrates, Galen, and Descartes.

Smith, Roger. "The Background of Physiological Psychology in Natural Philoso-phy." HISTORY OF SCIENCE 11 (June 1973): 75-123.

Staum, Martin S. "Cabanis and the Science of Man." JOURNAL OF THE HISTORY OF THE BEHAVIORAL SCIENCES 10 (April 1974): 135-43.

> Reviews Cabanis's contributions to a human science including his assumptions about human nature, the influence of the environment, the possibilities for growth, and the relationship between physio-logical and psychological processes.

Stratton, George Malcolm. THEOPHRASTUS AND THE GREEK PHYSIOLOGI-CAL PSYCHOLOGY BEFORE ARISTOTLE. London: George Allen & Unwin, 1917. Reprint. Chicago: Argonaut, 1967. 227 p.

> A translation of Theophrastus's ON THE SENSES accompanied by the Greek original and preceded by a lengthy introduction by Stratton, the translator. Extensive notes. Index.

Valenstein, Elliot S. "History of Brain Stimulation: Investigations Into the Physiology of Motivation." In BRAIN STIMULATION AND MOTIVATION: RESEARCH AND COMMENTARY, edited by Elliot S. Valenstein, pp. 1-43. Glenview, Ill.: Scott, Foresman, 1973.

> An overview of selected views of the nervous system beginning with Galen. Examines early cortical and later subcortical experi-mental and clinical investigations of stimulation of the brain. Ex-tensive bibliography.

Young, Robert Maxwell. MIND, BRAIN AND ADAPTATION IN THE 19TH CENTURY: CEREBRAL LOCALIZATION AND ITS BIOLOGICAL CONTEXT FROM GALL TO FERRIER. Oxford, Engl.: Clarendon Press, 1970. xiv, 278 p.

> A history from Franz Joseph Gall to David Ferrier on the mind-body problem, cerebral localization, and brain function. Covers contributions of such individuals as Flourens, Magendie, Bain, Johannes Mueller, Spencer, Fritsch, and Hitzig. Index.

b. Selected Textbooks, Anthologies, and Treatises

Beach, Frank A., et al., eds. THE NEUROPSYCHOLOGY OF LASHLEY. New York: McGraw-Hill, 1960. xx, 564 p.

> An anthology of thirty-one papers by Karl Spencer Lashley, a pioneer biopsychologist. Contains eulogies of Lashley by a psy-chologist (E.G. Boring) and a neurologist (Stanley Cobb). Lists Lashley's publications. Index.

Bennett, Thomas L. BRAIN AND BEHAVIOR. Monterey, Calif.: Brooks/Cole

Publishing Co., 1977. ix, 341 p.

> A brief but comprehensive text for college courses in physiological psychology. Historical perspective is provided for the various content areas.

Jacobson, E. "The Electro-physiology of Mental Activities." AMERICAN JOURNAL OF PSYCHOLOGY 44 (October 1932): 677-94.

Ladd, George T[rumbull]. ELEMENTS OF PHYSIOLOGICAL PSYCHOLOGY: A TREATISE OF THE ACTIVITIES AND NATURE OF THE MIND, FROM THE PHYSICAL AND EXPERIMENTAL POINTS OF VIEW. New York: Charles Scribner's Sons, 1887. xii, 696 p.

> A classic, comprehensive survey of the physiological psychology of the time. Discusses the gross anatomy of the nervous system and the senses, the localization of cerebral function, psychophysics, quality of sensations, feelings and emotions, the development of the mind, and the mind-brain problem. Bibliographical materials in footnotes. Index.

Ladd, George Trumbull, and Woodworth, Robert Sessions. ELEMENTS OF PHYSIOLOGICAL PSYCHOLOGY: A TREATISE OF THE ACTIVITIES AND NATURE OF THE MIND, FROM THE PHYSICAL AND EXPERIMENTAL POINTS OF VIEW. Rev. ed. New York: Charles Scribner's Sons, 1911. xix, 704 p.

> A revision of Ladd's classic text (see preceding entry). This edition is more thoroughly physiological and less speculative; its goal is to summarize the major findings of physiological psychology. Bibliographical materials in footnotes. Index.

Lotze, Hermann. OUTLINES OF PSYCHOLOGY. Translated by C.L. Herrick. 1885. Reprint. New York: Arno Press, 1973. ix, 150 p.

> Derives from dictated portions of Lotze's lectures, intended as a first book in psychology with a physiological emphasis. Concludes with a chapter on the anatomy of the brain.

Luria, A.R.,and Majouski, Lawrence V. "Basic Approaches Used in American and Soviet Clinical Neuropsychology." AMERICAN PSYCHOLOGIST 32 (November 1977): 959-68.

McDougall, William. PHYSIOLOGICAL PSYCHOLOGY. London: J.M. Dent, 1905. viii, 172 p.

> A brief, semi-popular primer intended to supplement James's PRINCIPLES OF PSYCHOLOGY, to help integrate physiology and psychology. Index.

Morgan, Clifford T. PHYSIOLOGICAL PSYCHOLOGY. 3d ed. New York: McGraw-Hill, 1965. ix, 627 p.

A major comprehensive textbook and reference source in physiological psychology. The 1943 and 1950 editions contain more complete reference lists than the 1965 edition. Index.

Sherrington, Charles S. THE INTEGRATIVE ACTION OF THE NERVOUS SYSTEM. 1911. Reprint. New Haven, Conn.: Yale University Press, 1947. xvi, 411 p.

Discusses simple and compound reflexes and the structural and functional characteristics of the brain. Based on a series of ten lectures given in 1906.

Troland, Leonard Thompson. THE PRINCIPLES OF PSYCHOPHYSIOLOGY. New York: D. Van Nostrand, 1929. xx, 430 p.

See section, C14, p. 235, for annotation.

Wundt, Wilhelm. PRINCIPLES OF PHYSIOLOGICAL PSYCHOLOGY. Vol. 1. Translated by E[dward].B[radford]. Titchener from 5th German edition (1902). London: Swan Sonnenschein; New York: Macmillan, 1910. Reprint. New York: Krause Reprint Co., 1969. xvi, 347 p.

See section C2, p. 133, for annotation.

5. PERCEPTION, THINKING, AND LANGUAGE

The books by Boring, by Beardslee and Wertheimer (eds.), and by Mandler and Mandler (eds.) provide fairly comprehensive historical overviews of developments in sensation, perception, and thinking; numerous articles treat specific topical areas in the histories of these fields. For general orientation, see relevant chapters in Stevens's HANDBOOK or in Osgood's or Woodworth's texts (all in section D2).

Ariotti, Piero. "Benedetto Castelli and George Berkeley as Anticipators of Recent Findings on the Moon Illusion." JOURNAL OF THE HISTORY OF THE BEHAVIORAL SCIENCES 9 (October 1973): 328-32.

Shows how Castelli and Berkeley anticipated modern findings on the effects of posture on the moon illusion (Boring, Holway, and Taylor) and on the effects of blocking the horizon on the moon illusion (Rock and Kaufman).

_____. "On the Apparent Size of Projected After Images: Emmert's or Castelli's Law? A Case of 242 Years Anticipation." JOURNAL OF THE HISTORY OF THE BEHAVIORAL SCIENCES 9 (January 1973): 18-28.

Notes that Benedetto Castelli demonstrated the law of the apparent size of projected afterimages by 1639. Multiple rediscovery of the law occurred over 200 years later.

Bain, A[lexander]. THE SENSES AND THE INTELLECT. 4th ed. London: Longmans, Green, 1894. xxxii, 703 p.

The first volume of Bain's massive and influential systematic work on "the Science of Mind" (the other volume is on the emotions and the will, see in section D7b, p. 303). An important early text in psychology.

Baumrin, Judith Marti. "Active Power and Causal Flow in Aristotle's Theory of Vision." JOURNAL OF THE HISTORY OF THE BEHAVIORAL SCIENCES 12 (July 1976): 254-59.

Clarifies terms such as "acting upon" and "active power" in Aristotle's theory of vision. Argues that with an understanding of these terms, Aristotle's theory is more sophisticated and modern than heretofore thought and hence deserves more attention.

Beardslee, David C., and Wertheimer, Michael, eds. READINGS IN PER-CEPTION. Princeton, N.J.: D. Van Nostrand, 1958. xiii, 751 p.

An anthology of fifty-two classic papers published between 1910 and 1957 on biological factors in perception, psychophysics, perception of objects and events, imagery and fantasy, and recognition and identification of figures. Index.

Berkeley, George. A NEW THEORY OF VISION AND OTHER WRITINGS. Introduction by A.D. Lindsay. New York: Everyman's Library, 1969. xxiv, 303 p.

In this classic (1709) psychological monograph (pp. 1-86), Berkeley argues for his empiristic theory of space perception. A second work reprinted in this volume is THE PRINCIPLES OF HUMAN KNOWLEDGE, advancing Berkeley's well-known idealism in which he argues that knowledge comes from sense experience and that we can know only our own perceptions. The final work in this volume, THREE DIALOGUES BETWEEN HYLAS AND PHILONOUS, IN OPPOSITION TO SCEPTICS AND ATHEISTS, is of less interest to psychologists.

Berlyne, D.E. "Experimental Aesthetics." In NEW HORIZONS IN PSYCHOL-OGY 2, edited by P.C. Dodwell. Baltimore: Penguin Books, 1972. 287 p.

Bevan, William. "Perception: Evolution of a Concept." PSYCHOLOGICAL REVIEW 65 (January 1958): 34-55.

Blumenthal, Arthur L. LANGUAGE AND PSYCHOLOGY: HISTORICAL AS-PECTS OF PSYCHOLINGUISTICS. New York: John Wiley and Sons, 1970. xii, 248 p.

A historical study of psycholinguistics focusing on the development of theory over the past one hundred years. Sections devoted to language acquisition, reading, the new psycholinguistics, and nineteenth-century work in language. Considers the work of such pioneers as Wilhelm Wundt, J.R. Kantor, Clara and William Stern, Floyd Allport, Karl Lashley, and Noam Chomsky. Bibliographical materials in footnotes. Index.

Boring, Edwin G. "Did Fechner Measure Sensation?" PSYCHOLOGICAL REVIEW 35 (September 1928): 443-45.

_____. SENSATION AND PERCEPTION IN THE HISTORY OF EXPERIMENTAL PSYCHOLOGY. New York: Appleton-Century-Crofts, 1942. xv, 613 p.

A comprehensive review of major methodological and substantive discoveries, issues, and theories about the various senses and about perception. Probably the most complete source available on the history of research in sensation and perception up to about 1930. Notes and bibliographic sources. Index.

Brožek, Josef. "Contributions to the History of Psychology: XII. Wayward History: F.C. Donders (1818-1889) and the Timing of Mental Operations." PSYCHOLOGICAL REPORTS 26 (April 1970): 563-69.

Campbell, Donald T., and Tauscher, Herman. "Schopenhauer (?), Seguin, Lubinoff, and Zehender as Anticipators of Emmert's Law: With Comments on the Issues of Eponymy." JOURNAL OF THE HISTORY OF THE BEHAVIORAL SCIENCES 2 (January 1966): 58-63.

Documents some of the anticipations of Emmert's law of afterimage size and discusses possible reasons for eponymy (naming a law after the person who formulated it).

Carmichael, L.; Hogan, H.P.; and Walter, A.A. "An Experimental Study of the Effect of Language on the Reproduction of Visually Perceived Form." JOURNAL OF EXPERIMENTAL PSYCHOLOGY 15 (February 1932): 73-86.

Carter, Dorothy J., and Pollack, Robert H. "The Great Illusion Controversy: A Glimpse." PERCEPTUAL AND MOTOR SKILLS 27 (December 1968): 705-6.

Carterette, Edward C., and Friedman, Morton P., eds. HANDBOOK OF PERCEPTION. Vol. 1. HISTORICAL AND PHILOSOPHICAL ROOTS OF PERCEPTION. New York: Academic Press, 1974. xix, 431 p.

Twenty papers, some which are of particular historical interest: a paper on perceptual structure by Michael Wertheimer, "Association (and the Nativist-Empiricist Axis)" by Bruce Earhard, "Consciousness, Perception, and Action" by Wolfgang Metzger, "Attention" by D.E. Berlyne, "Cognition and Knowledge: Psychological Epis-

temology" by Joseph R. Royce, "Organization and the Gestalt
Tradition" by Julian Hochberg, "The Learning Tradition" by
William W. Rozeboom, and "The Historical and Philosophical Background of Cognitive Approaches to Psychology" by W.J. Dowling
and Kelyn Roberts. References. Index.

Chance, B. "Goethe and His Theory of Colors." ANNALS OF MEDICAL
HISTORY 4 (1933): 360-75.

Cohen, J. "History of a Three-Color Mixer." SCIENCE 104 (August 1946):
166.

Corso, John F. "A Theoretico-historical Review of the Threshold Concept."
PSYCHOLOGICAL BULLETIN 60 (July 1963): 356-70.

Davis, Audrey B., and Merzbach, Uta C. EARLY AUDITORY STUDIES:
ACTIVITIES IN THE PSYCHOLOGICAL LABORATORIES OF AMERICAN UNI-
VERSITIES. Washington, D.C.: Smithsonian Institution, 1975. v, 39 p.

> An illustrated pamphlet concentrating primarily on apparatus and
> discussing the history of research on hearing in the United States.
> Selected bibliography. Index of auditory apparatus. Index of
> names.

Epstein, William. "David Brewster's Observations on Perception When Touch
and Vision Conflict: An Historical Note." PERCEPTION AND PSYCHOPHYS-
ICS 10 (August 1971): 97.

Fechner, Gustav. ELEMENTS OF PSYCHOPHYSICS. Vol. 1. Translated by
Davis H. Howes and Edwin G. Boring. New York: Holt, Rinehart and Winston,
1966. xxxi, 286 p.

> A classic (1860) work on the exact quantitative relations between
> sensations and the physical properties of stimuli. The psychophysi-
> cal methods introduced here are viewed by some as the beginnings
> of psychology as a scientific discipline.

Figlio, Karl M. "Theories of Perception and the Physiology of Mind in the
Late Eighteenth Century." HISTORY OF SCIENCE 13 (September 1975): 177-
212.

Gardner, Mark B. "Historical Background of the Haas and/or Precedence
Effect." JOURNAL OF THE ACOUSTICAL SOCIETY OF AMERICA 43 (1968):
1243-48.

Geldard, Frank A. THE HUMAN SENSES. 2d ed. New York: John Wiley
and Sons, 1972. xi, 584 p.

Discusses experimental psychology of the senses, with information on gross anatomy, psychophysics, electrophysiology, theories, and experimental findings. Sections on pressure and pain, kinesthesis, skin senses, smell, taste, audition, and vision. References. Index.

Haber, Ralph Norman, comp. CONTEMPORARY THEORY AND RESEARCH IN VISUAL PERCEPTION. New York: Holt, Rinehart and Winston, 1968. xi, 814 p.

Eighty research and theoretical papers covering most of the major topics in visual perception as of the 1960s.

_____. INFORMATION-PROCESSING APPROACHES TO VISUAL PERCEPTION. New York: Holt, Rinehart and Winston, 1969. ix, 418 p.

A companion anthology to the preceding entry. Reprints forty-seven then-recent contributions to the branch of experimental psychology indicated in the title.

Haber, Ralph Norman, and Hershenson, Maurice. THE PSYCHOLOGY OF VISUAL PERCEPTION. New York: Holt, Rinehart and Winston, 1973. xviii, 398 p.

A text for advanced undergraduate courses examining human visual perception primarily from the point of view of an information processing model. Index.

Hayes, John R. COGNITIVE PSYCHOLOGY: THINKING AND CREATING. Homewood, Ill.: Dorsey Press, 1978. xiii, 254 p.

First 4 chapters of this book trace the historical roots of cognitive psychology from early Greek thought to twentieth-century developments in such systems as behaviorism and Gestalt psychology. Index.

Humphrey, George. THINKING: AN INTRODUCTION TO ITS EXPERIMENTAL PSYCHOLOGY. New York: John Wiley and Sons, 1963. xi, 331 p.

Provides an exposition and critical treatment of experimental work on thinking with materials on association, the Wuerzburg school, the Gestalt theory of thought, the work of Selz, language and thought, and generalization. References. Index.

Hymes, Dell H., ed. STUDIES IN THE HISTORY OF LINGUISTICS: TRADITIONS AND PARADIGMS. Bloomington: Indiana University Press, 1974. viii, 519 p.

Twenty-one articles exploring such topics in the history of linguistics as views of various philosophers, sixteenth- and seventeenth-century grammars, and views on the history of linguistics.

Johannsen, Dorothea E. "Early History of Perceptual Illusions." JOURNAL OF THE HISTORY OF THE BEHAVIORAL SCIENCES 7 (April 1971): 127-40.

Describes "real world" as opposed to paper-and-pencil illusions, and the history of research on them. Discusses architectural illusions, movement illusions, the moon illusion, size-weight illusions, and binocular illusions.

Johnson, H.M. "Did Fechner Measure 'Introspectional' Sensations?" PSYCHOLOGICAL REVIEW 36 (July 1929): 257-84.

Argues that Fechner's formula for just noticeable differences is definitional rather than empirical. Argues that just noticeable differences in sensations are based on a census of responses classified by the experimenter rather than on introspective comparisons.

Kantor, J.R. "Newton's Influence on the Development of Psychology." PSYCHOLOGICAL RECORD 20 (Winter 1970): 83-92.

See B5bvii, p. 73, for annotation.

MacLeod, Robert B. "What Is a Sense?" In THE PHYSIOLOGICAL AND BEHAVIORAL ASPECTS OF TASTE, edited by Morley R. Kare and Bruce P. Halpern, pp. 1-5. Chicago: University of Chicago Press, 1961.

Mandler, Jean Matter, and Mandler, George, eds. THINKING: FROM ASSOCIATION TO GESTALT. New York: John Wiley and Sons, 1964. x, 300 p.

Excerpts major works in the history of the psychology of thinking from Aristotle through British and Scottish associationists, psychologists representing the Wuerzburg school and structuralism, and the Gestalt school. Bibliographical materials in footnotes. Index.

O'Neil, W.M. "Mueller's Theory of the Specific Energies of the Sensory Nerves." PSYCHOLOGIA: AN INTERNATIONAL JOURNAL OF PSYCHOLOGY IN THE ORIENT 14 (December 1971): 131-35.

Pastore, Nicholas. "Helmholtz's 'Popular Lectures on Vision.'" JOURNAL OF THE HISTORY OF THE BEHAVIORAL SCIENCES 9 (July 1973): 190-202.

Corrects errors in Phillip H. Pye-Smith's 1893 translation of Helmholtz's series of three articles entitled "Recent Progress in the Theory of Vision." Discusses concepts from Helmholtz's theory which are of current interest, such as the constancy hypothesis and illusions.

_____. "Samuel Bailey's Critique of Berkeley's Theory of Vision." JOURNAL OF THE HISTORY OF THE BEHAVIORAL SCIENCES 1 (October 1965): 321-37.

Outlines the essential features of Berkeley's theory of vision followed by a description of Samuel Bailey's little-known critique and alternative theory. Discusses possible reasons for the neglect of Bailey's work.

_____. "Sebastien Le Clerc on Retinal Disparity." JOURNAL OF THE HISTORY OF THE BEHAVIORAL SCIENCES 8 (July 1972): 336-39.

Shows that Le Clerc in 1679 used the notion of retinal disparity to dispute Descartes's theory of single vision.

_____. SELECTIVE HISTORY OF THEORIES OF VISUAL PERCEPTION 1650-1950. New York: Oxford University Press, 1971. vii, 454 p.

Outlines theories advanced by such writers as Descartes, Malebranche, Locke, Berkeley, Condillac, Helmholtz, and James, and more recent developments within the Gestalt, connectionist, and functionalist traditions. Index.

Pfaffmann, Carl. "Sensory Processes and Their Relation to Behavior: Studies on the Sense of Taste as a Model S-R System." In PSYCHOLOGY: A STUDY OF A SCIENCE, edited by Sigmund Koch, volume 4, pp. 384-416. New York: McGraw Hill, 1962.

Pikler, Andrew G. "History of Experiments on the Musical Interval Sense." JOURNAL OF MUSIC THEORY 10 (Spring 1966): 54-95.

Pliskoff, Stanley S. "Antecedents to Fechner's Law: The Astronomers J. Herschel, W.R. Dawes, and N.R. Pogson." JOURNAL OF THE EXPERIMENTAL ANALYSIS OF BEHAVIOR 28 (September 1977): 185-87.

Astronomers working with brightness or magnitude of stars formulated "Fechner's Law" by 1850.

Pollack, Robert H., and Zetland, Frances K. "A Translation of 'New Measurements of Visual Illusions in Adults and Children' by Jean-Jacques Van Biervliet." JOURNAL OF THE HISTORY OF THE BEHAVIORAL SCIENCES 2 (April 1966): 148-58.

A brief statement provides historical context for the translation of an article describing Van Biervliet's empirical work and his theoretical explanation of the Mueller-Lyer illusion.

Raman, C.V. "Newton and the History of Optics." CURRENT SCIENCE 11 (1942): 453-56.

Ribot, Th[éodule Armand]. ESSAY ON THE CREATIVE IMAGINATION. Translated by Albert H.N. Baron. New York: Arno Press, 1973. xix, 370 p.

A classic (1906) analysis of the components, characteristics, and development of constructive imagination. A final section and appendices explore manifestations of imagination in such areas as art and music. Index.

Siegel, Rudolph E. GALEN ON SENSE PERCEPTION. HIS DOCTRINES, OBSERVATIONS AND EXPERIMENTS ON VISION, HEARING, SMELL, TASTE, TOUCH AND PAIN, AND THEIR HISTORICAL SOURCES. New York: S. Karger, 1970. 216 p. Bibliography. Index.

Skaggs, E.B. "Atomism versus Gestaltism in Perception." PSYCHOLOGICAL REVIEW 47 (July 1940): 347-54.

Smith, Myra O. "History of the Motor Theories of Attention." JOURNAL OF GENERAL PSYCHOLOGY 80 (April 1969): 243-57.

Examines traditional theories of attention advanced by G.E. Mueller and Wilhelm Wundt, and motor theories advanced by Alexander Bain, David Ferrier, Théodule Ribot, and William McDougall.

Spearman, C. THE NATURE OF 'INTELLIGENCE' AND THE PRINCIPLES OF COGNITION. London: Macmillan, 1923. viii, 358 p.

Stam, James H. "The Sapir-Whorf Hypothesis in Historical Perspective." ANNALS OF THE NEW YORK ACADEMY OF SCIENCES 291 (18 April 1977): 306-16.

Stratton, George M. "Vision Without Inversion of the Retinal Image." PSYCHOLOGICAL REVIEW 4 (July 1897): 341-60; (September 1897): 463-81.

Stumpf, C. "Hermann von Helmholtz and the New Psychology." PSYCHOLOGICAL REVIEW 2 (January 1895): 1-12.

Sullivan, John. "On Cartesian Linguistics." ANNALS OF THE NEW YORK ACADEMY OF SCIENCES 291 (April 1977): 287-305.

Tinklepaugh, O.L. "An Experimental Study of Representative Factors in Monkeys." JOURNAL OF COMPARATIVE PSYCHOLOGY 8 (1928): 197-236.

Turbayne, Colin M. "Berkeley and Molyneux on Retinal Images." JOURNAL OF THE HISTORY OF IDEAS 16 (June 1955): 339-55.

Tweney, Ryan D. "American Psycholinguistics in the Nineteenth Century." ANNALS OF THE NEW YORK ACADEMY OF SCIENCES 291 (18 April 1977): 277-86.

Wallin, J.E.W[allace]. "An Historical Conspectus on the Existence of Congenital Wordblindness." JOURNAL OF SPECIAL EDUCATION 2 (Winter 1968): 203-7.

Wasserman, Gerald S. COLOR VISION: AN HISTORICAL INTRODUCTION. New York: Wiley, 1978. 242 p.

Wertheimer, Max. PRODUCTIVE THINKING. See annotation in section C11d, p. 197.

Wilinsky, Gloria F., and Ayre, Elizabeth. "Contributions to the History of Psychology: V. Translation of 'Stereognostic Perception' by E. Claparède." PERCEPTUAL AND MOTOR SKILLS 24 (February 1967): 35-41.

Zubek, John P., ed. SENSORY DEPRIVATION: FIFTEEN YEARS OF RESEARCH. New York: Appleton-Century-Crofts, 1969. ix, 522 p.

> A comprehensive and critical review of experimental findings and theoretical formulations on such topics as the biochemical, intellectual, and perceptual effects of sensory deprivation. Extensive bibliography. Index.

6. LEARNING

There are no historical works in learning comparable to Boring's SENSATION AND PERCEPTION IN THE HISTORY OF EXPERIMENTAL PSYCHOLOGY. Warren's A HISTORY OF THE ASSOCIATION PSYCHOLOGY provides a historical overview of one topic of interest to learning psychologists, but the book is not a comprehensive text. Major developments in twentieth-century learning theory are discussed in Hilgard's THEORIES OF LEARNING (1st and 2d eds.); the third edition (with Bower) presents more contemporary theories. For general orientation, see relevant chapters in Stevens's HANDBOOK or in Osgood's or Woodworth's texts (all in section D2, p. 255).

a. Histories of the Psychology of Learning

Abel, Theodora M., and Von Grunbaum, G.E. "A Contribution of a Medieval Arab Scholar to the Problem of Learning." JOURNAL OF PERSONALITY 15 (September 1946): 59-69.

> Outlines views on learning of Az-Zarnuji, a late twelfth- and early thirteenth-century scholar who lived in Persia.

Boguslavsky, G.W. "Conditioning: A Historical Note." AMERICAN PSYCHOLOGIST 17 (May 1962): 264-65.

> Describes the change in Pavlov's theoretical orientation from a psychological to a physiological interpretation of salivary secretion.

Bricke, John. "Hume's Associationist Psychology." JOURNAL OF THE HIS-TORY OF THE BEHAVIORAL SCIENCES 10 (October 1974): 397–409.

Presents Hume's five laws of association and an examination of the scope and limits of those laws.

Brown, Evan, and Deffenbacher, Kenneth. "Forgotten Mnemonists." JOUR-NAL OF THE HISTORY OF THE BEHAVIORAL SCIENCES 21 (October 1975): 342–49.

Reviews early experimental studies of persons with unusual memories conducted by such individuals as Binet, Georg Elias Mueller, and Susukita.

Cohen, Jozef. "Salivary Conditioning in the Seventeenth Century." AMERI-CAN PSYCHOLOGIST 18 (January 1963): 69.

Describes the work of Regnier De Graaf, who in 1664 collected saliva from a food–deprived dog via fistulas inserted in the parotid and pancreatic ducts.

Dallenbach, Karl M. "Twitmyer and the Conditioned Response." AMERICAN JOURNAL OF PSYCHOLOGY 72 (December 1959): 633–38.

Calls attention to Twitmyer's research in which "the discovery of the conditioned response was announced and the phenomenon first described."

Diamond, Solomon. "Seventeenth Century French 'Connectionism': La Forge, Dilly, and Regis." JOURNAL OF THE HISTORY OF THE BEHAVIORAL SCI-ENCES 5 (January 1969): 3–9.

Points out that La Forge, Dilly, and Regis "developed in the late seventeenth century a physiological theory of learning which was in essential respects similar to those of the late nineteenth and early twentieth century."

English, Horace B. THE HISTORICAL ROOTS OF LEARNING THEORY. New York: Random House, 1954. 21 p.

A brief sketch highlighting selected contributions to learning theory from the time of the Greeks to early twentieth–century developments.

Kimble, Gregory A., ed. FOUNDATIONS OF CONDITIONING AND LEARN-ING. New York: Appleton–Century–Crofts, 1967. xii, 696 p.

A section on historical foundations contains articles by Kimble on such topics as Sechenov and the experimental study of conditioned reflexes, and the objectivist climate: Bekhterev, Watson, and Tolman. Hull's article, "A Functional Interpretation of the Condi-

tioned Reflex," is also included. Other selections devoted to
theoretical, methodological, and substantive issues.

Knotts, Josephine R., and Miles, W.R. "Notes on the History and Construction of the Stylus Maze." JOURNAL OF GENETIC PSYCHOLOGY 35 (September 1928): 415-27.

Lowry, Richard. "The Reflex Model in Psychology: Origins and Evolution."
JOURNAL OF THE HISTORY OF THE BEHAVIORAL SCIENCES 6 (January 1970):
64-69.

> A brief sketch of the development of the reflex model emphasizing
> the thought of Descartes, Pavlov, and Hull.

Mowrer, O. Hobart. "How Does the Mind Work?" AMERICAN PSYCHOLO-
GIST 31 (December 1970): 843-57.

> Provides an overview of the life of Jerzy Konorski and reviews
> some of his contributions to learning theory.

Murray, D.J. "Research on Human Memory in the Nineteenth Century."
CANADIAN JOURNAL OF PSYCHOLOGY 30 (December 1976): 201-20.

Pratt, Kenneth J. "Motivation and Learning in Medieval Writings." AMERI-
CAN PSYCHOLOGIST 17 (July 1962): 496-500.

> See section D7a, p. 301, for annotation.

Rosenzweig, Mark R. "Pavlov, Bechterev, and Twitmyer on Conditioning."
AMERICAN JOURNAL OF PSYCHOLOGY 73 (June 1960): 312-16.

> A comment on two earlier papers, one by Rosenweig (see next item)
> and one by Dallenbach (see this section, p. 291) on the discovery
> of the conditioned reflex.

_____. "Salivary Conditioning Before Pavlov." AMERICAN JOURNAL OF
PSYCHOLOGY 72 (December 1959): 628-33.

> Relates accounts of the evocation of unconditioned responses by
> appropriate stimuli, dating from the sixteenth century, and men-
> tions investigations of conditioned reflexes in the nineteenth cen-
> tury.

Tighe, Louise S., and Tighe, Thomas J. "Discrimination Learning: Two Views
in Historical Perspective." PSYCHOLOGICAL BULLETIN 66 (November 1966):
353-70.

> Reviews early views of discrimination learning advanced by such
> theorists as William James, I.A. Krechevsky, and John B. Watson

in relation to more recent mediation theory and differentiation theory.

Touchette, Paul. "Ivanov-Smolensky and Operant Conditioning: An Historical Note." JOURNAL OF THE EXPERIMENTAL ANALYSIS OF BEHAVIOR 28 (September 1977): 181-84.

> Describes the work of Ivanov-Smolensky with children, done about 1927, which anticipated operant conditioning.

Verhave, Thom. "Contributions to the History of Psychology: III. G.W. Leibniz (1646-1716) on the Association of Ideas and Learning." PSYCHOLOGICAL REPORTS 20 (February 1967): 111-16.

_____. "Contributions to the History of Psychology: IV. Joseph Buchanan (1785-1829) and the 'Law of Exercise' (1812)." PSYCHOLOGICAL REPORTS 20 (February 1967): 127-33.

Warren, Howard C. A HISTORY OF THE ASSOCIATION PSYCHOLOGY. New York: Charles Scribner's Sons, 1921. Reprint. New York: Johnson Reprint Corp., 1967. ix, 328 p.

> Traces associationism from earliest times to the twentieth century. Chapters devoted to contributions from various countries, experimental investigations, and the laws of association. Bibliography. Index.

b. Selected Major Textbooks and Articles in the Psychology of Learning

Bartlett, F.C. REMEMBERING: A STUDY IN EXPERIMENTAL AND SOCIAL PSYCHOLOGY. New York: Macmillan, 1932. x, 317 p.

> A classic work on remembering. Includes major experimental methods for studying memory and analyses of the conditions influencing remembering.

Ebbinghaus, Hermann. MEMORY: A CONTRIBUTION TO EXPERIMENTAL PSYCHOLOGY. Translated by Henry A. Ruger and Clara E. Bussenius. New York: Columbia University Teachers College, 1913. 123 p.

Estes, William K., ed. HANDBOOK OF LEARNING AND COGNITIVE PROCESSES. 4 vols. New York: Halsted Press, vols. 1 and 2, 1975; vols. 3 and 4, 1976.

> Covers concepts and issues (volume 1), conditioning and behavior theory (volume 2), human learning and motivation (volume 3), and attention and memory (volume 4). Chapters prepared by dozens of prominent figures in the psychology of learning discuss both theoretical and practical issues and problems.

Gibson, J.J. "The Reproduction of Visually Perceived Forms." JOURNAL OF EXPERIMENTAL PSYCHOLOGY 12 (February 1929): 1-39.

Glaze, J. Arthur. "The Association Value of Nonsense Syllables." JOURNAL OF GENETIC PSYCHOLOGY 35 (June 1928): 255-69.

Guthrie, Edwin R. "Pavlov's Theory of Conditioning." PSYCHOLOGICAL RE-VIEW 41 (March 1934): 199-206.

> Responds to an earlier article by Pavlov entitled "The Reply of a Physiologist to Psychologists" (see section C10, p. 180) and discusses disagreements with Pavlov.

_____. THE PSYCHOLOGY OF HUMAN CONFLICT: THE CLASH OF MOTIVES WITHIN THE INDIVIDUAL. New York: Harper, 1938. ix, 408 p.

> Presents a systematic psychology of motivation based in large part on the writings of Pierre Janet, Walter B. Cannon, and E.J. Kempf. Also integrates Guthrie's own influential learning theory. Suggested readings. References. Index.

_____. THE PSYCHOLOGY OF LEARNING. Rev. ed. New York: Harper, 1952. x, 310 p.

> Presents a behavioristic analysis of traditional topics of interest to learning theorists including generalization, habit, reinforcement, forgetting, and punishment. References. Index.

Guthrie, Edwin R., and Horton, George P. CATS IN A PUZZLE BOX. New York: Rinehart, 1946. ix, 67 p.

> Reports the classic experiments undertaken to support Guthrie's influential theory of learning as association by contiguity.

Hilgard, Ernest R. THEORIES OF LEARNING. 2d ed. New York: Appleton-Century-Crofts, 1956. vii, 563 p.

> Revision of a classic (1948) exposition and analysis of the major learning theories which dominated the first half of the twentieth century. Suggested readings. References. Index.

Hilgard, Ernest R., and Bower, Gordon H. THEORIES OF LEARNING. 3d ed. New York: Appleton-Century Crofts, 1966. vii, 661 p.

> Presents descriptions and critical evaluations of major contemporary theories of learning and chapters on the neurophysiology of learning and the technology of instruction. Omits the chapter on Kurt Lewin included in the first two editions. References. Index.

Hull, Clark Leonard. A BEHAVIOR SYSTEM; AN INTRODUCTION TO BE-HAVIOR THEORY CONCERNING THE INDIVIDUAL ORGANISM. 1952. Reprint. New York: John Wiley and Sons, 1964. ix, 372 p.

> See section C9a, p. 161, for annotation.

_____. ESSENTIALS OF BEHAVIOR. New Haven, Conn.: Yale University Press, 1951. viii, 145 p.

> See section C9a, p. 161, for annotation.

_____. "A Functional Interpretation of the Conditioned Reflex." PSYCHO-LOGICAL REVIEW 36 (November 1929): 498-511.

> A discussion of the biological and behavioral significance of the conditioned reflex.

_____. PRINCIPLES OF BEHAVIOR: AN INTRODUCTION TO BEHAVIOR THEORY. New York: Appleton-Century-Crofts, 1943. x, 422 p.

> See section C9a, p. 161, for annotation.

Hulse, Stewart H.; Deese, James; and Egeth, Howard. THE PSYCHOLOGY OF LEARNING. 4th ed. New York: McGraw-Hill Book Co., 1975. xx, 456 p.

> A leading text since the publication of Deese's first edition in 1952. Surveys selected findings from the experimental literature in learning on such problems as reinforcement, extinction, motiva-tion, retention, transfer, and thinking. Also emphasizes theories. References. Index.

Kimble, Gregory A. HILGARD AND MARQUIS' CONDITIONING AND LEARNING. 2d ed. New York: Appleton-Century-Crofts, 1961. ix, 590 p.

> In the tradition of the first edition (1940), this text, long a stan-dard source in learning, presents results of key experiments from such areas within learning as classical and instrumental conditioning, reinforcement, secondary reinforcement, extinction, generalization, and discrimination. Examines alternative theoretical interpretations of factual material in the light of supporting evidence. Extensive references. Index.

Krueger, Wm. C.F. "The Effect of Overlearning on Retention." JOURNAL OF EXPERIMENTAL PSYCHOLOGY 12 (February 1929): 71-78.

McGeoch, John A. "The Influence of Associative Value Upon the Difficulty of Nonsense-Syllable Lists." JOURNAL OF GENETIC PSYCHOLOGY 37 (September 1930): 421-26.

McGeoch, John A., and McDonald, William T. "Meaningful Relation and Retroactive Inhibition." AMERICAN JOURNAL OF PSYCHOLOGY 43 (October 1931): 579-88.

Meltzer, H. "Individual Differences in Forgetting Pleasant and Unpleasant Experiences." JOURNAL OF EDUCATIONAL PSYCHOLOGY 21 (September 1930): 399-409.

Pavlov, Ivan Petrovitch. LECTURES ON CONDITIONED REFLEXES. 3d ed. Vol. 1. Translated and edited by W. Horsley Gantt. New York: International Publishers, 1963. 414 p.

A classic work containing an account of the historical development of Pavlov's work on conditioned reflexes as well as the major laboratory findings. Includes a brief biography of Pavlov's life to 1928. Bibliography. Index.

_____. LECTURES ON CONDITIONED REFLEXES: CONDITIONED REFLEXES AND PSYCHIATRY. 3d ed. Vol. 2. Translated and edited by W. Horsley Gantt. New York: International Publishers, 1963. 199 p.

Discusses applications of Pavlov's work on conditioned reflexes to the understanding and treatment of human psychological problems. A brief biography deals with the last phase of Pavlov's life (1928 to 1936). Appendixes. Minimal bibliographical materials. Index.

Pressey, S.L. "A Simple Apparatus Which Gives Tests and Scores--and Teaches." SCHOOL AND SOCIETY 23 (March 1926): 373-76.

Describes what may have been the first teaching machine.

Thorndike, Edward L. THE FUNDAMENTALS OF LEARNING. New York: Teachers College, Columbia University, 1932. xvii, 638 p.

Deals with "fundamental facts and forces in learning." Numerous experiments illustrate such topics as readiness, reward, punishment, and practice. Appendixes present selected details of experiments. Written with the collaboration of the division of psychology of the Institute of Educational Research of Teachers College, Columbia University. References. Index.

_____. HUMAN LEARNING. New York: Century, 1931. 206 p.

Twelve lectures present experimental data and principles on such topics as aftereffects of a connection, conditioned reflexes, Gestalt theory and learning, and thinking. Bibliography. Index.

Tolman, Edward Chase. PURPOSIVE BEHAVIOR IN ANIMALS AND MEN. New York: Century, 1932. xiv, 463 p.

See section C9, p. 163, for annotation.

Tolman, E[dward].C[hase]., and Honzik, C.H. "Introduction and Removal of Reward and Maze Performance in Rats." UNIVERSITY OF CALIFORNIA PUBLICATIONS IN PSYCHOLOGY 4 (1930): 257-75.

Watson, John B., and Rayner, Rosalie. "Conditioned Emotional Reactions." JOURNAL OF EXPERIMENTAL PSYCHOLOGY 3 (February 1920): 1-14.

Woodrow, Herbert. "The Effect of Type of Training Upon Transference." JOURNAL OF EDUCATIONAL PSYCHOLOGY 18 (March 1927): 159-72.

Yerkes, R[obert].M., and Dodson, J.D. "The Relation of Strength of Stimulus to Rapidity of Habit-Formation." JOURNAL OF COMPARATIVE NEUROLOGY 18 (November 1908): 459-82.

7. MOTIVATION AND EMOTION

Cofer and Appley's MOTIVATION: THEORY AND RESEARCH and Bolles's THEORY OF MOTIVATION contain chapters providing historical overviews of motivational concepts. Twentieth-century developments are outlined in chapters 2 and 3 of Marx and Tombaugh's MOTIVATION. For general orientation, see relevant chapters in Stevens's HANDBOOK or in Osgood's or Woodworth's texts (all in section D2, p. 255).

a. General and Specific Histories

Angell, James R. "A Reconsideration of James' Theory of Emotion in the Light of Recent Criticisms." PSYCHOLOGICAL REVIEW 23 (July 1916): 251-61.

Claims that arguments advanced by Sherrington and Cannon do not disprove James's theory of emotion.

Bolles, Robert C. THEORY OF MOTIVATION. New York: Harper and Row, 1967. 546 p.

A textbook on motivation containing chapters on such topics as the history of the field, instinct, dynamic psychology, drive theory, punishment, and reinforcement theories. References. Index.

Brooks, C.McC., Koizumi, K., and Pinkston, J.O., eds. THE LIFE AND CONTRIBUTIONS OF WALTER BRADFORD CANNON, 1871-1945. Brooklyn, N.Y.: State University of New York Downstate Medical Center, 1975. xxii, 264 p.

Cardno, J.A. "Instinct: Some Pre-experimental Landmarks." AUSTRALIAN JOURNAL OF PSYCHOLOGY 10 (December 1958): 329-40.

Carlson, Earl R. "The Affective Tone of Psychology." JOURNAL OF GEN-
ERAL PSYCHOLOGY 75 (July 1966): 65-78.

> A content analysis of 172 general introductory psychology texts
> published between 1900 and 1960. Shows an increasing tendency
> to focus on negative or unpleasant emotions.

Cassel, Russell N. "Critical Contributions to Human Motivation Theory."
PSYCHOLOGY 11 (February 1974): 58-64.

> Provides brief summaries of contributions to human motivation the-
> ory from such sources as instinct theory, evolutionary theory,
> depth psychology, conditioning psychology, topological psychology,
> and cognitive theories.

Cofer, Charles N. "Motivation." In ANNUAL REVIEW OF PSYCHOLOGY,
vol. 10, 1959, edited by P.R. Farnsworth and Quinn McNemar, pp. 173-202.
Palo Alto, Calif.: Annual Reviews, Inc.

Cofer, C[harles].N., and Appley, M.H. MOTIVATION: THEORY AND
RESEARCH. New York: John Wiley and Sons, 1964. 958 p.

> A comprehensive textbook on motivation. Includes historical per-
> spective, description and evaluation of the status of various con-
> cepts and theories, and extensive summaries of research literature.
> Lengthy bibliography. Index.

CURRENT RESEARCH AND THEORY IN MOTIVATION. See NEBRASKA SYM-
POSIUM ON MOTIVATION in section D7b, p. 305.

Darwin, Charles. THE EXPRESSION OF THE EMOTIONS IN MAN AND ANI-
MALS. New York: Greenwood Press, 1955. xi, 372 p.

> One of the pioneer works in comparative psychology (1872). De-
> scribes various emotions and advances explanations or theories of
> their origin and function. This edition includes illustrations and
> photographs from work on emotional expression by Konrad Lorenz,
> Gregory Bateson, and Margaret Mead. Index.

Diamond, Solomon. "Four Hundred Years of Instinct Controversy." BEHAVIOR
GENETICS 4 (September 1974): 237-52.

> An erudite article tracing the vicissitudes of instinct theory from
> the seventeenth century to the present. Emphasizes particular
> times and places in which the instinct concept was accepted or
> rejected. More than eighty references.

————. "Gestation of the Instinct Concept." JOURNAL OF THE HISTORY
OF THE BEHAVIORAL SCIENCES 7 (October 1971): 323-36.

> Traces uses of the term "instinct" and related terms in the writings

of scholars from the Greek period to the seventeenth century.
Cites writers from numerous countries.

Dickie, George. "Francis Hutcheson and the Theory of Motives." AMERICAN
JOURNAL OF PSYCHOLOGY 74 (December 1961): 625-29.

Dunlap, Knight, ed. THE EMOTIONS. Baltimore: Williams and Wilkins,
1922. 135 p.

    Reprints classic articles by William James ("What Is An Emotion?"
    and "The Emotions") and by Carl Georg Lange ("The Emotions")
    preceded by a brief editorial preface that provides historical per-
    spective.

Gardiner, H.M. "Affective Psychology in Ancient Writers After Aristotle."
PSYCHOLOGICAL REVIEW 26 (May 1919): 204-29.

    Examines ancient thought on emotions with primary emphasis on
    the Epicureans and the Stoics.

Gardiner, H.M.; Metcalf, Ruth Clark; and Beebe-Center, John G. FEELING
AND EMOTION: A HISTORY OF THEORIES. New York: American Book
Co., 1937. xiii, 445 p.

    A scholarly volume presenting a critical and historical discussion
    of theories of emotion beginning with the ancient Greeks. De-
    scribes patristic, medieval, renaissance, and post-renaissance
    thought. A final chapter discusses twentieth-century theories in
    affective psychology. Extensive bibliography. Index.

Gilbert, Albin R. "Phenomenology of Willing In Historical View." JOURNAL
OF THE HISTORY OF THE BEHAVIORAL SCIENCES 8 (January 1972): 103-8.

    Presents the views of a number of theorists (e.g., Wilhelm Wundt,
    William James, Hermann Ebbinghaus, René Descartes) on willing.
    Comments on some requirements for an adequate account of willing.

Haber, Ralph Norman, ed. CURRENT RESEARCH IN MOTIVATION. New
York: Holt, Rinehart and Winston, 1966. xii, 800 p.

    Seventy-six papers in motivation theory and research. Topics in-
    clude instinct, punishment, exploratory behavior, conflict, anxiety,
    and dreams. References. Index.

Hutcheson, Francis. AN ESSAY ON THE NATURE AND CONDUCT OF THE
PASSIONS AND AFFECTIONS; WITH ILLUSTRATIONS ON THE MORAL SENSE.
3d ed. Gainesville, Fla.: Scholars' Facsimiles and Reprints, 1969. xviii,
xx, 339 p.

    A facsimile reproduction of an early, influential, eighteenth-century
    work on motivation. An introduction by Paul McReynolds provides

some biographical materials on Hutcheson as well as orientation
to the work and its philosophical background.

Joffe, J.M. "The Peromyscus Papers." AMERICAN PSYCHOLOGIST 28 (June
1973): 527-29.

Discusses the twentieth-century history of the instinct concept in
psychology. Draws parallels to "biological boundaries of learning"
and the classic instinct doctrine of McDougall.

Krantz, David L., and Allen, David. "The Rise and Fall of McDougall's
Instinct Doctrine." JOURNAL OF THE HISTORY OF THE BEHAVIORAL SCI-
ENCES 3 (October 1967): 326-38.

Reviews arguments raised against instinct theory in the 1920s and
factors responsible for the decline of the theory. Discusses contemporary implications of McDougall's theory.

McMahon, C.E. "Images as Motives and Motivators: A Historical Perspective." AMERICAN JOURNAL OF PSYCHOLOGY 86 (September 1973): 465-
90.

McReynolds, Paul. "The Motivational Psychology of Jeremy Bentham: I.
Background and General Approach." JOURNAL OF THE HISTORY OF THE
BEHAVIORAL SCIENCES 4 (July 1968): 230-44.

Provides a biographical sketch of Bentham followed by an exposition of selected topics in his general psychology and in his motivation.

_____. "The Motivational Psychology of Jeremy Bentham: II. Efforts To-
ward Quantification and Classification." JOURNAL OF THE HISTORY OF
THE BEHAVIORAL SCIENCES 4 (October 1968): 349-64.

Explores details of Bentham's theory of motivation including his
attempts to quantify pleasure and pain and his motivational taxon-
omy.

_____. "The Motives to Attain Success and to Avoid Failure: Historical
Note." JOURNAL OF INDIVIDUAL PSYCHOLOGY 24 (November 1968):
157-61.

_____, ed. FOUR EARLY WORKS ON MOTIVATION. Gainesville, Fla.:
Scholars' Facsimiles and Reprints, 1969. xxxii, 512 p.

Includes eighteenth-century works by Francis Hutcheson on our
ideas of beauty and virtue (2d ed., 1726), the constitution of
human nature and the supreme good (1755), and human appetite
and affection (1747) presumably by James Long, followed by an

early nineteenth-century work by Jeremy Bentham on the springs of human action (1815). Editorial comments introduce the four works and provide perspective.

Marx, Melvin H., and Tombaugh, Tom N. MOTIVATION: PSYCHOLOGICAL PRINCIPLES AND EDUCATIONAL IMPLICATIONS. San Francisco: Chandler, 1967. xiii, 285 p.

Explores motivation in terms of research in physiological psychology, learning, and personality, and discusses implications. Opening chapters characterize recent historical developments. Bibliography. Index.

Mischel, Theodore. "Affective Concepts in the Psychology of J.F. Herbart." JOURNAL OF THE HISTORY OF THE BEHAVIORAL SCIENCES 3 (July 1967): 262-68.

Reviews Herbart's position on such concepts as feeling, emotion, and desire. Notes that Herbart's theory can be seen in the context of his desire to refute Kant's claim that psychology can never be a science.

Moore, John Robert. "Defoe's Project for Lie-Detection." AMERICAN JOURNAL OF PSYCHOLOGY 68 (December 1955): 672.

A brief note on an early eighteenth-century physiological theory for detecting guilt.

Mowrer, O.H. "Motivation." In ANNUAL REVIEW OF PSYCHOLOGY, edited by Calvin P. Stone and Donald W. Taylor, 3 (1952), pp. 419-438.

Pratt, Kenneth J. "Motivation and Learning in Medieval Writings." AMERICAN PSYCHOLOGIST 17 (July 1962): 496-500.

Outlines thoughts of medieval thinkers (e.g., Abelard, Dante, and James of Vitry) on such topics as stimulus substitution, rationalization, and effects of early experience.

Reymert, Martin L., ed. FEELINGS AND EMOTIONS: THE MOOSEHEART SYMPOSIUM IN COOPERATION WITH THE UNIVERSITY OF CHICAGO. New York: McGraw-Hill, 1950. xxiii, 603 p.

Forty-seven papers by distinguished scholars representing a variety of scientific disciplines. Focuses on the following topics in the psychology of feelings and emotions: theories, experiments, reviews, psychosomatics, methodology, and emotions in human development, social behavior, and applied fields. Appendixes contain additional addresses given at the symposium. Bibliographical materials. Index.

_____. FEELINGS AND EMOTIONS: THE WITTENBERG SYMPOSIUM. Worcester, Mass.: Clark University Press, 1928. xvi, 454 p.

An international symposium on feelings and emotions. Thirty-four papers by eminent scholars in such areas as the history of the psychology of feelings and emotions, theories of and the physiology of feelings and emotions, pathology and psychoanalysis of feeling and emotion, and training of emotions. Appendixes contain additional addresses given at the symposium. Minimal bibliographical materials. Index.

Ribot, Th[éodule Armand]. THE PSYCHOLOGY OF THE EMOTIONS. 2d ed. Translator not named. London: Walter Scott, 1911. xix, 455 p.

Examines general characteristics of emotion from the point of view of a systematic position influenced by Bain, Spencer, Maudsley, James, and Lange. Attempts to characterize a variety of emotions including fear, anger, sympathy, humility, and certain moral and religious emotions. Index.

Ruckmick, Christian A. THE PSYCHOLOGY OF FEELING AND EMOTION. New York: McGraw-Hill, 1936. xiii, 529 p.

A broad but dated overview of research literature and theories. Chapter 2 presents a brief history of work on feeling and emotion from the time of the early Greeks. Bibliographical materials in footnotes. Index.

Russell, Wallace A., ed. MILESTONES IN MOTIVATION: CONTRIBUTIONS TO THE PSYCHOLOGY OF DRIVE AND PURPOSE. New York: Appleton-Century-Crofts, 1970. xi, 572 p.

Contains classical and recent papers on such topics as instinct, drive, purpose, clinical and descriptive approaches to motivation, and measurement of motivation. Editorial comments provide a framework for understanding developments in motivation theory. References.

Selye, Hans. "The Evolution of the Stress Concept." AMERICAN SCIENTIST 61 (November-December 1973): 692-99.

Sully, James. AN ESSAY ON LAUGHTER: ITS FORMS, ITS CAUSES, ITS DEVELOPMENT AND ITS VALUE. New York: Longmans, Green, 1902. xvi, 441 p.

The first large-scale work on the subject. Explores theories of laughter advanced by such thinkers as Aristotle, Hobbes, Bain, Kant, and Schopenhauer; the value of laughter; developmental aspects of laughter; cultural aspects of laughter; degrees of laughter; and the varieties of occasions for and causes of laughter. Bibliographical materials in footnotes. Index.

Troland, Leonard Thompson. THE FUNDAMENTALS OF HUMAN MOTIVATION. 1928. Reprint. New York: Hafner, 1967. xvi, 521 p.

> A comprehensive text in motivation. Includes much historical material especially in early chapters covering classical (Greek, Christian, Utilitarian) views. Discusses psychoanalytic approaches and early views emerging from the behaviorist tradition. References. Index.

Wallace, K.R. FRANCIS BACON ON COMMUNICATION AND RHETORIC, OR, THE ART OF APPLYING REASON TO IMAGINATION FOR THE BETTER MOVING OF THE WILL. Chapel Hill: University of North Carolina Press, 1943. 286 p.

Wilm, Emil Carl. THE THEORIES OF INSTINCT: A STUDY IN THE HISTORY OF PSYCHOLOGY. New Haven, Conn.: Yale University Press, 1925. xiv, 188 p.

> Traces the history of instinct doctrines from before Plato through scholasticism and the Enlightenment to the "modern" (Darwinian) period. Index.

Woods, Ralph L., and Greenhouse, Herbert B., eds. THE NEW WORLD OF DREAMS. New York: Macmillan, 1974. xix, 439 p.

b. Selected Major Works

Bain, Alexander. THE EMOTIONS AND THE WILL. 3d ed. New York: Appleton, 1875. xxxii, 604 p.

> Supplements Bain's book on the senses and the intellect (see section D5, p. 283) and completes his classic "Systematic Exposition of the Human Mind."

Bard, P.A. "A Diencephalic Mechanism for the Expression of Rage with Special Reference to the Sympathetic Nervous System." AMERICAN JOURNAL OF PHYSIOLOGY 84 (April 1928): 490-515.

Cannon, Walter B. "Again the James-Lange and the Thalamic Theories of Emotion." PSYCHOLOGICAL REVIEW 38 (July 1931): 281-95.

> Reviews the James-Lange and the thalamic (Cannon-Bard) theories of emotion and criticizes an interpretation of the two theories made earlier by Newman, Perkins, and Wheeler.

_____. BODILY CHANGES IN PAIN, HUNGER, FEAR AND RAGE: AN ACCOUNT OF RECENT RESEARCHES INTO THE FUNCTION OF EMOTIONAL EXCITEMENT. New York: Appleton, 1915. xiii, 311 p. Index.

_____. "The James-Lange Theory of Emotions: A Critical Examination and an Alternative Theory." AMERICAN JOURNAL OF PSYCHOLOGY 39 (December 1927): 106-24.

_____. THE WISDOM OF THE BODY. Rev. ed. New York: W.W. Norton, 1963. xviii, 333 p.

An influential work outlining Cannon's research and theory on physiological homeostasis as the primary mechanism in motivation. Bibliography. Index.

Cannon, W[alter].B., and Washburn, A.L. "An Explanation of Hunger." AMERICAN JOURNAL OF PHYSIOLOGY 29 (March 1912): 441-54.

_____. "What Strong Emotions Do to Us." HARPER'S MAGAZINE, July 1922, pp. 234-41.

A popular account emphasizing that the bodily changes induced by strong emotions prepare us for action.

Davis, C.M. "Self-Selection of Diet by Newly Weaned Infants." AMERICAN JOURNAL OF DISEASES OF CHILDHOOD 36 (October 1928): 651-79.

Dollard, John, et al. FRUSTRATION AND AGGRESSION. New Haven, Conn.: Yale University Press, 1939. viii, 209 p.

A classic systematic work in which the authors discuss the research literature on aggression, arguing that "aggression is always a consequence of frustration." Discusses implications. References. Index.

Guthrie, Edwin R. THE PSYCHOLOGY OF HUMAN CONFLICT: THE CLASH OF MOTIVES WITHIN THE INDIVIDUAL. New York: Harper, 1938. ix, 408 p.

See section D6b, p. 294, for annotation.

James, W[illiam]. "What Is An Emotion?" MIND 9 (April 1884): 188-205.

Sets forth James's thesis that "the bodily changes follow directly the _perception_ of the exciting fact, and that our feeling of the same changes as they occur _is_ the emotion."

Jones, Mary Cover. "A Laboratory Study of Fear: The Case of Peter." PEDAGOGICAL SEMINARY 31 (December 1924): 308-15.

A classic study on extinction of fear in a small child; a sequel to the Watson and Rayner study (see section D6b, p. 297).

Luckhardt, A.B., and Carlson, A.J. "Contributions to the Physiology of the

Stomach: XVII. On the Chemical Control of the Gastric Hunger Mechanism."
AMERICAN JOURNAL OF PHYSIOLOGY 36 (December 1914): 37-46.

Morgan, C. Lloyd. INSTINCT AND EXPERIENCE. New York: Macmillan,
1912. ix, 299 p.

    A systematic treatment of instinct and experience exploring their
    evolutionary origins and associated philosophical problems such as
    finalism vs. mechanism. Presents a penetrating analysis of con-
    trasting views among such theorists as McDougall, Bergson,
    Titchener, and Morgan. Limited bibliographical materials. Index.

NEBRASKA SYMPOSIUM ON MOTIVATION. Lincoln: University of Nebraska
Press, 1953-- . Annual.

    Contains papers on both laboratory research and theories dealing
    with a great range of topics, e.g., artificial induction of biologi-
    cal drives via electrical stimulation of the brain, and theoretical
    papers which challenge the concept of motivation. James Cole
    and Theo Sonderegger (eds.) note in the 1974 volume that the
    topics discussed over the years "parallel the history of major theo-
    retical concerns in the area of motivation."

Troland, Leonard Thompson. THE FUNDAMENTALS OF HUMAN MOTIVATION.
New York: Van Nostrand, 1928. Reprint. New York: Hafner, 1967. xvi,
521 p.

    See section D7a, p. 303, for annotation.

Wangensteen, O.H., and Carlson, H.A. "Hunger Sensations in a Patient After
Total Gastrectomy." PROCEEDINGS OF THE SOCIETY FOR EXPERIMENTAL
BIOLOGY AND MEDICINE 28 (February 1931): 545-47.

8. PERSONALITY

Few works are devoted to the history of the scientific study of personality. A
brief treatment of the topic may be found in chapter 3 of Baughman and Welsh's
PERSONALITY: A BEHAVIORAL SCIENCE, and more recent historical developments are discussed in Hall and Lindzey's THEORIES OF PERSONALITY. There
have been some very useful histories of specific topics in personality. Examples
include Linda Viney's "Self: The History of a Concept" and Allport's analysis
of the origin of the term personality in his book PERSONALITY.

Adorno, T.W.; Frenkel-Brunswik, Else; Levinson, Daniel J.; and Sanford, R.
Nevitt. THE AUTHORITARIAN PERSONALITY. New York: Harper, 1950.
xxxiii, 990 p.

    A classic work developed in collaboration with Betty Aron, Maria

Hertz Levinson, and William Morrow; an early example of multi-disciplinary cooperation. Presents a major theory of authoritarian and ethnocentric ideology, ways to measure the ideology, and a discussion of the implications of that ideology for the modern world. References. Index.

Allport, Gordon W. THE NATURE OF PREJUDICE. Cambridge, Mass.: Addison-Wesley, 1954. xviii, 537 p.

A classic eclectic work which draws from motivation, perception, learning, and social psychology. Integrates the major empirical findings and theoretical approaches to prejudice. Notes and references. Index.

_____. "The Personalistic Psychology of William Stern." CHARACTER AND PERSONALITY 5 (March 1937): 231-46.

_____. PERSONALITY: A PSYCHOLOGICAL INTERPRETATION. New York: Holt, 1937. xiv, 588 p.

A comprehensive eclectic text surveying studies in the field of personality. Advances a broad systematic framework for understanding personality. Chapters 2 and 3 contain important historical discussions of meanings of the term "personality" and early approaches to the study of characterology. Notes and bibliographical materials. Index.

_____. THE USE OF PERSONAL DOCUMENTS IN PSYCHOLOGICAL SCIENCE. Bulletin 49 prepared for the Committee on Appraisal of Research. New York: Social Science Research Council, 1942. xix, 210 p.

Explores strengths and weaknesses of various techniques for research with personal documents and describes such forms as autobiographies, diaries, letters, confessions, and interviews. Provides historical perspective and comments on the place of idiographic methods in psychological research. References. Index.

Angyal, Andras. FOUNDATIONS FOR A SCIENCE OF PERSONALITY. New York: Commonwealth Fund, 1941. xii, 398 p. Index.

Baughman, E. Earl, and Welsh, George Schlager. PERSONALITY: A BEHAVIORAL SCIENCE. Englewood Cliffs, N.J.: Prentice-Hall, 1962. 566 p.

An undergraduate text in personality covering topics in standard content areas such as development and assessment. Emphasizes the scientific study of personality and includes a chapter on the historical background of the study of personality. Notes and bibliography. Index.

Bischof, Ledford J. INTERPRETING PERSONALITY THEORIES. New York: Harper and Row, 1964. ix, 694 p.

Provides an overview of eighteen major theories of personality including those of Freud, Sheldon, Moreno, Rogers, Eysenck, Mowrer, Goldstein, and Fromm. Index.

Broughton, John M., and Riegel, Klaus F. "Developmental Psychology and the Self." ANNALS OF THE NEW YORK ACADEMY OF SCIENCES 291 (18 April 1977): 149-69.

Traces numerous early conceptions of the self and outlines a developmental approach to self.

Cattell, Raymond B., and Dreger, Ralph M., eds. HANDBOOK OF MODERN PERSONALITY THEORY. New York: Halsted Press, 1977. 804 p.

Explores methods and such substantive content areas as development, perception, learning, and social influence in relation to personality. Index.

Cohen, John. "The Concept of Personality: A Symposium." JOURNAL OF PSYCHOLOGICAL RESEARCHES 17 (1973): 85-98.

Ekehammar, Bo. "Interactionism in Personality from a Historical Perspective." PSYCHOLOGICAL BULLETIN 81 (December 1974): 1026-48.

Gilbert, Albin R. "Bringing the History of Personality Theories Up To Date: German Theories of Personality Stratification." JOURNAL OF THE HISTORY OF THE BEHAVIORAL SCIENCES 9 (April 1973): 102-14.

Traces the historical development of the strata model of personality developed in Germany in the 1930s. It failed to achieve recognition elsewhere, probably because of communication barriers associated with the political climate of the time.

Hall, Calvin S., and Lindzey, Gardner. THEORIES OF PERSONALITY. 2d ed. New York: John Wiley and Sons, 1970. xiv, 622 p.

A standard reference source and text presenting the major theories of personality in terms of their key constructs and characteristic research. Exposition of each theory is followed by an evaluation and an estimate of current status. Bibliography. Index.

Huarte de San Juan, Juan. EXAMEN DE INGENIOS: THE EXAMINATION OF MEN'S WITS. Translated by M. Camillo Camilli and Richard Carew. Reprint of 1594 ed. Delmar, N.Y.: Scholars' Facsimiles and Reprints, 1976. xvi, 332 p.

One of the first attempts to show the relationship between physiological and psychological functioning.

Irwin, James R. "Galen on the Temperaments." JOURNAL OF GENERAL
PSYCHOLOGY 36 (1947): 45-64.

> Traces "Hippocrates' ideas of humours, or bodily fluids, as part of
> character, through the modification of the later physician, Galen,
> into a doctrine of 'temperaments' as a semi-scientific study of the
> larger field of character study."

Jaensch, E.R. EIDETIC IMAGERY: AND TYPOLOGICAL METHODS OF IN-
VESTIGATION. 2d ed. Translated by Oscar Oeser. New York: Harcourt,
Brace, 1930. 136 p.

> A classic work exploring the development of research on eidetic
> imagery as well as its psychological, physiological, and educa-
> tional implications. Bibliographical materials in footnotes. Index.

Jastrow, Joseph. CHARACTER AND TEMPERAMENT. New York: Appleton,
1921. xviii, 596 p.

> A text on the psychology of temperament and traits. Examines
> "the psychological sources of human quality." Categories of in-
> quiry include the scientific approach to the study of character,
> the sensibilities, emotions and conduct, higher stages of psychic
> control, temperament and individual differences, abnormal tenden-
> cies of mind, psychology of group traits, and character and envi-
> ronment. Detailed notes and minimal bibliographical materials.
> Index.

Krantz, David L. "Nineteenth and Twentieth Century Trends in the Psychology
of the Self." ANNALS OF THE NEW YORK ACADEMY OF SCIENCES 291
(18 April 1977): 178-80.

Prince, Morton. CLINICAL AND EXPERIMENTAL STUDIES IN PERSONALITY.
Cambridge, Mass.: Sci-Art Publishers, 1929. xvi, 559 p.

> An anthology of major articles by a pioneer investigator of person-
> ality and psychopathology. Index.

Schettler, Clarence. "Some Antecedent Concepts of Personality Trait."
PSYCHOLOGICAL REVIEW 48 (March 1941): 165-75.

> An article "based upon an historical survey of 145 writers whose
> modes of thought are related to personality trait." Discusses such
> individuals as Darwin, Locke, Herbart, Kant, and Galton.

Sheldon, William [Herbert]. "The New York Study of Physical Constitution and
Psychotic Pattern." JOURNAL OF THE HISTORY OF THE BEHAVIORAL SCI-
ENCES 7 (April 1971): 115-26.

> Reviews selected themes in the history of constitutional psychology
> and examines and refutes four major criticisms of somatotyping.

Sheldon, William Herbert, with the collaboration of S.S. Stevens. THE VARIETIES OF TEMPERAMENT: A PSYCHOLOGY OF CONSTITUTIONAL DIFFERENCES. New York: Harper, 1942. x, 520 p.

This book, together with the next one, presents the case for Sheldon's influential thesis that physique and temperament can be specified quantitatively on three dimensions each, and that physique and temperament are closely related. Index.

Sheldon, William Herbert; Stevens, S.S.; and Tucker, W.B. THE VARIETIES OF HUMAN PHYSIQUE. New York: Harper, 1940. xii, 347 p.

Spranger, Eduard. TYPES OF MEN: THE PSYCHOLOGY AND ETHICS OF PERSONALITY. Halle (Salle), The Netherlands: Max Niemeyer Verlag, 1928. xii, 402 p.

A classic attempt to isolate six basic character types: theoretical, economic, aesthetic, social, political, and religious.

Smith, M. Brewster. "Allport, Murray, and Lewin on Personality Theory: Notes on a Confrontation." JOURNAL OF THE HISTORY OF THE BEHAVIORAL SCIENCES 7 (October 1971): 353-62.

Smith paraphrases notes he took at meetings in December 1946 and January 1947 in which Allport, Murray, and Lewin presented their personality theories and exchanged views.

Spearman, C. THE ABILITIES OF MAN: THEIR NATURE AND MEASUREMENT. New York: Macmillan, 1927. 415 p.

Spearman, C., and Jones, L. Wynn. HUMAN ABILITY: A CONTINUATION OF "THE ABILITIES OF MAN." London: Macmillan, 1950. vii, 198 p.

A posthumous work continuing the preceding entry.

Viney, Linda. "Self: The History of a Concept." JOURNAL OF THE HISTORY OF THE BEHAVIORAL SCIENCES 5 (October 1969): 349-59.

Reviews the history of the concept of self from selected definitions advanced by the Greeks to contemporary definitions. Discusses phenomenological, social, and empirical approaches.

Winthrop, Henry. "A Contribution Towards a Scientific Program for a Systematic Constitutional Psychology." JOURNAL OF GENERAL PSYCHOLOGY 37 (1947): 139-58.

Seeks solid bases for constitutional psychology through multiple constitutional schemata and quantitative techniques.

Wolf, S. Jean. "Historic Background of the Study of Personality as it Relates to Success or Failure in Academic Achievement." JOURNAL OF GENERAL PSYCHOLOGY 19 (1938): 417-36.

Young, Kimball. PERSONALITY AND PROBLEMS OF ADJUSTMENT. New York: Appleton-Century-Crofts, 1952. x, 716 p.

9. INDIVIDUAL DIFFERENCES

This section lists items on the history of psychological testing; selected major works including texts, books of readings, and treatises; and entries on the social history of testing.

a. Histories of Psychological Testing

Beck, Samuel J. "How the Rorschach Came to America." JOURNAL OF PERSONALITY ASSESSMENT 36 (April 1972): 105-8.

Bondy, Milos. "Psychiatric Antecedents of Psychological Testing (Before Binet)." JOURNAL OF THE HISTORY OF THE BEHAVIORAL SCIENCES 10 (April 1974): 180-94.

> Describes nonstandardized tests developed during the mid-nineteenth century by such individuals as Joseph Guislain, Ludwig Snell, and Hubert von Grashey for purposes of assisting with psychiatric diagnosis.

Brigham, Carl C. A STUDY OF AMERICAN INTELLIGENCE. Princeton, N.J.: Princeton University Press, 1923. xxv, 210 p.

> A reexamination of the data gathered during the massive testing of recruits during World War I. Emphasizes differences in measured intelligence among native whites, immigrant whites, and blacks.

Burt, Cyril. "Francis Galton and His Contributions to Psychology." BRITISH JOURNAL OF STATISTICAL PSYCHOLOGY 15 (May 1962): 1-41.

Cassel, Russell N. "Eleven Great Tests That Have Made Major Contributions to Measurement Theory." PSYCHOLOGY: A JOURNAL OF HUMAN BEHAVIOR 5 (November 1968): 17-22.

> A brief overview of contributions of the Simon-Binet Intelligence Test, the U.S. Army Alpha-Beta Tests, Rorschach's Inkblot Test, Terman's study of a thousand gifted children, Gesell's Developmental Schedules, the Strong Vocational Interest Test, the OSS Assessment of Men in World War II, the Minnesota Multiphasic

Personality Inventory, Q-Methodology, the Talent Project by Flanagan, and the Structure of Intellect by Guilford.

_____. "Historical Review of Theories on Nature of Intelligence." PSYCHOLOGY: A JOURNAL OF HUMAN BEHAVIOR 6 (November 1969): 39-46.

A brief overview of eleven theories including those of Stern, Spearman, Thorndike, Thurstone, Guilford, and Cattell.

Doyle, Kenneth O., Jr. "Theory and Practice of Ability Testing in Ancient Greece." JOURNAL OF THE HISTORY OF THE BEHAVIORAL SCIENCES 10 (April 1974): 202-12.

Outlines Greek tests of physical achievement, mental achievement, physical aptitude, and mental aptitude. Discusses ancient notions of reliability and validity.

DuBois, Philip H. A HISTORY OF PSYCHOLOGICAL TESTING. Boston: Allyn and Bacon, 1970. xii, 173 p.

A brief history of varieties of psychological testing from early (2200 B.C.) Chinese civil service examinations through the twentieth century testing movement to contemporary criticisms of testing. Concludes with a chronology of psychometrics. Appendixes contain tests of historical interest. Bibliography. Index.

_____. "A Test Dominated Society: China 1115 B.C.-1905 A.D." In READINGS IN PSYCHOLOGICAL TESTS AND MEASUREMENTS, edited by W. Leslie Barnette, Jr., pp. 249-55. Rev. ed. Homewood, Ill.: Dorsey Press, 1968. xi, 393 p.

Describes early civil service test procedures in China.

Edwards, Allen J. INDIVIDUAL MENTAL TESTING: PART I: HISTORY AND THEORIES. Scranton, Pa.: Intext Educational Publishers, 1971. x, 209 p.

The first of three paperback volumes intended to help in the training of psychometrists. Discusses the history of the intelligence-testing movement and the events leading to our current measures, assumptions, and score expressions. Chapters devoted to Binet, Terman, Thorndike, Spearman, the Thurstones, Wechsler, Guilford, Piaget, and an introduction and an evaluative epilogue. Index.

Ellson, Douglas G., and Ellson, Elizabeth Cox. "Historical Note on the Rating Scale." PSYCHOLOGICAL BULLETIN 50 (September 1953): 383-84.

Discusses evidence that a personality rating scale was used in America as early as 1826, over fifty years prior to Galton's use of rating scales.

Engen, Trygg, and Levy, Nissin, comp. SELECTED READINGS IN THE HISTORY OF MENTAL MEASUREMENT. Providence, R.I.: Brown University, 1955. 106 p.

Forrest, D.W. FRANCIS GALTON: THE LIFE AND WORK OF A VICTORIAN GENIUS. New York: Taplinger, 1974. x, 340 p.

> This first bibliography of Francis Galton since Karl Pearson's massive work (1914-30, see below, this section, p. 314). Covers Galton's early childhood achievements, his accomplishments as a geographer and meteorologist, and his work on heredity and eugenics. Appendixes include lists of inventions, stimulus materials for word-association tests, and a bibliography of his published works. References. Index.

Friedmann, Alfred. "The History of Rorschach." BRITISH JOURNAL OF PROJECTIVE PSYCHOLOGY AND PERSONALITY STUDY 13 (1968): 3.

Goodenough, Florence L. MENTAL TESTING: ITS HISTORY, PRINCIPLES AND APPLICATIONS. New York: Rinehart, 1949. xix, 609 p.

> A brief overview of the history of mental testing from Aristotle to the mid-twentieth century followed by a nontechnical discussion of test principles and methods, types of tests, and applications. References. Glossary. Index.

Guilford, J.P. "Creativity: Yesterday, Today, and Tomorrow." JOURNAL OF CREATIVE BEHAVIOR 1 (January 1967): 3-14.

Gulliksen, Harold. "Looking Back and Ahead in Psychometrics." AMERICAN PSYCHOLOGIST 29 (April 1974): 251-61.

> Provides a sketch of some of the significant developments, primarily from the early 1930s, in test theory, scaling, factor analysis, and mathematical learning theory. Emphasizes major investigators and includes many reminiscences, adding to the historical interest of the paper.

Hoover, Thomas O., and McPherson, Marion W. "A Few Paradoxes in the History of Inkblots." PROCEEDINGS OF THE ANNUAL CONVENTION OF THE AMERICAN PSYCHOLOGICAL ASSOCIATION 7, pt. 2 (1972): 779-80.

Jarl, Vidkunn Coucheron. "Historical Note on the Term Differential Psychology." ACTA PSYCHOLOGICA 14 (1958): 158-60.

Klopfer, Walter G. "The Short History of Projective Techniques." JOURNAL OF THE HISTORY OF THE BEHAVIORAL SCIENCES 9 (January 1973): 60-65.

> Notes that although informal use of projective techniques may go

back to the beginnings of human history, their formal use began
with Galton's work on word associations. Traces the landmark
developments in projective testing from 1921, the date of publication of Rorschach's PSYCHODIAGNOSTIK, to the present. Speculates about future developments.

Laosa, Luis M. "Nonbiased Assessment of Children's Abilities: Historical
Antecedents and Current Issues." In PSYCHOLOGICAL AND EDUCATIONAL
ASSESSMENT OF MINORITY CHILDREN, edited by Thomas Oakland, pp. 1-
20. New York: Brunner/Mazel Publishers, 1977.

Outlines the history of attempts to develop unbiased methods for
psychological testing of children and discusses the difficulties in-
herent in any such endeavor.

Levine, Murray. "The Academic Achievement Test: Its Historical Content and
Social Functions." AMERICAN PSYCHOLOGIST 31 (March 1976): 228-38.

Examines a range of issues and topics related to achievement testing
such as philosophical and political issues, contributions of early pioneers in achievement testing, and the development of test technology.

McReynolds, P. "Historical Antecedents of Personality Assessment." In his
ADVANCES IN PSYCHOLOGICAL ASSESSMENT, vol. 3, pp. 477-532.
San Francisco: Jossey-Bass, 1975.

Mancuso, James C., and Dreisinger, Milton. "A View of the Historical and
Current Development of the Concept of Intelligence." PSYCHOLOGY IN THE
SCHOOLS 6 (April 1969): 137-51.

Meltzer, H. "Contributions to the History of Psychology: VI. Dr. William
Healey--1869-1963--The Man in His Time." PSYCHOLOGICAL REPORTS 20,
pt. 2 (June 1967): 1028-30.

Newman, Edwin B. "On the Origin of Scales of Measurement." In SENSATION
AND MEASUREMENT: PAPERS IN HONOR OF S.S. STEVENS, edited by
Howard R. Moskowitz, Bertram Scharf, and Joseph C. Stevens, pp. 137-45.
Boston: D. Reidel, 1974. xiii, 469 p. Index.

Oberholzer, Emil. "Rorschach--The Man and the Test." JOURNAL OF PRO-
JECTIVE TECHNIQUES AND PERSONALITY ASSESSMENT 32 (December 1968):
502-8.

Pearson, Karl. "The Contributions of Giovanni Plana to the Normal Bivariate
Frequency Surface." BIOMETRIKA 20A, pts. 3 and 4 (December 1928): 295-
98.

_____. THE LIFE, LETTERS AND LABORS OF FRANCIS GALTON. 3 vols. in 4 bound books. Cambridge: At the University Press, 1914, 1924, 1930.

A classic and extensive biographical work covering Galton's ancestry, childhood, and education (volume 1); his anthropological research, study of heredity, psychological investigations, and statistical investigations (volume 2); application of statistics to the study of heredity, and eugenics (volume 3a); and his character as revealed in letters (volume 3b). Extensive illustrations and notes. Index.

Porteus, Stanley D. PORTEUS MAZE TEST: FIFTY YEARS' APPLICATION. Palo Alto, Calif.: Pacific Books, 1965. v, 320 p.

Discusses selected themes in the history of testing from the early twentieth century, and Porteus's work on such topics as mental deficiency, measurement of performance differences among various ethnic groups, and relationships between organic conditions and maze performance.

_____. PRIMITIVE INTELLIGENCE AND ENVIRONMENT. New York: Macmillan, 1937. viii, 325 p.

Describes the field work of Porteus who compared the physical and mental abilities of races from a variety of geographical regions including Australia, Africa, and Hawaii. Minimal reference materials. Index.

Ryans, David G. "Francis Galton's Statistical Contributions." SCHOOL AND SOCIETY 48 (3 September 1948): 312-16.

Samelson, Franz. "World War I Intelligence Testing and the Development of Psychology." JOURNAL OF THE HISTORY OF THE BEHAVIORAL SCIENCES 13 (July 1977): 274-82.

The contributions of psychologists in the second decade of the twentieth century to science and to the war effort are not clearcut, but the work of psychologists in the war effort brought much needed publicity to the discipline.

Seagoe, May V. TERMAN AND THE GIFTED. Los Altos, Calif.: William Kaufmann, 1975. xiii, 258 p.

Sears, Robert R. "Sources of Life Satisfactions of the Terman Gifted Men." AMERICAN PSYCHOLOGIST 32 (February 1977): 119-28.

A fifty-year follow-up on a famous longitudinal study which began in 1922 (see in next section, p. 318). Outlines predictors of occupational satisfaction and family-life satisfaction.

Sundberg, Norman D. "A Note Concerning the History of Testing." AMERI-
CAN PSYCHOLOGIST 9 (April 1954): 150-51.

> Uses numbers of references to twelve psychological tests as a
> method for exploring the history of psychometrics.

Wolf, Theta H. ALFRED BINET. Chicago: University of Chicago Press, 1973.
xiii, 376 p.

> Based partly on interviews with Theodore Simon and Henri Piéron,
> this biography presents the development of Binet's thought, his
> work, and his personal qualities and circumstances. References
> include letters, unpublished manuscripts, a chronological list of
> Binet's publications, and publications about Binet before 1911.
> Index.

_____. "Alfred Binet: A Time of Crisis." AMERICAN PSYCHOLOGIST 19
(September 1964): 762-71.

> An account of Binet's early scientific work focusing on the decade
> from 1880 to 1890.

_____. "The Emergence of Binet's Conception and Measurement of Intelligence:
A Case History of the Creative Process." JOURNAL OF THE HISTORY OF THE
BEHAVIORAL SCIENCES 5 (April 1969): 113-34.

> Describes Binet's lengthy search from about 1890 to 1905 for ade-
> quate measures of intelligence.

_____. "The Emergence of Binet's Conception and Measurement of Intelligence:
A Case History of the Creative Process. Part II." JOURNAL OF THE HISTORY
OF THE BEHAVIORAL SCIENCES 5 (July 1969): 207-37.

> A continuation of an article in the previous issue of the same
> journal. Explores, in addition to the emergence of Binet's concept
> of intelligence, such topics as the development of interest in spe-
> cial education in France, Binet's views of the work of other early
> theorists, and likely directions of Binet's thought had he lived
> longer.

_____. "An Individual Who Made a Difference." AMERICAN PSYCHOLOGIST
16 (May 1961): 245-48.

> A brief article based on conversations which took place between
> Wolf and Theodore Simon in 1959 and 1960. Describes selected
> topics in the lives and works of Binet and Simon.

Yerkes, Robert M. "Testing the Human Mind." ATLANTIC MONTHLY, March
1923, pp. 358-70.

> Discusses misconceptions of the results of army mental tests and
> points to the value and benefits of mental testing.

b. Selected Major Works

Anastasi, Anne. DIFFERENTIAL PSYCHOLOGY: INDIVIDUAL AND GROUP DIFFERENCES IN BEHAVIOR. 3d ed. New York: Macmillan, 1958. xii, 664 p.

> An opening chapter, somewhat condensed in the third edition, provides an overview of the history of differential psychology, followed by chapters on heredity and environment, physique and behavior, constitutional types, age differences, intelligence, sex, race, and social class differences, and the roles of training and culture. Index.

_____. "Heredity, Environment and the Question 'How'?" PSYCHOLOGICAL REVIEW 65 (May 1958): 197-208.

_____. PSYCHOLOGICAL TESTING. 4th ed. New York: Macmillan, 1976. xiii, 750 p.

Barnett, W. Leslie, Jr., ed. READINGS IN PSYCHOLOGICAL TESTS AND MEASUREMENTS. Homewood, III.: Dorsey Press, 1964. xi, 393 p.

> Contains articles in such areas as general measurement problems, test administration, norms, response set, reliability, factor analysis, validity, intelligence, personality, and interests, abbreviated and edited for students enrolled in a first course in psychological testing. Index.

Binet, Alfred, and Simon, Theodore. THE DEVELOPMENT OF INTELLIGENCE IN CHILDREN. Translated by Elizabeth S. Kite. Baltimore: Williams and Wilkins, 1916. Reprint. Arno Press, 1973. 336,[1] p.

> Contains translations of five classic papers: upon the necessity of establishing a scientific diagnosis of inferior states of intelligence (1905), new methods for the diagnosis of intellectual level of subnormals (1905), applications of the new method to the diagnosis of the intellectual level among normal and subnormal children in institutions and in the primary schools (1905), the development of intelligence in the child (1908), and new investigations upon the measure of the intellectual level among school children (1911).

Buros, Oscar Krisen, ed. MENTAL MEASUREMENTS YEARBOOK. Highland Park, N.J.: Gryphon Press, 1938-- . Irregular. 7th ed., 1972, in 2 vols. Title and publisher vary.

> See section A2, p. 9, for annotation.

Cattell, J[ames].McK[een]. "Mental Tests and Measurements." MIND 15 (July 1890): 373-80.

Cattell, James McKeen, and Farrand, Livingston. "Physical and Mental Measurement of the Students of Columbia University." PSYCHOLOGICAL REVIEW 3 (November 1896): 618-48.

Crovitz, Herbert F. GALTON'S WALK: METHODS FOR THE ANALYSIS OF THINKING, INTELLIGENCE, AND CREATIVITY. New York: Harper and Row, 1970. xxi, 159 p.

Dearborn, Walter Fenno. INTELLIGENCE TESTS: THEIR SIGNIFICANCE FOR SCHOOL AND SOCIETY. New York: Houghton Mifflin, 1928. xxiv, 336 p.

Explores such topics as the background of intelligence testing, the role of heredity and environment in intelligence (with cautions against undue emphasis on heredity), intelligence and school achievement, use of intelligence tests in education selection programs, and intelligence and social policy. Bibliography. Index.

Galton, Francis. HEREDITARY GENIUS: AN INQUIRY INTO ITS LAWS AND CONSEQUENCES. Rev. ed. New York: Appleton, 1900. xii, 390 p.

A classic work demonstrating that accomplishment and genius run in families. Galton concluded that intelligence, like physical attributes, is inherited.

_____. INQUIRIES INTO HUMAN FACULTY AND ITS DEVELOPMENT. 2d ed. New York: E.P. Dutton, 1911. xix, 261 p.

Describes Galton's classic work on individual differences in such dimensions as height, weight, pain sensitivity, audition, character traits, and intellectual characteristics. Discusses twin studies, domestication of animals, and population problems.

Guilford, J.P. "Human Abilities." PSYCHOLOGICAL REVIEW 47 (September 1940): 367-94.

_____. PSYCHOMETRIC METHODS. 2d ed. New York: McGraw-Hill, 1954. ix, 597 p.

An early textbook on quantitative methods in psychology, serving for decades as a classic work on applied statistics. Contains portraits of pioneers in the field and useful tables in the appendix. Index.

Gulliksen, Harold. THEORY OF MENTAL TESTS. New York: John Wiley and Sons, 1950. xix, 486 p.

A technical presentation of such basic topics in test theory as reliability, validity, standardization, scoring methods, and item analysis. Intended primarily for those working in test development. References. Appendixes. Index.

Hull, Clark L. APTITUDE TESTING. New York: World, 1928. xiv, 535 p.

An early college text on principles of aptitude testing and test construction. Statistical tables in appendix. References. Index.

Jackson, Douglas N., and Messick, Samuel, eds. PROBLEMS IN HUMAN ASSESSMENT. New York: McGraw-Hill, 1967. xvi, 873 p.

A massive anthology reprinting seventy-four major contributions to the psychology of individual differences.

Popplestone, John A., and McPherson, Marion White. "The Prolonged Avoidance of Intellectual Behavior." PSYCHOLOGICAL RECORD 24 (Fall 1974): 549-57.

Spearman, Charles [Edward]. "'General Intelligence' Objectively Determined and Measured." AMERICAN JOURNAL OF PSYCHOLOGY 15 (April 1904): 201-93.

_____. THE NATURE OF 'INTELLIGENCE' AND THE PRINCIPLES OF COGNITION. London: Macmillan, 1923. viii, 358 p.

A full statement of Spearman's influential two-factory theory of intelligence. Index.

Stoddard, George D. THE MEANING OF INTELLIGENCE. New York: Macmillan, 1943. ix, 504 p.

Provides an overview of research on intelligence including a brief chapter on the historical background of mental testing. Index.

Strong, E.K., Jr. VOCATIONAL INTERESTS OF MEN AND WOMEN. Stanford, Calif.: Stanford University Press, 1943. 746 p.

Super, Donald E., and Crites, John O. APPRAISING VOCATIONAL FITNESS BY MEANS OF PSYCHOLOGICAL TESTS. Rev. ed. New York: Harper, 1962. 688 p.

Taine, H. ON INTELLIGENCE. Rev. ed. Translated by T.D. Haye. 2 vols. New York: Holt, 1884.

A classic work attempting to present the facts of cognition. Chapters deal with topics such as ideas, images, sensations, functions of nervous centers, illusions, education of the senses, and the concept of self.

Terman, Lewis M., ed. GENETIC STUDIES OF GENIUS. 5 vols. Stanford, Calif.: Stanford University Press, 1925-59.

These volumes constitute a continuing report on the life development of members of a gifted group of children. The study began in 1921 when the children were eleven years old and followed their development including schooling, interests, vocations, families, and achievements.

_____. THE MEASUREMENT OF INTELLIGENCE. Boston: Houghton Mifflin, 1916. xviii, 362 p.

Contains Terman's revision of the Binet-Simon intelligence scale and its extension and adaptation for use in the United States. Covers such topics as uses of intelligence tests, sources of error in judging intelligence, description of the Binet-Simon method, reliability, analysis of one thousand intelligence quotients, and detailed instructions for test administration. References. Index.

Terman, Lewis M., et al. THE STANFORD REVISION AND EXTENSION OF THE BINET-SIMON SCALE FOR MEASURING INTELLIGENCE. Baltimore, Md.: Warwick and York, 1917. 179 p.

Originally published as an Educational Psychology Monograph (No. 18). The revised and extended Binet scale was administered to nearly one thousand unselected school children, and the results are summarized here. Includes materials on distribution of IQ, sex differences, validity, and intelligence and social status. Appendix contains statistical information.

Terman, Lewis M., and Merrill, Maud A. MEASURING INTELLIGENCE: A GUIDE TO THE ADMINISTRATION OF THE NEW REVISED STANFORD-BINET TESTS OF INTELLIGENCE. New York: Houghton Mifflin, 1937. xiv, 461 p.

Contrasts the revised Stanford-Binet with its predecessor (1916), describes the details of the construction of the revision, and includes instructions for administration and scoring standards for forms L and M. Index.

Thorndike, E[dward].L. "Measurement of Intelligence: The Present Status." PSYCHOLOGICAL REVIEW 31 (May 1924): 219-52.

Thorndike, Edward L.; Bregman, E.O.; Cobb, M.V.; and Woodyard, Ella. THE MEASUREMENT OF INTELLIGENCE. New York: Teachers College, Columbia University, n.d. Reprint. New York: Arno Press, 1973. xxvi, 616 p.

Presents results of investigations into such basic topics as measurement of difficulty, transformation of scores, distributions, problems of scaling, the meaning of scores on standardized intelligence tests, and age and intelligence. References. Index.

Thurstone, L.L. "The Vectors of Mind." PSYCHOLOGICAL REVIEW 41 (January 1934): 1-32.

Urbach, Peter. "Progress and Degeneration in the 'I.Q. Debate.'" BRITISH JOURNAL FOR THE PHILOSOPHY OF SCIENCE 25 (June 1974): 99-135; (September 1974): 235-49.

Wechsler, David. THE MEASUREMENT OF ADULT INTELLIGENCE. 3d ed. Baltimore, Md.: Williams and Wilkins, 1944. vii, 258 p. Index.

_____. THE RANGE OF HUMAN CAPACITIES. 2d ed. Baltimore: Williams and Wilkins, 1952. ix, 190 p.

> Examines the distribution and range of human perceptual, physical, and mental capacities. Explores measurement problems, the effects of age, and genius and deficiency. Appendixes contain statistical tables on physical and mental differences. References. Index.

Whipple, Guy Montrose. MANUAL OF MENTAL AND PHYSICAL TESTS. 2d ed., rev. and enl. 2 vols. Baltimore, Md.: Warwick and York, 1914, 1915.

> Volume 1, on "simpler processes," outlines the nature and purpose of mental tests, rules for administration of tests, and statistical treatment. Introduces tests of such attributes as strength of grip, motor steadiness, quickness of movement, visual acuity, and attention. Provides normative data. Volume 2, on "complex processes," introduces tests and normative data for such dimensions as memory, mirror-drawing skill, linguistic invention, and size of vocabulary. References. Index.

c. Social History of Testing

Block, N.J., and Dworkin, Gerald, eds. THE I.Q. CONTROVERSY: CRITICAL READINGS. New York: Pantheon, 1976. xiii, 557 p.

> Includes primarily papers which are critical of well-known papers by Arthur Jensen and Richard Herrnstein concerning the inheritance of intelligence (see below, this section). Includes some replies, but the editors sought a critical rather than a balanced perspective. Also contains papers on larger philosophical issues surrounding the IQ debate.

Brigham, Carl C. A STUDY OF AMERICAN INTELLIGENCE. Princeton, N.J.: Princeton University Press, 1923. xxv, 210 p.

> An analysis by race and national origin of the measured intelligence of tens of thousands of military recruits during World War I.

Buss, Allan R. "Galton and Sex Differences: An Historical Note." JOURNAL OF THE HISTORY OF THE BEHAVIORAL SCIENCES 12 (July 1976): 283-85.

> Claims that Galton's Victorian sexist attitudes colored his interpretation of his early work on sex differences.

_____. "Galton and the Birth of Differential Psychology and Eugenics: So-
cial, Political, and Economic Forces." JOURNAL OF THE HISTORY OF THE
BEHAVIORAL SCIENCES 12 (January 1976): 47-58.

Argues that the liberal, democratic, and capitalistic characteristics
of nineteenth-century Britain contributed to the birth of eugenics
and the study of individual differences, and that these same social
and political forces opposed the practical application of the principles of eugenics.

Cronbach, Lee J. "Five Decades of Public Controversy Over Mental Testing."
AMERICAN PSYCHOLOGIST 30 (January 1975): 1-14.

Outlines controversies over mental testing in the 1920s and 1940s,
and more recently around the heritability of intelligence. Explores
relations between scientists and the popular press, and the general
problem of the scientist and the public.

_____. "Mental Tests and the Creation of Opportunity." PROCEEDINGS
OF THE AMERICAN PHILOSOPHICAL SOCIETY 114 (December 1970): 480-87.

Goddard, Henry Herbert. HUMAN EFFICIENCY AND LEVELS OF INTELLI-
GENCE. Princeton, N.J.: Princeton University Press, 1920. vii, 128 p.

A summary of lectures delivered at Princeton University in 1919.
Typifies the "new-found faith" in intelligence tests of that time.
Explores implications of intellectual differences for education, em-
ployment, delinquency, and democracy.

Herrnstein, Richard [J.]. "I.Q." ATLANTIC MONTHLY, September 1971,
pp. 43-64.

A popular controversial attempt to summarize the empirical evidence
about the role of nature and nurture in intelligence. Concludes
that a very substantial proportion of variation in IQ is genetic.

_____. I.Q. IN THE MERITOCRACY. Boston: Little, Brown, 1973. x,
235 p.

An expanded version of Herrnstein's ATLANTIC MONTHLY article
(see preceding entry). Argues that assessments of human intelligence
should be made dispassionately and without regard to ideology.
Much variation in IQ is genetic. People and groups differ in innate ability, and society should recognize this fact. References.
Index.

Jensen, Arthur R. "How Much Can We Boost IQ and Scholastic Achievement?"
HARVARD EDUCATION REVIEW 39 (Winter 1969): 1-123.

A controversial analysis of environmental and genetic contributions to IQ and scholastic achievement. Concludes that the evidence suggests that racial and social class variability in intelligence cannot be due solely to environmental differences but must be attributed at least in part to genetic differences.

Kamin, Leon J. THE SCIENCE AND POLITICS OF IQ. Potomac, Md.: Lawrence Erlbaum, 1974. vii, 183 p.

A brief overview of the history of IQ testing in America followed by an examination of major studies investigating the heritability of IQ performance. Challenges the conclusion that IQ test scores are heritable and explores the social and political assumptions of persons involved in IQ testing. Index.

Karier, Clarence J. "Testing for Order and Control in the Corporate Liberal State." EDUCATIONAL THEORY 22 (Spring 1972): 154-80.

Pastore, Nicholas. "In Defense of Walter Lippmann." AMERICAN PSYCHOLOGIST 30 (September 1975): 940-42.

_____. THE NATURE-NURTURE CONTROVERSY. New York: King's Crown Press, 1949. xvi, 213 p.

Discusses major figures in the history of the nature-nurture controversy concentrating on their concomitant social, political, and economic attitudes. Extensive bibliography. Index.

Samelson, Franz. "On the Science and Politics of the I.Q." SOCIAL RESEARCH 42 (Autumn 1975): 467-88.

Thorndike, Edward L. "Intelligence and its Uses." HARPER'S MAGAZINE, January 1920, pp. 227-35.

10. DEVELOPMENTAL PSYCHOLOGY

Developmental psychology originally meant child psychology. In recent years it has grown to encompass studies of infancy, childhood, adolescence, early adulthood, maturity, and old age. The references included here are devoted to practical topics, such as the history of attitudes toward child rearing, and theoretical issues in the history of developmental psychology. This section is divided into histories of developmental psychology and selected major works in developmental psychology.

a. General and Special Histories

Anandalakshmy, S., and Grinder, Robert E. "Conceptual Emphasis in the History of Developmental Psychology: Evolutionary Theory, Teleology, and the Nature-Nurture Issue." CHILD DEVELOPMENT 41 (December 1970): 1113-23.

Aries, Philippe. CENTURIES OF CHILDHOOD: A SOCIAL HISTORY OF FAMILY LIFE. Translated by Robert Baldick. New York: Knopf, 1962. Reprint. New York: Vintage Books, 1965. 447 p.

> Explores historical and modern conceptions of the nature of the family, the child, and the school. Emphasizes developments since the Middle Ages. Notes. Index.

Borstelmann, L.J. "Classics in Developmental Psychology: Historical Persons and Studies of Common Textbook Reference." DEVELOPMENTAL PSYCHOLOGY 10 (September 1974): 661-64.

Bremmer, Robert H., ed. CHILDREN AND YOUTH IN AMERICA: A DOCU-MENTARY HISTORY. 3 vols. bound in 5 books. Cambridge, Mass.: Harvard University Press, 1970-74.

> A large work exploring the history of public policy toward children in America from 1600 to 1865 in volume 1; 1866 to 1932 in volume 2; and since 1932 in volume 3. Covers such topics as child pro-tection, education, health, care of dependent children, child labor, and juvenile delinquency.

Burstein, S.R. "Gerontology: A Modern Science With a Long History." POST-GRADUATE MEDICAL JOURNAL 22 (1946): 185-90.

> Traces gerontological thought from Biblical and classical times to the mid-twentieth century.

Cable, Mary. THE LITTLE DARLINGS: A HISTORY OF CHILD REARING IN AMERICA. New York: Charles Scribner's Sons, 1972. x, 214 p.

> Traces major assumptions about the nature of children and methods of treating children in middle-class America from the colonies to the present time. Bibliography. Index.

Carmichael, Leonard. "William Preyer and the Prenatal Development of Behav-ior." PERSPECTIVES IN BIOLOGY AND MEDICINE 16 (Spring 1973): 411-17.

Cassel, Russell N. "Critical Contributions of Piaget to Developmental Psychol-ogy." PSYCHOLOGY 10 (1973): 42-45.

Charles, Don C. "Historical Antecedents of Life-Span Developmental Psychol-ogy." In LIFE-SPAN DEVELOPMENTAL PSYCHOLOGY: RESEARCH AND THEORY, edited by L.R. Goulet and Paul B. Baltes, pp. 23-52. New York: Academic Press, 1970.

Traces emerging interest in life-span development and notes that such interest has been stimulated by longitudinal studies. Index.

Collins, J.K. "Some Attitudes to Adolescents Over the Centuries." MENTAL HEALTH IN AUSTRALIA 1 (1975): 108-10.

Dasen, Pierre R. PIAGETIAN PSYCHOLOGY: CROSS CULTURAL CONTRIBU-TIONS. Preface by Jean Piaget. New York: Gardner Press, 1977. xiv, 379 p.

"Intended as a reference work for students and professionals in child psychology, education, anthropology, and international development." Discusses topics in cognitive development across cultures. Index.

deMause, Lloyd, ed. THE HISTORY OF CHILDHOOD. New York: Psycho-History Press, 1974. iv, 450 p. Sponsored by the Association for Applied Psychoanalysis.

Ten chapters written primarily by historians exploring basic attitudes toward children and methods of treating children in selected western cultures. Chapter topics include late Roman and early medieval childhood, childrearing in seventeenth-century England and America, childhood in Imperial Russia, and middle-class childhood in nineteenth-century Europe. References. Index.

Dennis, Wayne. "Historical Notes on Child Animism." PSYCHOLOGICAL REVIEW 45 (May 1938): 257-66.

_____, ed. HISTORICAL READINGS IN DEVELOPMENTAL PSYCHOLOGY. New York: Appleton-Century-Crofts, 1972. x, 355 p.

A collection of thirty-seven articles attempting to include "the most important contributions to child psychology, chronologically arranged from 1728 to 1948." Editorial comments provide perspective for each article. Index.

Eisdorfer, C., and Lawton, M. Powell, eds. THE PSYCHOLOGY OF ADULT DEVELOPMENT AND AGING. Washington, D.C.: American Psychological Association, 1973. xiv, 718 p.

An anthology selected by a task force on aging organized by the American Psychological Association. Covers a broad range of topics representing experimental, clinical, social, and developmental aspects of aging. Includes materials on the history of psychological gerontology. References. Index.

Elkind, David. "Piaget and Montessori." HARVARD EDUCATIONAL REVIEW 37 (Fall 1967): 535-45.

Friedman, Erwin. "A Historical Note to 'The Wild Boy of Kronstadt.'" JOUR-NAL OF THE HISTORY OF THE BEHAVIORAL SCIENCES 1 (July 1965): 284.

Recent evidence corroborates claims that "the wild boy of Kron-stadt" is one of the better documented cases of "feral humans."

Gray, Philip Howard. "Spalding and His Influence on Research in Developmental Behavior." JOURNAL OF THE HISTORY OF THE BEHAVIORAL SCIENCES 3 (April 1967): 168-79.

An overview of Spalding's research followed by an assessment of his theoretical influence in developmental psychology.

Grinder, Robert E. A HISTORY OF GENETIC PSYCHOLOGY: THE FIRST SCIENCE OF HUMAN DEVELOPMENT. New York: John Wiley and Sons, 1967. xii, 247 p.

Discusses theories of change and development from antiquity to the early twentieth-century genetic psychology of G. Stanley Hall. Includes excerpts from classical sources. Bibliographical materials in footnotes. Index.

Groffman, Karl J. "Life-Span Developmental Psychology in Europe: Past and Present." In LIFE-SPAN DEVELOPMENTAL PSYCHOLOGY: RESEARCH AND THEORY, edited by L.R. Goulet and Paul B. Baltes, pp. 53-68. New York: Academic Press, 1970.

A brief examination of both prescientific and scientific interest in life-span development.

Haffter, Carl. "The Changeling: History and Psychodynamics of Attitudes to Handicapped Children in European Folklore." JOURNAL OF THE HISTORY OF THE BEHAVIORAL SCIENCES 4 (January 1968): 55-61.

Traces European attitudes toward deformed children from the Middle Ages to the Enlightenment.

Inhelder, Barbel. "Genetic Epistemology and Developmental Psychology." ANNALS OF THE NEW YORK ACADEMY OF SCIENCES 291 (18 April 1977): 332-41.

Reviews the development of Piaget's thought and describes some of his major concerns.

Iowa University. PIONEERING IN CHILD WELFARE: A HISTORY OF THE IOWA CHILD WELFARE RESEARCH STATION, 1917-1933. Iowa City: University of Iowa, 1933. 80 p.

Iowa University. Institute of Child Behavior and Development. FIFTY YEARS OF RESEARCH 1917-1967. Iowa City: University of Iowa, 1967. vii, 129 p.

Kanner, Leo. "Emotionally Disturbed Children: A Historical Review." CHILD DEVELOPMENT 33 (March 1962): 97-102.

Kessen, William. THE CHILD. New York: John Wiley and Sons, 1965. xii, 301 p.

> Covers the contributions of such major pioneers in the history of the study of the child as Thomas Martin, John Locke, Jean-Jacques Rousseau, Charles Darwin, G. Stanley Hall, James Mark Baldwin, Alfred Binet, Arnold Gesell, John B. Watson, Sigmund Freud, and Jean Piaget. Index.

Krause, Irl B., Jr. "A Comparison of the Psychological Views of Piaget and Gesell." JOURNAL OF THOUGHT 3 (1968): 168-76.

Kroll, Jerome. "The Concept of Childhood in the Middle Ages." JOURNAL OF THE HISTORY OF THE BEHAVIORAL SCIENCES 13 (October 1967): 384-93.

> In contrast to the thesis put forth by Aries (see in this section, p. 323), argues that there was a concept (however ambivalent) of childhood in the Middle Ages.

Lane, Harlan C. THE WILD BOY OF AVEYRON. Cambridge, Mass.: Harvard University Press, 1976. 351 p.

> See section D12b, p. 349, for annotation.

Lomax, Elizabeth. "The Laura Spelman Rockefeller Memorial: Some of Its Contributions to Early Research in Child Development." JOURNAL OF THE HISTORY OF THE BEHAVIORAL SCIENCES 13 (July 1977): 283-93.

> Describes some of the research supported between 1925 and 1940 by the Laura Spelman Rockefeller Memorial.

McCullers, John C. "G. Stanley Hall's Conception of Mental Development and Some Indications of Its Influence on Developmental Psychology." AMERICAN PSYCHOLOGIST 24 (December 1969): 1109-14.

> A brief summary of Hall's accomplishments and his theory of mental development. Emphasizes his evolutionary bias and his idea of recapitulation. Notes that Hall's ideas are not well accepted today, but suggests that a reexamination of his ideas would be valuable to assess his influence and to determine whether his theory of mental development was rejected for valid reasons.

Munnichs, J.M. "A Short History of Psychogerontology." HUMAN DEVELOPMENT 9, no. 4 (1966): 230-45.

Nance, R. Dale. "G. Stanley Hall and John B. Watson as Child Psychologists." JOURNAL OF THE HISTORY OF THE BEHAVIORAL SCIENCES 6 (October 1970): 303-16.

> Contains selected biographical materials on Hall and Watson as well as an account of their contrasting approaches to child psychology.

Pascual-Leone, Juan. "On Learning and Development, Piagetian Style: II. A Critical History Analysis of Geneva's Research Programme." CANADIAN PSYCHOLOGICAL REVIEW 17 (October 1976): 289-97.

Phillips, Shelley. "Psychological Antecedents to Piagetian Concepts." PSYCHOLOGIA 20 (March 1977): 1-14.

> Explores anticipations of Piagetian theory in the work of James Ward, George Frederick Stout, John Dewey, Maria Montessori, James Mark Baldwin, and others.

Pollack, Robert H. "Binet on Perceptual-Cognitive Development, or Piaget-Come-Lately." JOURNAL OF THE HISTORY OF THE BEHAVIORAL SCIENCES 7 (October 1971): 370-74.

> Referring to experiments Binet conducted on his own children, Pollack shows that "Binet anticipated Piaget's classification of illusions as primary and secondary by nearly 50 years."

Riegel, Klaus F. "Developmental Psychology and Society: Some Historical and Ethical Considerations." In LIFE-SPAN DEVELOPMENTAL PSYCHOLOGY: METHODOLOGICAL ISSUES, edited by John R. Nesselroade and Hayne W. Reese, pp. 1-23. New York: Academic Press, 1973.

> Presents historical conceptualizations of human beings and their development found in pre-Grecian civilizations and the scholastic period (400 to 800 A.D.), and more contemporary views coming out of the western sciences, including some of Piaget's work and selected work in the Soviet Union. Index.

_____. "On the History of Psychological Gerontology." In THE PSYCHOLOGY OF ADULT DEVELOPMENT AND AGING, edited by Carl Eisdorfer and M. Powell Lawton, pp. 37-68. Washington, D.C.: American Psychological Association, 1973.

Riegel, Klaus F., and Meacham, John A. THE DEVELOPING INDIVIDUAL IN A CHANGING WORLD: I. HISTORICAL AND CULTURAL ISSUES. Chicago: Aldine, 1976. xvii, 409 p.

Ross, B., and Kastenbaum, R.K. "Care of the Aged: Some Historical Perspectives." In MODERN PERSPECTIVES IN PSYCHO-GERIATRICS, edited by J.G. Howells, pp. 421-49. New York: Brunner-Mazel, 1975.

Ross, Dorothy. G. STANLEY HALL: THE PSYCHOLOGIST AS PROPHET. Chicago: University of Chicago Press, 1972. xix, 482 p.

> Describes the life, psychological development, intellectual struggles, and selected works of one of the founders of American psychology. Concludes with selections from Hall's published works. Bibliography. Index.

Schlossman, Steven L. "G. Stanley Hall and the Boys' Club: Conservative Applications of Recapitulation Theory." JOURNAL OF THE HISTORY OF THE BEHAVIORAL SCIENCES 9 (April 1973): 140-47.

> Shows how Hall's psychology, and particularly his recapitulation theory, was used by social reformers in their attempts to control behavior.

Sears, Robert R. "Your Ancients Revisited." In REVIEW OF CHILD DEVELOPMENT RESEARCH, edited by Mavis Hetherington, vol. 5, pp. 1-73. Chicago: University of Chicago Press, 1975.

Senn, Milton J.E. INSIGHTS ON THE CHILD DEVELOPMENT MOVEMENT IN THE UNITED STATES. Monographs of the Society for Research in Child Development, vol. 4, nos. 3-4, monograph no. 161. Chicago: University of Chicago Press, 1975. 107 p.

> An overview of the contributions of such pioneers as G. Stanley Hall, John Dewey, John B. Watson, Arnold Gesell, Lewis M. Terman, Sigmund Freud, Kurt Lewin, and Jean Piaget followed by a consideration of contributions from pediatrics and child psychiatry. Includes a discussion of the child development movement. Much of the material based on interviews with experts. Minimal reference materials.

Voyat, Gilbert. "In Tribute to Piaget: A Look at His Scientific Impact in the United States." ANNALS OF THE NEW YORK ACADEMY OF SCIENCES 291 (18 April 1977): 342-49.

Wellman, B.L. "Contributions of Bird Baldwin to Child Development." JOURNAL OF JUVENILE RESEARCH 14 (1930): 1-7.

Wiltse, Sara E. "A Preliminary Sketch of the History of Child Study in America." PEDAGOGICAL SEMINARY 3 (October 1895): 189-212.

Wolf, Theta H. "Intuition and Experiment: Alfred Binet's First Efforts in Child Psychology." JOURNAL OF THE HISTORY OF THE BEHAVIORAL SCIENCES 2 (July 1966): 233-39.

> Focuses on three papers Binet published in 1890 which "present the initial intuitions and groping hypotheses about development and in-

dividual differences characteristic of many of Binet's later contributions."

b. Selected Major Works

Baldwin, Alfred Lee. BEHAVIOR AND DEVELOPMENT IN CHILDHOOD.
2d ed. New York: Holt, Rinehart and Winston, 1962. xvii, 619 p.

Bridges, Katharine M. Banham. "Emotional Development in Early Infancy."
CHILD DEVELOPMENT 3 (December 1932): 324-41.

Carmichael, Leonard. MANUAL OF CHILD PSYCHOLOGY. See Mussen,
Paul H., ed., CARMICHAEL'S MANUAL OF CHILD PSYCHOLOGY, below,
this section, p. 331.

Elkind, David. CHILD DEVELOPMENT AND EDUCATION: A PIAGETIAN
PERSPECTIVE. New York: Oxford University Press, 1976. xiii, 274 p.

> Summarizes the basic ideas of Piaget's system and offers implica-
> tions for educational practice. Index.

Flavell, John H. THE DEVELOPMENTAL PSYCHOLOGY OF JEAN PIAGET.
Princeton, N.J.: D. Van Nostrand, 1963. xvi, 472 p.

> A major systematic overview of Piaget's influential work. Con-
> tains a foreword by Piaget indicating that the book provides ex-
> cellent coverage up to about 1960. Index.

Gesell, Arnold Lucius. INFANT DEVELOPMENT: THE EMBRYOLOGY OF
EARLY HUMAN BEHAVIOR. New York: Harper, 1952. Reprint. Westport,
Conn.: Greenwood Press, 1972. xi, 108 p.

> A concise overview of the methodological and conceptual ap-
> proaches to Gesell's well-known research on human development.
> Suggested readings. Index.

_____. THE MENTAL GROWTH OF THE PRE-SCHOOL CHILD: A PSYCHO-
LOGICAL OUTLINE OF NORMAL DEVELOPMENT FROM BIRTH TO THE
SIXTH YEAR, INCLUDING A SYSTEM OF DEVELOPMENTAL DIAGNOSIS.
New York: Macmillan, 1930. x, 447 p. Index.

Gesell, Arnold L[ucius], and Amatruda, Catherine S[trunk]. DEVELOPMENTAL
DIAGNOSIS: NORMAL AND ABNORMAL CHILD DEVELOPMENT, CLINICAL
METHODS, AND PRACTICAL APPLICATIONS. New York: Paul B. Hoeber,
1941. xiii, 447 p.

> A general overview of diagnostic procedures followed by a de-
> tailed examination of sensory, motor, and intellectual defects

and deviations. Final section devoted to supervision of infant development. Appendices on examination equipment and techniques, case studies, and growth trend charts. Index.

_____. THE EMBRYOLOGY OF BEHAVIOR: THE BEGINNINGS OF THE HUMAN MIND. New York: Harper, 1945. Reprint. Westport, Conn.: Greenwood Press, 1971. xix, 289 p.

Traces the genesis and development of behavior in the embryo, fetus, and neonate. Emphasizes the unity of structure and function. References. Index.

Gesell, Arnold [Lucius]; Ilg, Frances L.; and Ames, Louise B.; in collaboration with Glenna E. Bullis. THE CHILD FROM FIVE TO TEN. Rev. ed. New York: Harper and Row, 1977. xviii, 461 p.

Gesell, Arnold Lucius; and Ilg, Frances L.; in collaboration with Louise B. Ames, Janet Learned, [and] Glenna E. Bullis. CHILD DEVELOPMENT: AN INTRODUCTION TO THE STUDY OF HUMAN GROWTH. 2 vols. New York: Harper, 1949.

Volume 1 presents materials on early growth, the effects of family and culture on individuals' cycles and stages of development, and behavior profiles over successive periods from birth to age five. Volume 2 presents behavior profiles, interests, and general developmental characteristics for children from five to ten years of age. Bibliography. Index.

Gesell, Arnold [Lucius], and Thompson, Helen, with the assistance of Catherine Strunk Amatruda. THE PSYCHOLOGY OF EARLY GROWTH INCLUDING NORMS OF INFANT BEHAVIOR AND A METHOD OF GENETIC ANALYSIS. New York: Macmillan, 1938. ix, 290 p.

Intended as a practical manual dealing with "the normative and diagnostic aspects of the psychology of early growth." Index.

Gillis, John R. YOUTH AND HISTORY: TRADITION AND CHANGE IN EUROPEAN AGE RELATIONS, 1770 TO THE PRESENT. New York: Academic Press, 1974. 240 p.

Ginsburg, Herbert, and Opper, Sylvia. PIAGET'S THEORY OF INTELLECTUAL DEVELOPMENT: AN INTRODUCTION. Englewood Cliffs, N.J.: Prentice-Hall, 1969. xi, 237 p.

Goodenough, Florence L. DEVELOPMENTAL PSYCHOLOGY: AN INTRODUCTION TO THE STUDY OF HUMAN BEHAVIOR. 2d ed. New York: Appleton-Century, 1945. xxii, 723 p.

Revision of the author's classic (1934) text covering development from birth to old age. References in footnotes. Index.

Hall, G. Stanley. ADOLESCENCE AND ITS PSYCHOLOGY, AND ITS RE-
LATIONS TO PHYSIOLOGY, ANTHROPOLOGY, SOCIOLOGY, SEX, CRIME,
RELIGION AND EDUCATION. 2 vols. New York: Appleton, 1905. Index.

Hilgard, Josephine Rohrs. "Learning and Maturation in Preschool Children."
PEDAGOGICAL SEMINARY AND JOURNAL OF GENETIC PSYCHOLOGY 41
(September 1932): 36-56.

Inhelder, B., and Chipman, H.H., eds. PIAGET AND HIS SCHOOL: A
READER IN DEVELOPMENTAL PSYCHOLOGY. New York: Springer-Verlag,
1976. xiii, 301 p.

Koffka, Kurt. THE GROWTH OF THE MIND: AN INTRODUCTION TO
CHILD PSYCHOLOGY. 2d rev. ed. Translated by Robert Morris Ogden.
New York: Harcourt Brace, 1928 (1925). xix, 427. Index.

    See section C11a, p. 186, for annotation.

Maier, Henry W. THREE THEORIES OF CHILD DEVELOPMENT: THE CON-
TRIBUTIONS OF ERIK H. ERIKSON, JEAN PIAGET, AND ROBERT R. SEARS,
AND THEIR APPLICATIONS. New York: Harper and Row, 1965. xvi, 314 p.

    Presents an exposition and comparison of the psychoanalytic theory
    of Erikson, the cognitive theory of Piaget, and the learning
    theory of Sears. Bibliographies of the writings of the three theo-
    rists. Index.

Mead, Margaret, and MacGregor, Frances Coke. GROWTH AND CULTURE:
A PHOTOGRAPHIC STUDY OF BALINESE CHILDHOOD. New York: G.P.
Putnam's Sons, 1951. xvi, 223 p.

    Mead and MacGregor's well-known work on the development of
    Balinese children compares the development of Balinese and Ameri-
    can children and describes the child-rearing practices of the Bali-
    nese. Appendix on methodological matters. Notes. References.
    Index.

Murchison, Carl, ed. HANDBOOK OF CHILD PSYCHOLOGY. Rev. ed.
Worcester, Mass.: Clark University Press, 1933. 956 p.

    An exposition and analysis of four major research areas within
    child psychology: development before birth, development after
    birth, factors that modify child behavior, and studies of special
    groups. Introductory chapter explores methods in child psychol-
    ogy. References. Index.

Mussen, Paul H., ed. CARMICHAEL'S MANUAL OF CHILD PSYCHOLOGY.
3d ed. 2 vols. New York: John Wiley and Sons, 1970.

A massive handbook containing chapters on selected subareas of the field, each written by an expert. Extensive bibliographic materials. Index.

Piaget, Jean. This influential Swiss psychologist has written dozens of books on the development of thought in children. Many of these are available in English translation. Rather than listing them all here, we refer the reader to one of the secondary sources on Piaget (e.g., Elkind, Flavell, or Ginsburg and Opper in this section), which can provide access to Piaget's many contributions.

Preyer, William. THE MIND OF THE CHILD: OBSERVATIONS CONCERNING THE MENTAL DEVELOPMENT OF THE HUMAN BEING IN THE FIRST YEARS OF LIFE. Translated by H.W. Brown. New York: Appleton, 1893. Reprint. New York: Arno Press, 1973.

A classic work in child psychology exploring the development of the senses and the will in part 1 and the development of language and of the self in part 2.

Ribot, Th[éodule Armand]. THE EVOLUTION OF GENERAL IDEAS. Translated by Frances A. Welby. Chicago: Open Court, 1899. xi, 231 p.

An early pre-Piagetian work in genetic epistemology. Outlines in lecture format three critical stages in the evolution of intellectual processes: inferior abstraction (preverbal period), intermediate abstraction (words gradually become instruments of thought), and superior abstraction (characterized by scientific ideas).

Shock, Nathan Wetheril. A CLASSIFIED BIBLIOGRAPHY OF GERONTOLOGY AND GERIATRICS. Stanford, Calif.: Stanford University Press, 1951. xxvii, 599 p. Supplements 1 and 2: 1957, 1963.

A major reference resource for works in the earlier literature on aging and the problems associated with the process of aging.

Smith, Theodate L., ed. ASPECTS OF CHILD LIFE AND EDUCATION BY G. STANLEY HALL AND SOME OF HIS PUPILS. Boston: Ginn, 1907. ix, 326 p.

An anthology of nine papers by a major early developmental psychologist and some of his students on such areas of practical interest as curiosity, daydreams, the collecting instinct, and fetishism in children. References. Index.

Stoddard, George D., and Wellman, Beth L. CHILD PSYCHOLOGY. New York: Macmillan, 1934. xii, 419 p.

A classic work which draws extensively from the research literature to establish a psychology of the child. References. Index.

Sully, James. OUTLINES OF PSYCHOLOGY: WITH SPECIAL REFERENCE TO THE THEORY OF EDUCATION. Rev. ed. New York: Appleton, 1908. xvii, 524 p.

> Intended both as an introduction to psychology and as a source for teachers wishing to apply the principles of psychology in educational settings. Covers traditional content areas of the time. Index.

11. SOCIAL PSYCHOLOGY

There is a marked paucity of work on the history of social psychology. One of the better sources is Allport's chapter (see below) in Lindzey and Aronson's HANDBOOK OF SOCIAL PSYCHOLOGY. Additionally, chapter 16 of Chaplin and Krawiec's SYSTEMS AND THEORIES OF PSYCHOLOGY (see section B, p. 33) examines the history of social psychology as well as more contemporary trends. A few relevant items can also be found in section E4, p. 413. This section lists sources in the history of social psychology and representative major works from the early part of the century to the 1950s.

a. General and Specific Histories

Allport, Gordon W. "The Historical Background of Modern Social Psychology." In HANDBOOK OF SOCIAL PSYCHOLOGY, 2d ed., edited by Gardner Lindzey and Elliot Aronson, vol. 1, pp. 1-80. Reading, Mass.: Addison-Wesley, 1968-70.

> Traces major trends, concepts, and methods in social psychology from antiquity to the twentieth century. Over 250 references.

Baumgardner, Steve R. "Critical Studies in the History of Social Psychology." PERSONALITY AND SOCIAL PSYCHOLOGY BULLETIN 3 (Fall 1977): 681-87.

Cardno, J.A. "Bain As A Social Psychologist." AUSTRALIAN JOURNAL OF PSYCHOLOGY 8 (1956): 66-76.

Cook, Gary A. "G.H. Mead's Social Behavioralism." JOURNAL OF THE HISTORY OF THE BEHAVIORAL SCIENCES 13 (October 1977): 307-16.

> Outlines differences in the orientations of Mead and Watson and argues that Mead's social behaviorism is a logical extension of his earlier functionalism.

Dewey, John. "The Need for Social Psychology." PSYCHOLOGICAL REVIEW 24 (July 1917): 266-77.

> See section C6, p. 151, for annotation.

Heidbreder, Edna. "William McDougall and Social Psychology." JOURNAL OF ABNORMAL AND SOCIAL PSYCHOLOGY 34 (April 1939): 150-60.

Hollander, Edwin P., and Hunt, Raymond G., eds. CLASSIC CONTRIBUTIONS TO SOCIAL PSYCHOLOGY: READINGS WITH COMMENTARY. New York: Oxford University Press, 1972. 430 p.

    A collection emphasizing early twentieth-century theoretical and empirical contributions of such individuals as Gordon Allport, Charles Cooley, George Herbert Mead, and Talcott Parsons.

Jensen, Howard E. "William McDougall's Doctrine of Social Psychology." JOURNAL OF SOCIAL PHILOSOPHY 4 (April 1939): 206-19.

Oberschall, Anthony. "Paul F. Lazarsfeld and the History of Empirical Social Research." JOURNAL OF THE HISTORY OF THE BEHAVIORAL SCIENCES 14 (July 1978): 199-206.

    Describes Lazarsfeld's contributions to the history of empirical social research; characterizes these works as complementing standard histories of sociology which focus on theory.

Sahakian, William S. SYSTEMATIC SOCIAL PSYCHOLOGY. New York: Chandler, 1974. xiii, 589 p.

    Traces the history of social psychology from antiquity to contemporary developments with emphasis on national trends and systematic positions advanced by such theorists as McDougall, Allport, Sherif, Lewin, Heider, and Festinger. Discusses contributions from psychoanalysis, sociology, cultural anthropology, Gestalt psychology, and learning theory. Index.

Samelson, Franz. "From 'Race Psychology' to 'Studies in Prejudice': Some Observations on the Thematic Reversal in Social Psychology." JOURNAL OF THE HISTORY OF THE BEHAVIORAL SCIENCES 14 (July 1978): 265-78.

    Traces external influences (e.g., Immigration Restriction Law of 1924, influx of ethnics into psychology, and the Great Depression) responsible for the shift from the belief in mental differences between races characteristic of the 1920s to the search for irrational prejudice characteristic of the 1940s.

_____. "History, Origin Myth and Ideology: 'Discovery' of Social Psychology." JOURNAL FOR THE THEORY OF SOCIAL BEHAVIOR 4 (October 1974): 217-31.

Smoke, Kenneth L. "The Present Status of Social Psychology in America." PSYCHOLOGICAL REVIEW 42 (November 1935): 537-43.

    Examines research trends and topics covered in major social-psychological textbooks.

Truzzi, Marcello. "Adam Smith and Contemporary Issues in Social Psychology." JOURNAL OF THE HISTORY OF THE BEHAVIORAL SCIENCES 2 (July 1966): 221-24.

> Shows how some of Smith's early writings anticipated such concepts in modern social psychology as balance theory, norms and sanctions, conformity, and status.

Walker, Ronald E., and Foley, Jeanne M. "Social Intelligence: Its History and Measurement." PSYCHOLOGICAL REPORTS 33 (December 1973): 839-64.

> Examines the history of measurement of social intelligence and considers issues associated with the concept such as the relationship between social intelligence and abstract intelligence. Analyzes briefly the relationship between social intelligence and related concepts such as person perception, interpersonal judgment, and interpersonal competence. References.

Wright, William Kelley. "McDougall's Social Psychology in the Light of Recent Discussion." JOURNAL OF PHILOSOPHY 18 (March 1921): 141-52.

> A comment on the importance of McDougall to the development of social psychology followed by a discussion of McDougall's central conceptions: instincts, sentiments, and development of character and volition.

b. Selected Major Works

Allport, Floyd Henry. SOCIAL PSYCHOLOGY. Boston: Houghton Mifflin, 1924. xiv, 453 p. Index.

Asch, Solomon E. SOCIAL PSYCHOLOGY. New York: Prentice-Hall, 1952. xvi, 646 p.

> A systematic overview of the phenomena of social psychology from an explicitly Gestalt orientation. Includes an account of Asch's famous experiments on the influence of group pressure on judgment processes. Index.

Baldwin, James Mark. THE INDIVIDUAL AND SOCIETY: OR PSYCHOLOGY AND SOCIOLOGY. Boston: R.G. Badger, 1911. 210 p.

Bogardus, Emory S. FUNDAMENTALS OF SOCIAL PSYCHOLOGY. New York: Century, 1924. xiv, 479 p. Index.

Bonner, Hubert. SOCIAL PSYCHOLOGY: AN INTERDISCIPLINARY APPROACH. New York: American Book Co., 1953. iv, 439 p. Index.

Dewey, John. HUMAN NATURE AND CONDUCT: AN INTRODUCTION

TO SOCIAL PSYCHOLOGY. New York: Holt, 1922. vii, 336 p.

> Not intended as a treatment of social psychology in today's sense.
> Discusses such topics as the place of habit, impulse, and intelligence
> in conduct. Also covers such issues as freedom and morality.
> Dewey attempts to demonstrate that "an understanding of habit
> and of different types of habit is the key to social psychology,
> while the operation of impulse and intelligence gives the key to
> individualized mental activity." Index.

Dunlap, Knight. SOCIAL PSYCHOLOGY. Baltimore: Williams and Wilkins,
1925. 261 p.

> An eclectic introduction to social psychology with chapters on the
> field of social psychology, sex differences, marriage and the
> family, religious organization, civil and martial organization, the
> conditions of social progress, principles of social organization, and
> propaganda. Minimal references. Index.

Krech, David, and Crutchfield, Richard S. THEORY AND PROBLEMS OF
SOCIAL PSYCHOLOGY. New York: McGraw-Hill, 1948. xv, 639 p.
Index.

Lindesmith, Alfred R., and Strauss, Anselm L. SOCIAL PSYCHOLOGY.
New York: Dryden Press, 1949. xvi, 549 p. Index.

Lindzey, Gardner, and Aronson, Elliot, eds. HANDBOOK OF SOCIAL
PSYCHOLOGY. 2d ed. 5 vols. Reading, Mass.: Addison-Wesley, 1968-
69.

> A major sourcebook which covers history, theory, and method
> and specific fields and applications of social psychology. Exten-
> sive references.

McDougall, William. THE GROUP MIND: A SKETCH OF THE PRINCIPLES
OF COLLECTIVE PSYCHOLOGY, WITH SOME ATTEMPT TO APPLY THEM TO
THE INTERPRETATION OF NATIONAL LIFE AND CHARACTER. 2d ed. New
York: G.P. Putnam's Sons, 1927.

_____. AN INTRODUCTION TO SOCIAL PSYCHOLOGY. 1926. Reprint.
Kennebunkport, Maine: Milford House, 1973. xxix, 524 p.

> A classic (1908) treatise which emphasizes the central role of in-
> stincts in human life. Minimal bibliographical materials in foot-
> notes. Index.

_____. "The Use and Abuse of Instinct in Social Psychology." JOURNAL
OF ABNORMAL AND SOCIAL PSYCHOLOGY 16 (December 1921-March 1922):
285-333.

Murchison, Carl, ed. A HANDBOOK OF SOCIAL PSYCHOLOGY. 2 vols.
New York: Russell and Russell, 1967.

> Forty-six articles representing a cross-section of methods and areas
> of inquiry in the first major systematic attempt (1935) to charac-
> terize the state of social psychology. References. Index.

Newcomb, Theodore M. SOCIAL PSYCHOLOGY. New York: Dryden Press,
1950. xi, 690 p. Index.

Queener, E. Llewellyn. INTRODUCTION TO SOCIAL PSYCHOLOGY. New
York: Dryden Press, 1951. xiv, 493 p. Index.

Radvanyi, Laszlo, ed. INTERNATIONAL DIRECTORY OF OPINION AND
ATTITUDE RESEARCH. Mexico: Social Sciences, 1948. xiv, 292 p.

> Contains brief biographies including such information as education,
> professional activities, fields of interest and research, and list of
> publications for researchers and teachers worldwide in fields de-
> fined in the preface. Includes some psychologists and social psy-
> chologists. Includes an institutional list of research organizations
> and educational institutions, and a geographical list of persons,
> both arranged alphabetically by country.

Sherif, Muzafer, and Sherif, Carolyn W. GROUPS IN HARMONY AND
TENSION: AN INTEGRATION OF STUDIES ON INTERGROUP RELATIONS.
New York: Harper, 1953. xiii, 316 p.

> A review of traditional and more recent approaches to the study of
> group relations followed by an appeal for a more comprehensive
> approach illustrated in detailed description of a now-classic "boys'
> camp" experiment on intergroup cooperation and conflict. Refer-
> ences. Index.

Young, Kimball, ed. SOURCE BOOK FOR SOCIAL PSYCHOLOGY. New
York: Alfred A. Knopf, 1927. xxiii, 844 p.

> Examines social behavior under six major subheadings: general
> features, psychological foundations, personality, social attitudes
> and the subjective environment, leadership and prestige, and col-
> lective behavior. Each subdivision includes integrative introduc-
> tions by the editor and excerpts from pertinent classic and lesser-
> known papers. Bibliographical materials. Index.

12. PSYCHOPATHOLOGY

A great deal has been written on abnormal psychology but not so much specifically on the history of study of the field. A problem in categorizing articles

on psychopathology is that much of the material could also be classified as relevant to clinical psychology (the psychological specialty that attempts to apply basic psychological principles and techniques to the alleviation of human suffering caused by emotional disorders) or to psychiatry (the medical specialty dealing with the treatment of people with emotional problems). For purposes of convenience, we have included in the section on clinical psychology (D13) and on psychiatry (E2) items that refer specifically to those professions and to the application of basic knowledge to the alleviation of psychopathology. This section contains general and specific histories of psychopathology, a few major works on psychopathology, and works on the social history of psychopathology.

a. General and Specific Histories

Altschule, Mark D. THE DEVELOPMENT OF TRADITIONAL PSYCHOPATHOL-OGY: A SOURCEBOOK. New York: John Wiley and Sons, 1976. vi, 330 p.

> Presents key thoughts of approximately one hundred leading histori-cal figures on such topics as the meaning of psychotic thinking, multiple personality, affective disorders, and thought disorders. Quotes such notables as Hippocrates, Burton, Cabanis, Locke, Hume, Esquirol, Rush, Binet, Freud, Charcot, and Pinel. Biblio-graphical materials in footnotes. Index.

_____. "Whichophrenia, or the Confused Past, Ambiguous Present, and Dubious Future of the Schizophrenia Concept." JOURNAL OF SCHIZOPHRE-NIA 1, no. 1 (1967): 8-17.

Anastasi, Anne, and Foley, John P., Jr. "A Survey of the Literature on Artistic Behavior in the Abnormal: 1. Historical and Theoretical Background." JOURNAL OF GENERAL PSYCHOLOGY 25 (July 1941): 111-42.

> Presents historical materials on the literary and artistic works of persons suffering from various psychopathologies in several countries, including Italy, France, Germany, Russia, England, and the United States.

Baldessarini, Ross J. "Frequency of Diagnoses of Schizophrenia versus Affec-tive Disorders From 1944 to 1968." AMERICAN JOURNAL OF PSYCHIATRY 127 (December 1970): 759-63.

Barr, Martin W. MENTAL DEFECTIVES: THEIR HISTORY, TREATMENT AND TRAINING. Philadelphia: P. Blakiston's Sons, 1904. x, 368 p. Index.

Berger, David M. "The Return of Neurasthenia." COMPREHENSIVE PSYCHI-ATRY 14 (November/December 1973): 557-62.

Bromberg, Walter. FROM SHAMAN TO PSYCHOTHERAPIST: A HISTORY OF

THE TREATMENT OF MENTAL ILLNESS. 4th ed. Chicago: Henry Regnery, 1975. vii, 360 p.

> Focuses on healing by mental means from earliest times to the present. Specific chapters devoted to such topics as rationalism and religion, demonology, early asylums, Mesmerism, emergence of psychological psychotherapies, the Freudian reign, and the breadth of psychotherapy. References. Index.

Bullough, Vern L. "Homosexuality and the Medical Model." JOURNAL OF HOMOSEXUALITY 1 (Fall 1974): 99-110.

Bullough, Vern L., and Voght, Martha. "Homosexuality and Its Confusion With the 'Secret Sin' in Pre-Freudian America." JOURNAL OF THE HISTORY OF MEDICINE AND ALLIED SCIENCES 28 (April 1973): 143-55.

Cancro, Robert, and Pruyser, Paul W. "A Historical Review of the Development of the Concept of Schizophrenia." BULLETIN OF THE MENNINGER CLINIC 34 (March 1970): 61-70.

Cardno, J.A. "The Aetiology of Insanity: Some Early American Views." JOURNAL OF THE HISTORY OF THE BEHAVIORAL SCIENCES 4 (April 1968): 99-108.

> Discusses the etiology of insanity as found in several early American sources: Ripley and Dana's AMERICAN CYCLOPAEDIA, a general textbook of medicine written in 1847 by George Bacon Wood, a work written by James Rush in 1865, and Thomas Cogswell Upham's text on "disordered mental function" (lst ed. 1831; reprinted 1840).

_____. "Idiocy, Imbecility: An Early American Contrast." PSYCHOLOGICAL RECORD 18 (April 1968): 241-45.

Carlson, Eric T., and Simpson, Meribeth M. "The Definition of Mental Illness: Benjamin Rush (1745-1813)." AMERICAN JOURNAL OF PSYCHIATRY 121 (September 1964): 209-14.

Chatel, John C., and Peele, Roger. "A Centennial Review of Neurasthenia." AMERICAN JOURNAL OF PSYCHIATRY 126 (April 1970): 1404-13.

Chertok, Leon. "Hysteria, Hypnosis, Psychopathology: History and Perspectives." JOURNAL OF NERVOUS AND MENTAL DISEASE 161 (December 1975): 367-78.

_____. "Psychosomatic Medicine in the West and in Eastern European Countries." PSYCHOSOMATIC MEDICINE 31 (November-December 1969): 510-21.

Clark, Robert A. MENTAL ILLNESS IN PERSPECTIVE: HISTORY AND SCHOOLS OF THOUGHT. Pacific Grove, Calif.: Boxwood Press, 1973. vii, 106 p.

Clausen, J. "Mental Deficiency: Development of a Concept." AMERICAN JOURNAL OF MENTAL DEFICIENCY 71 (March 1967): 727-45.

Crissey, Marie Skodak. "Mental Retardation: Past, Present, and Future." AMERICAN PSYCHOLOGIST 30 (August 1975): 800-808.

de Saussure, Raymond. "The Magnetic Cure." BRITISH JOURNAL OF MEDI-CAL PSYCHOLOGY 42, no. 2 (June 1969): 141-63.

d'Estrube, Pierre. "Diagnostic Labels in the History of Schizophrenia." CA-NADIAN PSYCHIATRIC ASSOCIATION JOURNAL 11 (1966): 356-57.

Deutsch, Albert. THE MENTALLY ILL IN AMERICA: A HISTORY OF THEIR CARE AND TREATMENT FROM COLONIAL TIMES. 2d ed. New York: Columbia University Press, 1949. xxi, 555 p.

    Traces the evolution of American culture in terms of the way people thought about, felt about, and treated the insane from ancient times to colonial America and through World War II. Takes the perspective of psychiatry rather than clinical psychology. Bibliography. Index.

Diethelm, Oskar. "The Medical Teaching of Demonology in the 17th and 18th Centuries." JOURNAL OF THE HISTORY OF THE BEHAVIORAL SCIENCES 6 (January 1970): 3-15.

    Discusses the widespread belief in demonology and the influence of demonology on medical writings during medieval times. Documents the growing skepticism regarding demonology in the seventeenth and eighteenth centuries.

Doll, Eugene E. "A Historical Survey of Research and Management of Mental Retardation in the United States." In READINGS ON THE EXCEPTIONAL CHILD: RESEARCH AND THEORY, 2d ed., edited by E. Philip Trapp and Philip Himelstein, pp. 47-97. New York: Appleton-Century-Crofts, 1972.

Durkin, Helen E. "Current Problems of Group Therapy in Historical Context." In GROUP THERAPY 1974: AN OVERVIEW, edited by Lewis R. Wolberg and Marvin L. Aronson, pp. 116-41. New York: Stratton Intercontinental Medical Book Corp., 1974.

Ellenberger, Henri F. "Mesmer and Puységur: From Magnetism to Hypnotism." PSYCHOANALYTIC REVIEW 52 (Summer 1965): 137-53.

Foucault, Michel. MADNESS AND CIVILIZATION: A HISTORY OF IN-SANITY IN THE AGE OF REASON. Translated by Richard Howard. New York: Pantheon Books, 1965. xii, 299 p.

> A literary and historical treatment of madness in the sixteenth, seventeenth, and eighteenth centuries, described as both "creative" and "complex" by José Barchilon in his introduction. Deals with various facets of madness including theories, symptoms, and treatments, and provides religious, artistic, sociological, and general historical perspective.

Fox, Ronald E. "Family Therapy." In CLINICAL METHODS IN PSYCHOLOGY, edited by Irving B. Weiner, pp. 451-515. New York: John Wiley and Sons, 1976.

Galen. ON THE PASSIONS AND ERRORS OF THE SOUL. Translated by Paul W. Harkins and interpreted by Walther Riese. Columbus: Ohio State University Press, 1963. 136 p.

> Translations of Galen's treatises THE DIAGNOSIS AND CURE OF THE SOUL'S PASSIONS, dealing with topics such as excessive anger, lust, drunkenness, and gluttony, and THE DIAGNOSIS AND CURE OF THE SOUL'S ERRORS, dealing with a theory of knowledge. Introduced by historical and biographical perspective and followed by an interpretation written by Walther Riese.

Hare, E.H. "Masturbatory Insanity: The History of an Idea." JOURNAL OF MENTAL SCIENCE 108 (January 1962): 1-25.

Haskell, R.H. "Mental Deficiency Over a Hundred Years." AMERICAN JOURNAL OF PSYCHIATRY 100 (1944): 107-18.

Havens, Leston L. "Charcot and Hysteria." JOURNAL OF NERVOUS AND MENTAL DISEASE 141 (November 1965): 505-16.

Hill, Christopher, and Sheperd, Michael. "The Case of Arise Evans: A Historico-Psychiatric Study." PSYCHOLOGICAL MEDICINE 6 (August 1976): 351-58.

> A mental aberration in mid-seventeenth century England. Emphasizes importance of the sociocultural background and the available clinical information.

Holsopple, James Q. "William McDougall and Abnormal Psychology." JOURNAL OF ABNORMAL AND SOCIAL PSYCHOLOGY 34 (April 1939): 161-65.

Hunt, W.A., and Landis, Carney. "The Present Status of Abnormal Psychology." PSYCHOLOGICAL REVIEW 42 (January 1935): 78-90.

Hunt and Landis analyzed the content of fifteen abnormal psychology textbooks and seven psychiatric textbooks to determine experimental content and percent of material devoted to various subjects.

Jackson, Stanley W. "Galen--On Mental Disorders." JOURNAL OF THE HISTORY OF THE BEHAVIORAL SCIENCES 5 (October 1969): 365-84.

Covers such topics as Galen's views on physiology, pathology, psychology, madness, and related nosological categories.

Janet, Pierre. PSYCHOLOGICAL HEALING: A HISTORICAL AND CLINICAL STUDY. 2 vols. Translated by Eden Paul and Cedar Paul. New York: Macmillan, 1925. 1265 p.

Jelliffe, S.E. "Some Historical Phases of the Manic-Depressive Synthesis." JOURNAL OF NERVOUS AND MENTAL DISEASE 73 (April-May 1931): 353-74, 499-521.

Provides an overview of the historical development of the concept of the manic-depressive psychoses.

Jones, Mary Cover. "A 1924 Pioneer Looks at Behavior Therapy." JOURNAL OF BEHAVIOR THERAPY AND EXPERIMENTAL PSYCHIATRY 6 (April 1975): 181-87.

Kanner, Leo. "Childhood Psychosis: A Historical Overview." JOURNAL OF AUTISM AND CHILDHOOD SCHIZOPHRENIA 1 (January-March 1971): 14-19.

_____. A HISTORY OF THE CARE AND STUDY OF THE MENTALLY RETARDED. Springfield, Ill.: Charles C Thomas, 1964. vii, 150 p.

Kauffman, James M. "Nineteenth Century Views on Children's Behavior Disorders: Historical Contributions and Continuing Issues." JOURNAL OF SPECIAL EDUCATION 10 (Winter 1976): 335-49.

Keller, Mark. "Alcohol in Health and Disease: Some Historical Perspectives." ANNALS OF THE NEW YORK ACADEMY OF SCIENCES 133 (1966): 820-27.

Kelly, Barry N. SIGNIFICANT TRENDS AND THEMES IN THE HISTORY OF MENTAL HEALTH. Philadelphia: Bureau of Research and Training, Mental Health, Commonwealth of Pennsylvania, 1975. 68 p.

Klaf, Franklin S., and Hamilton, John G. "Schizophrenia: A Hundred Years Ago and Today." JOURNAL OF MENTAL SCIENCE 107 (September 1961): 819-27.

Knoff, William F. "Four Thousand Years of Hysteria." COMPREHENSIVE PSYCHIATRY 12 (March 1971): 156-64.

_____. "A History of the Concept of Neurosis, With a Memoir of William Cullen." AMERICAN JOURNAL OF PSYCHIATRY 127 (July 1970): 80-84.

Kopell, Bert S., trans. "M. Pierre Janet's Report of Some Phenomena of Somnambulism." JOURNAL OF THE HISTORY OF THE BEHAVIORAL SCIENCES 4 (April 1968): 124-31.

    A translation of a paper presented by Janet in 1885 to the Society of Physiological Psychology. Relates Janet's early work on hypnosis with a hysterical patient named Leonie B.

Lewis, Aubrey. "Paranoia and Paranoid: A Historical Perspective." PSYCHOLOGICAL MEDICINE 4 (1974): 2-12.

_____. Psychopathic Personality: A Most Elusive Category." PSYCHOLOGICAL MEDICINE 4 (1974): 133-40.

Mackler, Bernard, and Bernstein, Elinor. "Contributions to the History of Psychology: II. Philippe Pinel: The Man and His Time." PSYCHOLOGICAL REPORTS 19 (December 1966): 703-20.

Mackler, Bernard, and Hamilton, Kay. "Contributions to the History of Psychology: VII. Benjamin Rush: A Political and Historical Study of the 'Father of American Psychiatry.'" PSYCHOLOGICAL REPORTS 20 (June 1967): 1287-1306.

McMahon, C.E. "Psychosomatic Concepts in the Works of Shakespeare." JOURNAL OF THE HISTORY OF THE BEHAVIORAL SCIENCES 12 (July 1976): 275-82.

    Selections from Shakespeare's plays illustrate late sixteenth- and early seventeenth-century European medical thought on such topics as cardiovascular involvement in emotion, experiential causes of psychosomatic disorders, and the pathological effects of emotional suppression.

_____. "The Role of Imagination in the Disease Process: Pre-Cartesian History." PSYCHOLOGICAL MEDICINE 6 (May 1976): 179-84.

Macmillan, M.B. "Beard's Concept of Neuroasthenia and Freud's Concept of the Actual Neuroses." JOURNAL OF THE HISTORY OF THE BEHAVIORAL SCIENCES 12 (October 1976): 376-90.

    Compares and criticizes Freud's and Beard's theories for their notions of etiology, their "vacuous" central theoretical concepts, and their "inadequate methods of assessing the strengths of the causal factors."

_____. "Extra-Scientific Influences in the History of Childhood Psychopathology." AMERICAN JOURNAL OF PSYCHIATRY 116 (June 1960): 1091-96.

Major, Rene. "The Revolution of Hysteria." INTERNATIONAL JOURNAL OF PSYCHO-ANALYSIS 55 (August 1974): 385-92.

Martindale, Colin. "Degeneration, Disinhibition, and Genius." JOURNAL OF THE HISTORY OF THE BEHAVIORAL SCIENCES 7 (April 1971): 177–82.

> Traces early theories on the presumed relationship between insanity and genius with emphasis on the theories of Lombroso and of Nordau.

Marx, Otto M. "Morton Prince and the Dissociation of a Personality." JOURNAL OF THE HISTORY OF THE BEHAVIORAL SCIENCES 6 (April 1970): 120–30.

> Examines the popular and scientific reaction to the influential book, DISSOCIATION OF A PERSONALITY, by Morton Prince.

Mason, John W. "A Historical View of the Stress Field." JOURNAL OF HUMAN STRESS 1 (1975): 22–36.

Micklem, Niel. "On Hysteria: The Mythical Syndrome." SPRING (1974): 147–65.

Mitchell, Alexander R. SCHIZOPHRENIA: THE MEANINGS OF MADNESS. New York: Taplinger, 1972. 158 p.

Moreno, Zerka T. "Origins of the Group Psychotherapy Movement." HAND-BOOK OF INTERNATIONAL SOCIOMETRY 7 (1974): 5–13.

Mowrer, O. Hobart. "Changing Conceptions of Neurosis and the Small-Groups Movement." EDUCATION 97 (Fall 1976): 24–62.

Parkin, A. "Neurosis and Schizophrenia: I. Historical Review." PSYCHIA-TRIC QUARTERLY 40 (1966): 203–16.

Platt, Anthony Michael, and Diamond, Bernard L. "The Origins and Develop-ment of the 'Wild Beast' Concept of Mental Illness and Its Relation to Theories of Criminal Responsibility." JOURNAL OF THE HISTORY OF THE BEHAVIORAL SCIENCES 1 (October 1965): 355–67.

> Traces the history of attempts to compare insane persons with wild beasts and discusses the perpetuation of the comparison in law.

Riese, Walther. THE LEGACY OF PHILIPPE PINEL: AN INQUIRY INTO THOUGHT ON MENTAL ALIENATION. New York: Springer, 1969. xii, 194 p.

> An analysis of Pinel's work. Strives to show that his approach to the mentally ill was a logical consequence "of his Hippocratic view of disease as an historical chapter in an individual's life." Riese holds that Pinel's thesis was that the causes of insanity can

be derived from the passions. Extensive references. Index.

Roberts, Kimberley S., and Sacks, Norman P. "Dom Duarte and Robert Burton: Two Men of Melancholy." JOURNAL OF THE HISTORY OF MEDICINE AND ALLIED SCIENCES 9 (January 1954): 21-37.

Rosen, George. "Mental Disorder, Social Deviance, and Culture Pattern: Some Methodological Issues in the Historical Study of Mental Illness." In PSYCHIATRY AND ITS HISTORY: METHODOLOGICAL PROBLEMS IN RESEARCH, edited by George Mora and Jeanne L. Brand, pp. 172-94. Springfield, Ill.: Charles C Thomas, 1970.

Rosen, Marvin; Clark, Gerald R.; and Kivitz, Marvin S., eds. THE HISTORY OF MENTAL RETARDATION: COLLECTED PAPERS. 2 vols. Baltimore: University Park Press, 1976.

> A two-volume anthology of writings on mental retardation. Ten sections sample the history of humanitarian concern about retardates from 1843 (a paper by Dorothea Dix and a description of Seguin's school) to the early 1970s, with commentary and head notes by the editors for each selection. References. Index.

Rotenberg, Mordechai, and Diamond, Bernard L. "The Biblical Conception of Psychopathy: The Law of the Stubborn and Rebellious Son." JOURNAL OF THE HISTORY OF THE BEHAVIORAL SCIENCES 7 (January 1971): 29-38.

> Surveys thought on psychopathy from Pinel to the present followed by a discussion of Biblical approaches.

Sarbin, Theodore R., and Juhasz, Joseph B. "The Historical Background of the Concept of Hallucination." JOURNAL OF THE HISTORY OF THE BEHAVIORAL SCIENCES 3 (October 1967): 339-58.

> Traces the historical roots of the concept of hallucination through the views of early church fathers, early physicians such as Galen, and representative views held in various time periods from the sixteenth century to the present. A larger theme of the paper is to demonstrate "the lack of scientific utility of medical models for describing behavioral disorders."

Schoenman, Thomas J. "The Role of Mental Illness in the European Witch Hunts of the Sixteenth and Seventeenth Centuries: An Assessment." JOURNAL OF THE HISTORY OF THE BEHAVIORAL SCIENCES 13 (October 1977): 337-51.

> Argues that historians of psychiatry have overestimated the role of mental illness in the witch hunts of the sixteenth and seventeenth centuries.

Scobie, A., and Taylor, A.J.W. "Perversions Ancient and Modern: I. Agalmatophilia, The Statue Syndrome." JOURNAL OF THE HISTORY OF THE BEHAVIORAL SCIENCES 11 (January 1975): 49-54.

> Reviews the history of agalmatophilia, a sexual attraction to statues, and speculates about the disappearance of this disorder in modern times.

Sharma, Sohan Lal. "A Historical Background of the Development of Nosology in Psychiatry and Psychology." AMERICAN PSYCHOLOGIST 25 (March 1970): 248-53.

> Traces the historical and sociological backgrounds of nosology and examines its utility and role in psychiatric thought.

Sicherman, Barbara. "The Uses of a Diagnosis. Doctors, Patients, and Neurasthania." JOURNAL OF THE HISTORY OF MEDICINE AND ALLIED SCIENCES 32 (January 1977): 33-54.

> Traces the history of neurasthania as a diagnostic category from 1869.

Small, S. Mouchly. "Hysteria: Concept of Hysteria: History and Re-Evaluation." NEW YORK STATE JOURNAL OF MEDICINE 69 (1969): 1866-72.

Stephenson, Pamela. "Society's Changing Attitude to the Idiot." CANADIAN PSYCHIATRIC ASSOCIATION JOURNAL 12 (1967): 83-84.

Stone, Calvin P. ABNORMAL PSYCHOLOGY GLOSSARY. Stanford, Calif.: Stanford University Press, 1954. 24 p.

> A glossary of 650 technical terms intended for beginning students in abnormal psychology, mental hygiene, and medical social service. Includes names, dates, and major contributions of significant figures in the history of psychopathology.

Sugerman, Shirley. "Sin and Madness: A Transformation of Consciousness." PSYCHOANALYTIC REVIEW 61 (Winter 1974-75): 497-516.

Tseng, Wen-Shing, and McDermott, John F., Jr. "Psychotherapy: Historical Roots, Universal Elements, and Cultural Variations." AMERICAN JOURNAL OF PSYCHIATRY 132 (April 1975): 378-84.

van den Berg, Jan Hendrik. DIVIDED EXISTENCE AND COMPLEX SOCIETY: AN HISTORICAL APPROACH. Pittsburgh: Duquesne University Press, distributed by Humanities Press, New York, 1974. xii, 306 p.

> An erudite discussion of multiple selves. Begins with a discussion of the history of writings on the subject and progresses into philosophical analyses of multiple individual existence.

Veith, Ilza. HYSTERIA: THE HISTORY OF A DISEASE. Chicago: University of Chicago Press, 1965. xvi, 301 p.

> Discusses the variety of explanations of the etiology, nature, symptoms, and treatment of hysteria, a widely studied human disorder. Provides historical perspective by examining theories of hysteria prominent in such times and places as ancient Egypt, Greece, and Rome, the Far East, the Middle Ages, the Victorian era, and the psychoanalytic era. Bibliography. Index.

Wallin, J.E. Wallace. "Training of the Severely Retarded, Viewed in Historical Perspective." JOURNAL OF GENERAL PSYCHOLOGY 74 (January 1966): 107-27.

> Traces the training of the severely retarded from ancient times through the Christian and medieval periods, the first European schools in the early nineteenth century and the beginnings of institutional provisions in the United States, to early twentieth-century developments in the United States.

Walter, Richard D. "What Became of the Degenerate? A Brief History of a Concept." JOURNAL OF THE HISTORY OF MEDICINE AND ALLIED SCIENCES 11 (October 1956): 422-29.

Zubin, David, and Zubin, Joseph. "From Speculation to Empiricism in the Study of Mental Disorder: Research at the New York State Psychiatric Institute in the First Half of the Twentieth Century." ANNALS OF THE NEW YORK ACADEMY OF SCIENCES 291 (18 April 1977): 104-35.

b. Selected Major Works and Sourcebooks

Beers, Clifford Whittingham. A MIND THAT FOUND ITSELF: AN AUTOBIOGRAPHY. Garden City, N.Y.: Doubleday, 1950 (1908): xx, 380 p.

> A classic and popular autobiography describing the mental illness of Beers and his recovery. One of the pivotal forces in initiating humanitarian reforms in the early twentieth-century treatment of psychiatric patients.

Bleuler, Eugen. DEMENTIA PRAECOX; OR THE GROUP OF SCHIZOPHRENIAS. Translated by Joseph Zinkin. New York: International Universities Press, 1950. 548 p.

> A classic and influential work examining the symptomatology of schizophrenia, schizophrenic subgroups, the course of the disease and its relation to other psychoses, problems of diagnosis, prognosis, and etiology. Also presents a theory of schizophrenia. Bibliography. Index.

Coleman, James C. ABNORMAL PSYCHOLOGY AND MODERN LIFE. 5th ed. Glenview, Ill.: Scott, Foresman and Co., 1976. 816 p.

A major comprehensive text covering the historical background, etiology, major classifications, and therapeutic procedures for the mentally ill'.

Ellis, Norman R., ed. HANDBOOK OF MENTAL DEFICIENCY: PSYCHOLOGICAL THEORY AND RESEARCH. New York: McGraw-Hill, 1963. xv, 722 p.

Explores behavioral dimensions of mental deficiency in ten papers on theory and eleven papers on empirical findings. Areas of inquiry include sensory and perceptual processes, motor skills, language, varieties of learning, genetic aspects of intelligence, field theory, social learning theory, Hull-Spence behavior theory, and studies of mental deficiency in the Soviet Union. References. Index.

Goddard, Henry Herbert. FEEBLE-MINDEDNESS: ITS CAUSES AND CONSEQUENCES. New York: Macmillan, 1914. xii, 559 p.

Reports a five-year study of 327 cases of feeble-mindedness and discusses various causes of feeble-mindedness with considerable attention to inheritance. Concludes with chapters on eugenics and practical considerations such as treatment, diagnosis, and training programs. Index.

_____. THE KALLIKAK FAMILY: A STUDY IN THE HEREDITY OF FEEBLE-MINDEDNESS. New York: Macmillan, 1912. xv, 121 p.

A classic and controversial book. Attempts to establish the hereditary basis of mental deficiency by comparing the descendants of Martin Kallikak, Sr. (fictitious name) and his wife with the descendants of Martin Kallikak, Sr., and a feeble-minded girl. Index.

Heber, Rick, et al., eds. BIBLIOGRAPHY OF WORLD LITERATURE ON MENTAL RETARDATION: JANUARY 1940-MARCH 1963. Washington, D.C.: U.S. Department of Health, Education and Welfare (published for the President's Panel on Mental Retardation), 1963. vii, 564 p. Supplement, 1966. vii, 99 p.

A bibliography limited to "that scientific and professional literature which directly discusses mental retardation and to literature on conditions and diseases known to be associated with retardation." Two sections: the first lists publications alphabetically by author, and the second is an author-subject index. Supplement covers March 1963 to December 31, 1964.

Krafft–Ebing, Richard von. PSYCHOPATHIA SEXUALIS. Translated and with an introduction by L.T. Woodward. Evanston, Ill.: Greenleaf, 1965. 384 p. Index.

Lane, Harlan L. THE WILD BOY OF AVEYRON. Cambridge, Mass.: Harvard University Press, 1976. 351 p.

> An intellectual biography of Jean–Marc–Gaspard Itard concentrating on the famous case of Victor, the "feral boy," found at the end of the eighteenth century, whom Itard tried to train for five years. Analyzes the legacies of Itard's handling of the case that resulted in major improvements in the treatment of mental retardates and children with sensory handicaps. Chronology of relevant events from 1712 to 1952. Notes. Bibliography. Index.

McDougall, William. OUTLINE OF ABNORMAL PSYCHOLOGY. New York: Charles Scribner's Sons, 1924. xvi, 572 p.

> McDougall intended this text as an extension (or part 2) of his 1924 OUTLINE OF PSYCHOLOGY (see section C8, p. 159). Discusses major psychopathological problems and seeks to integrate relevant findings of academic psychology with the theories of various schools of abnormal psychology. Includes a paper on the definition of the sexual instinct. Bibliographical materials in footnotes. Index.

Miller, J.L. "Burton's 'Anatomy of Melancholy.'" ANNALS OF MEDICAL HISTORY 8 (1936): 14–53.

Pillsbury, W[alter].B[owers]. AN ELEMENTARY PSYCHOLOGY OF THE ABNORMAL. New York: McGraw-Hill, 1932. x, 375 p.

> An early text on psychopathology using a chronological outline to cover its subject matter even though it was not intended as a history of abnormal psychology. References. Index.

Podolsky, Edward, ed. ENCYCLOPEDIA OF ABERRATIONS: A PSYCHIATRIC HANDBOOK. New York: Philosophical Library, 1953. viii, 550 p.

> An alphabetized encyclopedia containing brief definitions, short articles, and a few lengthy articles on a range of human disorders: the neuroses, alcoholism and drug addiction, the psychoses, epilepsy, and various character disturbances. Discusses topics in historical perspective. Occasional notes and references.

Prichard, James Cowles. A TREATISE ON INSANITY AND OTHER DISORDERS AFFECTING THE MIND. London: Sherwood, Gilbert, and Piper, 1835. 483 p.

> An early British attempt to write a systematic medical work on

psychopathology including extensive discussions of definition, nosology, prognosis, etiology, treatment, and legal aspects of insanity.

Prince, Morton. THE DISSOCIATION OF A PERSONALITY, A BIOGRAPHI-CAL STUDY IN ABNORMAL PSYCHOLOGY. 2d ed. New York: Longmans, Green, 1908. Reprint. New York: Johnson Reprint, 1968. x, 575 p.

A classic description of a case of multiple personality.

Ribot, Th[éodule Armand]. DISEASES OF MEMORY: AN ESSAY IN THE POSITIVE PSYCHOLOGY. Translated by William Huntington Smith. New York: Appleton, 1882. 209 p.

A classic monograph describing various forms of amnesia and for-getfulness as well as various anomalies of memory. Minimal bib-liographical materials in footnotes. Index.

_____. THE DISEASES OF THE WILL. 2d enl. English ed. Translated from the 8th French ed. by Merwin-Marie Snell. Chicago: Open Court, 1896. vi, 137 p.

A classic work describing pathological problems such as incapacity for effort, irresistible impulses, impairments of attention, and somnambulism. Suggests explanations. Bibliographical materials in footnotes. Index.

Seguin, Edward. IDIOCY: AND ITS TREATMENT BY THE PHYSIOLOGICAL METHOD. Rev. English ed. New York: William Wood, 1866. xi, 457 p.

Seguin's classic outlines the then-current knowledge about mental deficiency, the methods and practices for its treatment, and pre-sumed directions for scientific and educational efforts. A lengthy appendix includes notes on case histories. Bibliography.

Suinn, Richard M. FUNDAMENTALS OF BEHAVIOR PATHOLOGY, 2d ed. New York: John Wiley and Sons, 1975. 595 p.

A comprehensive text with a historical introduction. The author emphasizes "empirical discussion regarding the possible dynamics and treatment of the various disorders."

Talmey, Max. PSYCHE: A CONCISE AND EASILY COMPREHENSIBLE TREATISE ON THE ELEMENTS OF PSYCHIATRY AND PSYCHOLOGY FOR STUDENTS OF MEDICINE AND LAW. New York: Medico-Legal Publishing Co., 1910. viii, 282 p. Index.

Upham, Thomas Cogswell. OUTLINES OF IMPERFECT AND DISORDERED MENTAL ACTION. New York: Harper, 1840. Reprint. New York: Arno Press, 1973. 399 p.

An early (1840) American popular account of abnormal psychology
by a prominent philosopher-psychologist of the time.

White, Robert W. THE ABNORMAL PERSONALITY. 3d ed. New York:
Ronald Press, 1964. ix, 619 p.

A widely-used text in psychopathology, first published in 1948.
Chapter 1 provides an historical introduction to the origins of
abnormal psychology. References in footnotes. Suggestions for
further reading. Index.

c. Social History of Psychopathology

Bieliauskas, Vytautas J. "Mental Health Care in the USSR." AMERICAN
PSYCHOLOGIST 32 (May 1977): 376-79.

See annotation in section B5bxi, p. 79.

Bockover, J. Sanbourne. MORAL TREATMENT IN COMMUNITY MENTAL
HEALTH. New York: Springer, 1972. xii, 305 p.

The first nine chapters reprint Bockover's 1963 MORAL TREAT-
MENT IN AMERICAN PSYCHIATRY, largely a historical account
of some mental hospitals in the United States. Six new chapters
discuss more recent developments and practices with a plea for
recognition of the value of modern versions of moral treatment.

Brockett, L.P. "Cretins and Idiots: What Has Been and What Can Be Done
for Them." ATLANTIC MONTHLY, February 1858, pp. 410-19.

Brown, Bertram S. "The Federal Mental Health Program: Past, Present, and
Future." HOSPITAL AND COMMUNITY PSYCHIATRY 27 (1976): 512-14.

Dain, Norman. "Nineteenth Century Institutional Mental Care." ANNALS
OF THE NEW YORK ACADEMY OF SCIENCES 291 (April 1977): 74-82.

Dreher, Robert H. "Origin, Development, and Present Status of Insanity as
a Defense to Criminal Responsibility in the Common Law." JOURNAL OF THE
HISTORY OF THE BEHAVIORAL SCIENCES 3 (January 1967): 47-57.

Traces the development of insanity as a defense in criminal responsibility trials and clarifies the different approaches and assumptions
in the law and in the behavioral sciences.

Duffy, John. "Mental Strain and 'Over Pressure' in the Schools: A Nineteenth-
Century Viewpoint." JOURNAL OF THE HISTORY OF MEDICINE AND AL-
LIED SCIENCES 23 (January 1968): 63-79.

Grob, Gerald N. "Class, Ethnicity, and Race in American Mental Hospitals, 1830-75." JOURNAL OF THE HISTORY OF MEDICINE 28 (July 1973): 207-29.

_____. MENTAL INSTITUTIONS IN AMERICA: SOCIAL POLICY TO 1875. New York: Free Press, 1973. xiii, 458 p.

> Focuses on the growth of public mental hospitals and the evolution of public policy in America. Covers such topics as class and ethnicity in hospitals, mental illness in colonial America, and the development of psychiatry. Appendixes provide statistics on annual admissions, 1820-70; total patients treated, 1820-70; recoveries; deaths; and the founding of hospitals. Extensive bibliography. Index.

_____. "The State Mental Hospital in Mid-nineteenth Century America: A Social Analysis." AMERICAN PSYCHOLOGIST 21 (June 1966): 510-23.

Parsons, Gail Pat. "Equal Treatment for All: American Medical Remedies for Male Sexual Problems: 1850-1900." JOURNAL OF THE HISTORY OF MEDICINE AND ALLIED SCIENCES 32 (January 1977): 55-71.

Quen, Jacques M. "Anglo-American Criminal Insanity: An Historical Perspective." BULLETIN OF THE AMERICAN ACADEMY OF PSYCHIATRY AND THE LAW 2 (1974): 115-23.

_____. "Issac Ray and Mental Hygiene in America." ANNALS OF THE NEW YORK ACADEMY OF SCIENCES 291 (18 April 1977): 83-93.

Rieder, Ronald O. "The Origins of Our Confusion about Schizophrenia." PSYCHIATRY 37 (August 1974): 197-208.

Rosen, George. "The Mentally Ill and the Community in Western and Central Europe During the Late Middle Ages and the Renaissance." JOURNAL OF THE HISTORY OF MEDICINE AND ALLIED SCIENCES 19 (October 1964): 377-88.

> Discusses selected social, political, medical, and religious attitudes toward mental illness during the times indicated in the title.

_____. "Social Attitudes to Irrationality and Madness in 17th and 18th Century Europe." JOURNAL OF THE HISTORY OF MEDICINE AND ALLIED SCIENCES 18 (July 1963): 220-40.

Rosenberg, Charles E. "The Place of George M. Beard in Nineteenth Century Psychiatry." BULLETIN OF THE HISTORY OF MEDICINE 36 (1962): 245-59.

Ruphuy, Rodrigo Sanchez. "Psychology and Medicine: A New Approach for Community Health Development." AMERICAN PSYCHOLOGIST 32 (November 1977): 910-13.

> Describes a team approach to mental health care services in Costa Rica.

Shakow, David. "The Worcester State Hospital Research on Schizophrenia (1927-1946)." JOURNAL OF ABNORMAL PSYCHOLOGY MONOGRAPH 80 (1972): 67-110.

Sicherman, Barbara. "The Paradox of Prudence: Mental Health in the Gilded Age." JOURNAL OF AMERICAN HISTORY 62 (March 1976): 890-912.

13. CLINICAL PSYCHOLOGY

Clinical psychology started just before the turn of the century, received major impetus during both world wars, and is now among the largest specialties in psychology. Included in this section are references that deal specifically with clinical psychology. Items dealing with psychopathology that are not specifically addressed to clinical psychology as a specialty are found in section D12, p. 337 (psychopathology), while items dealing specifically with the medical specialty, psychiatry, are found in section E2, p. 397, on psychiatry. This section is divided into items that are general or specific histories of clinical psychology, and items on the historical development of psychotherapy.

a. General and Specific Histories of Clinical Psychology

Beck, Samuel J., and Molish, Herman B., eds. REFLEXES TO INTELLIGENCE: A READER IN CLINICAL PSYCHOLOGY. Glencoe, Ill.: Free Press, 1959. xiv, 669 p.

> Presents historical and recent thought on theoretical and applied issues in clinical psychology in seventy-four articles. Includes editorial comments and suggested readings. References.

Blank, Leonard, and David, Henry P., eds. SOURCEBOOK FOR TRAINING IN CLINICAL PSYCHOLOGY. New York: Springer, 1964. ix, 337 p.

> See section D16, p. 374, for annotation.

Brotemarkle, Robert A. "Clinical Psychology 1896-1946." JOURNAL OF CONSULTING PSYCHOLOGY 11 (January-February 1947): 1-4.

> Reviews the work and thought of Lightner Witmer in a commemorative address celebrating the fiftieth anniversary of the founding of the psychological clinic at the University of Pennsylvania.

Davis, Harold. "Clinical Psychology: A Historical Perspective." BULLETIN OF THE BRITISH PSYCHOLOGICAL SOCIETY 27 (1974): 135-39.

Garfield, Sol L. CLINICAL PSYCHOLOGY: THE STUDY OF PERSONALITY AND BEHAVIOR. Chicago: Aldine, 1974. xi, 461 p.

A survey of the field of clinical psychology. The first chapter provides a brief historical introduction to the field. Bibliographies. Index. Published as INTRODUCTORY CLINICAL PSYCHOLOGY, Chicago: Aldine, 1957.

Hersch, Charles. "From Mental Health to Social Action: Clinical Psychology in Historical Perspective." AMERICAN PSYCHOLOGIST 24 (September 1969): 909-16.

Provides a brief overview of selected topics in the history of clinical psychology from World War II to the late 1960s. Discusses trends including attempts to establish an autonomous profession "freed from the constraints of both medicine and academic psychology." Emphasizes community mental health and increased social and political action.

Kurland, Morton L. "Oneiromancy: An Historical Review of Dream Interpretation." AMERICAN JOURNAL OF PSYCHOTHERAPY 26 (July 1972): 408-16.

Levine, Murray, and Wishner, Julius. "The Case Records of the Psychological Clinic at the University of Pennsylvania (1896-1961)." JOURNAL OF THE HISTORY OF THE BEHAVIORAL SCIENCES 13 (January 1977): 59-66.

Describes the work done in the first psychological clinic for the periods 1896-1907, 1907-19, 1920-45, and 1946-61. Case records from the clinic are now on microfilm and available to qualified researchers.

Lubin, Bernard, and Levitt, Eugene E., eds. THE CLINICAL PSYCHOLOGIST: BACKGROUND, ROLES, AND FUNCTIONS. Chicago: Aldine, 1967. xii, 370 p.

Contains fifty-one articles written by leading authorities on such topics as the historical background of clinical psychology, education of clinical psychologists, roles and functions of clinical psychologists, relations between clinical psychology and other professions, and international aspects of clinical psychology. Information on ethical standards and various certification and licensing procedures. References. Index.

Meltzer, H. "Clinical Psychology in the PSYCHOLOGICAL ABSTRACTS, 1927-1970." JOURNAL OF PSYCHOLOGY 81 (July 1972): 209-24.

Miner, J.B. "The Significance and History of the Clinical Section of the A.P.A." PSYCHOLOGICAL EXCHANGE 1 (1932): 7-11.

Nawas, M. Mike. "Landmarks in the History of Clinical Psychology from Its Early Beginnings Through 1971." JOURNAL OF PSYCHOLOGY 82 (September 1972): 91-110.

Newbrough, J. Robert. "Community Psychology, 1973: With a View Backward and Forward." In CURRENT AND FUTURE TRENDS IN COMMUNITY PSYCHOLOGY, edited by S.E. Golann and J. Baker, pp. 13-40. New York: Human Sciences Press, 1975.

> A brief discussion of historical roots of community psychology followed by some theoretical exploration and speculation about future research strategies.

Reisman, John M. THE DEVELOPMENT OF CLINICAL PSYCHOLOGY. New York: Appleton-Century-Crofts, 1966. ix, 374 p.

> Examines some of the early roots of clinical psychology and traces significant historical developments through each of the decades from 1890 to 1959. References. Index.

_____. A HISTORY OF CLINICAL PSYCHOLOGY. 2d ed. New York: Irvington Publishers, 1976. ix, 420 p.

> A revised edition of Reisman's 1966 THE DEVELOPMENT OF CLINICAL PSYCHOLOGY (see preceding entry). Traces the growth of the field from its inception late in the eighteenth century through the development of theoretical systems and practices to the emergence of recent professional organizations. Extensive references. Index.

Rotter, Julian B. CLINICAL PSYCHOLOGY. 2d ed. Englewood Cliffs, N.J.: Prentice-Hall, 1971. x, 117 p.

> A nontechnical and comprehensive overview of the work, difficulties, and problems of clinical psychology. Includes a brief chapter on the history of clinical psychology. A few references. Index.

Seeman, Julius. "The Psychological Center: A Historical Note." AMERICAN PSYCHOLOGIST 23 (July 1968): 522-23.

> Outlines some of Lightner Witmer's ideas about clinical psychology and talks about their current relevance.

Sexton, Virginia S. "Clinical Psychology: An Historical Survey." GENETIC PSYCHOLOGY MONOGRAPHS 72 (1965): 401-34.

Shakow, David. "Clinical Psychology Seen Some Fifty Years Later." AMERI-
CAN PSYCHOLOGIST 33 (February 1978): 148-58.

A major historian of clinical psychology examines recommendations
of selected reports and conferences which influenced the development of clinical psychology. Emphasizes historical developments
in training and in clinical psychology's relation to other disciplines.

_____. "Reflections on a Do-It-Yourself Training Program in Clinical Psychol-
ogy." JOURNAL OF THE HISTORY OF THE BEHAVIORAL SCIENCES 12 (January 1976): 14-30.

An overview of the training, influential teachers, and professional
life of Shakow, an eminent clinical psychologist.

_____. What Is Clinical Psychology?" AMERICAN PSYCHOLOGIST 31
(August 1976): 553-60.

A reaffirmation of the scientist-professional model of the clinical
psychologist, with suggested training goals.

Stevenson, I. "A Bibliography of Naval Clinical Psychology." PSYCHOLOGI-
CAL BULLETIN 42 (June 1945): 390-92.

Wallin, J.E. Wallace. THE ODYSSEY OF A PSYCHOLOGIST: PIONEERING
EXPERIENCES IN SPECIAL EDUCATION, CLINICAL PSYCHOLOGY, AND
MENTAL HYGIENE, WITH A COMPREHENSIVE BIBLIOGRAPHY OF THE AU-
THOR'S PUBLICATIONS. Wilmington, Del.: Author, 1955. xvii, 243 p.

A narrative of the work of a pioneer in education and clinical
psychology. Discusses such topics of historical interest as conditions in early twentieth-century institutions for mental patients and
in departments of psychology.

Watson, Robert I. "A Brief History of Clinical Psychology." PSYCHOLOGI-
CAL BULLETIN 50 (September 1953): 321-46.

Traces the people and ideas that shaped the development of clinical psychology beginning with Galton and the psychometric tradition. Discusses the work of clinical psychologists in the armed
services and in clinics and hospitals as well as origins of professional activities. Over one hundred references.

_____. "The Experimental Tradition and Clinical Psychology." In EXPERI-
MENTAL FOUNDATIONS OF CLINICAL PSYCHOLOGY, edited by Arthur J.
Bachrach, pp. 3-25. New York: Basic Books, 1962.

Traces the impact on the development of clinical psychology of
such individuals as Charles Darwin, Ivan P. Pavlov, Emil Kraepelin,
and Shepard Ivory Franz. Discusses the effect on clinical psy-

chology of early experimental work in psychophysics, learning,
and communication.

Wolman, Benjamin B., ed. HANDBOOK OF CLINICAL PSYCHOLOGY.
New York: McGraw-Hill, 1965. xv, 1596 p.

Provides representative coverage of the research methods, theories,
diagnostic methods, mental disorders, and methods of treatment
which characterized clinical psychology in the mid-1960s. A
final section devoted to clinical psychology as a profession. References. Index.

Zilboorg, Gregory. A HISTORY OF MEDICAL PSYCHOLOGY. In collaboration with George W. Henry. New York: W.W. Norton, 1941. 606 p.

A thorough survey of the history of medical psychology from primitive and early Oriental thought to the early twentieth century.
Provides a comprehensive treatment of both basic and applied problems. Bibliographical materials in footnotes.

b. Historical Development of Psychotherapy

Abse, D[avid].W[ilfred]. CLINICAL NOTES ON GROUP-ANALYTIC PSYCHO-
THERAPY. Charlottesville: University of Virginia Press, 1974. ix, 192 p.

Barron, Jules. "Group Psychotherapy: Evolution and Process." JOURNAL
OF CONTEMPORARY PSYCHOTHERAPY 3 (1970): 27-30.

Berger, Philip A.; Hamburg, Beatrix; and Hamburg, David A. "Mental Health:
Progress and Problems." DAEDALUS 106 (Winter 1977): 261-76.

Describes twentieth-century development in understanding and
treatment of mental illness.

Bergin, Allen E., and Garfield, Sol. L. HANDBOOK OF PSYCHOTHERAPY
AND BEHAVIORAL CHANGE: AN EMPIRICAL ANALYSIS. New York: John
Wiley and Sons, 1971. xviii, 957 p.

A massive work reviewing the state of empirical knowledge in such
areas as client-centered, psychoanalytic, and eclectic therapies;
the behavior therapies; and therapies for family, home, school,
group, organization, and community. Examines methodological,
experimental, and theoretical issues and includes a chapter on historical perspectives. The final section evaluates the training of
therapists. References. Index.

Bringman, Wolfgang G.; Krichev, Alan; and Balance, William. "Goethe as
Behavior Therapist." JOURNAL OF THE HISTORY OF THE BEHAVIORAL SCI-
ENCES 6 (April 1970): 151-55.

Shows, from autobiographical sources, how Goethe anticipated behavior modification techniques to cure himself of fears of loud noises, heights, and objects that he presumed were carriers of disease.

Bromberg, Walter. FROM SHAMAN TO PSYCHOTHERAPIST: A HISTORY OF THE TREATMENT OF MENTAL ILLNESS. Chicago: Henry Regnery, 1975. vii, 360 p.

The fourth edition of Bromberg's earlier work (THE MIND OF MAN [1937], MAN ABOVE HUMANITY [1954], and THE MIND OF MAN [1958]. A comprehensive history of mental healing from early witchcraft and magic to twentieth-century developments. Includes chapters on early asylums, Mesmerism, the Freudian period, the breadth of psychotherapy, and shock and drug therapy. Index.

Carlson, Eric T. "Charles Poyen Brings Mesmerism to America." JOURNAL OF THE HISTORY OF MEDICINE AND ALLIED SCIENCES 15 (April 1966): 121-32.

Carlson, Eric T., and Simpson, Meribeth M. "Perkinism vs. Mesmerism." JOURNAL OF THE HISTORY OF THE BEHAVIORAL SCIENCES 6 (January 1970): 16-24.

Provides a brief overview of Mesmerism and of a similar treatment procedure developed by Elisha Perkins in the United States.

Davies, Martin H. "The Origins and Practice of Psychodrama." BRITISH JOURNAL OF PSYCHIATRY 129 (September 1976): 201-6.

Dreger, Ralph Mason. "Aristotle, Linnaeus, and Lewin, or the Place of Classification in the Evaluative-Therapeutic Process." JOURNAL OF GENERAL PSYCHOLOGY 78 (January 1968): 41-59.

Reviews historical approaches to classification and argues that classification is unavoidable in the evaluative-therapeutic process. Calls for improvement rather than rejection of classification schemes.

Ellis, Albert. "An Informal History of Sex Therapy." COUNSELING PSYCHOLOGIST 5, no. 1 (1975): 9-13.

Eng, Erling. "Modern Psychotherapy and Ancient Rhetoric." PSYCHOTHERAPY AND PSYCHOSOMATICS 24 (1974): 493-96.

Frank, George H. "On the History of the Objective Investigation of the Process of Psychotherapy." JOURNAL OF PSYCHOLOGY 51 (January 1961): 89-95.

Freedberg, E.J. "Behaviour Therapy: A Comparison Between Early (1890–1920) and Contemporary Techniques." CANADIAN PSYCHOLOGIST 14 (July 1973): 225–40.

Goldsmith, M.L. FRANZ ANTON MESMER; A HISTORY OF MESMERISM. Garden City, N.Y.: Doubleday, 1934. 308 p.

See annotation in section A5bviii, p. 74.

Graham, Thomas F. PARALLEL PROFILES: PIONEERS IN MENTAL HEALTH. Chicago: Franciscan Herald Press, 1966. xv, 245 p.

Provides brief biographies and describes the contributions of such mental health pioneers as Philippe Pinel, Benjamin Rush, Dorothea Dix, Sigmund Freud, Alfred Adler, and Carl Jung. Presents accomplishments of selected more recent pioneers.

Graziano, Anthony M. "An Historical Note: J. Stanley Gray's 'Behavior Modification,' 1932." JOURNAL OF THE HISTORY OF THE BEHAVIORAL SCIENCES 6 (April 1970): 156–58.

Excerpts from Gray's article, "A Biological View of Behavior Modification," show that he advocated applications of behavioral techniques to educational settings in a manner surprisingly similar to those developed more than a quarter of a century later.

Harms, Ernest. "Historical Background of Psychotherapy as a New Scientific Field." DISEASES OF THE NERVOUS SYSTEM 31 (1970): 116–18.

Havens, Leston L. "Charcot and Hysteria." JOURNAL OF NERVOUS AND MENTAL DISEASE 141 (November 1965): 505–16.

Henle, Mary. "Gestalt Psychology and Gestalt Therapy." JOURNAL OF THE HISTORY OF THE BEHAVIORAL SCIENCES 14 (January 1978): 23–32.

See annotation in section C11d, p. 194.

Hovec, Frank J. "Hypnosis Before Mesmer." AMERICAN JOURNAL OF CLINICAL HYPNOSIS 17 (April 1975): 272–76.

Examines use of hypnotic-like states in pre-Columbian America.

Kaplan, Harold I., and Sadock, Benjamin J., eds. THE ORIGINS OF GROUP PSYCHOANALYSIS. New York: Jason Aronson, 1972. x, 100, xlix p.

Among the four papers in this collection is one on the history of group psychotherapy, which explores pioneer theoretical and practical contributions of such individuals as LeBon, McDougall, Freud, Burrow, Lewin, Moreno, and Slavson. Other papers focus on psychoanalysis and group therapy. Glossary.

Katz, Alfred H., and Bender, Eugene I. "Self-help Groups in Western Society: History and Prospects." JOURNAL OF APPLIED BEHAVIORAL SCIENCE 12 (July-August-September 1976): 265-82.

Kazdin, Alan E. HISTORY OF BEHAVIOR MODIFICATION. Baltimore: University Park Press, 1978. 480 p.

Kazdin, Alan E., and Pulaski, Joan L. "Joseph Lancaster and Behavior Modification in Education." JOURNAL OF THE HISTORY OF THE BEHAVIORAL SCIENCES 13 (July 1977): 261-66.

> Describes a learning system used in England in the early 1800s which employed a type of token economy and student monitors who were responsible for small groups. Discusses criticisms and the demise of the system.

Kovacs, Arthur L. "Perspectives on Psychotherapy in the United States." REVISTA INTER-AMERICANA DE PSICOLOGIA 9 (1975): 59-88.

Kudlien, Fridolf. "The Old Greek Concept of 'Relative' Health." JOURNAL OF THE HISTORY OF THE BEHAVIORAL SCIENCES 9 (January 1973): 53-59.

> Traces themes in Greek thought on the concepts of perfect health and relative health. Reinforces the notion that society conditions our concept of health.

Leitenberg, Harold, ed. HANDBOOK OF BEHAVIOR MODIFICATION AND BEHAVIOR THERAPY. Englewood Cliffs, N.J.: Prentice-Hall, 1976. 688 p.

> A major work containing contributions from many well-known authorities. Outlines recent clinical developments and research in such areas as alcoholism, eating disorders, behavioral treatment of the neuroses, depression, sexual disorders, behavior modification with psychotic children, mental retardation, juvenile delinquency, behavioral intervention in the preschool, behavior modification in school, behavioral technology, and ethical issues and future trends in behavior modification.

Levine, Murray, and Levine, Adeline. "The More Things Change: A Case History of Child Guidance Clinics." JOURNAL OF SOCIAL ISSUES 26 (Summer 1970): 19-34.

Lindner, Robert. THE FIFTY-MINUTE HOUR; A COLLECTION OF TRUE PSYCHOANALYTIC TALES. New York: Bantam Books, 1955. xiv, 207 p.

Lubin, Bernard, and Lubin, Alice W. GROUP PSYCHOTHERAPY: BIBLIOGRAPHY OF THE LITERATURE FROM 1956 THROUGH 1964. East Lansing: Michigan State University Press, 1966. v, 186 p.

Lists some two thousand items published during the period 1956–1964 in the area of group psychotherapy. Arranged alphabetically by author for each year. Contains short supplementary lists for each year. Name and subject indexes.

Machovec, Frank J. "Hypnosis Before Mesmer." AMERICAN JOURNAL OF CLINICAL HYPNOSIS 17 (April 1975): 215–20.

Martin, Alexander R. "Old and New Psychotherapy: A Heuristic Approach." AMERICAN JOURNAL OF PSYCHOANALYSIS 36 (Winter 1976): 291–310.

Reviews the history of psychotherapy in terms of such categories as etymology of the term, exorcism, vitalism, and technology.

May, Rollo. "Historical and Philosophical Presuppositions for Understanding Therapy." In PSYCHOTHERAPY THEORY AND RESEARCH, by O. Hobart Mowrer et al., pp. 9–43. New York: Ronald Press, 1953.

Explores historical developments in psychotherapy with emphasis on attitudes toward therapy and types of therapies in Greek, Hellenistic, medieval, renaissance, and twentieth-century periods.

Moreno, J.L. "The Viennese Origins of the Encounter Movement, Paving the Way for Existentialism, Group Psychotherapy and Psychodrama." GROUP PSYCHOTHERAPY 22, nos. 1–2 (1969): 7–16.

Mowrer, O. Hobart. "Changing Conceptions of Neurosis and the Small Groups Movement." EDUCATION 97 (Fall 1976): 24–62.

Neugebauer, Richard. "Treatment of the Mentally Ill in Medieval and Early Modern England: A Reappraisal." JOURNAL OF THE HISTORY OF THE BEHAVIORAL SCIENCES 14 (April 1978): 158–69.

Claims that standard histories of psychiatry have often failed to give a representative picture of early views of mental illness. Shows that many early English legal records indicate humane and benevolent attitudes toward the mentally ill. Historians, however, have neglected these and other sources and presented a truncated view of attitudes toward the mentally ill.

Papageorgiou, Michael G. "Forms of Psychotherapy in Use in Ancient Greece and Among the Population of Modern Greece." PSYCHOTHERAPY AND PSYCHOSOMATICS 17 (1969): 114–18.

Parad, Libbie G. "Short-term Treatment: An Overview of Historical Trends, Issues, and Potentials." SMITH COLLEGE STUDIES IN SOCIAL WORK 41 (February 1971): 119–46.

Patch, Ian L. "Treatment or Punishment? A Nineteenth-Century Scandal." PSYCHOLOGICAL MEDICINE 6 (February 1976): 143-49.

Paterson, Gerry. "A Historical Review and Classification System of the New Group Therapies." WESTERN PSYCHOLOGIST 4 (1973): 79-87.

Pattie, Frank A. "Mesmer's Medical Dissertation and Its Debt to Mead's DE IMPERIO SOLIS AC LUNAE." JOURNAL OF THE HISTORY OF MEDICINE AND ALLIED SCIENCES 11 (July 1956): 275-87.

Pivnickie, D. "The Beginnings of Psychotherapy." JOURNAL OF THE HISTORY OF THE BEHAVIORAL SCIENCES 5 (July 1969): 238-47.

> Explores early Greek psychotherapeutic practices and theories, the emergence of the term "psychotherapy" in the late nineteenth century, and ambiguities regarding the role of the therapist.

Poulsen, Henrik. "Materialistic Conceptions of Cognition, the Principle of Reinforcement, and Skinnerian Behavior Therapy." SCANDINAVIAN JOURNAL OF PSYCHOLOGY 18, no. 1 (1977): 1-9.

Quen, Jacques M. "Case Studies in Nineteenth Century Scientific Rejection: Mesmerism, Perkinism, and Acupuncture." JOURNAL OF THE HISTORY OF THE BEHAVIORAL SCIENCES 11 (April 1975): 149-56.

> Provides historical background on Perkinism and acupuncture and notes that the three therapies--Mesmerism, Perkinism, and acupuncture--share the common fate of an absence of any "scientifically orthodox theory" which can explain their action.

Reik, Theodor. LISTENING WITH THE THIRD EAR: THE INNER EXPERIENCE OF A PSYCHOANALYST. New York: Grove Press, 1948. xiv, 514 p.

Rimm, David C., and Masters, John C. BEHAVIOR THERAPY: TECHNIQUES AND EMPIRICAL FINDINGS. New York: Academic Press, 1974. xvi, 513 p.

Rogers, Carl R. ON BECOMING A PERSON: A THERAPIST'S VIEW OF PSYCHOTHERAPY. Boston: Houghton Mifflin, 1961. xi, 420 p. Appendix. References. Index.

Rosen, George. "Mesmerism and Surgery: A Strange Chapter in the History of Anesthesia." JOURNAL OF THE HISTORY OF MEDICINE AND ALLIED SCIENCES 1 (October 1946): 527-50.

> Discusses contributions of Mesmerism, especially in shaping public attitudes on the concept of painless surgery.

Rosen, Gerald M., and Orenstein, Herbert. "A Historical Note on Thought Stopping." JOURNAL OF CONSULTING AND CLINICAL PSYCHOLOGY 44 (December 1976): 1016–17.

Rosenbaum, Max, and Snadowsky, Alvin. THE INTENSIVE GROUP EXPERIENCE: A GUIDE. New York: Free Press, 1976. xiv, 210 p.

Includes discussion of the historical roots of the group movement.

Ryan, Bruce A. "Jean-Jacques Rousseau and Behavior Control: The Technology of a Romantic Behaviorist." BEHAVIORISM 4 (Fall 1976): 245–56.

Sacks, James. "The Psychodramatic Approach." In GROUP PROCESS TODAY: EVALUATION AND PERSPECTIVE, edited by Donald S. Milman and George D. Goldman, pp. 137–45. Springfield, Ill.: Charles C Thomas, 1974.

Sager, Clifford J. "The Development of Marriage Therapy: An Historical Review." AMERICAN JOURNAL OF ORTHOPSYCHIATRY 36 (April 1966): 458–67.

Schneck, Jerome M. "Jean-Martin Charcot and the History of Experimental Hypnosis." JOURNAL OF THE HISTORY OF MEDICINE AND ALLIED SCIENCES 16 (July 1961): 297–305.

Contends that a generally high quality biography of Charcot by G. Guillain (J.M. CHARCOT, 1825–1893, SA VIE--SON OEUVRE, Paris: Masson et Cie, Libraries de l'Académie de Médecine, 1955) misrepresents Charcot's active contributions to experimental hypnosis.

Shafil, Mohammad. "A Precedent for Modern Psychotherapeutic Techniques: One Thousand Years Ago." AMERICAN JOURNAL OF PSYCHIATRY 128 (June 1972): 1581–84.

Smith, Edward. THE GROWING EDGE OF GESTALT THERAPY. New York: Mazel, 1976. xvi, 239 p.

Includes, among other material, a discussion of the history of gestalt therapy.

Smith, Edward W. "The Role of Early Reichian Theory in the Development of Gestalt Therapy." PSYCHOTHERAPY: THEORY, RESEARCH AND PRACTICE 12 (Fall 1975): 268–72.

Stone, Michael H. "Mesmer and His Followers: The Beginnings of Sympathetic Treatment of Childhood Emotional Disorders." HISTORY OF CHILDHOOD QUARTERLY: THE JOURNAL OF PSYCHOHISTORY 1 (Spring 1974): 659–79.

Thompson, Travis. "History of Treatment and Misconceptions Concerning the Mentally Retarded." In BEHAVIOR MODIFICATION OF THE MENTALLY RETARDED, edited by Travis Thompson and John Grabowski, pp. 3-15. New York: Oxford University Press, 1972.

> A brief history of the treatment and misconceptions concerning retardation. Emphasizes recent historical developments. References. Index.

Thoreson, Richard W. "The Evolution of Counselling." BRITISH JOURNAL OF GUIDANCE AND COUNSELING 2 (1974): 171-81.

Towery, O.B. "In Loco Parentis: The Child Model of Psychiatry, a Critique." INTERNATIONAL JOURNAL OF SOCIAL PSYCHIATRY 21 (Autumn 1975): 166-75.

> Discusses the history of a model in which the psychiatrist functions as the good parent while the patient functions as a child.

Wallin, J.E. Wallace. "Ph.D.s in Psychology Who Functioned As Clinical Psychologists Between 1896 and 1910." PSYCHOLOGICAL RECORD 11 (October 1961): 339-41.

> Lists fourteen individuals who served as clinicians during the period 1896-1910, giving school where PhD was earned and place of employment.

Weber, Robert J. "Contributions to the History of Psychology: XV. Uniformitarianism in Geology and Behavior Modification." PSYCHOLOGICAL REPORTS 34 (April 1974): 439-44.

Weyant, Robert G. "Lycurgus: The Father of Applied Psychology." AMERICAN PSYCHOLOGIST 22 (June 1967): 432-34.

> Relates the story of Lycurgus who is reputed to have served as king of Sparta and to have used a form of behavior modification to maintain discipline among his people during hardship.

Wolpe, Joseph, and Theriault, Norman. "Francois Leuret: A Progenitor of Behavior Therapy." JOURNAL OF BEHAVIOR THERAPY AND EXPERIMENTAL PSYCHIATRY 2 (March 1971): 19-21.

14. EDUCATIONAL PSYCHOLOGY

Psychology, with its emphasis on the study of such topics as learning, memory, and discrimination processes, has had a profound impact on educational theory and practice. Conversely, the educator's classroom has provided a natural laboratory for the psychologist interested in the application of the psychology of learning. Accordingly, the alliance between education and psychology produced the emergence of the interdisciplinary area of educational psychology. This section contains a small selection of articles on the history of educational psychology and major earlier texts in educational psychology.

Cameron, Edward Herbert, ed. VIEWPOINTS IN EDUCATIONAL PSYCHOLOGY: A BOOK OF SELECTED READINGS. New York: Century, 1930. xxv, 511 p.

> A valuable work both to educational and to systematic psychology. Presents contrasting treatments of a broad range of problems in educational psychology such as the nature and scope of psychology, original human nature, individual differences, intelligence, and topics in learning. An example of the approach is found in chapter 1, which contains statements by Titchener, Angell, Watson, Judd, and William James on the nature and scope of psychology. Index.

Dewey, John. PSYCHOLOGY AND SOCIAL PRACTICE. Chicago: University of Chicago Press, 1901. 42 p.

> Explores the relation of psychology to education with an emphasis on the objectivity psychology can bring to educational practice. Presidential address delivered to the American Psychological Association in 1899.

Guthrie, Edwin Ray, and Powers, Francis F. EDUCATIONAL PSYCHOLOGY. New York: Ronald Press, 1950. vi, 530 p.

> A comprehensive text drawing heavily from learning theory. Presents psychological principles which are applicable to educational settings. Index.

James, William. TALKS TO TEACHERS ON PSYCHOLOGY: AND TO STUDENTS ON SOME OF LIFE'S IDEALS. 1899. Reprint. New York: Dover Publications, 1962. xi, 301 p.

> Based on lectures originally delivered to Cambridge teachers on such practical educational concerns as habit, association, attention, and memory. Talks to students are on topics in relaxation, perceptual selectivity, and the significance of life.

Johanningmeier, Erwin V. "William Chandler Bagley's Changing Views on the Relationship Between Psychology and Education." HISTORY OF EDUCATION QUARTERLY 9 (Spring 1969): 3-27.

Judd, Charles H[ubbard]. EDUCATIONAL PSYCHOLOGY. New York: Houghton Mifflin, 1939. xx, 566 p.

> A major comprehensive text covering the traditional content areas

of educational psychology. Emphasizes the importance of group influence on development. Index.

Kagan, Jacob M. "How Psychology Stimulates Education Now (B.F. Skinner) and Then (William James)." PSYCHOLOGY IN THE SCHOOLS 8 (October 1971): 368-73.

Kaur, Amrit. "History of Educational Psychology in the U.S.A. during 1880-1940." INDIAN EDUCATIONAL REVIEW 7 (1972): 123-40.

McMurray, J.G. "Two Decades of School Psychology: Past and Future." CANADIAN PSYCHOLOGIST 8 (1967): 207-17.

Morgan, C[onwy].Lloyd. PSYCHOLOGY FOR TEACHERS. 2d ed. New York: Charles Scribner's Sons, 1906. xiii, 307 p.

Attempts to outline psychological principles which may be applied to the teaching-learning process. Index.

Muensterberg, Hugo. PSYCHOLOGY AND THE TEACHER. New York: Appleton, 1910. xii, 330 p.

Applies the principles of psychology to assist the teacher in understanding such topics as memory, attention, will, feeling, individual differences, and association. Includes a lengthy section on ethics and values and a final section on the work of the school (instruction, curriculum development, school organization). Index.

Muschinske, David. "The Nonwhite as Child. G. Stanley Hall on the Education of Nonwhite Peoples." JOURNAL OF THE HISTORY OF THE BEHAVIORAL SCIENCES 13 (October 1977): 328-36.

Hall proposed education for nonwhite peoples, but nevertheless, reflected the spirit of the times which advocated subservience.

Nance, R. Dale. "Contributions to the History of Psychology: XVIII. William H. Burnham: Forgotten Psychologist and Educational Pioneer." PSYCHOLOGICAL REPORTS 35 (August 1974): 147-51.

NATIONAL COUNCIL ON MEASUREMENT USED IN EDUCATION YEARBOOK. East Lansing, Mich.: 1939-63. 20 vols. National Council on Measurement in Education, 1939-63. 20 vols.

Contains reports or proceedings of meetings of the council. Subject matter pertains to tests and testing in education. Volumes 1939/41-59 published under the title NATIONAL COUNCIL ON MEASUREMENTS USED IN EDUCATION. Membership list. Superceded by JOURNAL OF EDUCATIONAL MEASUREMENT.

National Herbart Society. See National Society for the Study of Education (next entry).

NATIONAL SOCIETY FOR THE STUDY OF EDUCATION: YEARBOOK. Chicago: University of Chicago Press, 1895-- .

> 1895-1909 published by Society under its earlier names: National Herbart Society and National Society for the Scientific Study of Education. Each yearbook deals with a particular issue or problem in education, many of which pertain to psychology. For example, Twenty-seventh Yearbook, 1928, part I "Nature and Nurture: Their Influence Upon Intelligence" and part II "Nature and Nurture: Their Influence Upon Achievement"; Forty-first Yearbook, 1942, part II "The Psychology of Learning"; Seventy-fifth Yearbook, 1976, part I "Psychology of Teaching Methods."

Ogden, Robert Morris. PSYCHOLOGY AND EDUCATION. New York: Harcourt, Brace, 1926. xiii, 364 p.

> A textbook for educational psychology explicitly based on the then-relatively new Gestalt psychology, especially Koffka's thought in his THE GROWTH OF THE MIND (see section C11a, p. 331), which Ogden had translated from the German two years earlier. Index.

Pillsbury, Walter Bowers. EDUCATION AS THE PSYCHOLOGIST SEES IT. New York: Macmillan, 1925. 342 p.

Sully, James. OUTLINES OF PSYCHOLOGY, WITH SPECIAL REFERENCE TO THE THEORY OF EDUCATION. Rev. ed. New York: D. Appleton, 1895. xvii, 524 p.

> See annotation in section D10b, p. 333.

Thorndike, Edward L. EDUCATIONAL PSYCHOLOGY. 3 vols. New York: Teachers College, Columbia University, 1913-14.

> A large classic work intended to cover the facts of educational psychology. Deals with inherited capacities in volume 1, the laws of learning in volume 2, and individual differences in volume 3. Part 2 of volume 3 is a revision of Thorndike's EDUCATIONAL PSYCHOLOGY, first published in 1903, revised in 1910. Bibliography.

_____. EDUCATIONAL PSYCHOLOGY. New York: Teachers College, Columbia University, 1914. xii, 422 p.

> An abbreviated version of Thorndike's three-volume EDUCATIONAL PSYCHOLOGY (see preceding entry) covering inherent capacities, the psychology of learning, and individual differences. Bibliography. Index.

Van Fleet, Alanson A. "Charles Judd's Psychology of Schooling." ELEMEN-TARY SCHOOL JOURNAL 76 (May 1976): 455–63.

> Reviews Judd's contributions to educational psychology.

Venezky, Richard L. "Research on Reading Processes: A Historical Perspective." AMERICAN PSYCHOLOGIST 32 (May 1977): 339–45.

> Provides a brief historical overview of research on reading from the 1880s to post-1950s developments.

Watson, Robert I. "A Brief History of Educational Psychology." PSYCHO-LOGICAL RECORD 11 (October 1961): 209–42.

> Reviews ideas on educational psychology prior to the founding of psychology as a separate discipline and developments between 1880 and 1900, focusing on the contributions of such pioneers as Galton, Hall, James, Cattell, Binet, and Dewey. An "incubation period" from 1900 to 1918 saw the first specialists in educational psychology--Edward L. Thorndike and Charles H. Judd. Summarizes major events from 1918 (research, development of tests, influence of schools of psychology, development of courses) to 1941. Comments on the practical application and breadth of educational psychology and the paucity of sources on the history of educational psychology.

15. INDUSTRIAL PSYCHOLOGY

Psychology has been applied to practical problems in business, industry, and organizations for more than two-thirds of a century. The entries in this section include items specifically relevant to the history of industrial psychology, a few standard early texts, works about major contributors to the field, and characterizations of industrial psychology in various geographic locations.

Achilles, Paul S[trong]. "Commemorative Address on the Twentieth Anniversary of the Psychological Corporation and to Honor Its Founder, James McKeen Cattell." JOURNAL OF APPLIED PSYCHOLOGY 25 (December 1941): 609–18.

_____. COURSE IN PSYCHOLOGY IN BUSINESS. New York: Columbia University Press, 1929. 12 pamphlets.

> Each of twelve separately bound brief paperbacks ranging in length from thirteen to thirty-one pages, includes a monthly lesson, supplementary reading, and occasional exercises. A home study extension course organized into an introduction and four major parts: psychological foundations (three lessons), production psychology (two lessons), employment psychology (three lessons), and financial and marketing psychology (three lessons).

Anastasi, Anne. FIELDS OF APPLIED PSYCHOLOGY. New York: McGraw-Hill, 1964. xi, 621 p.

Provides a comprehensive overview of the work of applied psychologists, discussing their professional activities in business, industry, advertising and marketing, education, clinical practice, counseling, law, medicine, government, and the military services.

ANNALS OF THE AMERICAN ACADEMY OF POLITICAL AND SOCIAL SCIENCE 110 (November 1923): entire issue.

The entire issue is devoted to articles on "Psychology in Business" divided into three parts: psychology and the worker; psychology and the consumer; and agencies for psychological research in business.

Baritz, Loren. THE SERVANTS OF POWER: A HISTORY OF THE USE OF SOCIAL SCIENCE IN AMERICAN INDUSTRY. Middletown, Conn.: Wesleyan University Press, 1960. 273 p.

Bartlett, F.C. "Fifty Years of Psychology." OCCUPATIONAL PSYCHOLOGY 29 (1955): 203-16.

Beach, Leslie R[obert]., and Elon, L. Clark. PSYCHOLOGY IN BUSINESS. New York: McGraw-Hill, 1959. ix, 313 p. Index.

Chapanis, Alphonse. MAN-MACHINE ENGINEERING. Belmont, Calif.: Wadsworth, 1965. ix. 134 p.

A brief, popular survey of human factors engineering and engineering psychology. References. Index.

Chapanis, Alphonse; Garner, Wendell R.; and Morgan, Clifford T. APPLIED EXPERIMENTAL PSYCHOLOGY: HUMAN FACTORS IN ENGINEERING DESIGN. New York: John Wiley and Sons, 1949. xi, 434 p.

Cumming, Gordon, and Corkindale, Kenneth. "Human Factors in the United Kingdom." HUMAN FACTORS 11 (February 1969): 75-79.

Dear, Tom Hatherley. "Industrial Psychology As I Have Seen It." OCCUPATIONAL PSYCHOLOGY, LONDON 22 (1948): 107-17.

A brief history of industrial psychology in England.

Dunnette, Marvin D., ed. HANDBOOK OF INDUSTRIAL AND ORGANIZATIONAL PSYCHOLOGY. Chicago: Rand McNally, 1976. xxvii, 1,740 p.

A massive work attempting to present the domain of industrial and organizational psychology. Thirty-seven chapters written by forty-five authors. Presents materials on theory, issues, methodology, research findings in major content areas of industrial and organizational psychology, and the practice of industrial and organizational psychology. References. Index.

Erdely, Michael, and Grossman, Frank. DICTIONARY OF TERMS AND EXPRESSIONS OF INDUSTRIAL PSYCHOLOGY ("PSYCHOTECHNICS") IN GERMAN, ENGLISH, FRENCH, HUNGARIAN. New York: Pitman, 1939. viii, 98 p.

A four-language dictionary of some 1,800 words and phrases arranged alphabetically for the German version of each term. Presents by implication an impression of the state of industrial psychology as of the late 1930s. Indexes in English, French, and Hungarian.

Ewer, Bernard C. APPLIED PSYCHOLOGY. New York: Macmillan, 1923. xii, 480 p.

A relatively early textbook with questions, exercises, and a list of books on applied psychology. Organized into four parts: aims, principles, and methods; education and everyday life; mind and health; and industry and commerce. Index.

Ferguson, Leonard W. THE HERITAGE OF INDUSTRIAL PSYCHOLOGY. Hartford, Conn.: Finlay Press, 1963-1968.

A series of paperbound pamphlets constituting chapters in the history of industrial psychology, mostly devoted to individuals who made a major contribution to the field.

_____. "A Look Across the Years 1920 to 1950." In APPLICATIONS OF PSYCHOLOGY, edited by L.L. Thurstone, pp. 1-17. New York: Harper, 1952.

A brief history of applications of industrial psychology in the life insurance business.

Frisby, C.B. "The Development of Industrial Psychology at the NIIP." OCCUPATIONAL PSYCHOLOGY 44 (1970): 35-50.

Provides "a brief account of the research and advisory work of the National Institute of Industrial Psychology as it developed over fifty years."

Fryer, D.H., and Henry, E.R. HANDBOOK OF APPLIED PSYCHOLOGY. 2 vols. New York: Rinehart, 1950.

Over one hundred papers organized into eighteen chapters. Presents materials on a broad range of topics in applied psychology including personnel, industrial, business, educational, clinical, and consulting psychology. Extensive bibliography.

Guilford, J.P., ed. FIELDS OF PSYCHOLOGY   New York: D. Van Nostrand, 1940. 3rd ed., 1966.

See annotation in section D1, p. 251.

Kappauf, William E. "History of Psychological Studies of the Design and Operation of Equipment." AMERICAN PSYCHOLOGIST 2 (March 1947): 83-86.

Provides a brief account of the involvement of psychologists during World War II in human engineering and human factors research.

Kavruck, Samuel. "Thirty-three Years of Test Research: A Short History of Test Development in the U.S. Civil Service Commission." AMERICAN PSYCHOLOGIST 11 (July 1956): 329-34.

Kuna, David P. "The Concept of Suggestion in the Early History of Advertising Psychology." JOURNAL OF THE HISTORY OF THE BEHAVIORAL SCIENCES 12 (October 1976): 347-53.

Outlines some of the early work on the psychology of advertising in the United States with special attention to the theory of Walter Dill Scott, who emphasized the role of suggestion and the irrational aspects of consumer behavior.

Landauer, Ali A., and Cross, Michael J. "A Forgotten Australian: Muscio's Contribution to Industrial Psychology." AUSTRALIAN JOURNAL OF PSYCHOLOGY 23 (December 1971): 235-40.

Likert, Rensis. NEW PATTERNS OF MANAGEMENT. New York: McGraw-Hill, 1961. ix, 271 p.

Focuses on problems of business enterprises. Presents a theory of organization, administration, and management based on the psychology of group dynamics. Index.

Louttit, C.M. "An Historical Note on the Application of Psychology." JOURNAL OF APPLIED PSYCHOLOGY 18 (April 1934): 304-5.

Lynch, Edmund C. WALTER DILL SCOTT: PIONEER IN PERSONNEL MANAGEMENT. Austin: University of Texas. Studies in Personnel and Management No. 20, Bureau of Business Research, 1968. ix, 51 p.

An appreciation of Scott concentrating on his contributions to personnel management and the social conditions under which they were made.

McCollom, Ivan N. "Industrial Psychology Around the World: I. America and Western Europe." INTERNATIONAL REVIEW OF APPLIED PSYCHOLOGY 17 (1968): 3-16.

McCormick, Ernest J., and Tiffin, Joseph. INDUSTRIAL PSYCHOLOGY. 6th ed. Englewood Cliffs, N.J.: Prentice-Hall, 1974. xii, 625 p.

> A comprehensive, widely-used text emphasizing the scientific and applied dimensions of industrial psychology. Index.

McGregor, Douglas. THE HUMAN SIDE OF ENTERPRISE. New York: McGraw-Hill, 1960. x, 246 p.

> Attempts to support the thesis that "the theoretical assumptions management holds about controlling its human resources determine the whole character of enterprise [and] the quality of its successive generations of management." Contrasts Theory X, the traditional view of direction and control as the function of management with the newer Theory Y, which strives to integrate individual and organizational goals.

Moskowitz, Merle J. "Hugo Muensterberg: A Study in the History of Applied Psychology." AMERICAN PSYCHOLOGIST 32 (October 1977): 824-42.

> Reviews Muensterberg's intellectual background and examines his contributions to such areas as psychotherapy, educational psychology, and industrial psychology.

Muensterberg, Hugo. PSYCHOLOGY AND INDUSTRIAL EFFICIENCY. New York: Houghton Mifflin, 1913. viii, 321 p.

> The English version of a German book published a few months earlier. One of the first relatively thorough expositions of the field of industrial psychology focusing on applied experimental psychology and the psychology of work. Index.

Muensterberg, Margaret. HUGO MUENSTERBERG: HIS LIFE AND WORK. New York: Appleton, 1922. xiii, 449 p.

> Contains an account of Muensterberg's life from early childhood through his years at Harvard. Appendices summarize his major work including his contributions to industrial psychology during specific periods of his life. Index.

Risse, Guenter B. "Vocational Guidance During the Depression: Phrenology versus Applied Psychology." JOURNAL OF THE HISTORY OF THE BEHAVIORAL SCIENCES 12 (April 1976): 130-40.

> Describes the development, design, and use of a "psychograph" for measuring phrenological divisions of the head. Outlines the

conflicts between the advocates of the psychograph and members of the psychological community.

Roethlisberger, Fritz Jules, and Dickson, William J., with the assistance of Harold A. Wright. MANAGEMENT AND THE WORKER. Cambridge, Mass.: Harvard University Press, 1967. xxiv, 615 p.

Provides a detailed account of the classic "Hawthorne Studies," experiments conducted for fifteen years at the Hawthorne works of the Western Electric Company in Chicago, showing that the quality of human relations is a far more important determinant of industrial productivity than illumination, pay rate, length of work day, or rest pauses.

Scott, Walter D[ill]. "The Psychology of Advertising." ATLANTIC MONTHLY, January 1904, pp. 29-36.

Outlines some of the history of advertising in magazines and discusses advantages (e.g., lowered cost) and principles of advertising.

Seashore, Carl Emil. PSYCHOLOGY IN DAILY LIFE. New York: Appleton, 1916. xviii, 226 p.

Presents applications of psychology to such areas as play, memory, mental efficiency, and mental health. Uses the measurement of singing ability as a prototype to demonstrate the significance of mental measurement. Lecture format.

Thorndike, Edward L. "The Psychology of Labor." HARPER'S MAGAZINE, May 1922, pp. 799-806.

Discusses trends in human nature which can be satisfied by work-related activities.

U.S. Personnel System. War Department. PERSONNEL SYSTEM OF UNITED STATES ARMY. Vol. 1: HISTORY OF PERSONNEL SYSTEM DEVELOPED BY COMMITTEE ON CLASSIFICATION OF PERSONNEL IN ARMY. Washington, D.C.: [Government Printing Office], 1919. viii, 713 p. Vol. 2: PERSONNEL MANUAL DEVELOPED BY COMMITTEE ON CLASSIFICATION OF PERSONNEL IN ARMY. Washington, D.C.: Government Printing Office, 1919. viii, 342 p.

16. DEVELOPMENT OF PSYCHOLOGY AS A PROFESSION

Psychology emerged as a separate academic discipline in the last quarter of the nineteenth century. Its identity as a distinct profession is much more recent. Several of the items listed in this section document psychology's efforts to define itself as an area of practice in the human service field, primarily in clinical settings. Additional relevant entries may be found in section D13, p. 353, on clinical psychology.

American Psychological Association. CASEBOOK ON ETHICAL STANDARDS OF PSYCHOLOGISTS. Washington, D.C.: 1967. x, 94 p.

> Presents cases of practices that raise ethical questions, organized around nineteen basic ethical principles that constituted the APA's 1963 Code of Ethics.

American Psychological Association. Committee for Ethical Standards in Psychology, eds. ETHICAL STANDARDS OF PSYCHOLOGISTS. Washington, D.C.: 1973. 8 p.

Blank, Leonard, and David, Henry P., eds. SOURCEBOOK FOR TRAINING IN CLINICAL PSYCHOLOGY. New York: Springer, 1964. ix, 337 p.

> Summarizes "evolving trends in clinical psychology training since World War II." Examines conclusions of previous training conferences (Boulder, Stanford, Miami, and Princeton) along with major training issues and growth trends in training resources. Appendixes include criteria for evaluating training programs in clinical and counseling psychology, and lists of APA-approved training programs and internships. Bibliography on clinical training 1955-63. References. Index.

Brown, A.W., et al. "Report of Committee of Clinical Section of American Psychological Association: I. The Definition of Clinical Psychology and Standards of Training for Clinical Psychologists. II. Guide to Psychological Clinics in the United States." PSYCHOLOGICAL CLINIC 23 (1935): 1-140.

Camfield, Thomas M. "The Professionalization of American Psychology, 1870-1917." JOURNAL OF THE HISTORY OF THE BEHAVIORAL SCIENCES 9 (January 1973): 66-75.

> Traces the professionalization of psychology in terms of the work of such key figures as Wundt, James, and Hall; the establishment of journals; the funding of associations; the production of PhDs; and the establishment of ties with the rest of the scientific community.

Carlson, Harold S. "The AASPB Story: The Beginnings and First Sixteen Years of the American Association of State Psychology Boards, 1961-1977." AMERICAN PSYCHOLOGIST 33 (May 1978): 486-95.

Cattell, J[ames]. McK[een]. "Retrospect: Psychology as a Profession." JOURNAL OF CONSULTING PSYCHOLOGY 1 (January-February 1937): 1-3.

Clark, Kenneth E. AMERICA'S PSYCHOLOGISTS. A SURVEY OF A GROW-
ING PROFESSION. Washington, D.C.: American Psychological Association,
1957. ix, 247 p.

> Report of a study carried out by the American Psychological Asso-
> ciation with the support of the National Science Foundation on
> variables influencing the productivity of psychologists. Includes
> an overview of the development and status of American psychology
> as of the mid-1950s. Index.

Clark, Kenneth E., and Miller, George A. PSYCHOLOGY. Englewood
Cliffs, N.J.: Prentice-Hall, 1970. ix, 146 p.

> Reports the results of a survey sponsored by the National Academy
> of Sciences and the Social Science Research Council focusing on
> the nature and usefulness of various fields of psychology, the
> growth of the discipline, support for psychological research, and
> education and training needs. Intended to provide data for na-
> tional policy decisions. Appendix lists departments participating
> in the survey.

Daniel, Robert S., and Louttit, C[hauncey].M. PROFESSIONAL PROBLEMS
IN PSYCHOLOGY. Englewood Cliffs, N.J.: Prentice-Hall, 1953. xv,
416 p. Index.

> Prepared primarily for graduate students. Covers topics such as
> literature sources in psychology, reporting psychological research,
> psychological organizations and professional fields of psychology.
> Includes appendixes covering reference books, journals, and
> sources of tests, equipment, and supplies. Index.

Finison, Lorenz J. "Unemployment, Politics, and the History of Organized
Psychology." AMERICAN PSYCHOLOGIST 31 (November 1976): 747-55.

> Discusses attempts to deal with the problem of unemployment of
> psychologists during the 1930s. Solutions polarized around attempts
> to reduce the number of PhDs produced versus attempts to expand
> job opportunities. Organizations such as the Psychologists' League
> and the Society for the Psychological Study of Social Issues had
> their origin in efforts to expand employment opportunities.

_____. "Unemployment, Politics, and the History of Organized Psychology,
II: The Psychologists' League, the WPA, and the National Health Program."
AMERICAN PSYCHOLOGIST 33 (May 1978): 471-77.

> Complementing Finison's previous work on the same topic (see
> preceding item), examines unemployment of psychologists during
> the Depression, and the rise and fall and contributions of the
> Psychologists' League.

Finn, Michael H.P., and Brown, Fred, eds. TRAINING FOR CLINICAL

PSYCHOLOGY: PROCEEDINGS OF THE SPRINGFIELD-MOUNT SINAI CON-
FERENCES ON INTERN TRAINING IN CLINICAL PSYCHOLOGY. New York:
International Universities Press, 1959. viii, 186 p.

> Fourteen papers exploring such topics as selection of interns,
> supervisor-intern relationships, university training of clinical psy-
> chologists, research training during the internship, psychotherapy
> and the intern, and evaluation of intern training. References.

Hoch, Erasmus L.; Ross, Alan V.; and Winder, C.L., eds. PROFESSIONAL
PREPARATION OF CLINICAL PSYCHOLOGISTS (THE CHICAGO CONFER-
ENCE). Washington, D.C.: American Psychological Association, 1966. viii,
154 p.

Kelly, Lowell E., and Fiske, Donald W. THE PREDICTION OF PERFOR-
MANCE IN CLINICAL PSYCHOLOGY. Ann Arbor: University of Michigan
Press, 1951. xv, 311 p.

> A thorough report of an early five-year research project studying
> graduate school selection procedures for clinical psychologists.
> Several objective and clinical selection procedures were evaluated
> for their ability to predict such skills as therapeutic competence,
> diagnostic competence, and academic achievement. Appendixes.
> Bibliography. Index.

Korman, Maurice, ed. LEVELS AND PATTERNS OF PROFESSIONAL TRAIN-
ING IN PSYCHOLOGY: CONFERENCE PROCEEDINGS, VAIL, COLORADO,
JULY 25-30, 1973. Washington, D.C.: American Psychological Association,
1976. viii, 163 p.

Raimy, Victor C., ed. and comp. TRAINING IN CLINICAL PSYCHOLOGY.
Englewood Cliffs, N.J.: Prentice-Hall, 1950. xix, 253 p.

> Seventy-three persons experienced in the training of clinical psy-
> chologists met in Boulder, Colorado, in 1949 to discuss problems
> of training clinical psychologists. Topics considered include levels
> of training, professional ethics, undergraduate background training,
> research training, training in psychotherapy, relations with other
> professions, accreditation, licensing, and current issues. The
> conference recommended a scientist/professional training model.
> Appendixes include a list of participants and the 1947 Report of
> the Committee on Clinical Training of the American Psychological
> Association (the Shakow Report.) Bibliography. Index.

Roe, Anne, et al. GRADUATE EDUCATION IN PSYCHOLOGY. Washington,
D.C.: American Psychological Association, 1959. 97 p.

> Report of a conference sponsored by the Education and Training
> Board of the American Psychological Association. Explores roles
> of psychologists; core topics in the training of psychologists in-

cluding languages, ethics, and research; such specialty training areas as practicum and postdoctoral training; nondoctoral training; and controls of training such as accreditation. Appendixes include a list of conference participants and data on participants. References.

Strother, Charles R., ed. PSYCHOLOGY AND MENTAL HEALTH: A REPORT OF THE INSTITUTE ON EDUCATION AND TRAINING FOR PSYCHOLOGICAL CONTRIBUTIONS TO MENTAL HEALTH, HELD AT STANFORD UNIVERSITY IN AUGUST, 1955. Washington, D.C.: American Psychological Association, 1956. v, 154 p.

Wallin, J.E. W[allace]. "History of the Struggles Within the American Psychological Association to Attain Membership Requirements, Test Standardization, Certification of Psychological Practitioners, and Professionalization." JOURNAL OF GENERAL PSYCHOLOGY 63 (October 1960): 287-308.

> Discusses major disputes, deliberations, and actions pertaining to the professional issues indicated in the title, which occurred within the APA during its first sixty years of operation.

_____. "A Red-Letter Day in APA History." JOURNAL OF GENERAL PSYCHOLOGY 75 (July 1966): 107-14.

> Describes an early attempt to form a professional organization in clinical psychology and the influence of that attempt on the subsequent development of a clinical section (later called division) of the APA. Outlines the historical development of other professional organizations such as the American Board of Examiners in Professional Psychology.

Webb, Wilse B., ed. THE PROFESSION OF PSYCHOLOGY. New York: Holt, Rinehart and Winston, 1962. viii, 291 p.

> Separate chapters by experts characterize psychology and psychologists in colleges and universities, clinics, institutions, independent practice, schools, industry, government agencies, and other professions. Discusses misconceptions of psychology, antecedents of modern psychology, training and employment of psychologists, and psychology and the public. Appendix on psychology in other countries. Index.

Wellner, Alfred M., ed. EDUCATION & CREDENTIALING IN PSYCHOLOGY: PROPOSAL FOR A NATIONAL COMMISSION ON EDUCATION AND CREDENTIALING IN PSYCHOLOGY. Washington, D.C.: American Psychological Association, 1978. iv, 137 p.

Section E

HISTORIES OF RELATED FIELDS

Psychology grew out of developments in other disciplines, particularly physiology and philosophy. The parentage of the young science is, however, sufficiently broad that histories, not only of physiology and philosophy, but also of education, statistics, sociology, and general science are relevant to an understanding of its origins. The works included in this section further elucidate the historical development of psychology by clarifying contributions of other disciplines.

1. PHILOSOPHY

Philosophers struggled with psychological problems centuries before the birth of psychology as an independent discipline. Accordingly, inquiry into the history of psychology cannot be separated from inquiry into the history of philosophy. The following materials include some standard comprehensive textbooks in the history of philosophy, a few specialized histories, and numerous articles describing the contributions and positions of philosophers on specific psychological issues. Special attention is called to Edwards's eight-volume encyclopedia of philosophy (p. 380) and Copleston's nine-volume history of philosophy (this page), both useful historical sources for psychologists.

a. Histories of Philosophy

Cassirer, Ernest. THE PHILOSOPHY OF THE ENLIGHTENMENT. Translated by Fritz C.A. Koelln and James R. Pettegrove. Princeton, N.J.: Princeton University Press, 1951. xiii, 366 p. Bibliographical materials in footnotes.

Copleston, Frederick Charles. A HISTORY OF PHILOSOPHY. Rev. ed. 9 vols. New York: Newman Press, 1966-75. Originally published in 8 vols., 1946-66.

> Acclaimed by many as the standard work on the history of western philosophy. Covers Greece and Rome (volume 1); medieval philosophy, Augustine to Bonaventure in part 1 and Albert the Great to

Duns Scotus in part 2 (volume 2); late medieval and renaissance philosophy, Ockham to the speculative mystics in part 1 and the revival of Platonism to Suarez in part 2 (volume 3); modern philosophy, Descartes to Leibniz (volume 4); modern philosophy, the British philosophers, Hobbes to Paley in part 1 and Berkeley to Hume in part 2 (volume 5); modern philosophy, the French enlightenment to Kant in part 1 and Kant in part 2 (volume 6); modern philosophy, Fichte to Hegel in part 1 and Schopenhauer to Nietzsche in part 2 (volume 7); and modern philosophy, Bentham to Russell, British empiricism and the idealist movement in Great Britain in part 1 and idealism in America, the pragmatist movement, the revolt against idealism in part 2 (volume 8); and Maine de Biran to Sartre (volume 9). Notes. Bibliography. Index.

Durant, Will. THE STORY OF PHILOSOPHY: THE LIVES AND OPINIONS OF THE GREAT PHILOSOPHERS. New York: Simon and Schuster, 1926. xiii, 586 p.

Not intended as a comprehensive history. Focuses on the contributions of selected great philosophers. Chapters on Plato, Aristotle, Herbert Spencer, William James, and John Dewey of special interest to psychologists. Notes. Bibliographical materials. Index.

Edwards, Paul, ed. THE ENCYCLOPEDIA OF PHILOSOPHY. 8 vols. New York: Macmillan, 1967.

A major authoritative reference work containing over 1,500 articles by some five hundred contributors. Includes articles on contributions of individual thinkers, interface between philosophy and other disciplines, historical development of many topics, contributions to philosophy by people representing other disciplines, and major constructs and theories in philosophy. Cross references. Biographical and bibliographical materials. Index.

Merz, John Theodore. A HISTORY OF EUROPEAN THOUGHT IN THE 19TH CENTURY. PART II: PHILOSOPHICAL THOUGHT. Vols. 3-4. London: William Blackwood, 1904-12.

Provides a thorough overview of nineteenth-century philosophical writings. Index. (For first two volumes, see section E5, p. 417).

Persons, Stow. AMERICAN MINDS; A HISTORY OF IDEAS. New York: Holt, 1958. xii, 467 p.

A history of American thought divided into five parts: the colonial religious mind 1620-1660, the mind of the American enlightenment 1740-1812, the mind of nineteenth-century democracy 1800-1860, the naturalistic mind 1865-1929, and the contemporary neodemocratic mind. Suggestions for further reading. Index.

Riley, I. Woodbridge. AMERICAN PHILOSOPHY: THE EARLY SCHOOLS. New York: Russell and Russell, 1958. x, 595 p.

An overview of American puritanism, idealism, deism, materialism, and realism with a presentation of some of the major constructs of selected important philosophers in these traditions. Notes. Bibliographic materials in footnotes. Index.

Runes, Dagobert D. PICTORIAL HISTORY OF PHILOSOPHY. New York: Philosophical Library, 1959. x, 406 p.

Presents brief biographical statements followed by highlights of the philosophical views of over seven hundred philosophers representing ancient Greek, Indian and Judaic cultures, the Middle Ages, the world of Islam, and modern countries including France, Italy, Great Britain, Germany, Russia, and America. Over nine hundred pictures and illustrations accompany the text. Includes many early psychologists. Index.

_____, ed. TWENTIETH CENTURY PHILOSOPHY: LIVING SCHOOLS OF THOUGHT. New York: Philosophical Library, 1947. 571 p.

Includes twenty-two papers on a diversity of topics. Among those of interest to psychologists are "The Development of American Pragmatism" by John Dewey, "Phenomenology" by Marvin Farber, "Logical Empiricism" by Herbert Feigl, "Philosophy of the Twentieth Century" by Bertrand Russell, and "Philosophy of Science" by Victor F. Lenzen. References.

Russell, Bertrand. A HISTORY OF WESTERN PHILOSOPHY, AND ITS CONNECTION WITH POLITICAL AND SOCIAL CIRCUMSTANCES FROM THE EARLIEST TIMES TO THE PRESENT DAY. New York: Simon and Schuster, 1945. xxiii, 895 p.

A comprehensive history of philosophy emphasizing heritages which shaped philosophical thought as well as the influence of philosophical thought. Rich in general history. Minimal bibliographic materials in footnotes. Index.

_____. WISDOM OF THE WEST: A HISTORICAL SURVEY OF WESTERN PHILOSOPHY IN ITS SOCIAL AND POLITICAL SETTING. Edited by Paul Foulkes. New York: Crescent Books, 1959. 320 p.

A richly-illustrated work tracing the development of Western thought from the pre-Socratic philosophers to major trends in twentieth-century philosophy.

Schneider, Herbert W. A HISTORY OF AMERICAN PHILOSOPHY. New York: Columbia University Press, 1946. xiv, 646 p.

Explores major trends in American philosophic thought from the platonic heritage of the puritans to radical empiricism. Includes materials on liberty, nationalism and democracy, faculty psychology, transcendentalism, idealism, and evolution and human progress. Bibliographical materials. Index.

Tsanoff, Radoslav A. THE GREAT PHILOSOPHERS. 2d ed. New York: Harper and Row, 1964. x, 581 p.

A text in the history of Western philosophy covering the thought of the great philosophers from the early Greek cosmologists to twentieth-century contributors. Index.

b. Psychological Teachings of Selected Philosophers and the Influence of Philosophy on the Development of Psychology

Special attention is called to the book compiled by Benjamin Rand, THE CLASSICAL PSYCHOLOGISTS (see below, this section; also listed in section B4, p. 51), which provides an excellent overview of the psychological teachings of many philosophers.

Altschule, Mark D. "The Pneuma Concept of the Soul." JOURNAL OF THE HISTORY OF THE BEHAVIORAL SCIENCES 1 (October 1965): 314-20.

Traces the pneuma and closely related concepts of soul in writings representing such cultures as the early Greek, Hindu, Chinese, Egyptian, Christian, and Roman.

Aquinas, St. Thomas. See Gardeil, H.D., p. 387.

Augustine, Saint. BASIC WRITINGS OF SAINT AUGUSTINE. 2 vols. Edited by Whitney Oates. New York: Random House, 1948. Vol. 1, xl, 847 p.; Vol. 2, 898 p.

Provides a comprehensive portrait of St. Augustine's thought. An editorial introduction provides a background on St. Augustine's life and a basis for interpreting his writings. Of particular interest to psychologists is THE CONFESSIONS (volume 1). Editorial notes. Index.

Bacon, Francis. THE WORKS OF FRANCIS BACON. 14 vols. Edited by James Spedding et al. 1874. Reprint. New York: Garrett Press, 1968.

Divided into three major parts: philosophy and general literature (in Latin), volumes 1-3; (translated) volumes 4-5; literary and professional works, volumes 6-7; and letters, speeches, and other occasional matters, volumes 8-14. Brief biography in volume 1. Extensive notes and editorial comments. Indexes for each of the three major divisions.

Bain, Bruce. "Goethe is Different Things to Different People: A Note." JOURNAL OF THE HISTORY OF THE BEHAVIORAL SCIENCES 8 (October 1972): 418.

Cites claims that Goethe anticipated behavior therapy, Adlerian therapy, psychoanalytic therapy, and other psychological concepts, and comments on the problem of selective perception when scientists claim that earlier figures anticipated later developments.

Baumrin, Judith Marti. "Aristotle's Empirical Nativism." AMERICAN PSYCHOLOGIST 30 (April 1975): 486-94.

Points to similarities between Aristotelian thought and such modern theories as "Piaget's stages in the development of ideas about objects" and "Chomsky's theory of innate linguistic structures." Argues that "Aristotelian psychology is grounded in both empiricist and nativist principles." This interpretation is in contrast to that in an earlier article by Weimer (AMERICAN PSYCHOLOGIST, see below, this section, p. 397).

Beare, John I. GREEK THEORIES OF ELEMENTARY COGNITION FROM ALCMAEON TO ARISTOTLE. Oxford, Engl.: Oxford University Press, 1906. Reprint. New York: Irvington Publishers, 1977. 354 p.

Bentham, Jeremy. THE WORKS OF JEREMY BENTHAM. 11 vols. Edited by John Bowring. New York: Russell and Russell, 1962.

Among the material of special interest to psychologists in this eleven-volume set are articles on the springs of action (volume 1), principles of penal law (volume 1), the rationale of reward (volume 2), principles of international law (volume 2), an essay on language (volume 8), memoirs of Bentham (volume 10), and autobiographical materials (volume 11). Specific works introduced with helpful editorial comments. Index.

Bernard, Walter. "Spinoza's Influence on the Rise of Scientific Psychology: A Neglected Chapter in the History of Psychology." JOURNAL OF THE HISTORY OF THE BEHAVIORAL SCIENCES 8 (April 1972): 208-15.

Suggests that Spinoza's position on the mind-body problem, commitment to psychic determinism, views on psychological issues, and strong influence on some of the eminent individuals directly involved in the founding of psychology indicate that he made a greater contribution than Descartes to the founding of psychology.

Bidney, David. THE PSYCHOLOGY AND ETHICS OF SPINOZA: A STUDY IN THE HISTORY AND LOGIC OF IDEAS. 2d ed. New York: Russell and Russell, 1962. xv, 454 p.

A comprehensive and critical examination of Spinoza's treatment of the psychology of emotions and an assessment of Spinoza's impact on modern thought. Index.

Bongie, Laurence L. "A New Condillac Letter and the Genesis of the Traité des Sensations." JOURNAL OF THE HISTORY OF PHILOSOPHY 16 (January 1978): 83-94.

Brecher, Edward M. "Conatus in Spinoza's Ethics." PSYCHOLOGICAL REVIEW 40 (July 1933): 288-90.

Brennan, R.E. THOMISTIC PSYCHOLOGY; A PHILOSOPHIC ANALYSIS OF THE NATURE OF MAN. New York: Macmillan, 1941. xxvi, 401 p.

Brooks, Garland P. "The Faculty Psychology of Thomas Reid." JOURNAL OF THE HISTORY OF THE BEHAVIORAL SCIENCES 12 (January 1976): 65-77.

Compares previous interpretations of Thomas Reid's use of the term "faculty," attempts to clarify Reid's use of the term, and presents his enumeration and classification of mental powers.

Broughton, Janet, and Mattern, Ruth. "Reinterpreting Descartes on the Notion of the Union of Mind and Body." JOURNAL OF THE HISTORY OF PHILOSOPHY 16 (January 1978): 23-32.

Brown, S.C., ed. PHILOSOPHY OF PSYCHOLOGY. New York: Barnes and Noble, 1974. xi, 351 p.

Papers and remarks from a 1971 conference at the University of Kent on such topics as free will and determinism, computer models in psychology, perception, human learning, action theory, and psychology as science. Index.

Buchner, Edward Franklin. "A Study of Kant's Psychology With Reference to the Critical Philosophy." PSYCHOLOGICAL REVIEW MONOGRAPH SUPPLEMENTS 1 (January 1897): viii, 208 p.

Burns, R.J. "Plato and the Soul." NEW SCHOLASTICISM 20 (1946): 334-43.

Cantor, G.N. "Berkeley, Reid, and the Mathematization of Mid-Eighteenth-Century Optics." JOURNAL OF THE HISTORY OF IDEAS 38 (July-September 1977): 429-48.

Cardno, J.A. "Auguste Comte's Psychology." PSYCHOLOGICAL REPORTS 4 (September 1958): 423-30.

Notes on Comte's rejection of introspection and a discussion of his "view of the soul" (e.g., motivational, emotional, and intel-

lectual processes), his ideas on phrenology, and his position on
the relative importance of studying overt and covert behavior.

Carini, Louis. "Ernst Cassirer's Psychology: A Unification of Perception and
Language." JOURNAL OF THE HISTORY OF THE BEHAVIORAL SCIENCES 9
(April 1973): 148-51.

> Cassirer's three-volume work, PHILOSOPHY OF SYMBOLIC FORM,
> contains much material on psychology. Carini's article presents
> some of Cassirer's ideas about perception and language and their
> unification.

_____. "Ernst Cassirer's Psychology: II. The Nature of Thinking." JOUR-
NAL OF THE HISTORY OF THE BEHAVIORAL SCIENCES 9 (July 1973): 266-
69.

> Explores Cassirer's theory of thinking with emphasis on inferential
> processes.

Charms, George de. "Swedenborg's Psychology." NEW PHILOSOPHY 43
(July 1940): 328-41.

Church, R.W. HUME'S THEORY OF THE UNDERSTANDING. Ithaca, N.Y.:
Cornell University Press, 1935. Reprint. Hamden, Conn.: Archon Books,
1968.

> An elucidation of Hume's theory of causal inference, basic ele-
> ments in his philosophy, and his analysis of knowledge and belief.
> An appendix presents materials on Hume's epistemology and his
> analysis of experience. Index.

Collier, Rex Madison. "The Minima Sensibilia in the History of the Threshold Concept." JOURNAL OF GENERAL PSYCHOLOGY 43 (October 1950):
231-43.

> Traces the history of the threshold concept from Aristotle through
> such writers as Leibniz, Herbart, Descartes, Hooke, and Berkeley.

Condillac, Etienne Bonnot de. AN ESSAY ON THE ORIGIN OF HUMAN
KNOWLEDGE. Translated by Thomas Nugent. London: J. Nourse, 1756.
Reprint. Gainesville, Fla.: Scholars' Facsimiles and Reprints, 1971. xx, liv
(translator's preface), 339 p.

> Condillac's classic defense and extension of Locke's ESSAY CON-
> CERNING HUMAN UNDERSTANDING.

_____. TREATISE ON THE SENSATIONS. Translated by Geraldine Carr.
Los Angeles: University of California School of Philosophy, 1930. xxvii,
250 p.

A classic work developing the tabula rasa approach to the origin of knowledge by an elaborate analogy of a statue imbued with a single sense in which all the usual human varieties of mental processes are aroused by appropriate sensory experiences.

Corbet, Hildegard, and Marshall, Marilyn E., trans. "The Comparative Anatomy of Angels. A Sketch by Dr. Mises: 1825." JOURNAL OF THE HISTORY OF THE BEHAVIORAL SCIENCES 5 (April 1969): 135-51.

Translates the text written by Fechner under the pseudonym Dr. Mises. Typical of Fechner's humorous and satirical discussions of the methods of speculative philosophy.

Day, Willard F. "On Certain Similarities Between the Philosophical Investigations of Ludwig Wittgenstein and the Operationalism of B.F. Skinner." JOURNAL OF THE EXPERIMENTAL ANALYSIS OF BEHAVIOR 12 (May 1969): 489-506.

Dempsey, Peter J.R. THE PSYCHOLOGY OF SARTRE. Cork, Ireland: Cork University Press, 1950. 174 p.

Denton, George Bion. "Early Psychological Theories of Herbert Spencer." AMERICAN JOURNAL OF PSYCHOLOGY 32 (January 1921): 5-15.

Descartes, René. DESCARTES' PHILOSOPHICAL LETTERS. Edited by Anthony Kenny. Translated by Anthony Kenny. Oxford, Engl.: Clarendon Press, 1970. xiii, 270 p.

One hundred letters, some reproduced in full and some in part, selected for their philosophical interest, presented with helpful editorial comment. An index identifies persons to whom the letters were sent.

_____. THE PHILOSOPHICAL WORKS OF DESCARTES. 2 vols. Translated by Elizabeth S. Haldane and G.R.T. Ross. New York: Dover, 1955.

Diamond, Solomon. "The Debt of Leibniz to Pardies." JOURNAL OF THE HISTORY OF THE BEHAVIORAL SCIENCES 8 (January 1972): 109-14.

Demonstrates that contacts between Leibniz and Pardies in Paris between 1672 and 1676 resulted in an "uncommon friendship," and that Pardies very likely had a profound influence on the concepts of petites perceptions and apperception later developed by Leibniz.

Feigl, Herbert, Scriven, Michael, and Maxwell, Grover, eds. MINNESOTA STUDIES IN THE PHILOSOPHY OF SCIENCE. Vol. 1. THE FOUNDATIONS OF SCIENCE AND THE CONCEPTS OF PSYCHOLOGY AND PSYCHOANALYSIS. Vol. 2. CONCEPTS, THEORIES, AND THE MIND-BODY PROBLEM. Minneapolis: University of Minnesota Press, 1956. xiv, 346 p.; xv, 553 p.

Ferguson, H.H. "Locke's Theory of Knowledge." AUSTRALASIAN JOURNAL OF PSYCHOLOGY AND PHILOSOPHY 12 (1934): 107-18, 186-98.

Fialko, Nathan. "Hegel's Views on Mental Derangement." JOURNAL OF ABNORMAL AND SOCIAL PSYCHOLOGY 25 (October-December 1930): 241-67.

Gardeil, H.D. INTRODUCTION TO THE PHILOSOPHY OF ST. THOMAS AQUINAS. 4 vols. Translated by John A. Otto. St. Louis, Mo.: B. Herder, 1967.

   Four volumes exploring the logic of St. Thomas (volume 1), his cosmology (volume 2), psychology (volume 3), and metaphysics (volume 4).

Garforth, Francis W., ed. JOHN LOCKE'S "OF THE CONDUCT OF UNDERSTANDING." New York: Teachers College Press, Columbia University, 1966. viii, 133 p.

Gavin, Eileen A. "The Causal Issue in Empirical Psychology from Hume to the Present, with Emphasis on the Work of Michotte." JOURNAL OF THE HISTORY OF THE BEHAVIORAL SCIENCES 8 (July 1972): 302-20.

   A brief statement of Hume's views on causality followed by a more detailed exposition of Albert Michotte's intellectual background and his research on the perception of causation. Bibliography of Michotte's published works.

Gouaux, Charles. "Kant's View on the Nature of Empirical Psychology." JOURNAL OF THE HISTORY OF THE BEHAVIORAL SCIENCES 8 (April 1972): 237-42.

   A description of Kant's analysis of natural science followed by his observations on empirical psychology and his conclusion that psychology could not use objective observation or experimentation.

Goudge, Thomas A. "The Views of Charles Peirce on the Given in Experience." JOURNAL OF PHILOSOPHY 32 (September 1935): 533-44.

Gray, Philip H. "The Nature of Man or Man's Place in Nature? Bruno, Spinoza, and LaMettrie." JOURNAL OF GENERAL PSYCHOLOGY 76 (April 1967): 183-92.

   Contains selected biographical materials on Bruno, Spinoza, and La Mettrie as well as brief accounts of their positions on the lawfulness of behavior and the relation of nature to the human species.

_____. "The Problem of Free Will in a Scientific Universe: René Descartes to John Tyndall." JOURNAL OF GENERAL PSYCHOLOGY 80 (January 1969): 57-72.

Histories of Related Fields

Examines selected topics in the free will–determinism controversy with emphasis on positions advanced by Descartes, Geulincx, Spinoza, Leibniz, La Mettrie, and Tyndall.

Griffin, A.K. ARISTOTLE'S PSYCHOLOGY OF CONDUCT. London: Williams Norgate, 1931. 186 p.

Hammond, Lewis M. "Plato on Scientific Measurement and the Social Sciences." PHILOSOPHICAL REVIEW 44 (September 1935): 435–47.

Hansing, O. "The Doctrine of Recollection in Plato's Dialogs." MONIST 38 (April 1928): 231–62.

Hinrichs, Gerard. "Maine de Biran on Psychology and Metaphysics." PERSONALIST 34 (April 1953): 124–32.

Hobbes, Thomas. LEVIATHAN: OR THE MATTER, FORME AND POWER OF A COMMONWEALTH ECCLESIASTICALL AND CIVIL. Edited with an introduction by Michael Oakeshott. Oxford, Engl.: Basil Blackwell, 1960. lxvii, 468 p.

A major treatise by Hobbes on political philosophy and also a classic (1651) in social psychology.

Jager, Marga, and Hoorn, Willem van. "Aristotle's Opinion on Perception in General." JOURNAL OF THE HISTORY OF THE BEHAVIORAL SCIENCES 8 (July 1972): 321–27.

A review of Aristotle's theory of perception followed by a discussion of its relationship to his theories of matter and form and of potentiality and actuality.

Johnson, A.H. "The Psychology of Alfred North Whitehead." JOURNAL OF GENERAL PSYCHOLOGY 32 (April 1945): 175–212.

Explores Whitehead's treatment of such psychological topics as the experiencing person, the relationship of mind and body, perception, consciousness, thinking, language, the importance of the environment, and freedom.

Kant, Immanuel. CRITIQUE OF PURE REASON. 2d ed. Translated by Norman Kemp Smith. London: Macmillan, 1963. xiii, 681 p.

Kant's classic systematic essay on the problem of human knowledge. Index.

Kaufman, M. Ralph. "The Greeks Had Some Words For It." PSYCHIATRIC QUARTERLY 40 (January 1966): 1–33.

An outline of early Greek psychological concepts.

Kenny, Anthony. THE ANATOMY OF THE SOUL: HISTORICAL ESSAYS IN THE PHILOSOPHY OF MIND. New York: Barnes and Noble, 1973. ix, 147 p.

Six essays exploring such topics as mental health in Plato's republic, Aristotle on happiness, Aquinas on intellect and imagination, and Descartes on the will. Bibliographical materials.

King, C. Daly. "The Lockean Error in Modern Psychology." JOURNAL OF GENERAL PSYCHOLOGY 38 (April 1948): 129-38.

Laing, B.M. "Hume and the Contemporary Theory of Instinct." MONIST 36 (October 1926): 645-66.

Laird, John. HUME'S PHILOSOPHY OF HUMAN NATURE. Hamden, Conn.: Archon Books, 1967 (1932). ix, 312 p.

Covers Hume's thoughts on such topics as memory, association, custom, imagination, abstract ideas, mind and body, ethics, politics, and economics. Brief biographical sketch in the introduction. Index.

Landes, Margaret W. "Thomas Brown: Associationist (?)." PHILOSOPHICAL REVIEW 35 (September 1926): 447-64.

Laughlin, Charles D., Jr. "Discussion: The Influence of Whitehead's Organism Upon Murray's Personology." JOURNAL OF THE HISTORY OF THE BEHAVIORAL SCIENCES 9 (July 1973): 251-57.

Traces the influence of Whitehead on Murray in such areas as ontology, the nature of time, and the essence of self or personality.

Leary, David E. "Berkeley's Social Theory: Context and Development." JOURNAL OF THE HISTORY OF IDEAS 38 (October-December 1977): 635-49.

_____. "The Philosophical Development of the Conception of Psychology in Germany, 1780-1850." JOURNAL OF THE HISTORY OF THE BEHAVIORAL SCIENCES 14 (April 1978): 113-21.

See annotation in section B5biv, p. 67.

Leibniz, Gottfried Wilhelm. GOTTFRIED WILHELM LEIBNIZ: PHILOSOPHICAL PAPERS AND LETTERS. 2d ed. Edited and translated by Leroy E. Loemker. Dordrecht, The Netherlands: D. Reidel, 1970. xii, 736 p.

Selections from a broad range of Leibniz's papers and letters preceded by a helpful introduction which discusses such topics as Leibniz's life and work; the seventeenth century; Leibniz's method,

psychology, ethics, biology, and theology; and his influence.
References. Index.

Lincourt, John M., and Hare, Peter H. "Neglected American Philosophers in
the History of Symbolic Interactionism." JOURNAL OF THE HISTORY OF THE
BEHAVIORAL SCIENCES 9 (October 1973): 333-38.

 Traces the contributions of such philosophers as Josiah Royce,
 Charles S. Peirce, and Chauncey Wright to symbolic interactionism.

Locke, John. AN ESSAY CONCERNING HUMAN UNDERSTANDING. Edited
by Peter H. Nidditch. Oxford, Engl.: Clarendon Press, 1975. liv, 867 p.

 The fourth edition of Locke's classic work presents his well-known
 position that all knowledge is derived from sensation. Index.

Loemker, L[eroy].E. "Leibniz's Search for Adequate Psychological Categories."
PSYCHOLOGICAL BULLETIN 37 (October 1940): 548-49.

Loukas, Christ. "The Psychology of Aristotle: A Logical Arrangement of his
De Anima and Allied Treatises (in Synoptic Form)." JOURNAL OF GENERAL
PSYCHOLOGY 6 (January 1932): 157-89.

 A brief description of Aristotle's life, metaphysics, and position on
 such psychological topics as the soul, the senses, memory, association, imagination, reason, emotions, and dreams.

Loveday, T. "Studies in the History of British Psychology." MIND 17 (1908):
493-501.

 An early criticism of Thomas Hobbes.

Mack, Robert D. THE APPEAL TO IMMEDIATE EXPERIENCE: PHILOSOPHIC
METHOD IN BRADLEY, WHITEHEAD AND DEWEY. New York: Kings
Crown Press, 1945. Reprint. Freeport, N.Y.: Books for Libraries Press,
1968. vi, 86 p.

 Explores the role of immediate experience in philosophic method,
 specifically the treatment of immediate experience by Bradley,
 Whitehead, and Dewey. Notes. Bibliographical materials.

MacKenzie, Brian. "Darwinism and Positivism as Methodological Influences
on the Development of Psychology." JOURNAL OF THE HISTORY OF THE
BEHAVIORAL SCIENCES 12 (October 1976): 330-37.

 Comments about the broadening effects of Darwinism on methodology in psychology and about the restricting effects of positivism
 followed by speculation concerning the possible beneficial effects
 that might have resulted if psychology had placed a higher priority
 upon substantive problems than methodology.

Mackie, R. Andrew. "John Locke's Leading Doctrines." SCHOOL AND SOCIETY 52 (December 1940): 573-79.

Describes Locke's views in such disciplines as psychology, education, religion, politics, and philosophy.

McReynolds, Paul. "Jeremy Bentham and the Nature of Psychological Concepts." JOURNAL OF GENERAL PSYCHOLOGY 82 (January 1970): 113-27.

Presents the views of several early theorists (e.g., Galen, Hobbes, and Locke) on the nature and function of psychological concepts. Discusses details of the position of Jeremy Bentham.

Mall, Ram Adhar. HUME'S CONCEPT OF MAN: AN ESSAY IN PHILOSOPHICAL ANTHROPOLOGY. New York: Allied Publishers, 1967. v, 165 p.

Explores selected themes in Hume's analysis of belief, his concept of imagination, and his views on human nature. Bibliography. Index.

Maniou-Vakali, Mary. "Some Aristotelian Views on Learning and Memory." JOURNAL OF THE HISTORY OF THE BEHAVIORAL SCIENCES 10 (January 1974): 47-55.

Comments on the significance of Aristotle for psychology and on his method followed by a discussion of his views of learning (distinction between innate and acquired powers, and perception and its effect on learning), and of memory (types of memory, effects of intentional factors, and the physiological basis of memory).

Marshall, Marilyn E. "Gustav Fechner, Dr. Mises, and the Comparative Anatomy of Angels." JOURNAL OF THE HISTORY OF THE BEHAVIORAL SCIENCES 5 (January 1969): 39-58.

Explores themes in works by Fechner written under the pseudonym Dr. Mises. Describes the materials and offers comments which provide insights into Fechner's world view.

Marston, W.M. "Materialism, Vitalism and Psychology." PSYCHE 8 (1928): 15-34.

Martinez, Julio A. "Galileo on Primary and Secondary Qualities." JOURNAL OF THE HISTORY OF THE BEHAVIORAL SCIENCES 10 (April 1974): 160-69.

Describes Galileo's ideas about primary and secondary qualities and contrasts his position with those of Locke and Descartes.

Meerloo, Joost A.M "Spinoza: A Look At His Psychological Concepts." AMERICAN JOURNAL OF PSYCHIATRY 121 (March 1965): 890-94.

Meissner, W.W. "A Historical Note on Retention." JOURNAL OF GENERAL PSYCHOLOGY 59 (October 1958): 229-36.

Outlines Aristotle's theory of retention.

Miller, Eugene F. "Hume's Contribution to Behavioral Science." JOURNAL OF THE HISTORY OF THE BEHAVIORAL SCIENCES 7 (April 1971): 154-68.

Reviews some of the ideas set forth in Hume's A TREATISE OF HUMAN NATURE which justify an empirical science of behavior.

Misiak, Henryk. THE PHILOSOPHICAL ROOTS OF SCIENTIFIC PSYCHOLOGY. New York: Fordham University Press, 1961. 142 p.

A concise examination of the philosophical background of psychology with emphasis on the mind-body problem, empirical philosophy, philosophical study of sensation and perception, and associationism. Suggested readings. Index.

Moore-Russell, Martha E. "The Philosopher and Society: John Locke and the English Revolution." JOURNAL OF THE HISTORY OF THE BEHAVIORAL SCIENCES 14 (January 1978): 65-73.

Analyzes the development of Locke's thought in terms of his active and often contradictory attempts to understand and explain seventeenth-century life.

Morgan, J. THE PSYCHOLOGICAL TEACHING OF ST. AUGUSTINE. London: Stock, 1932. 264 p.

Mossner, Ernest C. "The Continental Reception of Hume's TREATISE, 1739-1741." MIND 56 (January 1947): 31-43.

A review of French and German journals of the time reveals a critical reception for Hume's TREATISE.

Mountjoy, Paul T., and Smith, Noel W. "A Reply to Thornton's: 'Socrates and the History of Psychology.'" JOURNAL OF THE HISTORY OF THE BEHAVIORAL SCIENCES 7 (April 1971): 183-86.

Examines major points raised in previous publications by Kantor and Thornton which advance conflicting interpretations of the psychology of Socrates. Offers a critical treatment of the article by Thornton.

Murphy, Gardner. "Pythagorean Number Theory and Its Implications for Psychology." AMERICAN PSYCHOLOGIST 22 (June 1967): 423-31.

A review of the Pythagorean tradition followed by a discussion of its implications in the works of such thinkers as Galileo and Herbart and in modern psychology.

Needham, J. MAN A MACHINE. New York: Norton, 1928. 103 p.

> Reviews La Mettrie's classic L'HOMME MACHINE and argues
> that the mechanistic position has been greatly strengthened since
> La Mettrie's time.

Oberg, Barbara Bowen. "David Hartley and the Association of Ideas." JOUR-
NAL OF THE HISTORY OF IDEAS 37 (July–September 1976): 441–54.

Ouellet, James V. "On Locke's Counter-Cartesianism." AMERICAN PSYCHOL-
OGIST 31 (January 1976): 93.

> Argues that Locke's refutation of the theory of innate ideas was
> directed not at Descartes but at English Platonists.

Prothro, E. Terry. "Ibn Sina: Tenth Century Empiricist." JOURNAL OF
GENERAL PSYCHOLOGY 51 (July 1954): 3–9.

> Outlines the psychological thought of Ibn Sina, a scientist of
> high reputation among Islamic students.

Rahman, F. AVICENNA'S PSYCHOLOGY. London: Oxford University Press,
1952. xii, 127 p.

> A translation of a classic work by an early Arabic scholar (980–
> 1037) with detailed introductory and appended notes.

Rand, Benjamin. "The Early Development of Hartley's Doctrine of Association."
PSYCHOLOGICAL REVIEW 30 (July 1923): 306–20.

_____, comp. THE CLASSICAL PSYCHOLOGISTS: SELECTIONS ILLUSTRAT-
ING PSYCHOLOGY FROM ANAXAGORAS TO WUNDT. Boston: Houghton
Mifflin, 1912. xxi, 734 p. Index.

> See section B4, p. 51, for annotation.

Rasmussen, E. Tranekjaer. "Berkeley and Modern Psychology." BRITISH
JOURNAL FOR THE PHILOSOPHY OF SCIENCE 4 (May 1953): 2–12.

Ratner, J. THE PHILOSOPHY OF JOHN DEWEY. New York: Holt, 1928.
xii, 560 p.

Reid, Thomas. AN INQUIRY INTO THE HUMAN MIND. Edited with an
introduction by Timothy Duggan. Chicago: University of Chicago Press, 1970.
li, 279 p.

> A text based on the 1813 American edition. Covers Reid's work
> on sensation and perception. An introduction by the editor pro-
> vides brief biographical details and an orientation to the work.

First published in 1764, with subsequent editions in 1765, 1769, and 1785. Index.

Ritter, Wm. E. "Why Aristotle Invented the Word Entelecheia." QUARTERLY REVIEW OF BIOLOGY 7 (December 1932): 377-404; 9 (March 1934): 1-35.

Robinson, T.M. PLATO'S PSYCHOLOGY. Toronto, Canada: University of Toronto Press, 1970. ix, 202 p.

Drawing from such sources as the PHAEDO, the REPUBLIC, the TIMAEUS, and the POLITICUS, Robinson presents Plato's thought on many psychological topics including the senses, desire, development, and intelligence. Bibliography.

Rooney, M.T. "Fifty Years Ago." NEW SCHOLASTICISM 19 (1945): 353-68.

Outlines the contributions of Edward Pace, one of Wundt's students, who was associated with the development of Thomistic philosophy.

Rosenfield, L.C. FROM BEAST-MACHINE TO MAN-MACHINE; ANIMAL SOUL IN FRENCH LETTERS FROM DESCARTES TO LA METTRIE. New York: Oxford University Press, 1941. xxviii, 353 p.

For annotation, see section D3a, p. 264.

Ross, Sir William David, ed. THE WORKS OF ARISTOTLE TRANSLATED INTO ENGLISH. 12 vols. Vols. 4, 5, and 8 co-edited by J.A. Smith and William David Ross. Oxford, Engl.: Clarendon Press, 1908-52.

Each of these volumes has subtitles, and many were published separately. Of particular interest to psychologists are volume 3 (containing DE ANIMA and DE SPIRITU) and volume 9 (containing ETHICA NICOMACHEA, MAGNA MORALIA, and ETHICA EUDEMIA).

Royce, James E. "Historical Aspects of Free Choice." JOURNAL OF THE HISTORY OF THE BEHAVIORAL SCIENCES 6 (January 1970): 48-51.

Provides a very brief overview of the positions on free choice of selected poets, dramatists, philosophers, physical scientists, and psychologists.

Rubenstein, S.L. "Consciousness in the Light of Dialectical Materialism." SCIENCE AND SOCIETY 10 (Summer 1946): 252-61. Translated by N.J. Nelson from BULLETIN OF THE ACADEMY OF SCIENCES OF THE USSR/ SERIES HISTORY AND PHILOSOPHY 3 (1945): 148-57.

Ryan, Bruce A. "Jean-Jacques Rousseau and Behavior Control: The Technology of a Romantic Behaviorist." BEHAVIORISM 4 (Fall 1976): 245-56.

Schmitt, Richard. "Nietzsche's Psychological Theory." JOURNAL OF EXISTENTIAL PSYCHIATRY 2 (1971): 71-92.

Schoen, Edward L. "Aristotle's Modern Conception of Man: A Reply to Basil Jackson." JOURNAL OF PSYCHOLOGY AND THEOLOGY 3 (1975): 109-15.

Shute, Clarence. "Aristotle's Interactionism and Its Transformations By Some 20th Century Writers." PSYCHOLOGICAL RECORD 23 (Summer 1973): 283-93.

_____. THE PSYCHOLOGY OF ARISTOTLE; AN ANALYSIS OF THE LIVING BEING. New York: Columbia University Press, 1941. xi, 148 p.

Skinhøj, Erik, and Skinhøj, Kirsten. "Søren Kirkegaard in American Psychology." ACTA PSYCHIATRICA KOBENHAVN 30 (1955): 315-25.

Smith, Noel W. "Aristotle's Dynamic Approach to Sensing and Some Current Implications." JOURNAL OF THE HISTORY OF THE BEHAVIORAL SCIENCES 7 (October 1971): 375-77.

> Reviews Aristotle's theory and concludes that his approach, despite its errors, is objective and naturalistic, and that it "overcomes the pernicious effects of our dualistic heritage from medieval theosophy and shows the way out of the resulting jungle of phenomenology and ghostly creations that has pervaded the work in perception."

_____. "Comments on Baumrin's Analysis of Shute and Aristotle." JOURNAL OF THE HISTORY OF THE BEHAVIORAL SCIENCES 14 (January 1978): 20-22.

> A brief critique of Judith Marti Baumrin's paper "Active Power and Causal Flow in Aristotle's Theory of Vision" (see in section C5, p. 283).

Spinoza, Benedict de. THE CHIEF WORKS OF BENEDICT DE SPINOZA. 2 vols. New York: Dover, 1955.

Spoerl, Howard Davis. "Dynamic Aspects of Swedenborg's Psychology." NEW PHILOSOPHY 46 (January 1943): 257-68.

_____. "Swedenborg: A Psychological Pioneer." PSYCHOLOGY DIGEST 2 (1937): 70-75.

Stierlin, Helm. "Karl Jaspers' Psychiatry in the Light of His Basic Philosophic Position." JOURNAL OF THE HISTORY OF THE BEHAVIORAL SCIENCES 10 (April 1974): 213-26.

Outlines the influence on Jaspers of such scholars as Max Weber and Immanuel Kant. Discusses Jaspers's basic philosophical orientation, his work as a psychiatrist, his relevance to modern psychiatry, and his reaction to psychoanalysis, including critical comment on that reaction.

Stillman, Peter G. "Hegel's Idea of Punishment." JOURNAL OF THE HISTORY OF PHILOSOPHY 14 (April 1976): 169-82.

Sullivan, John. "On Cartesian Linguistics." ANNALS OF THE NEW YORK ACADEMY OF SCIENCES 291 (18 April 1977): 287-305.

Swabey, William Curtis. "Locke's Theory of Ideas." PHILOSOPHICAL REVIEW 42 (November 1933): 573-93.

Swift, Louis J., and Block, Stanley L. "Classical Rhetoric in Vives' Psychology." JOURNAL OF THE HISTORY OF THE BEHAVIORAL SCIENCES 10 (January 1974): 74-83.

Explores Vives's thought on memory and association with special emphasis on how his ideas on these topics were conditioned by his views on rhetoric.

Tanner, Amy E. "Spinoza and Modern Psychology." AMERICAN JOURNAL OF PSYCHOLOGY 18 (October 1907): 514-18.

Briefly outlines Spinoza's thought on selected psychological topics.

Thomas Aquinas. See Gardeil, H.D., p. 387.

Tibbetts, Paul. "An Historical Note on Descartes' Psychophysical Dualism." JOURNAL OF THE HISTORY OF THE BEHAVIORAL SCIENCES 9 (April 1973): 162-65.

Cites correspondence between Princess Elizabeth and Descartes and observes that Descartes probably took the position that a rational and intellectually satisfying solution to the mind-body problem may be impossible.

Trainor, J.C. "The Contributions of Alfred Korzybski." PSYCHE 16 (1936): 165-77.

A tribute to an imaginative and influential semanticist.

Warren, Howard C. "Mental Association from Plato to Hume." PSYCHOLOGICAL REVIEW 23 (May 1916): 208-30.

Briefly outlines contributions to associationism of such scholars as Aristotle, St. Augustine, Vives, Descartes, Hobbes, Locke, and Berkeley.

Weimer, W.B. "Psycholinguistics and Plato's Paradoxes of the Meno." AMERI-
CAN PSYCHOLOGIST 28 (January 1973): 15-33.

Wisdom, J.O. "The Unconscious Origin of Schopenhauer's Philosophy."
INTERNATIONAL JOURNAL OF PSYCHO-ANALYSIS 26 (1945): 44-52.

Zakapoulos, Athenagoras N. PLATO ON MAN. New York: Philosophical
Library, 1975. 142 p.

> Subtitle indicates that this book is "A Summary and Critique of
> [Plato's] Psychology With Special Reference to Pre-Platonic,
> Freudian, Behavioristic and Humanistic Psychology." Index.

2. PSYCHIATRY

Psychiatry is the medical specialty that focuses on psychopathology. This section includes only articles that are addressed specifically to this medical field.
Articles on psychopathology as such are found in section D12, p. 337, and
items about clinical psychology are included in section D13, p. 353. Psychiatry and the applied branches of psychology, particularly psychopathology and
clinical psychology, share a variety of concerns. Accordingly, the history of
psychiatry is of considerable interest to many psychologists. The materials
which follow are intended to be only representative of the vast literature in
the history of psychiatry. Included are several comprehensive texts in section
E2a, this page, and references to numerous articles which focus on the development of psychiatry in specific times and places (section E2b, p. 401).

a. Selected Major Works and Articles

Ackerknecht, Erwin H. A SHORT HISTORY OF PSYCHIATRY. 2d rev. ed.
Translated by Sula Wolff. New York: Hafner, 1968. xii, 109 p.

> A brief history covering selected topics in psychiatric thought
> from Greek and Roman times to twentieth-century developments.
> Minimal references in footnotes. Index.

Alexander, Franz G., and Selesnick, Sheldon T. THE HISTORY OF PSYCHIA-
TRY: AN EVALUATION OF PSYCHIATRIC THOUGHT AND PRACTICE FROM
PREHISTORIC TIMES TO THE PRESENT. New York: Harper and Row, 1966.
xvi, 471 p.

> A comprehensive work surveying major trends of thought and treat-
> ment procedures from earliest times. Emphasis is on the psycho-
> analytic movement, but a large section on recent developments
> covers such topics as the organic and psychological approaches,
> social psychiatry, child psychiatry, and the psychosomatic orienta-
> tion in medicine. Appendixes cover the founders of the American
> Psychiatric Association, Jung and the National Socialists, and the

organization of psychoanalytic and psychiatric teaching practice and research. Notes. Bibliography. Index.

Altschule, Mark D., with the collaboration of Evelyn Russ Hegedus. PSYCHIATRY: ESSAYS IN THE HISTORY OF PSYCHIATRY. 2d ed. New York: Grune and Stratton, 1965. viii, 208 p.

Galdston, Iago, ed. HISTORIC DERIVATIONS OF MODERN PSYCHIATRY. New York: McGraw-Hill, 1967. xiv, 241 p.

> An introduction on medical historiography followed by eight essays treating such selected topics in the history of psychiatry as psychiatry and ancient medicine, psychiatry in the Middle Ages, evolution of depth psychology, and Descartes to Pavlov. References. Index.

Goshen, Charles E., ed. DOCUMENTARY HISTORY OF PSYCHIATRY: A SOURCE BOOK ON HISTORICAL PRINCIPLES. New York: Philosophical Library, 1967. x, 904 p.

> Reprints excerpts from classic writings in psychiatry from Plato through Freud with brief annotations.

Hall, J.K., gen. ed. ONE HUNDRED YEARS OF AMERICAN PSYCHIATRY. New York: Columbia University Press for the American Psychiatric Association, 1944. xxiv, 649 p.

> Written in commemoration of the hundredth anniversary of the American Psychiatric Association. Characterizes the growth and development of psychiatric thought in America. Chapters devoted to such topics as the founding of the American Psychiatric Association, the history of American mental hospitals, a century of psychiatric research, the history of psychiatric therapies, military psychiatry, legal aspects of psychiatry, the influence of psychiatry on anthropology, and (of special interest to psychologists) a chapter on a century of psychology and its relationship to American psychiatry. Illustrations. Bibliographical materials in footnotes. Index.

Harms, Ernest. ORIGINS OF MODERN PSYCHIATRY. Springfield, Ill.: Charles C Thomas, 1967. xiv, 256 p.

> A history of psychiatry covering selected topics from Paracelsus to William Alanson White. Early chapters provide critical comment on earlier histories of psychiatry. Many chapters previously published as articles in psychiatric journals. Index.

Howells, John G., ed. WORLD HISTORY OF PSYCHIATRY. New York: Brunner/Mazel, 1975. 770 p.

Presents overviews of milestones in psychiatric thought and practice. Twenty-nine articles deal with different countries or groups of countries. Major trends and common viewpoints in editor's introduction. References. Index.

Hunter, Richard, and Macalpine, Ida, author-eds. THREE HUNDRED YEARS OF PSYCHIATRY 1535-1860. London: Oxford University Press, 1963. xxvi, 1,107 p.

A valuable resource in the history of psychiatry. Presents over 325 excerpts, letters, documents, case studies, and self-reports written by philosophers, ministers, reformers, lawyers, and physicians on theories, etiology, care, and treatment of mental illness. Extensive comment by author-editors provides perspective and connection among the various excerpts. Cites original sources. Index.

Leigh, Denis. THE HISTORICAL DEVELOPMENT OF BRITISH PSYCHIATRY. Vol. 1. 18TH AND 19TH CENTURY. New York: Pergamon Press, 1961. xiv, 277 p.

An illustrated account of the evolution of psychiatry in England written by a practicing psychiatrist. Reviews eighteenth-century British psychiatry followed by separate chapters on John Haslam, James Prichard, and John Connolly, all of whose careers continued well into the nineteenth century. Bibliography. Index.

Lewis, Nolan D.C. A SHORT HISTORY OF PSYCHIATRIC ACHIEVEMENT, WITH A FORECAST FOR THE FUTURE. New York: W.W. Norton, 1941. 275 p.

A brief history of psychiatry. Begins with demonology and ancient medicine, touches on early Greek and Roman developments, and discusses the Middle Ages, the seventeenth and eighteenth centuries, the nineteenth century, "modern psychiatry," and the future. Short bibliography. Index.

McNeill, John T. A HISTORY OF THE CURE OF SOULS. New York: Harper, 1951. Reprint. New York: Harper Torchbooks, 1965. xii, 371 p.

A thorough work documenting the history of efforts to produce healthy souls by means of religious healing practices from ancient times through the early Christian Church to Protestantism and the emergence of psychiatry as a medical specialty. Index.

Menninger, R.W. "The History of Psychiatry." DISEASES OF THE NERVOUS SYSTEM 5 (1944): 52-55.

Menninger, William C. PSYCHIATRY: ITS EVOLUTION AND PRESENT STA-

TUS. Ithaca, N.Y.: Cornell University Press, 1948. xi, 138 p.

The first fifteen pages of this small book contain a brief overview of the history of psychiatry up to Freud.

Mora, George. "The History of Psychiatry: A Cultural and Bibliographical Survey." INTERNATIONAL JOURNAL OF PSYCHIATRY 2 (1966): 335-56.

Mora, George, and Brand, Jeanne L., eds. PSYCHIATRY AND ITS HISTORY: METHODOLOGICAL PROBLEMS IN RESEARCH. Springfield, Ill.: Charles C Thomas, 1970. xviii, 283 p.

Based on a symposium on methodological problems in the history of psychiatry held at Yale University in 1967. Papers cover such topics as problems in writing the history of psychoanalysis, bibliographic foundations for an emergent history of the behavioral sciences, the interdisciplinary approach to the history of American psychiatry, and comparative methods in the history of psychiatry. References. Index.

Overholser, Winfred. "An Historical Sketch of Psychiatry." JOURNAL OF CLINICAL PSYCHOPATHOLOGY 10 (April 1949): 129-46.

_____. "Jacksonville 1847--Psychiatry Then and Now." JOURNAL OF THE HISTORY OF MEDICINE AND ALLIED SCIENCES 3 (Summer 1948): 381-94.

A memorial centennial address in 1947 providing a brief overview of significant developments in psychiatry from the founding of the Jacksonville State Hospital in Illinois in 1847. Index.

Ray, Marie Beynon. DOCTORS OF THE MIND: WHAT PSYCHIATRY CAN DO. Rev. ed. Boston: Little Brown, 1946. xxxi, 356 p.

A popular account of selected developments in the history of psychiatry. Likely to have high interest value for a novice, but to be of less value to a more sophisticated student. Index.

Riese, Hertha, ed. HISTORICAL EXPLORATIONS IN MEDICINE AND PSYCHIATRY. New York: Springer, 1978. 256 p.

Roback, A[braham].A[aron]., and Kiernan, Thomas. PICTORIAL HISTORY OF PSYCHOLOGY AND PSYCHIATRY. New York: Philosophical Library, 1969. 294 p.

See section B1, p. 38, for annotation.

Santos, Elvin H., and Stainbrook, Edward. "A History of Psychiatric Nursing in the Nineteenth Century." JOURNAL OF THE HISTORY OF MEDICINE AND ALLIED SCIENCES 4 (Winter 1949): 48-74.

Whitewell, J.R. HISTORICAL NOTES ON PSYCHIATRY: EARLY TIMES--END OF THE 16TH CENTURY. Philadelphia: P. Blakiston's Son, 1937. xii, 252 p.

> Explores psychiatric thought in such ancient civilizations as China, India, Babylonia, Egypt, Greece, and Israel. Sketches the medical thought characteristic of the Roman era and Middle Ages. Presents translations and extracts of the thought of over sixty major contributors and a chronological table of major contributions to psychiatric thought. Bibliographical materials in footnotes.

Zilboorg, Gregory, and Henry, G.W. A HISTORY OF MEDICAL PSYCHOLOGY.

> See section D13a, p. 357, for annotation.

b. Selected Topics

Altschule, Mark D. ROOTS OF MODERN PSYCHIATRY: ESSAYS IN THE HISTORY OF PSYCHIATRY. 2d rev. and enl. ed. New York: Grune and Stratton, 1965. viii, 208 p.

> A collection of essays on such themes as eighteenth-century British ideas about anxiety, the early development of ego psychology, the growth of the concept of the unconscious before 1890, the history of beliefs about the role of sexual drives in mental disorders, and early treatment techniques. References. Index.

Amdur, M.K., and Messinger, E. "Jean-Etienne-Dominique Esquirol: His Work and Importance for Modern Psychiatry." AMERICAN JOURNAL OF PSYCHIATRY 96 (1939): 129-35.

Baruk, Henri. "Psychiatry in France." PSYCHIATRIC OPINION 10 (1973): 27-30.

Bleuler, Manfred. "Some Aspects of the History of Swiss Psychiatry." AMERICAN JOURNAL OF PSYCHIATRY 130 (September 1973): 991-94.

Braceland, Francis J. "Historical Perspectives of the Ethical Practice of Psychiatry." AMERICAN JOURNAL OF PSYCHIATRY 126 (August 1969): 230-37.

_____. "Kraepelin: His System and His Influence." AMERICAN JOURNAL OF PSYCHIATRY 113 (April 1957): 871-76.

Brady, John Paul, ed. CLASSICS OF AMERICAN PSYCHIATRY. St. Louis, Mo.: Warren H. Green, 1975. ix, 281 p.

> A brief anthology (eleven authors, fourteen papers) consisting of the writings of such significant nineteenth- and early twentieth-

century figures in the history of American psychiatry as Benjamin
Rush, Amariah Brigham, Morton Prince, Dorothea Dix, and Clifford
Beers.

Brill, A.A. FREUD'S CONTRIBUTION TO PSYCHIATRY. New York: W.W.
Norton, 1944. 244 p.

An overview of progress in psychiatry from 1903 with emphasis on
Brill's personal experiences and the impact of psychoanalysis.
Bibliographical materials in footnotes. Index.

Bry, Ilse. "Bibliographic Foundations for an Emergent History of the Behavioral
Sciences." In PSYCHIATRY AND ITS HISTORY: METHODOLOGICAL PROB-
LEMS IN RESEARCH, edited by George Mora and Jeanne L. Brand, pp. 82-
118. Springfield, Ill.: Charles C Thomas, 1970. xviii, 283 p.

Discusses primary and secondary sources for the history of the behavioral sciences, concentrating primarily on the history of psychiatry.

Caplan, Ruth B. PSYCHIATRY AND THE COMMUNITY IN NINETEENTH
CENTURY AMERICA: THE RECURRING CONCERN WITH THE ENVIRONMENT
IN THE PREVENTION AND TREATMENT OF MENTAL ILLNESS. New York:
Basic Books, 1969. xx, 360 p.

Written in collaboration with Gerald Caplan, this history of American psychiatry from 1800 to 1900 emphasizes such problems as
changing hospital environments, community and hospital relationships, government involvement, the psychiatric guild, and theories of nineteenth-century psychiatric leaders. Notes. Bibliographical materials.

Chang, Suk C., and Kim, Kwang-Iel. "Psychiatry in South Korea." AMERI-
CAN JOURNAL OF PSYCHIATRY 130 (June 1973): 667-69.

Chatel, John, and Joe, Barbara. "Psychiatry in Spain: Past and Present."
AMERICAN JOURNAL OF PSYCHIATRY 132 (November 1975): 1182-86.

Cleghorn, R.A. "The Shaping of Psychiatry By Science and Humanism."
CANADIAN MEDICAL ASSOCIATION JOURNAL 103 (October 1970): 933-41.

Cobb, Stanley. "One Hundred Years of Progress in Neurology, Psychiatry and
Neurosurgery." ARCHIVES OF NEUROLOGY AND PSYCHIATRY, CHICAGO
59 (1948): 63-98.

Curran, William J. "Legal Psychiatry in the 19th Century." PSYCHIATRIC
ANNALS 4 (August 1974): 8-14.

Dain, Norman. CONCEPTS OF INSANITY IN THE UNITED STATES, 1789-1865. New Brunswick, N.J.: Rutgers University Press, 1964. xv, 304 p.

A highly readable book tracing psychiatric, public, and religious views of insanity for the period 1789-1865. Extensive notes. Bibliography. Index.

Delia, Donald J. BENJAMIN RUSH: PHILOSOPHER OF THE AMERICAN REVOLUTION. TRANSACTIONS OF THE AMERICAN PHILOSOPHICAL SOCIETY. Vol. 64, no. 5. Philadelphia: American Philosophical Society, 1974. 113 p.

_____. "Benjamin Rush, David Hartley and the Revolutionary Uses of Psychology." PROCEEDINGS OF THE AMERICAN PHILOSOPHICAL SOCIETY 114 (April 1970): 109-18.

Ehrentheil, Otto F. "The Almost Forgotten Feuchtersleben: Poet, Essayist, Popular Philosopher, and Psychiatrist." JOURNAL OF THE HISTORY OF THE BEHAVIORAL SCIENCES 11 (January 1975): 82-86.

Ehrenwald, Jan, ed. FROM MEDICINE MAN TO FREUD: AN ANTHOLOGY. New York: Dell, 1956. 416 p.

A paperback book of readings in the history of psychiatry. Contains useful introductory and interpretive comments. Excerpts many major writers in three sections: Magic, religion, and science.

Evans, B. THE PSYCHIATRY OF ROBERT BURTON. New York: Columbia University Press, 1944. ix, 129 p.

Provides a modern analysis of Burton's famous work, THE ANATOMY OF MELANCHOLY.

Ewalt, Jack R., and Ewalt, Patricia L. "History of the Community Psychiatry Movement." AMERICAN JOURNAL OF PSYCHIATRY 126 (July 1969): 43-52.

Farr, C.B. "Benjamin Rush and American Psychiatry." AMERICAN JOURNAL OF PSYCHIATRY 100 (1944): 3-15.

Feinstein, Howard M. "Benjamin Rush: A Child of Light for the Children of Darkness." PSYCHOANALYTIC REVIEW 58 (Summer 1971): 209-22.

Flor-Henry, P. "Psychiatric Surgery--1936-1973: Evolution and Current Perspectives." CANADIAN PSYCHIATRIC ASSOCIATION JOURNAL 20 (1975): 157-67.

Freeman, Walter. THE PSYCHIATRIST: PERSONALITIES AND PATTERNS. New York: Grune and Stratton, 1968. x, 293 p.

Contains brief accounts of accomplishments and biographical sketches
of over twenty psychiatrists (including Freud), all of whom were
prominent figures in the historical development of psychiatry.
Presents materials on personality patterns of psychiatrists and the
so-called psychiatric dynasties, e.g., the Menningers and the
Woods. References. Index.

Goldstein, Abraham. "The Moral Psychiatry of Imperial Rome as Practiced by
Soranus of Ephesus." PSYCHIATRIC QUARTERLY 43 (July 1969): 535-54.

Gruner, O. Cameron. A TREATISE ON THE CANON OF MEDICINE OF
AVICENNA. 1930. Reprint. New York: Augustus M. Kelley, 1970. vii,
612 p.

Presents both a translation of Book 1 of Avicenna's canon of medicine (a major eleventh-century Arabic work) and a discussion of
its philosophical and biological significance. Includes brief summaries of books 2, 3, 4, and 5 of the canon and a translation
of "De Viribus Cordis." References. Index.

Hart, Bernard. "Psychology and Psychiatry." MENTAL HYGIENE 16 (April
1932): 177-201.

Explores the roles of selected psychologies in the development of
psychiatry.

Havens, Leston L. APPROACHES TO THE MIND: MOVEMENT OF THE PSY-
CHIATRIC SCHOOLS FROM SECTS TOWARD SCIENCE. Boston: Little,
Brown, 1973. xiii, 385 p.

_____. "Emil Kraepelin." JOURNAL OF NERVOUS AND MENTAL DIS-
EASE 141 (1965): 16-28.

Jelliffe, S.E. "Some Random Notes on the History of Psychiatry of the Middle
Ages." AMERICAN JOURNAL OF PSYCHIATRY 10 (1930): 275-86.

Kanner, L[eo]. "American Contributions to the Development of Child Psychiatry." PSYCHIATRIC QUARTERLY SUPPLEMENT 35 (1961): 1-12.

_____. "History of Child Psychiatry." In THE CHILD: HIS PSYCHOLOGI-
CAL AND CULTURAL DEVELOPMENT, edited by Alfred M. Freedman and
Harold I. Kaplan, pp. 3-7. New York: Atheneum, 1972. Index.

Kao, John J. "Psychiatry in the People's Republic of China: A Prospectus."
AMERICAN JOURNAL OF CHINESE MEDICINE 2 (1974): 441-44.

Kelly, Barry N. "Significant Trends and Themes in the History of Mental

Health." CONTEMPORARY ISSUES OF MENTAL HEALTH (MONOGRAPH SERIES) 1 (May 1975): 1-78.

> Traces scientific, political, and altruistic themes over the past one hundred years.

Knoff, William F. "A History of the Concept of Neurosis, with a Memoir of William Cullen." AMERICAN JOURNAL OF PSYCHIATRY 127 (July 1970): 80-84.

Kraepelin, Emil. LECTURES ON CLINICAL PSYCHIATRY. 2d ed. Translated from 2d German ed. Translator not named. Revised and edited by Thomas Johnstone. New York: William Wood, 1906. xvii, 352 p.

> These lectures by one of the foremost psychiatrists of the late nineteenth and early twentieth century focus primarily on individual case histories representing a considerable range of emotional disturbance. Emphasizes diagnostic description but does not neglect etiology and treatment. Includes materials on mental deficiency and criminal behavior. Index.

Laughlin, Henry P. "European Psychiatry: England, Denmark, Italy, Greece, Spain and Turkey." AMERICAN JOURNAL OF PSYCHIATRY 116 (March 1960): 769-76.

Le Gassicke, John. "Early History of Psychiatry in Newcastle Upon Tyne." BRITISH JOURNAL OF PSYCHIATRY 120 (April 1972): 419-22.

Leon, Carlos A. "Psychiatry in Latin America." BRITISH JOURNAL OF PSYCHIATRY 121 (August 1972): 121-36.

Lidz, Theodore. "Adolf Meyer and the Development of American Psychiatry." AMERICAN JOURNAL OF PSYCHIATRY 123 (September 1966): 320-32.

Mackler, Bernard, and Hamilton, Kay. "Contributions to the History of Psychology: VII. Benjamin Rush: A Political and Historical Study of the 'Father of American Psychiatry.'" PSYCHOLOGICAL REPORTS 20 (June 1967): 1287-1306.

Marx, Otto M. "What Is the History of Psychiatry?" AMERICAN JOURNAL OF ORTHOPSYCHIATRY 40 (July 1970): 593-605.

Meier, C.A. "Dynamic Psychology and the Classical World." In PSYCHIATRY AND ITS HISTORY: METHODOLOGICAL PROBLEMS IN RESEARCH, edited by G[eorge]. Mora and J.L. Brand, pp. 159-71. Springfield, Ill.: Charles C Thomas, 1970. xviii, 283 p.

Menninger, Karl. A GUIDE TO PSYCHIATRIC BOOKS IN ENGLISH. 3d ed. New York: Grune and Stratton, 1972. xviii, 238 p.

> Lists over three thousand books on psychiatry including texts and general reference materials and works on history, treatment, and special fields such as child psychiatry, geriatrics, and criminology. Also includes related fields such as neurology, philosophy of science, psychoanalysis, sociology, anthropology, and psychology (its history and such special fields as experimental, physiological, developmental, social, and clinical psychology). Index.

Mora, George. "The History of Psychiatry: A Cultural and Bibliographical Survey." PSYCHOANALYTIC REVIEW 52 (Summer 1965): 154-84.

_____. "Paracelsus' Psychiatry: On the Occasion of the 400th Anniversary of His Book 'Diseases That Deprive Man of His Reason' (1567)." AMERICAN JOURNAL OF PSYCHIATRY 124 (December 1967): 803-14.

Mullahy, Patrick, ed. THE CONTRIBUTIONS OF HARRY STACK SULLIVAN. A SYMPOSIUM ON INTERPERSONAL THEORY IN PSYCHIATRY AND SOCIAL SCIENCE. New York: Hermitage House, 1952. 238 p.

> Discusses Sullivan's major theories and conceptions, clinical work, and contributions to the social sciences. Bibliography of Sullivan's works.

Oliver, J.R. "The Psychiatry of Hippocrates: A Plea for the Study of the History of Medicine." AMERICAN JOURNAL OF PSYCHIATRY 5 (1925): 107-15.

Overholser, Winfred. "Cox and Trotter--Two Psychiatric Precursors of Benjamin Rush." AMERICAN JOURNAL OF PSYCHIATRY 110 (May 1954): 825-30.

Runes, Dagobert D., ed. THE SELECTED WRITINGS OF BENJAMIN RUSH. New York: Philosophical Library, 1947. xii, 433 p.

> An anthology of writings on politics, education, medicine, science, etc., by a distinguished eighteenth-century U.S. physician. Brief introduction. List of Rush's published works. Bibliography. Index.

Rush, Benjamin. MEDICAL INQUIRIES AND OBSERVATIONS UPON THE DISEASES OF THE MIND. 2d ed. Philadelphia: John Richardson, 1818. vi, 367 p.

> A classic work by a pioneer American psychiatrist. Presents Rush's theories and recommended treatments for a variety of mental disorders.

Rusk, George Yeisley. "Gestalt Psychiatry." JOURNAL OF ABNORMAL AND SOCIAL PSYCHOLOGY 29 (January–March 1935): 376–84.

> Argues that older psychologies have not provided a sound foundation for psychiatry. Examines implications of the work of Koehler and Sherrington and comments on its implications for psychiatry.

Saussure, Raymond de. "French Psychiatry of the Eighteenth Century." CIBA SYMPOSIA 11 (Summer 1950): 1222–52.

> Focuses on Pinel's work as a reformer and a psychiatrist. Includes materials on Pinel's disciples and on eighteenth-century psychiatric literature. Bibliography.

Savino, Michael T., and Mills, Alden B. "The Rise and Fall of Moral Treatment in California Psychiatry: 1852–1870." JOURNAL OF THE HISTORY OF THE BEHAVIORAL SCIENCES 3 (October 1967): 359–69.

> Shows how hospital documents of the early 1860s indicate that treatment programs were comparable to modern milieu therapy. With insufficient training of physicians and crowded conditions, however, the trend moved back to custodialism. Discusses effects of general social conditions and philosophy on treatment programs.

Scull, Andrew T. "Cyclical Trends in Psychiatric Practice: The Case of Bettelheim and Tuke." SOCIAL SCIENCE AND MEDICINE 9 (1975): 633–40.

Shakow, David. "The Development of Orthopsychiatry: The Contributions of Levy, Menninger, and Stevenson." AMERICAN JOURNAL OF ORTHOPSYCHIATRY 38 (October 1968): 804–9.

Siegel, Rudolph E. GALEN ON PSYCHOLOGY, PSYCHOPATHOLOGY AND FUNCTION AND DISEASES OF THE NERVOUS SYSTEM: AN ANALYSIS OF HIS DOCTRINES, OBSERVATIONS AND EXPERIMENTS. New York: S. Karger, 1973. ix, 310 p.

> Explores such topics in Galen's psychology as memory, sleeping, temperament, and free will, and such topics in psychopathology as the causes of disease, speech disturbances, headache, paralysis, madness, and dementia. Examines psychotherapeutic concepts. The psychology section complements Siegel's earlier book on Galen's views on sense perception (see below). Bibliography. Index.

_____. GALEN ON SENSE PERCEPTION: HIS DOCTRINES, OBSERVATIONS AND EXPERIMENTS ON VISION, HEARING, SMELL, TASTE, TOUCH AND PAIN, AND THEIR HISTORICAL SOURCES. New York: S. Karger, 1970. 216 p.

_____. GALEN'S SYSTEM OF PHYSIOLOGY AND MEDICINE: AND ANAL-

YSIS OF HIS DOCTRINES AND OBSERVATIONS ON BLOODFLOW, RESPIRA-
TION, HUMORS, AND INTERNAL DISEASES. New York: S. Karger, 1968.
419 p.

> A brief overview of Galen's life followed by a detailed examina-
> tion of topics listed in the subtitle. The first book in a three-
> volume work. Subsequent volumes explore Galen's analysis of
> sense perception (see above, this section) and his psychology and
> psychopathology (see above, this section). Index.

Stainbrook, Edward. "The Use of Electricity in Psychiatric Treatment During
the Nineteenth Century." BULLETIN OF THE HISTORY OF MEDICINE 22
(1948): 156-77.

Stanka, Hugo. "Psychiatry and Neurology One Hundred and Fifty Years
Ago." JOURNAL OF NERVOUS AND MENTAL DISEASE 98 (September 1943):
294-96.

Stone, Michael H. "Child Psychiatry Before the Twentieth Century." INTER-
NATIONAL JOURNAL OF CHILD PSYCHOTHERAPY 2 (1973): 264-308.

Tourney, Garfield. "History of Biological Psychiatry in America." AMERICAN
JOURNAL OF PSYCHIATRY 126 (July 1969): 29-42.

_____. "A History of Therapeutic Fashions in Psychiatry, 1800-1966."
AMERICAN JOURNAL OF PSYCHIATRY 124 (December 1967): 784-96.

Wilmer, Harry A., and Scammon, Richard E. "Neuropsychiatric Patients
Reported Cured at St. Bartholomew's Hospital in the Twelfth Century." JOUR-
NAL OF NERVOUS AND MENTAL DISEASE 119 (January 1954): 1-22.

Winslow, Walker. THE MENNINGER STORY. Garden City, N.Y.: Doubleday, 1956. 350 p.

> A biography of Dr. Charles Frederick Menninger (1862-1953) ac-
> companied by an account of the development of the Menninger
> Clinic and the contributions of the Menninger family in the many
> areas in which they have been active.

Wittels, Fritz. "The Contribution of Benjamin Rush to Psychiatry." BULLETIN
OF THE HISTORY OF MEDICINE 20 (1946): 157-66.

> Written in celebration of the 200th anniversary of Benjamin
> Rush's birth. Explores such topics as Rush's assumptions regarding
> mental illness, his nomenclature, and his treatment procedures.

Woods, Evelyn A., and Carlson, E.T. "The Psychiatry of Philippe Pinel."
BULLETIN OF THE HISTORY OF MEDICINE 35 (1961): 14-25.

Wortis, Joseph. SOVIET PSYCHIATRY. Baltimore: Williams and Wilkins, 1950. xv, 314 p.

A relatively brief yet thorough, dispassionate, and scholarly description of psychiatry in the Soviet Union during the first half of the twentieth century.

Zilboorg, Gregory. "The Dark Ages of Psychiatric History." JOURNAL OF NERVOUS AND MENTAL DISEASE 74 (November 1931): 610-35.

Surveys psychiatric practice during the Middle Ages.

_____. "Russian Psychiatry, Its Historical and Ideological Background." BULLETIN OF THE NEW YORK ACADEMY OF MEDICINE 19 (1943): 713-28.

3. BIOLOGICAL SCIENCES

Historical developments in physiology and neurology contributed to the emergence of psychology as an independent discipline. The early work of physiologists on such topics as the reflex, thresholds, and sensory processes led directly to the establishment of the new science of psychology. The following materials include mainly references to major historical works on a variety of topics in the biological sciences including the reflex, general neurology, heredity, and such relevant philosophical topics as vitalism and materialism.

Allen, Garland E. LIFE SCIENCE IN THE TWENTIETH CENTURY. New York: John Wiley and Sons, 1975. xxv, 258 p.

A study of the emergence of modern biology. Concentrates on selected issues in the growth of biology between 1890 and 1965: embryonic development, heredity, evolution, general physiology, biochemistry, and molecular biology. Bibliography. Index.

Bodenheimer, F.S. THE HISTORY OF BIOLOGY: AN INTRODUCTION. London: Wm. Dawson and Sons, 1958. 465 p.

Part 1 of this three-part book deals with problems in the history and philosophy of science; part 2 presents a brief factual history of biology; part 3 presents 133 sources in the history of science that describe the contributions of important scientific figures, list significant works, and contain excerpts. Index.

Brooks, Chandler Mc., et al. HUMORS, HORMONES, AND NEUROSECRETIONS: THE ORIGINS AND DEVELOPMENT OF MAN'S PRESENT KNOWLEDGE OF THE HUMORAL CONTROL OF BODY FUNCTION. New York: State University of New York, 1962. x, 313 p.

Discusses the history of physiology in three major sections: the development of endocrinology, chemical transmission of neuronal activity, and the central nervous system and humoral control of body function.

Cole, F.J. A HISTORY OF COMPARATIVE ANATOMY, FROM ARISTOTLE TO THE EIGHTEENTH CENTURY. London: Macmillan, 1944. viii, 524 p.

Most chapters of this overview devoted to the contributions of individual workers. Sections on academies and societies and on anatomical museums. Appendix contains brief biographies. Bibliography. Index.

Coleman, William R. BIOLOGY IN THE 19TH CENTURY: PROBLEMS OF FORM, FUNCTION, AND TRANSFORMATION. New York: John Wiley and Sons, 1971. vii, 187 p. Bibliography.

_____. GEORGES CUVIER, ZOOLOGIST: A STUDY IN THE HISTORY OF EVOLUTION THEORY. Cambridge, Mass.: Harvard University Press, 1964. x, 212 p.

An overview of Cuvier's work in comparative anatomy, his influential classification of animals, and his arguments against the transmutation of biological species. References. Index.

Dunn, L.C. "Cross Currents in the History of Human Genetics." AMERICAN JOURNAL OF HUMAN GENETICS 14 (March 1962): 1-13.

Eiseley, Loren Corey. DARWIN'S CENTURY: EVOLUTION AND THE MEN WHO DISCOVERED IT. Garden City, N.Y.: Doubleday, 1958. xvii, 378 p. Suggested readings. Index.

Foster, Sir M. LECTURES ON THE HISTORY OF PHYSIOLOGY DURING THE SIXTEENTH, SEVENTEENTH, AND EIGHTEENTH CENTURIES. Cambridge: At the University Press, 1901. Reprint. New York: Dover, 1970. vii, 310 p.

These lectures, with liberal quotations from original sources, cover selected individuals and their discoveries dating from Vesalius. A final chapter on older doctrines of the nervous system of particular interest to psychologists.

Franklin, K.J. A SHORT HISTORY OF PHYSIOLOGY. 2d ed. New York: Staples Press, 1949. iv, 122 p.

A brief, semipopular overview of the history of physiology from ancient times to the nineteenth century.

Fulton, John F., and Wilson, Leonard G., eds. SELECTED READINGS IN THE HISTORY OF PHYSIOLOGY. 2d ed., rev., enlarged and reset. Springfield, Ill.: Charles C Thomas, 1966. xxvi, 492 p.

Initially compiled by the late J.F. Fulton and completed by
L.G. Wilson (1930). Presents classic papers in traditional areas
of physiology such as digestion, circulation, endocrinology, and
the vascular system. Of particular interest to psychology are
sections on the central nervous system, homeostasis, muscle and
peripheral nerves, sexual generation, and endocrinology. Classical works preceded by brief biographical sketches. Index.

Gardner, Eldon J. HISTORY OF BIOLOGY. 3d ed. Minneapolis, Minn.:
Burgess Publishing Co., 1972. vii, 464 p.

An overview of major landmark contributions to biology from
ancient Greece to twentieth-century developments. Index.

Jacob, Francois. THE LOGIC OF LIFE: A HISTORY OF HEREDITY. Translated by Betty E. Spillman. New York: Pantheon Books, 1973. vii, 348 p.

Written by one of France's major scientists. Presents a nontechnical history of thought in heredity and reproduction from the sixteenth century to modern developments in molecular biology.
Bibliographical materials. Index. (Together with Lwoff and
Monod, Jacob received the Nobel Prize in 1965).

Koshtoyants, Kh. S. ESSAYS ON THE HISTORY OF PHYSIOLOGY IN RUS-
SIA. Translated by David P. Boder, Kristan Hanes, and Natalie O'Brien.
Edited by Donald B. Lindsley. Washington, D.C.: American Institute of
Biological Sciences, cosponsored by the American Psychological Association,
1964. xv, 321 p.

Explores selected topics in the history of Russian physiology and
psychology from the early eighteenth century through the first half
of the twentieth century, with emphasis on the work of Sechenov
and Pavlov. Bibliographical materials in footnotes. Index and
bibliography omitted in the English translation.

Lange, Friedrich Albert. THE HISTORY OF MATERIALISM: AND CRITICISM
OF ITS PRESENT IMPORTANCE. 3 vols. 3d ed. Translated by Ernest Chester
Thomas. New York: Humanities Press, 1950.

A classic (1865) work covering the history of materialism from the
early Greeks to its emergence in scientific physiology and psychology. Covers the positions of leading proponents of materialism in
England, France, and Germany; major criticisms of materialism;
and implications for morality and religion. Bibliographical materials in footnotes.

Lanham, Url. ORIGINS OF MODERN BIOLOGY. New York: Columbia
University Press, 1968. x, 273 p.

Outlines historical developments in biological thought from Greek times to the beginning of the twentieth century, with emphasis on the sixteenth, seventeenth, eighteenth, and nineteenth centuries. Bibliographical notes. Index.

McHenry, Lawrence C. GARRISON'S HISTORY OF NEUROLOGY. Springfield, Ill.: Charles C Thomas, 1969. xv, 552 p.

A revision and extension of Garrison's 1925 work. Covers the development of neurological thought from antiquity to nineteenth-century neuroanatomy, neurochemistry, and clinical neurology. Bibliography of classical, original, and standard works in neurology. References. Index.

Nordenskioeld, Erik. THE HISTORY OF BIOLOGY: A SURVEY. Translated by Leonard B. Eyre. New York: Tudor, 1936. ix, 629, xv p.

A substantial book relating the history of biology from classical antiquity to the early twentieth century, with some emphasis on European, especially Scandinavian, work. The original Swedish lectures on which it is based were written in 1916 and 1917.

Poynter, Frederick Noel Lawrence, ed. THE HISTORY AND PHILOSOPHY OF KNOWLEDGE OF THE BRAIN AND ITS FUNCTIONS; ANGLO-AMERICAN SYMPOSIUM, LONDON, JULY 15TH-17TH 1957. Oxford, Engl.: Blackwell, 1958. Reprint. Amsterdam: B.M. Israel, 1973. x, 272 p.

Riese, Walther. A HISTORY OF NEUROLOGY. New York: MD Publications, 1959. 223 p.

A brief but thorough general history of neurology. Contains chapters on the nervous impulse, reflex action, and cerebral localization. Useful chronological chart and lists of journals and neurological societies. Index.

Rothschuh, Karl E. HISTORY OF PHYSIOLOGY. Translated and edited by Guenter B. Risse. Huntington, N.Y.: Robert E. Kriefer, 1973 (1953). xxi, 379 p.

A translation and revision of the German text. Presents the history of physiology from fifth-century B.C. Greek thought to early twentieth-century developments. Describes the work of individuals important in the history of psychology such as Helmholtz, Magendie, Hering, Sherrington, Pavlov, and Johannes Mueller. Includes 151 pictures and figures. References. Index.

Singer, Charles. A SHORT HISTORY OF ANATOMY FROM THE GREEKS TO HARVEY. 2d ed. New York: Dover, 1957. xii, 209 p. Index.

_____. A SHORT HISTORY OF BIOLOGY: A GENERAL INTRODUCTION

TO THE STUDY OF LIVING THINGS. Oxford, Engl.: Clarendon Press, 1931. xxiv, 572 p.

An illustrated, semipopular work presenting an account of the historical development of biology from classical antiquity to the early twentieth century. Index.

Viets, Henry R. "The History of Neurology in the Last One Hundred Years." BULLETIN OF THE NEW YORK ACADEMY OF MEDICINE 24 (1948): 772–83.

Walker, A. Earl, ed. A HISTORY OF NEUROLOGICAL SURGERY. 1951. Reprint. New York: Hafner, 1967. xii, 582 p.

Contains fifteen chapters presenting historical materials on surgery in specific areas such as the hypophysis and the third ventricle, and for specific problems such as pain, epilepsy, and vascular anomalies. Includes a chapter on the history of diagnostic procedures. Bibliography. Index.

Wheeler, L.R. VITALISM: ITS HISTORY AND VALIDITY. London: H.F. and G. Witherby, 1939. xii, 275 p.

See annotation in section E5, p. 419.

4. SOCIOLOGY

The growth of sociological thought and psychological thought are often complementary. The following selected works are representative histories of sociological thought.

Abraham, J.H. THE ORIGINS AND GROWTH OF SOCIOLOGY. Baltimore: Penguin Books, 1973. 648 p.

A brief overview of the history of sociological thought followed by extracts from the writings of the great social theorists and sociologists from ancient and medieval times to the present. Theorists covered include Plato, Aristotle, Rousseau, Comte, de Tocqueville, Durkheim, Spencer, Marx, Weber, Sumner, Parsons, Mills, and Malinowski. Index.

Barnes, Harry Elmer, ed. AN INTRODUCTION TO THE HISTORY OF SOCIOLOGY. Chicago: University of Chicago Press, 1948. xvi, 960 p.

The result of the collaborative work of twenty-six contributors including Talcott Parsons and C. Wright Mills. Intended "as a comprehensive summary and critical appraisal of the growth of sociological thought from the ancient Near East to our own day." Chapters on the social-psychological thought of Wilhelm Wundt, Gustav Le Bon, and William Isaac Thomas of interest to psychologists. Notes. Bibliographical materials. Index.

Coser, Lewis A. MASTERS OF SOCIOLOGICAL THOUGHT: IDEAS IN HISTORICAL AND SOCIAL CONTEXT. New York: Harcourt Brace Jovanovich, 1971. xxi, 485 p.

Examines the work of twelve major sociological theorists: Auguste Comte, Karl Marx, Herbert Spencer, Emile Durkheim, Georg Simmel, Max Weber, Thorstein Veblen, Charles Horton Cooley, George Herbert Mead, Robert Ezra Park, Vilfredo Pareto, and Karl Mannheim. Explores the intellectual and social context influencing the work of each theorist. Biographical materials. References in footnotes. Index.

Fletcher, Ronald. THE MAKING OF SOCIOLOGY: A STUDY OF SOCIOLOGICAL THEORY. 2 vols. New York: Charles Scribner's Sons, 1971.

Explores the foundations of sociology in the works of such theorists as Comte, Spencer, John Stuart Mill, Marx, Ward, Sumner, and Giddings in volume 1 and more recent developments (theories of social evolution; evolution, development, and purpose; objective and subjective epistemologies; psychological aspects of society; social behaviorism and functionalism) in volume 2. Bibliography. Index.

Hinkle, Roscoe C. "Basic Orientations of the Founding Fathers of American Sociology." JOURNAL OF THE HISTORY OF THE BEHAVIORAL SCIENCES. 11 (April 1975): 107-22.

In response to historiography which treats early sociologists as a "gallery of intellectual luminaries or great men," Hinkle seeks a schema for making systematic comparisons among historic figures and applies that schema to such founding fathers of American sociology as Lester Frank Ward, William Graham Sumner, Franklin Henry Giddings, Albion Woodbury Small, Edward Alsworth Ross, and Charles Horton Cooley.

Maus, Heinz. A SHORT HISTORY OF SOCIOLOGY. New York: Philosophical Library, 1962. viii, 226 p.

A historical survey emphasizing national trends in the history of sociology. Index.

Mueller, Ronald H. "A Chapter in the History of the Relationship Between Psychology and Sociology in America: James Mark Baldwin." JOURNAL OF THE HISTORY OF THE BEHAVIORAL SCIENCES 12 (July 1976): 240-53.

Establishes the eminence of Baldwin and outlines some of his contributions in areas such as social psychology, philosophy, developmental processes, and biology. Selected biographical information.

Vine, Margaret Wilson. AN INTRODUCTION TO SOCIOLOGICAL THEORY. New York: Longmans, Green, 1959. xviii, 350 p.

Provides biographical materials, reviews of methods and central concepts, and evaluations of such major figures in sociological thought as Comte, Spencer, Ward, Sumner, Cooley, Ross, Weber, Sorokin, and Toynbee. Index.

5. SCIENCE, EDUCATION, AND STATISTICS

A history of science text can provide a sense of the scientific context in which psychology developed. Histories of education can clarify long-standing complementary interests of psychologists and educators. The history of statistics, written partly by the contributions of psychologists, clarifies the development of important research tools.

Bernal, J.D. SCIENCE IN HISTORY. 3d ed. 4 vols. London: C.A. Watts, 1965; Cambridge: M.I.T. Press, 1971.

A large-scale history of science from a Marxist perspective. Volume 1 covers the emergence and character of science, science in the ancient world, and science in the age of faith; volume 2 discusses the birth of modern science, and science and industry; volume 3, concentrating on the theme "science in our time," has lengthy chapters on twentieth-century physical and biological sciences; volume 4 discusses the social sciences before and after the world war, ending with a philosophical discussion of science and history. Notes, bibliography, acknowledgments, and index in each volume.

Bowen, James. A HISTORY OF WESTERN EDUCATION. 2 vols. Vol. 1, London: Methuen, 1972; Vol. 2, New York: St. Martin's Press, 1975.

Covers the history of education from early cultures in Mesopotamia and Egypt through Greek, Roman, and early Christian thought (volume 1), to the emergence of the European universities and the development of trends in specific European countries (volume 2). Bibliographical materials. Index.

Butterfield, H. THE ORIGINS OF MODERN SCIENCE, 1300-1800. Rev. ed. London: G. Bell and Sons, 1957. x, 242 p.

A history of European science written from the broad perspective of a historian concentrating on the evolution of ideas. Suggestions for further reading. Index.

Butts, R. Freeman, and Cremin, Lawrence A. A HISTORY OF EDUCATION IN AMERICAN CULTURE. New York: Holt, Rinehart and Winston, 1953. xi, 628 p.

Traces the history of education in America from colonial times with emphasis on social and industrial influences, philosophical

conflicts, and educational practices. Briefly discusses the influence of psychology. Suggestions for further reading. Index.

Cremin, Lawrence A. THE TRANSFORMATION OF THE SCHOOL: PROGRES-
SIVISM IN AMERICAN EDUCATION, 1876–1957. New York: Alfred A.
Knopf, 1964. xi, 387, xxiv p.

A study in the history of education detailing the growth, maturity,
and decline of the progressive movement in education. Lengthy
bibliographical note. Index.

Crombie, A.C. MEDIEVAL AND EARLY MODERN SCIENCE. Rev. 2d ed.
2 vols. New York: Doubleday, 1959.

See section B5a, p. 54, for annotation.

Curti, Merle E. THE SOCIAL IDEAS OF AMERICAN EDUCATORS, WITH A
NEW CHAPTER ON THE LAST TWENTY-FIVE YEARS. Rev. ed. Paterson,
N.J.: Littlefield, Adams, 1959. xliv, 613 p.

A history of the social thought of leaders in U.S. education, a
volume in the Report of the American Historical Association Commission on the Social Studies in the Schools. Traces the subject
from the early seventeenth century to the mid-twentieth century,
with chapters on such psychologists as G. Stanley Hall, William
James, E.L. Thorndike, and John Dewey. Bibliographical notes.
Index.

Dampier, Sir William Cecil. A HISTORY OF SCIENCE AND ITS RELATION
WITH PHILOSOPHY AND RELIGION. 4th ed., rev. and enl. New York:
Macmillan, 1949. xxvii, 527 p.

Gillispie, Charles Coulston. THE EDGE OF OBJECTIVITY: AN ESSAY IN
THE HISTORY OF SCIENTIFIC IDEAS. Princeton, N.J.: Princeton University
Press, 1960. vii, 562 p.

A major interpretation of selected scientific developments with
emphasis on the last two hundred years. Index.

Heath, A.E., ed. SCIENTIFIC THOUGHT IN THE TWENTIETH CENTURY:
AN AUTHORITATIVE ACCOUNT OF FIFTY YEARS' PROGRESS IN SCIENCE.
London: Watts, 1951. xvi, 387 p.

Fifteen relatively brief chapters, each by an expert, providing an
overview of the history of the various sciences (primarily in England) during the first half of the twentieth century. Includes
a chapter on psychology by Sir Cyril Burt.

Hofstadter, Richard, and Metzger, Walter P. THE DEVELOPMENT OF ACA-
DEMIC FREEDOM IN THE UNITED STATES. New York: Columbia University

Press, 1955. xvi, 527 p.

This analytical history of higher education from the Middle Ages through the colonial U.S. to the middle of the twentieth century, while concentrating on intellectual freedom in colleges and universities, is far broader in its treatment than its title suggests. Index.

Hofstadter, Richard, and Smith, Wilson, eds. AMERICAN HIGHER EDUCATION: A DOCUMENTARY HISTORY. 2 vols. Chicago: University of Chicago Press, 1961. xv, 1016, vii p.

An anthology of excerpts from major writings in the history of American higher education from 1633 to 1948. Headnotes for each section and thorough introductions to each of eleven sections. Index.

Knight, David. SOURCES FOR THE HISTORY OF SCIENCE 1660-1914. Ithaca, N.Y.: Cornell University Press, 1975. 223 p.

A helpful resource for those wishing to do historical research in science. Explores the uses of such sources as manuscripts, journals, histories of science, antique scientific equipment, and nonscientific books. Notes. Bibliographical sources. Index.

Lovejoy, Arthur O. THE GREAT CHAIN OF BEING: A STUDY OF THE HISTORY OF AN IDEA. Cambridge, Mass.: Harvard University Press, 1936. Reprint. New York: Harper Torchbooks, 1960. x, 376 p.

An erudite history of Western thought on ontology, cosmology, and science from a philosophical perspective. Index.

Mason, Stephen F. A HISTORY OF THE SCIENCES. Rev. ed. New York: Collier Books, 1962. 638 p.

A comprehensive text covering scientific thought from ancient cultures to the twentieth century. Emphasizes developments in the physical and biological sciences. Bibliography. Index.

Merz, John Theodore. A HISTORY OF EUROPEAN THOUGHT IN THE 19TH CENTURY. PART I: SCIENTIFIC THOUGHT. Vols. 1 and 2. London: William Blackwood, 1904-12.

A comprehensive, philosophically-oriented history of European science. Index. (For last two volumes, see section E1a, p. 380).

Royce, Joseph R. "The Development of Factor Analysis." JOURNAL OF GENERAL PSYCHOLOGY 58 (1958): 139-64.

A nontechnical paper tracing selected historical themes, recent advances, and applications of factor analysis.

Rudolph, Frederick. THE AMERICAN COLLEGE AND UNIVERSITY: A HIS-TORY. New York: Alfred A. Knopf, 1962. xii, 516, xxxvii p.

> Provides an answer to the question, "How and why and with what consequences have the American colleges and universities developed as they have?," beginning with the colonial college and ending in the mid-twentieth century. Thorough bibliography. Index.

Schachner, Nathan. THE MEDIAEVAL UNIVERSITIES. New York: Frederick A. Stokes, 1938. viii, 388 p.

> Traces the genesis and development of one of the important institutions in human intellectual history, the European universities in such places as Paris, Bologna, Oxford, Montpellier, and Cambridge. Bibliography. Index.

Thorndike, Lynn. HISTORY OF MAGIC AND EXPERIMENTAL SCIENCE, DURING THE FIRST THIRTEEN CENTURIES OF OUR ERA. 8 vols. New York: Columbia University Press, 1923-58.

> A mammoth undertaking, more than six thousand pages long, providing a history of science from the first century A.D. through the seventeenth century. Index.

Todhunter, Isaac. A HISTORY OF THE MATHEMATICAL THEORY OF PROBA-BILITY: FROM THE TIME OF PASCAL TO THAT OF LAPLACE. 1865. Reprint. New York: Chelsea, 1965. xvi, 624 p.

> A thorough work with numerous quotations. Covers the historical development of such topics as combinations, mortality and life insurance, and the area under a curve. Includes the contributions of Kepler, Galileo, Pascal, the Bernoullis, Montmort, DeMoivre, Euler, D'Alembert, Bayes, Lagrange, Condorcet, Trembley, and Laplace. A common notation system facilitates reading and the making of comparisons. Appendix describes lesser-known works. Index.

Usher, Abbott Payson. A HISTORY OF MECHANICAL INVENTIONS. Rev. ed. Cambridge, Mass.: Harvard University Press, 1954. xi, 450 p.

> See section C11d, p. 196, for annotation.

Veysey, Laurence R. THE EMERGENCE OF THE AMERICAN UNIVERSITY. Chicago: University of Chicago Press, 1965. xiv, 505 p.

> A thorough study based on a doctoral dissertation in history. Details the conflict of rival conceptions of higher learning from 1865 to 1910 and pursues the emergence of the leading U.S. universities between 1890 and 1910. Chronology of principal university administrations. Bibliographical note. Note on manuscript collections. Index.

Walker, Helen M. STUDIES IN THE HISTORY OF STATISTICAL METHOD, WITH SPECIAL REFERENCE TO CERTAIN EDUCATIONAL PROBLEMS. Baltimore: Williams and Wilkins, 1929. viii, 229 p.

Focuses on the early discoveries of theorists such as DeMoivre, Bernoulli, Galton, Pearson, Gauss, Fechner, and Ebbinhaus. Covers such major statistical topics as the normal curve, moments, percentiles, and correlation. One chapter outlines the development of the teaching of statistics in American universities. Pictures and illustrations. Table on the origins of technical terms. Index.

Wheeler, L. Richmond. VITALISM: ITS HISTORY AND VALIDITY. London: H.F. and G. Witherby, 1939. xii, 275 p.

Traces animistic thought in its various meanings from ancient times to nineteenth-century developments. Of particular interest to psychologists is a section on early twentieth-century vitalistic thought in psychology. Index.

Wieruszowksi, Helene. THE MEDIEVAL UNIVERSITY. Princeton, N.J.: D. Van Nostrand, 1966. 207 p.

Outlines the development of universities in France, Germany, England, and Italy. Reproduces excerpts of letters which refer to such matters as early rules and regulations, student life, relations of the universities to the church, and the manner in which certain subjects were taught. Bibliographical materials in footnotes. Index.

Woolf, Harry, ed. QUANTIFICATION: A HISTORY OF THE MEANING OF MEASUREMENT IN THE NATURAL AND SOCIAL SCIENCES. Indianapolis: Bobbs-Merrill, 1961. 224 p.

Proceedings of a conference on the history of quantification in the sciences. Includes papers on the history of quantification in such disciplines as physics, chemistry, medical science, psychology, sociology, biology, and economics. The paper on the history of quantification in psychology, by Edwin G. Boring, covers such topics as historical developments in psychophysics, reaction time, learning and remembering and individual differences. References.

NAME INDEX

This index includes all names of authors, editors, translators, and historical figures in psychology that are cited in this bibliography. Also included are the names of some well-known organizations which are responsible for the publication of works cited in this volume. All entries are alphabetized letter by letter. The reader interested in writings about particular individuals is urged to consult appropriate entries in the subject index, p. 475.

A

Abdi, Yusuf Omer 58
Abel, Theodora M. 148, 290
Abelard, Peter 301
Abraham, Hilda C. 208, 219
Abraham, J.H. 413
Abraham, Karl 201, 208, 219
Abse, D.W. 357
Abt, Lawrence Edwin 60, 62, 77
Achilles, Paul S. 368
Ackerknecht, Erwin H. 397
Adams, Grace 40, 135
Adams, James F. 65, 84
Aderman, Morris 241
Adler, Alfred 201, 202, 211, 215-16, 221, 240, 245, 262, 359, 383
Adler, Gerhard 216, 218
Adler, Helmut E. 84
Adler, Kurt A. 215
Adler, Leonore L. 262
Adorno, T.W. 305
Akhilanda, Swami 59
Albee, George 4
Albert, Peter 175
Albert the Great 379
Albrecht, Frank M. 127, 128

Alcmaeon 383
Aldrich, E.P. 141
Alexander, Franz 208, 209, 220, 397
Alibert, Jean Louis 75
Alighieri, Dante 301
Allee, W.C. 265
Allen, David 158, 159, 175, 300
Allen, Garland E. 409
Allen, Thomas W. 215
Allport, Floyd 284
Allport, Gordon W. 48, 50, 59, 85, 100, 115, 141, 142, 148, 209, 226, 227, 305, 306, 309, 333, 334, 335
Alonzo, Thomas M. 237
Alston, William P. 169
Altmann, Margaret 262
Altschule, Mark D. 338, 382, 398, 401
Amacher, Peter 200
Amatruda, Catherine 329, 330
Amdur, M.K. 401
American Psychological Association 1, 23, 25, 29
Ames, Louise B. 330
Ames, Van Meter 141
Anandalakshmy, S. 322

Name Index

Ananiev, B. 78
Anastasi, Anne 316, 338, 369
Anaxagoras 51, 393
Anderson, Richard J. 130
Anderson, Robert M. 182, 274
Andersson, Ola 200
Angel, Ernest 226
Angell, Frank 135
Angell, James Rowland 52, 130, 142, 147, 148, 149, 175, 237, 297, 365
Angermeir, W.F. 65
Angier, R.P. 142
Angyal, Andras 306
Annan, Gertrude L. 7, 11
Annin, Edith L. 109, 111, 112, 114
Anokhin, P.K. 83
Anrep, G.V. 180
Ansbacher, Heinz L. 24, 26, 215, 216
Ansbacher, Rowena 215
Anthony, E. James 200
Anthony, James 229
Appley, M.H. 70, 297, 298
Aquinas, St. Thomas 48, 55, 382, 384, 387, 389, 394, 396
Ardila, Ruben 77
Aries, Philippe 323, 326
Ariotti, Piero 282
Aristotle 34, 38, 48, 49, 55, 56, 58, 167, 169, 175, 186, 187, 190, 192, 205, 262, 280, 283, 287, 299, 302, 312, 358, 380, 383, 385, 388, 389, 390, 391, 392, 394, 395, 396, 410, 413
Armstrong, Andrew C. 155
Arnheim, R. 194
Arnold, Magda B. 221
Arnold, W. 20
Aron, Betty 305
Aronson, Elliot 333, 336
Aronson, Lester R. 262
Aronson, M.L. 340
Arvidson, Robert M. 70
Asch, Solomon E. 182, 335
Asher, H. 83, 180
Assigny, Marius d' 56
Astin, Helen S. 102
Atkinson, Richard C. 40

Augustine, Aurelius. See Augustine, Saint, of Hippo
Augustine, Saint, of Hippo 48, 54, 56, 379, 382, 392, 396
Aurelius Augustine. See Augustine, Saint, of Hippo
Averill, James R. 48
Avicenna 56, 393, 404
Ayman, Iraj 59
Ayre, Elizabeth 290
Az-Zarnuji, Burhan ad-Din 290

B

Bachrach, Arthur J. 356
Bachtold, Louise M. 103
Bacon, Francis 303, 382
Baerends, Gerard 265
Bagchi, Amalendu 59
Bagley, William Chandler 365
Bailey, P. 200
Bailey, Samuel 74, 287, 288
Bailyn, Bernard 67
Bain, Alexander 51, 73, 74, 86, 153, 249, 275, 280, 283, 289, 302, 303, 333
Bain, Bruce 383
Baines, Cecil 220
Bakan, David 84, 128, 129, 130, 165, 200, 209, 229
Baker, J. 355
Balance, William D.G. 49, 51, 115, 131, 357
Baldessarini, Ross J. 338
Baldick, Robert 323
Baldwin, Alfred Lee 329
Baldwin, Bird T. 130, 328
Baldwin, James Mark 15, 19, 31, 35, 41, 42, 68, 70, 85, 86, 89, 149, 234, 242, 249, 256, 326, 327, 335, 414
Ballou, Robert O. 146
Baltes, Paul B. 323, 325
Baltimore, Gertrude 224
Bancroft, Mary 216
Banerji, Manmatha Nath 60
Barchilon, José 341
Barclay, James R. 133
Bard, P.A. 303
Baritz, Loren 369

C

Eisenstein, Samuel 220
Eissler, K.R. 124
Ekehammer, Bo 307
Ekstein, Rudolf 202, 220
Eliasberg, Wladimir G. 209
Elkind, David 324, 329, 332
Ellenberger, Henri F. 202, 226, 340
Elliott, Charles K. 28
Ellis, Albert 240, 358
Ellis, Norman R. 348
Ellis, Willis Davis 189, 194, 276
Ellison, D.R. 219
Ellson, Douglas G. 311
Ellson, Elizabeth Cox 311
Elon, L. Clark 369
Emmert, E. 282, 284
Eng, Erling W. 54, 101, 189, 193, 228, 358
Engen, Trygg 312
Engle, T.L. 250, 251
English, Eva Champney 19
English, Horace B. 19, 231, 240, 291
Engreen, Evelyn K. 240
Engreen, Fred E. 240
Epstein, William 285
Erdely, Michael 370
Erickson, Ralph Waldo 10, 107, 134, 137, 170, 231, 240
Erigena, Johannes Scotus 56
Erikson, Erik H. 220, 221, 331
Erikson, R.W. 223
Ertle, Jutta E. 117, 257
Esper, Erwin A. 33, 119
Esquirol, Jean-Etienne-Dominique 338, 401
Estes, William K. 293
Estey, Helen Grace 10
Euler, Leonard 418
Evans, B. 403
Evans, Elizabeth Glendower 143
Evans, Rand B. 49, 98, 101, 131, 137, 140
Evans, Richard I. 48, 49, 115, 217, 266
Ewalt, Jack R. 403
Ewalt, Patricia L. 403
Ewer, Bernard C. 370
Eyre, Leonard B. 412

Eysenck, H.-J. 20, 170, 231, 307

F

Fancher, Raymond E. 134, 202, 240
Farber, Marvin 223, 381
Farnsworth, P.R. 298
Farr, C.B. 403
Farrand, Livingston 97, 317
Fay, Jay Wharton 86, 118
Fearing, Franklin 107, 274, 276
Fechner, Gustav Theodor 49, 50, 66, 67, 68, 69, 84, 144, 146, 202, 262, 284, 285, 287, 288, 386, 391, 418
Federn, Ernest 216
Fehr, Robert C. 70
Feifel, Herman 226
Feigl, Herbert 172, 381, 386
Feinstein, Howard M. 124, 403
Feldman, S. 131
Feldman, W.T. 151
Felter, Jacqueline W. 7, 11
Ferenczi, Sandor 201
Ferguson, H.H. 387
Ferguson, Leonard W. 370
Fernberger, Samuel W. 54, 87, 97, 131, 240, 256
Ferrier, David 49, 52, 280, 289
Festinger, Leon 231, 334
Feuchtersleben, Ernst von 205, 403
Feuer, Lewis S. 151, 240
Fialko, Norman 387
Fichte, Johann Gottlieb 51, 68, 380
Field, John 275
Figlio, Karl M. 285
Fine, B. 199
Fine, Reuben 170, 197
Finison, Lorenz J. 87, 98, 375
Finn, Michael H.P. 375
Fischer, Constance T. 118, 223
Fischer, Ronald A. 266
Fisher, Donald 33
Fisher, Seymour 213
Fishman, Stephen M. 143
Fisk, Margaret 98
Fiske, Donald W. 376
Fite, Warner 151

Name Index

Fitzpatrick, John J. 123
Flanagan, J.C. 311
Flavell, John H. 329, 332
Fleming, Donald 67, 167
Fletcher, Ronald 414
Flor-Henry, P. 403
Flourens, Pierre 52, 279, 280
Flournoy, Theodore 146
Fluckiger, Fritz A. 223
Flugel, John Carl 31, 33, 73, 108
Focht, Mildred 188
Fodor, Jerry A. 231
Fodor, Nandor 198
Foley, Jeanne M. 335
Foley, John P., Jr. 338
Ford, Adelbert 34
Fordham, Frieda 217
Fordham, Michael 218
Forescue, G.K. 8
Forest, Louise C. Turner 54
Forrest, D.W. 312
Forrest, Derek 257
Foss, B.M. 73
Foster, G. 143
Foster, Sir M. 410
Foster, William S. 257
Foucault, Michael 341
Foulkes, Paul 381
Fox, Dixon Ryan 45
Fox, Ronald E. 341
Fraisse, Paul 75, 166
Frank, George H. 358
Frank, Jerome D. 190, 193
Frankl, Viktor E. 223
Franklin, K.J. 410
Franz, Shepard Ivory 87, 356
Freedberg, E.J. 359
Freedman, Alfred M. 404
Freeman, Frank S. 182
Freeman, G.L. 190
Freeman, Lucy 209
Freeman, Walter 403
Freides, Thelma 10
Freigius, Johannes Thomas 96
Frenkel-Brunswik, Else 209, 305
Freud, Anna 210, 220
Freud, Ernest L. 208
Freud, Sigmund 37, 42, 53, 57,
   80, 91, 124, 133, 134, 165,
   174, 182, 197, 198, 199, 200,

201, 202, 203, 204, 205, 206,
207, 208, 209, 210, 211, 212,
213, 214, 215, 216, 217, 218,
219, 220, 221, 229, 234, 238,
239, 240, 242, 243, 245, 246,
307, 326, 328, 338, 339, 343,
358, 359, 397, 398, 400, 402,
403, 404
Frey-Rohn, Liliane 240
Friedman, Erwin 325
Friedman, Lawrence 202, 203
Friedman, Morton 284
Friedmann, Alfred 312
Fries, Jakob Friedrich 67
Frisby, C.B. 370
Fritsch, Gustav 280
Froebel, F. 51
Froebes, Joseph 99
Frolov, Y.P. 178
From, F. 95
Fromm, Eric 115, 211, 213, 221,
   240, 307
Frost, Elliot Park 137
Fryer, D.H. 370
Fuchs, Alfred H. 64, 136, 240,
   242
Fujita, Osamu 188
Fulcher, J. Rodney 87, 128
Fulton, John F. 273, 410, 411
Furfey, P.H. 241

G

Galdston, Iago 398
Galen 56, 277, 278, 279, 280,
   289, 308, 341, 342, 391, 407,
   408
Galileo 54, 186, 187, 192, 391,
   392, 418
Gall, Franz Joseph 128, 129, 153,
   288
Galton, Francis 51, 52, 72, 86,
   153, 308, 310, 311, 312, 313,
   314, 317, 320, 321, 356, 368,
   418
Galvani, Luigi 279
Ganguli, Harish C. 60
Gantt, W. Horsley 180, 296
Gardeil, H.D. 382, 387, 396
Gardiner, Harry W. 60

Name Index

Gardiner, H.M. 299
Gardiner, Judith Kegan 55
Gardner, Eldon J. 411
Gardner, Mark B. 285
Garfield, Sol L. 354, 357
Garforth, Francis W. 387
Garner, Wendell R. 369
Garrett, Henry E. 190, 257
Garrison, Fielding Hudson 412
Garvey, C.R. 87, 257
Gates, Arthur I. 194
Gaub, Jerome 279
Gauss, Christian 418
Gavin, Eileen A. 223, 387
Gaynor, F. 198
Gedo, John E. 203
Geissler, L.R. 241
Gelb, Adhémar 224
Geldard, Frank A. 285
Gengerelli, J.A. 87
Gerard, Eugene O. 55
Gesell, Arnold 310, 326, 328, 329, 330
Geulincx, Arnold 388
Ghiselli, Edwin 4
Giannitrapani, Duilio 277
Gibbons, J. 81, 179
Gibson, James J. 183, 294
Gibson, W.R.B. 224
Giddings, Franklin Henry 414
Gifford, G. 147
Gifford, Sanford 67
Gilbert, Albin R. 60, 223, 232, 299, 307
Gillis, John R. 330
Gillispie, Charles C. 3, 416
Ginsburg, Herbert 330, 332
Giorgi, Amedeo 224, 241
Glaze, J. Arthur 294
Goddard, Henry Herbert 321, 348
Goeckel, Rudolf 96
Goethe, Johann Wolfgang von 285, 357, 358, 383
Golann, S.E. 355
Goldenson, Robert M. 20
Goldman, George D. 363
Goldsmith, M.L. 359
Goldsmith, Margaret 74
Goldstein, Abraham 404
Goldstein, Kurt 67, 183, 187, 194, 224, 307

Goldstein, Melvin L. 277
Golomb, Jacob 224
Goodenough, Florence L. 42, 312, 330
Goodman, Elizabeth S. 113
Goodson, Felix H. 234
Goshen, Charles E. 75, 398
Goss, Albert E. 174
Gottfurcht, James W. 109
Gottlieb, Gilbert 166
Gouaux, Charles 387
Goudge, Thomas A. 387
Gould, Julius 20
Gould, Silas E. 250
Goulet, L.R. 323, 325
Grabowski, John 364
Graham, C.H. 63, 174
Graham, Thomas F. 359
Granit, R.A. 137
Grashey, Hubert von 310
Gray, George W. 174
Gray, H. 217
Gray, J. Stanley 174, 359
Gray, Philip Howard 174, 263, 272, 325, 387
Graziano, Anthony M. 359
Greenberg, Roger P. 213
Greenhouse, Herbert B. 303
Greenspoon, Joel 175
Greenstein, Fred 123
Gregg, F.M. 190
Gregory, J.C. 170
Gregson, E.D. 273
Gregson, R.A.M. 273
Griffin, A.K. 388
Griffin, Donald R. 266
Griffith, Coleman R. 34, 42, 118
Grinder, Robert E. 322, 325
Grinstein, Alexander 11, 198
Grob, Gerald N. 352
Groffman, Karl J. 325
Grossman, Frank 370
Grotjahn, Martin 203, 210, 220
Grove, Carl 110
Gruba-McCallister, Frank P. 119
Gruner, O. Cameron 404
Guilford, J.P. 93, 241, 251, 311, 312, 317, 371
Guillain, Georges 363
Guislain, Joseph 310

431

Name Index

Johanningmeier, Erwin V. 365
Johannsen, Dorothea E. 287
Johnson, A.H. 388
Johnson, Allen 3
Johnson, Alvin 19, 22
Johnson, H.M. 287
Johnson, Hiram K. 210
Johnson, Rochelle J. 170
Johnson, Samuel 87
Johnson Associates, Inc. 46
Johnstone, Thomas 405
Joncich, Geraldine M. 155, 156
Jones, Ernest 204, 209, 211
Jones, L. Wynn 309
Jones, Mary Cover 175, 304, 342
Josey, Charles C. 195
Jousset, P. 49
Joynt, Robert J. 129
Judd, Charles Hubbard 130, 133, 252, 258, 365, 368
Juhasz, Joseph B. 56, 274, 345
Jung, Carl Gustav 113, 115, 201, 202, 211, 216-19, 221, 240, 241, 246, 359, 397

K

Kagan, Jacob M. 366
Kahn, Eugen 224
Kahn, Samuel 198
Kaketa, Katsumi 61
Kallikak, Martin 348
Kamin, Leon J. 322
Kaminsky, Jack 152
Kanner, Leo 326, 342, 404
Kant, Immanuel 48, 49, 67, 68, 187, 201, 224, 301, 302, 308, 380, 384, 387, 388, 396
Kantor, Jacob R. 34, 58, 73, 119, 145, 152, 162, 167, 174, 184, 232, 284, 287, 392
Kao, John J. 404
Kaplan, Harold I. 200, 204, 359, 404
Kappauf, William E. 371
Karamyan, A.I. 80
Kare, Morley R. 287
Karier, Clarence J. 322
Kashiwagi, K. 63
Kassinove, Howard 110

Kastenbaum, R.K. 327
Katz, Alfred H. 360
Katz, David 184
Kauffman, James M. 342
Kaufman, Lloyd 282
Kaufman, M. Ralph 388
Kaur, Amrit 366
Kavruck, Samuel 371
Kawai, Hayao 218
Kawash, George F. 240, 242
Kazdin, Alan E. 360
Keehn, J.D. 169, 170
Kellaway, Peter 277
Keller, Fred S. 34, 35
Keller, Mark 342
Kelly, Barry N. 342, 404
Kelly, Lowell E. 376
Kelman, Harold 218, 224
Kempf, E.J. 294
Kendler, Howard H. 162
Kenny, Anthony 386, 389
Kepler, Johannes 54, 418
Kern, Stephen 204
Kessen, William 326
Kido, Mantaro 61
Kierkegaard, Søren 240, 395
Kiernan, Thomas 38, 400
Kilby, Richard W. 61
Killam, Keith F. 277
Kim, Kwang-Iel 402
Kimble, Gregory A. 81, 179, 291, 295
Kimmel, E. 104
King, C. Daly 138, 389
King, Lester S. 277
King, William P. 171
Kingsbury, Forrest A. 93
Kinnaird, Lucia Burk 78
Kircher, A. 273
Kirihara, Shigemi H. 61
Kirsch, Irving 120, 233, 258
Kirsch, James 218
Kisch, Ruth 83, 180
Kissinger, Henry 123
Kite, Elizabeth S. 316
Kivitz, Marvin S. 345
Klaf, Franklin S. 342
Klein, Barry T. 21
Klein, David B. 31, 35, 211, 213, 233

Name Index

Klemm, Otto 35
Klibbe, Helene 278
Klinghammer, Erich 266
Klix, Friedhart 66
Klopfer, Peter H. 263, 267
Klopfer, Walter G. 312
Knight, David 417
Knight, Rex 73
Knoff, William F. 342, 343, 405
Knopfelmacher, F. 171
Knotts, Josephine R. 292
Knox, G.W. 184, 190
Koch, Sigmund 233, 252, 277, 288
Kockelmans, Joseph J. 89, 224
Koehler, Wolfgang 37, 66, 67, 89,
    142, 180, 183, 184, 185, 187,
    188, 189, 190, 191, 195, 241,
    243, 267, 407
Koellin, Fritz C.A. 379
Koffka, Kurt 37, 67, 87, 116,
    183, 186, 187, 189, 190, 191,
    331, 367
Kohlberg, Lawrence 48
Kohyama, Iwao 225
Koizumi, K. 297
Kolb, W.L. 20
Konorski, Jerzy 292
Kopell, Bert S. 75, 343
Korman, Maurice 376
Kornilov, Konstantin N. 82, 179,
    181
Korzybski, Alfred 396
Koshtoyants, Kh. S. 180, 411
Kovach, Joseph K. 31, 37
Kovacs, Arthur L. 360
Kraepelin, Emil 49, 356, 401,
    404, 405
Krafft-Ebing, Richard von 49, 349
Krantz, David L. 31, 35, 106, 136,
    158, 159, 175, 242, 300, 308
Krasner, Leonard 242
Kraus, Karl 212
Kraus, Oskar 134
Krause, Irl B., Jr. 326
Kraushaar, Otto F. 145
Krawiec, T.S. 3, 31, 33, 121, 333
Krech, David 336
Krechevsky, I.A. 292
Kren, George M. 124
Krenzel, K. 76

Krichev, Alan 357
Kroll, Jerome 326
Krueger, J.C. 258
Krueger, Wm. C.F. 295
Kubie, Lawrence S. 242
Kudlien, Fridolf 360
Kuelpe, Oswald 133, 134, 135,
    182, 240
Kuenzli, Alfred E. 225
Kuhn, Ronald 226
Kuhn, Thomas 112
Kult, Milton 117
Kuna, David P. 371
Kuo, You-Yuh 61, 159
Kuo, Zing Yang 166, 175, 176
Kurland, Morton L. 354
Kussmaul, Adolf 49

L

LaCagnina, Giulia R. 237
La Chambre, Marin Cureau de 54
Lachman, Sheldon J. 176, 277
Ladd, George Trumbull 89, 92,
    252, 258, 261, 281
La Fave, Lawrence 191
La Forge, Louis de 291
Lagrange, Joseph Louis, Comte 418
Laing, B.M. 389
Laird, John 389
Lamarck, Jean-Baptiste de Monet,
    Chevalier de 86
Lambert, Johann Heinrich 260
La Mettrie, Julien Offray de 168,
    175, 264, 387, 388, 393, 394
Lampl-de Groot, Jeanne 204
Lana, Robert E. 233
Lancaster, Joseph 360
Landauer, A.A. 192, 371
Landes, Margaret W. 389
Landis, Carney 209, 341, 342
Landsman, Ted 225
Lane, Harlan C. 326, 349
Lang, Frederick R. 56
Lange, Carl Georg 299, 302, 303,
    304
Lange, Friedrich Albert 411
Langer, Walter C. 67
Langfeld, Herbert S. 3, 12, 67,
    89, 101, 138, 159, 243, 249,
    250, 258

Name Index

Lonsdale, Kathleen 104
Lorand, Sandor 199, 204
Lorenz, Konrad 48, 245, 264, 266,
268, 298
Lotze, Rudolph Hermann 66, 68,
92, 145, 281
Loughnan, H.B. 155
Loukas, Christ 390
Louttit, Chauncey M. 10, 13, 43,
371, 375
Loveday, T. 390
Lovejoy, Arthur O. 417
Lowenberg, Peter 204
Lowie, Robert H. 104
Lowry, Richard 31, 35, 179, 204,
292
Lubin, Alice W. 360
Lubin, Bernard 354, 360
Lubinoff, M.N. 284
Luce, R. Duncan 4
Luchins, Abraham S. 191, 195
Luchins, Edith H. 195
Luckhardt, A.B. 304
Ludwig, Emil 211
Lund, Frederick H. 191
Lundholm, Helge 191
Lundin, Robert W. 31, 35
Luria, A.R. 48, 78, 83, 281
Lwoff, Andre 411
Lycurgus 364
Lyman, Richard 123
Lynch, Edmund C. 371
Lynch, J.A. 152
Lyons, Joseph 226

M

McAlister, Linda L. 134
Macalpine, Ida 214, 399
McClelland, David 231
McCollom, Ivan N. 372
McCormick, Ernest J. 372
McCullers, John C. 326
McDermott, John F., Jr. 346
McDonald, William T. 296
McDougall, William 37, 42, 89,
158–60, 163, 173, 175, 191,
193, 243, 244, 245, 252, 264,
281, 289, 300, 305, 334, 335,
336, 341, 349, 359

Mace, C.A. 73, 74
Mace, Marjorie 74
McElwain, D.W. 64
McFarland, Ross A. 78
McGaugh, J.L. 173
McGeoch, John A. 233, 295, 296
McGill, Raymond D. 5
McGill, V.J. 225, 244
McGinnies, Elliott 62
McGregor, Douglas 372
MacGregor, Frances Coke 331
McGuire, William J. 120, 218
Mach, Ernst 135, 267
McHenry, Lawrence C. 412
Machovec, Frank J. 361
Mack, Robert D. 390
McKeachie, Wilbert J. 89
MacKenzie, Brian D. 120, 171,
390
MacKenzie, S. Lynne 120
Mackie, R. Andrew 391
McKinney, Fred 43, 153
Mackler, Bernard 343, 405
McLeish, John 82, 179
MacLeod, Robert B. 35, 70, 71,
140, 222, 223, 225, 244, 287
McMahon, C.E. 300, 343
McMalton, Carol E. 277
MacMillan, M.B. 343
McMurray, J.G. 366
McNeill, John T. 399
McNemar, Quinn 298
McPherson, Marion White 102, 115,
116, 117, 259, 312, 318
McReynolds, Paul 299, 300, 313,
391
Madden, Edward H. 153, 196, 233
Maddi, Salvatore R. 225
Magendie, Francois 52, 280, 412
Magoun, H.W. 275
Mahan, A. 86
Maher, Brendan 191
Maier, Barbara M. 268
Maier, Henry W. 331
Maier, Norman R.F. 196, 268
Maier, Richard A. 268
Maine de Biran, Marie Francois
Pierre Gonthier 380, 388
Major, Rene 343
Majovsky, Lawrence V. 281

Name Index

Miller, Anne C. 114
Miller, Arthur I. 186, 196
Miller, Eugene F. 392
Miller, George A. 36, 253, 375
Miller, H.C. 220
Miller, James G. 82
Miller, Jessie L. 82, 349
Miller, Julian A. 205
Miller, Neal E. 231
Mills, Alden B. 407
Mills, C. Wright 413
Milman, Donald S. 363
Miner, J.B. 99
Minkowski, Eugene 226
Mintz, Alexander 82, 258
Mischel, Theodore 74, 171, 301
Mises, Dr. 386, 391
Mishler, Elliot G. 171
Misiak, Henryk 31, 36, 52, 58,
    77, 99, 226, 392
Mitchell, Alexander R. 344
Mitchell, Mildred B. 104
Mitra, S.C. 62
Miyaka, K. 63
Molish, Herman B. 48, 353
Mollinger, Robert N. 124
Molyneux, William 72, 289
Monod, Jacques 411
Montaigne, Michel de 167
Montessori, Maria 77, 324, 327
Montmort, Pierre Raymond de 418
Moore, Burness 199
Moore, Clyde B. 97
Moore, Jared Sparks 36, 211, 253
Moore, John Robert 301
Moore, Kate Gordon 56, 57
Moore, Thomas V. 99, 187
Moore-Russell, Martha E. 392
Mora, George 345, 400, 402, 405,
    406
Morales, Manuel 78
More, Thomas 262
Moreno, J.L. 307, 359, 361
Moreno, Zerka T. 344
Morgan, Clifford T. 119, 281, 369
Morgan, Conwy Lloyd 52, 187, 262,
    264, 269, 274, 305, 366
Morgan, J. 392
Moritz, Karl Philipp 101
Morris, Charles W. 153

Morrison, James C. 226
Morrow, William 306
Mosak, Harold H. 216
Moskowitz, Howard R. 313
Moskowitz, Merle J. 372
Moss, R.A. 269
Mossner, Ernest C. 392
Motoyoshi, Ryoji 62
Mott, Frank Luther 14
Mountjoy, Paul T. 113, 264, 273,
    392
Moustgaard, I.K. 226
Mowrer, O. Hobart 162, 292, 301,
    307, 344, 361
Muckler, Fredrick A. 167
Mudge, Isadore Gilbert 11
Mueller, Georg Elias 68, 187,
    255, 289, 291
Mueller, Johannes 278, 280, 287,
    412
Mueller, Ronald H. 70, 414
Mueller-Freienfels, Richard 36, 66,
    108
Muensterberg, Hugo 42, 115, 142,
    253, 366, 372
Muensterberg, Margaret 372
Mukhopadhyay, P.K. 62
Mullahy, Patrick 211, 406
Muller, P.H. 95
Munn, Norman L. 264, 269, 273
Munnichs, J.M. 326
Munroe, Ruth L. 205, 220
Murakami, Eiji 60
Murase, Takao 60
Murchison, Carl 3, 4, 36, 37,
    47, 94, 155, 157, 159, 215,
    259, 331, 337
Murphy, Emma 178
Murphy, Gardner 31, 37, 43, 51,
    62, 108, 120, 146, 187, 192,
    193, 214, 392
Murphy, Lois B. 4, 37, 51, 62
Murphy, William 178
Murray, D.J. 292
Murray, Henry A. 142, 209, 226,
    309, 389
Mursell, James L. 171
Muschinske, David 366
Muscio, Bernard A. 371
Mussen, Paul H. 329, 331

Name Index

Papageorgiou, Michael G. 361
Papanek, Helene 216
Paracelsus 398, 406
Parad, Libbie G. 361
Pardies, Ignace 386
Pareek, Udai 63
Pareto, Vilfredo 414
Park, Dorothy G. 214
Park, Robert Ezra 414
Parkin, Alan 205, 344
Parsons, Gail Pat 352
Parsons, Talcott 334, 413
Pascal, Blaise 418
Pascual-Leone, Juan 327
Pastore, Nicholas 120, 146, 187, 278, 287, 288, 322
Patch, Ian L. 362
Paterson, Garry 362
Patrick, George T.W. 94
Patterson, C.H. 227
Pattie, Frank A. 362
Paul, Cedar 342
Paul, Eden 342
Pavlov, Ivan Petrovitch 50, 72, 79, 81, 82, 116, 160, 178, 179, 180, 181, 182, 242, 243, 290, 291, 292, 294, 296, 356, 398, 411, 412
Payne, T.R. 180
Pearson, Karl 312, 313, 314, 418
Peatman, John G. 193
Peele, Roger 339
Peirce, Charles S. 149, 152, 153, 154, 387, 390
Peixotto, Helen E. 94
Penfield, Wilder 137, 278
Pennington, L.A. 253
Pepper, Stephen C. 162
Perkins, Elisha 358, 362
Perkins, F. Theodore 193, 303
Perloff, Linda S. 108
Perloff, Robert 108
Perls, Frederick 182, 195
Perry, Jon 56
Perry, Ralph Barton 142, 143, 146, 147, 159, 176
Persons, Stow 85, 380
Pestalozzi, J.H. 51
Peterfreund, Emanuel 124
Peterman, B. 187

Peters, R.S. 31, 32, 38
Pettegrove, James R. 379
Peyre, Henri 89
Pfaffmann, Carl 288
Phillips, Shelley 181, 327
Piaget, Jean 76, 83, 224, 229, 311, 323, 324, 325, 326, 327, 328, 329, 331, 332, 383
Piéron, Henri 75, 76, 166, 315
Pikler, Andrew G. 288
Pillsbury, Walter Bowers 38, 44, 90, 93, 135, 192, 244, 253, 349, 367
Pinel, Phillippe 52, 338, 343, 344, 345, 359, 407, 408
Pinkston, J.O. 297
Pintner, Rudolph 35, 132
Pitres, A. 49
Pivnicki, D. 362
Plana, Giovanni 313
Plato 48, 56, 57, 58, 206, 245, 303, 380, 382, 384, 388, 389, 394, 396, 397, 398, 413
Platt, Anthony Michael 344
Platt, Charles E. 71, 91
Platt, Gerald M. 125
Pliskoff, Stanley S. 288
Plotinus 48
Plottke, Paul 77
Ploucquet, Gottfried 260
Podolsky, Edward 349
Poffenberger, A.T. 99, 154, 155
Pogson, N.R. 288
Pollack, Robert H. 75, 284, 288, 327
Pollock, George H. 203
Pontalis, J.B. 198
Poppen, Paul 246
Popplestone, John A. 102, 115, 116, 117, 259, 318
Porter, James P. 269
Porter, Langley 278
Porterfield, William 120
Porteus, Stanley D. 314
Poser, Ernest G. 74
Postman, Leo 48, 51, 119, 259
Potts, Louis W. 123
Poulsen, Henrik 362
Powers, Francis F. 365
Poyen, Charles 358

Poynter, Frederick Noel Lawrence
  412
Prabhu, G.G. 63
Prandtl, Antonin 66
Pratola, Stephanie 104
Pratt, Carroll C. 127, 128, 185
Pratt, Kenneth J. 292, 301
Pressey, S.L. 296
Preyer, William 323, 332
Prichard, James Cowles 349, 399
Prince, Morton 37, 49, 308, 344,
  350, 402
Progoff, Ira 219, 221
Prothro, E. Terry 59, 393
Proust, Marcel 168
Pruyser, Paul W. 339
Prytula, Robert E. 171
Pubols, Benjamin H., Jr. 278
Pulaski, Joan L. 360
Purdy, D.M. 187
Putnam, James Jackson 147
Puységur, Marquis Amand Marie
  Jacques Chastenet de 340
Pye-Smith, Phillip H. 287
Pythagoras 37, 56, 392

Q

Queener, E. Llewellyn 337
Quen, Jacques M. 352, 362

R

Radford, John 110, 139
Radner, Joseph 152
Radvanyi, Laszio 337
Raehlmann, E. 168, 169
Rahman, F. 393
Rahmani, Levy 83, 181
Rahn, Carl 244
Raimy, Victor C. 376
Raman, C.V. 288
Ramsay, Andrew Michael 260
Ramul, Konstantin 57, 259
Ramzy, Ishak 205
Rancurello, Antos C. 134
Rand, Benjamin 7, 15, 19, 51,
  112, 256, 382, 393
Rank, Otto 210, 211, 220, 221,
  240

Rapaport, David 91, 214
Raphelson, Alfred C. 94, 132, 153
Rapoport, Anatol 71
Rappoport, Leon H. 124
Rashevsky, N. 192
Rasmussen, Edgar Tranekjaer 192,
  244, 393
Rathbauer-Vincie, Margreta 219
Rather, L.J. 279
Ratner, J. 393
Ratner, Stanley C. 265
Ray, Isaac 352
Ray, Marie Beynon 400
Rayner, Doris 216
Rayner, Rosalie 297, 304
Razran, Gregory H.S. 83, 181
Read, Herbert 218
Rees, R.A. 13
Reese, Hayne W. 327
Reeves, Joan Wynn 38
Reeves, Margaret Pegram 245
Régis, Pierre-Sylvain 291
Reich, Wilhelm 124, 221, 363
Reid, Thomas 72, 86, 127, 384,
  393
Reidel, Robert G. 108
Reik, Theodor 220, 362
Reimarus, Hermann Samuel 55, 56
Reingold, Nathan 113
Reinmuth, O.W. 57
Reiser, Oliver L. 187, 245
Reisman, John M. 355
Reitman, Walter R. 11
Rescher, Nicholas 192
Rethlingshafer, D.A. 272
Reuchlin, M. 75
Reymert, Martin L. 301, 302
Rhine, J.B. 4
Rhine, Louisa E. 4
Ribes-Iñesta, Emilio 78
Ribot, Théodule Armand 51, 68, 74,
  76, 279, 288, 289, 302, 332,
  350
Richards, Angela 210
Richards, Robert J. 264
Richardson-Robinson, F. 254
Richelle, Marc 171
Richemont, Baron de 49
Rickman, John 198, 199
Ricks, David 246

Name Index

Rickwood, Jean 70
Rieber, Robert W. 90
Rieder, Ronald O. 352
Riegel, Klaus F. 65, 94, 121, 307, 327
Riese, Hertha 400
Riese, Walther 279, 341, 344, 412
Riess, Bernard F. 60, 62, 77
Rife, David C. 172
Riggs, Lorrin 4
Riley, I. Woodbridge 153, 381
Rimm, David C. 362
Ripley, George 339
Risse, Guenter B. 372, 412
Ritter, Wm. E. 394
Ritvo, Lucille B. 205
Riviere, Joan 202
Roazen, Paul 211, 221
Roback, Abraham Aaron 10, 38, 90, 107, 108, 115, 118, 147, 172, 254, 400
Robert, Marthe 206
Roberts, Kelyn 285
Roberts, Kimberley S. 345
Robinson, D.M. 32
Robinson, Daniel N. 31, 38, 44, 51
Robinson, Edward S. 254
Robinson, T.M. 394
Robson-Scott, Elaine 209
Robson-Scott, William 209
Rock, Irvin 193, 282
Rockefeller, Laura Spelman 326
Roe, Anne 376
Roeckelein, Jon E. 113
Roethlisberger, F.J. 373
Rogers, Carl R. 225, 226, 240, 307, 362
Romanes, George John 264, 270
Romanyshyn, Robert D. 227
Rooney, M.T. 394
Rorschach, Hermann 19, 310, 312, 313
Rosca, Al 71
Rosen, George 206, 345, 352, 362
Rosen, Gerald M. 363
Rosen, Marvin 345
Rosenbaum, Max 363
Rosenberg, Charles 104, 352
Rosenfield, Leonora Cohen 168, 264, 394

Rosenzweig, Mark R. 292
Rosenzweig, Saul 43, 245
Ross, Alan O. 376
Ross, Barbara 107, 109, 147, 327
Ross, Dorothy 44, 121, 328
Ross, Edward Alsworth 414, 415
Ross, G.R.T. 386
Ross, Helen 220
Ross, William David 394
Rossiter, Margaret W. 104
Rotenberg, Mordechai 345
Rothgeb, Carrie Lee 199
Rothschuh, Karl E. 412
Rotter, Julian B. 355
Rouček, J.S. 72
Rousseau, Jean-Jacques 124, 326, 363, 394, 413
Royal Society of London, The 16
Royce, James E. 394
Royce, Joseph 4, 285, 417
Royce, Josiah 234, 390
Rozeboom, William W. 285
Rubenshtein, S.L. 78, 79, 83, 179, 180, 181, 394
Rubin, Edgar 192, 226
Ruch, Floyd L. 254, 255
Ruch, T.C. 273
Ruckmich, Christian A. 90
Ruckmick, Christian A. 90, 102, 260, 302
Rudolph, Frederick 418
Ruger, Henry A. 293
Ruitenbeek, Hendrik M. 212
Runes, Dagobert D. 381, 406
Ruphuy, Rodrigo Sanchez 353
Rush, Benjamin 86, 87, 127, 128, 338, 339, 343, 359, 402, 403, 405, 406, 407
Rush, James 339
Rush, Norwin 88
Rusk, George Yeisley 407
Russell, Bertrand 380, 381
Russell, Wallace A. 68, 302
Russo, Nancy Felipe 103
Ryan, Bruce A. 363, 394
Ryans, David G. 314
Ryback, David 245
Rychlak, Joseph F. 227
Rycroft, Charles 199, 200

Name Index

Shafii, Mohammad 363
Shakespeare, William 54, 343
Shaklee, Alfred B. 109
Shakow, David 91, 209, 214, 353, 356, 407
Shannon, Claude E. 192
Shapiro, S.I. 114
Sharma, Sohan Lal 346
Sheehan, Mary R. 31, 40, 127, 147
Sheehy, Eugene P. 11
Sheer, Daniel E. 279
Sheldon, H.D. 94
Sheldon, William Herbert 307, 308, 309
Sheperd, Michael 341
Sherif, Carolyn W. 337
Sherif, Muzafer 334, 337
Sherman, Murray H. 206
Sherrington, Charles S. 73, 279, 282, 297, 407, 412
Shields, Stephanie A. 105, 153
Shipley, Thorne 48, 52
Shirley, Norma 27, 29
Shock, Hathan Wetheril 332
Shute, Clarence 395
Sibinga, Maarten S. 258
Sicherman, Barbara 346, 353
Siegel, Michael H. 260
Siegel, Rudolph E. 289, 407
Sills, David L. 21, 22
Silverman, Hirsch Lazaar 76, 221
Silverman, Lloyd H. 212
Simmel, Georg 414
Simmons, Roger D. 207
Simon, Bennett 57, 206
Simon, Brian 83
Simon, Robert I. 245
Simon, Theodore 76, 310, 315, 316, 319
Simpson, Meribeth M. 107, 339, 358
Sina, Ibn 393
Singer, Charles 412
Sinofsky, Faye 123
Skaggs, E.B. 289
Skinhøj, Erik 395
Skinhøj, Kirsten 395
Skinner, B.F. 48, 52, 115, 158, 160, 162, 165, 167, 168, 170,

171, 172, 174, 212, 231, 239, 245, 362, 366, 386
Skrupskelis, Ignas K. 147
Slavson, Samuel Richard 359
Slobin, Dan I. 80, 84, 178
Small, Albion Woodbury 414
Small, Marvin 209
Small, S. Mouchly 346
Smedslund, Jan 172
Smirnov, A.A. 83
Smith, Adam 335
Smith, Edward W. 363
Smith, J.A. 394
Smith, M. Brewster 225, 309
Smith, Myra O. 289
Smith, Noel W. 57, 58, 392, 395
Smith, Norma Kemp 388
Smith, Roger 280
Smith, Stevenson 245
Smith, Theodate L. 332
Smith, William Huntington 350
Smith, Wilson 417
Smith-Rosenberg, Carroll 104
Smoke, Kenneth L. 334
Snadowsky, Alvin 363
Snell, Ludwig 310
Snell, Merwin-Marie 350
Snellgrove, Louis 251
Snyder, Laurence H. 172
Snygg, Donald 225
Sociological Abstracts 17, 27
Socrates 56, 58, 392
Sohn, David 153
Sokal, Michael M. 74, 97, 102, 117, 155
Sokolov, E.N. 83
Sonderegger, Theo 305
Sonnemann, Ulrich 227
Soper, Kate 212
Soranus of Ephesus 404
Sorokin, Pitirim 415
Spalding, Douglas A. 174, 175, 325
Spearman, Charles Edward 39, 108, 193, 243, 289, 309, 311, 318
Spedding, James 382
Spence, Janet T. 162
Spence, Kenneth W. 158, 162, 163, 230, 348
Spencer, Herbert 45, 74, 144,

Name Index

T

Taillepied, Noel 96
Taine, H. 318
Talmey, Max 350
Tanaka, Yashihisa 63
Tanner, Amy E. 396
Tauscher, Herman 284
Tausk, Viktor 211, 212
Tausky, Curt 173
Taylor, A.J.M. 346
Taylor, Donald W. 282, 307
Taylor, H. 188
ten Hoor, Marten 139
Teplov, Boris M. 78, 82, 83
Terman, Lewis Madison 49, 310,
    311, 314, 318, 319, 328
Terrell, D.B. 134
Teuber, Hans Lukas 69, 137
Theophrastus 280
Theriault, Norman 364
Thomas, Ernest Chester 411
Thomas, Milton H. 154
Thomas, William Isaac 413
Thomas Aquinas. See Aquinas, Thomas
Thompson, Clara 207
Thompson, Helen 330
Thompson, Robert 31, 39
Thompson, Travis 364
Thoreson, Richard W. 364
Thorndike, Edward L. 51, 86, 101,
    142, 154, 155, 156, 157, 160,
    174, 193, 270, 296, 311, 319,
    322, 367, 368, 373, 416
Thorndike, Lynn 418
Thorne, Frederick C. 121, 157
Thornton, Harry 58, 392
Thornton, Henry 65
Thorpe, W.H. 270, 271
Throne, John M. 176
Thurstone, Louis Leon 92, 172, 214,
    257, 311, 319, 370
Thwin, Hla 63
Tibbetts, Paul 396
Tiebout, H.M. 245
Tiffin, Joseph 372
Tighe, Louise S. 292
Tighe, Thomas J. 292
Tillich, Paul 51, 89
Timpanaro, Sebastiano 212

Tinbergen, Niko 231, 264, 265,
    271, 273
Tinker, M.A. 132
Tinklepaugh, O.L. 289
Tissot, Simon-Andred 204
Titchener, Edward Bradford 35, 45,
    47, 49, 64, 92, 98, 130, 132,
    133, 134, 135, 136, 137, 138,
    139, 140, 141, 155, 172, 175,
    242, 243, 244, 245, 246, 261,
    282, 305, 365
Titus, Edna Brown 17
Tobach, Ethel 262
Tocqueville, Alexis de 413
Todhunter, Isaac 418
Tolman, Edward Chase 158, 159,
    160, 162, 163, 165, 170, 174,
    177, 233, 291, 296, 297
Tombaugh, Tom N. 297, 301
Tomoda, Fujio 64
Tompkins, Margaret 27, 29
Topoff, Howard R. 270
Touchett, Paul 293
Tourney, Garfield 207, 408
Towery, O.B. 364
Townsend, H.G. 154
Toynbee, Arnold 114, 415
Trainor, J.C. 396
Trapp, E. Philip 340
Trembley, Jean 418
Tridon, Andre 207
Troland, Leonard Thompson 235,
    246, 282, 303, 305
Trosman, Harry 207
Trotter, Thomas 406
Truzzi, Marcello 335
Tsanoff, Radoslav A. 382
Tseng, Wen-Shing 346
Tsushima, Tadashi 64
Tuchman, Barbara 123
Tucker, W.B. 309
Tuke, Daniel H. 22, 407
Turbayne, Colin M. 289
Turner, Merle B. 177
Turner, R. Steven 68
Tweney, Ryan D. 289
Twitmyer, E.B. 291, 292
Tyler, Leona 4
Tyndall, John 175, 387, 388
Tyson, Alan 210

Name Index

TITLE INDEX

This index includes titles of books. Since titles of articles in periodicals are not listed, the reader is advised to check the subject index, p. 475, for relevant entries. Subtitles of books are deleted unless they are necessary for identification of a particular work. When two or more books have the same title, the title is entered only once, with page references to each of the entries. This index is alphabetized letter by letter.

Title Index

Title Index

Title Index

Title Index

Title Index

SUBJECT INDEX

This index includes both names of individuals when they are mentioned in annotations or titles, and substantive topical areas. This subject index is alphabetized letter by letter.

Subject Index

Subject Index

Dynamic psychology 154, 156, 157, 159, 244. See also Psychoanalysis

E

Earhard, Bruce 284
Eastern Europe, psychology in 71-72
Ebbinghaus, Hermann 259, 299, 418
Eccles, J.C. 137
Eclecticism vs. system making 233
Edinburgh, University of 145
Education 173, 260, 356, 366, 367, 369, 370
  behaviorism and 174
  child development and 323, 329, 331
  functionalist contributions to 150
  Gestalt contributions to 186
  history of 415-19
  and intelligence tests 317, 321
  Locke's views on 391
  psychoanalysis and 211
  Rush's views on 406
  Thorndike on 156
  Vives's thought on 276
Educational psychology 236, 238, 251, 253, 254, 294, 308, 333, 354, 359, 360, 371, 372
  in British psychology 74
  Gestalt theory of 194
  histories of 366, 368
  selected texts, readers, and classic works on 364, 365, 366, 367, 368
  in the Soviet Union 79, 84
  in Sweden 95
Education and Training Board of APA 376
Edwards, Jonathan 87
Edwards, Paul 379
Effect, law of 156, 157
Efficiency 250
Ego 206, 220, 401
Egyptian psychology 56, 57, 58, 59, 347, 401
Ehrenfels, Christian von 183
Eidetic imagery 308
Einstein, Albert 186, 188, 196

Eire, psychology in 58
Electroencephalogram 275
Elizabeth, Princess 396
Elizabethan psychology 54, 55
Elkind, David 332
Eminent psychologists 2, 6, 7, 10, 18, 50, 52, 98, 108, 109-12, 119, 121
Emmert, E. 284
Emmert's law 282, 284
Emotion 235, 244, 249, 251, 253, 254, 255, 256, 259, 260, 269, 276, 277, 281, 283, 308, 329, 343, 384, 390
  Aristotle's views on 302, 389, 390
  behavioristic interpretations of 162, 163, 164, 174, 177, 178
  Cannon-Bard theory of 303, 304
  in English psychology 74
  functionalist views on 148, 150, 152, 158
  James-Lange theory of 118, 145, 303, 304
  histories of 297-303
  Puritan views of 128
  Russian materialistic interpretations of 180, 181
  selected major works on 303-5
  Wundt's stance on 131
Empathy 66
Empiricism 380, 381, 382, 387, 392, 393
Employment of psychologists 375, 377.
Employment psychology 368
Encounter movement 361
Encyclopaedia Britannica 21
Engineering psychology 251, 369, 371
England, psychology in 58, 68, 72-74, 108, 116, 120, 134, 180, 220, 257, 287, 361, 369, 390
Entelecheia 394
Epicureans 299
Epistemology 118, 152, 172, 233, 325, 385, 387, 388, 414
Eponymy 113, 284

Subject Index

316, 317, 321, 348, 367, 409, 411
Hering, Ewald 187, 412
Herrick, Charles Judson 267
Herrnstein, R.J. 272, 320
Herschel, J. 288
Hervey, W.L. 89
Hickok, Laurens Perseus 88
High school, teaching of psychology in 249, 250, 251
Hilgard, Ernest 115, 290, 295
Hillix, William A. 117
Hindu psychology 59, 60
Hinkle, Roscoe C. 414
Hipp chronoscope 102
Hippocrates 56, 57, 277, 279, 308, 338, 344, 406
Historicism 121
Historic psychological apparatus 102
Histories of psychology, general 31-40
Histories of psychology, reviews of 10
Historiography
    contemporary Western European 8
    definition of 105
    philosophical issues in 117-23, 306
    of psychology 8, 18, 70, 71, 76, 77, 79, 80, 95, 105-25, 398, 400, 402, 414, 417
History of Education Society 46
History of ideas 35, 38, 47, 49, 217, 271, 415, 416
History of Psychology, APA Division of 105, 106
History of psychology as a specialty 105-6
History of science 12
Hitler, Adolf 69, 202
Hitzig, Eduard 280
Hobbes, Thomas 51, 302, 380, 388, 391, 396
Hochberg, Julian 285
Hocking, William Ernest 142
Hoffman, Fridericus 277
Holland, psychology in 95, 116
Hollingworth, Harry Levi 93
Hollingworth, Leta 103, 105
Holt, Robert R. 199

Holway, A.H. 282
Homeostasis 304, 411
Homer 57
Homing behavior 272
Homosexuality 339
Hooke, Robert 385
Hopkins, Johns, University 97, 153, 256
Hormic psychology 158-60, 163
Horney, Karen 211, 220, 221, 240
Hsi-liang, Chu 188
Hull, Clark L. 19, 49, 87, 158, 160, 161, 167, 169, 174, 230, 291, 292, 348
Human factors 369, 371
Humanism, science and 203, 207, 402
Humanistic psychology 50, 118, 144, 171, 197, 221-29, 231, 237, 238, 397
    and behaviorism 242, 246
    Marxist critique of 227
    and the research tradition 222
Hume, David 48, 72, 167, 291, 338, 380, 385, 387, 389, 391, 392, 396
Humor 196, 240, 302
Hunger 304, 305
Hunt, Joseph McVicker 93
Hunt, W.A. 342
Hunter, Thomas 136
Hunter, Walter S. 165, 174
Husserl, Edmund 222, 223, 224, 225, 226, 228, 229, 240
Hutcheson, Francis 299, 300
Huxley, T.H. 52, 166, 175
Hypnosis 75, 76, 145, 179, 180, 203, 205, 206, 339, 340, 343, 359, 361, 363
Hysteria 75, 205, 339, 341, 342, 343, 344, 346, 347, 359

I

Ibn Sina 393
Ideas 148, 177, 224, 270, 318, 332, 389, 396
Ideas, history of 35, 38, 47, 49, 217, 271, 415, 416
Idiocy. See Mental deficiency

Subject Index

Subject Index

Subject Index

Subject Index

and McDougall 335
Muensterberg on 366
phenomenology in 299
Ribot on 279, 350
Soviet views on 181
Upham on 91
U.S. psychology on 235
William Alanson White Psychoanalytic
Society 198
William of Ockham 380
Willoughby, Raymond B. 209
Wilson, L.G. 411
Windsor, University of 70
Wisconsin, University of 87, 89,
147
Wisconsin at Milwaukee, University
of 108
Witchcraft 358
Witch hunts 345
Witmer, Lightner 353, 355
Wittenberg Symposium 302
Wittgenstein, Ludwig 244, 386
Wolf, Theta H. 315
Wolfe, H.K. 89
Wolff, Christian von 260
Women, psychology of 153
Women in psychology 102-5
Wood, George Bacon 339
Wood family 404
Woodworth, Robert S. 147, 154,
155, 157, 193, 235, 274,
290, 297
Worcester State Hospital 353
Work, psychology of 368-73

Wright, Chauncey 153, 390
Wuerzburg school 68, 133, 134,
135, 137, 223, 240, 286,
287
Wundt, Wilhelm 66, 68, 100, 116,
182, 252, 261, 262, 374,
394
on attention 289
and Brentano 134
Husserl on 224
on psycholinguistics 284
on social psychology 413
Titchener on 140
and U.S. psychology 85
on willing 299
works of and secondary sources on
49, 51, 52, 130-33, 393

Y

Yale University 86, 92, 93, 199,
262, 400
Yugoslavia, psychology in 71

Z

Zehender, W. 284
Zeitgeist 121
Zeller, Eduard 66
Zen 141, 218
Zimbardo, Philip G. 254
Zurich, University of 115
Zusne, Leonard 109
Zweig, Arnold 209